Fodor's 92 Japan

S0-BYO-264

Fodor's Travel Publications, Inc.
New York and London

Fodor's Japan

Editor: Caroline V. Haberfeld
Contributors: Susan Bain, Helen Brower, Diane Durston, Nigel Fisher, Tara Hamilton, Kiko Itasaka, Jared Lubarsky, Dale Northrup, Marcy Pritchard, Timon Screech, Oliver Statler, Jon Spayde
Art Director: Fabrizio La Rocca
Cartographer: David Lindroth
Illustrator: Karl Tanner
Cover Photograph: Wing/Stock Boston

Design: Vignelli Associates

Special Sales

Fodor's Travel Publications are available at special discounts for bulk purchases (100 copies or more) for sales promotions or premiums. Special editions, including personalized covers, excerpts of existing guides, and corporate imprints, can be created in large quantities for special needs. For more information write to Special Marketing, Fodor's Travel Publications, 201 East 50th St., New York, NY 10022; or call 800/800–3246. Inquiries from the United Kingdom should be sent to Fodor's Travel Publications, 20 Vauxhall Bridge Rd., London, England SW1V 2SA.

MANUFACTURED IN THE UNITED STATES OF AMERICA
10 9 8 7 6 5 4 3 2 1

Contents

Foreword

We wish to express our gratitude to those who helped prepare this guide: Grace Herget and the New York staff of the Japan National Tourist Organization (JNTO); the JNTO Tokyo staff; Toshino Ikubo and Seiko Taniguchi of Morris Simoncelli of Japan Airlines; and Ron Doughty of United Airlines.

While every care has been taken to ensure the accuracy of the information in this guide, the passage of time will always bring change, and consequently, the publisher cannot accept responsibility for errors that may occur.

All prices and opening times quoted here are based on information supplied to us at press time. Hours and admission fees may change, however, and the prudent traveler will avoid inconvenience by calling ahead.

Fodor's wants to hear about your travel experiences, both pleasant and unpleasant. When a hotel or restaurant fails to live up to its billing, let us know and we will investigate the complaint and revise our entries where the facts warrant it.

Send your letters to the editors of Fodor's Travel Publications, 201 E. 50th Street, New York, NY 10022.

Highlights '92 and Fodor's Choice

Highlights '92

Though three times as many Japanese (10.9 million) traveled overseas in 1990 as foreigners visited their country, both domestic and foreign tourism in Japan is increasing. While Koreans have displaced Americans for the highest number of visitors from a single country, the yen's decline against the dollar may reverse this trend. Certainly the cost of visiting Japan is not more expensive than traveling in Western Europe.

Inexpensive Accommodations Tokyo, to be sure, is an expensive city, but visitors can safely reduce expenditures by traveling on the subways, staying in a hotel away from midtown, and eating at small, inexpensive restaurants. And out of Tokyo, prices decline, as they do out of large American metropolises. There are a number of cost-cutting techniques you can practice that are detailed in free brochures published by the Japanese National Tourist Organization (JNTO). One such booklet lists business hotels with small double rooms, priced around ¥11,000 ($73), that are invariably clean and absolutely safe. Another lists inexpensive ryokans (like B&Bs with tatami matting on the floors) that cost about ¥4,000 ($35), though unlike the business hotels, many do not have rooms with private toilet facilities.

Another type of accommodation, which combines value and the opportunity to meet Japanese people is the minshuku, or private home, where a night's stay, including two meals, costs between ¥6,000 and ¥10,000. Travelers are treated like honored guests, and meals are often far superior and more extensive than those at a reasonably priced restaurant. Minshukus are usually located away from the big towns.

More and more visitors to Japan are recognizing that the countryside has more to offer than the big cities, which accounts for the success of the Okayama International Villas. Beginning with one traditional farmhouse in 1988, the chain now has six, tucked away in villages sheltered by the Chugoku mountain range in Western Japan. Each villa can accommodate up to eight people, with a shared bath. One night costs ¥3,000; the rate declines for longer stays. Reservations are made through the Okayama Prefectural Office, Okayama 700, tel. 0862/24–2111.

Getting to Japan Major airlines are continually upgrading their services and adding more nonstop flights between the United States and Japan. Japan Airlines has recently taken delivery of the state of the art Boeing 747–400 aircraft, and the major U.S. carrier, United Airlines, has recently added another nonstop route between Tokyo's Narita Airport and New York's Newark International, continuing to Dulles International in Washington, DC, and also serves San Francisco and Dallas/Ft. Worth. All Nippon Airways has added service out of New York to its West Coast and Washington, DC, routes. Remember, too, that additional flight segments to other Asian countries can be added to your ticket at marginal cost.

Tokyo's international airport, Narita, is the worst in Asia. It will get worse before it improves. Permission has been granted to increase the number of daily flights to 325, the absolute maximum tolerable for its one 4,000-meter runway. For passengers, this means long lines, crowded waiting rooms, pushing and shoving at the transportation desk, and general mass confusion in unpleasant surroundings. Plans are afoot to improve the situation, but local farmers are unwilling to give up their land for runway extensions and new facilities. Activists supporting the farmers have resorted to violent demonstrations and car bombing, which has led to the heavy security and the time-consuming police checks of all travelers entering the airport.

Congestion getting to and from Narita eased in 1991 when East Japan Railways (JR East) began operating its new Narita Special Express. The one-hour nonstop service departs from an underground station beneath the air terminal. Shinjuku and Tokyo stations are the only two stops in Tokyo. There are three trains an hour.

Domestic Travel The celebrated Shinkansen (bullet) trains are being spruced up. In every other car there is now a pay telephone for domestic calls. The Green Cars (first class) have earphones for classical and pop music, and on some trains there are private rooms for business travelers. New double-decker coaches have dining cars with elongated windows for "scenic dining."

The traveler's best buy remains the Japan Rail Pass. It offers one, two, or three weeks of unlimited rail travel and permits seat reservations without additional charge. Using a week's rail pass to travel from Tokyo to Kyoto, Kanazawa, Hiroshima and Nagasaki, and back to Tokyo can save you more than ¥23,730 ($170.00) over individual fares.

Without the Japan Rail Pass, trains are expensive. Long-distance buses called *chokyori basu* are a popular alternative. They offer considerable savings, though they take twice the time of a train. Since these buses often travel through the night, the hardy traveler also saves on a hotel accommodation. Details on the bus routes are available from JNTO offices.

Big Business Travel and tourism are booming in Japan and new forms of entertainment are always sought. Now there are submarine safaris—in Kasari Bay off Kagoshima and in the Okinawa Marine National Park, where for $75, 40 passengers visit Japan's only unpeopled park on 35-minute underwater excursions. Big Bird is also big business. Plans are underway to build several theme parks along the lines of the 11-year old Sesame Place amusement park in Langhorne, Pennsylvania. It should succeed; Sony Creative Products chalked up ¥6 billion in a year's sales of Sesame Street muppets. Outer space is popular, too. At Kitakyushu City, just outside Fukuoka, Space World opened in the summer of 1990, with six pavilions, eight amusement facilities, three plazas, seven stores and five restaurants. Meanwhile, Tokyo's Disneyland's new Star Tours odyssey to the unknown planet Endor is meeting with great success—perhaps because it is billed as "not for the faint hearted and pregnant women should consider twice before embarking."

Gender imbalance is showing up in the population. In the 20 to 39 age bracket, there are 8,318,000 single men and 5,263,000 single women. That's not all. While women are enjoying the beginnings of women's rights, the pampered sons of overprotective mothers have forgotten how to court. This has spawned the Bachelors Academy in Osaka to teach the "code": don't fawn over women; don't patronize them; be understanding; be open; be confident.

Fads and Status Presenting one's business card is more than just a ritual; it is a proclamation of status. The latest fad is to have custom-designed cards. One such card is made of stainless steel meishi the thickness of a newspaper, with the characters engraved with chemicals. (Cost: $240 for 100 cards.) Another type, made of resin, becomes pliant and rubbery as the temperature rises, but returns to its original shape when cooled. (Cost: $70 for 20 cards.) The pièce de résistance is the card made from one gram of pure gold, with characters impressed on the surface in plastic. (Cost: $42 for one card.) More than 50,000 have been sold.

Golf is Japan's number one pastime of prestige. A membership at a top-ranking club costs an average of $30,000. The 1,709 courses (315 more are under construction) are just not enough to go around. The popularity of the game has caused a shortage of caddies. Caddying is strictly a woman's job, but women are not volunteering, though the salary is considerably higher than a typical office job. To attract more applicants, one club advertised for "course mates." Meanwhile, environmentalists concerned about damage to the environment from weed-control chemicals, have successfully halted construction of 20 new golf courses.

New Attraction In July 1990 the brand new $133 million Osaka Aquarium opened in the most exciting effort yet to bring new attractions to a city known previously only for its industry. The aquarium contains an overwhelming 1.4-million-gallon tank approximately 90 feet high. Visitors view a slice of the Pacific ocean while descending spiral ramps enabling them to see all different angles of the underwater environment. A giant whale shark and other exotic sea creatures from around the world are featured.

Fodor's Choice

No two people will agree on what makes a perfect vacation, but it's fun, and it can be helpful, to know what others think. We hope you'll have a chance to experience some of Fodor's Choices yourself while visiting Japan. We have tried to offer something for everyone and from every price category. For more information about each entry, refer to the appropriate chapters (listed in the margin) within this guidebook.

Sights

Tokyo	Noh by Torchlight
	Omotesando
	Tsukiji Fish Market
	Isamu Noguchi's Plaza, Sogetsu Hall
Kamakura	Daibutsu (Great Buddha)
Fuji-Hakone-Izu	Dogashima, Izu Peninsula
	Mt. Fuji reflected in Lake Kawaguchi
	Togendai Ropeway, Hakone
Nagoya	Dorokyo Gorge, Kii Peninsula
	Cherry Blossoms at Mt. Yoshino
	Ukai Fishing, Gifu and Kiso River
Japan Alps	Chubu-Sangaku National Park, Kamikochi
	Kiso Valley Old Post Villages
	Sado Skyline Drive, Sado Island
	Shirakawago-mura, Hida Prefecture
	Takayama
Kyoto	Gion Corner
	Arashiyama
	Old Nishila Street Market
Osaka	National Bunraku Theater
	Cherry Blossoms at the Mint
Kobe	Kitano
	Portliner
Western Honshu	Carp in the Tsuwanogawa River
	Torii Gate, Itsukushima Jinja Shrine, Miyajima
	Hagi Pottery Town

Kurashiki

Kyushu Mt. Aso

Tohoku Matsushima Bay

Tono Basin (old farmhouses)

Hokkaido Akan Traverse, Akan National Park

Ice Floes in the Sea of Ohkutsk

Mating Dance of the Red-crested Crane (Tancho), Kushiro Great Marsh

Orofure Pass, Skikotu-Toya National Park

Sounkyo Gorge, Daisetsuzan National Park

Temples and Shrines

Tokyo Hie Jinja Shrine

Sengakuji Temple

Sensoji Temple

Yasukuni Jinja Shrine

Nikko Toshogu Shrine

Futaarasan Jinja Shrine

Rinnoji Temple

Kamakura Engakuji Temple

Hasedera Temple

Kenchoji Temple

Tsurugaoka Hachimangu Shrine

Nagoya Grand Shrines at Ise (Ise Jingu Shrine), Ise

Mt. Koya Temples

Tagata Jinga Shrine, Tagata

Japan Alps Myoryuji Temple (Ninjadera), Kanazawa

Zenkoji Temple, Nagano

Kyoto Ginkakuji Temple (Silver Pavilion)

Jakko-in Temple

Kinkakuji Temple (Gold Pavilion)

Kiyomizudera Temple

Ryoanji Temple

Nara Horyuji Temple

Kasuga Taisha Shrine

Todaiji Temple

Osaka Shintennoji Shrine

Western Honshu	Dashoin Temple, Hagi
	Itsukushima Jinja Shrine, Miyajima
	Izumo Taisha Shrine
	Taikodani-Inari Jinja Shrine, Tsuwano
Shikoku	Kotohiragu Shrine, Kotohira
Tohoku	Yamadera Temple, Yamagata

Buildings and Monuments

Tokyo	Imperial Palace
	Kabuki-za Theater
Nagoya	Inuyamajo Castle, Inuyama
Japan Alps	Matsumotojo Castle, Matsumoto
	Samurai Houses, Kanazawa
Kyoto	Katsura Imperial Villa
	Kawai Kanjiro Memorial House
	Nijojo Castle
Osaka	Osakajo Castle
Western Honshu	Atomic Bomb Dome, Hiroshima
	Himejijo Castle, Himeji
	Matsuejo Castle, Matsue
	Meimeian Tea House, Matsue
Shikoku	Kochijo Castle, Kochi
	Kompira O-Shibai Kabuki Theater, Kotohira
Kyushu	Glover Mansion, Nagasaki
	Kumamotojo Castle, Kumamoto
Tohoku	Hirosakijo Castle, Hirosaki
	Samurai Houses, Kakunodate
	Storehouses, Kitakaka

Museums

Tokyo	Horyuji Treasure Hall, Tokyo National Museum
	Nezu Institute of Fine Arts
	Yamatane Museum of Art
Kamakura	Treasure House, Tsurugaoka Hachimangu Shrine
Fuji-Hakone-Izu	Hakone Open Air Museum, Chokoku-no-mori
	MOA Museum, Atami
Japan Alps	Hida-Minzoku-mura (Folk Village), Takayama

Japan Ukiyo-e Museum, Matsumoto

Kusakabe Mingeikan Folkcraft Museum, Takayama

Seisonkaku Villa, Kanazawa

Kyoto Kyoto Museum of Traditional Industrial Arts

Kyoto National Museum

Western Honshu Kurashiki Folkcraft Museum, Kurashiki

Ohara Art Museum, Kurashiki

Peace Memorial Museum, Hiroshima

Hokkaido Shiraoi Ainu Museum, Shiraoi

Parks and Gardens

Tokyo Denbo-in Temple Garden

Hama Rikyu Detached Palace Garden

New Otani Hotel

Shinjuku Gyoen Garden

Kamakura Hokokuji Temple Gardens

Yokohama Sankeien Garden

Japan Alps Gyokusenen Garden, Kanazawa

Kenrokuen Garden, Kanazawa

Kyoto Old Imperial Palace Grounds

Shugakuin Villa Garden

Nara Nara Park

Western Honshu Korakuen Garden, Okayama

Shizuki-Koen Park, Hagi

Shikoku Ritsurin-Koen Garden, Takamatsu

Kyushu Suizenji Gardens, Kumamoto

Dining

Tokyo Attore *(Very Expensive)*

Inakaya *(Very Expensive)*

Gold Leaf *(Expensive)*

Edo-Gin *(Moderate–Expensive)*

Kamakura Tori-ichi *(Very Expensive)*

Fuji-Hakone-Izu Fujiya Hotel Restaurant, Miyanoshita *(Expensive)*

Nagoya Koraku Restaurant, Nagoya *(Very Expensive)*

Torikyu Restaurant, Nagoya *(Expensive)*

Japan Alps Tsubajin Ryokan, Kanazawa *(Very Expensive)*

Kincharyo Restaurant, Kanazawa *(Expensive)*

Suzaki, Takayama *(Expensive)*

Kyoto Ashiya Steak House *(Expensive)*

Heihachi-Jaya *(Moderate–Expensive)*

Yagenbori *(Moderate–Expensive)*

Divo diva *(Moderate)*

Nishiki *(Moderate)*

Rokusei Nishimise *(Moderate)*

Sagano *(Moderate)*

Nara Tsukihitei *(Very Expensive)*

Uma no me *(Moderate)*

Osaka Ron *(Very Expensive)*

Rose Room *(Very Expensive)*

The Seasons *(Very Expensive)*

Kobe A-1 *(Moderate)*

Salaam *(Moderate)*

Wang Thai *(Inexpensive)*

Western Honshu Ryokan Mitakiso, Hiroshima *(Expensive)*

Kanawa Restaurant, Hiroshima *(Moderate)*

Kyushu Togasaku Honten, Kumamoto *(Very Expensive)*

Fugumatsu, Beppu *(Moderate–Expensive)*

Shikairo, Nagasaki *(Inexpensive–Moderate)*

Tohoku Iwashiya, Sendai *(Expensive)*

Hokkaido Izakaya Karumaya, Sapporo *(Moderate)*

Uoisshin, Otaru *(Expensive)*

Lodging

Tokyo Capitol Tokyu Hotel *(Very Expensive)*

Hotel Okura *(Very Expensive)*

Hotel Atamiso *(Expensive)*

Palace Hotel *(Expensive)*

Hotel Ginza Ocean *(Moderate)*

Fuji-Hakone-Izu Ryokan Sanyoso, Shizuoka *(Very Expensive)*

Taikanso Ryokan, Atami *(Very Expensive)*

Fujiya Hotel, Miyanoshita *(Expensive)*

Ryokan Naraya, Miyanoshita *(Expensive)*

Japan Alps	Ryokan Asadaya, Kanazawa *(Very Expensive)*
	Ryokan Kinkikan, Takayama *(Very Expensive)*
	Hotel Fujiya (Royal Suite), Nagano *(Very Expensive)*
Kyoto	Tawaraya *(Very Expensive)*
	Kyoto Brighton Hotel *(Expensive)*
	Hotel Fujita Kyoto *(Expensive)*
	Kinmata *(Moderate)*
Nagoya	Nagoya Hilton *(Expensive)*
	Asanaro Minshuku, on Ago Bay *(Inexpensive)*
Osaka	Hotel New Otani Osaka *(Very Expensive)*
	Osaka Hilton International *(Very Expensive)*
Kobe	Kobe Portopia Hotel *(Very Expensive)*
	Oriental Hotel *(Expensive)*
Nara	Edo-San *(Very Expensive)*
	Kankaso *(Expensive)*
	Nara Hotel *(Expensive)*
Western Honshu	Hokumon Yashiki, Hagi *(Expensive)*
	Iwaso Ryokan, Miyajima *(Expensive–Very Expensive)*
	Ryokan Kurashiki, Kurashiki *(Expensive)*
	Minshuku Genroku Bekkan, Kundani *(Inexpensive)*
Kyushu	Sakamoto-ya, Nagasaki *(Very Expensive)*
	Clio Court Hotel, Fukuoka *(Moderate)*
	Sakaeya, Beppu *(Inexpensive)*
Tohoku	Ryokan Matsushimajo, Matsushima *(Moderate–Expensive)*
Hokkaido	Grand Hotel, Sapporo *(Very Expensive)*
	Harbor View, Mombetsu *(Moderate)*

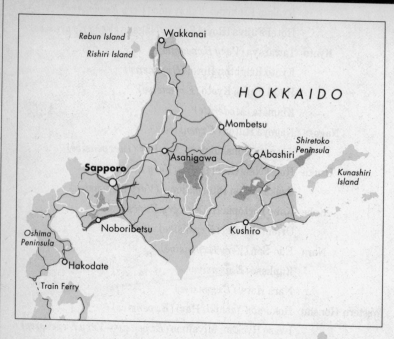

HOKKAIDO
(see inset)

Hakodate

Tsugaru
Peninsula

Shimokita
Peninsula

Sea of Japan

Aomori

Akita Morioka

Sado
Island

Niigata

Yamagata

Sendai

Noto
Peninsula

Fukushima

Kanazawa

Toyama

Nikko

Utsunomiya

Fukui

Nagano

Takayama

Matsumoto

Oyama

Maebashi

Mito

Gifu

Kofu

Kyoto

Tokyo

Nagoya

Chiba

Yokohama

Nara

Tsu

Mt. Fuji

Shizuoka

Izu
Peninsula

Oshima Island

H O N S H U

P A C I F I C   O C E A N

0   50 miles

0   75 km

Numbers below vertical bands relate each zone to Greenwich Mean Time (0 hrs.).
Local times frequently differ from these general indications,
as indicated by light-face numbers on map.

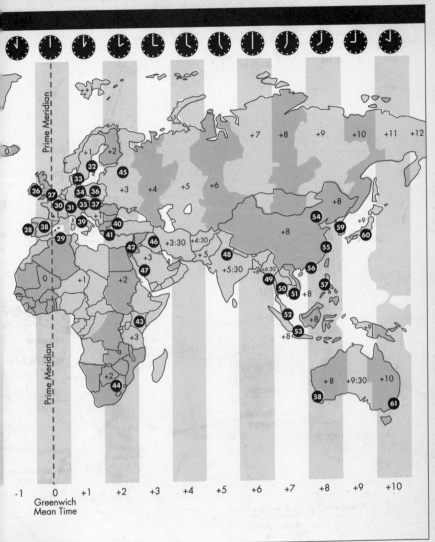

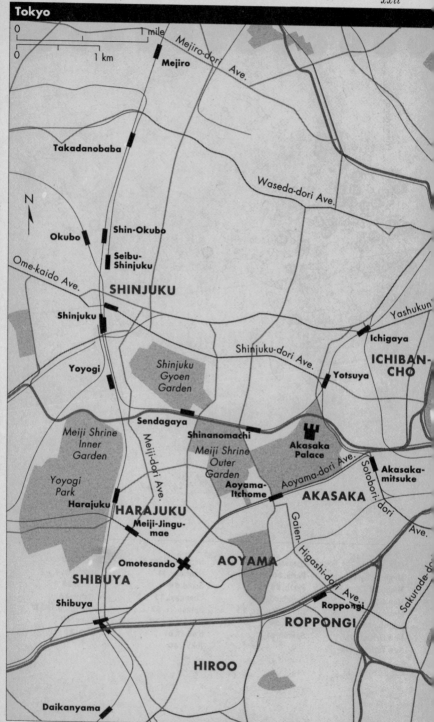

Tokyo

0   1 mile
0   1 km

N

Mejiro-dori Ave.

Mejiro

Takadanobaba

Waseda-dori Ave.

Okubo

Shin-Okubo

Seibu-Shinjuku

Ome-kaido Ave.

SHINJUKU

Shinjuku

Yoyogi

Shinjuku Gyoen Garden

Shinjuku-dori Ave.

Yashukun

Ichigaya

Yotsuya

ICHIBAN-CHO

Meiji Shrine Inner Garden

Sendagaya

Shinanomachi

Meiji Shrine Outer Garden

Akasaka Palace

Akasaka-mitsuke

Yoyogi Park

Harajuku

Meiji-dori Ave.

HARAJUKU

Meiji-Jingu-mae

Aoyama-Itchome

Aoyama-dori Ave.

AKASAKA

Sotobori-dori

Ave.

Omotesando

AOYAMA

Gaien-Higashi-dori Ave.

Roppongi

Sakurade-do

SHIBUYA

Shibuya

ROPPONGI

HIROO

Daikanyama

Kansai

Lake Biwa

KOSEI LINE

Meishin Expwy.

SHINKANSEN

KYOTO

Ujitawara

Wazuka

Yamashiro

KANSAI MAIN LINE

Uji

Joyo

SANIN MAIN LINE

Kameoka

Muko

Nagaokakyo

Yawata

Takatsuki

Katano

Shijonawate

Neyagawa

Kadoma

Daito

Moriguchi

Yodo River

SHINKANSEN

Ibaraki Hirakata

Settsu

OSAKA

Nose

Minoo

Toyonaka

Itami

Amagasaki

Kawanishi

Inagawa

Ashiya

Takarazuka

Mt. Rokko

SHINKANSEN

Sanda

Chugoku

Expwy.

FUKUCHIYAMA LINE

N

KOBE
Port Kobe

Port Osaka

Osaka Bay

NARA

Ikoma

Yamatokoriyama

Tenri

Sakurai

Higashi Osaka

Yao

Kashihara

Gose

Oyodo

Mt. Yoshino

Kashiwara

Fujidera

Habikino

Tonda Bayashi

Mt. Kongo

Gojo

Kinokawa River

Matsubara

Kawachi-Nagano

Hashimoto

Sakai

Izumi

Uchita

Takaishi

Kumatori

Izumiotsu

Kishiwada

Kaizuka

Izumi-Sano

Hannan

Nishi-Meihan Expwy.

HANWA LINE

WAKAYAMA LINE

Hanwa Expwy.

6 miles
9 km

Introduction

by Oliver Statler

Currently a resident of Honolulu, Oliver Statler has lived in Japan, off and on, for more than 18 years. His several books include Japanese Inn, Shimoda Story, *and* Japanese Pilgrimage.

I first came to Japan when it was an occupied country after World War II. My most vivid memory is of the industrial area between Yokohama and Tokyo. As far as the eye could see on both sides of the highway, the flat earth was black. The only structures standing were the chimneys of factories the firebombs had consumed.

Like everyone else in the occupying force, I was comfortably housed and amply fed. But for the Japanese, food and clothing were scarce, and housing was at a premium. Faces were gray, and foreign correspondents reported an air of hopelessness. Those close to Prime Minister Shigeru Yoshida have told how, after a day of coping with Japan's problems and occupation officials, he sometimes smoked his postprandial cigar while pacing the garden of his official residence, looking out over ruined Tokyo, and muttering, "Will it ever be rebuilt? Will it ever be rebuilt?"

I came with curiosity about the nation I had been fighting against, but with precious little knowledge of it. I intended to stay only the two years called for by my contract. The two years stretched to 11. My involvement with Japan became lifelong.

Looking back, I can trace three paths that drew me into this fascinating, beautiful, and exasperating country. The first was Japan's contemporary prints. The moment I saw a small exhibition, I fell in love with them. I began collecting, I was able to meet many of the artists, and I formed bonds of friendship that endure to this day. My first book, *Modern Japanese Prints*, grew out of this enthusiasm.

The second path led to the Minaguchi-ya, the *ryokan*, the Japanese inn whose story I eventually set down. Frustrated because I never could get a reservation at any of the Western-style resort hotels the occupation authorities had taken over (they had overlooked none and had declared every other hostelry in the country off-limits to us), I found, one lucky day, a small advertisement announcing that the Minaguchi-ya had been placed "on-limits" (by the small detachment of American military police stationed in the nearby city, I learned later; they wanted to use the inn). The Minaguchi-ya was a considerable distance from Yokohama, where I was based, and the red tape encountered in getting there was formidable, but I made it, and another love affair began. That was my introduction to the ryokan, and I remain addicted to the special delights of those uniquely Japanese retreats: the quiet elegance of traditional Japanese architecture; the personal service that eschews lobbies and restaurants to coddle you in your rooms, where all attention is focused on you; and the fine food, beautifully served.

It may be wise to add a cautionary note. Like other breeds of hotels, there are good and bad ryokans, expensive and inexpensive. The most expensive are just as costly as a luxury hotel, but they can pamper you in ways no hotel can match.

The third path took me to the Kabuki theater, which, not at first but at second or third sight, enthralled me and still does. There I found glorious stagecraft put to dramatizing the long and engrossing history of Japan. I had been lured into that history by the story of the Minaguchi-ya; Kabuki quickened my interest by showing me, in action, the princely feudal lords called *daimyo*, their samurai, and commoners of every calling—merchants, farmers, artisans, gamblers, ruffians, and acquiescent waitresses.

I mention my own experiences because I am convinced that pursuing one's personal interests is the best way of meeting Japan. Japan's culture is unique. So is that of every other country, but with Japan, few of us share the kind of cultural linkage that bonds us to Europe and the Middle East. For most of us, our heritage is Western civilization. Our ancestors, our language, our heroes, our folklore, and our way of thinking are Western, and it takes some effort to appreciate the equally great civilizations of the East. The handiest bridge is an interest already formed. Whatever it may be, from baseball to pottery or the food the Japanese nestle in it, from religion to railroads, music, gardens, or marketing, pursuing it can add depth and zest to travel. Whenever someone asks me how to plan a trip to Japan, I ask, "What are your interests?"

The Japanese themselves have always been avid tourists: you must not be surprised to find yourself vastly outnumbered at any popular spot. The Japanese think of travel as education. "If you love your son, let him travel," says one of their proverbs, and there is a corollary: "A traveler is without shame." Travel offers a release from the inhibitions and restraints at home; it's a license to misbehave that is sometimes exercised.

In days past, when travel was difficult—almost entirely on foot and sometimes sharply restricted by feudal regulation—most literate travelers kept a diary (a practice I suggest to you). Most, of course, were personal efforts to waken memories later or to share with family or friends. But some were "public diaries" meant to be published, like the diaries of Samuel Pepys and Daniel Defoe. Among these are some of the masterpieces of Japanese literature. Two favorites of mine are *The Tosa Diary*, about a journey in 935, and *The Narrow Road to the Deep North* (as the title is commonly translated), written 754 years later, in 1689.

The first is by a nobleman and distinguished poet named Tsurayuki, about his journey home to the capital after serving for five years as the governor of the distant province of Tosa (now Kochi Prefecture) on the Pacific side of the island of Shikoku. The second was written by Japan's most famous haiku poet, Basho, the man who raised the 17-syllable verse into art.

Basho shaped and even fictionalized his diary to reflect the landscape of his mind as well as the landscape he journeyed through. Tsurayuki, too, used fictional techniques; he pretended that his diary was written by a woman, perhaps because he considered that a central theme—sorrow over the loss of a little daughter who had died in Tosa—could best be expressed by a mother, and perhaps because he chose to write in colloquial Japanese instead of the elevated style expected of an educated man.

Both are poetic diaries. Both men turned to poetry when their feelings were too intense to be expressed in prose. This was not unusual, for in their times any cultured man was supposed to be able to toss off a poem when the occasion called for it. Even today a great deal of poetry is written by amateurs—shopkeepers, politicians, housewives, businessmen—just for the love of it.

Both diaries have been translated, and I highly recommend them. They are the testimonies of sensitive travelers, which we all aspire to be.

I do not put much faith in analyses that attempt to explain the Japanese character and personality. Of course, in some ways the Japanese are different from us because their history and their culture are different, but human beings are human beings, and we have much more in common than we have differences.

Still, the Japanese do have their particular hang-ups and idiosyncrasies. They explain many of these by the fact that they are a homogeneous people. Certainly just about everybody has black hair (unless henna or age has intervened), which, as a friend has remarked, makes for a neat-looking crowd—no confusion of sundry variations on blond, red, brown, and black.

Because of their homogeneity and because they have lived so closely together for so long, they maintain that they are so attuned to each other that much need not be said: nuance in tone or phrase conveys unspoken meaning. There is truth in this, but if it were totally true there would be no misunderstandings between the Japanese, which is not the case. It is also true that in the West what is unspoken is often more meaningful than what is said, and we, too, have our formulas for avoiding the overt. When casual acquaintances part by saying, "Let's get together sometime," they both understand that they have no intention of planning another meeting.

Because the Japanese have their own nuances, the foreigner would do well to listen carefully; if there is a shadow of a doubt, it's best to probe a bit for the real meaning. The Japanese may consider this gauche, but it is preferable to a misunderstanding. As has been pointed out, the Japanese often say yes to mean that they understand you, not that they agree with you.

Inscrutable is an adjective that has long been applied to the Japanese; in my opinion, it's misapplied. Some of this is because they speak with their own brand of nuance. But to describe the Japanese face as an expressionless mask makes no sense to me. The Japanese have their conventions of hiding those feelings they think will make other people uncomfortable, just as we do, but the faces of the Japanese I know are as revealing as those of my Caucasian friends. And the faces of complete strangers—on a commuter train, for example—often betray their mood. I consider the Japanese a passionate people, rather akin to the Spanish. Their emotions lie close to the surface and incline to bubble over, as Kabuki and movie audiences demonstrate. I have found that my Japanese friends are at least as likely as my American friends to confide to me their heartaches or aspirations. Sometimes they find it easier to open up to a foreigner than to another Japanese.

It is true enough that the Japanese are a homogeneous people, but what that means is that the mix occurred so long ago that it is past remembering.

The Japanese are a blend of immigrants who originated in regions all the way from the South Pacific to the frozen steppes and who wore every skin color known to mankind. (Note the variety of facial types on the street or in a subway car.) And while Japanese civilization is heavily indebted to China, it is not just a variation on the Chinese. It contains basic elements—such as the traditional architecture of the home, or the emphasis on the daily hot bath—that certainly did not come from China.

Some of those immigrants of long ago simply walked, for during the Ice Age so much of the oceans' water was frozen at the poles that the rest was far shallower than it is today. Great stretches that are now ocean bottom were then exposed, including a wide bridge linking the Asian continent with what is now northern Kyushu and western Honshu. When people reached Japan, their march ended: There was no place farther to go.

The ice melted, and the oceans rose. The land bridge is now under the waters of the Sea of Japan, which is quite shallow as seas go. But along the east coasts of Japan, the floor of the Pacific Ocean plunges five or six miles to one of the deepest of all submarine trenches. The Japanese islands are the tops of volcanic mountains that rise from that trench to heights of more than two miles. These heights and depths create enormous strains and stresses; this is a very unstable part of the earth's crust. Earthquakes of varying intensity average about four a day. In Tokyo, shocks that one can *feel* occur on average every three days.

Japan is all islands—more than 3,300 of them, of which about 440 are inhabited. The four biggest are Hokkaido, in the north; Honshu, curving south and west; Kyushu, in the west; and Shikoku, smallest of the four, cradled between Honshu and Kyushu across the Inland Sea. The mountaintops that are these islands are themselves very mountainous. Plains are few: The Japanese can cultivate only about 16% of the land they live on. Today that 16% is crowded, but in early centuries it was more than adequate and very attractive to immigrants. And so, long after the land bridge had disappeared, people kept coming in boats. A hundred miles of dangerous sea divide southern Korea and northern Kyushu, but that is the part of Japan closest to the Asian continent, and it was the gateway for both people and culture entering from the continent. Its ports were busy with a continuing flow of settlers and innovations. In that area, metals first replaced stone for making tools and weapons, and hunting and foraging gave way to the cultivation of rice in wet fields. Farming made people stop roaming and settle down in communities—little "kingdoms"—which promptly started to fight each other. As the strong conquered the weak, a few powerful fiefdoms emerged. For a long time, northern Kyushu was the most advanced area of Japan. It is where Japan began.

L egends tell us that the group of clans that produced the imperial family originated in Kyushu and fought their way eastward along the Inland Sea to the inviting plain where eventually rose the cities of Nara, Osaka, and Kyoto. In an area called Yamato, they dug in and asserted their right to rule all Japan.

The early history of Japan is still shrouded in mist that archaeologists and historians are patiently working to disperse, but we know that the Yamato group was not unchallenged. There were other centers of power. Had those others combined, Japan would have had a different imperial dynasty, but they did not combine. Separately, they gave way, some to force of arms, some to persuasion and concession.

What remains for all to see are two great Shinto shrines, which symbolize forces once surely locked in conflict. The Ise Shrine on the Pacific coast is the shrine of the imperial family; one complex of the shrine is dedicated to the family's legendary ancestress, the Sun Goddess, and is the shrine of the victors. The Izumo Shrine on the Sea of Japan, the opposite side of Honshu, is dedicated to the legendary adversary of the Sun Goddess, her unruly brother; it is usually considered the shrine of a people who yielded politically but held on to their gods and their identity. Both shrines are magnificent, but they are different. Ise celebrates light, while Izumo embodies brooding power. Ise and Izumo are high on my list of important places.

The northern Kyushu ports not only teemed with trade and immigration but also were the ports of embarkation for Japanese armies that were sent to the Korean peninsula in an attempt to maintain a foothold there in the age when Korea, like Japan, was divided among small states warring each other.

After a couple of centuries of struggle, that Japanese effort ended in decisive failure. In 663, a sizable Japanese fleet and army were all but annihilated by the combined forces of Tang China and the dominant Korean kingdom.

The Japanese were understandably fearful that they in turn would be invaded by the victors. With the help of Korean engineers who had fled to Japan, they built impressive fortifications and prepared to repel an attack. But, as it turned out, the Chinese had no interest in invading Japan. Instead, they moved to establish friendly relations and commerce. Imperial China labeled imports from other countries as "tribute," but, whatever it was called, it and the "gifts" the Chinese returned in exchange constituted profitable trade, and the trade flourished.

Faced with the necessity to receive foreign delegations with no less ceremony than the Chinese did, the Japanese scrapped their hastily built military headquarters and on the same site built a grand complex of pillared halls, resplendently red and gold under heavy tile roofs. These housed a major arm of the government, which for centuries was in the forefront of diplomatic and trade relations. This was Dazaifu, Japan's "distant capital." Here, foreign embassies were received and entertained, and Japanese missions to the continent were sent off.

This was a time of enormous energy in Japan. As it steadily moved toward becoming a centralized nation, Japan's rulers sought the skills in government and law that the Chinese had mastered, and along with them all of the arts and learning that would give at least the capital and its nobility a culture that in its own way would rival China's. There was a continuing flow of Japanese officials, scholars, and priests dispatched to learn in China and bring home its knowledge.

The art of writing had been imported, bringing at once the boon of literacy and a heavy burden of difficulty. It was bad luck that the only system of writing the Japanese were exposed to was Chinese, with its infinitely complex system of characters—wholly unsuited to the Japanese language, which is very different from Chinese. But there it was, and for centuries Chinese was the language of learned men in Japan, as Latin was in Europe.

Buddhism had already entered Japan. Coming from India by way of China and Korea, it reached Japan in the 6th century, bringing its vast heritage of architecture, sculpture, painting, metalworking, music, and dance, together with new concepts of morality and man's place in the universe. To those who are puzzled when they hear that most Japanese are both Buddhist and Shintoist, I can offer my own views.

Shintoism is native to Japan. Its beliefs can be described as awe in the face of nature and reverence for the ancestral spirits of the nation, the clan, and the family. It expresses these feelings simply and directly; it has no elaborate doctrines or hierarchies that lay down dogma. Buddhism, one of the great world religions, is highly organized, profound, and complex.

The arrival of Buddhism raised no conflict with Shintoism. They complemented each other and found it easy to coexist. Mutual accommodation set in—and a slow process of fusion. Buddhist temples and Shinto shrines were built side by side. People worshiped at either or both, as they chose; they saw the two religions as two paths to the same goal. Most Japanese are indifferent to sectarian differences and cannot accept the view that any one religion monopolizes the truth.

Buddhism and Shintoism have now mingled and merged in Japanese minds for more than 13 centuries. Together they have formed a religion that is uniquely Japanese. The deities of each retain their identities and their appeal. Their services are distinct. Their architecture is different. Each has its own priests. But few laymen can define the boundaries that separate them. They are part of a whole, two aspects of a faith and credo that the Japanese carry inside themselves. These beliefs mold their lives, whether or not they ever pause at an altar or send up a prayer.

The governors and major officials of Dazaifu held positions of great responsibility, but, for most, it was a hardship post. To the nobility, any place more than 10 miles from the capital was remote, rural, and uncivilized. At distant Dazaifu, a man was certainly out of the swim of things. Sometimes the people in power sent men there to get them out of the way. Even when done politely, it was banishment.

The most notable exile was a scholar, poet, and official named Michizane. He had the misfortune to become the favorite of the reigning emperor, who raised him to one of the highest positions in the government. When that emperor retired, Michizane was at the mercy of the jealous ruling clique, which quickly concocted false charges of treason and bundled him off like a criminal to Dazaifu. After two years of privation, illness, and melancholy, he died there in 902.

Beyond question, there were some guilty consciences in Kyoto; Moreover, it was a very superstitious age with a powerful belief in vengeful spirits. It seemed clear that Michizane's vengeful spirit had gone to work; with alarming rapidity, death struck down his chief enemy and his progeny. There was a calamitous drought, broken by a violent storm during which lightning struck the imperial palace, killing another conspirator. There were ill omens and prophetic revelations. After each shocking event, greater posthumous honors were heaped on Michizane. In a last, desperate move, the court made him a deity. They could do no more.

Thus was Michizane transformed from the terrible to the benevolent, to one of the heavenly deities of the Shinto pantheon. He became Tenjin, the guiding spirit of scholarship and literature. It behooves any young person who aspires to an education in the best schools to seek his blessing; every year, millions come to his thousands of shrines, along with their concerned relatives and friends. Throngs are drawn to the celebrated shrine that rises above his grave at Dazaifu. Among the deities, Tenjin is one of Japan's great success stories.

Waves of influence from the continent swelled and ebbed. The government weakened, and rebellion flared: A member of the nobility dispatched by the court to quell piracy in the Inland Sea sized up the situation and joined the pirates as their leader. In 941, he pillaged Dazaifu for its treasure gained in trade and left it in flames. It was reconstructed on the same noble scale; the foundation stones one sees today date from the reconstruction, while, a couple of feet down, the older stones lie buried, along with a layer of burned and blackened earth.

Rebuilt Dazaifu was the command post when Kublai Khan mounted his invasions of Japan in 1274 and 1281. After conquering Korea and most of China, he twice sent huge armies of Chinese and Koreans across the strait. In bitter fighting, the Japanese repulsed them, both times helped by storms that devastated the invasion fleets. The Japanese thanked their gods for those divine winds—called *kamikaze*—but the defense effort sapped the strength of the shogunate, the military government based in Kamakura, and the country began a slide into civil war. Rivals for power fought for control of Kyushu, and Dazaifu's authority disintegrated. There was no place for the outpost of a government that could not govern. The site is now a quiet place, a grassy field where the foundation stones of ancient buildings testify to their grandeur. But during the centuries that those buildings stood, Dazaifu played a major role in the history of Japan.

It used to take a Dazaifu official about two weeks of hard travel to go home to the capital, Nara, or, later, Kyoto. Nowadays it's a fast trip by air or bullet train, but a pleasant alternative is to cruise the busy waterway through the Inland Sea.

Your ferry will thread its way through three clumps of islands, mostly sleepy now but once the bases of sailors who lived largely by extorting fees to navigate the narrow channels. This was more profitable than fishing, because almost all cargo moved by water; there were no roads or vehicles able to handle freight, including the vital transport of rice. And when the authority of the central government weakened, as it did in the 10th century, the islanders turned to piracy, and travel on the Inland Sea became perilous.

Later, these men of the Inland Sea joined the seafarers of northern Kyushu to raid the coasts of Korea and China. From the 13th to the 17th centuries, they were the terrors of the China Sea. On the other hand, they were not always pirates. They were legitimate traders when trade was permitted; piracy was their mode when unsocial Chinese and Korean governments restricted trade or banned it altogether. Nor were they exclusively Japanese: Chinese and Korean freebooters joined and sometimes outnumbered the Japanese 10 to 1; their knowledge of their own shores helped them strike deep and with impunity.

In time they were joined by Southeast Asians and some newcomers, the Portuguese. In the late 15th century, the Portuguese found their way to Asia by navigating around Africa. They were after the spices of the East, spices that were vital in an age that lacked refrigeration. They soon made themselves quite at home in the South China Sea, but it took them until 1543 to reach Japan, where they introduced the gun and Christianity.

The gun revolutionized warfare in Japan and hastened the reunification of the country. At this point a strong new shogunate imposed peace and decreed isolation: From the early 17th to the mid-19th century, Japan was sealed off from the Western world, save for a handful of Dutch merchants who were tolerated at Nagasaki. Those two centuries saw the Japanese turn their backs on the gun—it was not a gentleman's weapon. (Not keeping up with the technology of slaughter cost Japan years of tribulation when, in the 1850s, Westerners came battering at the gates.)

The other import, Christianity, flourished during the same decades that the gun dominated, but, once civil strife ended, the new strongmen banned it: it was clearly subversive to the established order.

Moving eastward through the Inland Sea, Shikoku lies on the right. Shikoku is the island I feel most at home on, for I have walked its perimeter following the thousand-mile trail of its ancient Buddhist pilgrimage. For centuries pilgrims have sought the physical, mental, and spiritual benefits that pilgrimage brings. Through farmlands and villages and cities, along the sea and deep in the mountains, they have traced the paths that tradition says were walked by Kobo Daishi, a beloved saint.

Kobo Daishi was born on Shikoku. He lived from 774 to 835 and was one of those who went to China; the doctrine he brought back transformed Japanese Buddhism. Kobo Daishi became one of Japan's greatest scholars, a fine artist, a distinguished poet, a great calligrapher, a pioneer educator, a social worker, a religious philosopher, and, among other things, a first-rate civil engineer. In 816, he founded the great monastery called Koyasan (Mt. Koya) in the mountains of the Kii peninsula, across the channel east of Shikoku. Koyasan is a place I feel deeply about. I return whenever I can, and I usually try to insert at least an overnight stay into the itinerary of any traveler who consults me.

There are reasons less esoteric than a pilgrimage for visiting Shikoku. Takamatsu has the beauties of Ritsurin Park, once the villa of a feudal lord. Near that city is the mountaintop shrine of seafarers, Kotohira, and near that is the temple—numbered 75 among the 88 temples of the pilgrimage—that marks the birthplace of Kobo Daishi. In Matsuyama is Dogo hot spring, celebrated since ancient times. The midsummer bash called Awa Odori brings the citizens of Tokushima into the streets for antic dances. And I happen to think that Kochi Prefecture, which stretches along Shikoku's Pacific coast and nurtures great independence of spirit among its people, provides some of the best food in Japan.

Moving through one group of islands, you will pass beneath an island-hopping bridge that for the first time links Shikoku and the main island of Honshu. Eventually two more will be built, bridges that Shikoku's people hope will speed their island's commercial development, which has lagged.

One can only hope that they manage development well. The Japanese have followed the course of every other industrialized country, fouling many of their streams and savaging great areas of their land. To their credit, they have shown the will to clean up some messes. A few years ago, the air of cities like Tokyo, Osaka, and Kobe was chokingly polluted; today, it is remarkably clean. But the absence of zoning has caused havoc all over the country. I would hate to count the places I once thought idyllic but which are now unlivable.

If the ferry docks at Kobe, I will head for one of the city's fine restaurants. Today's city, pleasantly situated on a narrow strand between the mountains and the sea, came into existence around 1868 as the result of foreign pressure to open a port, and during all its short life it has been an international city. Its restaurants reflect that, offering just about every fare a person might yearn for. And if you don't mind hills, almost everyplace is within walking distance of the city's heart, Sannomiya.

But if we dock at Osaka—second only to Tokyo as a center of commerce and industry—I will hurry to that virile city's lively entertainment district, Dotonbori. I can amuse myself for hours wandering its streets and alleys through a kaleidoscope of theaters, bars, coffeehouses, restaurants, and other temptations. If I am lucky, the Bunraku puppet troupe will be at home in its handsome National Theater, and I will delight in one of Japan's great theatrical arts.

Osaka grew as the port for the old capitals of Nara and Kyoto, but today it dwarfs them. Nara and Kyoto, both rich in history, are cities of temples and shrines. Kyoto also offers shopping streets that are fun to stroll along even if you don't have the money to buy, some fine inns and, like Osaka, good Japanese food in the style of that part of the country— sweeter and, to me, less appealing than the food of Tokyo.

Kyoto was the seat of government for more than six centuries (there was a break from 1185 to 1333, when the shogunate at Kamakura called the tune), but in 1600, power resumed its eastward march: Ieyasu, the first shogun of the Tokugawa line, carried it up the Tokaido Road to his castle at Edo (now Tokyo).

Thereafter, the Tokaido was Japan's Main Street. Even those in the provinces who never had a chance to set foot on it knew its route and its 53 stations from stories of ribald adventure and the woodblock prints of artists like Hiroshige. History's pageant traveled that road: peddlers, priests, poets, and pilgrims; businesslike officials and merchants on business; schemers and dreamers; each spring's first crop of new tea for the shogun; the Dutch on their journeys from Nagasaki to carry exotic European gifts to the shogun (part of the taxes they paid for the privilege of conducting trade); the daimyo (feudal lords) moving to and from attendance at the shogun's court.

The daimyo provided the best show. A great lord's strutting entourage might stretch for miles (but his lackeys strutted only in the towns; where nobody important was watching, they went slack). For the sake of the daimyo, the Tokaido was ingeniously designed. If a lesser daimyo met a greater, the de rigueur deference would be ego-bruising, and so, at each station, a lane led to a spot that furnished an excuse to get off the highway—a temple or a shrine, a scenic view, or a stone commemorating a bit of history. There the inferior would tarry until his superior had passed and the road was clear.

When the daimyo ceased to make their journeys and the shogunate was at last toppled, the men who wrested power in the name of the emperor bowed to reality. Rather than try to take the government to the emperor's city, they brought the emperor to the shogun's city and, in 1868, installed him in what had been the shogun's castle. They salved their feelings by renaming the place Tokyo, the Eastern Capital.

Today, almost nothing remains of the old Tokaido, but along the alternate road, the Nakasendo, which wound through the mountains while the Tokaido bordered the sea, is a stretch that has scarcely changed. There, two stations, Tsumago and Magome, were bypassed when a railroad was built; modernization passed them by. They remained just as they had been and for decades were nearly destitute; now their heritage is a powerful attraction. One can walk a few miles of the old road, rest under the deep eaves of weather-worn shops, and stay at inns that have been lovingly preserved for two centuries.

The Tokaido is still Main Street. Along its relatively short span of about 300 miles (one-sixth of the distance from one end of Japan to the other, not including Okinawa) are all of the nation's great cities (Tokyo, Yokohama, Nagoya, Kyoto, Osaka), 40% of its population, and 70% of its industry.

Politically, economically, socially, everything heads up in Tokyo. There is much talk of decentralization and of invigorating the provincial cities, but decentralization seems mostly to end with extending Tokyo's sprawl by pushing some government installations to satellite cities.

Today, Tokyo is more than ever the heart of things; it's the site of government, the financial center, the preeminent headquarters for business, the magnet for intellectuals, the focus of the arts. It is Washington, New York, and Boston rolled into one. It pulses with energy and runs on split-second schedules, yet turn a corner and you find a neighborhood where housewives trade gossip as they shop for the day's groceries in mom-and-pop stores that spill into the street. The city has been called ugly, but I do not agree. It has grand vistas, spacious parks, inviting residential areas, and a giddy mix of architecture that ranges from the cheerfully vulgar and outrageously fantastic to the strong and innovative. It offers more to do than any resident can possibly keep up with, much less a visitor. Above all, Tokyo is exciting; it is never dull.

When people ask me, "Where can I find the *real* Japan?" they usually have in mind the idyllic: thatch-roofed farmhouses set in verdant paddy fields. My answer probably surprises them. "Tokyo," I say. "Today, Tokyo is the real Japan."

1 Essential Information

Before You Go

Government Tourist Offices

For information about traveling in Japan, contact the nearest branch of the **Japan National Tourist Organization** (JNTO):

In the U.S. 630 Fifth Ave., Suite 2101, New York, NY 10111, tel. 212/757–5640; 401 North Michigan Ave., Chicago, IL 60601, tel. 312/222–0874; 2121 San Jacinto St., Suite 980, Dallas, TX 75201, tel. 214/754–1820; 360 Post St., Suite 401, San Francisco, CA 94108, tel. 415/989–7140; 624 South Grand Ave., Suite 2640, Los Angeles, CA 90017, tel. 213/623–1952.

In Canada 165 University Ave., Toronto M5H 3B8, Ontario, tel. 416/366–7140.

In the U.K. 167 Regent St., London W1R 7FD England, tel. 071/734–9638.

JNTO provides a variety of helpful pamphlets, booklets, and publications that offer a wealth of information on travel in Japan and that answer many questions you will have before departure. Separate publications give detailed advice on transportation, dining, lodging, culture, and itineraries. These publications include *Your Guide to Japan*, *Your Traveling Companion: Japan*, and *The Tourist's Handbook*, which contains useful phrases for getting around the country. JNTO distributes pamphlets on specific cities and areas of Japan; these pamphlets include information on sights, festivals, and local crafts and cuisine. The organization also offers booklets on accommodations, which list hotels, ryokans, and youth hostels, and tourist maps of Japan and some of the major cities.

Tour Groups

With the continuing strength of the yen, no trip to Japan will be cheap. Some relief may be found with package tours, which tend to offer lower airfares and hotel rates than you can get on your own. Savvy tour operators are also shifting more of their itineraries to less-traveled areas within the country, which lowers costs and introduces travelers to sites less frequented by tourists. One warning: Stick with the established operators, as costs are squeezing some smaller companies out of the market. Listed below is a sampling of experienced operators who specialize in Japan and the Orient.

When considering a tour, be sure to find out (1) exactly which expenses are included (particularly tips, taxes, side trips, additional meals, and entertainment); (2) government ratings of all hotels on the itinerary and the facilities they offer; (3) cancellation policies for both you and for the tour operator; and (4) if you are traveling alone, what the single supplement is. Most tour operators request that bookings be made through a travel agent; there is no additional charge for doing so.

General-Interest Tours **Japan and Orient Tours** (3131 Camino del Rio North, Suite 1080, San Diego, CA 92108, tel. 619/282–3131 or 800/877–8777) has arranged tours to the Orient for 31 years. **TBI Tours** (787 7th Ave., New York, NY 10019, tel. 212/489–1919 or 800/223–0266) benefits from an affiliation with the Japan Travel Bureau, one of the oldest travel agencies in Japan. Both offer a variety of packages. The 16-day "Highlights of the Orient" tour from **Glo-**

bus-Gateway (150 S. Los Robles Ave., Suite 860, Pasadena, CA 91101, tel. 818/449–0919 or 800/556–5454) takes in Tokyo, Bejing, Bangkok, Singapore, and Hong Kong. **American Express Vacations** (Box 5014, Atlanta, GA 30302, tel. 800/241–1700 or, in Georgia, 800/282–0800) offers an 18-day "Ancient Treasures" tour, which stops in Kyoto, Hakone, and Tokyo before heading to Bejing, Xian, Kunming, and Hong Kong. Several of the tours offered by **Olson-Travelworld** (100 N. Sepulveda Blvd., Suite 1010, El Segundo, CA 90245, tel. 800/421–2255, 800/421–5785 in CA. or 213/615–0711) and **Maupintour** (Box 807, Lawrence, KA 66044, tel. 800/255–4266 or 913/843–1211) feature stops in Japan.

Special-Interest Tours

Art **Esplanade Tours** (581 Boylston St., Boston, MA 02116, tel. 617/266–7465) delves into the art and cultural treasures of Japan in a 19-day tour.

Country Inns "Ryokans of Japan" from **Abercrombie and Kent International** (1420 Kensington Road, Oak Brook, IL 60521, tel. 312/954–2944 or 800/323–7208) uses traditional Japanese inns for accommodations in several ancient cities.

Music **Dailey-Thorp Travel** (315 W. 57th St., New York, NY 10019, tel. 212/307–1555) offers deluxe opera and music tours scheduled around special appearances by native or visiting performers.

Sports **InterPacific Tours International** (111 E. 15th St., New York, NY 10003, tel. 212/953–6010) has jogging, bicycling, and increasingly popular golf tours; most team up Japan with a stay in Hong Kong and/or China. For the adventurous, **Sobek Expeditions** (Angels Camp, CA 95222, tel. 209/736–4524 or 800/426–7794) leads a trek through the Japan Alps.

Package Deals for Independent Travelers

InterPacific (*see* Special-Interest Tours, above) has a "Pacific à la Carte" program, providing four-day and six-day Japan options. **Japan Airlines** (tel. 800/JALFONE) and **American Express** (*see* General-Interest Tours, above), among others, can create custom air/land packages for independent travelers. **Japan and Orient Tours** (*see* General-Interest Tours, above) offers the budget-minded "Tokyo Travel Bargain," with accommodations for six nights, round-trip airfare, and a sightseeing tour. **Globus-Gateway** (*see* General-Interest Tours, above) has a nine-day independent package joining Tokyo with Hong Kong. **United Airlines** (tel. 800/328–6877) offers an 11-day "Seasons of Japan" tour that includes Tokyo, Kamakura, Hakone, Kashikojima, Kyoto, and Nara. The airline also serves up several air-inclusive eight-day packages, as well as hotel packages in Kyoto, Osaka, and Tokyo.

When to Go

The best seasons to travel to Japan are spring and fall, when the weather is at its best. In the spring, the country is warm, with only occasional showers. Japan is at its loveliest in this season, with flowers gracing landscapes in both rural and urban areas. The first harbingers of spring are plum blossoms in early March; cherry blossoms follow in late March and early April. Summer brings on the rainy season, with particularly heavy rains and mugginess in July. Fall is a welcome relief after the humid summer, with clear blue skies and beautiful foliage.

Occasionally a few surprise typhoons occur in early fall, but the storms are usually as quick to leave as they are to arrive. Winter is gray and chilly, with little snow in most areas. Temperatures rarely fall below freezing.

For the most part, the climate of Japan is temperate and resembles the East Coast of the United States. The exceptions are the subtropical southern islands of Okinawa, located south of Kyushu, and the northern island of Hokkaido, where it snows for several months in the winter and is pleasantly cool in the summer.

It is best not to travel at times when most Japanese are vacationing. For the most part, Japanese cannot select when they want to take their vacations; they tend to do so on the same holiday dates. As a result, airports, planes, trains, and hotels are booked far in advance and are extremely crowded. Many businesses, shops, and restaurants are closed during holidays. The first major holiday each year is a few days before and after New Year's. In the week just following Greenery Day, which falls on April 29, there is a holiday known as Golden Week. The main summer holiday is in the middle of August at the time of the Obon festivals, when it is traditionally believed that spirits of ancestors return to earth. Many Japanese return to their hometowns during this week. Travel at these times should be avoided as much as possible.

Climate What follows are the average daily maximum and minimum temperatures for major cities:

Tokyo	Jan.	46F	8C	May	72F	22C	Sept.	78F	26C
		29	-2		53	12		66	19
	Feb.	48F	9C	June	75F	24C	Oct.	70F	21C
		30	-1		62	17		56	13
	Mar.	53F	12C	July	82F	28C	Nov.	60F	16C
		35	2		70	21		42	6
	Apr.	62F	17C	Aug.	86F	30C	Dec.	51F	11C
		46	8		72	22		33	1

Kyoto	Jan.	48F	9C	May	75F	24C	Sept.	82F	28C
		35	2		56	13		68	20
	Feb.	53F	12C	June	82F	28C	Oct.	74F	23C
		32	0		66	19		53	12
	Mar.	59F	15C	July	93F	34C	Nov.	62F	17C
		40	4		72	22		46	8
	Apr.	65F	18C	Aug.	89F	32C	Dec.	53F	12C
		44	7		74	23		33	1

Fukuoka	Jan.	53F	12C	May	74F	23C	Sept.	80F	27C
		35	2		57	14		68	20
	Feb.	58F	14C	June	80F	27C	Oct.	74F	23C
		37	3		68	20		53	12
	Mar.	60F	16C	July	89F	32C	Nov.	65F	18C
		42	6		75	24		48	9
	Apr.	62F	17C	Aug.	89F	32C	Dec.	53F	12C
		48	9		75	24		37	3

Sapporo	Jan.	29F	−2C	May	60F	16C	Sept.	72F	22C
		10	−12		40	4		51	11
	Feb.	30F	−1C	June	70F	21C	Oct.	60F	16C
		13	11		50	10		40	4
	Mar.	35F	2C	July	75F	24C	Nov.	46F	8C
		20	−7		57	14		29	−2
	Apr.	51F	11C	Aug.	78F	26C	Dec.	33F	1C
		32	0		60	16		18	−8

Updated hourly weather information in more than 750 cities in the United States and around the world is only a phone call away. Dialing WeatherTrak at 900/370–8728 will connect you to a computer, with which you can communicate by touch tone—at a cost of 95¢ per minute. The number plays a taped message that tells you to dial the three-digit access code for the destination you're interested in. The code is either the area code (in the United States) or the first three letters of the foreign city. For a list of all access codes, send a stamped, self-addressed envelope to Cities, 9B Terrace Way, Greensboro, NC 27403. For more information, call 800/247–3282.

National Holidays

When a holiday falls on a Sunday, it is celebrated on the following Monday.

Jan. 1. New Year's Day is the "festival of festivals" for the Japanese. Some women dress in traditional kimonos, and many people visit shrines and hold family reunions. Although the day is observed with solemnity, streets are often decorated with pine twigs, plum branches, and bamboo stalks.

Jan. 15. Adults' Day honors those who have reached voting age—20.

Feb. 11. National Foundation Day celebrates accession to the throne by the first emperor.

Mar. 21 (or 20). Vernal Equinox Day celebrates the start of spring.

Apr. 29. Greenery Day. The first day of **Golden Week,** when many people are taking vacation and hotels, trains and attractions are crowded. Not a good week to visit Japan.

May 3. Constitution Memorial Day. This anniversary recalls the enforcement of the Japanese constitution.

May 5. Children's Day. Families with little boys display paper or cloth carp on bamboo poles outside the house or a set of warrior dolls inside the home.

Aug. 13–16. The Bon Festival, a time of Buddhist ceremonies in honor of ancestors. Many Japanese take off the entire week to travel to their home towns. Tourists should avoid this time.

Sept. 15. Respect for the Aged Day.

Sept. 23 (or 24). Autumnal Equinox Day.

Oct. 10. Health-Sports Day commemorates the Tokyo Olympics of 1964.

Nov. 3. Culture Day is expected to encourage the Japanese to cherish peace, freedom, and culture, both old and new.

Nov. 23. Labor Thanksgiving Day is recognized by harvest celebrations in some parts of the country.

Dec. 23. The Emperor's Birthday.

Dec. 27. Osho-Gatsu, the first day of the week long New Year celebrations. Travel not recommended.

Festivals and Seasonal Events

Festivals and seasonal events are very important to the Japanese, and a large number are held throughout the year all over the country. Many of these festivals originated in folk and religious rituals and date back hundreds of years. Gala festivals take place annually at Buddhist temples and Shinto shrines. Because festivals offer a unique glimpse into Japanese culture and traditions, you are advised to consider dates and places for festivals when you are planning your trip. Contact the nearest branch of the Japan National Tourist Organization (see Government Tourist Offices, above) for further information about festivals in Japan.

What to Pack

Pack light, because porters can be hard to find and baggage restrictions are tight on international flights. What you pack depends more on the time of year than on any particular dress code. For travel in the cities, pack as you would for an American or European city. At more expensive restaurants and nightclubs, men will usually need to wear a jacket and tie, and women will need a dress or skirt. Conservative-colored clothing is recommended for both men and women to wear at business meetings. Casual clothes are fine for sightseeing. Jeans are as popular in Japan as in the United States and are perfectly acceptable for informal dining and sightseeing. Although there are no strict dress codes for visiting temples and shrines, you will be out of place in shorts or immodest outfits. For sightseeing, leave sandals and open-toe shoes behind; you'll need sturdy walking shoes for the gravel pathways that surround the temples and fill the parks. Make sure to bring comfortable clothing that isn't too tight to wear in traditional Japanese restaurants, where you may need to sit on tatami-matted floors.

For beach and mountain resorts, pack informal clothes for both day and evening wear. Although sunglasses, sunscreen lotions, and hats are readily available, you're better off buying them at home, because they're much more expensive in Japan.

Japanese do not wear shoes in private homes or in many of the temples and traditional inns. Having shoes you can quickly slip in and out of is a decided advantage. For winter visits, take some wool socks along to help you through those shoeless occasions.

If you're a morning coffee addict, take along packets of instant coffee. Hotels often provide a thermos of hot water and bags of green tea in every room, but coffee is expensive and hard to find, especially in rural areas. You won't need an electrical adapter. The current in Japan is 100 volts and 50 cycles. American hair dryers, shavers, and other small appliances work on this system, although they run a bit slower, but you will need a plug adapter.

Tipping is not the custom in Japan. You may like to take along small gift items, such as scarves or perfume sachets, to reward someone who has been attentive to you.

Taking Money Abroad

Traveler's checks and major U.S. credit cards—particularly Visa—are accepted in larger cities and resorts. In smaller towns and rural areas, you'll need cash. Small restaurants and shops in the cities also tend to operate on a cash basis. Most U.S. banks will change your money into yen. If your local bank can't provide this service, you can exchange money through Thomas Cook Currency Services. To find the office nearest you, contact them at 29 Broadway, New York, NY 10006 (tel. 212/757–6915). It is not necessary, however, to change money before you leave. Rates are considerably better at the exchange booths at Japanese airports than they are in the United States.

For safety and convenience, it's always best to take traveler's checks. You also receive a slightly better exchange rate for traveler's checks than you do for cash. The most recognized traveler's checks are American Express, Barclay's, Thomas Cook, and those issued through major commercial banks such as Citibank and Bank of America. Some banks will issue the checks free to established customers, but most charge a 1% commission fee. Buy part of the traveler's checks in small denominations to cash toward the end of your trip. This will save your having to cash a large check and ending up with more foreign money than you need. You can also buy traveler's checks in yen, a good idea if the dollar is falling and you want to lock in the current rate. Remember to take the addresses of offices where you can get refunds for lost or stolen traveler's checks.

Getting Money from Home

There are at least three ways to get money from home:

1) Have it sent through a large commercial bank with a branch in the city or town where you're staying. The only drawback is that you must have an account with the bank; if not, you'll have to go through your own bank, and the process will be slower and more expensive.

2) Have it sent through American Express. If you are a cardholder, you can cash a personal check or a counter check at an American Express office for up to $1,000 (2,500 for gold cardholders) in cash or traveler's checks. There is a 1% commission on the traveler's checks. You can also get money through American Express MoneyGram and you don't have to be a cardholder. Through this service, you can receive up to $10,000 cash. It works this way: You call home and ask someone to go to an American Express office or an American Express MoneyGram agent located in a retail outlet and fill out an American Express MoneyGram. It can be paid for with cash, MasterCard, Visa, or the Optima card. The person making the payment is given a reference number and telephones you with that number. The American Express MoneyGram agent calls an 800 number and authorizes the transfer of funds to an American Express office or a participating agency in the town where you're staying. In most cases, the money is available in 15 minutes on a 24-hour basis. You pick it up by showing identification and giving the reference number. Fees vary according to the amount of money sent. For sending $300, the fee is $30; for $5,000, $195. For the American Express MoneyGram location nearest your home, and to find out where the service is available overseas, call 800/

543–4080. You do not have to be a cardholder to use this service.

3) Have it sent through Western Union (tel. 800/325–6000). If you have a MasterCard or Visa, you can have money sent for any amount up to your credit limit. If not, have someone take cash or a certified cashier's check to a Western Union office. The money will be delivered in two business days to a bank in the city where you're staying. Fees vary with the amount of money sent and where it is being sent. For $1,000, the fee is $69; for $500, $59. Add $10 if you use credit cards.

Currency

The unit of currency in Japan is the yen (¥). There are bills of ¥10,000, ¥5,000, and ¥1,000. Coins are ¥500, ¥100, ¥50, ¥10, ¥5, and ¥1. Japanese currency floats without a fixed official exchange rate. At press time, the exchange rate was about ¥137 to the U.S. dollar, ¥127 to the Canadian dollar, and ¥277 to the pound sterling.

What It Will Cost

By now you have heard many horror stories about exorbitant prices in Japan. The dollar has dropped more than 50% in value against the yen since 1986. With the continuing strength of the yen, imported goods, in particular, are shockingly expensive. One American freelance writer, upon arriving in Tokyo, said, "I feel as though I am from a Third World country. I can't afford anything. Everything seems so expensive and inaccessible." This is, of course, an exaggeration, and while a melon can easily cost the equivalent of U.S. $100, remember that this is because melons are imported luxury goods or specially cultivated on the island of Kochi.

It is undeniable that Japan is expensive, but there are ways to cut corners. This requires, to some extent, an adventurous spirit and the courage to stray from the standard tourist paths. Avoid taxis (they tend to get stuck in traffic anyway), and try the inexpensive and incredibly efficient subway and bus systems; instead of going to a restaurant with menus in English and Western-style foods, go to places where you can rely on your good old index finger to point at the dish you want and try food that the Japanese eat.

There is an across-the-board, nonrefundable 3% consumer tax levied on all sales. Since the tax was introduced in April 1989, vendors have either been absorbing the tax in their quoted retail prices or adding it on to the sale. Always inquire which is the case if you are planning a major purchase.

The following are some sample prices:

a cup of coffee: ¥350–¥600; a bottle of beer: ¥350–¥1,000; a 2-km taxi ride: ¥470; a McDonald's hamburger: ¥180; a bowl of noodles: ¥500; a double room in Tokyo—Very Expensive: over ¥21,000; Expensive: ¥16,000–¥21,000; Moderate: ¥10,000–¥16,000; Inexpensive: under ¥10,000.

Passports and Visas

American All U.S. citizens require a passport to enter Japan. Applications for a new passport must be made in person; renewals can be obtained in person or by mail (*see* below). First-time applicants should apply well in advance of their departure date to one of the 13 U.S. Passport Agency offices. In addition, local county courthouses, many state and probate courts, and some post offices accept passport applications. Necessary documents include: (1) a completed passport application (Form DSP-11); (2) proof of citizenship (birth certificate with raised seal or naturalization papers); (3) proof of identity (unexpired driver's license, employee ID card, or any other document with your photograph and signature); (4) two recent, identical, two-inch-square photographs (black-and-white or color); (5) $42 application fee for a 10-year passport (those under 18 pay $27 for a 5-year passport). If you pay in cash, you must have the right amount. No change is given. Passports are mailed to you in about 10 working days.

To renew your passport by mail, you'll need completed Form DSP-82, two recent, identical passport photographs, a recent passport less than 12 years old, and a check or money order for $35.

U.S. leisure and business travelers do not need a visa for a visit to Japan of 90 days or less. Visas are necessary for those U.S. citizens who plan to work or study in Japan. Contact the nearest Consulate General of Japan for details:

Atlanta: 100 Colony Square Bldg., 1175 Peachtree St., Suite 2000, Atlanta, GA 30361, tel. 404/892-2700; **Boston:** Federal Reserve Plaza, 600 Atlantic Ave., 14th Fl., Boston, MA 02210, tel. 617/973-9772; **Chicago:** 737 N. Michigan Ave., Chicago, IL 60611, tel. 312/280-0400; **Honolulu:** 1742 Nuuanu Ave., Honolulu, HI 96817, tel. 808/536-2226; **Houston:** 1000 Louisiana, First Interstate Bank Plaza, Suite 5300, Houston, TX 77002, tel. 713/652-2977; **Kansas City:** 2519 Commerce Tower, 911 Main St., Kansas City, MO 64105, tel. 816/471-0111; **Los Angeles:** 250 E. 1st St., Suite 1507, Los Angeles, CA 90012, tel. 213/624-8305; **New Orleans:** 639 Loyola Ave., Suite 2050, New Orleans, LA 70113, tel. 504/529-2101; **New York:** 299 Park Ave., 16th fl., New York, NY 10171, tel. 212/888-0889; **Portland:** 2400 First Interstate Tower, 1300 S.W. 5th Ave., Portland, OR 97201, tel. 503/221-1811; **San Francisco:** 50 Fremont St., 23rd fl., San Francisco, CA 94105, tel. 415/777-3533; **Seattle:** 1301 5th Ave., Seattle, WA 98101, tel. 206/682-9107; **Washington, DC:** Embassy of Japan, 2520 Massachusetts Ave., NW, Washington, DC 20008, tel. 202/939-6700.

Canadian All Canadians require a passport to enter Japan. Send completed application (available at any post office or passport office) to the Bureau of Passports, Suite 215, West Tower, Guy Lévesque Blvd. W, Montreal, Quebec H2Z 1X4. Include $25, two photographs, a guarantor, and proof of Canadian citizenship. Applications can be made in person at the regional passport offices in many locations, including Edmonton, Halifax, Montreal, Toronto, Vancouver, or Winnipeg. Passports are valid for five years and are nonrenewable.

Canadian nationals are exempted from visa requirements for stays up to three months.

Customs and Duties

On Arrival　Japan is strict about bringing firearms, pornography, and narcotics other than alcohol into the country. Anyone caught with drugs is liable to detention, deportation, and refusal of reentry into Japan. Certain fresh fruits, vegetables, plants, and animals are also illegal. Nonresidents are allowed to bring in duty-free: (1) 400 cigarettes or 100 cigars or 500 grams of tobacco; (2) 3 bottles of alcohol; (3) 2 ounces of perfume; (4) other goods up to ¥200,000 value.

On Departure　If you are bringing any foreign-made equipment from home, such as cameras, it is wise to carry the original receipt with you or register it with U.S. Customs before you leave (Form 4457). Otherwise you may end up paying duty on your return.

U.S. residents may bring home duty-free up to $400 worth of foreign goods, so long as they have been out of the country for at least 48 hours and have not made an international trip in 30 days. Each member of the family is entitled to the same exemption, regardless of age, and exemptions can be pooled. For the next $1,000 worth of goods, a flat 10% rate is assessed; above $1,400, duties vary with the merchandise. Included for travelers 21 or older are one liter of alcohol, 100 cigars (non-Cuban), and 200 cigarettes. Only one bottle of perfume trademarked in the United States may be imported. However, there is no duty on antiques or art more than 100 years old. Anything exceeding these limits will be taxed at the port of entry and may be taxed additionally in the traveler's home state. Gifts valued at under $50 may be mailed to friends or relatives at home duty-free, but must not exceed one package per day to any one addressee and must not include perfumes costing more than $5, tobacco, or liquor.

Canadian residents have an exemption ranging from $20 to $300, depending on the length of stay out of the country. For the $300 exemption, you must have been out of the country for one week. For any given year, you are allowed one $300 exemption. You may also bring in duty-free: (1) up to 50 cigars, 200 cigarettes, or 2.2 pounds of tobacco; and (2) 40 ounces of liquor, provided these are declared in writing to customs on arrival and accompany the traveler in hand or checked-through baggage. Personal gifts should be mailed as "Unsolicited Gift— Value under $40." Request the Canadian Customs brochure, *I Declare*, for further details.

Tips for British Travelers

Passports and Visas　You will need a valid 10-year passport (cost: £15). Visas are not required. Vaccinations against typhoid are recommended.

Customs　**On Arrival.** See previous section.

On Departure. Returning to Britain, you may bring home: (1) 200 cigarettes or 100 cigarillos or 50 cigars or 250 grams of tobacco; (2) 2 liters of table wine with additional allowances for (a) 1 liter of alcohol over 22% by volume or 38.8 proof (most spirits) or (b) 2 liters of alcohol under 22% by volume (fortified or sparkling wine) or (c) two more liters of table wine; (3) 60 milliliters of perfume and 250 milliliters of toilet water; and (4) other goods up to a value of £32, but not more than 50 liters of beer or 25 lighters.

Insurance We recommend that you insure yourself against sickness and motoring mishaps with **Europ Assistance** (252 High St., Croydon, Surrey CRO 1NF, tel. 081/680–1234). It is also wise to take out insurance to cover loss of luggage (though check that this isn't already covered through your existing home-owner policy. Trip-cancellation insurance is another wise buy. The **Association of British Insurers** (Aldermary House, 10–15 Queen St., London EC4N 1TT, tel. 071/248–4477) will give comprehensive advice on all aspects of vacation insurance.

Tour Operators Among the many companies offering packages to Japan and the Orient are the following:

Japan Travel Bureau (10 Maltravers St., London WC2R 3EX, tel. 071/836–9367) runs several packages to Japan. For the adventurous, the "Freedom of Japan" package is ideal, with a Rail Pass, hotel vouchers offering a choice of over 100 hotels throughout Japan, and a "go-as-you-please" itinerary. A 12-day "Imperial Japan" tour shows you three distinct areas of Japan: the Pacific side, including Tokyo, Kyoto, Mt. Fuji, and other sights; the scenic Japan Sea coast in the north; and secluded castle towns in the Japan Alps.

Kuoni Travel Ltd. (Kuoni House, Dorking, Surrey RH5 4AZ, tel. 0306/740888) offers a 15-day escorted "Japan and the Orient" tour, with three nights in Tokyo spent visiting the Imperial Palace, the Toshugu Shrine, and Nikko National Park, among other sights. Travel by bullet train to Kyoto for three nights, and visit the Nijo Castle, the Imperial Palace, and the village of Nara. Then on to Osaka and Bangkok. Kuoni also operates a 16-day tour of Japan and the Orient, beginning in Tokyo and taking in Kyoto, Bali, and Singapore.

Speedbird Holidays (Pacific House, Hazelwick Ave., Three Bridges, Crawley, W. Sussex RH10 1NP, tel. 0293/611611) offers an 18-day "Japan Contrasts" tour featuring the sights in and around Tokyo and Kyoto, with four nights in Hong Kong and four nights in Bangkok. Stays in Bali and Singapore are other options.

Stopovers (Atlantic House, Hazelwick Ave., Three Bridges, Crawley, W. Sussex RH10 1NP, tel. 0533/461000), a division of British Airways Leisure Traveller, offers hotel packages in Tokyo, Osaka, and Kyoto, with optional sightseeing tours of these cities and the surrounding areas.

Traveling with Film

If your camera is new, shoot and develop a few rolls of film before leaving home. Pack some lens tissue and an extra battery for your built-in light meter. Invest about $10 in a skylight filter and screw it onto the front of your lens. It will protect the lens and also reduce haze.

Film doesn't like hot weather. If you're driving in summer, don't store film in the glove compartment or on the shelf under the rear window. Put it behind the front seat on the floor, on the side opposite the exhaust pipe.

On a plane trip, never pack unprocessed film in check-in luggage; if your bags get X-rayed, say good-bye to your pictures. Always carry undeveloped film with you through security, and ask to have it inspected by hand. (It helps to isolate your film in a plastic bag, ready for quick inspection.) Inspectors at American airports are required by law to honor requests for hand inspection; Japanese airport security also will hand inspect cameras and film.

The old airport scanning machines—still in use in some countries—use heavy doses of radiation that can turn a family portrait into an early-morning fog. The newer models—used in all U.S. airports—are safe for many more scans, depending on the speed of your film. But the effects are cumulative; you can put the same roll of film through several scans without worry. After five scans, though, you're asking for trouble.

If your film gets fogged and you want an explanation, send it to the **National Association of Photographic Manufacturers** (550 Mamaroneck Ave., Harrison, NY 10528). They will try to determine what went wrong. The service is free.

Staying Healthy

No serious health risks are associated with travel through Japan. If you have a health problem that might require purchasing prescription drugs while in Japan, have your doctor write a prescription using the drug's generic name. If you plan to spend a lot of time in the rural areas, have the prescription translated into Japanese before you go. Finding a pharmacy that will fill an English-language prescription is not a problem in the cities but could be difficult in the rural areas.

The International Association for Medical Assistance to Travelers (IAMAT) is a worldwide association offering a list of approved English-speaking physicians and clinics whose training meets British and American standards. In Japan, IAMAT has member hospitals or clinics in Tokyo, Yokohoma, Osaka, Kyoto, Kobe, Hiroshima, and Okinawa. For more information, write IAMAT, 417 Center St., Lewiston, NY 14092, tel. 716/754–4883. In Canada: 40 Regal Rd., Guelph, Ontario N1K1B5. In Europe: 57 Voirets, 1212 Grand-Lancy, Geneva, Switzerland. Membership is free.

Shots and Medications. Inoculations are not necessary unless you are entering Japan from an infected country. For information on these countries and the necessary inoculations, call the Japanese Consulate nearest you or the visa section of the Japanese Embassy in Washington, DC (tel. 202/939–6800).

Insurance

Travelers may seek insurance coverage in three areas: health and accident, lost luggage, and trip cancellation. Your first step is to review your existing health and home-owner policies. Some health insurance plans cover health expenses incurred while traveling, some home-owner policies cover luggage theft, and some major medical plans cover emergency transportation.

Health and Accident Several companies offer coverage designed to supplement existing health insurance for travelers:

Carefree Travel Insurance (Box 310, 120 Mineola Blvd., Mineola, NY 11501, tel. 516/294–0220 or 800/323–3149) provides coverage for emergency medical evacuation and accidental death and dismemberment. It also offers 24-hour medical advice by phone.

International SOS Assistance (Box 11568, Philadelphia, PA 19116, tel. 215/244–1500 or 800/523–8930), a medical assistance company, provides emergency evacuation services, worldwide medical referrals, and optional medical insurance.

Travel Guard International, underwritten by Transamerica Occidental Life Companies (1145 Clark St., Stevens Point, WI 54481, tel. 715/345–0505 or 800/782–5151), offers reimbursement for medical expenses with no deductibles or daily limits, and emergency evacuation services.

Wallach and Company, Inc. (243 Church St., NW, Suite 100D, Vienna, VA 22180, tel. 703/281–9500 or 800/237–6615) offers comprehensive medical coverage, including emergency evacuation services worldwide.

Flight Insurance Flight insurance is often included in the price of a ticket when paid for with American Express, Visa, and other major credit and charge cards. It is usually included in combination travel-insurance packages available from most tour operators, travel agents, and insurance agents.

(For information on insurance for lost luggage, *see* Getting to Japan, below).

Renting and Hiring Cars

Driving in the built up areas of Japan or along the Tokyo-Kyoto-Hiroshima corridor is not advisable. Trains and subways will get you to your destinations faster and more comfortably. The roads are congested, highway tolls are exorbitant, and gas is expensive. In major cities, parking is a nightmare.

Even though public transport is far more efficient and comprehensive in Japan than in America, to explore the rural parts of Japan, more and more foreign visitors are discovering that a car can be the best way. On major roads, there are sufficient markers in the Roman alphabet for directions, and on country roads there is usually someone to ask for help. However, it's a good idea to have a detailed map with towns written in Ganji and the Roman alphabet. As in the United Kingdom, driving in Japan is on the left side.

Those who do wish to rent a car require an international or a Japanese license. Both Avis and Hertz have offices in Tokyo. (It is also possible to reserve the car from overseas.) The **Avis-Nissan** office is located at 1-5-7 Azabudai, Minato-ku (tel. 03/587–4000). The **Hertz-Nippon** office is in the Jinnan Building, 4-3 Udagawacho, Shibuya-ku (tel. 03/469–0919). In general it costs ¥8,000–¥9,000 per day to rent a car.

In most cities it is possible to make arrangements for a hired car and guide. Cars with drivers cost around ¥8,500 per hour. The cost of an English-speaking guide is approximately ¥20,000–¥30,000 a day, plus expenses. Arrangements can be made through major hotels, or by calling the **Japan Guide Association** (tel. 03/213–2706) for a list of guides. Prices are negotiated directly with the guides.

Japan Rail Pass

The Japan Rail Pass is an exceptionally good value for tourists who are planning to do extensive train traveling while in Japan.

Holders of the pass may travel on any Japan Railways train or bus for unlimited miles during one, two, or three weeks. The passes must be purchased before departure for Japan. (For more information, *see* Getting Around Japan by Train, below).

Student and Youth Travel

The **International Student Identity Card** entitles students to youth rail passes, special fares on local transportation, and discounts at museums, theaters, sports events, and many other attractions. If purchased in the United States, the $14 cost of the ISIC also includes $3,000 in emergency medical insurance, plus $100 a day for up to 60 days of hospital coverage, and a phone number to call collect in case of emergencies. Apply to the **Council on International Educational Exchange** (CIEE; 205 E. 42nd St., New York, NY 10017, tel. 212/661–1414). In Canada, the ISIC is available from **Travel Cuts** (187 College St., Toronto, Ont. M5T 1P7, tel. 416/979–2406).

The **Youth International Educational Exchange Card** (YIEE), issued by the Federation of International Youth Travel Organizations (FIYTO; 81 Islands Brugge, DK-2300 Copenhagen S, Denmark), provides similar services to nonstudents under the age of 26. In the United States, the card is available from CIEE (address above). In Canada, the YIEE is available from the **Canadian Hostelling Association** (CHA, 1600 James Naismith Dr., Suite 608, Gloucester, Ont. K1B 5N4, tel. 613/748–5638).

An **International Youth Hostel Federation** (IYHF) membership card is the key to inexpensive dormitory-style accommodations at thousands of youth hostels around the world. Hostels provide separate sleeping quarters for men and women at rates of $7–$20 a night per person and are situated in a variety of facilities, including converted farmhouses, villas, and restored castles, as well as specially constructed modern buildings. There are more than 5,000 hostel locations in 68 countries. Apply through **American Youth Hostels** (Box 37613, Washington, DC 20013, tel. 202/783–6161). The first-year cost is $25 for adults 18 to 54; annual renewal is $15; youths 17 and under pay $10; seniors 55 and older, $15. Family membership costs $35. Every national hostel association offers special reductions such as discounted rail fares or free bus travel, so be sure to ask for the list when you apply.

Economical **bicycle tours** for small groups of adventurous, energetic students are another popular AYH student travel service. For information on these and other AYH services and publications, contact the above address.

Council Travel, a CIEE subsidiary, is the foremost U.S. student-travel agency, specializing in low-cost charters and serving as the exclusive U.S. agent for many student airfare bargains and student tours. CIEE's 80-page *Student Travel Catalog* and *Council Charter* brochure are available free from any Council Travel office in the United States (enclose $1 postage if ordering by mail). In addition to CIEE headquarters at 205 E. 42nd St. and a branch office at 35 W. 8th St. in New York City (tel. 212/254–2525), there are Council Travel offices in Berkeley, La Jolla, Long Beach, Los Angeles, San Diego, San Francisco, and Sherman Oaks, CA; Boulder, CO; New Haven, CT; Washington, DC; Atlanta, GA; Chicago and Evanston, IL; New Orleans, LA; Amherst, Boston, and Cambridge, MA;

Minneapolis, MN; Durham, NC; Portland, OR; Providence, RI; Austin and Dallas, TX; Seattle, WA; and Milwaukee, WI.

The **Educational Travel Center,** another student travel specialist worth contacting for information on student tours, bargain fares, and bookings, may be reached at 438 N. Frances St., Madison, WI 55703 (tel. 608/256–5551).

Students who would like to work abroad should contact **CIEE's Work Abroad Department** (205 E. 42nd St., New York, NY 10017, tel. 212/661–1414, ext. 1130). The council arranges various types of paid and voluntary work experiences overseas for up to six months. CIEE also sponsors study programs in Europe, Latin America, and Asia; it also publishes many books of interest to the student traveler: these include *Work, Study, Travel Abroad: The Whole World Handbook* ($10.95, plus $1 book-rate or $2.50 first-class postage); and *Volunteer! The Comprehensive Guide to Voluntary Service in the U.S. and Abroad* ($6.95, plus $1 book-rate or $2.50 first-class postage).

The Information Center (809 U.N. Plaza, New York, NY 10017, tel. 212/984–5413) at the **Institute of International Education** (IIE) has reference books, foreign university catalogues, study-abroad brochures, and other materials, which may be consulted by students and nonstudents alike, free of charge. The Information Center is open weekdays 10–4. It is not open on weekends or holidays. For a current list of IIE publications, prices, and ordering information, write to Institute of International Education Books at the Information Center address above. Books must be purchased by mail or in person; telephone orders are not accepted. General information on IIE programs and services is available from the institute's regional offices in Atlanta, Chicago, Denver, Houston, San Francisco, and Washington, DC.

Traveling with Children

Publications *Family Travel Times* is an 8- to 12-page newsletter published 10 times a year by TWYCH (Travel with Your Children, 80 8th Ave., New York, NY 10011, tel. 212/206–0688). The $35 yearly subscription includes access to back issues and twice-weekly opportunities to call in for specific information. Send $1 for a sample issue. See also *A Parent's Guide to Tokyo: Tokyo Treats for Tots, Teens and Tourists* by N. Hartzenbusch and A. Shabecoff (Shufunotomo Co., Ltd., Tokyo; $14.20).

Hotels The **New Otani Hotel and Tower** (4-1 Kioi-cho, Chiyoda-ku, Tokyo 102, tel. 03/265–1111; in the United States, 800/421–8795; or in California, 800/252–0197) supervises a Tiny Tots room and facilitates baby-sitting arrangements. The **Miyako Hotel** (Sanjo Keage, Higashiyama-ku, Kyoto 605, tel. 075/771–7111; in the United States, 800/336–1136) offers a family plan, children's menu, and baby-sitting (reserve a week in advance).

Home Exchange Exchanging homes is a low-cost way to enjoy a vacation abroad, especially a long one. The largest organization, **International Home Exchange Service** (Box 190070, San Francisco, CA 94119, tel. 415/435–3497), publishes three directories a year. Membership costs $45 and entitles you to one listing and all three directories. **Loan-a-Home** (2 Park Lane, 6E, Mount Vernon, NY 10552, 914/664–7640) is popular with academics on sabbatical and businesspeople on temporary assignment. There's no annual membership fee or charge for listing your home; one directory and a supplement costs $35.

Getting There On international flights, children under two not occupying a seat pay 10% of adult fare. Various discounts apply to children two to 12 years of age. Regulations about infant travel on airplanes are in the process of changing. Until they do, however, if you want your infant secured in a safety seat, you must buy a separate ticket and bring your own infant car seat. Some airlines do not charge if there's a spare seat available; if there isn't, your infant seat will be stored and the child will have to be held by an adult. (Check with the airline in advance; certain seats aren't allowed; for the booklet *Child/Infant Safety Seats Acceptable for Use in Aircraft*, write to the Federal Aviation Administration, APA-200, 800 Independence Ave. SW, Washington, DC 20591, tel. 202/267–3479.) If you hold your baby on your lap, do so with the infant outside the seatbelt.

Also inquire about about special children's meals or snacks. The February issue of Family Travel Times, *TWYCH's Airline Guide*, is always devoted to travel with children and contains a rundown of the children's services offered by 46 airlines.

Baby-sitting Services Many of the Western-style hotels throughout Japan have supervised playrooms where you can drop children off. Child-care arrangements can be made through the concierge; however, some properties require up to a week's notice.

Hints for Older Travelers

The **American Association of Retired Persons** (AARP, 1909 K St. NW, Washington, DC 20049, tel. 202/662–4850) has two programs for independent travelers: (1) The Purchase Privilege Program, which offers discounts on hotels, airfare, car rentals, and sightseeing; and (2) the AARP Motoring Plan, provided by Amoco, which offers emergency aid and trip-routing information for an annual fee of $33.95 per person or married couple. **American Express Vacations** (Box 5014, Atlanta, GA 30302, tel. 800/241–1700 or, in GA, 800/637–6200) arranges group tours and cruises for AARP members. AARP members must be at least 50 years old or be the spouse of someone who is. Annual dues are $5 per person or per couple.

When using an AARP or other identification card, ask for a reduced hotel rate when you make your reservation, not when you check out. At participating restaurants, show your card to the maître d' before you're seated, because discounts may be limited to certain set menus, days, or hours. Your AARP card will identify you as a retired person but will not ensure a discount in all hotels and restaurants. When renting a car, be sure to ask about special promotional rates which may offer greater savings than the available discounts.

Elderhostel (75 Federal St., 3rd floor, Boston, MA 02110–1941, tel. 617/426–7788) is an innovative program for people 60 and older. Participants live in dorms on 1,200 campuses around the world. Mornings are devoted to lectures and seminars; afternoons, to sightseeing and field trips. The all-inclusive fee for three-week trips, including room, board, tuition, and round-trip transportation, ranges from $1,800 to $4,500.

Mature Outlook (6001 N. Clark St., Chicago, IL 60660, tel. 800/336–6330), a subsidiary of Sears, Roebuck & Co., is a travel club for people over 50 years of age, offering hotel discounts and a bimonthly newsletter. Annual membership is $9.95 per person or couple. Instant membership is available at participating Holiday Inns.

The National Council of Senior Citizens (925 15th St. NW, Washington, DC 20005, tel. 202/347–8800) is a nonprofit advocacy group with some 5,000 local clubs across the country. Annual membership is $12 per person or per couple. Members receive a monthly newspaper with travel information and an ID card for reduced rates on hotels and car rentals.

Hints for Disabled Travelers

The **Information Center for Individuals with Disabilities** (Fort Point Place, 1st floor, 27-43 Wormwood St., Boston, MA 02210, tel. 617/727–5540; TDD 617/727–5236) offers useful problem-solving assistance, including lists of travel agents that specialize in tours for the disabled.

Moss Rehabilitation Hospital Travel Information Service (1200 W. Tabor Rd., Philadelphia, PA 19141–3009, tel. 215/456–9600; TDD 215/456–9602) provides information on tourist sights, transportation, and accommodations in destinations around the world for a small fee.

Mobility International USA (Box 3551, Eugene, OR 97403, tel. 503/343–1284) is an international organization with 500 member affiliates. For a $20 annual fee, it coordinates exchange programs for disabled people around the world and offers information on accommodations and organized study programs.

The **Society for the Advancement of Travel for the Handicapped** (26 Court St., Penthouse Suite, Brooklyn, NY 11242, tel. 718/858–5483) offers access information. Annual membership costs $45, $25 for senior travelers and students. Send $1 and a stamped, self-addressed envelope for a list of tour operators who arrange travel for the disabled.

Travel Industry and Disabled Exchange (TIDE, 5435 Donna Ave., Tarzana, CA 91356, tel. 818/368–5648) is an industry-based organization with a $15-per-person annual membership fee. Members receive a quarterly newsletter and information on travel agencies and tours.

The Itinerary (Box 2012, Bayonne, NJ 07002, tel. 201/858–3400) is a bimonthly travel magazine for the disabled. A subscription costs $10 for one year, $20 for two.

Further Reading

History Fourteen hundred years of history is rather a lot to take in when going on a holiday, but two good surveys make the task much easier: Richard Storry's *A History of Modern Japan* (by modern, he means everything post-prehistoric) and George Sansom's *Japan: A Short Cultural History.* Both books were written several years ago but have not been superseded, and the same can be said of Sansom's three-volume *History of Japan.* Edwin O. Reischauer's more recent *Japan: The Story of a Nation* utilizes the author's knowledge gained from serving as a U.S. ambassador to Japan and as a Harvard University professor of Japanese studies.

For those interested in earlier times, a classic work is Ivan
Morris's *The World of the Shining Prince*, which uses diaries
and literature of the time to reconstruct life in the ancient city
of Heian (Kyoto) from 794 to 1192. It is required reading for
anyone wishing to tour old Kyoto. For a collection of studies on
Japan's civil wars during the 16th century, see *Warlords, Artists and Commoners*, edited by George Elison. *The Culture of
the Meiji Period*, by Irokawa Daikichi, covers Japan's 19th century encounter with the West. Oliver Statler's *Japanese Inn*
deals with 400 years of Japanese social history.

Religion   Anyone wanting to read a Zen Buddhist text should try *The
Platform Sutra of the Sixth Patriarch*, one of the Zen classics,
written by an ancient Chinese head of the sect and translated
by Philip B. Yampolsky. Another Zen text of high importance
is the Lotus Sutra; it has been translated by Leon Hurvitz as
*The Scripture of the Lotus Blossom of the Fine Dharma: The
Lotus Sutra*. Stuart D. Picken has written books on both major
Japanese religions: *Shinto: Japan's Spiritual Roots* and *Buddhism: Japan's Cultural Identity*. Joseph Kitagawa traces the
full history of Japanese Buddhism and Shinto in *Religion in
Japanese History*. William R. LaFleur traces how Buddhism
actually affected the mentality and behavior of people in the
Japanese medieval period in *Karma of Words: Buddhism and
the Literary Arts in Medieval Japan*, which is highly recommended. In *Japanese Pilgrimage*, Oliver Statler recounts the
story of Kobo Daishi, a Buddhist saint, deity, and miracle
worker.

Literature   The great classic of all Japanese fiction is the *Tale of Genji*
(Genji or the Shining Prince has long been taken as the arche-
type of ideal male behavior). The novel was written by a woman
of the court, Murasaki Shikibu, around the year 1000; two
translations are available, by Arthur Waley and by Edward
Seidensticker. Of the same period, reckoned as Japan's Golden
Age, is *The Pillow Book of Sei Shonagon*, the diary of a
woman's courtly life, eloquently translated by Ivan Morris.

The Edo period is well covered by literary translations. How-
ard Hibbett's *Floating World in Japanese Fiction* gives an excellent selection with commentaries. The racy prose of Saikaku
Ihara, who lived at the end of the 17th century and embodied
the rough bravura of the growing merchant class, is translated
in various books: *Some Final Words of Advice*, *Life of an Amorous Man*, *Five Women Who Loved Love*, and others. More serious literature of the same period are *haikai* poems. Basho
produced great examples of these 17-syllable verses, and his
Narrow Road to the Deep North and Other Travel Sketches is
available in translation. A general overview of poetry may be
found in the *Penguin Book of Japanese Verse*. Basho's other
travel diaries (a major genre in Japanese literature) are translated by Earl Miner in *Japanese Poetic Diaries*.

Several modern Japanese novelists have been translated into
English. One of the best-known fiction writers among West-
erners is Yukio Mishima, author of a series of novels called *The
Sea of Fertility* trilogy. His works often deal with the effects of
Westernization on Japanese culture as experienced by postwar
Japanese. Two superb prose stylists are Junchiro Tanizaki, au-
thor of *The Makioka Sisters*, *Some Prefer Nettles*, and *Seven
Japanese Tales*, and Nobel Prize winner Yasunari Kawabata,
whose novels include *Snow Country*, *Beauty and Sadness*, and

The Sound of the Mountain. Kobe Abe is a Japanese novelist who writes in an experimental vein; his books include *The Woman in the Dunes* and *The Ruined Map.*

Sociology The Japanese have a genre they refer to as *nihonjin-ron,* or studies of "Japaneseness." Western-style studies of the Japanese way of life in relation to the West also abound. Perhaps the best is Ezra Vogel's *Japan As Number One: Lessons for America.* A fine study of the Japanese mind is found in Takeo Doi's *The Anatomy of Dependence* and Chie Nakane's *Japanese Society.* Edwin O. Reischauer's *The Japanese* and his more recent *The Japanese Today* are general overviews of Japanese society.

Two other highly recommended looks at modern Japanese life and culture are Robert Christopher's *The Japanese Mind* and John David Morley's *Pictures from the Water Trade.* An exceptionally enlightening book on the Japanese socio-political system, especially for diplomats and business people intending to work with the Japanese, is *The Enigma of Japanese Power* by Harel van Wolferen.

Art/Architecture Not surprisingly, a wealth of literature exists on Japanese art. Much of the early writing has not withstood the test of time, but R. Paine and Alexander Soper's *Art and Architecture of Japan* remains a good place to start. A more recent survey, though narrower in scope, is Joan Stanley-Smith's *Japanese Art.* Japanese art can also be appreciated before traveling to Japan by making a trip to a local museum (for example, Boston, Cleveland, Kansas City, and Washington have excellent collections). Museum catalogues can also provide additional information.

The *Japan Arts Library* is a multivolume survey published by Kodansha, and covers most of the famous styles and personalities of Japanese art, including architecture. The series has volumes on castles, teahouses, screen painting, and wood-block prints. *The Heibonsha Survey of Japanese Art* is a similar series. A more detailed look at the architecture of Tokyo is Edward Seidensticker's *Low City, High City. What is Japanese Architecture?* by Kazuo Nishi and Kazuo Hozumi is full of information on the history of Japanese architecture, with examples of buildings you will actually see on your travels.

Film Several excellent volumes about Japanese film are available. Audie Bock's *Japanese Film Directors* studies the careers of major contemporary Japanese filmmakers. *The Japanese Film: Art and Industry,* by Joseph L. Anderson and Donald Richie, is a classic study of Japanese film history. *The Films of Akira Kurosawa* and *Ozu: His Life and Films,* both by Donald Richie, investigate the works of two of Japan's most highly regarded film directors.

Getting to Japan

From North America by Plane

Airlines More than 40 international carriers offer regular flights to Tokyo. Fares vary with the airline, season, and type of ticket.

Japan Airlines (JAL; tel. 800/525–3663) has the most flights between North America (New York, Chicago, Los Angeles) and Tokyo and because JAL has increased its coverage of domestic routes within Japan, the traveler can more easily construct his itinerary on one airline ticket. JAL has also enhanced its services, particularly by increasing passenger comfort in the business class. **All Nippon Airways** (tel. 800/235–9262) is the other major Japanese international carrier with flights from the east and west coasts of the United States.

United Airlines (tel. 800/538–2929) is the major U.S. carrier, with direct flights to Tokyo from the east and west coasts of the United States; it hopes to have the rights soon to fly between Chicago and Tokyo and Sydney and Tokyo.

The following are some other major airlines with regular routes to Japan, followed by toll-free U.S. telephone numbers: **Canadian Airlines International** (tel. 800/426–7000), **Korean Air** (tel. 800/223–1155), **Northwest Orient Airlines** (tel. 800/447–4747), **American Airlines** (tel. 800/433–7300), and **Continental Airlines** (tel. 800/231–0856). Continental's record for delays and lack of concern for this market puts it at a disadvantage. **Thai International Airlines** also flies nonstop to Tokyo from Seattle en route to Bangkok.

Flying Time The flight time to Tokyo from North America varies slightly with the airline's route. From New York: 13 hours, 45 minutes; from Chicago: 12 hours, 45 minutes; from L.A.: 9 hours, 30 minutes.

Flights to Japan are long and trying. Because of time difference, jet lag and fatigue are nearly inevitable. Try to get as much sleep and rest as possible on the plane. Wear comfortable clothing, drink lots of nonalcoholic liquids, and relax.

Discount Flights Many airlines offer discounts on seats depending on travel time restrictions on the ticket. One type of inexpensive ticket is the APEX fare, whereby you generally must remain in your country of destination for at least seven days but no more than 90 days. These tickets must be reserved and paid for 21 days in advance. Contact the individual airlines for information. Discount-travel agents often sell surprisingly inexpensive tickets; it is possible to get a round-trip New York–Tokyo ticket for less than $1,000.

Smoking As of late February 1990, smoking was banned on the domestic legs of all foreign routes but the rule does not affect international flights. If cigarette smoke bothers you, request a seat far away from the smoking section.

Luggage Regulations
Carry-on Luggage On U.S. airlines, passengers are limited to two carry-on bags. For a bag you wish to store under the seat, the maximum dimensions are 9″ + 14″ + 22″, a total of 45″. For bags that can be hung in a closet or on a luggage rack, the maximum dimensions are 4″ + 23″ + 45″, a total of 72″. For bags you wish to store in an overhead bin, the maximum dimensions are 10″ + 14″ + 36″, a total of 60″. Your two carryons must each fit one of these sets of dimensions, and any item that exceeds the specified dimensions will generally be rejected as a carryon and handled as checked baggage. Keep in mind that an airline can adapt these rules to circumstances, so on an especially crowded flight, don't be surprised if you are only allowed one carry-on bag.

In addition to the two carryons, passengers may also carry aboard a handbag (pocketbook or purse); an overcoat or wrap; an umbrella; a camera; a reasonable amount of reading material; an infant bag; and crutches, a cane, braces, or other prosthetic device upon which the passenger is dependent. Infant/ child safety seats can also be brought aboard if parents have purchased a ticket for the child or if there is space in the cabin.

Note that these regulations are for U.S. airlines only. Foreign airlines generally allow one piece of carry-on luggage in tourist class, in addition to handbags and bags filled with duty-free goods. Passengers in first and business class are also allowed to carry on one garment bag. It is best to check with your airline ahead of time to find out what its exact rules are regarding carry-on luggage.

Checked Luggage On international flights, passengers are generally allowed to check two pieces of luggage, neither of which can exceed 62" (length + width + height) or weigh more than 70 pounds. Baggage allowances vary slightly among airlines, so check with the carrier of your travel agent before departure.

Luggage Insurance On international flights, airlines are responsible for lost or damaged property only up to $9.07 per pound ($20 per kilo) for checked baggage, and up to $400 per passenger for unchecked baggage on international flights. If you're carrying valuables, either take them with you on the airplane or purchase additional insurance for lost luggage. Some airlines will issue additional luggage insurance when you check in, but many do not. Insurance for lost, damaged, or stolen luggage is available through travel agents or directly through various insurance companies. Two that issue luggage insurance are **Tele-Trip** (Box 31685, 3201 Farnam St., Omaha, NE 68131, tel. 800/228–9792), a subsidiary of Mutual of Omaha, and **The Travelers Corporation** (Ticket and Travel Dept., 1 Tower Sq., Hartford, CT 06183, tel. 203/277–0111 or 800/243–3174). Tele-Trip operates sales booths at airports and also issues insurance through travel agents. Tele-Trip will insure checked luggage for up to 180 days; rates vary according to the length of the trip. The Travelers Corporation will insure checked or hand luggage for $500– $2,000 valuation per person, also for a maximum of 180 days. The rate for 1–5 days for $500 valuation is $10; for 180 days, $85.

Other companies with comprehensive policies include **Access America Inc.,** a subsidiary of Blue Cross–Blue Shield (Box 11188, Richmond, VA 23230, tel. 800/334–7525 or 800/284– 8300); **Near Services** (450 Prairie Ave., Suite 101, Calumet City, IL 60409, tel. 708/868–6700 or 800/654–6700).

Before you go, itemize the contents of each bag in case you need to file an insurance claim. Be certain to put your home address on each piece of luggage, including carry-on bags. If your luggage is lost or stolen and later recovered, the airline will deliver the luggage to your home free of charge.

From North America by Ship Although it is possible to travel to Japan by sea, most boats stop at the port cities of Kobe or Yokohama, not at Tokyo. Consult your local travel agent for more information.

From the United Kingdom

By Plane **British Airways** (Box 10, London-Heathrow Airport, Hounslow, Middlesex TW6 2JA, tel. 081/897–4000) and **Japan Airlines** (5 Hanover Sq., London W1R ODR, tel. 071/629–9244) are the major operators serving Japan. They have daily flights to Tokyo's Narita Airport, some nonstop (flight time 11½ hrs.), others stopping at Anchorage (flight time 17½ hrs.). Other airlines serving Japan include **All Nippon Airways** (tel. 7667/081/750–3000); **Korean Air** (tel. 071/930–6513); **Lufthansa** (tel. 071/408–0442); **Swissair** (tel. 071/439–4144); and **Thai Airways International** (tel. 071/499–9113), with one or more transfers.

At press time, an APEX round-trip flight costs £962–£1,003. Check with airlines for the latest information on fares.

By Ship   Among the companies offering cruises to Japan is **Ocean Cruises/Pearl Cruises** (10 Frederick Close, Stanhope Pl., London W2 2HD, tel. 071/262–3017), which has a "China Explorer" tour that includes stops at Kobe and the Inland Sea. There are five departures a year in May, September, and October; you spend 15 nights on board. **Princes Cruises** (P&O) (77 New Oxford St., London WC1A 1PP, tel. 071/831–1881) operates two cruises. One, the "Sea Princes," takes in Hiroshima, Kyoto, and Tokyo, as well as China and Korea. Three of the 22 nights are spent in Japan. Departures are March–April. The other tour is the "Kobe-Vancouver." Stops in Japan include Tokyo, Kyoto, Kobe, and Yokohama. Again, three of the 22 nights are spent in Japan. Departures are in May.

Getting Around Japan

By Train

Japanese trains are both efficient and convenient. The Shinkansen (bullet train), one of the fastest trains in the world, offers services between major cities both north and south of Tokyo. The trains run frequently and are on time within minutes. The Shinkansen is only slightly less expensive than flying but is in many ways more convenient, because train stations are more centrally located than airports.

Other trains are not as fast but are convenient. There are basically three types of train services: *futsu* (local service), *tokkyu* (limited express service), and *kyuko* (express service). Both the tokkyu and the kyuko offer a first-class compartment known as the Green Car.

Japan Rail Pass   The **Japan Rail Pass** is the Japanese version of the Eurailpass. These passes are recommended for anyone who plans to travel extensively by rail in Japan. With this pass, you can travel on any Japan Railways (JR) train for unlimited miles. Japan Railways, now a privately owned company, was formerly a government-operated service. It is possible to purchase a one-, two-, or three-week pass. A one-week pass is less expensive than a regular round-trip ticket from Tokyo to Kyoto.

Japan Rail Passes are available in coach class and first class (Green Car); a one-week pass costs ¥27,800 coach class, ¥37,000 first class; a two-week pass costs ¥44,200 coach class, ¥60,000 first class; and a three-week pass costs ¥56,600 coach class, ¥78,000 first class.

The Japan Rail Pass must be bought prior to departure for Japan and must be used within three months of purchase. It is also available only to people with tourist visas, as opposed to business, student, and diplomatic visas. It can be purchased through travel agents or any of the following: **Japan Airlines** (JAL) (655 Fifth Ave., New York, NY 10022, tel. 212/838–

4400), **Japan Travel Bureau** (JTB) (787 7th Ave., New York, NY 10019, tel. 212/246–8030), or **Nippon Travel Agency** (NTA) (120 W. 45th St., New York, NY 10036, tel. 212/944–8660). JAL, JTB, and NTA also have bureaus in other major cities throughout the United States.

When you arrive in Japan, you exchange your voucher for the Rail Pass. You can do this at the Japan Railways (JR) desk in the Arrivals Hall at Narita Airport or at the JR Stations of major cities. When you make this exchange, you determine the day that you want the rail pass to begin—and, by definition, when it ends. Time it to maximize its use. The Rail Pass allows you to travel on all JR operated trains (which cover most destinations in Japan), but not lines owned by other companies. It also allows you to use buses operated by Japan Railways. Furthermore, it allows you to make seat reservations on all trains that have reserved-seat coaches (usually the long-distance trains, for example, the Shinkansen and Limited Expresses). The Rail Pass does not cover the cost of sleeping compartments on the Blue trains.

Purchasing Tickets If you are using a Rail Pass, there is no need to buy individual tickets, but it is advisable to get a reservation. Not only does this guarantee you a seat, but it is a useful reference for the times of train departures and arrivals. You can reserve up to two weeks in advance or just minutes before the train departs. If you fail to make the train, there is no penalty and you can reserve again. Seat reservations may be made at any JR Station except at the tiniest villages, for any JR route. The reservation windows or offices, *Midori-no-madoguchi*, have green signs in English and green-striped windows. For those traveling without a Japan Rail Pass, there is a surcharge of approximately ¥500 (depending upon distance traveled) for seat reservations. (Reservations are advised during peak travel times.) Sleeping berths, even with the Japan Rail Pass, are additions. Tickets and seat reservations can be purchased several days in advance of your trip or moments before the train is due to depart. Nonreserved tickets can be bought at regular ticket windows. There are no reservations made on local service trains. For traveling shorter distances, tickets are usually sold at vending machines.

Most clerks at train stations have a few basic words of English and can read Roman script. Moreover, they are invariably helpful in plotting your route. Traveling by train in Japan, you will find, is easier than travel in your own country. Trains are on time to the minute in 99% of the cases. The Japan National Tourist Organization's booklet, *The Tourist's Handbook*, provides helpful information about purchasing tickets in Japan.

By Plane

All major Japanese cities have airports connected by domestic flights. The two major services are **All Nippon Airways** (3-6-3 Irifunecho, Chuo-ku, Tokyo, tel. 03/3552–6311) and **Japan Airlines** (5-37-8 Shiba, Minato-ku, Tokyo, tel. 03/3456–2111).

By Bus

Japan Railways offers a number of overnight long-distance buses that are not very comfortable but are inexpensive. Japan

Rail Passes may be used on these buses. City buses are quite convenient, but be sure of your route and destination, because the bus driver will probably not speak English. Some buses have a set cost of ¥160, in which case you board at the front of the bus and pay as you get on. On other buses, cost is determined by the distance. In these cases, you take a ticket when you board at the rear door of the bus; it will bear the number of the stop at which you boarded. Your fare is indicated by a board with rotating numbers at the front of the bus. Under each boarding point, indicated by a number, the fare will increase the farther the bus travels.

By Ferry

Ferry services exist between many of the islands of Japan. The ferries are inexpensive and are a pleasant if slow way of traveling. Private cabins are available, but it is more fun (if less comfortable) to travel in the economy class, where everyone sleeps in one large room. Passengers eat, drink, and enjoy themselves, creating a convivial atmosphere. Ferries connect most of the islands of Japan. Some of the more popular routes are from Tokyo to Tomakomai or Kushiro in Hokkaido; from Tokyo to Shikoku; and from Tokyo or Osaka to Kyushu. You can purchase tickets in advance from travel agencies or before boarding.

By Taxi

Taxis are a convenient but expensive way of getting around cities in Japan. The first 2 kilometers cost ¥480, and it is ¥90 for every additional 370 meters (400 yards). If possible, avoid use of taxis during rush hours (8 AM–9 AM and 5:30 PM–6:30 PM).

In general, it is easy to hail a cab. Do not shout or wave wildly, but rather simply raise your hand. Do not try to open the taxi door, because all taxis have an automatic door-opening function. The door will slam in your face if you are too close to it. When you leave the cab, do not try to close the door. The driver will again use the automatic system. Only the curbside rear door opens. A red light on the dashboard indicates an available taxi, and a green light indicates an occupied taxi.

The drivers are for the most part courteous. Sometimes they will balk at the idea of a foreign passenger because they do not speak English. Unless you are going to a well-known destination such as a major hotel, it is advisable to have a Japanese person write out your destination in Japanese. Remember, there is no need to tip.

By Car

Road Conditions. It is possible for foreigners to drive in Japan with an international driving license, and though few select this option, it is becoming more popular. More and more, highways have transliterated signs, though the smaller roads do not. A good map really helps. Indeed, except in Tokyo and a few major cities, exploring in your own rented car can be rewarding. However, long-distance traveling by car is ill-advised. Except for the toll roads, (and they are frightfully expensive), highways tend to be congested, making driving frustrating and considerably slower than taking the train. Instead, consider renting a car locally for a day or even half a day in those areas where exploring the countryside will be the most interesting. Gas costs much more in Japan than it does in the United States.

Rules. Driving is on the left side of the street, opposite that of the United States. Speed limits vary, but generally the limit is 80 kilometers per hour (50 mph) on highways, 40 (25 mph) in cities.

Staying in Japan

Tourist Information

Tourist Information Centers In Japan, the Japan National Tourist Organization (JNTO) operates the **Tourist Information Centers** (TIC), whose services include travel information on Japan, free pamphlets, and suggestions for tour itineraries. Reservations, however, are not handled here. Either visit the TIC offices or call.

Tokyo Office. Kotani Building, 1-6-6 Yurakucho, Chiyoda-ku, tel. 03/3502–1461. Open weekdays 9–5, Saturday 9–noon; closed Sunday and national holidays.

Tokyo International Airport Office, Airport Terminal Building, Narita Airport, Chiba Prefecture, tel. 0476/32–8711. Open weekdays 9–8, Saturday 9–noon; closed Sunday and national holidays.

Kyoto Office. Kyoto Tower Building, Higashi-Shiokojicho, Shimogyo-ku, tel. 075/371–5549. Open weekdays 9–5, Saturday 9–noon; closed Sunday and national holidays.

Japan Travel-Phone If you have travel-related questions or need help in communicating, call the TIC's Travel-Phone service, daily 9–5. In Tokyo and Kyoto, call the TIC offices. Elsewhere, dial toll-free 0120/222–800 for information on eastern Japan and 0120/444–800 for western Japan. The Travel-Phone service is available through yellow, blue, or green telephones (not red ones) and through private phones. When using a public telephone, insert a ¥10 piece, which will be returned.

Teletourist Service Those who want to know of cultural activities and events going on in Tokyo can call tel. 03/3503–2911. In Kyoto, call tel. 075/361–2911. You will get a tape-recorded telephone information service in English.

Good-Will Guides This program was launched by JNTO to help visitors from overseas with any language problems. Volunteer Good-Will Guides can be identified by the distinctive Good-Will Guide badge that is worn on their clothing. They will happily answer questions and give directions in English. The program operates in many places in Japan, including Tokyo, Kyoto, Nara, Nagoya, Osaka, Hiroshima, and other cities.

Home Visit System Through the Home Visit System, travelers may visit a Japanese family in their home for a few hours to get a sense of Japanese domestic life. The program is voluntary on the homeowner's part, with no charge for a visit. It is active in many cities throughout the country, including Tokyo, Yokohama, Nagoya, Kyoto, Osaka, Hiroshima, Nagasaki, Sapporo, and others. An application in writing to make a home visit should be submitted at least a day in advance to the local tourist information office of the place you are visiting. The Japan

National Tourist Organization provides information on the program; contact them before leaving for Japan.

Language

Most Japanese study English for nearly a decade as a requirement in school. Unfortunately, this does not mean that everyone speaks English. The educational system in Japan emphasizes reading, writing, and grammar, with very little focus on spoken English. As a result, many Japanese can read English with fluency yet speak only the most basic phrases.

Sometimes even those who do speak a fair amount of English, in response to the question, "Do you speak English?" out of embarrassment will say, "No." You are probably better off simply assuming that they understand a little; speak slowly and clearly. You will probably have more luck communicating with younger people, because they tend to be more open and are more likely to remember their English lessons.

Japanese is not an easy language to learn, but your efforts to use a few phrases, such as *arigato* (thank you), will be appreciated. Pronunciation of Japanese Romanized words is fairly straightforward. The most common system of Romanization is the Hepburn system (followed in this book), which essentially spells out syllabically all of the sounds. Therefore, when you encounter a Japanese word, try to sound out each letter as much as possible, without emphasizing any syllable. For example, when saying the word for good-bye, say "sa-yo-na-ra" without using any inflection. Most English speakers say "sa-yo-NAH-ra," because English words have accents on particular syllables.

The vowel sounds are set in Japanese. *A* is pronounced like the "ah" sound in "father." *E* is pronounced like the "eh" sound in "men." *I* is pronounced like the sound in "it." *O* is pronounced like the "oh" sound in "only." *U* is pronounced like the "oo" sound in "boot." Sound out all of the vowels in Japanese, though sometimes the combinations may be confusing. When you see the "ei" combination in a word, it is pronounced "eh-i." An example of this is the first name of the well-known conductor, Seiji Ozawa. His name is pronounced not "see-ji" but "seh-i-ji."

When you have the combination of two of the same consonants in a row, such as in the word *Nippon*, say it as though it were two separate words, "Nip-pon," hesitating slightly between the syllables.

Geography

Japan consists of an arc-shaped archipelago of islands situated east of continental Asia. The islands extend for 1,734 miles and are situated in a part of the Pacific Ocean that is known as the Circum-Pacific zone, an area where earthquakes and volcano eruptions frequently occur. Japan consists of four main islands—Honshu, Hokkaido, Shikoku, and Kyushu—as well as thousands of small islands.

Most of Japan (four-fifths) is covered with mountains, many of which are volcanic. The highest mountain is Mt. Fuji, which stands 12,388 feet above sea level and is an active volcano, although it has not erupted in two centuries. There are as many as 67 active volcanoes in Japan, such as Mt. Usu in Hokkaido and Mt. Aso in Kyushu.

It is interesting to note that the combination of volcanic and seismic activity in Japan has created much of this country's natural beauty, including the graceful shapes of many of the volcanic mountains, such as Mt. Fuji, and the hot springs that cover all Japan.

Prefectures

Japan is divided into a total of 47 prefectures. The name of a prefecture is indicated by the suffix "*-ken.*" Some examples are Shizuoka-ken or Gifu-ken. These geographic demarcations are roughly equivalent to states in America and are essentially based on historic feudal divisions of land. Before the prefectures, which were domains of feudal lords, the divisions were known as *han*. At the time of the Meiji Restoration, these areas were slightly reorganized and called *ken*.

There are a few geographic areas in Japan that are not called ken. One is Hokkaido. The reason is that in feudal times, Hokkaido was not considered to be a domain with a recognized feudal lord, and it was therefore designated *do*. The other exceptions are greater Tokyo, which is called Tokyo-to, and Kyoto and Osaka, which are followed by the suffix "-fu"— Tokyo-to, Kyoto-fu, Osaka-fu.

Addresses

Japanese addresses are very simple if broken down into their various elements. The following is an example of a typical Japanese address: 6-chome 8–19, Chuo-ku, Fukuoka-shi, Fukuoka-ken. In this address the "chome" indicates a precise area, and the numbers following "chome" indicate the location within the area, not necessarily in sequential order—numbers may have been assigned when a building was erected. However, only the postmen in Japan seem to be familiar with the area defined by the chome. Sometimes, instead of a "chome," a "machi" is used. "Ku" refers to a ward, or in other words, a district of a city. "Shi" refers to a city name, and "ken" indicates a prefecture, which is roughly equivalent to states in America. It is not unusual for the prefecture and the city to have the same name, as in the above address.

Not all addresses will conform exactly to the above format. Rural addresses, for example, do not have "ku," because only urban areas are divided into wards.

It is important to note that often even Japanese people cannot find a building based on the address alone. Do not assume if you get in a taxi with an address written down, the driver will be able to find your destination. Usually, people provide very detailed instructions or maps to explain their exact locations. A common method is to give the location of your destination in relation to a major building or department store.

Telephones

Pay phones are one of the great delights of Japan. Not only are they conveniently located in hotels, restaurants, and on street corners; pay phones, at ¥10 for three minutes, have to be one of the few remaining bargains in Japan. Telephones come in three styles: pink, red, and green. Pink phones, for local calls, accept only ¥10 coins. Most red phones are only for local use, but some accept ¥100 coins and can be used for long-distance domestic calls. Domestic long distance rates are reduced as much as 50% after 9 PM (40% after 7 PM). Green phones take coins and often accept what are known as telephone cards—disposable cards of fixed value that you use up in increments of ¥10. Telephone cards, sold in vending machines, hotels, and a variety of stores, are tremendously convenient, because you will not have to search for the correct change. International calls can be placed from the many green phones that have gold plates indicating, in English, that the telephone can be used for these calls. Telephone credit cards are especially convenient for international calls. For operator assistance in English on long-distance calls, dial 0051.

An alternative method for making certain overseas calls is to use "Home Country Direct." By dialing the appropriate number (for Australia, dial 0039–611; for the United Kingdom, dial 0039–441; and for the United States, dial 0039–111), you are put in touch with an operator located within that country. The operator will then make your call collect or bill your telephone credit card.

Mail

The Japanese postal service is very efficient with both domestic and foreign mail. Although numerous post offices exist in any given city, it is probably best to take the trouble of going to central post offices that are located near the main train station in a city, because the workers speak English and can handle foreign mail. Some of the smaller post offices are not equipped to send packages. Post offices are open weekdays 8–5 and Saturday 8–noon. Some of the central post offices have longer hours, such as the one in Tokyo, located near Tokyo Station, which is open 24 hours, year-round.

Postal rates vary with destination. It costs ¥100 to send a letter by air to the United States or Canada; ¥120 to Europe. An airmail postcard costs ¥70 to North America; ¥70 to Europe. Aerograms cost ¥100. Hotels can assist you in sending telegrams.

It is possible to receive mail sent *poste restante* at the central post office in major cities, but unclaimed mail is returned after 30 days. American Express offices, located in all major Japanese cities, are other good places to have mail sent. The address of the main office in Tokyo is American Express, Halifax Building, 16-26 Roppongi 3-chome, Minato-ku, Tokyo.

Dining

Japanese food is not only delicious and healthy but also aesthetically pleasing. Even the most humble *bento* lunch box procured at a stand in a train station will be created with careful attention paid to the color combination and general presentation. Be warned that portions may be small, so you may feel that the price of beauty is a less-than-full stomach.

Food, as is the case with many things in Japan, is high-priced. Eating at hotels and famous restaurants is costly, but by looking for standard restaurants that may not have signs in English, you can eat well for reasonable prices. Many less-expensive restaurants have displays in their front windows of their menus, so you can always point to what you want to eat. A good place to look for moderately priced dining spots is in the restaurant concourse of department stores.

In general, Japanese restaurants are very clean. The water is safe, even when drawn from a tap. Most hotels have Western-style rest rooms, but restaurants may have Japanese-style toilets where you must squat.

There are many types of restaurants offering Japanese food. **Sushiya** usually offer only sushi. Beware of places that do not list their prices, because they can be extremely expensive. Some sushi places have revolving counters. Customers pick whatever dishes they want off the conveyor belt and are charged according to the number of plates. These automatic sushi places are both inexpensive and fun, but be cautious in the summer months, when the fish might not be fresh.

Noodle fans can go to a **ramenya,** where they can get an inexpensive but filling bowl of ramen (Japanese noodles). Ramenya also serve beer and **gyoza** (fried dumplings) for those who want a bit more. **Sobaya** are close relatives of ramenya and serve buckwheat noodles. These noodles are served hot or cold; they are a refreshing and light meal or snack.

Nomiya are bars, but in addition to beer, sake, and whiskey, they often serve simple but tasty food. You can identify many nomiya because they each have a red lantern hanging outside. These places are not sophisticated and fancy, but they often provide a glimpse of the life of the working man.

Outdoor food stalls are located on many urban street corners and offer a variety of food, including yakitori (chicken on skewers), noodles, or simple roast chestnuts. This food is safe to eat and inexpensive.

Japanese coffee shops, known as **kissaten,** are always good places for weary tourists to know about. Although you may be astonished by the high price of one cup of coffee (no, there are no refills), you can sit as long as you like, long after you have finished your coffee. Some coffee shops offer "morning set" breakfasts consisting of a hard-boiled egg, toast, and a small salad. Priced at only a few hundred yen, they are one of the few really inexpensive meals available in Japan.

For those who tire of Japanese food, Western, Chinese, and other types of food are available, particularly in urban areas. In recent years, ethnic food has become extremely popular, so those in need of a taco or a spicy Thai curry can fulfill their desires. The quality of ethnic food is surprisingly good.

Tipping, Tax, and Service Charge A 3% federal consumer tax is added to all restaurant bills. Another 3% local tax is added to the bill if it exceeds ¥5,000. At the more expensive restaurants, a 10%–15% service charge is added to the bill. Tipping is not the custom.

Lodging

Hotels Several major full-service, first-class hotels in Japan are similar to their counterparts all over the world. At these hotels, most of the staff will speak English, and the hotel will have full amenities. Particularly in peak tourist seasons, it is best to book far in advance.

For those who like the comforts of a hotel, but do not want to pay the steep prices of luxury hotels, business hotels are a reasonable alternative. These hotels are clean and comfortable, though the rooms vary from tiny to minuscule and the services are limited. They are often conveniently located near the railway station. The staff may not speak English, and there is usually no room service.

One unusual and not very comfortable hotel made for the modern Japanese urbanite is the capsule hotel. The rooms (capsules) are shaped so that the customer can only enter prone. The dimensions are 1.1 meters in width, 1.1 meters in height, and 2.2 meters in length. The capsules have an alarm clock, television, and phone, but little else. These hotels often are used by commuters who have had an evening of excess and cannot make the long journey home. Although these hotels are not the ideal place to spend a night, they certainly have a great deal of novelty value.

Ryokans Ryokans (Japanese-style inns), the traditional form of accommodation, are usually one- or two-story small wood structures with a garden or scenic view. Upon entering a Japanese ryokan, you take off your shoes, as you would in a Japanese household, and put on the slippers that are provided in the entryway. A maid, after bowing to welcome you, will escort you to your room, which will probably be partitioned off with *shoji* (sliding paper-paneled walls) and will feature *tatami* (strawmats) on the floor. Remove your slippers before entering your room; you should not step on the tatami with either shoes or slippers. The room will have little furniture or decoration—perhaps one small low table and cushions on the tatami, with a long simple scroll on the wall. Often the rooms overlook a garden. In this simple setting you will rest, eat, and sleep.

Most guests arrive in the late afternoon. After relaxing in their room with a cup of green tea, they have a long hot bath. In ryokans with thermal pools, you can take to the waters anytime (usually the doors to the pool are locked from 11 PM to 6 AM). In ryokans without thermal baths or private baths in guest rooms, guests must stagger their visit to the one or two public baths. Typically the maid will ask what time you would like your bath and fit you into a schedule. In Japanese baths, you wash and rinse off entirely before entering the tub. Because other guests will be using the same bathwater after you, it is important to observe these customs. After your bath, you change into a *yukata*, a simple cotton kimono, which will be provided in your room. Do not feel abashed at walking around in what is essentially a robe—all the guests will be doing the same.

Dinner, which is included in the price of the room, will be served in the room. After you are finished with your repast, a maid will discreetly come in, clear away the dishes, and lay out your futon bedding, which will consist of the bedding and heavy quilts. The less expensive ryokans (under ¥7,000 for one) have become slightly lackadaisical in changing the sheet cover over the quilt with each new guest. Feel free to complain. In the morning, a maid will gently wake you, clear away the futon, and bring in your Japanese-style breakfast. If you are not fond of Japanese breakfasts (often consisting of fish, raw egg, and rice among other delicacies), the staff will usually be able to rustle up some coffee and toast.

Because the staffs of most ryokans are usually small and dedicated, it is important to be considerate and understanding of their somewhat rigid schedules. Guests are expected to arrive in the late afternoon and eat around 6. Usually the doors to the inn are locked up at 10, so plan for early evenings. Breakfast is served around 8, and checkout is at 10.

Part of the charm of a ryokan is its simplicity. To the unaccustomed eye, the rooms may seem barren and the bedding rather Spartan. Ryokans are not for those who cannot stand the thought of sleeping on the floor with simple bedding, sharing a bath with others, or eating rice and fish for breakfast. But for those who are willing to try an evening in the Japanese spirit, they will find solace in the simple elegance of the inn.

Ryokans, as is the case with hotels, vary in price and quality. Some of the long-established older inns cost as much as ¥80,000 per person, whereas the humbler places are as low as ¥3,000. Unlike hotels, prices are per person and include the cost of breakfast, dinner, and tax. Some inns will allow guests to stay without having dinner and will lower the cost accordingly. However, this is not recommended, because the service and the meals are all part of the ryokan experience. Not all inns are willing to accept foreign guests because of language and cultural barriers. It is therefore important to make reservations in advance to ensure that you are welcome. To find the inn that best suits your needs, contact the **Japan Ryokan Association**, 1-8-3 Marunouchi, Chiyoda-ku, Tokyo, tel. 03/231-5310.

The genuine traditional ryokan with exemplary service is exorbitantly expensive—more than ¥30,000 a night with two meals. Many modern hotels with Japanese-style rooms are now referring to themselves as ryokans, and though meals may be served in the guests' rooms, these places are a far cry from the traditional ryokan. There are also small inns claiming the lofty status of ryokans, which are really nothing more than bed-and-breakfast establishments where meals are taken in a communal dining room and service is minimal. Prices are around ¥5,000 for a single room, ¥7,000 for a double. (JNTO offers a publication listing some of these.)

Minshukus Minshukus are private homes that accept guests. Usually they cost approximately ¥5000 per person, which includes the cost of two meals. Unlike in a ryokan, where you need not lift a finger and everything is there for you, in a minshuku you are expected to lay out and put away your own bedding and bring your own towels. The meals are often served in communal dining rooms. Minshukus vary in size and atmosphere. Some are literally private homes that take on only a few guests; others are more like inns that do not provide any frills. Those interested should contact the **Japan Minshuku Association** (1-29-5 Takadanobaba, Shinjuku-ku, Tokyo, tel. 03/3232-6561).

Youth Hostels Youth hostels cost approximately ¥2,500–¥3,000 per day, including two meals. The hostels provide little more than a bunk bed or a futon and have strictly enforced curfew hours at 9 PM. Some require a membership card from a youth-hostel association. Memberships and further information are available at the **Japan Youth Hostel Association**, Hoken Kaikan, 1-1, Ichigaya-

Sadohara-cho, Shinjuku-ku, Tokyo, tel. 03/3269–5831. JNTO has a free pamphlet listing every youth hostel in Japan, with their locations on a map.

Temples It is possible to arrange for accommodations in Buddhist temples. JNTO has lists of temples that accept guests. A stay at a temple generally costs around ¥3,000 a night, including the price of two meals. Some temples offer instruction in meditation or allow the guests to observe the temple religious practices, but others simply offer a room. The rooms are very basic and are not always very comfortable, but temples provide a taste of traditional Japan.

Inexpensive Accommodations The Japan National Tourist Organization (JNTO) publishes a listing of 143 accommodations that are reasonably priced. To make this category, the property must meet Japanese fire prevention codes and charge less than ¥8,000 per person without meals. For the most part, the properties charge ¥5,000 to ¥6,000. Since these properties agree to be listed, they welcome foreigners (many Japanese hotels and ryokans do not like to have foreign guests). These properties include business hotels, ryokans of very rudimentary nature, minshukus, and pensions. It's the luck of the draw whether you choose a good or less than good property. In most cases, the room are clean, but very small. The two meals usually included will be average. Except for the business hotels, private baths are not common and you will be expected to have your room lights out by 10 PM.

Many accommodations on the JNTO's list can be reserved through the non-profit organization Welcome Inn Reservation Center (International Tourism Center of Japan, 2nd. Floor, Kotani Bldg., 1–6–6 Yurakucho, Chiyoda-ku, Tokyo 100, tel. 03/3580–8353, fax. 03/3580–8256).

Tipping, Tax, and Service Charge Tipping at hotels is not necessary. However, a 3% federal consumer tax is added to all hotel bills. Another 3% local tax is added to the bill if it exceeds ¥10,000. You may save money if you pay for your hotel meals separately rather than charge them to your bill.

At first-class, full-service, and luxury hotels, a 10% service charge will be added to the bill in place of individual tipping. At the more expensive ryokans, where individualized maid service is offered, the service charge will usually be 15%. At business hotels, minshukus, youth hostels, and economy inns, no service charge will be added to the bill.

Tipping

Individual tipping is not common practice in Japan. No tip is necessary for taxi drivers. However, a chauffeur for a hired car will usually receive a tip of ¥500 for a ½-day excursion and ¥1,000 for a full-day trip. Tipping is not necessary at beauty parlors, barber shops, bars and nightclubs. Porters charge fees of ¥250–¥300 at railroad stations and ¥200 per piece of luggage at airports. Tipping at hotels, including the porter, is not the custom unless a special service beyond the normal practices of the hotel or ryokan has been rendered. In such cases, a gratuity of ¥2,000 or ¥3,000 should be placed in an envelope and handed to the staff member discreetly.

Shopping

Shopping is one of the great pleasures of a trip to Japan. Do not be frightened by the high value of the yen; you will not find many steals, but a clever shopper can find reasonably priced items. Do not look for items that you could easily buy at home for less. Japan is not the place to pick up a Gucci bag; instead, try to find items that are uniquely Japanese.

Crafts in Japan are good souvenirs and presents. Some of the traditional crafts such as lacquer ware are extremely expensive, but many folk-craft items, particularly those that are handmade, are affordable.

Those interested in seeing what Japanese actually buy in the course of their daily lives can venture into one of the shopping malls or arcades located underneath train stations. Here you can find anything—food, clothing, stationery items, records, and much else. This is a good place to pick up inexpensive knick-knacks as presents. For extremely organized and civilized shopping, go to department stores. They are well-organized and usually have someone on staff who speaks English. Department stores do not have higher prices than smaller shops, and they offer convenient and pleasant shopping.

Opening and Closing Times

General business hours in Japan are 9–5. Many offices are also open at least half of the day on Saturday but are generally closed on Sunday.

Banks are open 9–3 weekdays and 9–noon on the first and last Saturday of the month. They are closed on Sunday.

Department stores are open 10–7 but are closed one day a week, which varies with each department store. Other stores are usually open 10 or 11 to 7 or 8.

Sports

Participant Sports
Beaches

For a country that consists entirely of islands, Japan has surprisingly few good beaches. Outside of Tokyo there are some good beaches in areas such as Kamakura and the Izu Peninsula, though they are absolutely mobbed with high-school and college students during the summer. The beaches of Kyushu and Shikoku are less crowded, more pleasant, and have clear blue water. The best beaches in all of Japan are in the subtropical Ryukyu Islands. Keep in mind, however, that many Japanese find it less expensive to fly to Hawaii than to go to the Ryukyus.

Bicycling

Most of Japan does not offer ideal conditions for biking. The roads are narrow, and much of the terrain is mountainous. The best cycling is probably on some of the remote islands of Japan, such as Sado, on the Sea of Japan, or Iki, a small island off the coast of Kyushu. Cyclists should bear in mind that cars drive on the left side of the street in Japan. However, for exploring a more rural area or provincial towns such as Takayama or Hagi, bicycles can be an inexpensive way to travel from one site to another. Often in these areas, there will be a rental bicycle store in close proximity to the bus or railway station. The approximate charge for rental is ¥300 per hour.

Fitness Although health clubs and aerobic studios abound in most major Japanese cities, memberships are usually long-term and expensive. Many of the major hotels in Tokyo have excellent fitness facilities that are open to their guests.

Joggers will probably find Japanese streets too narrow and crowded. Many runners in Tokyo enjoy the jogging course around the Imperial Palace.

Skiing Japan's mountains are beautiful and snowy in the winter season, with very good skiing conditions. Many skiing grounds are located near hot springs, so it is possible to combine a day of skiing with a long, restful soak in a natural hot spring.

The major drawback of skiing in Japan is the crowds, particularly on weekends and holidays. Not only are the slopes crowded, but the trains and highways heading toward ski areas are congested, and the accommodations are nearly always full. Those determined to ski in Japan should probably try to go on weekdays, or else head for Hokkaido.

Spectator Sports

Baseball Baseball is so near and dear to the hearts of most Japanese that they probably do not even remember that it is American in origin. A baseball game in Japan is not all that different from one in the United States, complete with hot dogs and fans with baseball caps. The only difference is that the field is slightly smaller and crowds are a bit more orderly, with cheering done in unison. Do not be surprised to see a few non-Japanese on the fields. Japanese professional teams are allowed two foreign players per team. American baseball notables such as Reggie Smith and Bob Horner have played in Japan. In Tokyo, the place to see pro baseball is the Korakuen, a new dome-shaped indoor stadium. Bleacher seats are approximately ¥ 700.

Sumo The earliest recorded sumo matches were held around AD 200, and it is a sport that is deeply steeped in tradition. A Shinto-style roof is hung from the ceiling over a clay circular ring. The match begins when two wrestlers face each other in the ring and toss salt into the ring as a purification ritual. The match is concluded when any part of the sumo wrestler's body touches the ground or he is pushed out of the ring.

The wrestlers are of enormous girth, usually weighing 90–165 kilograms (200–365 pounds). During the match they are clad in loincloths that cover little of the massive bodies that push and shove during the match. Yet there is a certain elegance in their movements that is much enhanced by their top-knot hairstyles that are slicked down with linseed oil.

Although inexpensive seats can be purchased for ¥500, it is worthwhile to buy the more expensive seats (¥5,000–¥6,500) because you get a large carrier bag full of refreshments and souvenirs. The food is a tasty meal of generous portions, with sushi, yakitori chicken sticks, and other Japanese foods, along with bottles of beer. Souvenirs include tasteful ceramic items or small lamps with sumo-related patterns.

Bathhouses

The art of bathing has been an intrinsic part of Japanese culture for centuries. Baths are for washing and cleansing, but for many Japanese they are a form of relaxation and pleasure. Traditionally, Japanese went to communal bathhouses that served as centers for social gatherings. Although most Japanese houses and apartments in modern times have bathtubs, many Japanese still prefer the pleasures of communal bathing—either in hot springs on vacations or in public bathhouses. More social centers than anything else, baths are places where many a confidence is exchanged and many a joke is retold.

Private or communal, Japanese baths are meant for soaking and not for washing. The water in the bath is drawn only once and thrown away only after everyone has finished; bathers must wash and rinse before getting into the bath to keep the water clean. Because the water is used by more than one person, it is a cardinal rule that no soap gets into the bathwater. Unlike Western bathtubs, in which the bather reclines, Japanese tubs are deep enough that bathers can sit upright with water up to their necks. The water is as hot as the human body can endure, but the reward for a moment of unease upon entry is the pleasure of soaking in water that does not get tepid.

The procedures for taking a Japanese bath are simple. First you sit on a stool outside the bathtub and, using a pail with a long handle, dip water (either from the bath or from faucets) cleanse yourself with soap and then rinse thoroughly. Do not worry about spilling the water, because there is a drain outside the tub. In public baths it is common for one bather to wash other people's backs and to help them rinse off. If you are in a private home, remember to place the lid on top of the tub so that the water remains as hot as possible for the next bather.

Because most major hotels only offer Western-style reclining bathtubs, those in search of the quintessentially Japanese bathing experience should either stay in a Japanese-style inn or try going to a public bathhouse. Public baths are both clean and hygienic, and they are not hard to find. There is at least one in nearly every neighborhood. Although small towels are available for a small fee, it is best to bring your own. The bathhouses are divided into male and female areas. Simply do as all the other bathers do; undress in the front room, leave your clothes in small lockers or baskets, and venture into the washing area and from there into the bath. Be prepared to see another side of Japanese life. The retiring women, for example, that you encounter on the streets will be far more forward, far more ribald than they would be in other situations. If you are more interested in a peaceful soak than in experiencing the hubbub of bathhouse life, go in the middle of the afternoon, when you will probably encounter only a few subdued elderly folk.

Hot Springs

It is fortuitous for the Japanese, who are great aficionados of bathing, that natural hot springs, known as *onsen*, dot the entire Japanese archipelago. Many onsen are surrounded by resorts that vary in nature, ranging from large Western-style hotels to small, humble inns.

For the most part, onsen water is piped into hotel rooms or large communal baths, but some onsen are located outdoors. The onsen areas are usually open year-round, so it is even possible to soak in the onsen water while surrounded by snowy winter landscapes.

For years, going to onsen was considered to be for old men and women who wanted to rest their weary bones, but in the past five years there has been a great resurgence in the popularity of onsen for people of all ages. Onsen can be found all over Japan. Some of the more well-known spas near Tokyo are Atami, Hakone, Ito, and Nikko. Some of the more famous resorts in other parts of Japan are Beppu and Unzen in Kyushu; Arima, near Kobe, in Gunma Prefecture of Honshu; and Noboribetsu in Hokkaido.

Customs, Manners, and Etiquette

Propriety is an important part of Japanese society. Many Japanese expect foreigners to behave differently and are tolerant of faux pas. They are pleasantly surprised when people acknowledge and observe their customs. The easiest way to ingratiate yourself with the Japanese is by taking the time to learn and respect their ways.

It is customary upon meeting someone to bow. The art of bowing is not as simple as you might expect. The depth of your bow depends on your social position in respect to that of the other person. Younger people, or those of lesser status, must bow deeper in order to indicate their respect and acknowledge their position. Foreigners are not expected to understand the complexity of these rules, and a basic nod of the head will suffice. Many Japanese are familiar with Western customs and will offer their hand for a good old handshake.

Do not be offended if you are not invited to someone's home. In general, most entertaining is done outside of the home in restaurants or bars. It is an honor when you are invited to a home; this means that your host feels comfortable and close with you. If you do receive an invitation, follow Japanese custom and bring along a small gift—a souvenir from your country is always the best present, but food and liquor are always appreciated. Upon entering a home, remember to remove your shoes in the foyer and put on the slippers that are provided. As you can imagine, it is important to have socks or stockings that are in good condition, as you will have to remove your footwear.

Japanese restaurants often provide a small hot towel called an *oshibori*. This is to wipe your hands but not your face. You may see some Japanese wiping their faces with their oshibori, but generally this is considered to be bad form. When you are finished with your oshibori, do not just toss it back onto the table, but fold or roll it up. Those who are not accustomed to eating with chopsticks may ask for a fork instead. When eating from a shared dish, do not use the part of the chopsticks that have entered your mouth; instead, use the end that you have been holding in your hand.

Doing Business

As Japan's role in the global economy expands, the number of business travelers to Japan increases. Although international business practices are universal, certain customs remain unique to Japan. It is not necessary to observe these precepts, but Japanese will always appreciate observance of their customs.

Business cards are mandatory in Japan. Upon meeting someone for the first time, it is common to bow and to proffer your business card simultaneously. Do not worry about getting your cards printed in Japanese—English will do. In a sense, the cards are simply a means of convenience. Japanese sometimes have difficulty with Western names, and they like to refer to the cards. Also, in a society where hierarchy matters, Japanese like to ascertain job titles and rank, so it is useful if your card indicates your position in your company. Japanese often place the business cards they have received in front of them on a table or desk as they conduct their meetings. Follow suit, and do not simply shove the card in your pocket.

The concept of being fashionably late does not exist in Japan; it is extremely important to be prompt for both social and business occasions. Japanese addresses tend to be complicated, and traffic is often heavy, so allow for adequate travel time.

Most Japanese are not accustomed to using first names in business circumstances. Even workmates of 20 years' standing use surnames. Unless you are sure that the Japanese person is extremely comfortable with Western customs, it is probably better to stick to last names. Also, respect the hierarchy, and as much as possible address yourself to the most senior person in the room.

Don't be frustrated if decisions are not made instantly. Individual businessmen are rarely empowered to make decisions, but must constantly confer with their colleagues and superiors. Even if you are annoyed, don't express anger or aggression. Losing one's temper is equated with losing face in Japan.

A separation of business and private lives remains sacrosanct in Japan, and it is best not to ask about personal matters. Rather than asking about a person's family, it is better to stick to neutral subjects. This does not mean that you can only comment on the weather, but rather that you should be careful not to be nosy. Do not be offended if you are not invited to a Japanese businessman's home. Because of cramped housing, many Japanese entertain in restaurants or bars. It is not customary for Japanese to bring wives along. If you are traveling with your spouse, do not assume that an invitation includes both of you. You may ask if it is acceptable to bring your spouse along, but remember that it is awkward for a Japanese person to say no. Hence, you should pose the question carefully, or not at all.

Usually, entertaining is done over dinner, followed by an evening on the town. Drinking is something of a national pastime in Japan. If you would rather not suffer from a hangover the next day, do not refuse your drink—sip, but keep your glass at least half full. An empty glass is nearly the equivalent of requesting another drink. You should never pour your own drink or let your companions pour theirs.

A special note to women traveling on business in Japan: Remember that although the situation is gradually changing, most Japanese women do not have careers. Many Japanese businessmen do not yet know how to interact with Western businesswomen. They may be uncomfortable, aloof, or patronizing. Be patient and, if the need arises, gently remind them that, professionally, you expect to be treated as any man would be.

Great Itineraries

Each chapter in *Fodor's Japan* has, in fact, been described as an itinerary through a particular city or region of Japan. The following are suggestions for other itineraries that cross from one area to another and combine parts of the exploring sections of the various chapters.

Introduction to Traditional Japan (One Week)

Like every nation, Japan has some sights that are more famous than others. These sights tend to be in the major cities. The following itinerary covers the barest minimum, but it does include modern Tokyo; the splendor of Nikko; the temples and shrines of Kamakura, the power center of Japan's first shogunate; the temples of classical Kyoto; and Nara, Japan's first permanent capital. Be warned that this itinerary barely scratches the surface of Japan's heritage. A week does not begin to do justice to the complexity of Japan.

Day 1: Arrive in Tokyo. Flights from the United States tend to arrive in the late afternoon, which means that by the time you reach your hotel in downtown Tokyo, it is early evening.

Day 2: Visit the major Tokyo sites that appeal to you (*see* Chapter 3). Arrange it so that your evening is spent in one or two of the nighttime districts, such as Roppongi or Shinjuku.

Day 3: Visit Nikko either on your own or with a tour (*see* Chapter 4). Return to Tokyo for evening pleasures.

Day 4: Visit Kamakura on your own, traveling to Kamakura from Tokyo by train (*see* Chapter 4). If there is time left in the day, stop on the way back to Tokyo and visit Yokohama (*see* Chapter 4).

Day 5: Take one of the morning Shinkansen trains from Tokyo to Kyoto (*see* Chapter 7). Visit the sights in the Eastern District (Higashiyama) in the afternoon and enjoy the Gion District in the evening.

Day 6: In the morning visit more of the Eastern District sights and in the afternoon visit the Western District sights.

Day 7: Cover Central Kyoto in the morning and travel to Nara in the afternoon to see the sights (*see* Chapter 8).

Day 8: Return to Tokyo via Kyoto and go straight to the airport.

An Extended Introduction to Japan (Two Weeks)

Two weeks is obviously better than one week in Japan. Covering the same ground as the one-week itinerary of Japan, this itinerary also includes some of the Japan Alps, Hiroshima, and the Seto Inland Sea.

Day 1: Arrive in Tokyo. Flights from the United States tend to arrive in the late afternoon, which means that by the time you reach your hotel in downtown Tokyo it is early evening.

Day 2: Visit any of the major Tokyo sights that appeal to you (*see* Chapter 4). Arrange your itinerary so that your evening is spent in one or two of the nighttime districts such as Roppongi or Shinjuku.

Day 3: Visit Nikko either on your own or with a tour (*see* Chapter 4). Return to Tokyo for evening pleasures.

Day 4: Visit Kamakura on your own, traveling to Kamakura from Tokyo by train (*see* Chapter 4). If there is time left in the day, stop on the way back to Tokyo and visit Yokohama (*see* Chapter 4).

Day 5: Take the train to Nagano and visit Zenkoji Temple. Continue by train to Matsumoto and visit Karasujo Castle, the Japan Folklore Museum and the Japan Ukiyo-e Museum (*see* Chapter 6). 'Alps'

Day 6: Travel via Kamikochi to Takayama (*see* Chapter 6).

Day 7: Spend the day visiting Takayama sights and in the late afternoon travel by train via Toyama to Kanazawa (*see* Chapter 6).

Day 8: Spend the day visiting the sights of Kanazawa (*see* Chapter 6) and catch the late-afternoon train to Kyoto (*see* Chapter 7).

Day 9: Visit the sights in the Eastern District (Higashiyama) in the afternoon and enjoy the Gion District in the evening.

Day 10: In the morning visit more of the Eastern District sights and in the afternoon visit the Western District sights.

Day 11: Cover Central Kyoto in the morning and Northern Kyoto in the afternoon.

Day 12: Travel to Nara in the afternoon to see the sights there (*see* Chapter 8).

Day 13: Travel by train to Himeji to visit the castle (*see* Chapter 11). Continue on to Okayama and reach Kurashiki by early afternoon.

Day 14: Leave Kurashiki by train in time to be in Hiroshima for lunch. Visit the Peace Memorial Park and Museum and then take the train and ferry to Miyajima Island and spend the night there (*see* Chapter 11).

Day 15: Return to Tokyo in the morning and go straight to the airport.

Scenic Japan

Tohoku, in northern Honshu, is a mixture of modern cities and small villages, rustic farmhouses and glorious temples, and high mountain ranges and indented shorelines. Tohoku has yet to be commercialized; there is still the feeling that one is traveling in another era. The chapter on Tohoku is an itinerary in itself. Here we have shortened the itinerary so that it can easily be managed in a week and also include a visit to Nikko.

Day 1: Take the Shinkansen train from Tokyo to Sendai. See the sights in Sendai and then take the train to Matsushima (*see* Chapter 14).

Day 2: Spend most of the day exploring Matsushima and return to Sendai for the night (*see* Chapter 14).

Day 3: Take the train to Hiraizumi and visit the sights. Reboard the train to Morioka (*see* Chapter 14).

Day 4: Take the train north as far as Obuke and transfer to a bus to cross the Hachimantai Plateau. At the end of the Aspite Skyline Drive, change buses and head south to Tozawako (*see* Chapter 14).

Day 5: Take the train to Kakunodate to visit the samurai houses. Reboard the train to travel to Yamegata to visit Yamadera (*see* Chapter 14).

Day 6: Take the train south to Yamagata and on to Fukushima, where you can board the Shinkansen train for Utsonomiya. Here, rather than return to Tokyo, you can take a local train up to Nikko (*see* Chapter 4).

Day 7: Return to Tokyo.

Into the Northern Frontier

Northern Japan is rural Japan, steeped in folklore and natural beauty. Though tourist facilities are available throughout the area of northern Honshu and Hokkaido, the number of tourists is fewer. This itinerary gives the traveler the chance to see the other side of Japan—not the industry that has spawned the country's economic miracle or the aristocratic temples of Imperial Japan—but rustic Japan, with more of what the country looked like before it was swept into 20th-century Western technology.

The itinerary starts in Sapporo in Hokkaido, on the assumption that one arrives there by plane. (The cost of flying to Sapporo from Europe or the United States is no more if you fly to Sapporo via Tokyo than if you fly just to Tokyo.)

Day 1: Explore Sapporo (*see* Chapter 15).

Day 2: Visit the Shakotan Peninsula by rented car, or by a bus/train combination. Return to Sapporo in the evening, perhaps dining at Otaru on the way back (*see* Chapter 15).

Day 3: Take the train to Asahigawa and rent a car for the drive to Sounkyo in the Daisetsuzan Park. You can also travel by bus (*see* Chapter 15).

Day 4–5: Travel by car or bus to Akan National Park. You may want to spend two nights here exploring (*see* Chapter 15).

Day 6: Travel by car or by bus and train to Abashiri and go north to Mombetsu (*see* Chapter 15).

Day 7: Travel back to Ashigawa, return the car and take the train back to Sapporo. There is the option of traveling north from Mombetsu to Wakkanai and visiting Rebun and Rishiri islands (*see* Chapter 15).

Day 8: By bus travel to Lake Toya and onto Noboribetsu Onsen (*see* Chapter 15).

Day 9: By train travel to Hakodate, visit the town (*see* Hokkaido chapter) and then reboard the train for Aomori. Change trains and go on to Hirosaki (*see* Chapter 14).

Day 10: Travel south to Akita by train and then change for a train to Kakunodate to visit the samurai houses. Reboard the train and continue on to Tozawako (*see* Chapter 14).

Day 11: Travel by train to Morioka and farther west to Miyako, with a visit to Jodogahama Beach (*see* Chapter 14).

Day 12: By train travel to Kamaishi and then east to Tono (*see* Chapter 14).

Day 13: Continue by train to Hanamaki and change for the train going to Hiraizumi. Visit the temples and before nightfall catch the train on to Sendai (*see* Chapter 14).

Day 14: Visit Matsushima and spend the day exploring and visiting the scenery. You can either spend the night or return to Tokyo via Sendai (*see* Chapter 14).

Castles

Only 12 donjons from the feudal period have survived intact. The following is a tour designed to cover the best of them, though we have had to omit the one in Hirosaki since it is off by itself in northern Tohoku (northern Honshu). While this six-day tour travels from castle town to castle town, there are plenty of other sights to see in the vicinity of each castle. At certain places you will probably wish to stay longer than the itinerary below suggests, and make it a 10-day trip.

Day 1: Leaving Tokyo or Kyoto by Shinkansen train, the first stop is Himeji and its magnificent castle. Then continue on to Okayama to visit its castle. Rather than spend the night at Okayama, take the commuter train to Kurashiki and stay there (*see* Chapter 11).

Day 2: Cross over to Shikoku either by train or ferry, and continue by bus to Kochi and its castle (*see* Chapter 12).

Day 3: Using a combination of train and bus head for Uwajima and its castle, before continuing by train to Matsuyama and its castle (*see* Chapter 12).

Day 4: By ferry cross over the Inland Sea to Hiroshima and take the train north to Matsue and its castle (*see* Chapter 11).

Day 5: Take the train to Hikone in the direction of Kyoto, visit the castle, and then continue by train via Gifu to Inuyama (*see* Chapter 5).

Day 6: From Inuyama, return to Gifu and then take the train to Matsumoto to visit one of the most attractive feudal castles. From Matsumoto, return to Tokyo (*see* Chapter 6).

In the Shadow of the Mountains

Old traditional Japan is fast disappearing, but the north coast of Western Honshu has largely avoided the eyesore of modern industrialism. This area is ideal for anyone willing to go off the beaten track and take a leisurely trip through small villages, rustic countryside, and medieval castle towns. Minimally this itinerary will take five or six days, but it could easily be extended to a leisurely 10-day exploration (*see* Chapter 11).

Day 1: Head west from Kyoto on the Shinkansen to Ogori. From Ogori (west of Hiroshima) cross from the south coast of Western Honshu to Hagi on the north coast by bus. See Hagi's sights.

Day 2: Travel by bus to Tsuwano and spend the rest of the day here.

Day 3: Take the train to Masuda and begin heading northeast along the coast. If you have the time, you may want to make Matsue your first stop.

Day 4: Make sure that you visit the Izumo Taisha Shrine.

Day 5: Continue northwest along the coast to Tottori and the Tottori Sand Dunes, then on to Kasumi and Kirosaki for the night.

Day 6: The last major sight on the coast is Amanohashidate, one of the Big Three Scenic Wonders in Japan. From here Kyoto is less than three hours away by train.

Warm Weather Adventure

Starting from Kyoto, this itinerary covers the Inland Sea, Shikoku, and Kyushu. Both Shikoku and Kyushu have their southern coasts washed by the warm Black Current, which causes almost tropical weather. Since both Shikoku and Kyushu see fewer foreigners than the major tourist centers, such as Kyoto and Tokyo, this tour offers the opportunity to experience the less commercialized side of Japan. The itinerary also covers one of Japan's most scenic places, Miyajima Island, the beautiful Himejijo Castle, the museum town of Kurashiki, and Nagasaki and Hiroshima.

Day 1: From Kyoto travel by train to Himeji to visit the castle, and then, reboarding the train, continue to Okayama and its castle. Spend the night at Kurashiki, a short distance by commuter train from Okayama (*see* Chapter 11).

Day 2: Return to Okayama and transfer to the shuttle train for Uno, where you can take the JR ferry across the Inland Sea to Takamatsu on the island of Shikoku (*see* Chapter 12). Spend the day visiting the sights of Takamatsu, perhaps even taking a trip out to Shodo Island.

Day 3: From Takamatsu, first visit Kotohira and then continue by train to Kochi (*see* Chapter 12).

Day 4: Taking the train to Kubokawa and on to Nakamura before changing to the bus, travel southwest to Cape Ashizuri. Then go north by bus to Uwajima, or if by train, backtrack toward Kochi as far as Kubokawa and change there for the Uwajima train (*see* Chapter 12).

Day 5: Cross the Bungo Channel on the ferry to Usuki (*see* Kyushu chapter) and take the train to stops north to Beppu. Spend the rest of the day visiting the hot pools and geysers, and taking the mineral waters (*see* Chapter 13).

Day 6: Take the train across Kyushu (via Oita) to Mt. Aso. In the afternoon continue on to Kumamoto (*see* Chapter 13).

Day 7: Travel north to Nagasaki (*see* Chapter 13).

Day 8: Take the train across the island of Kyushu back via Fukuoka and Kokura to Hiroshima and visit the Peace Memorial Park, with a side trip to Miyajima (*see* Chapter 11) before returning to Kyoto. An alternative way back to Kyoto from Nagasaki is to travel first to Beppu by train and then take an overnight ferry boat that sails through the Seto Inland Sea to Kobe; then take the train to Kyoto or wherever your final destination may be.

2 Portraits of Japan

Japanese History

Origins: 10,000 BC–AD 500

by Jon Spayde

The coauthor of All Japan: The Catalogue of Everything Japanese, *Jon Spayde writes about Japanese culture for* Art News *and other publications.*

No one knows for certain how long human beings have lived in the Japanese islands. Stone tools excavated in many places can be dated to periods well before 10,000 BC, and archaeologists are convinced that the sheer variety of these artifacts suggests a well-established culture even in those early times. But who these people may have been and how they arrived on the Japanese islands are still matters of conjecture.

Just as uncertain is this pre-pottery culture's relationship with the fascinating pottery-making one that followed it after about 10,000 BC. The hand-shaped pots of the so-called Jomon culture teem with so much surface ornamentation that they look as if they had been overgrown with some uncanny form of plant life. Female figures with bulging, insectlike eyes and conical legs suggest the solemn religiosity of an earth cult. And Jomon men and women may very well have been deeply religious, because they depended on hunting and fishing luck to sustain them as they traveled from camp to camp and pitched by the seaside or next to mountain springs.

Wherever it appears, agriculture marks a revolution in man's control over his environment; with its arrival in Japan around 300 BC we also become aware for the first time of something that will be a major theme in Japanese history: the nearness and prestige of the continent of Asia, particularly of Korean and Chinese culture. The charred grains of rice found at the bottom of the pots of the Yayoi culture (300 BC–AD 200) originated in eastern China. The continent also gave Japan the other great technologies of the age: metalworking, and pottery-making with the wheel. Political turmoil was driving refugees across the Sea of Japan to the forested hills and fertile valleys of the eastern islands, and these exiles seem to have been the ones who first brought Japan into the orbit of the much older cultures of the continent. Then as now, weaponry led the way; bronze halberds and swords found in Yayoi sites are based directly on Chinese models. But metal mirrors—ritual objects based on entirely secular Chinese originals—have also been discovered in these burials.

Yayoi-era changes began shaping Japan into the sort of place it would remain for many centuries: an agricultural country of settled villages growing irrigated rice and dry-field crops—but also possessed of a restless military elite on horseback, doing its best to dominate, and then unify, Japan.

The history of the period between about AD 200 and 500 is chiefly the tale of a scattering of small independent kingdoms coming to recognize the power of one of their number, based in the Yamato lowlands south of Kyoto. By 300, the chieftains of the Yamato clan had managed to subordinate several of their neighbors; for the next 250 years, these chieftains combined negotiation, political marriage, and warfare to build their kingdom into the greatest power in the country. Their greatness is plain to see even today by examining the mammoth tumuli (artificial mounds) they created as final resting places. The largest *kofun*, as the tumuli are known, is the tomb of the leader whom a later age called the Emperor Nintoku. Outside of the city of Osaka, this 5th-century creation occupies some 80 acres; shaped like a giant keyhole, it resembles a forested mountain at ground level. Whoever the shadowy Nintoku may have been, he clearly had the clout to keep thousands of workers busy for some 20 years on a project of truly Egyptian proportions.

Classical Japan: 500–1156

As long as the rulers of Yamato were merely building kofun, forging swords, and riding down their enemies in cavalry raids, their fortunes were peripheral to the history of Asia. With the coming of literacy and the Buddhist religion in the 6th century, however, Japan entered the stage of history as a junior participant in a brilliant composite civilization that stretched from Iran to Korea and Vietnam; a civilization whose common denominator was Buddhism but which also included sculptural traditions from Hellenistic Greece, the political legacy of Confucius, and the music of the Persian court.

The Yamato rulers had for many years been powerful enough to meddle in Korean politics; in 553, according to later chroniclers, the king of the small Korean state of Paekche sent a copper-and-gold image of the Buddha and other religious paraphernalia, including scriptures, to the Yamato court as part of a petition for Japanese troops to fight against his enemies. This event (probably used by the chronicler to symbolize a more gradual process of importation and Korean immigration) set off a dispute at court between the Soga, a clan well disposed to the new religion, and the Mononobe and Nakatomi, families of hereditary priests and ritualists of the good old native faith that was later named Shintoism, "the way of the gods" (gods who, in their thousands, supposedly presided over and protected Japan).

After bitter struggles, the Soga triumphed. This parvenu family, without an ancient pedigree, hitched its wagon to the star of Buddhist culture and rode it to power. After 587, when the Mononobe were crushed, the Soga led Japan's ar-

istocracy in a wholesale adoption of Buddhism and Sino-Ko-
rean culture.

The man who has long stood as the outstanding symbol of
Japan's earnest apprenticeship in the opening years of the
7th century is Prince Shotoku (574–622), who, as regent for
an infant empress, was an ally of the Soga but no mere tool
in their hands. He supported the serious application of Confucian principles to the ruling of Japan and was a genuinely
devout student of Buddhism. Shotoku founded temples and
monasteries (including the beautiful Horyuji at Nara) and
penetrated beyond the power-conferring glamour of the
new religion to the vision of compassionate kingship that is
at the heart of Buddhist politics.

But Shotoku's humane vision didn't carry the day in this
still-rugged society. When the Soga tried to seize the em-
perorship, their long-suffering rivals, the Nakatomi,
struck back in a coup d'état that has resounded throughout
Japanese history: the Taika Reform of 645. The leaders of
the rebellion were imperial legitimists but were no longer
hostile to continental culture. Like the tough-minded prag-
matists who Westernized Japan 13 centuries later, they put
foreign ideas at the service of their Japanese goal: a centralized Japan under an emperor powerful enough to resist
both invaders and usurpers.

After several false starts and at least one serious rebellion,
the greatest concrete symbol of the new regime was completed in 710: the permanent capital at Nara, modeled on
glorious Changan, seat of China's Tang Dynasty and one of
the most gracious and cosmopolitan cities Asia had ever
seen. Nara may have been a sort of poor-man's Changan,
but the delight the Japanese took in their first real city
knew no bounds. Poets in Japan's first imperially commissioned anthology, the *Manyoshu*, took joyous pleasure in
the mere sight of "goodly green-red Nara" (green for the
tile roofs, red for the wooden walls of the sturdy city).

The good fortune that Buddhism enjoyed in the Nara period is symbolized by the Todaiji Temple, built by the pious
Emperor Shomu (reigned 724–749). The rebuilt temple
tourists see today is immense; the original was gargantuan,
occupying the equivalent of 16 city blocks, with twin pagodas over 300 feet high. The fact is that, in the Nara age, Japan belonged to a world culture no less than she does today.
The treasure-house museum called the Shoso-in, on the
grounds of the Todaiji, contains beautiful and useful objects enjoyed by Shomu during his lifetime. There is an
Iranian lute inlaid with a mother-of-pearl picture of a camel
under a palm tree; textiles from desert cities beyond the
last Chinese frontier forts; herbal medicines from Southeast Asia; and masks with superbly Persian noses. This was
an age in which Japanese monks traveled regularly to China and even India, and Chinese abbots and Korean sculptors held forth before crowds of eager young Japanese disci-

ples in the monasteries and workshops of the "goodly green-red" city.

In 784, a new capital marked the opening of a new era. In that year, the Emperor Kammu (737–806) took the court away from Nara to Nagaoka, about 20 miles to the northwest. Ten years later, he forced his courtiers to move again, this time to the spot on the Kamogawa River where Kyoto now stands. This resolute and politically savvy ruler was fleeing the very Buddhist power that Shomu had done so much to build up. Heian-kyo, as the new metropolis was named, would be a larger and more resplendent Nara, built on the same Chinese principles, a fit seat for an emperor who intended to rule unimpeded by ambitious clerics.

After 850, the cultural self-confidence of this regime was so great that government-sponsored voyages to China stopped; Japan declared herself a graduate of Chinese tutelage, and politics, the arts, and literature took a brilliant native turn.

Native politics had always meant family politics, and the main theme of the political history of the Heian era was the rise of the powerful Fujiwara family, the direct descendants of the Nakatomi, those enemies of Buddhism turned reformers in 645. Fujiwara grandees served as regents for youthful emperors, then stayed on as "mayors of the palace," exercising near-total control when, as eventually happened, weak rulers ascended the throne.

The courtiers of Heian were wealthy, supremely self-satisfied, and reverent toward the sitting emperor, but they were increasingly independent of him as they built up agricultural estates in the countryside. They created a culture that broke with the themes of the Nara age. The austere Buddhism of the earlier period gave way to sects that attuned themselves to the metropolitan values of the aristocrats; dour Buddhist doctors, venerated in Nara, became figures of fun to Heian's elite, who appreciated Buddhism for its ability to gratify their visual sense with gorgeous ceremonies and to deepen the literary melancholy that they treasured.

The literary and cultural high noon of this age was the regency of Michinaga Fujiwara (served 996–1027), and the masterpiece of Michinaga's heyday was *Genji Monogatari (The Tale of Genji)*. This enormous work of fiction was given to world literature by the greatest of Heian's many women authors and poets, the prim, scholarly court lady we know as Murasaki Shikibu (ca. 970–ca. 1030). Her book is an extended portrait of the age's beau ideal: Hikaru Genji, the complete courtier. Genji composes poetry with effortless brilliance, judges elegant handwriting with a connoisseur's eye, and plays the great drum or the flute beautifully at court music sessions. But mainly, Genji is a lover, and the novel is, among other things, a great catalogue of woman-

kind. Its sophisticated truthfulness and psychological subtlety easily survive 900 years and translation into another
tongue.

The Genji world, both fictional and real, was obsessed with
its own beauty and fragility, and when the Heian court lost
its power, it lost it in a manner we would call tragic. It fell on
the heels of a series of catastrophes that convinced many
sensitive thinkers and writers that the world itself was
coming to an end. Another elite had been flexing its muscles
while the snobbish courtiers of Heian carried on their elegant pastimes and spoke of the provinces as purgatory and
of commoners as animals. It was an elite of horse-riding
warriors, descended from aristocrats but brought up far
from Heian, both geographically and psychologically. As
they began to appear in the streets of the capital, they became *the* harbingers of the seven centuries to come, during
which—directly or indirectly—soldiers ruled Japan. It
was an era that, on one reckoning, didn't end until the signing of the instrument of surrender on board the U.S.S. *Mis-
souri* in 1945.

Feudal Japan: 1185–1600

For all the refinement of the capital, the Heian period was a
restless age in the country as a whole, especially after
about 1060. Banditry, piracy, and insurrection flared up,
and a succession of ambitious emperors tested the limits of
Fujiwara power. Japan became a place where disciplined
bands of armed men could be kept busy.

Such bands grew up in the provinces. Fiercely loyal to their
families and their commanders, they protected the agricultural estates of the aristocracy and were often called upon
to become de facto imperial armies fighting rebels or the
aboriginal Ainu. These bands were rewarded with land and
court titles.

In 1156, a succession dispute broke out between court factions, and the party led by the retired but still influential
Emperor Shirakawa (1053–1129) invited soldiers of the
Taira clan into the capital to crush the opposition. This was
easily managed; but after it was over, the Taira under
Kiyomori (1118–1181) refused to leave the city; in fact,
Kiyomori stayed on as virtual military dictator of the country, ruling in the circumspect Fujiwara style and marrying
his daughters to imperial princes.

To the Japanese, the Taira are symbols of the impermanence of worldly glory; their reign was short. In 1180, another great warrior family, the Minamoto (who had made
their name fighting rebels in northern Japan), rose up
against Kiyomori; thus began the most romanticized war in
the treasury of Japanese song and story. The Minamoto
clan leader Yoritomo (1147–1199) and his brilliant younger
brother Yoshitsune (1159–1189) capped a series of land vic-

tories with a great sea fight at Dannoura in the Inland Sea, in which the baby Emperor Antoku was drowned along with countless Taira seamen and warriors.

The renown of the victory, engineered by the dashing Yoshitsune (a hero who became the Prince Genji of a war-like age), roused the jealousy of the supremely unromantic and hardheaded Yoritomo, who had his brother hunted down and killed. The Taira-Minamoto war and Yoritomo's fratricide contributed to a new artistic sensibility: The great Buddhist theme of the impermanence of all earthly things, which in Heian had been treated with great subtlety in individual lives, was now played out on battlefields and in the histories of proud warrior clans. Prose literature turned from the courtly diary and the novel to the military epic, sung with the accompaniment of the *biwa* (lute) to audiences of warriors and common folk. Painters depicted the torments of Buddhist hells, and traveling evangelists preached salvation through simple faith in the Buddha Amida.

Yoritomo and his successors ruled this troubled and newly dynamic Japan not from Kyoto but from Kamakura on the great eastern plain called the Kanto (where Tokyo would one day stand), the heartland of the warrior class. The efficiency of this regime was not diminished—at least not for a while—by the rise within it of that familiar phenomenon, indirect rule by regents. The Hojo family, prominent retainers of the Minamoto, began playing the Fujiwara role, standing in the stead of the ruling *shoguns* (generals). A figurehead imperial house was now further removed from real power by a figurehead shogun and his regent, and a resolute, tragic emperor rose up to challenge this state of affairs.

The revolt in 1221 of the Emperor Go-Toba (1180–1239), who declared the Hojo regent an outlaw, was a test of the nerve of the entire warrior class. Spurred on by Yoritomo's widow Masako (1156–1225), the Minamoto vassals and allies stood firm. In this standoff between a samurai woman and the emperor of Japan, the emperor lost. He was exiled to the remote Oki Islands, where he spent his last days as the compiler of one of the greatest anthologies of classical verse, the *Shinkokinshu.*

An even greater test of *bakufu* (military government) strength was the seaborne invasion of Japan by Mongol troops of Kublai Khan's Yuan Dynasty in China. On two separate occasions (1274 and 1281), the bakufu's vassals in Kyushu did what Persian and Chinese armies had failed to do—they held back the horde. Both times, the Japanese were aided by their native gods, who saw fit to send devastating winds and high seas to swamp the Korean ships the invaders rode.

What Kublai could not engineer—the fall of the Hojo/Mina-
moto regime—was brought about at home through the
machinations of another of Japan's great rebel emperors,
Go-Daigo (1288–1339). In Go-Daigo, the bakufu had an imperial foe to reckon with. With a patience and a cunning
that contrasted sharply with Go-Toba's impulsiveness, Go-
Daigo strengthened the finances of the imperial house and
courted samurai who were unhappy with Hojo rule. But before the coup could be mounted, the bakufu struck, and another emperor was packed off to the desolate Okis.

Go-Daigo, however, had no intention of ending his days,
like his predecessor had, in a limbo of literature and regret.
With the aid of his son, he escaped from the Okis and returned to the mainland, raising the standard of legitimacy
and rebellion once more. This time the insurrection took.
Powerful families, led by the warrior Takauji Ashikaga
(1304–1358), forswore Kamakura. In 1333, Ashikaga's soldiers murdered the last Hojo regent and ushered in two full
centuries of political disintegration.

The next casualty of Go-Daigo's rebellion was Go-Daigo's
court. Takauji Ashikaga, who more than matched Yoritomo
in craft and ambition, declared himself displeased with the
new emperor's administration (it does seem to have been in-
ept). He turned on the sovereign and placed him under
house arrest in Kyoto. With his back to the wall once more,
Go-Daigo kept his nerve. When Takauji placed a rival emperor on the throne (who later declared Takauji shogun),
Go-Daigo fled south to the old imperial pleasure ground at
Yoshino, where he established a rival court. For the next 60
years, the enemy courts fought an inconclusive war. Incessant campaigning weakened the new bakufu and forced the
Ashikaga rulers to depend upon the powerful military families to keep order in the country at large. But the grandees
at the head of these families were evolving from the loyal
vassals of Kamakura days into practically autonomous local
lords who built up their castle towns into trade centers and
increasingly thought of their relationship with the bakufu
as an alliance between equals.

The Ashikaga years (1333–1523) could have been culturally
barren, at least if one thinks great art requires great
peace. But as in the roughly contemporary Italian Renaissance, a violent time produced an unprecedented inven-
tiveness and refinement in the arts. Paradoxically, the chief
arts of the Ashikaga period were those of tranquillity: garden design, ink painting, the tea ceremony, the Noh drama.
And even more paradoxically, the peak time for these arts,
which seem to us the essence of the Japanese spirit, was an
age of intense admiration for China. Medieval Japan was
back in touch with the continent, mainly via Zen, or medita-
tive, Buddhism.

The Zen sect had been established in Japan under the Kamakura regime—military men were attracted to its asceti-

cism and elitism—and under the Ashikaga (whose head-quarters in the Muromachi quarter of Kyoto has given its name to the age), Zen priests became diplomats and spiritual advisers of the elite. Although Zen rejects scripture in favor of direct perception of the Buddhist truth of universal emptiness—a perception reached during arduous medita-tion—in the Muromachi period (1338–1573), Zen priests were well-read intellectuals who imbued the arts they influ-enced with a continental up-to-dateness that was secular and deeply spiritual at the same time.

A cultural achievement such as the Japanese garden is a case in point. It is a rich hybrid of Zen practice (in that it is mainly intended to aid meditation), Chinese elegance (gar-dens re-create Chinese, not Japanese, beauty spots), and the classical Japanese cult of the changing seasons. Similar-ly, flower arrangement and the very popular tea ceremony, with roots in Sino-Buddhist culture, have blossomed into distinctly Japanese hybrids during this age.

The Ashikaga Shogun Yoshimasa (1436–1490) was the era's greatest patron of the arts, but he was no soldier, and he found himself presiding over a Japan slipping into anarchy. When the influential Yamana and Hosokawa families went to war over which family would determine shogunal succes-sion, the battleground was Kyoto. A decade of fighting, which the Ashikaga were utterly powerless to stop and which embroiled the armies of more and more provincial lords, left Kyoto a smoking ruin. When it was over, the *dai-myo* (as these lords were now known) who had been busy in the capital suddenly found themselves challenged by rebel-lious vassals back in the provinces, and they hurried home with flags flying. Those lords who had been entrusted with the responsibility of keeping order in the countryside found themselves holding the bag for an impotent bakufu.

In short, Japan was in a situation it had not faced since the 4th century: It was every clan for itself. The imperial house was bankrupt, the shogunate a formality. All bets were off, and an age was dawning when the shrewdest and most ruthless warrior, whatever his social origins or connections with traditional power, could be the ruler of the nation if he could hammer its pieces back together.

In the 16th century, Japan first made the acquaintance of European civilization in the humble guise of a handful of Portuguese sailors who were shipwrecked off the coast of Kyushu in 1543. These were expansive years for European power, and, by the 1560s, Portuguese and Spanish mission-aries had established themselves at Nagasaki and else-where in Japan, and Nagasaki was a regular port of call for Portuguese and Spanish merchant ships. But unlike many another country visited by Europeans in these years, Japan was in no danger of falling under their domination. Never in her history, before or since, has she had such forceful lead-ers as the triumvirate of Nobunaga Oda (1534–1582),

Hideyoshi Toyotomi (1536–1598), and Ieyasu Tokugawa (1546–1616), who together pulled their country out of the rubble of the Ashikaga collapse and forged a formidably self-protective and self-conscious Japan.

Nobunaga, who by 1560 had fought his way to the lordship of the Owari domain east of Lake Biwa, looked longingly at nearby Kyoto. Since 1156, military control of the capital had meant eventual overlordship of Japan. After securing his rear through campaigns and alliances with lords to his east and north, Nobunaga marched into the capital in 1568 in the company of Yoshiaki Ashikaga, whom he set up as shogun. But when Yoshiaki grew restive as lord of Owari's puppet, Nobunaga drove the last of the Ashikaga out of the city gates; thus passed the dynasty established by the fierce Takauji two centuries before.

Ruthless and practical, Nobunaga was also something of a Europhile; he affected a Spanish cape and liked red wine. Best of all of Europe's gifts he liked firearms, and he put them to devastating use when he moved east against the Takeda family, of Kai province in central Honshu, one of his allies during the Kyoto campaign. The Minamoto vassals had met Kublai Khan's Mongols as individual warriors, calling out their lineages and staking their lives on their superb swords, the world's best; Nobunaga's musketeers were peasant foot soldiers who mowed down the Takeda chivalry with massed firepower, rather in the manner of conquistadors versus Aztecs. (Not accidentally, this age saw the building of massive castles girded with stone to withstand such assaults.)

With the Kyoto heartland and the east under his belt, Nobunaga next dispatched two of his best generals, Mitsuhide Akechi (1528–1582) and Hideyoshi Toyotomi (1537–1598), to western Japan. In one of the greatest double-crosses in Japanese history, Mitsuhide reversed his line of march, reentered Kyoto, and murdered Nobunaga in 1582. Hideyoshi saw his opportunity, the perfect coalescence of feudal piety and naked self-interest. He assaulted Kyoto and destroyed his lord's destroyer, thus becoming paramount himself.

With a dogged prudence that matched Nobunaga's open ruthlessness, Hideyoshi campaigned in northern Honshu and Shikoku in 1585, then invaded the southernmost island of Kyushu, where he humbled the proud Shimazu house of Satsuma, a feudal state that was used to such independence that it even carried on its own foreign relations with China and Okinawa.

Hideyoshi's control of Japan was assured when, in 1590, he ousted the Hojo, the ancient family of regents, from their domains in the Kanto Plain. He bestowed this rich land upon his ally Ieyasu Tokugawa, who was to make good use of it in the next decades.

Hideyoshi Toyotomi was more than Japan's first unifier-by-force in 1,200 years; he was also a symbol of his age. This farmer's son was the first peasant to rule Japan (though his lineage prevented him from even attempting to have himself named shogun), and he had an unparalleled grasp of the nuts-and-bolts requirements of power. Among his most careful and effective plans was a nationwide "sword hunt" that disarmed the peasantry (thereby creating a gulf between the common people and the samurai and also ensuring that no upstart would follow in Hideyoshi's footsteps).

But Hideyoshi was capable of follies that were as great as his triumphs. The years 1592–1595 saw two of them. Childless, he appointed a capable 20-year-old nephew, Hidetsugu, as his heir; at the same time he launched an invasion of Korea and China from Kyushu. By 1593, one of his concubines had given birth. Two years later, he ordered the now superfluous Hidetsugu to commit suicide with his entire household. Even by the relaxed standards of this ruthless age, it was a cruel measure, and some of Hideyoshi's allies went so far as to question his sanity. Meanwhile, the continental campaign had bogged down in inconclusive fighting against a heroic Korean navy and the armies of the Ming Dynasty. Another assault fared no better, and, when the old dictator died in 1598, his forces were weary and ready to come home.

The council of regents that the dying Hideyoshi had convened to rule on behalf of his infant heir, Hideyori, saw to the repatriation of the troops at the end of 1598. It was practically the last thing they agreed on. The Kanto baron Ieyasu was the paramount regent, and, when a subordinate lord named Mitsunari Ishida stirred up jealousy against him Ieyasu realized he was no safer from treachery than Nobunaga had been. A lifetime of warfare had taught this plodding, prudent warrior of bland demeanor that there were times when the only safety was in ruthless action. He led an army of 80,000 Kanto region troops against Ishida and his western allies and crushed them on the plain of Sekigahara on October 21, 1600.

Tokugawa power was now unchallengeable. With the rise of the phlegmatic Ieyasu to the office of shogun in 1603 (a letter from the emperor was arranged, and Minamoto lineage was "discovered" in Ieyasu's undistinguished background), the era of great personalities was over. So were 300 devastating years of war. Ieyasu Tokugawa reversed the course of Japanese history by devising a political system so carefully balanced and set against disruption that the next 250 years would seem to some like a charmed era, a serene and changeless golden age of traditional Japan.

Tokugawa Japan: 1603-1853

Of course, the Tokugawa era was anything but changeless. In the 250 years between Ieyasu's assumption of the shogunate and the arrival of Commodore Matthew C. Perry at the harbor of Uraga in 1853, Ieyasu's system preserved a peace that allowed major changes at all levels of society and culture.

That system was a network of regulations applied to every one of the institutions that had disturbed Japan in the recent past. First among these, of course, were the great lords themselves. Ieyasu established trusted and long-term allies in the heartland of Japan, the capital region and the Kanto. Lords who had opposed him before Sekigahara were granted lands far away from this strategic central zone. All the lords were kept in a sort of genteel poverty by the requirement that they spend half of every year in attendance upon the shogun at his capital, Edo (today's Tokyo), and also by the periodic exactions that the Tokugawa bakufu made for road repairs and other public works. The idea was simple: the bakufu police could keep tabs on the daimyo, and the lords' coffers would be too bare to pay for revolt.

The Kyoto court that had once produced insurgent emperors was placed under polite but firm curbs; aristocrats were effectively forbidden from leaving the palace complex except on ceremonial errands.

The Buddhist establishment was supported, but only as a sort of vaccine against Christianity. Ieyasu was particularly anxious to remove the cancer of international religious politics from his dominions; he had no wish to see Japan made a battleground between Spanish and Portuguese traders, Franciscans and Jesuits, or Protestants and Catholics. He also feared domestic Catholics, and with reason; samurai converts who carried the cross into battle and invoked St. James as Spanish soldiers did had been among his opponents when he laid siege to the remnants of Hideyoshi's family in Osakajo Castle in 1615. So, in 1618, the shogunate began to torture and even crucify converts who would not abjure the faith, driving many underground to form secret Christian communities that preserved a strange Buddhist-tinged Catholicism for 200 years.

After 1639, the country was closed, not just to missionaries but also to most foreign trade. The Protestant Dutch (whose warships had helped the shogunate massacre Catholics) were permitted to maintain a cramped little outpost on an artificial island in Nagasaki harbor, which eventually became a window into (and out of) sealed Japan.

With the screws turned down so far on potential sources of disruption, change went on at a more stately pace than during the bloody centuries preceding Sekigahara. The military in Edo and the dominions turned into administrators instead of fighters; swordsmanship became only one of many samurai accomplishments, along with the tea ceremony, scholarship, philosophy, and poetry. The populace got slowly and steadily richer, as domestic markets grew in complexity and the banking and brokerage businesses developed.

The most unstable and exciting places in this stable society were the major cities: Kyoto, home of proud artisans; Osaka, the great city of sake brewers, rice brokers and moneylenders; and Edo, the Washington, DC, of Japan, which was filled with samurai bureaucrats of the central government and all the domains. Artisans and merchants were at the bottom of the Tokugawa social scale, but as these urban commoners grew rich during the course of the long peace, the whole society came to dance to their tune. Financially strapped samurai families found themselves in debt to their social inferiors, and some merchants were even granted samurai pedigrees and the right to wear two swords in exchange for discreet fiscal favors.

These proud and powerful merchants created one of the world's great urban cultures. In Kyoto, Osaka, and Edo, the licensed brothel quarters, teahouses, bathhouses, and restaurants teemed with stylishly dressed (and undressed) pleasure seekers. To belong to this world, you had to know your way around the ladies-for-hire, keep up with the latest topical puppet plays, and stay in tune with the trends in fashion and deportment set by the leading actors and the most elegant courtesans.

The prim official Confucianism of the authorities made little headway here—censorship was tightened periodically, but, after all, the pleasure quarters called as seductively to many sedentary samurai as they did to rice-brokerage apprentices and tattooed gamblers. The Balzac of this world was Saikaku Ihara (1642–1693), whose novels capture a new version of the great theme of impermanence. These middle-class high-livers call themselves the inhabitants of the *ukiyo*, the "floating world" of momentary wealth and passing pleasure. The falling cherry blossom meant the changeable heart of one's lover to a Heian aristocrat; to the poetic spirit of the feudal age, it suggested a warrior dying in battle; to Saikaku's heroes and heroines, who chase love and money with equal devotion and are proud of their modishness and savvy, the cherry's brief splendor is a reminder that joy, like fashion, is fragile and of the moment. Tokugawa-period hedonism and stylishness become profound when they remind us (ever so gently) of death.

In many respects, Tokugawa culture was a great summing-up of everything that had preceded it in Japanese art and thought. Puppet-play writers, novelists, and poets—such as the great Basho Matsuo (1644–1694), who elevated the witty poetry called *haikai* into high art—drew upon classical Chinese and Japanese learning even when they wrote comedies and parodies. A school of consummate craftsmen in Kyoto revived the palette and the sensibility of the Heian court. Cultured samurai amateurs painted like Chinese literati. And everywhere, great labors of essay writing, library building, and connoisseurship were carried on.

In Japanese thought, an obsession with the past is sometimes a means of moving forward. The most backward-looking of Tokugawa-era thinkers were the scholars of "national learning" *(kokugaku)*—philologists and linguists who worked on the oldest Japanese texts and who also cherished a political agenda. In a Sinophilic age, they boosted ancient Japan; in the era of shogunal bureaucracy, they looked back to the great ages of direct imperial rule and revered the medieval rebel emperors.

Their rivals included not only the Confucianists but also a tiny community of "Dutch-scholars," students allowed by the shogunate to examine Dutch books provided by the traders in Nagasaki harbor. These were iconoclastic men whose studies sometimes led them surprisingly far from Tokugawa ideals. As their command of Dutch grew greater and they explored mysteries such as copperplate etching, Western medicine, vanishing-point perspective, and even camera-obscura photography, they grew restless under Ieyasu's orderly system and longed to study the world face-to-face and to cast away all authorities—Chinese, Japanese, feudal, and familial—in the pursuit of a new body of science.

After 1853 and a grave political crisis, the Tokugawa peace came to a boil, and this time the disruption was more profound and interesting than simple war. A massive, self-confident urban population, a class of young idealists who revered the emperor, and inquirers into things Western joined together in a great backward leap that, with startling speed, produced modern Japan.

Modern Japan: 1853–Present

The profound political crisis after 1853 was not merely the result of the arrival of Commodore Perry and his "black ships" on their mission to set up trade and diplomatic relations with a closed Japan. It was the Tokugawa bakufu's response, seen by many as treasonous cowardice. Perry's 1853 voyage had been a simple show of force; as promised, he returned in 1854 and compelled a flustered shogunate to sign a diplomatic treaty. Full commercial relations with the United States, including a consulate on Japanese soil, followed in 1858. Similar treaties were soon signed with European nations, and Ieyasu's closed-country policy became a relic.

The result was an explosion of antiforeign violence and antibakufu agitation. Young samurai from the domains of Satsuma and Choshu in Kyushu and Tosa in Shikoku took up the great slogan of the age: *sonno-joi*, "revere the emperor and expel the barbarians." They struck up alliances with like-minded young courtiers in Kyoto, and from the conclaves of these radical "men of purpose" *(shishi)* emerged—or rather reemerged—the vision of a Japan united under a powerful emperor, with the bakufu swept away once and for all. Only such a Japan, they reasoned, could abrogate the humiliating and unequal treaties.

These activities eventually persuaded key daimyo and senior nobles to fall in with their plans, and a demoralized bakufu capitulated again, this time to the sonno-joi advocates. The last reigning shogun in Japanese history, Keiki Tokugawa (1837–1913), voluntarily stepped down in 1867. On the morning of January 3, 1868, the formal restoration of direct imperial rule was proclaimed by the 16-year-old Emperor Meiji (1852–1912).

One thing the Meiji Restoration was not, however, was a genuine return of the reins of government to the emperor. It was instead the accession to power of a remarkable young clique of ex-samurai officials from the western domains—men whose antiforeignism soon underwent a sea change. They clothed their policies in the language of imperial loyalism; they reorganized and promoted the native cult of Shintoism into a state religion; they built an educational system that stressed the personal loyalty of every Japanese to the imperial house; and, in many other ways, they fulfilled the agenda of the philosophers of "national learning" in the Tokugawa period. But they also set the country on the tracks of "civilization and enlightenment" *(bummei kaika)*—the thought and technology of the West. They intended to defend Japan's honor by joining the club of her potential enemies, the modern industrialized nations.

The Meiji period (1868–1912) was, therefore, a time of dizzying change, as the government sought the aid of foreign experts in many fields. With their help, a national-conscript army and a modern navy were created; Japanese industry grew up from silkworm culture to steel making; new modes of farming were tried in the virgin lands of Hokkaido; and even such things as the teaching of art and music were totally transformed.

The men and women of Meiji were experimenters: in dress, in cuisine (beef restaurants made their first appearance in this era), in art and literature (the heirs of Murasaki and Saikaku discovered Shakespeare and Shaw at the same time), in sexual relations. Twenty-five years after the fall of the last shogun, Tokyo had a municipal street railway, and Japan had a national parliament, which had been convened in 1890 after a decade of struggle between two factions of the ruling clique.

These authoritarian rulers of Japan, led by the first prime minister, Hirobumi Ito (1841–1909), had initiated the Meiji

changes not to create a more liberal society but to make a
stronger nation. The tests of their success were diplomacy
and warfare. In 1895, Japan humiliated the Chinese empire
in a brief war for control of Korea, but it was forced by a
consortium of European powers (which were themselves
busy gobbling up China) to give up their territorial claims
on the continent.

It was a bittersweet victory that fed Japanese resentment
of the Western powers. But Japan's smashing defeat of Russia in a 1904–1905 war (fought to keep the czarist state out
of Korea) was an unambiguous triumph. Japan, which had
been powerless before a handful of American sailors and
marines in 1853, had defeated a great (if ailing) European
power. She even acquired a colony on the mainland with the
annexation of Korea in 1910.

World War I may have been a tragedy for Europe, but it was
a boon for Japan. Her minimal participation in the Allied
cause left her unscathed, and war needs strengthened her
industry and expanded her trade with Asia. The postwar
era also saw a strengthening of representative government
as the influence of the elderly heroes of the Restoration
waned and the torch was passed to party politicians who
had never known feudalism.

Even the terrible earthquake that shook the Tokyo region
in 1923 became a symbol of renewal. The Tokyo that
emerged from the rubble and the ash in the ensuing years
had a more cosmopolitan look, and it struggled to become a
real world city, not just a modernized Edo. Japanese film
made its first substantial achievements in the 1920s, and
arts such as oil painting, poetry in the modern style, and
photography essentially caught up with Western developments. By the end of the decade, there were competent
Japanese futurists, surrealists, expressionists, and Freud-
ians, at least in Tokyo; even in Kyoto, young people danced
to "Tokyo Conga" by the rhumba band called the Tokyo
Cuban Boys.

Culturally, the 1930s were a deepening of this cosmo-
politanism, as well as the heyday of the Left in literature
and art. But politically, it was an increasingly dangerous
time for liberalism. Military influence over civilian cabinets
increased, and ultranationalist young officers called for a
second Restoration that would cleanse Japan, not of the
bakufu this time but of the scourges of capitalism, liberalism, Marxism, modernism, and other diseases that were
sapping Japan's will to fight and her single-minded devotion to the emperor. It goes without saying that the young
officers sought a greater role for Japan in Asia.

On September 18, 1931, a bomb planted by Japanese agents
exploded on the tracks of the Japanese-owned South Manchuria Railway. Local Chinese troops were blamed, and the
Japanese garrison seized control of Manchuria itself. Six

years later, Japanese troops stationed in Peking, Shanghai, and Nanking, under the terms of the settlement of the Boxer Rebellion of 1900, moved to protect Japanese interests against what they saw as a dangerously powerful Nationalist Chinese government. It escalated into a full-scale, protracted Japanese in-vasion of China.

To patriotic Japanese, the China campaign had an irrefutable logic: the territorial gains for which Japanese servicemen had shed their blood in 1895 and 1905 had been stolen by the jealous West; tiny Japan needed an overseas sphere of influence for her very survival; and those who sought to restrain Japanese expansion were really strangling her.

The other, and more tragic, consequence of the China campaign was that it required the Japanese to advance south into the tin-and-rubber-rich French, English, and Dutch colonies of Southeast Asia to obtain war materiel that could no longer be had from the United States, which was leading the international opposition to Japan's China adventure. And finally, as Japanese-American diplomacy broke down, the security of the sea-lanes required Japanese strategists to neutralize American power in the Philippines and at Pearl Harbor in Hawaii.

With the December 7, 1941, attack, liberalism in Japan came to a dead halt. Intellectuals fell in line, almost to a man; artists cooperated; and poets who had helped Japan discover her modern soul turned to praise-poems of the imperial house and the valor of Japanese arms. In the prevailing view, Pearl Harbor was really a sort of attack on Japan; exposed now to the full might of America, Japan was the one in danger. Propaganda touted glorious victories, of course, but what the Japanese really loved was the spirit of sacrifice, and that somber spirit characterized the Japanese attitude toward this unwinnable war almost from the beginning.

It was a realistic attitude. After the Japanese defeats at Midway and the Coral Sea in the very first year of the conflict, Japan had no real chance of turning back the American amphibious and airborne advance that ended with the firebombing of Tokyo and the dawn of the nuclear age. In an ironic footnote to Japan's troubled history of love and hate for the West, the cities chosen for atomic annihilation were Hiroshima, the headquarters of Protestantism in Japan, and Nagasaki, the Catholic city of the 16th century, graveyard of martyrs, and Japan's first window on the rest of the world.

The rebuilding of Japan after her destruction at American hands is one of the great success stories of the century. General Douglas MacArthur, who led the 1946–1952 occupation of the country, became the first foreign ruler of the Japanese islands—and a hero to millions of war-weary, genuinely disillusioned Japanese greatly in need of a strong hand in Tokyo. Ex-New Dealers in the occupation bureaucracy dismantled Japanese industry and rehabilitated the Japanese Left. With the escalating Cold War, and some careful prodding by Prime Minister Shigeru Yoshida (1878–1967), however, the Americans were persuaded to use their economic might to build Japan up into a reliable ally in the Pacific. With the end of the occupation in 1952, Japan embarked upon her career of economic growth, domestic political consensus, and expanding trade with Asia and the world.

Living under an American-drafted constitution that renounces war, and shielded by a 1952 treaty with the United States that makes the latter responsible for Japanese security in the event of a major war, Japan has been free to pursue the arts of peace for nearly 40 years now. She has become an economic giant (the world's leading creditor nation), and her architects, artists, and designers are at last taking positions of leadership in the creation of the international culture of the late 20th century. Her increasing international presence is bringing calls for her to adjust her inward-looking political attitudes and reassess her pacifism. All is not rosy for this successful nation. She faces challenges that could become dangers: absurdly crowded cities, an aging population, slower growth, the competition of an economically vibrant South Korea, and the resentment of an America hurt by Japanese exports. The outstanding spiritual problem for her wealthy younger generation will be finding a way to define itself as two things at once: the heirs of a rich and very particular tradition, self-involved and ambivalent about the outside world; and confident *kokusaijin* (international people), poised for something new in their history: world leadership.

Japan at a Glance: A Chronology

10,000–300 BC Neolithic Jomon hunting and fishing culture leaves richly decorated pottery.

300 AD Yayoi culture displays knowledge of farming and metallurgy imported from Korea.

After 300 The Yamato tribe consolidates power in the rich Kansai plain and expands westward, forming the kind of military aristocratic society that was to dominate Japan's history.

c. 500 Yamato leaders, claiming to be descended from the sun goddess, Amaterasu, take the title of emperor.

552 Buddhism, introduced to the Yamato court from China by way of Korea, complements rather than replaces the indigenous Shinto religion. Horyuji, a Buddhist temple built at Nara in 607, includes the oldest surviving wooden building in the world.

593–622 Prince Shotoku encourages the Japanese to embrace Chinese culture.

710–784 **Nara Period**

Japan has first permanent capital (at Nara); great age of Buddhist sculpture, piety, and poetry.

794–1160 **The Fujiwara or Heian Period**

The capital is moved from Nara to Heiankyo (Kyoto), where the imperial court is dominated by the Fujiwara family. Lady Murasaki's novel *The Tale of Genji*, written c. 1020, describes the elegant, ceremonious court life.

1185–1335 **The Kamakura Period**

Feudalism enters, with military and economic power in the provinces and the emperor a powerless, ceremonial figurehead in Kyoto. Samurai warriors welcome Zen, a new sect of Buddhism from China.

1192 After a war with the Taira family, Yoritomo of the Minamoto family becomes the first shogun; he places his capital in Kamakura.

1274, 1281 The fleets sent by Chinese emperor Kublai Khan to invade Japan are destroyed by typhoons, praised in Japanese history as *kamikaze*, or divine wind.

1336–1568 **Ashikaga Period**

The Ashikaga family assumes the title of shogun and settles in Kyoto. The Zen aesthetic flourishes in painting, landscape gardening, and tea ceremony. The Silver Pavilion on Ginkaku-ji in Kyoto, built in 1483, is the quintessential example of Zen-inspired architecture. The period is marked by constant warfare but also by increased trade with the mainland. Osaka develops into an important commercial city, and trade guilds appear.

1543   Portuguese sailors, the first Europeans to reach Japan, initiate trade relations with the lords of western Japan and introduce the musket, which changes Japanese warfare.

1549–1551   St. Francis Xavier, the first Jesuit missionary, introduces Christianity.

1568–1600   The Momoyama Period of National Unification

Two generals, Nobunga Oda and Hideyoshi Toyotomi, are the central figures of this period.

1592, 1597   Hideyoshi invades Korea. He brings back Korean potters, who rapidly develop a Japanese ceramic industry.

1600–1868   The Tokugawa Period

Ieyasu Tokugawa becomes shogun after the battle of Sekigahara. The military capital is established at Edo (Tokyo), which shows phenomenal economic and cultural growth. A hierarchy of four social classes—warriors, farmers, artisans, and merchants—is rigorously enforced. The merchant class, however, is increasingly prosperous and effects a transition from a rice to a money economy. Also, merchants patronize new, popular forms of art: kabuki, haiku, and the ukiyo-e school of painting. The life of the latter part of this era is beautifully illustrated in the wood block prints of the artist Hokusai (1760–1849).

1618   Persecution of Christians who refuse to recant.

1637–1638   Japanese Christians massacred in the Shimabara uprising. Japan is closed to the outside world except for a Dutch trading post in Nagasaki harbor.

1853   The American Commodore Perry reopens Japan to foreign trade.

1868–1912   The Meiji Restoration

Supporters of Emperor Meiji, calling for direct imperial rule, depose the shogun and move the capital to Edo, renaming it Tokyo. Japan is modernized along Western lines with a constitution proclaimed in 1889; a system of compulsory education and a surge of industrialization follow.

1902–1905   Japan defeats Russia in the Russo–Japanese War and achieves world-power status.

1910   Japan annexes Korea.

1914–1918   Japan joins the Allies in World War I.

1923   A catastrophic earthquake shakes Tokyo and Yokohama.

1931   Japan seizes the Chinese province of Manchuria.

1937   Following years of increasing military and diplomatic activity in northern China, open warfare breaks out (until 1945); it is resisted by both Nationalists and Communists.

1939–1945 Japan, having signed anti-Communist treaties with Nazi Germany and Italy (1936 and 1937), invades and occupies French Indochina.

1941 The Japanese attack on Pearl Harbor on December 7 brings the United States into war against Japan in the Pacific.

1942 Japan's empire extends to Indo-China, Burma, Malaya, the Philippines, and Indonesia. Defeat by U.S. forces at Midway in June turns the tide of Japanese military success.

1945 Tokyo and 50 other Japanese cities are devastated by U.S. bombing raids. The United States drops atomic bombs on Hiroshima and Nagasaki, precipitating Japanese surrender.

1945–1952 The American occupation under General Douglas MacArthur disarms Japan and encourages the establishment of a democratic government. Emperor Hirohito retains his position.

1953 After the Korean War Japan begins a period of great economic growth.

1964 Tokyo hosts the Summer Olympic games.

Late 1960s Japan develops into one of the major industrial nations in the world.

mid-1970s Japanese production of electronics, cars, cameras, and computers places her at the heart of the emerging "Pacific Rim" economic sphere and threatens to spark a trade war with the industrial nations of Europe and the United States.

1989 Emperor Hirohito dies.

The Discreet Charm of Japanese Cuisine

by Diane Durston

A resident of Kyoto for over 10 years, Diane Durston is the author of Old Kyoto: A Guide to Traditional Shops, Restaurants and Inns *and* Kyoto: Seven Paths to the Heart of the City.

Leave behind the humidity of Japan in summer and part the crisp linen curtain of the neighborhood *sushi-ya* some hot night in mid-July. Enter a world of white cypress and chilled sea urchin, where a welcome *oshibori* (hot towel) awaits your damp forehead, and a master chef stands at your beck and call. A cup of tea to begin. A tiny mound of ginger to freshen the palate, and you're ready to choose from the colorful array of fresh seafood on ice inside a glass case before you. Bite-size morsels arrive in friendly pairs. A glass of ice-cold beer. The young apprentice runs up and down making sure everyone has tea—and anything else that might be needed. The chef has trained for years in his art, and he's proud, in his stoic way, to demonstrate it. The *o-tsukuri* (sashimi) you've ordered arrives; today the thinly sliced raw tuna comes in the shape of a rose (Is it really your birthday?). The fourth round you order brings with it an unexpected ribbon of cucumber, sliced with a razor-sharp sushi knife into sections that expand like an accordion. The chef's made your day. . . .

Red paper lanterns dangling in the dark above a thousand tiny food stalls on the back streets of Tokyo. To the weary Japanese salaried man on his way home from the office, these *akachochin* lanterns are a prescription for the best kind of therapy known for the "subterranean homesick blues," Japanese style: one last belly-warming bottle of sake, a nerve-soothing platter of grilled chicken wings, and perhaps a few words of wisdom for the road. Without these comforting nocturnal way stations, many a fuzzy-eyed urban refugee would never survive that rumbling, fluorescent nightmare known as the last train home.

And where would half of Japan's night-owl college students be, if not for the local *shokudo*, as the neighborhood not-so-greasy spoon is known? Separated at last from mother's protective guidance (and therefore without a clue as to how an egg is boiled or a bowl of soup is heated), the male contingent of young lodging-house boarders put their lives in the hands of the old couple who runs the neighborhood café. Bent furtively over a platter of *kare-raisu* (curry and rice) or *tonkatsu teishoku* (pork cutlet set meal), these ravenous young men thumb through their baseball comics each night, still on the road to recovery from a childhood spent memorizing mathematical formulas and English phrases they hope they'll never have to use.

Down a dimly lit back street not two blocks away, a geisha in all her elaborate finery walks her last silk-suited customer out to his chauffeur-driven limousine. He has spent the

evening being pampered, feasted, and fan-danced in the
rarefied air of one of Tokyo's finest *ryotei*. (You must be invited to these exclusive eateries—or be a regular patron,
introduced years earlier by another regular patron who
vouched for your reputation with his own.) There has been
the most restrained of traditional dances, some samisen
playing—an oh-so-tastefully suggestive tête-à-tête. The
customer has been drinking the very finest sake, accompanied by a succession of exquisitely presented hors
d'oeuvres—what amounts to a seven-course meal in the end
is the formal Japanese *haute cuisine* known as *kaiseki*. His
grapes have all been peeled. If it were not for his company's
expense account, by now he would have spent the average
man's monthly salary. Lucky for him, he's not the average
man.

On a stool, now, under the flimsy awning of a street stall,
shielded from the wind and rain by flapping tarps, heated
only by a portable kerosene stove and the steam from a
vat of boiling noodles, you'll find neither tourist nor ptom-
aine. Here sits the everyday workingman, glass of
shochu (a strong liquor made from sweet potatoes) in sun-
baked hand, arguing over the Tigers' chances of winning
the Japan Series, as he zealously slurps down a bowl of
hot noodle soup sprinkled with red-pepper sauce—more
atmosphere, and livelier company than you're likely to find
anywhere else in Japan. The *yatai-san*, as these inimit-
able street vendors are known, are an amiable, if disappearing, breed.

Somewhere between the street stalls and the exclusive
ryotei, a vast culinary world exists in Japan. Tiny, over-
the-counter restaurants, each with its own specialty—from
familiar favorites, such as tempura, sukiyaki, or sushi, to
exotic delicacies like *unagi* (eel), or *fugu* (blowfish)—inhabit every city side street. Comfortable, countrystyle restaurants abound, serving a variety of different *nabemono*, the
one-pot stew dishes cooked right at your table. There are
also lively neighborhood *robatayaki* grills, where cooks in
happi coats wield skewered bits of meat, seafood, and vegetables over a hot charcoal grill as you watch.

Ten years ago, sukiyaki and tempura were exotic enough
for most Western travelers. Those were the days when raw
fish was still something a traveler needed fortitude to try.
But, with *soba* (noodle) shops and sushi bars popping up
everywhere from Los Angeles to Paris, it seems that—at
long last—the joy of Japanese cooking has found its way
westward . . . and it's about time.

There *is* something special, however, about visiting the tiger in his lair. Something no tame circus cat could ever
match. Although tours to famous temples and scenic places
can provide important historical and cultural background
material, there is nothing like a meal in a local restaurant—
be it under the tarps of the liveliest street stall, or within

the quiet recesses of an elegant Japanese inn—for a taste of the real Japan. Approaching a platter of fresh sashimi in Tokyo is like devouring a hot dog smothered in mustard and onions in Yankee Stadium. There's nothing like it in the world.

The Essentials of a Japanese Meal

As exotic as it might seem, the basic formula for a traditional Japanese meal is simple. It starts with soup, followed by raw fish, then the entrée (grilled, steamed, simmered or fried fish, chicken, or vegetables), and ends with rice and pickles, with perhaps some fresh fruit for dessert, and a cup of green tea. As simple as that, almost.

An exploration of any cuisine should begin at the beginning, with a basic knowledge of what it is you're eating. Rice, of course, the traditional staple. And seafood—grilled, steamed, fried, stewed, or raw. Chicken, pork, or beef, at times—in that order of frequency. A wide variety of vegetables (wild and cultivated), steamed, sautéed, blanched, or pickled, perhaps—but never overcooked. Soybeans in every form imaginable, from tofu to soy sauce. Seaweed, in and around lots of things.

The basics are just that. But there are, admittedly, a few twists to the story, as could be expected. Beyond the raw fish, it's the incredible variety of vegetation used in Japanese cooking that still surprises the Western palate: *take-no-ko* (bamboo shoots); *renkon* (lotus root); and the treasured *matsutake* mushrooms (which grow wild in jealously guarded forest hideaways and sometimes sell for over $60 apiece), to name but a few.

Tangy garnishes, both wild and domestic, such as *kinome* (leaves of the Japanese prickly ash pepper tree), *mitsuba* (trefoil, of the parsley family), and *shiso* (a member of the mint family) are used as a foil for oily foods. The more familiar sounding ingredients, such as sesame and ginger, appear in abundance, as do the unfamiliar—*wasabi* (Japanese horseradish), *uri-ne* (lily bulbs), *ginnan* (ginko nuts), and *daikon* (gigantic white radishes). Exotic? Perhaps, but delicious, and nothing here bites back. Simple? Yes, if you understand a few of the ground rules.

Absolute freshness is first. According to world-renowned Japanese chef Shizuo Tsuji, soup and raw fish are the two test pieces of Japanese cuisine. Freshness is the criterion for both: "I can tell at a glance by the texture of their skins—like the bloom of youth on a young girl—whether the fish is really fresh," Tsuji says in *The Art of Japanese Cooking*. A comparison as startling, perhaps, as it is revealing. To a Japanese chef, freshness is an unparalleled virtue, and much of his reputation relies on his ability to obtain the finest ingredients at the peak of season: fish brought in from the sea this morning (not yesterday), and vegetables from the earth (not the hothouse), if at all possible.

Simplicity is next. Rather than embellishing foods with heavy spices and rich sauces, the Japanese chef prefers his flavors au naturel. Flavors are enhanced, not elaborated; accented rather than concealed. Without a heavy dill sauce, fish is permitted a degree of natural fishiness—a garnish of fresh red ginger will be provided to offset the flavor rather than to disguise it.

The third prerequisite is beauty. Simple, natural foods must appeal to the eye as well as to the palate. Green peppers on a vermilion dish, perhaps, or an egg custard in a blue bowl. Rectangular dishes for a round eggplant. So important is the seasonal element in Japanese cooking that maple leaves and pine needles will be used to accent an autumn dish. Or two small summer delicacies, a pair of freshwater *ayu* fish, will be grilled with a purposeful twist to their tails to make them "swim" across a crystal platter to suggest the coolness of a mountain stream on a hot August night.

That's next: the mood. It can make or break the entire meal, and the Japanese connoisseur will go to great lengths to find the perfect yakitori stand—a smoky, lively place—an environment appropriate to the occasion, offering a night of grilled chicken, cold beer, and camaraderie. To a place like this, he'll take only friends he knows will appreciate the gesture.

Atmosphere depends as much on the company as it does on the lighting or the color of the drapes. In Japan, this seems to hold particularly true. The popularity of a particular *nomiya*, or bar, depends entirely on the affability of the *mama-san*, that long-suffering lady who's been listening to your troubles for years. In fancier places, mood becomes a fancier problem, to the point of quibbling over the proper amount of "water music" trickling in the basin outside your private room.

Culture: The Main Course

Sipping coffee at a sidewalk café on the Left Bank, you begin to feel what it means to be a Parisian. Slurping noodles on tatami in a neighborhood soba shop overlooking a tiny interior garden, you start to understand what it's like to live in Japan. Food, no matter which country you're in, has much to say about the culture as a whole.

Beyond the natural dictates of climate and geography, Japanese food has its roots in the centuries-old cuisine of the Imperial Court, which was imported from China—a religiously formal style of meal called *yusoku ryori*. It was prepared only by specially appointed chefs, who had the status of priests in the service of the emperor, in a culinary ritual

that is now nearly a lost art. Although it was never popularly served in centuries past (a modified version can still be
found in Kyoto), much of the ceremony and careful attention to detail of yusoku ryori is reflected today in the formal
kaiseki meal.

Kaiseki Ryori: Japanese Haute Cuisine

Kaiseki refers to the most elegant of all styles of Japanese
food available today, and *ryori* means cuisine. With its
roots in the banquet feasts of the aristocracy, by the late
16th century it had developed into a meal to accompany ceremonial tea. The word kaiseki refers to a heated stone
(seki) that Buddhist monks placed inside the folds *(kai)* of
their kimonos to keep off the biting cold in the unheated
temple halls where they slept and meditated.

Cha-kaiseki, as the formal meal served with tea *(cha)* is
called, is intended to take the edge off your hunger at the
beginning of a formal tea ceremony and to counterbalance
the astringent character of the thick green tea. In the tea
ceremony, balance—and the sense of calmness and well-being it inspires—is the keynote.

The formula for the basic Japanese meal derived originally
from the rules governing formal kaiseki—not too large a
portion, just enough; not too spicy, but perhaps with a savory sprig of trefoil to offset the bland tofu. A grilled dish is
served before a steamed one, a steamed dish before a simmered one; a square plate is used for a round food; a bright
green maple leaf is placed to one side to herald the arrival of
spring.

Kaiseki ryori appeals to all the senses at once. An atmosphere is created in which the meal is to be experienced. The
poem in calligraphy on a hanging scroll and the flowers in
the alcove set the seasonal theme, a motif picked up in the
pattern of the dishware chosen for the evening. The colors
and shapes of the vessels complement the dishes served on
them. The visual harmony presented is as vital as the balance and variety of flavors of the foods themselves, for
which the ultimate criterion is freshness. The finest ryotei
will never serve a fish or vegetable out of its proper season—no matter how marvelous a winter melon today's
modern greenhouses can guarantee. Melons are for rejoic-
ing in the summer's bounty . . . period.

Kaiseki ryori found its way out of the formal tearooms and
into a much earthier realm of the senses when it became the
fashionable snack with sake in the teahouses of the geisha
quarters during the 17th and 18th centuries. Not only the
atmosphere, but the Chinese characters used to write the
word *kaiseki* are different in this context; they refer to aristocratic "banquet seats." And banquets they are. To partake in the most exclusive of these evenings in a teahouse in
Kyoto still requires a personal introduction and a great deal

of money, though these days many traditional restaurants offer elegant kaiseki meals (without the geisha) at much more reasonable prices.

One excellent way to experience this incomparable cuisine on a budget is to visit a kaiseki restaurant at lunchtime. Many of them offer *kaiseki bento* lunches at a fraction of the dinner price, exquisitely presented in lacquered boxes, as a sampler of their full-course evening meal.

Shojin Ryori: Zen-Style Vegetarian Cuisine

Like an overnight stay in a Buddhist temple, *shojin ryori*, the Zen-style vegetarian cuisine, is another experience you shouldn't pass up if you have the opportunity. In traditional Japanese cuisine, the emphasis on the natural flavor of the freshest ingredients in season, without the embellishment of heavy spices and rich sauces, is an aspect perhaps influenced most strongly by the practice of zazen. Protein is provided by an almost limitless number of dishes made from soybeans—such as *yudofu*, or boiled bean curd, and *yuba*, sheets of pure protein skimmed from vats of steaming soy milk. The variety and visual beauty of a full-course shojin ryori meal offers new dimensions in dining to the vegetarian gourmet. *Gomadofu*, or sesame-flavored bean curd, for example, is a delicious taste treat, as is *nasu-dengaku*, grilled eggplant covered with a sweet *miso* sauce.

There are many fine restaurants (particularly in the Kyoto area) that specialize in shojin ryori, but for a real experience, seek out one of the many temples throughout Japan that open their doors to visitors who wish to try their special meals within the actual temple halls, which often overlook a traditional garden.

Sushi, Sukiyaki, Tempura, and Nabemono: A Comfortable Middle Ground

Leaving the rarefied atmosphere of teahouses and temples behind, an entire realm of more down-to-earth gastronomic pleasures waits to be explored.

Sushi, sukiyaki, and tempura are probably the three most commonly known Japanese dishes in the Western world. Restaurants serving these dishes are to be found in abundance in every major hotel in Japan. It is best, however, to try each of these in a place that specializes in just one.

An old Japanese proverb says *"Mochi wa mochi-ya e"*—if you want rice cakes, go to a rice-cake shop. The same goes for sushi. Sushi chefs undergo a lengthy apprenticeship, and the trade is considered an art form. Possessing the discipline of a judo player, the *itamae-san* (or "man before . . . or behind . . . the counter," depending on your point of view) at a sushi-ya is a real master. Every neighborhood has its own sushi shop, and everyone you meet has his own secret little place to go for sushi.

The Tsukiji Fish Market district in Tokyo is so popular for its sushi shops that you usually have to wait in line for a seat at the counter. Some are quite expensive, some are relatively cheap. "Know before you go" is the best policy; "ask before you eat" is next.

Among the dozens of kinds of sushi available, some of the most popular are *maguro* (tuna), *ebi* (shrimp), *hamachi* (yellowtail), *uni* (sea urchin), *anago* (conger eel), *tako* (octopus), and *awabi* (abalone). The day's selection is usually displayed in a glass case at the counter, which enables you to point at whatever catches your eye. (Try the *akagai*, or red shellfish. The word is a euphemistic expression for the female organ, for reasons blushingly recognizable.)

Tempura, the battered and deep-fried fish and vegetable dish, is almost certain to taste better at a small shop that serves nothing else. The difficulties of preparing this seemingly simple dish lie in achieving the proper consistency of the batter and the right temperature and freshness of the oil in which it is fried.

Sukiyaki is the popular beef dish that is sautéed with vegetables in an iron skillet at the table. The tenderness of the beef is the determining factor here, and many of the best sukiyaki houses also run their own butcher shops so that they can control the quality of the beef they serve. Although beef did not become a part of the Japanese diet until the turn of the century, the Japanese are justifiably proud of their notorious beer-fed and hand-massaged beef (e.g., the famous Matsuzaka beef from Kobe, and the equally delicious Omi beef from Shiga Prefecture). Though certainly a splurge, no one should pass up an opportunity to try a beef dinner in Japan.

Apart from sukiyaki and beef, *shabu-shabu* is another possibility, though this dish has become more popular with tourists than with the Japanese. It is similar to sukiyaki in that it is prepared at the table with a combination of vegetables, but it differs in that shabu-shabu is swished briefly in boiling water, while sukiyaki is sautéed in oil and, usually, a slightly sweetened soy sauce. The word *shabu-shabu* actually refers to this swishing sound.

Nabemono, or one-pot dishes, are not as familiar to Westerners as the three mentioned above, but the variety of possibilities is endless, and nothing tastes better on a cold winter's night. Simmered in a light, fish-base broth, these stews can be made of almost anything: chicken *(tori-nabe)*, oysters *(kaki-nabe)*, or the sumo wrestler's favorite, the hearty *chanko-nabe* . . . with something in it for everyone. Nabemono is a popular family or party dish. The restaurants specializing in nabemono often have a casual, country atmosphere.

Bento, Soba, Udon, and Robatayaki: Feasting on a Budget

Tales of horror floating around the world of unsuspecting tourists swallowed up by money-gobbling monsters disguised as quaint little restaurants on the back streets of Japan's major cities abound in these days of the high yen. There are, however, many wonderful little places that offer excellent meals and thoughtful service—and have no intention of straining anyone's budget. To find them, you must not be afraid to venture outside your hotel lobby or worry about the fact that the dining spot has no menu in English. Many restaurants have menus posted out front that clearly state the full price you can expect to pay. (Some do add on a 10% tax, and possibly a service charge, so ask in advance.)

Here are a few suggestions for Japanese meals that do not cost a fortune and are usually a lot more fun than relying on the familiar but unexciting international fast-food chains for quick meals on a budget: *bento* lunches, *soba* or *udon* noodle dishes, and the faithful neighborhood *robatayaki* grills, ad infinitum.

The Bento Box Lunch. The bento is the traditional Japanese box lunch. Available for take-out everywhere, they are usually comparatively inexpensive and can be purchased in the morning to be taken along and eaten later, either outdoors or on the train as you travel between cities. They consist of rice, pickles, grilled fish or meat, and vegetables, in an almost limitless variety of combinations to suit the season.

The basement level of most major department stores sell beautifully prepared bento lunches to go. In fact, a department store basement is a great place to sample and purchase the whole range of foods offered in Japan: among the things available are French bread, imported cheeses, traditional bean cakes, chocolate bonbons, barbecued chicken, grilled eel, roasted peanuts, fresh vegetables, potato salads, pickled bamboo shoots, and smoked salmon.

The *o-bento* (the "o" is honorific) in its most elaborate incarnation is served in gorgeous multilayered lacquered boxes as an accompaniment to outdoor tea ceremonies or for flower-viewing parties held in spring. Exquisite *bento-bako* (lunch boxes) made in the Edo period (1603–1868) can be found in museums and antiques shops. They are inlaid with mother-of-pearl and delicately hand-painted in gold. A wide variety of sizes and shapes of bento boxes are still handmade in major cities and small villages throughout Japan in both formal and informal styles. They make excellent souvenirs.

A major benefit to the bento lunch is its portability. Sightseeing can take you down many an unexpected path, and you need not worry about finding an appropriate place to stop for a bite to eat—if you bring your own bento. No Japanese family would ever be without one tucked carefully inside their rucksacks right beside the thermos bottle of tea on a cross-country train trip. If they do somehow run out of time to prepare one in advance—no problem—there are hundreds of wonderful options in the form of the beloved *eki-ben* ("train-station box lunch").

Each whistle-stop in Japan takes great pride in the uniqueness and flavor of the special box lunches, featuring the local delicacy, sold right at the station or from vendors inside the trains. The pursuit of the eki-ben has become a national pastime in this nation in love with its trains. Entire books have been written in Japanese explaining the features of every different eki-ben available along the 26,000 kilometers of railways in the country. This is one of the best ways to sample the different styles of regional cooking in Japan, and is highly recommended to any traveler who plans to spend time on the Japan Railway trains *(see* Regional Differences, below).

Soba and Udon Noodles. Soba and udon noodle dishes are another life-saving treat for stomachs (and wallets) unaccustomed to exotic flavors (and prices). Small shops serving soba (thin, brown, buckwheat noodle) and udon (thick, white, wheat noodle) dishes in a variety of combinations can be found in every neighborhood in the country. Both can be ordered plain (ask for *o-soba* or *o-udon)*, in a lightly seasoned broth flavored with bonito and soy sauce, or in combination with things like tempura shrimp (*tempura soba* or *udon*), or chicken (*tori-namba soba* or *udon*). For a refreshing change in summer, try *zaru soba*, cold noodles to be dipped in a tangy soy sauce. *Nabeyaki-udon* is a hearty winter dish of udon noodles, assorted vegetables, and egg served in the pot in which it was cooked.

Robatayaki Grill. The last and perhaps the most exuberant of these three inexpensive options is the robatayaki. Beer mug in hand, elbow-to-elbow at the counter of one of these popular neighborhood grills—that is the best way to relax and join in with the local fun. You'll find no pretenses here, just a wide variety of plain good food (as much or as little as you want) with the proper amount of alcohol to get things rolling.

Robata means fireside, and the style of cooking is reminiscent of old-fashioned Japanese farmhouse meals cooked over a charcoal fire in an open hearth. It's easy to order at a robatayaki shop, because the selection of food to be grilled is lined up behind glass at the counter. Fish, meat, vegetables, tofu—take your pick. Some popular choices are *yakizakana* (grilled fish), particularly *kare-shio-yaki* (salted and grilled flounder) and *asari saka-mushi* (clams simmered in sake, Japanese rice wine). Try the grilled Japanese *shiitake* (mushrooms), *ao-to* (green peppers), and the *hiyayakko* (chilled tofu sprinkled with bonito flakes, diced green onions, and soy sauce). Yakitori can be ordered in most robatayaki shops, though many inexpensive drinking places specialize in this popular barbecued chicken dish.

The budget dining possibilities in Japan don't stop there. *Okonomiyaki* is one popular choice. Somewhat misleadingly called the "Japanese pancake," it is actually a mixture of vegetables, meat, and seafood in an egg-and-flour batter grilled at your table, much better with beer than with butter. It's most popular for lunch or as an after-movie snack.

Another is *kushi-age*, skewered bits of meat, seafood, and vegetables battered, dipped in bread crumbs, and deep-fried. There are many small restaurants serving only kushi-age at a counter, and many of the robatayaki grills serve it as a sideline. It's another popular drinking snack.

Oden, the last inexpensive meal on the list, is a winter favorite. A variety of meats and vegetables slowly simmered in vats, it goes well with beer or sake. This, too, you may order piece by piece *(ippin)* from the assortment you see steaming away behind the counter, or *moriawase*, and the cook will serve you up an assortment.

Sake: The Samurai Beverage

With all this talk about eating and drinking, it would be an unforgivable transgression to overlook Japan's number one alcoholic beverage, sake (rice wine), the "beverage of the samurai," as one brewery puts it. The ancient myths call it the "drink of the gods." There are over 2,000 different brands of sake produced throughout Japan today, and a lifetime of serious scene-of-the-crime research would be necessary to explore all the possibilities and complexities of this interesting drink.

Like other kinds of wine, sake comes in sweet *(amakuchi)* and dry *(karakuchi)* varieties; these are graded *tokkyu* (superior class), *ikkyu* (first class), and *nikkyu* (second class) and are priced accordingly. (Connoisseurs say this ranking is for tax purposes and is not necessarily a true indication of quality.)

Best drunk at room temperature *(nurukan)* so as not to alter the flavor, sake is also served heated *(atsukan)* or with ice *(rokku de)*. It is poured from *tokkuri* (small ceramic vessels) into tiny cups called *choko*. The diminutive size of these cups shouldn't mislead you into thinking you can't drink too much. The custom of making sure that your drinking companion's cup never runs dry often leads the novice astray.

Junmaishu is the term for pure rice wine, a blend of rice, yeast, and water to which no extra alcohol has been added. Junmaishu has the strongest and most distinctive flavor, compared with various other methods of brewing, and is preferred by the sake *tsu*, as connoisseurs are known.

Apart from the *nomiya* (bars) and restaurants, the place to sample sake is the *izakaya*, a drinking establishment that serves only sake, usually dozens of different kinds, including a selection of *jizake*, the kind produced in limited quantities by small regional breweries throughout the country.

In the words of Ikkyu, one of Japan's most revered and notorious 15th-century imbibers (and one of its "highest" Buddhist priests):

> *I have been ten days in this temple*
> *and my heart is restless.*
> *The scarlet thread of lust at my feet*
> *has reached up long.*
> *If someday you come looking for me,*
> *I will be in a shop that sells fine seafood,*
> *a good drinking place,*
> *or a brothel.*

Regional Differences

Tokyo people are known for their candor and vigor, as compared with the refined restraint of people in the older, more provincial Kyoto. This applies as much to food as it does to language, art, and fashion. Foods in the Kansai district (including Kyoto, Nara, Osaka, and Kobe) tend to be lighter, the sauces less spicy, the soups not as hardy as those of the Kanto district, of which Tokyo is the center. How many Tokyoites have been heard to grumble about the "weak" soba broth on their visits to Kyoto? You go to Kyoto for the delicate and formal kaiseki; to Tokyo for sushi.

Nigiri-sushi, with pieces of raw fish on bite-size balls of rice (the form with which most Westerners are familiar), originated in the Kanto district, where there is a bounty of fresh fish. *Saba-sushi* is the specialty of landlocked Kyoto. Actually the forerunner of nigiri-sushi, it is made by pressing salt-preserved mackerel onto a bed of rice in a mold.

Every island in the Japanese archipelago has its specialty, and, within each island, every province has its own *meibutsu ryori*, or specialty dish. In Kyushu, try *shippoku-ryori*, a banquet-style feast of different dishes in which you eat your way up to a large fish mousse topped with shrimp. This dish is the local specialty in Nagasaki, for centuries the only port through which Japan had contact with the West.

On the island of Shikoku, try *sawachi-ryori*, an extravaganza of elaborately prepared platters of fresh fish dishes, the specialty of Kochi, the main city on the Pacific Ocean side of the island. In Hokkaido, where salmon dishes are the local specialty, try *ishikari-nabe*, a hearty salmon-and-vegetable stew.

The Bottom Line

There are a couple of things that take some getting used to. Things will be easier for you in Japan if you've had some experience with chopsticks. Some of the tourist-oriented restaurants (and of course all those serving Western food) provide silverware, but most traditional restaurants in Japan offer only chopsticks. It's a good idea to practice. The secret is to learn to move only the chopstick on top, rather than to try to move both chopsticks at once.

Sitting on the floor is another obstacle for many, including the younger generation of Japanese to whom the prospect of sitting on a cushion on tatami mats for an hour or so means nothing but stiff knees and numb feet. Because of this, many restaurants now have rooms with tables and chairs. The most traditional restaurants, however, have kept to the customary style of dining in tatami rooms. Give it a try. Nothing can compare with a full-course kaiseki meal brought to your room at a traditional inn. Fresh from the bath, robed in a cotton kimono, you are free to relax and enjoy it all, including the view. After all, the carefully landscaped garden outside your door was designed specifically to be seen from this position.

The service in Japan is usually superb, particularly at a *ryori-ryokan,* as restaurant/inns are called. A maid is assigned to anticipate your every need (even a few you didn't know you had). *"O-kyakusan wa kamisama desu"* (the customer is god), as the old Japanese proverb goes. People who prefer to dine in privacy have been known to say the service is too much.

Other problems? "The portions are too small" is a common complaint. The solution is an adjustment in perspective. In the world of Japanese cuisine, there are colors to delight in and shapes, textures, and flavors are balanced for your pleasure. Naturally, the aroma, flavor, and freshness of the foods have importance, but so do the dishware, the design of the room, the sound of water in a stone basin outside. You are meant to leave the table delighted—not stuffed. An appeal is made to all the senses through the food itself, the atmosphere, and appreciation for a carefully orchestrated feast in every sense of the word—these, and the luxury of time spent in the company of friends.

This is not to say that every Japanese restaurant offers aesthetic perfection. Your basic train-platform, stand-up, gulp-it-down noodle stall ("eat-and-out" in under six minutes) should leave no doubts as to the truth of the old saying that "all feet tread not in one shoe."

In the end, you'll discover that the joy of eating in Japan lies in the adventure of exploring the possibilities. Along every city street, you'll find countless little eateries specializing in anything you can name—and some you can't. In the major cities, you'll find French restaurants, British pubs, and little places serving Italian, Chinese, Indian, and American food, if you need a change of pace. In country towns, you can explore a world of regional delicacies found nowhere else.

There is something for everyone and every budget—from the most exquisitely prepared and presented formal kaiseki meal to a delicately sculpted salmon mousse à la nouvelle cuisine, from skewers of grilled chicken in barbecue sauce to a steaming bowl of noodle soup at an outdoor stall. And much to the chagrin of culinary purists, Japan has no dearth of international fast-food chains—from burgers to spareribs to fried chicken to doughnuts to 31 flavors of American ice cream.

Sometimes the contradictions of this intriguing culture— as seen in the startling contrast between ancient traditions and modern industrial life—seem almost overwhelming. Who would ever have thought you could face salad with lettuce, tomatoes, and seaweed . . . or green-tea ice cream? As the famous potter, Kawai Kanjiro, once said, "Sometimes it's better if you don't understand everything. . . . It makes life so much more exciting."

Manners

1) Don't point or gesture with chopsticks. Licking the ends of your chopsticks is rude, as is taking food from a common serving plate with the end of the chopstick you've had in your mouth.

2) There is no taboo against slurping your noodle soup, though women are generally less boisterous about it than men.

3) Pick up the soup bowl and drink directly from it, rather than lean over the table to sip it. Take the fish or vegetables from it with your chopsticks. Return the lid to the soup bowl when you are finished. The rice bowl, too, is to be picked up and held in one hand while you eat from it.

4) When drinking with a friend, don't pour your own. Take the bottle and pour for the other person. He will in turn reach for the bottle and pour for you. Japanese will attempt to top your drink off after every few sips. If you've had enough, try politely refusing, and good luck.

5) Japanese don't pour sauces on their rice in a traditional meal. Sauces are intended for dipping foods lightly, not for dunking or soaking.

6) Among faux pas that are considered nearly unpardonable, the worst is perhaps blowing your nose. It's better to excuse yourself and leave the room if this becomes necessary.

7) Although McDonald's and Hâagen-Dazs have made great inroads on the custom of never eating in public (except per-

haps on long-distance trains or at picnics), it is still considered gauche to munch on a hamburger (or an ice-cream cone) as you walk along a public street.

3 Tokyo

Introduction

by Jared Lubarsky
and Nigel Fisher

A resident of
Tokyo, Jared
Lubarsky has
lived in Japan
since 1973. His
articles have
appeared in the
New York Times,
Travel &Leisure,
Travel-Holiday,
and major
in-flight
magazines.

Nigel Fisher is the
editor of Voyager
International; he
has traveled
extensively in
Japan for over 20
years.

Tokyo: Of all the major cities in the world, it is perhaps the hardest to understand, to feel comfortable in, and to see in any single perspective. To begin with, consider the sheer, outrageous size of it. Tokyo incorporates 23 wards, 26 smaller cities, seven towns, and eight villages, together sprawling 55 miles east to west and 15 miles north to south. The wards alone enclose an area of 227 square miles—home to some 8.5 million people. Over two million of these residents pass through Shinjuku Station, one of the major hubs in the transportation network, every day.

It's staggering to think what the population density would be if Tokyo went up instead of out. Mile after mile, the houses rise only one or two stories above the ground, that low uniformity broken here and there by the sore thumb of an apartment building. Space, that most precious of commodities, is so scarce that pedestrians have to weave in and out around the utility poles as they walk along the narrow sidewalks—and everywhere, space is wasted. Begin with that observation, and you discover that the very fabric of life in this city is woven of countless, unfathomable contradictions.

Tokyo is a state-of-the-art financial marketplace, where billions of dollars are whisked electronically around the globe every day, in the blink of an eye—and where automatic cash dispensers shut down at 7 PM. (The machines levy a service charge of ¥103 for withdrawals after 6 PM.) It's a metropolis of exquisite politenesses, where the taxi drivers open the door for you when you get in and out—and where the man in the subway will push an old woman out of the way to get a seat. A city of astonishing beauty in its small details, Tokyo also has some of the ugliest buildings on the planet and generates 20,000 tons of garbage a day. It installed its first electric light in 1833, yet still has hundreds of thousands of households without a bathtub.

Life was simpler here in the 12th century, when Tokyo was a little fishing village called Edo, near the mouth of the Sumida River on the Kanto Plain. The Kanto was a strategic granary, large and fertile; over the next 400 years it was governed by a succession of warlords and other rulers. One of them, named Dokan Ota, built the first castle in Edo in 1457; that deed is still officially regarded as the founding of the city, but the honor really belongs to Ieyasu, the first Tokugawa shogun, who arrived in 1590. When the civil wars of the 16th century came to an end, Ieyasu was the vassal of Generalissimo Hideyoshi Toyotomi, who gave him the eight provinces of Kanto and eastern Japan in exchange for three provinces closer to Kyoto—the imperial capital and ostensibly the seat of power. Ieyasu was a farsighted soldier; the swap was fine with him. In place of Ota's stronghold, he built a mighty fortress of his own—from which, 10 years later, he was ruling the whole country.

By 1680, there were over a million people here, and a great city had grown up out of the reeds in the marshy lowlands of Edo Bay. Tokyo can only really be understood as a *joka-machi*—a castle town. Ieyasu had fought his way to the shogunate, and he had a warrior's concern for the geography of his capital. Edo Castle had the high ground, but that wasn't enough; all around it, at strategic points, he gave large estates to allies and

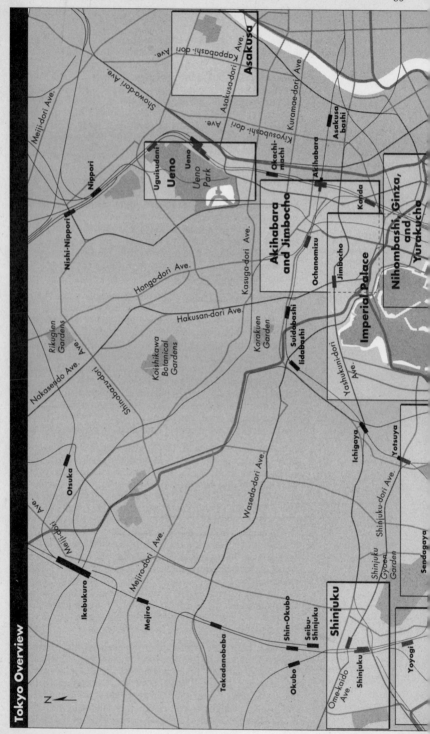

Tokyo Overview

N

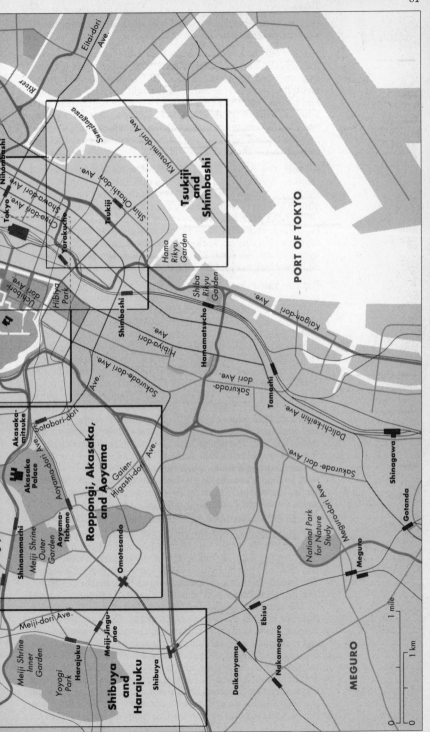

trusted retainers. These lesser lords' villas would also be garrisons, outposts on a perimeter of defense.

Farther out, he kept the barons he trusted least of all. Ieyasu had won the Battle of Sekigahara (1600), which made him shogun, only because someone had switched sides at the last moment; he controlled the barons who might one day turn against him by bleeding their treasuries. They were required to keep large, expensive establishments in Edo; to contribute generously to the temples he endowed; to come and go twice a year in great pomp and ceremony; and, when they returned to their estates, to leave their families—in effect, hostages—behind.

All this, the Edo of feudal estates, of villas and gardens and temples, lay south and west; it was called the *Yamanote*—the Bluff, the "uptown." Here, all was in its proper order, disciplined and ceremonious; every man had his rank and duties. (Within the garrisons were very few women.) Almost from the beginning, those duties were less military than bureaucratic; Ieyasu's precautions worked like a charm, and the Tokugawa dynasty enjoyed some 250 years of unbroken peace, during which nothing very interesting ever happened uptown.

But the Yamanote was only the demand side of the economy: somebody had to bring in the fish, weed the garden, weave the mats, and entertain the bureaucrats during their time off. To serve the noble houses, common people flowed into Edo from all over Japan; their allotted quarters of the city were jumbles of narrow streets, alleys, and culs-de-sac, in the low-lying estuarine lands to the north and east. Often enough, the land wasn't even there when it was assigned to them; they had to *make* it by draining and filling the marshes. (The first reclamation project in Edo dates to 1457.) The result was Shitamachi—the "downtown," the part below the castle. Bustling, brawling Shitamachi was the supply side: it had the lumber yards, markets, and workshops; the wood-block printers, kimono makers, and moneylenders. The people here gossiped over the back fence in the earthy, colorful Edo dialect. They supported the bathhouses and the Kabuki theaters, had fireworks festivals, and went to Yoshiwara, making it the biggest licensed brothel quarter in the world. The Edokko—the people of Shitamachi—haven't changed much; their city and its spirit have survived, and the great estates uptown are now mostly parks and hotels.

The shogunate was overthrown in 1867. The following year, the Emperor Meiji moved his court to Edo and renamed it Tokyo (Eastern Capital). By now it was home to nearly 2 million people, and the geography was vastly more complex than before. The broad divisions of Yamanote and Shitamachi remained. The Imperial Palace still provided a point of reference, a locus for the heart of the city, but Tokyo defied such easy organization. As it grew, it became not one but many smaller cities, with different centers of commerce, government, amusement, and transportation. In Yamanote rose the department stores, the office buildings, and public halls, which made up the architecture of an emerging modern state. The workshops of Shitamachi multiplied, some of them to become small jobbers and family-run factories. Still, there was no planning, no grid; the neighborhoods and subcenters were worlds unto themselves, and the traveler from one was soon hopelessly lost in another.

The firebombings of 1945 left Tokyo, for the most part, in rubble and ashes. Here was an opportunity to start again: to build a planned city, like Kyoto, Barcelona, or Washington, with a rational shape. It never happened. Tokyo reverted to type; it became once again an aggregation of small towns and villages. Author Donald Richie once described them as "separate, yet welded to the texture of the metropolis itself." One village was much like any other; the nucleus was always the *shoten-gai* (shopping arcade). Every arcade had a butcher, a grocer, a rice dealer, a mat maker, a barber, and a pinball parlor; every arcade also had a florist and a bookstore—sometimes two of each. You could live your whole life in the neighborhood of the shoten-gai; it was sufficient to your needs.

People seldom moved out of these villages; the vast waves of new residents who arrived after World War II (about three-quarters of the people in the Tokyo metropolitan area today were born elsewhere) just created more villages. Everybody who lived in one knew his way around; there was no particular need to name the streets. Houses were numbered, not in sequence, but in the order in which they were built; #3 might well share a mailbox with #12. People still take their local geography for granted; the closer you get to the place you're looking for, the harder it is to get coherent directions. Away from main streets and landmarks, a stranger, or even a taxi driver, can get hopelessly lost.

Fortunately, there are the *kobans:* small police boxes, or substations, usually with two or three officers assigned to each of them full time, to look after the affairs of the neighborhood. These kobans are one important reason for the legendary safety of Tokyo: On foot or on white bicycles, the police are a visible presence, covering the beat. (Burglaries are not unknown, but street crime is very rare.) You can't go far in any direction without finding a koban. The officer on duty knows where everything is, and is glad to point the way; like the samurai-bureaucrats of Edo, he seldom has anything more pressing to do.

Outsiders, however, seldom venture very far into the labyrinths of residential Tokyo; for the tourist, especially, the city is the sum of its districts and neighborhoods, such as Ueno, Asakusa, Ginza, Roppongi, Shibuya, and Shinjuku. Harajuku is a more recent addition to that list, and soon the waterfront will add another; the *attention* of Tokyo shifts constantly, seeking new patches of astronomically expensive land (you can't buy 3 square meters in Ginza today for $1 million) on which to realize its enormous commercial energy.

Tokyo is still really two areas, Shitamachi and Yamanote. The heart of Shitamachi, proud and stubborn in its Edo ways, is Asakusa; the dividing line is Ginza; to the west lie the boutiques and department stores, the banks and engines of government, the pleasure domes and swell cafés. Today there are 10 subway lines weaving the two areas together. Another special feature of Tokyo's geography is found where the lines intersect: vast underground malls, with miles of shops in fluorescent-lit, air-conditioned corridors. These stores sell anything you might want to buy between subway rides.

Up on the surface, confusion reigns, or seems to. Tokyo is the most *impermanent* of cities, constantly tearing itself down and building over. Whole blocks disappear overnight; the next day, a framework of girders is already rising on the empty lot. It's no longer possible to put up a single-family house in the eight central wards of the city; the plot to put it on costs more than the average person will earn in several lifetimes. Home owners live in the suburbs, an hour or more by train from their jobs. Only developers can afford the land closer in; they build office buildings, condominiums, and commercial complexes. Tokyo has no skyline, no prevailing style of architecture, nothing for a new building to measure itself against; every new project is an environment unto itself. World-famous architects like Arata Isozaki, Fumihiko Maki, and Kisho Kurokawa revel in this anarchy; so do the designers of neon signs, show windows, and interior spaces. The kind of creative energy you find in Tokyo could flower only in an atmosphere where there are virtually no rules to break.

Not all of that is for the best. Many of the buildings in Tokyo are merely grotesque; most of them are supremely ugly. In the large scale, Tokyo is not an *attractive* city; neither is it gracious, and it is certainly not serene. The pace of life is wedded to the one stupefying fact of population: Within a 20-mile radius of the Imperial Palace live almost 30 million souls, all of them in a hurry, and all of them ferocious consumers. They live in a city that went from rubble to dazzling affluence in a generation; they are very sure of what they have accomplished, but they are terribly uncertain about who they are. They consume to identify themselves—by what they wear, where they eat, and how they use their leisure time.

Tokyo is a magnet. Its attractive power, of course, is money— enormous amounts of it, looking for new ways of turning itself over. The health of the economy and the formidable new strength of the yen have made the Japanese the world's foremost consumers—not merely of things, but of culture and leisure. Everything shows up here, sooner or later: van Gogh's *Sunflowers*, the Berlin Philharmonic, Chinese pandas, Mexican food. Even the Coney Island carousel is here—lovingly restored to the last gilded curlicue on the last prancing unicorn, brought to life again at an amusement park called Toshima-en. And now, because you are reading this guide, the magnet is drawing you. What follows is an attempt to chart a few paths for you through this exasperating, exciting, movable feast of a city.

Essential Information

Arriving and Departing

By Plane   Tokyo has two airports, Narita and Haneda. Narita Airport is 50 miles northeast of Tokyo and serves all international flights, except for those operated by (Taiwan's) China Airways, which uses Haneda Airport. Ten miles southwest of Tokyo, Haneda Airport serves all domestic flights. While Haneda has ample terminal space (though it is uncomfortable for waiting around), Narita's passenger traffic has outgrown its facilities. Often the lobby for arrivals is jammed with passengers and luggage carts. Narita is the only Japanese airport that imposes a departure tax (¥2,000, ¥1,000 for children 2–11 years old; no tax for children under 2 or for transit passengers flying out the same day as their arrival).

Narita has more direct flights arriving from around the world than any other Japanese airport. Japan Airlines (JAL) and United Airlines are the major carriers between North America and Narita; Northwest, American Airlines, Continental, and All Nippon Airways (ANA) also link North American cities with Tokyo. Japan Airlines and British Airways fly between Narita and Great Britain; Japan Airlines, United Airlines, and Qantas fly between Narita and Australia; and Japan Airlines and Air New Zealand fly between Narita and New Zealand. An extensive network of domestic flights in and out of Haneda is operated by JAL, ANA, and Japan Air System. For information on arrival and departure times, call the individual airlines.

Narita has two wings, north and south, that adjoin each other. When you arrive, your first task should be to convert your money into yen; you'll need it for transport into Tokyo. In both wings, money exchange counters are located in the wall between the customs inspection area and the arrival lobby. Directly across from the customs area exit are the ticket counters for Airport Limousine Buses to Tokyo. (*See* By Bus, below.) In between the two wings is the Japan National Tourist Organization's Tourist Information Center, where maps, brochures, and information can be obtained free of charge. It is well worth visiting this center if you have extra time before your bus departs.

Between Narita Airport and Center City

By Bus. The Airport Limousine Bus is the best way to make the long, tedious trip into the city. The trip usually takes two hours because of traffic congestion, though the scheduled time is 90 minutes. Tickets for these buses are sold at the large ticket counter in the arrival lobby, directly across from the customs area exit. The buses depart right outside the terminal exit. They leave exactly on time; the departure time is stated on the ticket.

Two services, the Airport Limousine Bus and the Airport Express Bus, run from Narita to many of Tokyo's major hotels located in the city's different areas, such as Akasaka, Ginza, Ikebukuro, Shiba, and Shinagawa (cost: ¥2,700). These hotel buses are the best method of reaching your destination; even if you are not staying at one of the hotel drop-off points, take the bus going closest to your hotel, and then use a taxi for the remaining distance. Most of the hotels in the Very Expensive category (*see* Lodging, below) serve as drop-off points. However, these buses only run every hour, and they do not run after 10 or 10:30 PM. (The Airport Express Bus service also has a ticket counter in the arrival lobby.)

A regularly scheduled bus to the Tokyo City Air Terminal (TCAT) leaves approximately every 20 minutes from 6:50AM to 11:30 PM (cost: ¥2,500). The problem is that TCAT is located in Nihombashi in north-central Tokyo, which is far from most convenient destinations. From TCAT you can connect directly with the Suitengu station on the Hanzomon subway line, and then to anywhere in the subway network; if you take a taxi from TCAT, it will cost about ¥3,000 to reach most hotels.

By Train. Trains run every 30–40 minutes between Narita Airport Train Station and the Keisei-Ueno Station on the privately owned Keisei Line; the ride takes approximately an hour (cost: ¥1,630 on the Keisei Skyliner, taking 62 minutes; ¥910 on the Keisei limited express, taking 72 min). To reach the Narita Airport Train Station from the airport arrivals building, there is a shuttle bus (a 6-minute ride). Unless your final destination is around Ueno, you must change to the Tokyo subway system or the Japan Railways loop line at Ueno (the station is adjacent to the Keisei-Ueno Station) or take a cab to your hotel.

The latest and probably best rail connection is the new Japan Railways Narita Express, running directly between the airport and Tokyo Station approximately every 30 minutes—every hour from Tokyo Station between 10 and 4. The first train from Narita departs at 7:45 AM, the last at 9:45 PM. The ride takes 53 minutes; the one-way fare is ¥2,890 (¥4,890 for the first-class "Green Car" and ¥5,280 per person for a private compartment that seats four).

By Taxi. Taxis are rarely used between Narita Airport and central Tokyo, because the cost of approximately ¥20,000 is prohibitive. Also, because taxis have small trunks, your luggage may have to be placed in the front passenger seat, thus causing cramped conditions if there are three or more passengers. Station wagon taxis do exist, and the meter rates are the same as for the standard sedans, but they are not always available. Limousines are also very expensive; for example, a limousine ride from Narita Airport to the Imperial Hotel costs approximately ¥37,000.

Between Haneda Airport and Center City **By Monorail.** The monorail train from Haneda Airport to Hamamatsucho Station in Tokyo is the best and most frequently used method; the journey takes about 17 minutes and operates approximately every 10 minutes (cost: ¥300). From Hamamatsucho Station, change to the subway or take a taxi.

By Taxi. A taxi to the center of Tokyo takes about 40 minutes (cost: approximately ¥6,000).

From Out of Town **By Train.** The JR Shinkansen (bullet train) and JR express trains on the Tokaido Line (to Nagoya, Kyoto, Kobe, Osaka, Hiroshima, and the island of Kyushu) use Tokyo Station in central Tokyo. The JR Shinkansen and express trains on the Tohoku Line (to Sendai and Morioka) use Ueno Station, just north of Tokyo Station. The JR Shinkansen and express trains on the Joetsu Line (to Niigata) also use Ueno Station. JR trains to the Japan Alps (Matsumoto) use Shinjuku Station.

By Bus. Most bus arrivals and departures are at Tokyo Train Station or Shinjuku Bus Station.

Getting Around

Daunting in its sheer size, Tokyo is, in fact, an extremely easy city to negotiate. If you have any anxieties about getting from place to place, remind yourself first that a transportation system obliged to cope with 4 or 5 million commuters a day simply *has* to be efficient, extensive, and reasonably easy to understand. Remind yourself also that virtually anyplace you're likely to go as a visitor is within a five-minute walk of a train or subway station—and that station stops are always marked in English. Of course, exceptions to the rule exist; the system has its flaws. In the outline here you'll find a few things to avoid, and also a few pointers that will save you time—and money—as you go.

By Train　**Japan Railways (JR).** Trains are color-coded, making it easy to identify the different lines. The **Yamanote Line** (green or silver, with green stripes) makes a 35-kilometer (22-mile) loop around the central wards of the city in about an hour. The 29 stops include the major hub stations of Tokyo, Yurakucho, Shimbashi, Shinagawa, Shibuya, Shinjuku, and Ueno. The **Chuo Line** (orange) runs east to west through the loop from Tokyo to the distant suburb of Takao. During the day, however, these are limited express trains that don't stop at most of the stations inside the loop; for local crosstown service, which also extends west to neighboring Chiba Prefecture, you have to take the **Sobu Line** (yellow). The **Keihin Tohoku Line** (blue) goes north to Omiya in Saitama Prefecture and south to Ofuna in Kanagawa, running parallel to the Yamanote Line between Tabata and Shinagawa. Where they share the loop, the two lines usually use the same platform—Yamanote trains on one side, and Keihin Tohoku trains headed in the same direction on the other. This requires a little care. Suppose, for example, you want to take the loop line from Yurakucho around to Shibuya, and you board a blue train instead of a green one; four stops later, where the lines branch, you'll find yourself on an unexpected trip to Yokohama.

JR fares start at ¥120; you can get anywhere on the loop for ¥290 or less. Most stations have a chart in English somewhere above the row of ticket vending machines, so you can check the fare to your destination; if not, you can simply buy the cheapest ticket and pay the difference at the other end. In any case, hold on to your ticket: you'll have to turn it in at the exit. Tickets are valid only on the day you buy them, but if you plan to use the JR a lot, you can save time and trouble with an Orange Card, available at any station office. The card is electronically coded; at vending machines with orange panels, you insert the card, punch the cost of the ticket, and that amount is automatically deducted. ¥1,000 and ¥3,000 Orange Cards are worth their face values; ¥5,000 Cards are coded for ¥5,600 worth of fares.

Shinjuku, Harajuku, and Shibuya are notorious for the long lines that form at ticket dispensers. If you're using a card, make sure you've lined up at a machine with an orange panel; if you're paying cash, and have no change, make sure you've lined up at a machine that will change a ¥1,000 note—not all of them do!

Yamanote and Sobu trains begin running about 4:30 AM and stop around 12:30 at night. The last departures are indicated at each station—but only in Japanese. Bear in mind that 7–9:30 AM and 5–7 PM trains are packed to bursting with commuters; avoid the trains at these times, if possible. During these hours, smoking is not allowed in JR stations or on platforms.

By Subway　Tokyo is served by 10 subway lines, seven of them operated by the Rapid Transportation Authority (Eidan) and three by the Tokyo Municipal Authority (Toei). Maps, bilingual signs at entrances, and even the trains are color-coded for easy identification. Subway trains run about every five minutes from about 5 AM to midnight; except during rush hours, the intervals are slightly longer on the newer Toei lines. Your last train, of course, will depend on which station you use: It's a good idea to check beforehand.

The network of interconnections (subway-to-subway and train-to-subway) is particularly good; one transfer—two at most—

Tokyo Subways

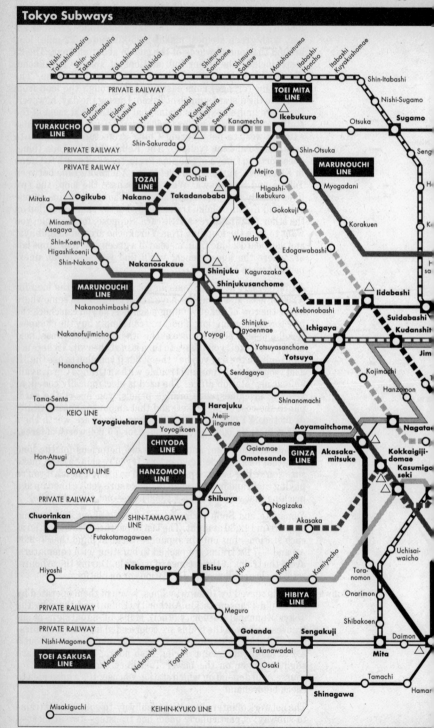

will take you in less than an hour to any part of the city you're likely to visit. At some stations—such as Otemachi, Ginza, and Iidabashi—long underground passageways connect the various lines, and it does take time to get from one to another. Directions, however, are clearly marked. Less helpful is the system of signs that tell you which of the 15 or 20 exits (exits are often numbered and alphabetized) from a large station will take you aboveground closest to your destination; only a few stations have such signs in English. Try asking the agent when you turn in your ticket; he may understand enough of your question to come back with the exit number and letter (such as A3 or B12), which is all you need.

Subway fares begin at ¥140. Toei trains are generally a bit more expensive than Eidan trains, but both are somewhat cheaper than the JR. From Ueno across town to Shibuya on the old Ginza Line (yellow), for example, is ¥150; the same ride on the Yamanote Line is ¥190. The Eidan (but *not* the Toei) has inaugurated an electronic card of its own, called Metrocard; the denominations are ¥1,000, ¥2,000, and ¥3,000. Automatic card dispensers are installed at some subway stations.

By Bus Because Tokyo has no rational order—no grid—the bus routes are impossibly complicated. The Tokyo Municipal Government operates some of the lines; private companies run the rest. There is no telephone number even a native Japanese can call for help. The buses all have tiny seats and low ceilings. With one exception, the red double-decker in Asakusa (*see* Exploring, below, for Asakusa), you should forget the buses.

By Taxi Tokyo taxi fares are among the highest in the world; the meter starts running at ¥540 and ticks away at the rate of ¥80 every 370 meters (about ⅕ mi). There are also smaller cabs, called *kogata*, which charge ¥520 and then ¥70 per 398 meters. If your cab is caught in traffic—hardly an uncommon event—the meter registers another ¥80 for every two minutes and 15 seconds of immobility. Between 11 PM and 5 AM, a 20% surcharge is added to the fare.

You do get very good value for the money, though. Taxis are invariably clean and comfortable. The doors open automatically for you when you get in and out. The driver takes you where you want to go by the shortest route he knows, and he does not expect a tip. Tokyo cabbies are not, in general, a sociable species (you wouldn't be either if you had to drive for 10–12 hours a day in Tokyo traffic), but you can always count on a minimum standard of courtesy. And if you forget something in the cab—a camera, a purse—your chances of getting it back are almost 100%.

Hailing a taxi during the day is seldom a problem; you would have to be in a very remote part of town to wait more than five minutes for one to pass by. In the Ginza, drivers are allowed to stop for passengers only in designated areas; elsewhere, you need only step off the curb and raise your arm. If the cab already has a fare, there will be a green light on the dashboard, visible through the windshield; if not, the light will be red.

Night changes the rules a bit, when everyone's been out drinking and wants a ride home. Don't be astonished if a cab with a red light doesn't stop for you: The driver may have had a radio call, or he may be heading for an area where he can pick up a

long, profitable fare to the suburbs. (Or he may simply not feel
like coping with a passenger in a foreign language. Refusing a
fare is against the law—but it's done all the time.) Between 11
PM and 2 AM on Friday and Saturday nights, you have to be very
lucky to get a cab in any of the major entertainment districts; in
Ginza, it is impossible.

By Ferry   The best ride in Tokyo, hands down, is the "river bus," operated by the Tokyo Cruise Ship Company from **Hinode Pier** (2-7-
104 Kaigan, Minato-ku, tel. 03/3457–7830), at the mouth of the
Sumida River, upstream to Asakusa. The pier is a seven-minute walk from the JR Hamamatsucho Station on the Yamanote
Line; the glassed-in double-decker boats depart roughly every
30 minutes, 9:50 AM–6:30 PM, Monday through Friday; extended weekday service to 7:35 July–Aug.). The trip takes 40
minutes, and costs ¥560; children ride at half-fare.

The Sumida River was once Tokyo's lifeline, a busy highway for
travelers and freight alike; the ferry service dates back to 1885.
Some people still take it to work, but today the passengers are
primarily tourists, most of them Japanese. On its way to
Asakusa, the boat passes under 11 bridges; though they are all
of modern construction, the guided tour (a recording on the
boat's loudspeaker) deems it worthy to comment upon them at
length. There are far more interesting things to see: **Tsukiji
Market,** the largest wholesale fish and produce market in the
world (*see* Exploring, below, for Tsukiji); the vast reclamation/
construction projects meant to sate the city's insatiable need
for high-tech office space; the old lumberyards and warehouses
upstream; and the Kokugikan (*see* Off the Beaten Track, below), with its distinctive green roof, which is the new arena and
headquarters of sumo wrestling.

Another place to catch the ferry is at the **Hamarikyu Gardens,** a
15-minute walk from Ginza. Once part of the Imperial Detached Palace, the gardens are open to the public, although you
will have to pay a separate ¥200 entrance fee; the ferry landing
is inside, a short walk to the left as you enter the main gate.
Boats depart at 45-minute intervals every weekday 10:15–4:05;
the adult fare to Asakusa is ¥520.

By Hired Car   Large and comfortable cars may be hired (the Japanese call
them *haiya*) for about ¥6,000 per hour for a midsize car and
¥13,000 per hour for a Cadillac limousine. Call **Hinomaru** (tel.
03/3505–0707). The Imperial, Okura, and Palace hotels also
offer limousine services.

By Rental Car   Congestion, lack of road signs in English, and the difficulty of
parking make driving in Tokyo impractical for the foreign visi-
tor. However, should you wish to rent a car, **Avis-Nissan Reservation Center** (Landlick Ikura Building, 1-5-7 Azabudai,
Minato-ku, tel. 03/3587–4123) and **Toyota Rent-a-Car** (Jinnan
Building, 4-2 Udagawacho, Shibuya-ku, tel. 03/3264–2834) are
national car-rental companies with offices all around Tokyo and
Japan. The cost is approximately ¥15,000 per day. An international driving license is required.

Maps   Excellent maps of the subway system, with the major JR lines
included, are available at any station office, free of charge;
you'll find the same map in the monthly *Tour Companion* magazine. Hotel kiosks and English-language bookstores stock a
wide variety of pocket maps, some of which have suggested
walking tours that also mark the locations of JR and subway

stations along the way. A bit bulkier to carry around, but by far the best and most detailed resource, is *Tokyo: A Bilingual Atlas* (Kodansha Publishing, ¥1,800; $14.95 in the United States), which contains subway and rail-system guides and area maps. Because all notations are in both English and Japanese, you can always get help on the street, even from people who do not speak your language, just by pointing at your destination.

Important Addresses and Numbers

Tourist Information
The **Tourist Information Center** (TIC) (1-6-6 Yurakucho, Chiyoda-ku, tel. 03/3502–1461) is an extremely useful office for free maps and brochures, as well as for planning any trip in Japan. It is definitely worth visiting this office early in your stay in Tokyo. The closest subway stations to the TIC are Hibiya and Yurakucho. The Hibiya station is on the same avenue, Harumi-dori, as the TIC (take exit A4, walk toward the railway bridge, and the TIC is on the right hand side of the street); Yurakucho Station is just to the north of the TIC; if you follow the overhead train tracks south one block, the TIC office is across the street. *Open weekdays 9–5, Sat. 9–noon.*

Travel Information. Information in English on all domestic travel, buses, and trains can be acquired by phoning the TIC (tel. 03/3502–1461). You may also call Japan Railways (tel. 03/3212–3579), though you may need to speak Japanese.

Current Events/Exhibitions. A taped recording in English (tel. 03/3503–2911) gives information on current events in Tokyo and vicinity. *The Tour Companion,* a free weekly newspaper available at hotels, provides some information on events, exhibitions, festivals, plays, etc. *The Tokyo Journal,* however, has a more comprehensive monthly listing of what's happening in Tokyo. It also lists services and stores that may have special interest for foreigners (cost: ¥500). *The Japan Times,* the country's daily English-language newspaper, is good for national and international news coverage, as well as for entertainment reviews and listings.

Embassies and Consulates
U.S. Embassy and Consulate, 1-10-5 Akasaka, Minato-ku, tel. 03/3224–5000. Consulate open 8:30–noon and 2–4; closed Sat.
Australian Embassy, 2–1–4 Mita, Minato-ku, tel. 03/5232–4111. Open 9 AM–noon and 1:30–5.
British Embassy and Consulate, 1 Ichiban-cho, Chiyoda-ku, tel. 03/3265–5511. Consulate open 9–noon and 2–4; closed Sat. and holidays.
Canadian Embassy, 7-3-38 Akasaka, Minato-ku, tel. 03/3408–2101. Open weekdays 9–12:30 and 1:30–5:30.
New Zealand Embassy, 20 Kamiyama-cho, Shibuya-ku, tel. 03/3467–2271. Open weekdays 9–noon and 1:30–5.

Telephone Directory
For Tokyo numbers, dial 104; for elsewhere in Japan, dial 105.

General Information
NTT (Japanese Telephone Corporation, tel. 03/3277–1010) will help find information (in English), such as telephone numbers, museum openings, and various other facts that it has in its data bases.

Emergencies
Ambulance and Fire, tel. 119; Police, tel. 110; Tokyo English Life Line (TELL; tel. 03/3264–4347) is a telephone service for anyone in distress who cannot communicate in Japanese. The

service will relay your emergency to the appropriate Japanese authorities and/or will serve as a counselor.

Doctors **International Catholic Hospital** (Seibo Byoin), 2-5-1 Naka Ochiai, Shinjuku-ku, tel. 03/3951–1111. Open Mon.–Sat. 8:30–11 AM.
International Clinic, 1-5-9 Azabudai, Roppongi, Minato-ku, tel. 03/3582–2646, 03/3583–7831. Accepts emergencies. Open weekdays 9–noon and 2:30–5, Sat. 10–noon.
St. Luke's International Hospital (Member of American Hospital Association), 10-1 Akashi-cho, Chuo-ku, tel. 03/3541–5151. Offers no emergency services. Open Mon.–Sat. 8:45–11 AM.
Tokyo Medical and Surgical Clinic, 32 Mori Building, 3-4-30 Shiba-Koen, Minato-ku, tel. 03/3436–3028. Open weekdays 9–4:45, Sat. 9AM–1PM.

Dentists **Yamauchi Dental Clinic** (member of American Dental Association), Shiroganedai Gloria Heights 1F, 3-16-10 Shiroganedai, Minato-ku, tel. 03/3441–6377. Open weekdays 9–1 and 3–6; Sat. 9–noon.

Pharmacies No drugstores in Tokyo are open 24 hours a day, but grocery stores carry basics such as aspirin. The **American Pharmacy** (Hibiya Park Building, 1-8-1 Yurakucho, Chiyoda-ku, tel. 03/3271–4034) and **Hill Pharmacy** (4-1-6 Roppongi, Minato-ku, tel. 03/3583–5044) both stock American products. The American Pharmacy is conveniently located near the Tourist Information Center (*see* above). **Nagai Yakkyoku** (1-8-10 Azabu-Juban, Minato-ku, tel. 03/3583–3889) will mix a Chinese and/or Japanese herbal medicine for you after a consultation. A little English is spoken.

English Bookstores Most of the top hotels have a bookstore with a modest selection of English-language books. However, for a wide selection of English and other non-Japanese-language books, the **Kinokuniya Bookstore** (10-7 Shinjuku 3-chome, Shinjuku-ku, tel. 03/3354–0131) has some 40,000 books and magazine titles (closed 3rd Wed. of each month, except Apr. and Dec.). Kinokuniya also has a branch store in the Tokyu Plaza Building (1-2-2 Dogenzaka, Shibuya-ku, tel. 03/3463–3241) across from the Shibuya Station. The **Jena Bookstore** (5-6-1 Ginza, Chuo-ku, tel. 03/3571–2980) also carries a wide range of books and is located near the Ginza and Marunouchi subway line exits in Ginza. **Yaesu Book Center** (2-5-1 Yaesu, Chuo-ku, tel. 03/3281–1811) is located near the Tokyo Train Station.

Travel Agencies **Japan Travel Bureau** (1-13-1 Nihombashi, Chuo-ku, tel. 03/3276–7803) has the most extensive network of agencies throughout Tokyo and Japan. This bureau organizes various tours conducted in English, in and around Tokyo; it will make arrangements for your travels throughout Japan and overseas, if you wish.

Other travel agencies include **American Express International** (4-3-13 Toranomon, Minato-ku, tel. 03/3469–6335) and **Japan Amenity Travel** (6-2-10 Ginza, Chuo-ku, tel. 03/3573–1011).

Lost and Found The **Central Lost and Found Office** of the Metropolitan Police is located at 1-9-11, Koraku, Bunkyo-ku, Tokyo, tel. 03/3814–4151. Open weekdays 8:30–5:15, Sat. 8:30–12:30; closed Sun. and holidays. If you have lost something on the train, report it to the lost and found office at any station. However, the main lost and found offices for Japan Railways are at the JR Tokyo

Station Lost Properties Office (tel. 03/3231–1880) and at Ueno Station (tel. 03/3841–8069).

If you leave something on the subways, contact **Teito Rapid Transit Authority** (TRTA) at its Ueno Lost Properties Office (tel. 03/3834–5577).

If you leave something in a taxi, contact the **Tokyo Taxi Kindaika Center** (Shinseikaikan Building, 33 Shinanomachi, Shinjuku-ku, tel. 03/3648–0300). Only Japanese is spoken here.

Currency Exchange and Banks
Most hotels will change both traveler's checks and notes into yen. However, their rates are always lower than banks. Because Japan is so safe and virtually free from street crime, one may consider exchanging large sums of money into yen at banks at any time. Most of the larger banks have a foreign exchange counter. Banking hours: weekdays 9–3, Saturday 9–noon; closed Sunday and national holidays.

The major banks can transfer funds to and from overseas. Two banks that may be familiar to you are **Bank of America** (Arc Mori Building, 1-12-32 Akasaka, Minato-ku, tel. 03/3587–3111) and **Chase Manhattan Bank** (1–2–1 Marunouchi, Chiyoda-ku, tel. 03/3287–4000). **American Express** has its main office at Mitsui Building, 3-8-1 Kasumigaseki, Chiyoda-ku, tel. 03/3508–2400 (open weekdays 10–4:30) and another office at Four Stars Building, 4-4-1 Ginza, tel. 03/3564–4381 (open Mon.–Sat. 10–4:30).

Post and Telegraph Offices
Most hotels have stamps and will mail your letters and post-cards; they will also give you directions to the nearest post office. The main **International Post Office** is on the Imperial Palace side of the JR Tokyo Station (2-33 Otemachi, tel. 03/3241–4891). For cables, contact the KDD International Telegraph Office (2–3–2 Nishi-Shinjuku, Shinjuku-ku, tel. 03/3344–5151).

Guided Tours

Orientation Tours
Organized by the Japan Travel Bureau, **Sunrise Tours** (tel. 03/3276–7777) offers guided tours in English around Tokyo. The sights on tours vary according to current popularity, but some recently offered tours are as follows: A morning tour (4 hours) includes the Tokyo Tower Observatory, a tea ceremony at Happo-en, the Imperial East Garden, flower arrangement at the Tasaki Pearl Gallery (cost: ¥3,910); a four-hour afternoon tour includes the Imperial Palace Plaza, the Furasato old farm-house- style restaurant with authentic folkcraft interior, the Meiji Shrine, and Tokyo Tower Observatory (cost: ¥3,910). A full-day tour (7 hours) combines most of what is covered in the morning and afternoon tours (cost: ¥9,980, lunch included). Tours are conducted in large, air-conditioned buses that set out from Hamamatsucho Bus Terminal, but there is also free pick-up and return from the major hotels. (If one travels independently and uses the subway, we estimate that the full-day tour's itinerary can be accomplished for about ¥2,250, including lunch.) **The Japan Gray Line** (tel. 03/3433–5745) offers tours similar to Sunrise's.

Special-Interest Tours
Sunrise Tours (tel. 03/3276–7777) has recently added two "Industrial Tours" that have become popular. One includes the Tokyo Stock Exchange and Isuzu Motors; the other tour includes a monorail trip to Haneda Airport to visit the Japan Air

Lines Maintenance Base, and a tour of Isuzu Motors. These tours offered only on Tuesdays and Thursdays, cost ¥9,980. Other tours include a full-day in Tokyo Disneyland (cost: ¥8,630) and a trip to several craft centers (cost: ¥10,300).

Nightlife Tours **Sunrise Tours** (tel. 03/3276–7777) offers night tours (6–11 PM) of Tokyo, which, depending on the one selected, include Kabuki drama at the Kabuki-za theater, a geisha show at Matsubaya, or a cabaret/floor show at the Shogun in Roppongi (cost: ¥12,970), depending on whether you join the tour for dinner. **The Japan Gray Line** (tel. 03/3433–5745) has similar programs.

Tours from Tokyo To Nikko, **Sunrise Tours** (tel. 03/3276–7777) offers one-day tours (cost: ¥18,500, lunch included) and two-day tours (cost: ¥28,000, 1 lunch and overnight accommodation included). **Tobu Travel** (tel. 03/3281–6622, a division of Tobu Railways) offers full-day (8–7:30) trips to Nikko with an English-speaking guide, reserved train travel, lunch and admission fees (cost: ¥18,500). **Sunrise Tours** (tel. 03/3276–7771), **Japan Amenity Travel** (tel. 03/3573–1417), and **The Japan Gray Line** (tel. 03/3433–1011) offer tours to Mt. Fuji and Hakone; one-day tours cost ¥18,500 (lunch included), and two-day tours cost ¥40,100 (meals and accommodation included). Some of these tours include a quick visit to Kamakura. There is also a two-day excursion to Kyoto via the Shinkansen for ¥75,000.

Personal Guides **The Japan Guide Association** (tel. 03/3213–2706) will introduce you to English-speaking guides. However, you will need to agree with the guide on the itinerary and price.

Exploring

Orientation

The distinctions of downtown (Shitamachi) and uptown (Yamanote) have shaped the character of Tokyo since the 17th century and will be your guide, too, as you explore the city. At the risk of an easy generalization, it might be said that downtown offers the visitor more to *see*, and uptown more things to *do;* another way of putting it is that Tokyo north and east of the Imperial Palace embodies more of the city's history, its traditional way of life, whereas the fruit of modernity—the glitzy, ritzy side of Tokyo as an international city—lies generally south and west.

The following exploring section has been divided into 10 tours of major areas of Tokyo. The first six tours follow a downtown loop which starts in central Tokyo at the Imperial Palace District and proceeds north to Akihabara and Jimbocho, and from there to Ueno. From Ueno, the tours turn east to Asakusa, then south to Tsukiji and Shimbashi, returning to the center of the city by way of Nihombashi, Ginza, and Yurakucho.

The four tours of Tokyo's uptown take you south to Roppongi and then north to Akasaka (which is west of the Imperial Palace district). The tours continue from Akasaka to the western part of Tokyo, through Aoyama, Shibuya, Harajuku, and finally Shinjuku.

Fortunately, no point on any of your 10 itineraries is very far from a subway station; you can use Tokyo's efficient subway system to hop from one area to another, to cut a tour short, or to return to a tour the next day. The areas in the 10 tours are not always contiguous—Tokyo is too spread out for that—but they generally border on each other to a useful degree. You will probably want to improvise; you can skip segments of tours according to your fancy, or combine parts of one tour with another in order to end your day exploring the area of your choice.

Let's begin, then, in central Tokyo, with the Imperial Palace District.

Imperial Palace District

Numbers in the margin correspond with points of interest on the Imperial Palace District map.

The **Imperial Palace** occupies what were once the grounds of Edojo Castle. The first feudal lord here, a local chieftain named Dokan Ota, was assassinated in 1486, and the castle he built was abandoned for more than 100 years. When Ieyasu Tokugawa chose the site for his castle in 1590, he had two goals in mind: first, it would have to be impregnable; second, it would have to reflect the power and glory of his position. He was lord of the Kanto, the richest fief in Japan, and would soon be shogun, the military head of state. The fortifications he devised called for a triple system of moats and canals, incorporating the bay and the Sumida River into a huge network of waterways that enclosed both the castle keep (the stronghold or tower) and the palaces and villas of his court—in all, an area of about 450 acres. The castle had 99 gates (36 in the outer wall), 21 watchtowers (of which 3 are still standing), and 28 armories. The outer defenses stretched from present-day Shimbashi Station to Kanda. Completed in 1640 and later expanded, it was at the time the largest castle in the world.

The walls of Edojo Castle and its moats were made of stone from the Izu Peninsula, about 60 miles to the southwest. The great slabs were brought by barge—each of the largest was a cargo in itself—to the port of Edo (then much closer to the castle than the present port of Tokyo is now), and hauled through the streets on sledges by teams of 100 men or more. Thousands of stonemasons were brought from all over the country to finish the work; under the gates and castle buildings, the blocks of stone are said to have been shaped and fitted so precisely that a knife blade could not be slipped between them.

The inner walls divided the castle into four main areas, called *maru.* The innermost (Hon Maru) area contained the shogun's audience halls, his private residence, and, for want of a better word, his seraglio: the O-oku, where the shogun kept his wife and concubines, with their ladies-in-waiting, attendants, cooks, and servants. (Concubines came and went; at any given time, as many as 1,000 women might be living in the O-oku. Intrigue, more than sex, was its principal concern, and tales of the seraglio provided a rich source of material for the Japanese literary imagination.) Below the Hon Maru was the second fortress (Ni-no-Maru), where the shogun lived when he transferred his power to an heir and retired. Behind it, to the north, was the Kita-no-maru, now a public park; south and west was the Nishi-no-maru, a subsidiary fortress.

Not much of the Tokugawa glory remains. The shogunate was abolished in 1868; the Emperor Meiji (1868–1912), restored to power, moved his court from Kyoto to Edo—renaming it Tokyo—and Edojo Castle was chosen for the site of the Imperial Palace. Many of the buildings had been destroyed in the turmoil of the Meiji Restoration (1868); others fell victim to fire in 1872; still others were simply torn down. Of the 28 original *tamon* (armories), only two survived. The present-day Imperial Palace is open to the public only twice a year: on January 2 (New Year's) and Dec. 23 (Emperor's Birthday), when many thousands of people assemble under the balcony to offer their good wishes to the imperial family. In 1968, to mark the completion of the current palace, the area that once encompassed the Hon Maru and Ni-no-Maru were opened to the public as the East Imperial Garden. There are three entrance gates— Otemon, Hira-kawamon, and Kita Hanebashimon. Each can easily be reached from the Otemachi or Takebashi subway stations.

❶ A good place to start this exploration of the Imperial Palace area is **Tokyo Station.** The Otemachi subway stop (Chiyoda, Marunouchi, Tozai, and Toei Mita lines) is a closer and handier connection, but the old redbrick Tokyo Station building is a more compelling place. The work of Kingo Tatsuno, one of Japan's first modern architects, it was completed in 1914; Tatsuno modeled his creation on the railway station of Amsterdam. The building lost its original top story in the air raids of 1945, but it was promptly repaired; more recent plans to tear it down entirely were scotched by a protest movement, and the idea now is to have it "remodeled"—which, to judge by the prevailing standards of architecture in Tokyo, can do it very little good. The best thing about the building is the **Tokyo Station Hotel,** which wanders along the west side on the second and third floors; the windows along the corridor look out over the station rotunda. The hotel's frosted glass, flocked wallpaper, and heavy red drapes have seen better days, but it still has enough pride of place—you couldn't ask for a more central location—to charge ¥18,000 for a double room without bath. The dining room serves a fairly decent breakfast for ¥1,900– ¥2,400. *1-9-1 Marunouchi, Chiyoda-ku, tel. 03/3231–2511.*

Leave the station by the Marunouchi Central exit, cross the street in front at the taxi stand, and walk up the broad divided avenue that leads to the Imperial Palace grounds. To your left is Marunouchi, to your right is Otemachi: you are in the heart of Japan, Incorporated—the home of its major banks and investment houses, its insurance and trading companies. Take the second right, at the corner of the New Marunouchi Building; walk two blocks, past the gleaming brown marble fortress of the Industrial Bank of Japan, and turn left. Ahead of you, across Uchibori (Inner Moat) Avenue from the Palace Hotel, is **❷** the **Otemon,** one of three entrances to the **East Imperial Garden.** *Admission free. Open 9–3. Closed Mon., Fri., and Dec. 25–Jan. 5.*

The Otemon was in fact the main entrance to the castle itself. The so-called *masu* (box) style was typical of virtually all the approaches to Ieyasu's impregnable fortress: the first portal (*mon* is Japanese for "gate") leads to a narrow enclosure with a second and larger gate beyond that offered the defenders inside a devastating field of fire upon any would-be intruders. Most of the Otemon was destroyed in 1945 but was rebuilt in 1967 on the original plans; the outer gate, however, survived.

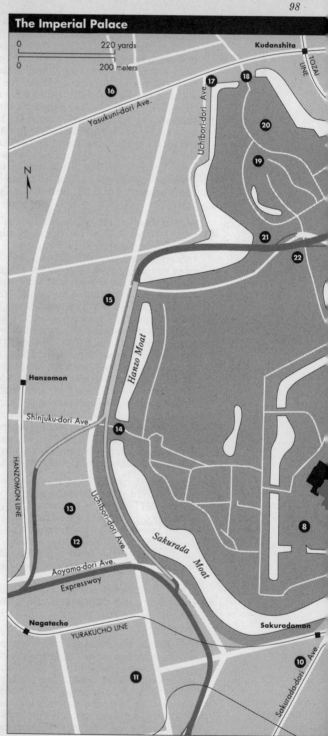

The Imperial Palace

98

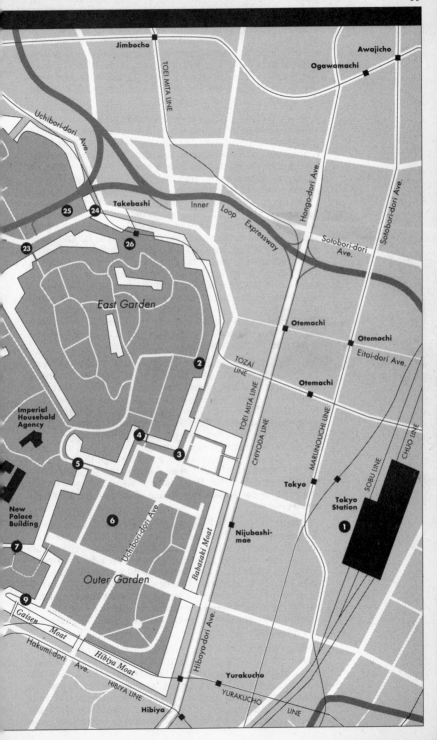

Go through the gate, collect a plastic token at the office on the other side (there's no admission fee), and walk up the driveway. The bloodcurdling shrieks and howls you may hear on your left are harmless; they come from the National Police Agency *dojo* (martial arts hall). The hall was built in the Taisho period (1912–1925) and is still used for *kendo* (Japanese fencing) practice. On the right is the Ote Rest House, where for ¥100 you can buy a simple map of the garden.

At the top of the drive was once another gate, where feudal lords summoned to the palace would descend from the palanquins and proceed on foot. The gate itself is gone, but two 19th-century guardhouses survive; one outside the massive stone supports on the right, and a longer one inside on the left. The latter was known as the Hundred-Man Guardhouse; this approach was defended by four shifts of 100 soldiers each. Past it, to the right, is the entrance to what was once the Ni-no-maru, now a grove and garden, its pathways defined by rows of rhododendrons manicured to within an inch of their lives, with a pond and a waterfall in the northwest corner. At the far end is the **Suwa Tea Pavilion,** an early 19th-century building relocated here from another part of the castle grounds. Dominating the west side of the garden are the steep stone walls of the Hon Maru, with the Moat of Swans below (the swans are actually elsewhere, in the outer waterways); halfway along, a steep path leads up to an entrance in the wall to the upper fortress. This is **Shio-mi-zaka,** which might be translated as "Briny View Hill," so named because in the Edo period one could see the ocean from this vantage point.

Walk back to the guardhouses, turn right, and follow the road for the main entrance to the Hon Maru. Nothing remains on the broad expanse of lawn to recall the scores of buildings that once stood here, connected by a network of corridors. The stone foundations of the castle keep may be found at the far end of the grounds. As you enter, turn left and explore the wooded paths that skirt the perimeter. There is shade and quiet and benches are available where you can sit, rest your weary feet, and listen to bird song. In the southwest corner, through the trees, you can see the back of the **Fujimi Yagura,** the only surviving watchtower of the Hon Maru; farther along the path, on the west side, is the **Fujimi Tamon,** one of the two remaining armories.

The foundations of the keep make a platform with a fine view of **Kitanomaru-Koen Park** and the city to the north. The view must have been even finer from the keep itself; built and rebuilt three times, it soared more than 250 feet over Edo, five stories high. The other castle buildings were all plastered white; the keep was black, unadorned but for a golden roof. In 1657, a fire destroyed most of the city. Strong winds carried the flames across the moat, where it consumed the keep in a heat so fierce that it melted the gold in the vaults underneath. The keep was never rebuilt.

Now it's time to review your priorities. You can abbreviate your tour of the palace area from here in one of two ways. To the left of the keep, there is an exit from the Hon Maru that leads to the **Kita Hanebashi Gate;** to the right, another road leads past the **Toka Music Hall** (an octagonal tower faced in mosaic tile, built in honor of the empress in 1966) down to the Ni-no-Maru and out of the gardens by way of the **Harakawa Gate.** Both these exits will bring you to **Takebashi** (Bamboo Bridge), which you encounter much later in the day on the longer course of this excursion.

To take a longer course, leave the Hon Maru the way you came in. Stop for a moment at the rest house on the west side of the park, and look at the pairs of before-and-after photographs along the wall; these are the same views of the castle, taken about 100 years apart. In the 1870s, much of the castle was in astonishing disrepair, and the warriors of the Hundred-Man Guardhouse were a trifle ragtag. Turn in your plastic token, turn to the right as you leave the Otemon, and walk along the moat.

❸ Where the wall makes a right angle, you will see the second of the three surviving watchtowers, the **Tatsumi** or **Niju** (Double-Tiered) **Yagura.** Here the sidewalk opens out to a parking lot for tour buses and the beginning of a broad promenade. In the far corner, where the angle of the wall straightens again, is the
❹ **Kikyomon,** a gate used primarily for deliveries to the palace. (Short and prestigious indeed is the roster of *Go-yotashi*—Purveyors to the Imperial Household.) At the far end of the park-
❺ ing lot is **Sakashitamon,** the gate used by the officials of the Imperial Household Agency itself.

❻ From here to **Hibiya-Koen Park,** along both sides of Uchibori-dori Avenue, stretches the concourse of the **Imperial Palace Outer Garden.** This whole area once lay along the edge of Tokyo Bay. Later, the shogun had his most trusted retainers build their estates here; these in turn gave way to the office buildings of the Meiji government. In 1899, the buildings were relocated; the promenade was planted with the wonderful stands of pine trees you see today. Walk along the broad gravel
❼ path to **Nijubashi** (Two-Tiered Bridge) and the **Seimon** (Main Gate).

This is surely the most photogenic spot on your tour of the Castle, though you can approach it no closer than the head of the short stone bridge called the **Seimon Sekkyo.** Cordoned off on the other side is the gate through which ordinary mortals may pass only on January 2 and Dec. 23; the guards in front of their little copper-roof octagon sentry boxes change every hour on the hour—alas, with nothing like the pomp and ceremony of Buckingham Palace. Nijubashi makes its graceful arch over the moat here from the area inside the gate; the building in the
❽ background, completing the picture, is the **Fushimi Yagura,** built in the 17th century and the last of the three surviving original watchtowers.

❾ Continue on the gravel walk past the Seimon, turn right, and pass through the **Sakuradamon** (Gate of the Field of Cherry Trees). (Before you do, turn and look back down the concourse: you will not see another expanse of open space like this anywhere else in Tokyo.) Sakuradamon is another masu gate; by hallowed use and custom, the little courtyard between the portals is where the joggers warm up for their 3-mile run around the palace. Many of them will already have passed you on your exploration; jogging around the palace is a ritual that begins as early as 6 AM and goes on all through the day, no matter what the weather. Almost everybody runs the course counterclockwise; now and then you may spot someone going the opposite way, but rebellious behavior of this sort is frowned upon in Japan.

Across the street as you pass through the gate is the beginning of Sakurada-dori Avenue, with the **Metropolitan Police Department** building on the north corner, by world-renowned architect Kenzô Tange; the older brick buildings on the south corner belong to the **Ministry of Justice.** Sakurada-dori runs through the heart of official Japan; between here and Kasumigaseki are the ministries—from Foreign Affairs and Education to International Trade and Industry—that comprise the central government. They inhabit, however, what are surely the most uninteresting buildings, architecturally, of any government center in the world; they should not tempt you from your course. Turn right, and follow the moat as you walk up the hill.

Ahead of you, where the road branches to the left, you will see the squat pyramid of the **National Diet Building,** which houses the Japanese Parliament. Completed in 1936 after 17 years of work, it is a building best contemplated from a distance; on a gloomy day, it might well have sprung from the screen of a German Expressionist movie. Bear right as you follow the moat, to the five-point intersection where it curves again to the north. Across the street are the gray stone slabs of the **Supreme Court;** this, and the **National Theater** next door, are worth a short detour.

The Supreme Court building, by architect Shinichi Okada, was the last in a series of open design competitions sponsored by the various agencies charged with the reconstruction of Tokyo after World War II. Completed in 1968, its fortresslike planes and angles speak volumes for the role of the law in Japanese society; here is the very bastion of the established order. Okada's winning design was one of 217 submitted; before it was finished, the open competition had generated so much controversy that the government did not hold another one for almost 20 years. *4-2 Hayabusa, Chiyoda-ku (nearest subway station: Hanzomon). Call the Public Relations Office (Kohoka) at 03/ 3264–8111 for permission to visit inside.*

Like the Supreme Court, Hiroyuki Iwamoto's National Theater (1966) was also a design-competition winner; the result was a rendition in concrete of the ancient *azekura* (storehouse) style, best exemplified by the 8th-century Shosoin Imperial Repository in Nara. The large hall seats 1,746 and features primarily Kabuki theater, ancient court music, and dance; the small hall seats 630 and is used primarily for Bunraku puppet theater and traditional music. *4-1 Hayabusa, Chiyoda-ku (nearest subway station: Hanzomon), tel. 03/3265–7411. Ticket prices vary considerably depending on the performance.*

Cross back to the palace side of the street. At the top of the hill, on your right, a police contingent guards the road to the **Hanzomon**—and beyond it, to the new Imperial Palace. At the foot of this small wooden gate was once the house of the legendary Hattori Hanzo, leader of the shogun's private corps of spies and infiltrators (and assassins, if need be)—the black-clad *ninja*, perennial material for historical adventure films and television dramas.

North from here, along the Hanzo-bori Moat, is a narrow strip of park; facing it, across the street, is the **British Embassy.** Along this western edge of his fortress, the shogun kept his personal retainers, called *hatamoto*, divided by district (*ban-cho*) into six regiments. Today these six bancho comprise one of the most sought-after residential areas in Tokyo, where high-rise apartments commonly fetch $1 million or more.

At the next intersection, review your priorities again. You can turn right, and complete your circuit of the palace grounds by way of the **Inuimon,** or you can continue straight north on Uchibori-dori Avenue to Kudanzaka and **Yasukuni Jinja** (Shrine of Peace for the Nation).

Time Out A good, moderately priced place for lunch, if you choose the latter course, is **Tony Roma's**—just past the intersection on the west side of the street. The specialty here, as it is in this chain's umpteen locations, from London to Okinawa, is charcoal-broiled spare ribs. *1 Sambancho, Chiyoda-ku, tel. 03/3239-0273. Open noon–10:30.*

Where Uchibori-dori Avenue comes to an end, cross the street to the grounds of the Yasukuni Jinja Shrine. Founded in 1869, Yasukuni enshrines the souls—worshiped as deities—of some 2.5 million people who gave their lives in the defense of the Japanese Empire. Since most of that "defense" took place in the course of what others regard as opportunistic wars abroad, Yasukuni is a very controversial place. It is a memorial out of keeping with the postwar constitution, which commits Japan to the renunciation of militarism forever; on the other hand, hundreds of thousands of Japanese visit the shrine every year, simply to pray for the repose of friends and relatives they have lost. Prime ministers and other high officials try to skirt this controversy, with no great success, by making their visits as private individuals, not in their official capacities.

Pick up a pamphlet and simplified map of the shrine in English from the guard station on the right as you enter. Just ahead of you, in a circle on the main avenue, is a statue of Masujiro Omura, commander of the imperial forces that subdued the Tokugawa loyalist resistance to the new Meiji government in 1868. From here, as you look down the avenue to your right, you see the enormous steel outer *torii* (arch) of the main entrance to the shrine at Kudan-shita; to the left, you see the bronze inner torii, erected in 1887. (The arches of Shinto shrines are normally made of wood and are painted red.) Beyond the inner torii is the gate to the shrine itself, with its 12 pillars and chrysanthemums—the imperial crest—embossed on the doors.

The shrine is not one structure but a complex of buildings that includes the **Main Hall** and the **Hall of Worship,** both built in the simple, unadorned style of the ancient shrines at Ise. In the complex are various reception halls, a museum, a Noh theater, and, in the far western corner, a sumo-wrestling ring. Both Noh and sumo have their origins in religious ritual, as performances offered to please and divert the gods; these performances are given at Yasukuni during the two main festivals of the year, April 21–23 and October 17–19.

Turn right in front of the Hall of Worship, and cross the grounds to the museum, called the **Yushukan.** None of the documents and memorabilia on display here are identified in English, although in some cases the meanings are clear enough; the rooms on the second floor house an especially fine collection of medieval swords and armor. Perhaps the most bizarre exhibit is the *Kaiten* (Human Torpedo) in the main hall on the first floor; this is the submarine equivalent of a kamikaze plane. The Kaiten was a black cylinder about 50 feet long and 3 feet in diameter, with 3,400 pounds of high explosives in the nose and a man in the center, squeezed into a seat, who peered into a periscope and worked the directional vanes with his feet. It was carried into battle on the deck of a ship and launched against the enemy; on its one-way journey, it had a maximum range of about 5 miles. *3-1-1 Kudan-kita, Chiyoda-ku, tel. 03/3261-8326. Admission: ¥200. Museum open Mar.–Sept., 9–5; Oct.–Feb., 9–4:30. Closed June 22–23, Dec. 28–31. Grounds of the shrine open 5:30 AM–7 PM.*

If time permits, turn right as you leave the Yushukan and walk past the other implements of war (cannons, ancient and modern; a tank, incongruously bright and gay in its green-and-yellow camouflage paint) arrayed out front of the pond at the rear of the shrine. There is, unfortunately, no admittance to the teahouses on the far side, but the pond is among the most serene and beautiful in Tokyo, especially in spring, when the irises are in bloom. If you are pressed, leave Yasukuni Jinja the way you came in, cross the street, turn left, and walk down the hill. About 50 yards from the intersection, on the right, is the entrance to **Chidori-ga-fuji-Koen Park;** it is time once again to review your priorities. The park is a pleasant green strip of promenade, high on the edge of the moat, lined with cherry trees. The park leads back in the direction of the Imperial Palace; halfway along, it widens, and opposite the **Fairmont Hotel** a path leads down to the **Chidori-ga-fuji Boathouse.** Long before Edojo Castle, there was a lovely little lake here, which Ieyasu Tokugawa incorporated into his system of defenses; now it's possible to rent a rowboat and explore it at your leisure. *Tel. 03/3234-1948. Open 9:30–4 (July and Aug. to 5). Closed Mon. and Dec. 16–Feb. 28. Boat rentals: ¥200 for 30 min.*

Leave the park the way you came in, turn right, and continue down the hill to the **Tayasumon,** the entrance to **Kitanomaru-Koen Park.** This is one of the largest and finest of the surviving masu gates to the castle; inside, you come first to the **Budokan** (2-3 Kitanomaru Koen, Chiyoda-ku, tel. 03/3216–5100), built as a martial arts arena for the Tokyo Olympics of 1964. The octagonal design was based on the Hall of Dreams of the Horyuji Temple in Nara. Apart from hosting tournaments and exhibitions of judo, karate, and kendo (fencing), this arena also serves as a concert hall, especially for visiting superstars. Tokyo rock promoters are fortunate in their audiences, who don't seem to mind that the ticket prices are exorbitant, the acoustics are unforgivable, and the overselling is downright hazardous.

Just opposite the main entrance to the Budokan, past the parking lot, a pedestrian walkway leads off through the park, back in the direction of the palace. Cross the bridge at the other end of the walk, turn right, and right again before you leave the park, on the driveway that leads to the **Kogeikan,** the **Crafts Gallery** of the National Museum of Modern Art. Built in 1910, the Kogeikan was once the headquarters of the Imperial Guard; it is a rambling redbrick building, neo-Gothic in style, with exhibition halls on the second floor. The gallery features work of traditional craftsmanship—primarily lacquer ware, textiles, pottery, and metalworking—by the modern masters. The exhibits are all too few, but many of the craftspeople represented here have been designated by the government as Living National Treasures—a recognition given only to lifetimes of the finest work in each of these fields. *1-1 Kitanomaru, Koen, Chiyoda-ku, tel. 03/3211–7781. Admission: ¥400; ¥500 on a joint ticket to the National Museum. Open 10–4:30. Closed Mon.*

Return to the park exit, and cross the street to the palace side.

㉒ Ahead of you is the **Inuimon** (Northwest Gate); a driveway here leads to the Imperial Household Agency and the palace. This gate is used primarily by members of the imperial family and by the fortunate few who have managed to obtain special permission to visit the palace itself. A bit farther down the hill is

㉓ the **Kita Hanebashi** (North Drawbridge) **Gate,** mentioned earlier as one of the entrances to the East Imperial Garden.

㉔ At the foot of the hill is **Takebashi** (Bamboo Bridge); the original bridge material has long since given way to reinforced concrete. Here, depending on how you have organized your our, you might want to cross and walk the short distance up the oth-

㉕ er side of the street to the **National Museum of Modern Art.** Founded in 1952 and moved to its present site in 1969, the museum mounts a number of major exhibitions of 20th-century Japanese and Western art throughout the year. The second through fourth floors house the permanent collection (painting, prints, and sculpture), which includes works by Rousseau, Picasso, Foujita, Ryuzaburo Umehara, and Taikan Yokoyama. *3 Kitanomaru, Koen, Chiyoda-ku, tel. 03/3214–2561. Admission: ¥400; ¥500 on a joint ticket to the Kogeikan Crafts gallery. Open 10–4:30. Closed Mon.*

㉖ Cross back to the palace side of the street. A short walk from Takebashi is **Hirakawamon,** the third entrance to the East Imperial Garden and the last stop on your tour. The approach to this gate, recently restored, is the only wood bridge that spans the moat; the gate itself is also a reconstruction, but an especially beautiful one—it looks much as it must have when the Hirakawamon was used by the shogun's ladies, on their rare excursions from the seraglio. From here, follow the moat as it turns south again; in a few minutes you will find yourself back at Otemon, tired but triumphant.

Akihabara and Jimbocho

Numbers in the margin correspond with points of interest on the Akihabara and Jimbocho map.

This is it: the greatest Sound and Light show on earth. **Akihabara** is a merchandise mart for anything—and everything—that runs on electricity, block after block of it, with a combined annual turnover well in excess of ¥30 *trillion*. Here you'll find microprocessors, washing machines, stereo systems, blenders, television sets, and gadgets that beep when your bathwater is hot. Wherever you go in the world, if people know nothing else about Japan, they recognize it as a cornucopia of electronics equipment and household appliances; about 10% of what that industry makes for the domestic market passes through Akihabara.

Just after World War II there was a black market here, around the railroad station, where the Yamanote Loop Line and the crosstown Sobu Line intersect. In time, most of the stalls were doing a legitimate business in radio parts, and in 1951 they were all relocated in one dense clump under the tracks. Retail and wholesale suppliers prospered there in less-than-peaceful coexistence, as they spread out into the adjacent blocks and made the area famous for cut-rate prices.

No visitor to Tokyo neglects this district; the mistake is to come here merely for shopping. Akihabara may be consumer heaven, but it is also the first stop on a walking tour through the general area known as Kanda (where the true Edokko, the born-and-bred Tokyoite of the old town, claimed his roots) to the book-stalls of Jimbocho. In a sense, this tour is a journey through time: it's a morning's walk from satellite-broadcast antennas to the sacred precincts of the printed word.

Start at the west exit of JR Akihabara Station. (There's also a stop nearby on the Hibiya subway line, but the JR provides much easier access.) Come out to the left into the station square, turn right, and walk to the main thoroughfare; ahead of you on the other side of the street you'll see the **LAOX** building, one of the district's major discount stores. *1-2-9 Soto Kanda, Chiyoda-ku, tel. 03/3255–9041. Open daily 10–7:30.*

Before you get to the corner, on the right, is a little warren of stalls and tiny shops that cannot have changed an iota since the days of the black market—except for their merchandise. Wander through the narrow passageways and see an astonishing array of switches, transformers, resistors, semiconductors, printed circuit cards, plugs, wires, connectors, and tools; this corner of Akihabara is for people who know—or want to know—what the latest in Japanese electronic technology looks like from the inside. (A lot of the foreign browsers here seem to confer in Eastern European languages.)

Turn right at the corner, and walk north on Chuo-dori Avenue. Music blares at you from hundreds of storefronts as you walk along; this is the heart of the district.

Just past the second intersection, on the right, is **Yamagiwa** (4-1-1 Soto Kanda, Chiyoda-ku, tel. 03/3253–2111), a store that stocks simply everything, from computer software to chandeliers to hearing aids, including a considerable selection of imported goods. There's also an annex for duty-free shopping (bring your passport). Rival **Minami,** at the far end of the block, offers a similar variety of goods, plus an entire sixth floor devoted to European antiques. *4-3-3 Soto Kanda, Chiyoda-ku, tel. 03/3255–3173.*

Cross the street, continue northward to the Soto Kanda 5-chome intersection (there's an entrance to the Suehiro-cho subway station on the corner), and turn left on Kuramaebashi-dori Avenue. Walk about five minutes—you will cross one more intersection with a traffic light—and in the middle of the next block you will see a flight of steps on the left, between two new brick buildings. Red, green, and blue pennants flutter from the handrails; this is the back entrance to the **Kanda Myojin Shrine.**

Kanda Myojin is said to have been founded in 730 in a village called Shibasaki, where the Otemachi financial district stands today. Three principle deities are enshrined here: Daikoku,

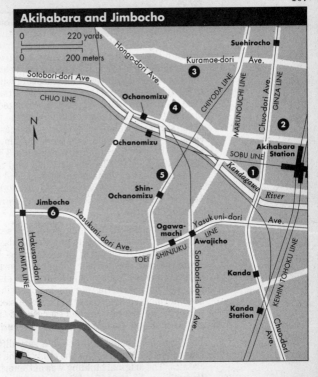

Ebisu, and Taira no Masakado. Daikoku looks after the well-being of farming and fishing villages and other small communities; one also appeals to him for the cure of various diseases. Ebisu is the god of success in business; he concerns himself as well with the prosperity of families and the happiness of marriages. Taira no Masakado was a 10th-century warrior whose contentious spirit earned him a place in the Shinto pantheon: he led a revolt against the Imperial Court in Kyoto, seized control of the eastern provinces, declared himself emperor—and was beheaded for his rebellious ways in 940.

In 1616, the shrine was relocated, a victim of Ieyasu Tokugawa's ever-expanding system of fortifications; the present site was chosen, in accordance with Chinese geomancy, to afford the best view from Edojo Castle and protect it from evil influences. The townspeople of Kanda, contentious souls in their own right, made Taira no Masakado a kind of patron saint, and even today (oblivious somehow to the fact that he lost) they appeal to him for victory when they face a tough encounter. The shrine itself was destroyed in the earthquake of 1923; the present buildings reproduce in concrete the style of 1616. Ieyasu preferred the jazzier decorative effects of Chinese Buddhism to the simple lines of traditional Shinto architecture; this is especially evident in the curved, copper-tile roof of the main shrine and in the two-story front gate.

Some of the smaller buildings you see as you come up the steps and walk around the main hall contain the *mikoshi*—portable shrines that are featured in one of Tokyo's three great blowouts, the Kanda Festival. (The other two are the Sanno Festival of the Hie Shrine in Nagatacho, and the Sanja Festival of the Asakusa Shrine.) The essential shrine festival is a procession in which the gods, housed for the occasion in their mikoshi, pass through the streets and get a breath of fresh air. The Kanda Festival began in the early Edo period; heading the procession then were 36 magnificent floats, most of which were destroyed in the fires that raged through the city after the earthquake of 1923. The floats that lead the procession today move in stately measure on wheeled carts, attended by the priests and officials of the shrine in Heian-period (794–1185) costume; behind them come the mikoshi, some 70 of them, bobbing and weaving, carried on the shoulders of the townspeople. The spirit of Taira no Masakado is channeled on this day into a determination to shout the loudest, drink the most beer, and have the best time. *2-16-2 Soto Kanda, Chiyoda-ku, tel. 03/3254–0753. The Kanda Festival takes place in odd-numbered years; it is next scheduled for May 1993.*

Leave the shrine by the main gate. The seated figures in the alcoves on either side are its guardian gods; carved in camphor wood, they are depicted in Heian costume, holding long bows. From the gate down to the copper-clad torii (arch) on Hongo-dori Avenue is a walk of a few yards; on either side are shops that sell the specialties famous in this neighborhood: pickles, miso (fermented bean paste), and sweet sake (rice wine) laced with ground ginger. On the other side of the avenue you will ❹ see the wall and wooded grounds of the **Yushima Seido.**

This, too, is a shrine, but one of a very different sort: It was founded in 1632 as a hall for the study of the Chinese Confucian classics. The original building was in Ueno; its headmaster was Razan Hayashi, the official Confucian scholar to the Tokugawa government. The Tokugawas found these Chinese teachings, with their emphasis on obedience and hierarchy, particularly attractive. Confucianism became a kind of state ideology, and the hall (moved to its present site in 1691) turned into an academy for the ruling elite. In a sense, nothing has changed: In 1872, the new Meiji government established the country's first teacher training institute here, and that, in turn, evolved into Tokyo University—the graduates of which still make up much of the ruling elite.

Cross Hongo-dori Avenue and turn left, following the wall downhill. Turn right at the first narrow side street, and right again at the bottom; the entrance to Yushima Seido is a few steps from the corner. Japan's first museum and its first national library were built on these grounds; both were soon relocated. As you walk up the path, you will see a statue of Confucius on your right; where the path ends, a flight of stone steps leads up to the main hall of the shrine—destroyed six times by fire, and each time rebuilt. The last repairs date to 1954. The hall could almost be in China; painted black, weathered and somber, it looks like nothing else you are likely to see in Japan. Confucian scholarship, it seems, did not lend itself to ornamentation. In May of odd-numbered years, when the Kanda Festival passes by, the spirit enshrined here must take a dim view of the frivolities on the other side of the wall. *1-4-25 Yushima, Bunkyo-ku, tel. 03/3251–4606. Admission free. Open daily 9:30–5.*

Retrace your steps, turn right as you leave the shrine, and walk up to **Hijiribashi** (Bridge of Sages), which spans the Kanda River at Ochanomizu Station on the JR Sobu Line. Cross the bridge (you're now back on Hongo-dori); ahead of you, just beyond the station on the right, you'll see the dome of **Nikolai Cathedral,** center of the Orthodox Church in Japan. Formally, this is the Holy Resurrection Cathedral; the more familiar name derives from its founder, St. Nikolai Kassatkin (1836–1912), a Russian missionary who came to Japan in 1861 and spent the rest of his life here propagating the Orthodox faith. The building, planned by a Russian engineer and executed by a British architect, was completed in 1891. Heavily damaged in the earthquake of 1923, the cathedral was restored with a dome much more modest than the original. Even so, it endows this otherwise featureless part of the city with the charm of the unexpected. *4-1 Surugadai, Kanda, Chiyoda-ku, tel. 03/3295–6879. Admission free. Open Tues.–Sat. 1–4.*

Continue south on Hongo-dori Avenue to the major intersection at Yasukuni-dori Avenue. Surugadai, the area to your right as you walk down the hill, is a kind of fountainhead of Japanese higher education: Two of the city's major private universities—Meiji and Nihon—occupy a good part of the hill. Not far from these is a score of elite high schools, public and private. In the 1880s, several other universities were founded in this area. They have since moved away, but the student population here is still enormous; Nihon University alone accepted some 9,000 freshmen this year to its four-year program.

Students are not as serious as they used to be. So saith every generation, but as you turn right on Yasukuni-dori Avenue, you encounter palpable proof. Between you and your objective—the **bookstores of Jimbocho**—are three blocks of stores devoted almost exclusively to electric guitars, records, travel bags, skis, and skiwear. The bookstores begin at the intersection called Surugadai-shita, and continue along Yasukuni-dori Avenue for about a ¼-mile, most of them on the south (left) side of the street. This area is to print what Akihabara is to electronics; browse here for art books, catalogs, scholarly monographs, secondhand paperbacks, and dictionaries in most known languages. Jimbocho is home as well to wholesalers, distributors, and many of Japan's most prestigious publishing houses.

A number of the antiquarian booksellers here carry not only rare typeset editions but also wood-block–printed books of the Edo period and individual prints. At shops like **Isseido** (1-7 Kanda Jimbocho, Chiyoda-ku, tel. 03/3292–0071) and **Ohya Shobo** (1-1 Kanda Jimbocho, Chiyoda-ku, tel. 03/3291–0062), it is still possible to find a genuine Hiroshige or Toyokuni print (granted, not in the best condition) at an affordable price.

What about that word processor or CD player you didn't buy at the beginning of your walk because you didn't want to carry it all this way? No problem. There's a subway station (Toei Mita Line) right on the Jimbocho main intersection; ride one stop to Suidobashi, transfer to the JR Sobu Line, and five minutes later you're back in Akihabara.

Ueno

Numbers in the margin correspond with points of interest on the Ueno map.

The JR station at **Ueno** is Tokyo's Gare du Nord: the gateway to (and from) the provinces. The single most important fact of Japanese life since the 17th century has been the pull of the cities, the great migration from the villages in pursuit of a better life; since 1883, when the station was completed, the people of Tohoku—the northeast—have begun that pursuit here.

Ueno was a place of prominence, however, long before the coming of the railroad. When Ieyasu Tokugawa established his capital here in 1603, it was merely a wooded promontory, called Shinobugaoka (The Hill of Endurance), overlooking the bay. The view was a pleasant one, and Ieyasu gave a large tract of land on the hill to one of his most important vassals, Todo Takatora, who designed and built Edojo Castle. Ieyasu's heir, Hidetada, later commanded the founding of a temple on the hill. Shinobugaoka was in the northeast corner of the capital; in Chinese geomancy, the northeast approach required a particularly strong defense against evil influences.

That defense was entrusted to Tenkai (1536–1643), a priest of the Tendai sect of Buddhism and an adviser of great influence to the first three Tokugawa shoguns. Tenkai turned for his model to Kyoto, guarded on the northeast by Mt. Hiei and the great temple complex of Enryakuji. The temple he built on Shinobugaoka was called Kaneiji, and he became the first abbot. Mt. Hiei was loftier, but the patronage of the Tokugawas and their vassal barons made Kaneiji Temple a seat of power and glory. By the end of the 17th century, it occupied most of the hill. To the magnificent Main Hall were added scores of other buildings—including a pagoda and a shrine to Ieyasu—and 36 subsidiary temples. The city of Edo itself expanded to the foot of the hill; most of present-day Ueno was once called Monzen-machi (the town in front of the gate).

The power and glory of Kaneiji came to an end in one day: April 11, 1868. An army of clan forces from the western part of Japan, bearing a mandate from Emperor Meiji, had marched on Edo and demanded the surrender of the castle. The shogunate was by then a tottering regime; it capitulated, and with it went everything that had depended on the favor of the Tokugawas. The Meiji Restoration began with a bloodless coup.

A band of some 2,000 Tokugawa loyalists then assembled on Ueno Hill and defied the new government. On May 15, the imperial army attacked; outnumbered and surrounded, the loyalists, known as the Shogitai, soon discovered that right was on the side of modern artillery. A few survivors fled; the rest committed ritual suicide—and took the Kaneiji with them; they put the temple and most of its outbuildings to the torch.

The new Meiji government turned Ueno Hill into one of the nation's first public parks. The intention was not merely to provide a bit of greenery, but to make the park an instrument of civic improvement and a showcase for the achievements of an emerging modern state. It would serve as the site of trade and industrial expositions; it would have a national museum, a library, a university of fine arts, and a zoo. That policy continued well into the present era, with the building of further galleries and concert halls, but Ueno is more than its museums. The Shogitai failed to take everything with them; some of the most important buildings in the temple complex have survived or been restored. The "town in front of the gate" is gone, but here and there, in the narrow streets below the hill, the way of life is much the way it was 100 years ago. Exploring Ueno can be one excursion, or two: It can be an afternoon of culture-browsing, or it can be a full day of discoveries in one of the great centers of the city.

The best way to begin, in either case, is to come to Ueno on the JR, and leave the station by the Park Exit (Koenguchi) on the upper level. Directly across from the exit is the **Tokyo Metropolitan Festival Hall** (Tokyo Bunka Kaikan), designed by architect Kunio Maekawa and completed in 1961. This is the city's largest and finest facility for classical music, the one most often booked for visiting orchestras and concert soloists. The large auditorium seats 2,327; the smaller one seats 661. *5-45 Ueno Koen, Taito-ku, tel. 03/3828-2111.*

Opposite the Festival Hall on the right is the **National Museum of Western Art.** The building was designed by Le Corbusier and houses what was once the private collection of a wealthy businessman named Kojiro Matsukata. The Rodins in the courtyard—*The Gate of Hell, The Thinker,* and the magnificent *Burghers of Calais*—are genuine; an admirer of French impressionism, Matsukata somehow acquired castings from Rodin's original molds, along with some 850 paintings, sketches, and prints by masters like Renoir, Monet, and Cézanne. He kept the collection in Europe; it was returned by the French government after World War II, left to the country in Matsukata's will, and opened to the public in 1959. Since then, the museum has diversified a bit; more recent acquisitions include works by Reubens, Tintoretto, El Greco, Max Ernst, and Jackson Pollock. *7-7 Ueno Koen, Taito-ku, tel. 03/3828-5131. Admission: ¥360 adults, ¥60 children under 12; ¥720/¥230 for special exhibitions. Open 9:30-4:30. Closed Mon.*

Just behind the National Museum of Western Art, to the right, is the **National Science Museum**—a natural-history museum very much in the conventional mode. That is, it has everything from dinosaurs to moon rocks on display, but it offers relatively little in the way of hands-on learning experiences. This is not a place to linger if your time is short. *7-20 Ueno Koen, Taito-ku, tel. 03/3822-0111. Admission: ¥360 adults, ¥70 children under 12. Open 9-4:30. Closed Mon.*

Beyond the National Science Museum, you will come to a broad street that cuts through the park; turn left, and you come almost immediately to the **Tokyo National Museum.** Here, you should plan to spend some time, even if you are not overly fond of museums: The Tokyo Kokuritsu Hakubutsukan, as it is called in Japanese, is one of the world's great repositories of oriental art and archaeology.

The museum consists of four buildings grouped around a courtyard; on this site once stood the temple-residence of the abbot of Kaneiji Temple. The building on the left is the **Hyokeikan,** the oldest and smallest of the three; completed in 1909, it has only nine exhibition rooms, all devoted to archaeological objects. Look especially for the flamelike sculptured rims and elaborate markings of Middle Jomon–period pottery (c. 3500–2000 BC), so different from anything produced in Japan before or since. Look also from the terra-cotta figures called *haniwa,* unearthed at burial sites dating from the 4th to the 7th centu-

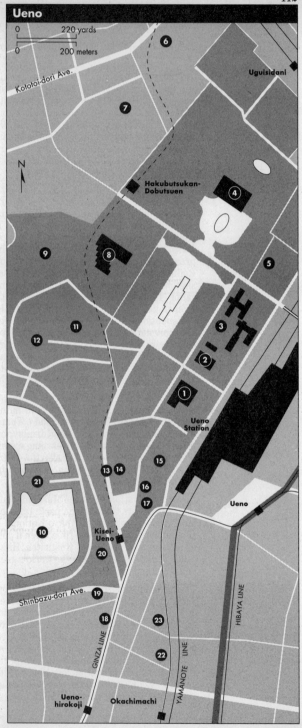

ry; these figures are deceptively simple in shape, and mysterious and comical at the same time in their effects.

Behind the Hyokeikan is a two-story building called the **Horyuji Treasure Hall** (Horyuji Homotsukan), which is open only on Thursdays. In 1878, the 7th-century Horyuji Temple in Nara presented 319 works of art in its possession—sculpture, scrolls, masks, and other objects—to the Imperial Household; these were later transferred to the National Museum, and in 1964 the Horyuji Treasure Hall was built to house them. If at all possible, schedule your visit to the museum on Thursday, but bear in mind that these works of wood and paper are more than 1,000 years old; if the weather is too hot or wet, the hall may not be open.

The central building in the complex, the **Honkan,** was built in 1937 and houses Japanese art exclusively: paintings, calligraphy, sculpture, textiles, ceramics, swords, and armor. The more attractive **Toyokan,** on the right, completed in 1968, is devoted to the art of other Asian cultures. Altogether, the museum has some 87,000 objects in its permanent collection, with several thousand more on loan from shrines, temples, and private owners. Among these are 84 objects designated by the government as National Treasures. The Honkan rotates the works on display several times during the year; it also hosts two special exhibitions a year, April–May and October–November, featuring important collections from foreign museums. These, unfortunately, can be an ordeal: The lighting in the Honkan is not particularly good, the explanations in English are sketchy at best, and the hordes of visitors make it impossible to linger over a work you especially want to study. *13-9 Ueno Koen, Taito-ku, tel. 03/3822–1111. Admission: ¥400 adults, ¥70 children under 12. Open 9–4:30. Closed Mon.*

Turn to the left as you leave the museum, walk east, and turn left again at the first corner. The building across the road on ❺ your right is the **Jigendo** (14-5 Ueno Koen), a memorial hall to Abbot Tenkai, who was given the posthumous title of Jigen Daishi (Great Master of the Merciful Eye). The six bronze lanterns in front, with their dragon faces, are especially fine. At the end of the road, turn left again and walk along the back of ❻ the museum; to your right is the cemetery of the **Kaneiji Temple.** Several of the Tokugawa shoguns had their mausoleums here; these were destroyed in the air raids of 1945, but you will see the gate that once led to the tomb of the fourth shogun, Ietsuna. At the end of the road, in the far northwest corner of the park, is the Kaneiji Temple itself.

The main hall of the Kaneiji, built in 1638, has covered a lot of territory in its day. Abbot Tenkai had it moved to Ueno from a temple in the town of Kawagoe, about 25 miles from Tokyo, where he had once been a priest; it was moved again, to its present site, in 1879, and looks a bit weary of its travels. Behind the temple is the ornately carved gate to what was once the mausoleum of Tsunayoshi, the fifth shogun; Tsunayoshi is famous in the annals of Tokugawa history first for his disastrous fiscal mismanagement, and second for his *Shorui Awaremi no Rei (Edicts on Compassion for Living Things)*, which, among other things, made it a capital offense for a human being to kill a dog. *1-14-11 Ueno Sakuragi, Taito-ku. Admission free. Open 9–sunset.*

Turn right as you leave the temple, and walk south until you come again to the main road through the park. If you turn right on this road, you will soon come to the **Tokyo University of Arts Exhibition Hall** on the left side of the road. The collection here has some interesting works, some of which are designated National Treasures, but it is not actually a museum. The exhibitions on display are intended primarily as teaching materials for courses in the school curriculum. *12-8 Ueno Koen, Taito-ku, tel. 03/3828–6111. Admission free. Open to the public 10–4 weekdays during the school year, mid-Apr.–mid-July and Sept.–mid-Dec.*

You may skip the Exhibition Hall and instead turn left when you reach the main road through the park. Return to the entrance of the National Museum, and cross the street to the long esplanade with its reflecting pool. At the opposite end, turn right and walk down the path to the **Tokyo Metropolitan Art Museum.**

There are three floors of galleries in the Tokyo Metropolitan; the museum displays its own collection of modern Japanese art on the lower level, and rents out the remaining spaces to various organizations. At any given time, there will be at least five different exhibitions in the building: work by promising young painters, for example, or new forms and materials in sculpture, or modern calligraphy. Completed in 1975, the museum was designed by Kunio Maekawa, who also did the nearby Metropolitan Festival Hall. *8-36 Ueno Koen, Taito-ku, tel. 03/3823–6921. Admission free to the permanent collection; varying fees (usually ¥400 to ¥700) for other exhibitions. Open 9–4:30. Closed 3rd Mon. of each month.*

Return to the south end of the esplanade, and you will see a sign for the entrance to the **Ueno Zoo.** Opened in 1882, the zoo gradually expanded to its present 35 acres, the original section on the hill connected to the one below, along the edge of **Shinobazu Pond,** by a bridge and a monorail. The zoo houses some 900 different species, most of which look less than enthusiastic about being there. Ueno is not among the most attractive zoos in the world. On the other hand, it does have a pair of giant pandas whose union gave birth to Yuyu in June 1988 (their quarters are near the main entrance). You might decide it's worth a visit on that score alone. On a pleasant Sunday afternoon, however, upwards of 20,000 Japanese are likely to share your opinion; don't expect to have a leisurely view. *9-83 Ueno Koen, Taito-ku, tel. 03/3828–5171. Admission: ¥400 adults, ¥100 children under 12. Open 9:30–4. Closed Mon.*

The zoo has one other attraction that makes it unusual; the process of expansion somehow left within its confines the fivestory **Pagoda of the Kaneiji Temple.** Built in 1631 and rebuilt after a fire in 1639, the 120-foot pagoda is painted vermilion and has a copper roof on the top level; most visitors find it a bit out of keeping with the bison cages next door.

A much better view of the pagoda is from the path that leads to the **Toshogu Shrine.** Return to the esplanade, and follow the sign to the shrine until you see a small police substation; just beyond it, on a narrow path, the entrance to the shrine is marked by a stone torii (arch), built in 1633. Ieyasu, the first Tokugawa shogun, died in 1616, and the following year was given the posthumous name Tosho-Daigongen (The Great Incarnation Who Illuminates the East). He was declared by the Imperial Court a divinity of the first rank, thenceforth to be worshiped at Nikko, in the mountains north of his city, at a shrine he had commissioned before his death. That shrine is the first and foremost Toshogu Shrine. The one here in Ueno dates to 1627; miraculously, it has survived the disasters that destroyed most of the other original buildings on the hill—the fires, the revolt of 1868, the earthquake of 1923, the bombings of 1945—and is thus one of the very few early Edo-period buildings left in Tokyo.

The path from the torii to the shrine is lined with 200 stone lanterns; another stone lantern *(obaketoro)*, inside the grounds, is more than 18 feet high—one of the three largest in Japan. Beyond these is a double row of bronze lanterns, presented by the feudal lords of the 17th century as expressions of their piety and loyalty to the regime; the lanterns themselves were arrayed in the order of the wealth and ranking of their donors. On the left, before you reach the shrine itself, is the **Peony Garden** (for which you must pay a separate entrance fee), where some 200 varieties are on display. *Admission: ¥800 adults, ¥400 children under 12. Open 9–5 Jan.–Feb. and Apr.–May.*

At the end of the path, pay your admission fee and walk around the shrine to the entrance. You'll notice, on the left, a graceful little tea-ceremony pavilion, where Ieyasu Tokugawa's vassal Todo Takatora (who built the shrine itself) is said to have entertained the second and third shoguns. The Toshogu, like its namesake in Nikko, is built in the ornate style called *gongenzukuri;* it is gilded, painted, and carved with motifs of plants and animals. The carpentry of roof supports and ceilings is especially intricate. The shrine and most of the works of art in it have been designated National Treasures.

The first room inside is the Hall of Worship; the four paintings in gold on wood panels are by Tan'yu, one of the famous Kano family of artists who enjoyed the patronage of emperors and shoguns from the late 15th century to the end of the Edo period. Tan'yu was appointed *goyo eshi* (official court painter) in 1617; his commissions included the Tokugawa castles at Edo and Nagoya, and the Nikko Toshogu Shrine. The framed tablet between the walls, with the name of the shrine in gold, is in the calligraphy of Emperor Go-Mizunoo (1596–1680); other works of calligraphy are by the abbots of the Kaneiji Temple. Behind the Hall of Worship, connected by a passage called the *haiden,* is the Sanctuary, where the spirit of Ieyasu is enshrined.

The real glories of the Toshogu are its so-called Chinese Gate, which you reach at the end of your tour of the building, and the fence on either side. Like its counterpart at Nikko, the fence is a kind of natural-history lesson, with carvings of birds, animals, fish, and shells of every description; unlike the one at Nikko, however, this fence was left unpainted. The two long panels of the gate, with their dragons carved in relief, are attributed to Jingoro Hidari—a brilliant sculptor of the early Edo period whose real name is unknown (*hidari* means "left"; Jingoro was reportedly left-handed). The lifelike appearance of his dragons have inspired a legend. Every morning they were found mysteriously dripping with water; finally it was discovered that they were sneaking out at night to drink from the nearby Shinobazu Pond, and wire cages were put up around them to curtail this disquieting habit. *9–8 Ueno Koen, Taito-ku, tel. 03/3822–3455. Admission: ¥200 adults, ¥100 children under 12. Open 9–5:30.*

Retrace your steps to the police substation, turn right, and follow the avenue south. Shortly you will see a kind of tunnel of red-lacquer torii, in front of a small shrine to Inari, a Shinto deity of harvests and family prosperity. Shrines of this kind are to be found all over the downtown part of Tokyo, tucked away in alleys and odd corners, always with their guardian statues of foxes—the mischievous creatures with which the god is associated. A few steps farther, down a small road that branches to the right, is a shrine to Michizane Sugawara (854–903), a Heian-period nobleman and poet worshiped as the Shinto deity Tenjin. Because he is associated with scholarship and literary achievement, Japanese students visit his various shrines by the hundreds of thousands in February and March to pray for success on their entrance exams.

Return to the main road and continue south. You will see on ⑬ your left a black gate called the **Kuromon,** a replica of one that once stood at the entrance to the entire Kaneiji Temple complex. The Kuromon, built in the early 17th century, was the main gate of the National Museum until it was moved to this site in 1937; the numerous bullet holes in it were made during the battle for Ueno Hill in 1868. Go through the gate and up the ⑭ stone steps to the **Kiyomizu Kannon Hall.**

Kiyomizu was part of Abbot Tenkai's grand attempt to echo the holiness of Kyoto; the model for it was the magnificent Kiyomizudera Temple in that city. The echo is a little weak. Where the original rests on enormous wood pillars over a gorge, the Kiyomizu Hall in Ueno merely perches on the lip of a little hill. The hall is known to afford a grand view of Shinobazu Pond—which itself was landscaped to recall Lake Biwa, near Kyoto—but in fact the trees in front of the terrace are too high and full most of the year to afford any view at all. The Kyoto original is maintained in perfect condition; the copy, much smaller, is a little down-at-the-heels. Another of the few buildings that survived the battle of 1868, Kiyomizu is designated a National Treasure.

The principal Buddhist image of worship here is the Senju Kannon (Thousand-Armed Goddess of Mercy). Another figure, however, receives greater homage; this is the Kosodate Kannon, who is believed to answer the prayers of women having difficulty conceiving children. If their prayers are answered, they return to Kiyomizu and leave a doll, as both an offering of thanks and a prayer for the child's health. In a ceremony held every September 25, the dolls that have accumulated during the year are burned in a bonfire. *1 Ueno Koen, Taito-ku. Admission free. Open 9–sunset.*

Leave the hall by the front gate, on the south side. As you look to your left, you will see a new two-story brick services/ ⑮ administration building; on the other side of this is the **Ueno no Mori Royal Museum.** This museum has no permanent collection of its own, but makes its galleries available to various groups, primarily for exhibitions of painting and calligraphy. A more professional museum staff could do some good things here; the Royal Museum has two floors of prime space, but accomplishes very little with it. *1-2 Ueno Koen, Taito-ku, tel. 03/3833–4191. Admission free. Open 10–5.*

If you continue south from the Kiyomizu Kannon Hall, you soon come to where the park narrows to a point, and two flights of steps lead down to the main entrance, on Chuo-dori Avenue.

16 Before you reach the steps, on the left, is the **Shogitai Memorial.** Time seems to heal wounds very quickly in Japan; only six years after they had destroyed most of Ueno Hill, the Meiji government permitted the Shogitai to be honored with a gravestone, erected on the spot where their bodies had been cremated. Descendants of one of the survivors still tend the memorial. A few steps away, with its back to the stone, stands

17 the **statue of Takamori Saigo** (1827–1877), chief of staff of the imperial army that took the surrender of Edo and overthrew the shogunate—the army that the Shogitai had died defying. Ironically, Saigo himself fell out with the other leaders of the new Meiji government and was killed in an unsuccessful rebellion of his own. The sculptor Koun Takamura's bronze, made in 1893, sensibly avoids presenting him in uniform.

Time Out Walk down the two flights of steps, leave the park, turn right on Chuo-dori Avenue, and right again at the second corner. One block in from the avenue brings you to the authentic part of shitamachi; off the beaten tourist path here is **Futaba,** an inexpensive *tonkatsu* (fried pork cutlet) restaurant. If you get lost in the narrow streets here, just ask for it by name; this part of Ueno is considered the original home of tonkatsu restaurants, and Futaba is one of the oldest and best. Anyone you stop will know it. Try the *teishoku* (set menu). *2-8-11 Ueno, Taito-ku, tel. 03/3831–6483. Open 11:30–2:30 and 5–7:30.*

Retrace your steps, keeping on the west side of Chuo-dori Avenue, to where Shinobazu-dori Avenue comes in on the left. About a block before this corner, you'll see a building hung with

18 banners; this is **Suzumoto,** a theater specializing in a traditional narrative comedy called *rakugo.* In Japan, a monologue comedian does not stand up to ply his trade: He sits on a purple cushion, dressed in a kimono, and tells stories that have been handed down for centuries. The rakugo storyteller has only a fan for a prop; he plays a whole cast of characters, with their different voices and facial expressions, by himself. The audience may have heard his stories 20 times already, and they still laugh in all the right places. Suzumoto dates back to about 1857, making it the oldest theater of its kind in Tokyo; the present building, however (in front of which, incidentally, is a stop on the red double-decker bus for Asakusa), is new. *2-7-12 Ueno, Taito-ku, tel. 03/3834–5906. Admission: ¥2,000. Continual performances daily noon–4:10 and 5–8:30.*

19 Turn left at the intersection, and walk west on Shinobazu-dori Avenue. A few doors from the corner is **Jusanya** (2-12-21 Ueno, Taiko-ku, tel. 03/3831–3238), a shop selling handmade boxwood combs. The business was started in 1736 by a samurai who couldn't support himself in the martial arts, and it has been in the same family ever since. Directly across the avenue is an entrance to the grounds of Shinobazu Pond; just inside, on the right, is the small black and white building that houses the

20 **Shitamachi Museum.**

Shitamachi (Town Below the Castle) lay originally between Ieyasu's fortifications on the west and the Sumida River on the east; as it expanded, it came to include what today constitute the Chuo, Taito, Sumida, and Koto wards. During the Edo period, some 80% of the city was allotted to the warrior class, the temples, and the shrines; in the remaining 20% lived the common people, who made up more than half the population. Well into the modern period, the typical residential units in this part of the city were the *nagaya:* long, single-story tenements, one jammed up against the next along narrow alleys and unplanned streets. The density of Shitamachi shaped the character of the people who lived there; they were gossipy, short-tempered, quick to help a neighbor in trouble, hardworking, and not overly inclined to save for a rainy day. Their way of life will soon be gone completely; the Shitamachi Museum was created to preserve and exhibit what it was still like as late as 1940.

The two main displays on the first floor are a merchant house and a tenement, intact with all their furnishings. Visitors can take their shoes off and step up into the rooms; this is a hands-on museum. On the second floor are displays of toys, tools, and utensils, which were donated, in most cases, by people who had grown up with them and used them all their lives. Photographs of Shitamachi and video documentaries of craftspeople at work may be seen; occasionally there are demonstrations of various traditional skills, and visitors are welcome to take part. The space in this museum is used with great skill, and there's even a passable brochure in English. Don't miss it. *2-1 Ueno Koen, Taito-ku, tel. 03/3823-7451. Admission: ¥200 adults, ¥100 children under 12. Open 9:30-4:30; closed Mon.*

In front of the museum, take the path that follows the western shore of Shinobazu Pond. During the first week of June, the path is lined on both sides with the stalls of the annual All-Japan Azalea Fair, a spectacular display of bonsai (miniature) flowering shrubs and trees; nurserymen in *happi* (workmen's) coats sell a variety of plants, seedlings, bonsai vessels, and ornamental stones.

Shinobazu was once an inlet of Tokyo Bay; reclamation turned it into a freshwater pond, and Abbot Tenkai had an island made **㉑** in the middle of it, on which he built the **Shrine to Benten,** a patron goddess of the arts. Later improvements included a causeway to the island, embankments, and even (1884-1893) a race course. Today the pond is in three sections. The first, with its famous lotus plants, is a sanctuary for about 15 species of birds, including pintail ducks, cormorants, great egrets, and grebes. Some 5,000 wild ducks migrate here from as far away as Siberia, remaining September-April. The second section, to the north, belongs to the Ueno Zoo; the third, to the west, is a small lake for boating.

Walk up the east side of the embankment to the causeway, and cross to the shrine. The goddess Benten is one of the Seven Gods of Good Luck, a pantheon that emerged sometime in the medieval period from a jumble of Indian, Chinese, and Japanese mythology; she is depicted holding a musical instrument called a *biwa*, and is thus associated with the lake of the same name, near Kyoto—which Abbot Tenkai wanted to recall in his landscaping of Shinobazu Pond. The shrine, with its distinctive octagonal roof, was destroyed in the bombings of 1945; the present version is a faithful copy.

Cross to the other side of the pond, turn left in front of the boat house (open 9-4:30; cycle boats: ¥500 for 30 min, rowboats ¥ 400 for 30 min), and follow the embankment back to Shinobazu-dori Avenue. Off to your right as you walk, a few blocks away and out of sight, begin the precincts of Tokyo University, the nation's most prestigious seat of higher learning, alma mater to generations of bureaucrats. Turn left as you leave the park, and walk back in the direction of the Shitamachi Museum. When you reach the intersection, cross Chuo-dori and turn right; walk past the ABAB clothing store and turn left at the second corner: at the end of this street is the **Tokudaiji Temple** and the heart of **Ameya Yokocho Market.**

The Tokudaiji (4-6-2 Ueno, Taito-ku) is a curiosity in a neighborhood of curiosities: a temple on the second floor of a supermarket. The principal image of worship is the Indian goddess Marishi, a daughter of Brahma, usually depicted with three faces and four arms; she is believed to help worshipers overcome various sorts of difficulties and to prosper in business. The other image is that of the bodhisattva Jizo; the act of washing this statue is believed to help safeguard one's health. Among the faithful visitors to the Tokudaiji are the merchants of Ameya Yokocho.

The history of Ameya Yokocho (often shortened to "Ameyoko") begins in the desperate days immediately after World War II. Ueno Station had survived; virtually everything around it was rubble; and anyone who could make his way here from the countryside with rice and other small supplies of food could sell them at exorbitant black-market prices. One thing not to be had in postwar Tokyo at any price was sugar; before long, there were hundreds of stalls in the black market selling various kinds of confections (*ame*), most of them made from sweet potatoes. These stalls gave the market its name: Ameya Yokocho means "Confectioners' Alley."

Shortly before the Korean War, the market was legalized, and soon the stalls were carrying a full array of watches, chocolate, ballpoint pens, blue jeans, and T-shirts that had somehow been "liberated" from American PXs. In the years to follow, the merchants of Ameyoko diversified still further—to fine Swiss timepieces and French designer luggage of dubious authenticity, cosmetics, jewelry, fresh fruit, and fish. The market became especially famous for the traditional prepared foods of the New Year, and during the last few days of December, as many as half a million people crowd into the narrow alleys under the railroad tracks to stock up for the holiday.

There are over 500 little shops and stalls in the market, stretching from Okachimachi at the south end (the *o-kachi*—"honorable infantry"—were the samurai of lowest rank in the shogun's service; this part of the city was allotted to them for their homes) to the beginning of Showa-dori Avenue at the north. Follow the JR tracks as you wander north; in a few minutes, you will find yourself in front of Ueno Station, your exploring done for the day.

Asakusa

Numbers in the margin correspond with points of interest on the Asakusa map.

In the year 628, so the legend goes, two brothers named Hamanari and Takenari Hinokuma were fishing on the lower reaches of the Sumida River when they dragged up a small gilded statue of Kannon—an aspect of the Buddha worshiped as the Goddess of Mercy. They took the statue to their master, Naji no Nakamoto, who enshrined it in his house. Later, a temple was built for it in nearby **Asakusa;** now called **Sensoji**, it was rebuilt and enlarged several times over the next 10 centuries—but Asakusa itself remained just a village on a river crossing a few hours' walk from Edo. Then Ieyasu Tokugawa made Edo his capital, and Asakusa blossomed. Suddenly, it was the party that never ended, the place where the free-spending townspeople of the new capital came to empty their pockets. Also, for the next 300 years it was the wellspring of almost everything we associate with Japanese popular culture.

The first step in that transformation came in 1657, when Yoshiwara—the licensed brothel quarter not far from Nihombashi—was moved to the countryside farther north: Asakusa found itself square in the road, more or less halfway between the city and its only nightlife. The village became a suburb and a pleasure quarter in its own right. In the narrow streets and alleys around Sensoji Temple, stalls sold toys, souvenirs, and sweets; there were acrobats, jugglers, and strolling musicians; there were sake shops and teahouses—where the waitresses often provided more than tea. (The Japanese have never worried much about the impropriety of such things; the approach to a temple is still a venue for very secular enterprises of all sorts.) Then, in 1841, the Kabuki theaters—which the government regarded as a source of dissipation second only to Yoshiwara—were also moved to Asakusa.

Highborn and lowborn, the people of Edo flocked to Kabuki. They loved its extravagant spectacle, its bravado and brilliant language; they cheered its heroes and hissed its villains. They bought wood-block prints, called *ukiyo-e*, of their favorite actors. Asakusa was home to the Kabuki theaters for only a short time, but that was enough to establish it as *the* entertainment quarter of the city—a reputation it held unchallenged until World War II.

When Japan ended its long, self-imposed isolation in 1868, where else would the novelties and amusements of the outside world first take root but in Asakusa? The country's first photography studios appeared here in 1875. Japan's first skyscraper, a 12-story mart called the Junikai, filled with shops selling imported goods, was built in Asakusa in 1890. The area around Sensoji Temple had by this time been designated a public park and was divided into seven sections; the sixth section, called Rokku, was Tokyo's equivalent of 42nd Street and Times Square. The nation's first movie theater opened here in 1903—to be joined by dozens more, and these in turn were followed by music halls, cabarets, and revues. The first drinking establishment in Japan to call itself a "bar" was started in Asakusa in 1880; it still exists.

Most of this area was destroyed in 1945. As an entertainment district, it never really recovered, but Sensoji Temple was rebuilt almost immediately. The people here would never dream of living without it—just as they would never dream of living anywhere else. This is the heart and soul of *Shitamachi* (downtown), where you can still hear the rich, breezy Tokyo accent of the 17th and 18th centuries. Where if you sneeze in the middle of the night, your neighbor will demand to know the next morning why you aren't taking better care of yourself. Where a carpenter will refuse a well-paid job if he doesn't think the client has the mother wit to appreciate good work when he sees it. Where you can still go out for a good meal and not have to pay through the nose for a lot of uptown pretentions. Even today, the temple precinct embraces an area of narrow streets, arcades, restaurants, shops, stalls, playgrounds, and gardens; it is home to a population of artisans and small entrepreneurs, neighborhood children and their grandmothers, hipsters and hucksters and mendicant priests. In short, if you have any time at all to spend in Tokyo, you really have to devote at least a day of it to Asakusa.

Start your exploration from Asakusa Station, at the end of the Ginza Line. (This was in fact Tokyo's first subway, opened from Asakusa to Ueno in 1927; it became known as the Ginza Line when it was later extended through Ginza to Shimbashi and Shibuya.) Take the stairway in the middle of the platform; when you come up to the street level, turn right and walk west on Asakusa-dori Avenue. In a few steps you will come to **Kaminarimon** (Thunder God Gate), with its huge red paper lantern hanging in the center. This is the main entrance to the grounds of Sensoji Temple. *Admission free. Temple grounds open 6 AM–sundown.*

(Two other means of transportation can take you to Kaminarimon. The "river bus ferry" from Hinode Pier stops in Asakusa at the south corner of **Sumida Park.** Walk out to the three-way intersection, cross two sides of the triangle, and turn right on Asakusa-dori Avenue. Kaminarimon is in the middle of the second block. Another way to get here is on the red double-decker bus that runs between Kaminarimon and the Suzumoto Theater in Ueno. The service began in 1981, when the Merchants' Association in Asakusa borrowed a London double-decker for a month to move the overflow crowds they expected for a street fair. The idea proved so popular that it was decided to inaugurate a regular service—but there was an unexpected hitch: by law, a commercial bus could be no higher than 3.8 meters, and the English double-decker was 70 centimeters (27½ inches) over the limit. The solution was to order three custom vehicles from a German company; a fourth was added later. The bus runs every ½-hour (every 20 min Sat.–Sun.), 10–7, from Ueno, and 10:25–7:25 from Asakusa. The fare is ¥200 for adults, ¥100 for children under 12.

Traditionally, two fearsome guardian gods are installed in the alcoves of a temple gate, to protect the temple from evil spirits. The Thunder God (*Kaminari no Kami*) of the Sensoji gate is on the left; he shares his duties with the Wind God (*Kaze no Kami*) on the right. Few Japanese visitors neglect to stop at **Tokiwado** (1-3 Asakusa), the shop on the west side of the gate, to buy some of Tokyo's most famous souvenirs: *kaminari okoshi* (thunder crackers), made of rice, millet, sugar, and beans. The original gate itself was destroyed by fire in 1865; the replica that stands here now was built after World War II.

From Kaminarimon to the inner gate of the temple runs a long, narrow avenue called **Nakamise-dori** (The Street of Inside Shops), once composed of stalls that were leased out to the townspeople who cleaned and swept the temple grounds. The rows of redbrick buildings now belong to the municipal government, but the leases are, in effect, hereditary: some of the shops have been in the same families since the Edo period. One

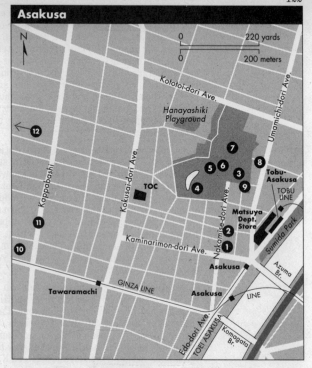

worth stopping at is **Ichiban-ya,** about 100 yards down on the right, for its handmade toasted *sembei* (rice crackers) and its seven-pepper spices in gourd-shape bottles of zelkova wood. Another recommended shop, on the left, is **Hyotanya,** which carries ivory carvings and utensils. At the end of the street, on the right, is **Sukeroku,** specializing in traditional handmade dolls and models clothed in the costumes of the Edo period.

From here, you enter the courtyard of Sensoji Temple through a two-story gate called the **Hozomon,** which serves as a repository for sutras (Buddhist texts) and other treasures of the temple. This gate, too, has its guardian gods; if either of them should decide to leave his post for a stroll, an enormous pair of sandals is hanging on the back wall—the gift of a village famous for its straw-weaving, in Yamagata Prefecture.

At this point, you must take an important detour. To the left of the gate is a two-story modern building that houses the temple's administrative offices: walk in, go down the corridor on the right to the third door on the left, and ask for permission to see the **Garden of Denbo-in Temple.** There is no charge; you simply enter your name and address in a register and receive a ticket. Hold on to the ticket; you'll get to the Denbo-in later on your excursion.

Two of the three most important buildings in the compound are the **Five-story Pagoda,** on the left side, and the **Main Hall of Sensoji Temple** (2-3-1 Asakusa, Taito-ku); both are faithful copies in concrete of originals that burned down in 1945. Most visitors stop at the huge bronze incense burner, in front of the Main

Hall, to bathe their hands and faces in the smoke—it's a charm to ward off illnesses—before climbing the stairs to offer a prayer to Kannon.

The Main Hall, about 115 feet long and 108 feet wide, is not an especially impressive piece of architecture; unlike in many temples, however, part of the inside has a concrete floor, so visitors come and go without removing their shoes. In this area hang the Sensoji's chief claims to artistic importance: a collection of votive paintings on wood, from the 18th and 19th centuries. Plaques of this kind, called *ema*, are still offered to the gods at shrines and temples, but they are commonly simpler and smaller; the worshiper buys a little tablet of wood with the picture already painted on one side, and inscribes his prayer on the other. The temple owns over 50 of these works, which were removed to safety in 1945 and so escaped the air raids; only eight of them, depicting various scenes from Japanese history and mythology, are on display. A catalogue of the collection is on sale in the hall, but the text is in Japanese only. The lighting is poor in the hall, and the actual works are difficult to see; this is also true of the ceiling, done by two contemporary masters of Nihonga (traditional Japanese-style painting): the dragon is by Ryushi Kawabata, and the motif of angels and lotus blossoms is by Insho Domoto. One thing that visitors cannot see at all is the holy image of Kannon itself, which supposedly lies buried somewhere deep under the temple. Not even the priests of Sensoji have ever seen it, and in fact there is no conclusive evidence that it really exists!

That doesn't seem to matter to the people of Shitamachi. It took 13 years, when most of them were still rebuilding their own bombed-out lives, to raise the money for the restoration of their beloved Sensoji; to them—and especially to those involved in the world of entertainment—it is far more than a tourist attraction. Kabuki actors still come here before a new season of performances, and sumo wrestlers come before a tournament, to pay their respects; the large lanterns in the Main Hall were donated by the geisha associations of Asakusa and nearby Yanagibashi.

Several structures in the temple complex survived the bombings of 1945; the largest, to the right of the Main Hall, is **❼ Asakusa Jinja** (2-3-1 Asakusa, Taito-ku)—a Shinto shrine to the Hikonuma brothers and their master Naji no Nakatomo. (In Japan, Buddhism and Shintoism have enjoyed a comfortable coexistence since the former arrived from China in the 6th century; it's the rule, rather than the exception, to find a Shinto shrine on the same grounds as a Buddhist temple.) The shrine, built in 1649, is also known as Sanja Samma (Shrine of the Three Guardians); the Sanja Festival, held every year on the third weekend in May, is the biggest, loudest, wildest party in Tokyo. Each of the neighborhoods under Sanja Samma's protection has its own *mikoshi* (portable shrine); on the second day of the festival, these palanquins are paraded through the streets of Asakusa, bouncing and swaying on the shoulders of the participants, to the shrine itself. Many of the "parishioners" take part naked to the waist, or with the sleeves of their tunics rolled up, to expose fantastic red-and-black tattoo patterns that sometimes cover their entire backs and shoulders. These are the tribal markings of the Japanese underworld.

Near the entrance to the shrine is another survivor of World War II: the east gate to the temple grounds, called the **Nitenmon,** built in 1618 and designated by the government as an Important Cultural Property. It was made originally for a shrine to Ieyasu Tokugawa, which was also part of Sensoji in the early 17th century.

From the Nitenmon, walk back in the direction of the Kaminarimon to the southeast corner of the grounds. On a small plot of ground stands the shrine to Kume no Heinai, a 17th-century outlaw who repented and became a priest of one of the subsidiary temples of Sensoji. Late in life he carved a stone statue of himself and buried it where many people would walk over it; in his will, he expressed the hope that his image would be trampled upon forever. Somehow, Heinai came to be worshiped as the patron god of lovers—as mystifying an apotheosis as you will ever find in Japanese religion.

Just beyond this shrine is the entrance to a narrow street that runs back to Asakusa-dori Avenue, parallel to Nakamise-dori Avenue. On the left as you enter this street is **Bentenyama** (2-3 Asakusa, Taito-ku), a tiny hillock with a shrine to the Goddess of Good Fortune perched on top. Next to it is the **Toki-no-kane Belfry,** built in the 17th century; the bell used to toll the hours, and it was said that you could hear it anywhere in Shitamachi—a radius of about four miles. The bell still sounds at 6 AM every day, when the temple grounds are opened to the faithful, and on New Year's Eve—108 strokes in all, beginning just before midnight, to "ring out" the 108 sins and frailties of mankind and make a clean start for the coming year.

Opposite Bentenyama is a shop called **Nakaya** (2-2-12 Asakusa, Taito-ku, tel. 03/3841-7877), where they sell all manner of regalia for the Sanja Festival. Best buys at Nakaya are the thick woven firemen's jackets, called *sashiko hanten*, and *happi* coats (cotton tunics printed in bright colors with Japanese characters or *ukiyo-e* wood-block pictures), available in children's sizes.

Next door is **Kuremutsu** (2-2-13 Asakusa, Taito-ku, tel. 03/ 3842-0906; open 4–10), a tiny old teahouse now turned into a fairly expensive *nomiya* (literally, "drinking place," the drink of choice in this case being sake), and next to Kuremutsu is **Hyakusuke** (2-2-14 Asakusa, Taito-ku, tel. 03/3841-7058); this is the last place in Tokyo that carries government-approved skin cleanser made from powdered nightingale droppings. Ladies of the Edo period—especially the geisha—swore by it; they mixed the powder with water and patted it on gently, as a boon to their complexions. There's only one source left in Japan for this powder—a fellow in the mountains of Aichi Prefecture who collects and dries the droppings from about 2,000 birds. (Nightingale ranching! Japan is a land of many vocations.) Hyakusuke is over 100 years old and has been in the same family for three generations; it sells relatively little nightingale powder now, but it still does a steady trade in cosmetics and theatrical makeup for Kabuki actors, geisha, and traditional weddings. Interesting things to fetch home from here are seaweed shampoo and camellia oil, as well as handmade wool brushes, bound with cherry wood, for applying cosmetics.

Three doors up, on the same side of the street, is **Fujiya** (2-2-15 Asakusa, Taito-ku, tel. 03/3841-2283), a shop that deals exclu-

sively in printed cotton hand towels called *tenugui*. Owner
Keiji Kawakami literally wrote the book on this subject; his
Tenugui fuzoku emaki is the definitive work on the hundreds of
traditional towel motifs that have come down from the Edo period: geometric patterns; scenes from Bunraku puppet theater,
Kabuki, and festivals; artifacts from folklore and everyday life;
plants and animals. The tenugui in the shop were all designed
and dyed by Kawakami himself. They unfold to about three
feet, and many people buy them to frame. Kawakami towels are
in fact collector's items; when he feels that he has made enough
of one, he destroys the stencil.

Turn right at the corner past Fujiya and walk west, until you
cross Nakamise-dori Avenue. On the other side of the intersection, on the left, is **Yonoya** (1-37-10 Asakusa, Taito-ku, tel. 03/
3844–1755), purveyors of very pricey handmade boxwood
combs. The shop itself is postwar, but the family business goes
back about 300 years. The present owner/master craftsman is
Mitsumasa Minekawa; his grandfather, he observes, was still
making combs when he retired at 85. Traditional Japanese coif-
fures and wigs are very complicated, and they need a lot of different tools; Yonoya sells combs in all sizes, shapes, and
serrations, some of them carved with auspicious motifs (peonies, hollyhocks, cranes) and all engraved with the family
benchmark.

Now it's time to cash in the ticket you've been carrying around.
Walk west another 50 feet or so, and on the right you will see an
old black wood gate; it's the side entrance to Denbo-in Temple.
The Abbot of Sensoji has his living quarters here; the only part
of the grounds you can visit is the garden, believed to have been
made in the 17th century by Enshu Kobori, the genius of Zen
landscape design. Go through the small door in the gate, across
the courtyard and through another door, and present your ticket to the caretaker in the house at the end of the alley; the entrance to the garden is down a short flight of stone steps to the
left.

This is the best-kept secret in Asakusa. The front entrance to
Denbo-in Temple can be seen from Nakamise-dori Avenue, behind an iron fence in the last block of shops, but the thousands
of Japanese visitors passing by seem to have no idea what it is;
if they do, it somehow never occurs to them to apply for an admission ticket. The garden of Denbo-in is usually empty and always utterly serene—an island of privacy in a sea of pilgrims.
As you walk along the path that circles the pond, a different vis-
ta presents itself at every turn; the only sounds are the cries of
birds and the splashing of carp. Spring is the ideal time to be
here; in the best of all possible worlds, you come on a Monday
when the wisteria is in bloom, and there's a tea ceremony in the
pavilion at the far end of the pond.

Retrace your steps, and turn to the right as you leave the black
gate; next door is a small Shinto shrine to the *tanuki* (raccoons)
who were displaced when Denbo-in was built. Japanese visitors
come here more often, however, to leave an offering at the statue of the bodhisattva Jizo, who looks after the well-being of
children.

Farther on, in the row of knockdown clothing stalls along the
right side of the street, is the booth of calligrapher Koji Matsumaru, who makes *hyosatsu*, the Japanese equivalent of door-

plates. A hyosatsu is a block of wood (preferably cypress) hung on a gatepost or an entranceway, with the family name on it in India ink. Enormous reverence still attaches in Japan to penmanship; opinions are drawn about you from the way you write. The hyosatsu is, after all, the first thing people will learn about a home; the characters on it must be well- and felicitously formed, so one comes to Matsumaru. Famous in Asakusa for his fine hand, he also does lanterns, temple signboards, certificates, and other weighty documents. Western names, too, can be rendered in the *katakana* syllabic alphabet, should you decide to take home a hyosatsu of your own.

Time Out   Opposite the row of clothing stalls mentioned above, on the corner of Orange Street, is the redbrick Asakusa Public Hall; performances of Kabuki and traditional dance are sometimes held here, as well as exhibitions of life in Asakusa before World War II. Across the street is **Nakase,** one of the best of Asakusa's many fine tempura restaurants; it's moderately priced. Founded about 120 years ago, it was destroyed in the war and rebuilt in the same style; the tatami-mat rooms look out on a perfect little interior garden—hung, in May, with great fragrant bunches of white wisteria. The pond is stocked with carp and goldfish; you can almost lean out from your room and trail your fingers in the water as you listen to the fountain. *1-39-13 Asakusa, Taito-ku, tel. 03/3841–4015. Open noon–8. Closed Tues.*

Now review your options. If you have the time and energy, you may want to explore the streets and covered arcades on the south and west sides of Denbo-in. Where Denbo-in-dori (the avenue you have been following along the south side of the garden) meets Sushiya-dori (the main avenue of Rokku), there is a small flea market; turn right here, and you are in what remains—alas!—of the old movie-theater district. East of the movie theaters, between Rokku and Sensoji, runs Nishi-sando-dori Avenue, an arcade where you can find kimonos and yukata fabrics, traditional accessories, fans, and festival costumes at very reasonable prices. If you turn to the left at the flea market, you soon come to the **ROX Building,** a misplaced attempt to endow Asakusa with a glitzy vertical mall; just beyond it, you can turn left again and stroll along Shin-nakamise-dori Avenue (New Street of Inside Shops). This arcade and the streets that cross it north–south are lined with stores selling clothing and accessories, restaurants and coffee shops, and purveyors of crackers, seaweed, and tea. This area is Asakusa's answer to the suburban shopping center.

When you have browsed to saturation, turn south, away from Denbo-in Temple on any of these side streets, return to Kaminarimon-dori Avenue, turn right, and walk to the end. Cross Kokusai-dori Avenue, turn left, and then right at the next major intersection; on the corner is the entrance to Tawaramachi Station on the Ginza Subway Line. At the second traffic light, you will see the **Niimi Building** across the street, and atop the Niimi Building is the guardian god of **Kappabashi:** an enormous chef's head in plastic, 30 feet high, beaming, mustachioed, and crowned (as every chef in Japan is crowned) with a tall white hat. Turn right.

Kappabashi is Tokyo's wholesale restaurant supply street: ½-mile of shops—more than 200 of them—selling everything the city's purveyors of food and drink could possibly need to do business, from paper supplies to bar stools, from signs to soup tureens. In their wildest dreams, the Japanese themselves would never have cast Kappabashi as a tourist attraction, but indeed it is.

For one thing, it is *the* place to buy plastic food. From the humblest noodle shop or sushi bar to neighborhood restaurants of middling price and pretension, it's customary in Japan to stock a window with models of what is to be had inside. The custom began, according to one version of the story, in the early days of the Meiji Restoration, when anatomical models made of wax first came to Japan as teaching aids in the new schools of Western medicine. A businessman from Nara decided that wax models would also make good point-of-purchase advertising for restaurants. He was right: the industry grew in a modest way at first, making models mostly of Japanese food, but in the boom years after 1960, restaurants began to serve all sorts of cookery ordinary people had never seen before, and the models offered much-needed reassurance. ("So *that's* a cheeseburger. It doesn't look as bad as it sounds; let's go in and try one.") By the mid-1970s, the makers of plastic food were turning out creations of astonishing virtuosity and realism, and foreigners had discovered them as pop art.

In the first two blocks of Kappabashi, at least a dozen shops sell plastic food; at the second intersection, on the right, is the main showroom of the **Maizuru Company,** one of the oldest and largest firms in the industry. They are virtuosos in the art of counterfeit cuisine. In 1960, models by Maizuru were included in the "Japan Style" Exhibition at London's Victoria and Albert Museum. Here, one can buy individual pieces of plastic sushi, or splurge on a whole Pacific lobster, perfect in coloration and detail down to the tiniest spines on its legs. *1-5-17 Nishi Asakusa, Taito-ku, tel. 03/3843–1686. Open 9–6.*

Across the street from Maizuru is **Nishimura,** a shop specializing in *noren*—the short divided curtains that hang from a bamboo rod over the door of a shop or restaurant to announce that it is open for business. The curtain is made of cotton, linen, or silk, and it is usually dyed to order with the name and logo of the shop or what it has for sale. Nishimura also carries readymade noren with motifs of all sorts, from landscapes in white-on-blue to geisha and sumo wrestlers in polychromatic splendor. Use your imagination; they make wonderful wall hangings and dividers. *1-10-10 Matsugaya, Taito-ku, tel. 03/3844–9954. Open 9–5:30. Closed Sun.*

In the next block is **Kondo Shoten,** which specializes in all sorts of bamboo trays, baskets, scoops, and containers. *3-1-13 Matsugaya, Taito-ku, tel. 03/3841–3372. Open 9:30–5:30. Closed Sun.*

Generally, however, the exploring is better on the Maizuru side of the street. A few doors down, for example, is **Biken Kogei,** a general supplier of signs, waterwheels, and assorted shop displays; this is a good place to look for the folding red paper lanterns (*aka-chochin*) that grace the front of inexpensive bars and restaurants. *1-5-16 Nishi Asakusa, Taito-ku, tel. 03/3842–1646. Open Mon.–Sat. 9–6, Sun. 11–4.*

In the middle of the next block is **Iida Shoten,** which stocks a good selection of embossed cast-iron kettles and casseroles, called *nambu* ware—craftwork certified by the Association for the Promotion of Traditional Craft Products. *2-21-6 Nishi Asakusa, Taito-ku, tel. 03/3842-3757. Open Mon.–Sat. 9–5:30, Sun. 10–5.*

On the next corner is the **Union Company,** which sells everything one needs to run a coffee shop: roasters, grinders, beans, flasks and filters of every description, cups, mugs, demitasse, sugar bowls, and creamers. Coffee lovers pronounce the coffee shops of Japan among the best in the world; here's where the professionals come for their apparatus. *2-22-6 Nishi Asakusa, Taito-ku, tel. 03/3842-4041. Open Mon.–Sat. 9–6, Sun. 10–5.*

The intersection here is about in the middle of Kappabashi; turn left, and just past the next traffic light, on the right, you come to **Sogenji Temple** (3-7-2 Matsugaya, Taito-ku, tel. 03/3841-2035)—better known as the Kappa Temple, with its shrine to the imaginary creature that gives this district its name. In the 19th century, so the story goes, there was a river here (and a bridge, back at the intersection where you took the left turn); the surrounding area was poorly drained and was often flooded. A local shopkeeper began a project to improve the drainage, investing all his own money, but met with little success until a troupe of *kappa*—mischievous green water sprites—emerged from the river to help him. The local people still come to the shrine at Sogenji to leave offerings of cucumber and sake—the kappa's favorite food and drink. (A more prosaic explanation for the name of the district points out that the lower-ranking retainers of the local lord used to earn money on the side by making straw raincoats, also called kappa, that they spread to dry on the bridge.)

Retrace your steps to the intersection; there is more of Kappabashi to the left, but you can safely ignore it and continue east, straight past Union Company down the narrow side street; in the next block, on the left, is **Tsubaya Hochoten.** A *hocho* is a knife; Tsubaya Hochoten sells cutlery for professionals—knives of every length and weight and balance, for every imaginable use, from slicing sashimi to making decorative cuts in fruit. The best of these, too, carry the Traditional Craft Association seal: hand-forged tools of tempered blue steel, set in handles banded with deer horn to keep the wood from splitting. *3-7-2 Nishi Asakusa, Taito-ku, tel. 03/3845-2005. Open Mon.–Sat. 9–6, Sun. 10–5.*

Continue on this street east to Kokusai-dori Avenue, and turn left; as you walk you will see several shops selling Buddhist household altars (*butsudan*). The most elaborate of these, hand-carved in ebony and covered with gold leaf, are made in Toyama Prefecture and can cost as much as ¥1 million. No proper Japanese household is without a butsudan, even if it is somewhat more modest; it is the spiritual center of the family, where reverence for one's ancestors and continuity of the family traditions are expressed. In a few moments, you will be back at Tawaramachi Station—the end of your excursion.

Tsukiji and Shimbashi

Numbers in the margin correspond with the points of interest on the Tsukiji and Shimbashi map.

Tsukiji reminds us of the awesome disaster of the great fire of 1657. In the space of two days, it leveled almost 70% of Ieyasu Tokugawa's new capital and killed more than 100,000 people. Ieyasu was not a man to be discouraged by mere catastrophe, however; he took it as an opportunity to plan an even bigger and better city, one that would incorporate the marshes east of his castle. Tsukiji, in fact, means "reclaimed land," and it was a substantial block of land, laboriously drained and filled, from present-day Ginza to the bay.

The common people in tenements and alleys, who had suffered most in the great fire, benefited not at all from this project; the land was first allotted to feudal lords and to temples. After 1853, when Japan opened its doors to the outside world, Tsukiji became Tokyo's first Foreign Settlement—the site of the American legation and an elegant two-story brick hotel, and home to a heroic group of missionaries, teachers, and doctors. Today, this area is best known for its astonishing fish market, the largest in Asia. This is where, if you are prepared to get up early enough, you should begin your exploration.

Take the Hibiya subway line to Tsukiji and exit by the stairs closest to the back of the train. Cross Shin-ohashi-dori Avenue to the **Tsukiji Honganji Temple** (which looks like a transplant from India), turn right, and walk west. Cross Harumi-dori Avenue to the next intersection, cross the bridge, and take the first left; walk to the end of the road, and turn right. If you reach this point at precisely 5 AM, you will hear a signal for the start of Tokyo's greatest ongoing open-air spectacle: the fish auction at the **Central Wholesale Market.**

The city's fish market used to be farther uptown, in Nihombashi; it was moved to Tsukiji after the Great Kanto Earthquake of 1923, and it occupies the site of what was once Japan's first naval training academy. Today the market sprawls over some 54 acres of reclaimed land; its warren of buildings houses about 1,200 wholesale shops, supplying 90% of the fish consumed in Tokyo every day and employing some 15,000 people. One would expect to see docks here, and unending streams of fish spilling from the holds of ships, but, in fact, most of the seafood sold in Tsukiji comes in by truck, arriving through the night from fishing ports all over the country.

What makes Tsukiji a great show is the auction system. The catch—over 100 varieties in all, including whole frozen tuna, Styrofoam cases of shrimp and squid, and crates of crabs—is laid out in the long covered area between the river and the main building; then the bidding begins. Only members of the wholesalers' association may take part; wearing license numbers fastened to the front of their caps, they register their bids in a kind of sign language, shouting to draw the attention of the auctioneer and making furious combinations in the air with their fingers. The auctioneer keeps the action moving in a hoarse croak that sounds like no known language; spot quotations change too fast for ordinary mortals to follow.

Different fish are auctioned off at different times and locations, but by 6:30 AM or so, this part of the day's business is over, and the wholesalers fetch their purchases back into the market in barrows. The restaurant owners and retailers arrive about 7, making the rounds of favorite suppliers for their requirements.

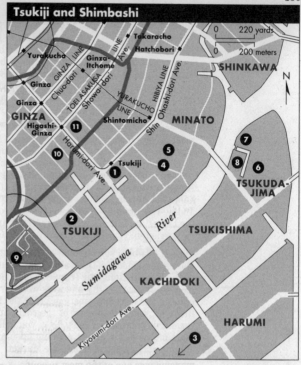

Chaos seems to reign, but everybody here knows everybody else, and they all have it down to a system.

A word to the wise: these people are not running a tourist attraction. They're in the fish business, and this is their busiest time of day; the cheerful banter they use with each other can turn snappish if you get in their way. Also bear in mind that they keep the market spotlessly clean, which means the water hoses are running all the time. Because you will be moving on in your exploration, you may not want to carry boots or a change of clothes. Some visitors bring a pair of heavy-duty trash bags to slip over their shoes and secure above their ankles.

If you come after 9 AM, there is still plenty to do and see. You'll have missed the auctions, but you may want to explore the maze of alleys between the market and Harumi-dori Avenue; there are fishmongers here by the score, of course, but also sushi bars, restaurants, and stores for pickles, tea, crackers, kitchen knives, baskets, and crockery. Markets like these are a vital counterpoint to the museums and monuments of conventional sightseeing; they bring you up close to the way people really live in the cities you visit. If you have time on your itinerary for just one market, this is the one to see.

Return to Shin-ohashi-dori Avenue, and walk back in the direction of Honganji Temple. When you reach Harumi-dori Avenue, you may want to make a detour; to the right, this road **③** will bring you (after a longish walk) to the **International Trade Center** (5-3-53 Harumi, Chuo-ku, tel. 03/3533–5314). The expositions presented here during the year—electronics and information systems, imported foods, toys, automobiles, recreation equipment—attract huge throngs of visitors; check the publication *Tour Companion* to see if there's a show running you'll want to catch.

If not, return to Tsukiji Honganji Temple. This is the main branch temple in Tokyo of the Nishi Honganji Temple in Kyoto; it was located here after the fire of 1657, but disaster seemed to follow it—the temple was destroyed again at least five times, and reconstruction in wood was finally abandoned after the Great Kanto Earthquake. The present stone building dates to 1935. It was designed by Chuta Ito, a pupil of Kingo Tatsuno, who built Tokyo Station. Ito's other credits include the Meiji Jingu Shrine in Harajuku; he also lobbied for Japan's first law for the preservation of historic buildings. Ito traveled extensively in the Orient; the evocations of classical Hindu architecture in the domes and ornaments of Honganji were his homage to India for being the cradle of Buddhism.

Turn right as you leave the main gate of the temple, and right again at the first corner; walk south until you cross a bridge, and turn left on the other side. When you cross another bridge, turn right: in the traffic island at the next intersection, you will see two stone memorials that mark the true importance of Tsukiji in the modern history of Japan.

4 The taller of the two is the **Monument to Ryotaku Maeno and Genpaku Sugita.** With a group of colleagues, these two men translated the first work of European science into Japanese. Maeno and his collaborators were samurai and physicians; Maeno himself was in the service of the Lord Okudaira, whose mansion was one of the most prominent in Tsukiji. In 1770, he acquired a book, a text in Dutch on human anatomy, in Nagasaki; it took his group four years to produce their translation. Remember that at this time Japan was still officially closed to the outside world; the trickle of scientific knowledge accessible through the Dutch trading post at Nagasaki—the only authorized foreign settlement—was enormously frustrating to the eager young scholars who wanted to modernize their country. Also bear in mind that Maeno and his colleagues began with barely a few hundred words of Dutch among them and had no reference works or other resources on which to base their translation, except the diagrams in the book. It must have been an agonizing task, but the publication in 1774 of *Kaitai shinsho*, as it was called in Japanese, in a sense shaped the world we know today. From this time on, Japan would turn away from classical Chinese scholarship and begin to take its lessons in science and technology from the West.

The other stone memorial commemorates the founding of Keio University by Yukichi Fukuzawa (1835–1901), the most influencial educator and social thinker of the Meiji period. Fukuzawa was the son of a low-ranking samurai in the same clan as Maeno; sent by his lord to start a school of Western learning, he began teaching classes at the Matsudaira residence in Tsukiji in 1858. Later the school was moved west to Mita, where the university is today. Engraved on the stone is Fukuzawa's famous statement: "Heaven created no man above another, nor below"; uttered when the Tokugawa feudal regime was still in power, this was an enormously daring and disturbing thought. It took Japan almost a century to catch up with Fukuzawa's liberal and egalitarian vision.

❺ Across the street to the left is **St. Luke's International Hospital,** founded in 1900 by Dr. Rudolf Teusler, an American medical missionary; the present building dates to 1933. In the several square blocks north of the hospital was the foreign settlement created after the signing of the U.S.–Japan Treaty of Commerce in 1858. (Among the residents here in the latter part of the 19th century was a Scottish surgeon and missionary named Henry Faulds. Intrigued by the Japanese custom of putting their thumbprints on documents for authentication, he began the research that established for the first time that no two person's fingerprints were alike. In 1880, he wrote a paper for *Nature* magazine, suggesting that this fact might be of some use in criminal investigation.)

Review your priorities. From here, you can retrace your steps to the subway, moving on to Higashi-Ginza and Shimbashi, or **❻** you can take a longish but rewarding detour to **Tsukudajima.** If you choose the latter, walk west from the monuments to the next corner, turn right, and walk north for two blocks. Cross the main intersection here, and turn right; the street rises to become the Tsukuda-ohashi Bridge, and just before it crosses the river you'll find a flight of steps leading up to the pedestrian walkway.

Built up from mud flats at the mouth of the Sumida River, Tsukudajima was first created in the early 17th century. Over the years, more and more land has been reclaimed from the bay, more than doubling the size of the island and adding other areas to the south and west; the part to explore is the original section: a few square blocks on your left as you cross the bridge. This neighborhood—its maze of narrow alleys, its profusion of potted plants and bonsai, its old houses with tile roofs—almost could have come straight out of the Edo period.

In 1613, the shogunate ordered a group of fishermen from Tsukuda (a village, now part of Osaka) to relocate on these flats. Officially, they were brought here to provide the castle with whitebait; unofficially, their role was to keep watch and report on any suspicious maritime traffic in the bay. They also developed a method of preserving the fish they caught, by boiling it in soy sauce and salt; this delicacy, called *tsukudani,* is **❼** still the island's most famous product. **Tsukugen** (1-3-13 Tsukuda, Chuo-ku), a shop on the first street along the breakwater as you leave the bridge, has been making tsukudani since the 17th century.

Go to the end of the breakwater, and turn right; from here it's a **❽** short walk to the torii of the **Sumiyoshi Myojin Shrine** (1-1 Tsukuda, Chuo-ku), established by the fishermen from Osaka when they first settled on the island. The god enshrined here is the protector of those who make their livelihoods from the sea; once every three years (most recently in 1990), the shrine celebrates its main festival. On the first weekend in August, the god is brought out for his procession in an unusual eight-side palanquin, preceded by huge golden lion heads carried high in the air, their mouths snapping in mock ferocity to drive any evil influences out of the path. As the palanquin passes, the people of the island douse it with water, recalling the custom, before the breakwater was built, of carrying it to the river for a high-spirited ducking.

If you have time, wander through the area bounded by the breakwater and the L-shape canal. It's ramshackle in places (even a little scruffy), but this is an authentic corner of Shitamachi that cannot last much longer. Having survived most of the natural disasters of the past three centuries, it faces a new threat—the huge development project on the north end of the island—that will eventually doom the village to modernity.

Time Out Retrace your steps to the Tsukiji subway station, and continue along Shin-ohashi-dori Avenue in the direction of the fish market. On the right side of the avenue is **Edo-Gin,** a sushi bar founded in 1924 that is legendary for its generous portions— slices of raw fish that almost hide the balls of rice underneath. Pricey for dinner; not bad at all for lunch. *4-5-1 Tsukiji, Chuo-ku, tel. 03/3543–4401. Open 11–9:30.*

Pass the market on your left and the Asahi Newspapers Building on your right. The avenue curves and brings you to an overhead bridge; on the left is the entrance to the **Hama Rikyu Detached Palace Garden.** The land here was originally owned by the Owari branch of the Tokugawa family from Nagoya, and it extended to part of what is now the fish market. When one of this family became shogun, in 1709, his residence was turned into a shogunal palace—complete with pavilions, ornamental gardens, groves of pine and cherry trees, and duck ponds. The garden became a public park in 1945, although a good portion of it (including the two smaller ponds) is fenced off as a nature preserve. None of the original buildings survives, but on the island in the large pond is a reproduction of the pavilion where former U.S. President Ulysses S. Grant and Mrs. Grant had an audience with the Emperor Meiji in 1879. The building can be rented for parties. (The path to the left as you enter the garden leads to the "river bus" ferry landing, from which you can leave this excursion and begin another: up the Sumida to Asakusa.) *Hama Rikyu Teien, Chuo-ku, tel. 03/3541–0200. Admission: ¥200. Open 9–4. Closed Mon.*

Retrace your steps, cross the overhead pedestrian bridge, and continue north on the street that brought you from Tsukiji. The next major intersection is Showa-dori Avenue; if you turned left here, across another overhead bridge, your route would take you past the huge JR Shiodome railroad yards (an "O" marker here and a section of the original tracks commemorate the starting point of Japan's first railway service, between Shimbashi and Yokohama, in 1872) and on to Shimbashi Station.

Almost nothing remains in **Shimbashi** to recall its golden age— the period after the Meiji Restoration, when this was one of the most famous geisha districts of the new capital. Its reputation as a pleasure quarter is even older. In the Edo period, when there was a network of canals and waterways here, it was the height of luxury to charter a covered boat (called a *yakata-bune*) from one of the Shimbashi boathouses for a cruise on the river; a local restaurant would cater the excursion, and a local geisha house would provide the companionship. After 1868, the geisha moved indoors; there were many more of them, and the pleasure quarter became much larger and more sophisticated—a reputation it still enjoys among the older (and wealthier) generation of Japanese men. There are perhaps 150 geisha still working in Shimbashi; they entertain at some 30 or 40 *ryotei* (traditional restaurants) tucked away on the back streets of the district, but you are unlikely to encounter any on your exploration. From time to time, the newspapers still delight in the account of some distinguished widower, a politician or captain of industry, who marries a Shimbashi geisha—in the vain expectation that he will be treated at home the way he was treated in the restaurant.

Turn right instead on Showa-dori Avenue, away from Shimbashi Station. At the next major intersection, turn right again, and left at the third corner; walk north by east in the direction of Higashi-Ginza Station. In the second block, on your right, is the **Shimbashi Embujo Theater** (*see* The Arts, below); on the left is the Nissan Motor Company headquarters. A brisk minute's walk from here will bring you to the intersection of Harumi-dori Avenue; turn left, and on the next block, on the right, you will see the **Kabuki-za Theater.**

Soon after the Meiji Restoration, Kabuki began to reestablish itself in this part of the city, from its enforced exile in Asakusa. The first Kabuki-za was built in 1889, with a European facade; here, two of the hereditary theater families, Ichikawa and Onoe, developed a brilliant new repertoire that brought Kabuki into the modern era. In 1912, the Kabuki-za was taken over by the Shochiku theatrical management company, and in 1925 the old theater building was replaced. Designed by architect Shin'ichiro Okada, it was damaged during World War II but was soon restored. (For information on performances, *see* The Arts, below). *4-12-15 Ginza, Chuo-ku, tel. 03/3541–8597.*

Just in front of the Kabuki-za is the Higashi-Ginza Station of the Hibiya subway line, where you can bring your exploration to a close.

Nihombashi, Ginza, and Yurakucho

Numbers in the margin correspond with points of interest on the Nihombashi, Ginza, and Yurakucho map.

Tokyo is a city of many centers. Now that the new City Hall is completed, the administrative center has shifted from Marunouchi to Shinjuku. For almost 350 years, the center of power was Edo Castle, and the great stone ramparts still define—for the visitor, at least—the heart of the city. History, politics, entertainment, fashion, traditional culture: Every tail we want to pin on the donkey goes in a different spot. Geographically speaking, however, there is one and only one center of Tokyo: a tall, black iron pole on the north side of **Nihombashi Bridge**—and if the tail you were pinning represented high finance, you would also have to pin it right here.

When Ieyasu Tokugawa had the first bridge built at Nihombashi (Bridge of Japan), he designated it the starting point for the five great roads leading out of his city, the point from which all distances were to be measured. His decree is still in force: The black pole on the present bridge, constructed in 1911, is the "Zero Kilometer" marker for all the national highways.

In the early days of the Tokugawa Shogunate, Edo had no port. As the city grew, almost everything it needed was shipped from the western part of the country, which was economically

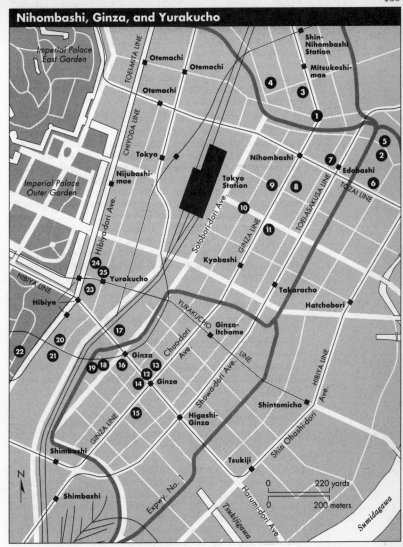

Nihombashi, Ginza, and Yurakucho

Imperial Palace
East Garden

Imperial Palace
Outer Garden

TOEI MITA LINE

CHIYODA LINE

Otemachi
Otemachi
Otemachi

Shin-Nihombashi Station

④ Mitsukoshi-mae
③
①

Tokyo

Nijubashi-mae

Nihombashi

⑤ ⑦ Edobashi
② ⑥

TOZAI LINE

Tokyo Station

⑨ ⑧
⑩
⑪

Sotobori-dori Ave.

GINZA LINE

TOEI ASAKUSA LINE

Kyobashi

Takaracho

Hatchobori

Hibiya-dori Ave.

HIBIYA LINE

② ②
②⑤ Yurakucho
②③
Hibiya

YURAKUCHO LINE

Ginza-Itchome

Chuo-dori Ave.

HIBIYA LINE

② ②
② ②
① ①⑧ ⑯ ⑬
⑫
⑭ Ginza
⑮

Ginza

Showa-dori Ave.

Shintomicho

Shimbashi

Higashi-Ginza

GINZA LINE

Tsukiji

Shin Ohashi-dori Ave.

Shimbashi

Expwy. No. 1

Harumi-dori Ave.

Tsukijigawa

Sumidagawa

N

0   220 yards
0   200 meters

Bank of Japan, **4**
Bridgestone Museum of Art, **11**
Dai-ichi Mutual Life Insurance Company Building, **23**
Hibiya-Koen Park, **22**
Idemitsu Museum of Arts, **25**

Imperial Hotel, **21**
Imperial Theater, **24**
International Shopping Arcade, **19**
Kabuto Jinja Shrine, **5**
Kite Museum, **7**
Kyukyodo, **14**
Maruzen, **9**
Matsuzakaya Department Store, **15**

Mikimoto, **13**
Mitsukoshi Department Store, **3**
Mullion Building, **17**
Nihombashi Bridge, **1**
Riccar Art Museum, **18**
Sukiyabashi, **16**

Takarazuka Theater, **20**
Takashimaya Department Store, **8**
Tokyo Stock Exchange, **2**
Wako, **12**
Yaesu Underground Arcade, **10**
Yamatane Museum of Art, **6**

11-5
Closed Sun

more developed; because the bay shore was marshy and full of tidal flats, the ships would come only as far as Shinagawa, a few miles down the coast, and unload to smaller vessels. These in turn would take the cargo into the city through a network of canals to wharves and warehouses at Nihombashi. The bridge and the area south and east became a wholesale distribution center, not only for manufactured goods but also for foodstuffs; te city's first fish market, in fact, was established at Nihombashi in 1628 and remained here until the great earthquake of 1923.

All through the Edo period, this was part of Shitamachi (downtown). Except for a few blocks between Nihombashi and Kyobashi, where the deputy magistrates of the city had their villas, it belonged to the common people—not all of whom lived elbow-to-elbow in poverty. There were huge fortunes to be made in the markets, and the early millionaires of Edo built their homes in the Nihombashi area. Some, like the legendary timber magnate Bunzaemon Kinokuniya, spent everything they made in the pleasure quarters of Yoshiwara and died penniless; others founded great trading houses—Mitsui, Mitsubishi, Sumitomo—that exist today and still have warehouses not far from Nihombashi.

❷ It was appropriate, then, that when Japan's first corporations were created and the Meiji government developed a modern system of capital formation, the **Tokyo Stock Exchange** (Shoken Torihikijo) would be built on the west bank of the Nihombashi River. Next to the exchange now are most of the country's major securities companies, which move billions of yen around the world electronically—a far cry from the early years of high finance, when they burned a length of rope on the floor of the exchange; trading was over for the day when it had smoldered down to the end.

A little farther west, money—the problems of making it and moving it around—shaped the area in a somewhat different way. In the Edo period, there were three types of currency in circulation: gold, silver, and copper, each with its various denominations. Determined to unify the system, Ieyasu Tokugawa started minting his own silver coins in 1598, in his home province of Suruga, even before he became shogun. In 1601, he established a gold mint; the building was only a few hundred yards from Nihombashi, on the site of what is now the Bank of Japan. In 1612, he relocated the Suruga plant to a patch of reclaimed land to the west of his castle; the area soon came to be known informally as the Ginza (Silver Mint).

The value of these various currencies fluctuated; there were profits to be made in the changing of money, and this business eventually came under the control of a few large merchant houses. One of the most successful of these merchants was a man named Takatoshi Mitsui, who had a dry-goods shop in Kyoto and opened a branch in Edo in 1673. The shop, called Echigoya, was just north of Nihombashi; by the end of the 17th century, it was the base of a commercial empire—in retailing, banking and trading—known today as the Mitsui Group. Not far from the site of Echigoya stands its direct descendant: the **❸ Mitsukoshi Department Store.**

Rui wa tomo wo yobu, goes the Japanese expression: "Like calls to like." From Nihombashi through Ginza to Shimbashi is the domain of all the Noble Houses that trace their ancestry back to the dry-goods and kimono shops of the Edo period: Mitsukoshi, Takashimaya, Matsuzakaya, Matsuya. All are intensely proud of their places at the upper end of the retail business, as purveyors of an astonishing range of goods and services. Together, they are but the latest expression of this area's abiding concern with money. Take some of it with you on your exploration: you may find an opportunity here and there to spend it.

Begin at Tokyo Station. Take the Yaesu Central exit, cross the main avenue in front of you (Sotobori-dori), and turn left. Walk north until you cross a bridge under the Shuto Expressway, and turn right at the second corner, between the Bank of Tokyo **❹** and the **Bank of Japan** (2-2 Nihombashi Hongokucho, Chuoku). The older part of the Bank of Japan is the work of Tatsuno Kingo, who also designed Tokyo Station; completed in 1896, the bank is one of the very few surviving Meiji-era Western buildings in the city.

Walk east two blocks to the main intersection at Chuo-dori Avenue. To your left is the Mitsui Bank, to your right is **Mitsukoshi;** this small area, formerly called Surugacho, is the birthplace of the Mitsui conglomerate. *1-7-4 Nihombashi Muromachi, Chuo-ku, tel. 03/3241–3311. Open Tues.–Sun. 10–6:30. Closed Mon.*

Takatoshi Mitsui made his fortune by revolutionizing the retail system for kimono fabrics. The drapers of his day usually did business on account, taking payment semiannually and adding various surcharges to the price of their goods. Mitsui started the practice of unit pricing, and his customers paid cash on the spot. As time went on, the store was always ready to adapt to changing needs and merchandising styles; these adjustments included garments made to order, home delivery, imported goods—and even, as the 20th century opened and Echigoya had become Mitsukoshi, the hiring of women to the sales force. The emergence of Mitsukoshi as Tokyo's first department store, or *hyakkaten* (hundred-kinds-of-goods emporium), actually dates to 1908, with a three-story Western building modeled on Harrods of London; this was replaced in 1914 by a five-story structure that boasted Japan's first escalator. The present flagship store is vintage 1935.

Turn right on Chuo-dori Avenue. As you walk south, you'll see on the left a shop founded in 1849, called **Yamamoto Noriten,** which specializes in *nori,* or dried seaweed, once the most famous product of Tokyo Bay. *16-4 Nihombashi Muromachi, Chuo-ku, tel. 03/3241–0261. Open 9–6:30.*

At the end of the next block is the Nihombashi Bridge. Why the expressway *had* to be routed directly over this lovely old landmark, back in 1962, is one of the mysteries of Tokyo and its city planning—or lack thereof. There were protests and petitions, but they had no effect. Planners argued the high cost of alternative locations; at that time Tokyo had only two years left to prepare for the Olympics, and the traffic congestion was already out of hand. So the bridge, with its graceful double arch and ornate lamps, its bronze Chinese lions and unicorns, was doomed to bear the perpetual rumble of trucks overhead—its claims overruled by concrete ramps and pillars.

Before you cross the bridge, notice on your left the small statue of a sea princess seated by a pine tree: a monument to the fish market. To the right is the Zero Kilometer marker, from which all the highway distances are measured. On the other side, also to the right, is a plaque depicting the old wood bridge; in the Edo period, the south end of the bridge was set aside for the posting of public announcements—and for displaying the heads of criminals.

Turn left as soon as you cross the bridge, and walk past the Nomura Securities building to where the expressway loops overhead and turns south. This area is called Kabuto-cho, after the small **Kabuto Jinja Shrine** here on the left, under the loop. Legend has it that a noble warrior of the 11th century, sent by the Imperial Court in Kyoto to subdue the barbarians of the north, stopped here and prayed for assistance. His expedition was successful, and on the way back he buried a golden helmet (*kabuto*) on this spot as an offering of thanks. Few Japanese are aware of this legend; "Kabuto-cho" invokes instead the world of brokers and securities. With good reason: Just across the street from the shrine is the **Tokyo Stock Exchange.** At the exchange's new Exhibition Plaza and Gallery, visitors may watch the fast and furious action on the trading floor. A robot, which resembles a character from *Star Wars*, demonstrates hand signals at the touch of a button. The robot also lectures on the daily trading of securities at the Tokyo Stock Exchange. An array of video exhibits introduces companies and offers worldwide stock news and trading terms. *2-1-1 Nihombashi Kayabacho, Chuo-ku, tel. 03/3666–0141. Admission: free. Open weekdays 9–4. Trading hours: weekdays 9–11 and 12:30–3.*

From the main entrance of the exchange, turn right; walk south two blocks to the intersection at Eitai-dori Avenue and turn right again. The black building on the corner is Yamatane Securities Building; on the eighth and ninth floors is the **Yamatane Museum of Art.** The museum specializes in *nihonga*, or painting in the traditional Japanese style, from the Meiji period and later; it was designed with an interior garden by architect Yoshiro Taniguchi, who also did the National Museum of Modern Art in Takebashi. The museum's own private collection includes masterpieces by such painters as Taikan Yokoyama, Gyoshu Hayami, Kokei Kobayashi, and Gyokudo Kawai; the exhibitions, which sometimes include works borrowed from other collections, change every two months. The decor and display at the Yamatane make it an oasis of quiet and elegance in the world of high finance; the chance to buy the lavish catalogue of the collection would be well worth the visit. *7-12 Nihombashi Kabutocho, Chuo-ku, tel. 03/3669–4056. Admission: ¥500 adults, ¥200 children under 12. Open 10–5. Closed Mon.*

Time Out Turn right as you leave the Yamatane Building, and continue west on Eitai-dori Avenue across the intersection with Showa-dori Avenue. Turn right, and left on the first small street behind the Bank of Hiroshima; just off the next corner is **Taimeiken,** a restaurant serving Western food at very reasonable prices. (A portion of cabbage salad and vegetable soup, for example, is only ¥50—the same price it was when the restaurant first opened, some 40 years ago.) At lunch, Taimeiken is packed with people from the nearby banks and securities companies; you buy a ticket for the meal you want at the counter to the left of the entrance, and then look for a table to share. *1-12-10 Nihombashi, Chuo-ku, tel. 03/3271–2463. Open 11–8. Closed Sun.*

After lunch, take the elevator from the Taimeiken restaurant to the fifth floor, where the late Shingo Motegi, who founded
❼ the restaurant, established a wonderful **Kite Museum.** Kite flying is an old tradition in Japan; the Motegi collection includes examples of every shape and variety, from all over the country, hand-painted in brilliant colors with figures of birds, geometric patterns, and motifs from Chinese and Japanese mythology. Call ahead, and the museum will arrange a kite-making workshop for groups of children. *1-12-10 Nihombashi, Chuo-ku, tel. 03/3271–2463. Admission: ¥100 adults, ¥30 children under 12. Open 11–5. Closed Sun.*

Retrace your steps to Eitai-dori Avenue, continue west to Chuo-dori Avenue, and turn left. One block south, on the left,
❽ is the **Takashimaya Department Store** (2-4-1 Nihombashi, Chuo-ku, tel. 03/3211–4111; open 10–6:30; closed Wed.); on the
❾ right is **Maruzen,** one of Japan's largest booksellers (2-3-10 Nihombashi, Chuo-ku, tel. 03/3272–7211; open 10–6:30; closed Sun.). Maruzen prospers in large part on its imports—at grossly inflated rates of exchange. On the third floor, you can find books in Western languages on any subject from Romanesque art to embryology. There's an extensive collection here of books about Japan, and also a small crafts center.

If you look to your right at the next intersection, you will see that you have come back almost to Tokyo Station; below the
❿ avenue from here to the station runs the **Yaesu Underground Arcade,** with hundreds of shops and restaurants. The whole area here, west of Chuo-dori Avenue, was named after Jan Joosten, a Dutch sailor who was shipwrecked on the coast of Kyushu with William Adams—hero of the recent novel *Shogun*—in 1600. Like Adams, Joosten became an adviser to Ieyasu Tokugawa, took a Japanese wife, and was given a villa not far from the castle; "Yaesu" (originally Yayosu) was as close as the Japanese could come to the pronunciation of his name. Adams, an Englishman, lived out his life in Japan; Joosten died at sea, off the coast of Indonesia, in an attempt to return home.

⓫ On the southeast corner of the intersection is the **Bridgestone Museum of Art,** one of Japan's best private collections of French impressionist art and sculpture and also of post-Meiji Japanese painting in Western styles, by such artists as Shigeru Aoki and Tsuguji Foujita. The collection, assembled by Bridgestone Tire Company founder Shojiro Ishibashi, also includes work by Rembrandt, Picasso, Utrillo, and Modigliani. In addition, the Bridgestone often organizes or co-organizes major exhibitions from private collections and museums abroad. *1-10-1 Kyobashi, Chuo-ku, tel. 03/3563–0241. Admission: ¥500 adults, ¥200 children under 12. Open 10–5:30. Closed Mon.*

Consider your feet. By now, they may be telling you that you would really rather not walk to the next point on your exploration; if so, get on the Ginza Line (there's a subway entrance right in front of the Bridgestone Museum) and ride one stop to **Ginza.** Take any exit for the *4-chome* intersection; when you come up the surface, you can orient yourself by the Ginza branch of the **Mitsukoshi Department Store** (4-6-16 Ginza) on the northeast corner and the round **Sanai Building** (5-7-2 Ginza) on the southwest.

Ieyasu's silver mint moved out of this area in 1800; the name *Ginza* remained, but it was not until much later that it began to acquire any cachet for wealth and style. The turning point was 1872, when a fire destroyed most of the old houses here; in the same year, the country's first railway line was completed, from nearby Shimbashi to Yokohama. This prompted the city to one of its periodic attempts at large-scale planning: the main street of Ginza, together with a grid of cross streets and parallels, was rebuilt as a Western *quartier*. It had two-story brick houses with balconies; it had the nation's first sidewalks and horse-drawn streetcars; and it had gas lights and, later, telephone poles. Before the turn of the century, Ginza had attracted the great mercantile establishments that still define its character. The **Wako** (4-5-11 Ginza) Department Store, for example, on the northwest corner of the 4-chome intersection, established itself here as Hattori, purveyors of clocks and watches; the clock on the present building was first installed in the Hattori clock tower, a Ginza landmark, in 1894.

Many of the shops nearby have lineages almost as old, or older. A few steps north of the intersection, on Chuo-dori Avenue, is **Mikimoto** (4-5-5 Ginza), selling the famous cultured pearls first developed by Kokichi Mikimoto in 1883; his first shop in Tokyo dates to 1899. On the south side, next door to the Sanai Building, is **Kyukyodo** (5-7-4 Ginza), with its wonderful variety of handmade Japanese papers, paper products, incense, brushes, and other materials for calligraphy; Kyukyodo has been in business since 1663, and on the Ginza since 1880. One block south is **Matsuzakaya** (6-10-1 Ginza), a department store that began as a kimono shop in Nagoya in 1611. Exploring this area (there's even a name for browsing: *Gin-bura*, or "Ginza-wandering") is best on Sundays, noon–6 or 7 (depending on the season), when Chuo-dori Avenue is closed to traffic, from Shimbashi all the way to Ueno, and becomes one long pedestrian mall. On Saturday afternoons, 3–6 or 7, the avenue is closed to traffic between Shimbashi and Kyobashi.

Walk west on Harumi-dori Avenue in the direction of the Imperial Palace. From Chuo-dori Avenue to the intersection at **Sukiyabashi,** your exploration should be free-form: the side streets and parallels north–south are ideal for wandering, particularly if you are interested in art galleries—of which there are 300 or more in this part of the Ginza. The art world works a bit differently here: a few of these establishments, like the venerable **Nichido** (7-4-12 Ginza), **Gekkoso** (6-3-17 Ginza), **Yoseido** (5-5-15 Ginza), **Yayoi** (7-6-61 Ginza), and **Kabutoya** (8-8-7 Ginza), actually function as dealers, representing particular artists, as well as acquiring and selling art; the vast majority, however, are nothing more than rental spaces. The artists or groups pay for the gallery by the week, publicize the show themselves, and in some cases even hang their own work. Not unreasonably, one suspects that a lot of these shows, even in so prestigious a venue as the Ginza, are "vanity" exhibitions by amateurs with money to spare—but that's not always the case. The rental spaces are also the only way for serious professionals, independent of the various art organizations that might otherwise sponsor their work, to get any critical attention; if they're lucky, they can at least recoup their expenses with an occasional sale.

West of Sukiyabashi, from Sotobori-dori Avenue to Hibiya-Koen Park and the Outer Gardens of the Imperial Palace, is the district called **Yurakucho.** The name derives from one Urakusai Oda, younger brother of the warlord who had once been Ieyasu Tokugawa's commander; Urakusai, a Tea Master of some note (he was a student of Sen no Rikyu, who developed the Tea Ceremony), had a town house here, beneath the castle ramparts, on land reclaimed from the tidal flats of the bay. He soon left Edo for the more refined comforts of Kyoto, but his name stayed behind, becoming Yurakucho—the *Quarter (cho)* where one can *Have (yu) Pleasures (raku)*—in the process. Sukiyabashi was the name of the bridge over the moat—both long gone in the course of modernization—by Urakusai's villa to the area of the Silver Mint.

The "pleasures" associated with this district in the early postwar period stemmed from the fact that a number of the buildings here survived the air raids of 1945 and were requisitioned by the Allied forces. Yurakucho quickly became the haunt of the so-called *pan-pan* girls, who provided the GIs with female company; because it was so close to the military Post Exchange in Ginza, the area under the railroad tracks became one of the city's largest black markets. Later, the black market gave way to clusters of cheap restaurants, most of them little more than counters and a few stools, serving yakitori (bits of grilled chicken on bamboo skewers) and beer. Office workers on meager budgets, and journalists from the nearby *Mainichi, Asahi,* and *Yomiuri* newspaper headquarters, would gather here at night; Yurakucho-under-the-tracks was smoky, loud, and friendly, a kind of open-air substitute for the local taproom. Alas, the area has long since moved upscale, and no more than a handful of the yakitori stalls survive.

From Sukiyabashi, keep on the left side of the avenue as you cross the intersection; on the opposite side, you will see the curved facade of the **Mullion Building,** a new shopping and entertainment complex of the sort that is rapidly turning Yurakucho into a high-fashion extension of the Ginza. (The Seibu Department Store, which occupies half the building, is a leader in marketing the fusion of modern and traditional Japanese design.) Take your first left down the narrow side street that runs along the west side of the Hankyu Department Store (the horned monstrosity in the pocket park on your right is by sculptor Taro Okamoto), cross at the corner, and turn right; at the end of the next block is the **Riccar Art Museum.**

This gallery, on the seventh floor of the Riccar Company building, houses some 5,000 *ukiyo-e* (wood-block prints), mostly from the 18th and 19th centuries, from the private collection of the late Shinji Hiraki, who was chairman of the company. Included are some of the most famous prints by Utamaro, Sharaku, Hokusai, and Hiroshige; the works on exhibit are changed every month. The depth of the collection makes it possible for the museum to organize exhibitions on a variety of interesting themes—Kabuki and the townspeople of Edo, for example, or how the Japanese portrayed the earliest visitors from other countries. *6-2-3 Ginza, Chuo-ku, tel. 03/3571-3254. Admission ranges from ¥400–¥1,000 depending on exhibition. Open 11–6. Closed Mon.*

From the Riccar building, take the street that goes under the JR tracks and walk west. On both sides of the street, just under the bridge, you will see entrances for the **International Shopping Arcade,** a collection of stores that feature kimonos and *happi* (workmen's) coats, pearls and cloisonné, prints, cameras, and consumer electronics—one-stop shopping for presents and souvenirs. In the next block, on the right, you will see the **Takarazuka Theater,** and on the left the **Imperial Hotel;** walk to the end of the street, where it runs into Hibiya-dori Avenue, and turn right.

Across the avenue is **Hibiya-Koen Park.** This was Japan's first Western-style public park and dates to 1903. With its lawns and fountains, it makes a pretty place for office workers in the nearby buildings to take their lunches on a warm spring afternoon, but there's nothing here to detain you on your exploration. Press on—across the Harumi-dori Avenue intersection, past the Marunouchi Police Station, to the **Dai-ichi Mutual Life Insurance Company** Building. Built like a fortress, it survived World War II virtually intact and was taken over by the Supreme Command of the Allied Powers; from his office here, General Douglas MacArthur directed the affairs of Japan for six years (1945–1951). The room is kept exactly as it was then, and can be visited on appointment. *1-1-13 Yurakucho, Chiyoda-ku, tel. 03/3216–1211. Admission free. Open 9–5.*

On the next corner is the International Building, with the **Imperial Theater** on the first floor. The original Imperial, built in 1911, was Japan's first purely Western-style theater; the present version, by architect Yoshiro Taniguchi, is the venue of choice for big-budget musicals, like the Japanese productions of *Man of La Mancha* and *Fiddler on the Roof.* Turn right here, and walk halfway down the block to the main entrance of the building; on the ninth floor is the **Idemitsu Museum of Arts.**

With its four spacious rooms, the Idemitsu is one of the largest private museums in Tokyo, and it is one of the best designed. The strength of the collection is in its Chinese porcelain of the Tang and Song dynasties, and in Japanese ceramics—including works by Ninsei Nonomura and Kenzan Ogata, and masterpieces of Old Seto, Oribe, Old Kutani, Karatsu, and Kakiemon ware; there are also outstanding examples of Zen painting and calligraphy, wood-block prints and genre paintings of the Edo period. Of special interest to scholars is the resource collection of shards from virtually every pottery-making culture of the ancient world. *3-1-1 Marunouchi, Chiyoda-ku, tel. 03/3213–9404. Admission: ¥500 adults, children under 12 free. Open 10–5. Closed Mon.*

Turn left as you leave the International Building, and right at the second corner. A minute's walk will bring you to the JR Yurakucho Station, the end of your exploration.

Roppongi

Numbers in the margin correspond with points of interest on the Roppongi, Akasaka, and Aoyama map.

The best way to arrive in **Roppongi,** in southern Tokyo, is to surface from the subway at Roppongi Station on the Hibiya Line. Street traffic, especially from the late afternoon through the evening, can be horrendously congested. Roppongi has two personalities. By day, the area is relatively quiet, with house-wives doing their shopping and delivery trucks restocking the bars and restaurants for another evening of revelry. By night, the neighborhood hums with people from all over Tokyo who come to enjoy the local discos, restaurants, and bars.

Once a sleepy suburban area, Roppongi has become a fashionable high-rent district. Many of the embassies that did not locate in Akasaka have settled here, and executives from overseas corporations often select the area for their Tokyo bases. Consequently, Roppongi is Tokyo's international and cosmopolitan neighborhood for both living and partying. Indeed, the district claims to have the best bars and nightclubs at affordable prices, compared with the exceedingly high cost of Ginza's nightlife. As a result, the area appeals to affluent university graduates working their way up the corporate ladder. Roppongi is Yuppieland, with entertainment considerably more sophisticated than that of raunchy Shinjuku and more polished than that of Shibuya.

1 The first stop on this tour is **Almond** (the Japanese omit the "l" in their pronunciation), just across from the Roppongi Station on the southwest corner of Roppongi-dori Avenue and Imoar-ai-zaka Slope. This multistory pink café is used by many as a meeting place, and that habit has not died, despite the inferior coffee and cakes served. Farther down (southwest) Roppongi-dori Avenue, on the left-hand side, is a huge outdoor video **2** screen. That belongs to **Wave** (6-2-27 Roppongi, Minato-ku), one of the most advanced record and home-electronics stores in the world. The first four floors sell records from a stock that exceeds 60,000; through a computer linkup, information on any recorded music is retrieved instantaneously. Downstairs in the basement of the building is an experimental movie theater.

A block farther down (southwest) Roppongi-dori Avenue is the **3** **Asahi Kogaku,** also known as the Pentax Gallery. Asahi, the parent company of Pentax, has 3,400 items in this museum, which traces the development of the camera from the daguerreotype to the most sophisticated modern cameras with electronic eyes. This exhibition includes novelty cameras, such as one disguised as a watch and another as a ballpoint pen. *3-21-20, Nishi-Azabu, Minato-ku, tel. 03/3401–2186. Admission free. Open 10–5. Closed Sun. and national holidays.*

Next, walk along Roppongi-dori Avenue and under the Shuto Expressway in the opposite direction (northeast) from Wave, and keep to the right-hand side of the avenue. If you take a right on the first small street after Gaien-higashi-dori Avenue, **4** and then an immediate left, you will reach the **Square Building,** (3-10-3 Roppongi, Minato-ku), which is the home of seven discos. Keep the location in mind when you return in the evening.

If you take the next left, you will soon be back on Roppongi-dori Avenue. Take a right and continue walking northeast for the **5** **Roppongi Prince Hotel** (3-2-7 Roppongi, Minato-ku). In about 200 yards, take a right up a small street, and immediately left up a steep slope is the hotel's entrance. Especially on a summer's afternoon, the café tables around the hotel's courtyard swimming pool are much in demand, perhaps not for refreshing drinks but rather for people-watching. The pool's sides are

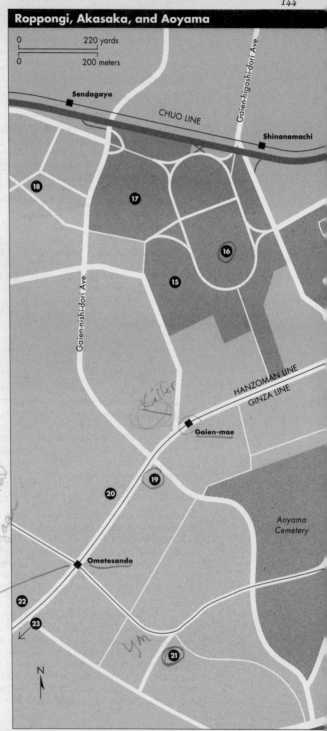

144

Roppongi, Akasaka, and Aoyama

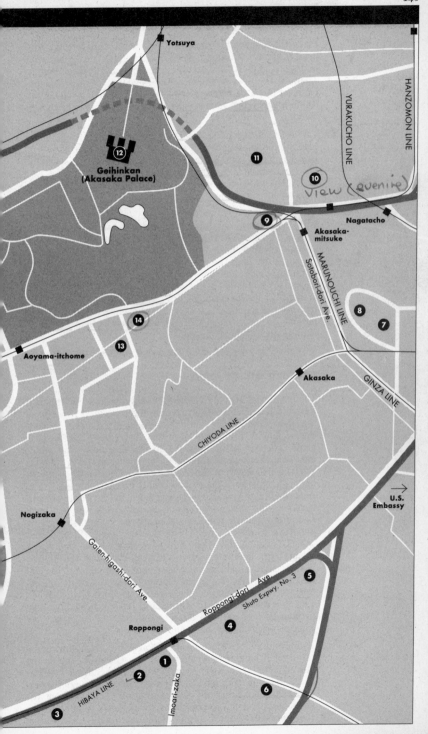

built with transparent acrylic; the swimmers look like wallowing whales in an aquarium.

From the Roppongi Prince, cut back southwest through the maze of streets to Gaien-higashi-dori Avenue. The easiest way is to take a left at the bottom of the Roppongi Prince's ramp. Then, at the first street after the Zengakuji Temple, take a right for 50 yards before going left. This will bring you out on Gaien-higashi-dori Avenue just south of the Roppongi Forum Building.

❻ Take a left on Gaien-higashi-dori Avenue; the **Axis Building** (5-17-1, Roppongi, Minato-ku) will be across the avenue. The Axis Building has a well-known collection of stores, with especially fine textiles and high-quality interior-design merchandise. Actually, the wares in Axis are more than just goods for sale; they make up an exhibition of creative design. You do not have to be a shopper to be inspired by a visit here.

Walk back (north) up Gaien-higashi-dori Avenue and you'll be back at Almond Café's entrance. Instead of keeping to the main avenue, try to wander down the back streets. Especially after six in the evening, the party mood is everywhere; discos, restaurants, clubs, and bars vie for space, and the streets are packed with trendy Japanese fun-seekers. This is a very safe area and, with its cosmopolitan flavor, is comfortable for the foreigner to explore. However, as the evening wears on, taxis become scarce, so consider leaving the district before the last subway does (soon after 11:30).

(For more information about Roppongi, *see* Nightlife, below).

Akasaka and Aoyama

Though **Akasaka** is only a 15-minute taxi ride from the Imperial Palace, not much more than a hundred years ago Akasaka grew tea bushes and *akane*, plants that produced a red dye. Indeed, that is how Akasaka, which means "red slope," received its name. Then, in 1936, when the mammoth granite Diet building, which houses the national government, moved to Nagata-cho (the area north of Akasaka), the neighborhood became an important pleasure quarter for politicos and their lobbyists. Accordingly, the geishas were upgraded, and so was the neighborhood. The geisha houses and *ryotei* (expensive traditional restaurants) with their unobtrusive signs are still to be found—a Mercedes or BMW in the courtyard will help spot them. As the neighborhood improved, it developed an international flair. Many foreign countries, including the United States, established their embassies here to be close to the National Diet. To service those visiting the area, new deluxe hotels sprang up, including the prestigious Hotel Okura. When TBS Television moved to Akasaka in 1960, it brought screen personalities of national fame to the district. In their wake came shops, cabarets, bars, and nightclubs.

Begin your visit to Akasaka at Kokkai Gijido-mae Subway Station (you'll have arrived on either the Chiyoda Line or the Marunouchi Line). If you started from Tokyo Station, you'll be on the Marunouchi Line and will need to walk through the passageways of Kokkai Gijido-mae Station to leave from the Chiyoda exit. When you reach the street, you'll be opposite the
❼ rear entrance of the **Capitol Tokyu Hotel** (2-10-3 Nagatacho,

Chiyoda-ku). To save yourself a climb up the hill and around the hotel, enter the building through this rear entrance and take the elevator to the main lobby. The Capitol Tokyu is a good place to start the day with breakfast, either Western or Japanese. In the breakfast room you can look on to a garden surrounding a pond. Then, leave the hotel by the main entrance, and the **Hie Jinja Shrine** will be before you.

As in so much of Tokyo, traditional Japan is hidden among the modern concrete structures. The Hie Jinja is an example of this old Japan. The entrance to the shrine is easily spotted by the large torii in front of the steps leading up to the shrine complex. Notice the archway before the shrine; it is distinctive for its unusual triangular roof. The present building was rebuilt in 1959, and the gates in 1962, but its inspiration is from the late 15th century, when a military commander dedicated the building to Oyamakuni-no-Kami, a tutelary deity of Edo. Later, the shrine became a favorite of the Tokugawa Shogunate, and some of the best festivals during the Edo period were held here. Several festivals a year still take place here, but by far the most important is Sanno Matsuri, held June 11–16, with processions of palanquins and marchers that recall the days of the Tokugawa Shogunate, when the event was known as the "Festival Without Equal." For the rest of the year, the shrine has a special appeal to those seeking protection against miscarriages; note the statue in the main courtyard of the female monkey holding her offspring. Recently, people have visited the shrine to protect themselves against traffic accidents; it is not unusual to see a Shinto priest blessing a new car. *2-10-5 Nagatacho, Chiyoda-ku. Admission free. Open sunrise–sunset.*

To the right of the Hie Jinja on Kasumigaseki Hill is the National Diet (*see* Imperial Palace District tour, above). Instead of climbing up the hill to the Diet, walk back down past the Capitol Tokyu to Akasaka's main avenue, Sotobori-dori, and turn right. Here is Akasaka's shopping area, with stores above and below ground flanking both sides of the street. On the left, running parallel to Sotobori-dori, are two smaller avenues, Tamachi-dori and Hitotsugi-dori. On these two streets, and their cross streets and alleys, are housed Akasaka's evening pleasures: lots of small bars, restaurants, and cafés. Nearby is the Cordon Bleu, a popular cabaret. The few remaining geisha houses are at the southern end of this area. However, unless you have affluent Japanese friends to invite you to a geisha party, you will only be able to note the houses' traditional architecture from the street, or perhaps spot a geisha, dressed in her elaborate kimono as she leaves for an assignment.

At the top end of Sotobori-dori Avenue is the Akasaka-mitsuke Station and the intersection with Aoyama-dori Avenue. Across the intersection on the left, on the other side of the overpass, is the Suntory Building. On its 11th floor is the **Suntory Museum**, which rotates in exhibition its own substantial collection of traditional art objects, which includes paintings, prints, lacquerware, glassware, and costumes; it also holds special loan exhibitions throughout the year. For the size of the museum, the admission charge is high; but the exhibits are carefully selected, extremely well displayed, and often are the finest of their kind. To one side of the museum is a teahouse, where you can experience a tea ceremony in the old-fashioned way. *1-2-3 Moto-Akasaka, Minato-ku, tel. 03/3470–1073. Admission:*

¥500 adults, ¥200 children under 12 (Sun. and holidays ¥300/ ¥100). Tea ceremony is an additional ¥500. Open Tues.- Thurs. and weekends, 10–4:30; Fri. 10–7. Closed Mon.

For those wanting something more than tea, Suntory opens a beer garden on its building's rooftop during the summertime (open 5–9). However, the beer garden's views are only of Akasaka's busy intersection, while from across the road, at the **Akasaka Prince Hotel** (1-2 Kioicho, Chiyoda-ku), the views include all of Tokyo.

You can't miss the Akasaka Prince Hotel. It's on the other side of Aoyama-dori Avenue from the Suntory Building. The 40-story half-moon structure stands on top of a small hill and dominates the landscape. Designed by Kenzo Tange, the building meets either with acclaim for its contemporary architecture or with criticism for being cold and sterile. Certainly the building's starkness, with nothing but the sky for its backdrop, stands out as a bold example of 20th-century architecture. Whatever your reaction to the building's design, you will not dispute the views from the hotel's upper floors. It's hard to surpass the view of Tokyo from its penthouse Gardenia Lounge (open 7–10 for dinner) or from the cocktail lounge, the Top of Akasaka (open 5 PM–2 AM). Indeed, it is worth making a special effort to come here just before twilight to see the sprawl of Tokyo turn into flickering lights against the night's darkening sky.

On the right-hand side of the Akasaka Prince is the **New Otani Hotel** (4-1 Kioicho, Chiyoda-ku), the largest hotel in Asia. Even if you abhor huge hotels, the New Otani holds a certain futuristic fascination as a minicity. Not only does it have 2,100 guest rooms, but there are also banquet facilities for any event, arcades of shops, a minisupermarket in its basement, and numerous bars and restaurants. At times, the New Otani seems more like a crowded subway at rush hour than a hotel, but it does have one area of tranquillity. The hotel's Garden Lounge looks on to a 400-year-old Japanese garden with vermilion bridges over ponds and winding paths—a little of traditional Japan, amid the endless stream of people pacing the hallways of the hotel and browsing through its high-fashion shops. Across the expressway and to the west of the New Otani are the gardens and fountains of **Geihinkan** (also known as the Akasaka Detached Palace; 2-1-1 Moto-Akasaka, Minato-ku). The palace was formerly the home of the crown prince, who was later to become the Taisho emperor (1912–1926); it is now an official state-guest house. The palace is a copy of Buckingham Palace, and the interior, which is not open to the public, imitates the style of Versailles.

Running along the south side of the Geihinkan gardens is Aoyama-dori Avenue, which goes all the way through the area to Shibuya. The distance is about three miles, or four subway stops on the Ginza Line if you use the Akasaka-mitsuke Station (opposite the Suntory Building and at the top end of Sotobori-dori Ave.). To give your feet a rest, we suggest taking the subway for two stops to Gaienmae Station. You'll miss walking past the **Canadian Embassy** and **Sogetsu Kaikan**, a famous Ikebana flower school where lessons are given in English on Tuesdays 10–noon. 7-2-21 Akasaka, Minato-ku, tel. 03/3408–1126. Cost: ¥4,490 for 1st lesson, ¥3,460 thereafter. Reservations must be made a day in advance.

The Gaienmae Station on Aoyama-dori Avenue takes you to the neighborhood of **Aoyama.** This is also the subway stop for the **Jingu Baseball Stadium** (13 Kasumigaoka, Shinjuku-ku tel. 03/3404–8999.), home field of the Yakult Swallows. You'll see it across the street from the Chichibunomiya Rugby and Football Ground. Actually, the stadium is in the **Meiji Jingu Shrine Outer Garden** (Jingu Gaien Park); on the other side of this park is the **National Stadium** (10 Kasumigaoka, Shinjuku-ku), the main venue of the 1964 Summer Olympics. The National Stadium is Japan's largest, with seating for 75,000 people. To the right of the stadium is the **Kaigakan Museum** (the Meiji Memorial Picture Gallery), which exhibits approximately 80 paintings depicting events in the life of Emperor Meiji. *9 Kasumigaoka, Shinjuku-ku, tel. 03/3401–5179. Admission: ¥300 adults, ¥100 children under 12. Open 9–4:30.*

Now you come to the real reason for getting off the subway at Gaienmae. If you walk about five minutes along Aoyama-dori Avenue toward Shibuya district (west), you'll spot the **Japan Traditional Craft Center** (Zenkoku Dentoteki Kogeihin Senta). It's located on the second floor of the Plaza 246 Building. This craft center promotes Japanese traditional crafts and exhibits a range of products that includes lacquer ware, ceramics, paper products, dolls, and metalwork. Some of the exhibits have English descriptions, others do not, but someone is usually available to ask a question if a particular item takes your fancy. A visit to this center gives one a head start to understanding different regional crafts and techniques before one leaves Tokyo to travel Japan's hinterland. *3-1-1 Minami Aoyama, Minato-ku, tel. 03/3403–2460. Admission free. Open 10–6. Closed Thurs.*

If you continue walking down (south) Aoyama-dori Avenue toward Shibuya, past a branch of America's **Brooks Brothers** on the right you'll reach the Omotesando Subway Station. If you take a left at the crossroads on to Omotesando-dori Avenue and walk another 10 minutes, you'll find the **Nezu Institute of Fine Arts.** The museum has a priceless collection of oriental art that includes superb examples of Japanese paintings and scrolls. An extremely attractive aspect of this museum is its small garden, with a traditional stream and five tea-ceremony houses. *6-5-36 Minami Aoyama, Minato-ku, tel. 03/3400–2536. Admission: ¥700 adults, ¥500 students. Open 9:30–4:30. Closed Mon. and the day after national holidays.*

The Nezu Institute of Fine Arts is about halfway between Roppongi and Shibuya. If it is still daytime, you might proceed to Shibuya, or even over to the area of Harajuku and the Meiji Shrine. If you do go directly to Shibuya from the Nezu Institute, it's about a 20-minute walk. Return first to Aoyama-dori Avenue and take a left. It will lead straight to Shibuya and the Hachiko statue, first passing the **National Children's Castle** (5-53-1 Jingumae, Shibuya-ku, tel. 03/3797–5666), an emporium designed to constructively entertain the young with its swimming pool, gym, concerts, theater, and audiovisual library. Another place to entertain children is the **Goto Planetarium** (2-21-12 Shibuya, Shibuya-ku, tel. 03/3407–7409). It is located right before Shibuya Station. While it has daily shows, plus a special Saturday-evening show that adds music to the stars, the narrative is in Japanese. At the north end of the Shibuya Station plaza is the statue of Hachiko.

Shibuya and Harajuku

Numbers in the margin correspond with points of interest on the Shibuya and Harajuku map.

Though **Shibuya** is a long way from being a commuter jungle like Shinjuku is, this district is a major transport hub. Almost a million commuters pass through Shibuya twice a day and travel on the two subways, three private railways, Japan Railways, and city buses. Much of this activity takes place aboveground—some of the subway platforms belie their name by being three stories above the street—so that the commuter congestion looks more confusing than in Shinjuku. As broad avenues intersect with a jumbled melee of vehicular traffic, pedestrian overpasses curve and snake their way to Shibuya Station. Surrounding the station are the inevitable department stores that cluster around Tokyo's major commuter areas.

❶ The flagship store of the Tokyu Department Store, **Tokyu Plaza** (1-2-2 Dogenzaka, Shibuya-ku), dominates the Shibuya Station neighborhood. If you select a window table at one of the two dozen restaurants on the top two floors of the building, you will find yourself gazing in awe at the seething flow of commuters around the station. On the seventh floor of Tokyu Plaza is a branch of **Kinokuniya Bookstore** (tel. 03/3463–3241), with a large selection of books written in English. The selection, however, is not as large as that of the Kinokuniya store in Shinjuku.

Unfortunately, from the restaurants' windows you cannot see ❷ the **Statue of Hachiko.** For that, you must return to the station plaza and go to the north exit. You'll spot the statue by the number of people who are standing around it waiting for someone. "Meet you by Hachiko" is an arrangement frequently made by Tokyoites. Hachiko was an Akita, a Japanese breed of dog. Every day he walked his master, a professor at Tokyo University, to Shibuya Station. In the evening, he would return to the station and greet his master off the train. One day in 1925, while at the university, the professor died of a stroke. Every evening for the next seven years, the dog went to the station and waited until the last train had pulled out of the station. Crestfallen, the dog would return to his home to try again the next evening. Then the dog died, too, and his story made the national newspapers. Gifts flooded in. A bronze statue was built, and the dog was stuffed to keep vigil in the Tokyo Museum of Art. The statue seen today is a replica; the original was melted down for its metal in World War II.

Shibuya has become a popular area for evening entertainment, such as shopping and going to restaurants and *nomiya* (inexpensive bars). It is not as international or cosmopolitan as Akasaka or Roppongi, but it is less expensive than those districts. Most places in Shibuya, however, are unaccustomed to foreigners, so be prepared to use one or two words of Japanese if you enter a small restaurant.

Time Out If you are a sashimi connoisseur, you may want to try **Kujiraya** ❸ (2-29-22 Dogenzaka, Shibuya-ku, tel. 03/3461–9145), which serves nothing but whale meat; this is best served raw and chilled, with ginger. To reach Kujiraya, take the avenue called Dogensaka, which goes off to the left from Hachiko's statue. Then take the first right fork, which leads to the main branch of the Tokyu Department Store. If you walk 100 yards farther

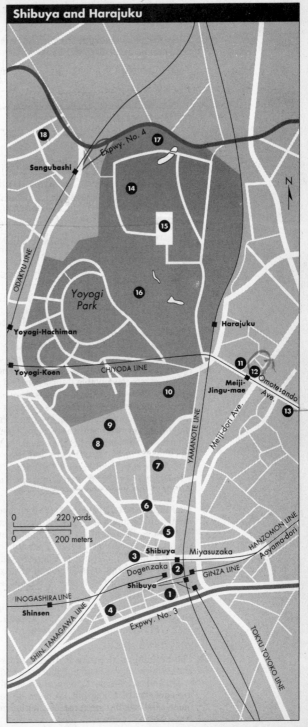

Shibuya and Harajuku

from the store on this same street, Kujiraya will be on your left. For the less adventurous, the well-known restaurant **④** **Furusato** (3-4-1 Aobadai, Meguro-ku, tel. 03/3463–2310) offers regional foods in a restored 300-year-old farmhouse transferred to Tokyo from the Hida region of the Japan Alps. To find Furusato, walk west from Shibuya Station past Tokyu Plaza and along Tamagawa-dori Avenue. After you cross Yamatedori Avenue, Furusato will be on your left.

From Shibuya Station, plaza department stores and shops are spread out along Aoyoma-dori Avenue and Meiji-dori Avenue. Tokyu has seven stores, Seibu has six, and Marui has two. For this tour, leave the station plaza in the direction that the **⑤** Hachiko statue is facing. On your left will be **Seibu Department Store** (21-1 Udagawacho, Shibuya-ku), which has a particularly good selection of European and Japanese designer-label fashions. Equally fascinating is a walk through Seibu's basement, which has one of Tokyo's most extensive food departments.

The street branching left after Seibu is Koen-dori Avenue, the smartest street in the neighborhood. A short way uphill, again **⑥** on the left, is **Parco**, owned by Seibu and said to be Tokyo's leading fashion complex. Parco actually comes in four parts. Parco 1 and Parco 2 (3 Udagawacho, Shibuya-ku) specialize in fashion, and on the top floor of Parco 1 is Parco Theater, for plays and performances. Parco 3 (14 Udagawacho, Shibuya-ku) has interior design merchandise and a floor devoted to visiting cultural exhibitions. Parco 4 (32–13 Udagawacho, Shibuya-ku) features young fashions, and has a performance hall called the Club Quattro on the fifth floor. Across Koen-dori Avenue, not far **⑦** from the Parco complex, is the **Tobacco and Salt Museum,** which houses every conceivable item associated with tobacco and salt since the days of the Maya. The displays of smoking utensils are fascinating, but the museum is perhaps more interesting for the Japanese, many of whom are inveterate smokers, than for the foreigner who may have seen similar exhibitions elsewhere. Of more interest is the special exhibit of ukiyo-e woodblock prints on the fourth floor depicting smokers' necessities. *1-16-8 Jinnan, Shibuya-ku, tel. 03/3476–2041. Admission: ¥100. Open 10–5:30. Closed Mon., 2nd Tues. of June, and New Year's.*

⑧ Walking farther up Koen-dori Avenue leads to **NHK Broadcasting Center** (Nippon Hoso Kyokai) for Japanese National Public Television. This 23-story building was originally built as the Olympic Information Center. Parts of the broadcasting complex are open to visitors. In the main building, a tour route is offered, and techniques for sound effects and film are shown. Explanations are given only in Japanese, so foreign tourists may be a little baffled. Perhaps the most exciting part of the tour permits you to watch an actual filming of a television scene and some of the stage sets. *2-2-1 Jinnan, Shibuya-ku, tel. 03/3465–1111. Admission free. Open 10–5. Closed 4th Mon. of each month.*

⑨ The building next to the NHK Broadcast Center is the **NHK Hall,** which serves as a multipurpose auditorium designed for opera and concert performances. It is quite large, with a seating capacity of 4,000, but its pièce de résistance is its 7,640-piece pipe organ, foremost of its kind in the world (*see* The Arts, below).

⑩ Across the street from NHK Hall is the **National Yoyogi Sports Center** (2-1-1 Jinnan, Shibuya-ku), consisting of two ultramodern structures designed by Kenzo Tange. His ability to work with ferro-concrete to evoke a templelike simplicity is impressive. The center was built for the 1964 Olympics, and both the stadium, which can accommodate 15,000 spectators for swimming and diving events, and the annex, which houses a basketball court with a seating capacity of 4,000, are open to visitors when there are no competitions (admission free; open 10–4). The bronze bust in the center of the Sports Center is of Yoshitoshi Tokugawa. In 1910, he became Japan's pioneer aviator by staying aloft for four minutes and traveling 230 feet. (His plane is on display at the Transportation Museum in the Koto ward.)

Across from the Sports Center are the green lawns of **Yoyogi-Koen Park.** It was once the barracks for the Japanese Army; then, after World War II, the U.S. Army took it over, and the area became known as Washington Heights. In 1964 it was used as the Olympic Village. Now it is public parkland lined with paths and, on Sundays, is often the venue for groups of young kids to dance, mime, or play their music to the amusement of spectators. This is **Harajuku,** a mini-downtown that attracts the youth of Tokyo.

Perhaps the presence of the U.S. occupation forces stationed in this area after World War II has caused Harajuku to permit a more liberal, Western-type behavior. In the late 1970s and early 1980s, the youth of Tokyo seemed to congregate every Sunday on the wide street between NHK and Harajuku Subway Station. The more exhibitionist youths formed groups that acted out their fantasies in dance, break dancing, skateboard antics, bands, or pantomime. The more inhibited would only watch. The youth were named the "bamboo-shoot children," Japan's counterpart to the flower children of America. Their numbers have since declined, but on Sundays, a variety of amusing performances is still offered.

Today's Japanese youth are the product of a new consumerism that is sweeping through the nation after decades of austerity. The young come here on Sundays to be anticorporate and to rebel against the pressure to succeed. They also come to consume. Dressed in the latest fashion fads, they seek out the bargains from the stalls and shops that remain open all day on Sunday.

The JR Harajuku Station is easy to recognize. The 1924 building looks more like an English village station than a metropolitan subway stop. Directly across the road from the station is **Omotesando Avenue,** bustling with pedestrians and shoppers. And, on Sundays, it seems that all the trendy Japanese young people are here, dressed in their finery. Up a small street, on **⑪** the left-hand side before Meiji-dori Avenue, is the **Ota Memorial Museum of Art.** On two floors, you'll find a rotating exhibit of *ukiyo-e* wood-block prints from the private collection of Seizo Ota. For anyone interested in ukiyo-e, some of Japan's best-known artists are represented here, including Hiroshige, Sharaku, and Utamaro. *1-10-10 Jingumae, Shibuya-ku, tel. 03/ 3403–0880. Admission: ¥800 adults, ¥250 children under 12. Open 10:30–5. Closed Mon., New Year's, and from the 25th to the end of each month.*

⑫ Across the road from the Ota Memorial Museum, on the corner of Omotesando Avenue and Meiji-dori Avenue, is **La Foret** (1-11-6 Jingumae, Shibuya-ku). This is the main fashion building in Harajuku. Inside La Foret are about 110 shops; most of them are high-price boutiques, and you can rest at one of the coffee shops in the building if you need time to decide on a purchase.

⑬ Lined with ginkgo trees, Omotesando Avenue is rich with boutiques and shops, including Paul Stewart from the United States. However, the one store that is really worth looking at for Japanese antiques is the **Oriental Bazaar** (next to Shakey's Pizza). Downstairs in the basement, salesmen set up their stalls and offer a range of old Japanese items, such as kimonos, jewelry, dolls, and wood-block prints. It's like a hands-on museum. *5-19-13 Jingumae, Shibuya-ku, tel. 03/3400-3933. Open 9:30–6:30. Closed Thurs.*

Backtrack about 100 yards to Meiji-dori Avenue, take a right, and more boutique and fashion stalls will greet you. If you are still not overwhelmed by the mass consumerism, walk a little farther along Meiji-dori Avenue and take a left onto **Takeshita-dori,** a 300-yard street that is crammed with fashion vendors, with names such as Rap City and Octopus Army, and youthful buyers. Takeshita-dori leads back to Harajuku Station, and on **⑭** the other side of the train tracks is the **Meiji Jingu Shrine Inner** **⑮** **Garden,** the grounds for the **Meiji Jingu Shrine.**

The Meiji Jingu Shrine is a welcome contrast of serene solemnity to the youthful consumerism exhibited on the shop-filled streets around Harajuku. The two torii gates, made from 1,700-year-old cypress trees from Mt. Ari in Taiwan, each tower 40 feet high. Indeed, they are the largest (but not the tallest) gates in Japan; here, more than ever, they fulfill their role of symbolizing the separation between the mundane, everyday world and the spiritual world of the Shinto shrine. Legend has it that the shape of the torii gates derives from the shape of a rooster's perch, and that it was the rooster whose crowing awoke the sun goddess, who thus brought light to the world. (The Meiji Jingu Shrine's two gates have perches spanning 56 feet.) The shrine was built in memory of Emperor Meiji, who died in 1912, and his wife, Empress Dowager Shoken, who died two years later. He was the emperor who brought Japan out from the isolationist policies of the Tokugawa Shogunate and opened the country's doors to the West. (Incidentally, Emperor Meiji would not be surprised by the behavior of the youth of Harajuku. In 1881, concerned about the influence of Western civilization, he issued a book on public morality.)

Even though the shrine is new (completed in 1920 and rebuilt in 1958 after being badly damaged by fire in 1945), it evokes the traditional asceticism of Japan's past. The buildings (the main hall forms a quadrangle with the outlying structures) are made with Japanese cypress, and the curving green copper roofs seem to symbolize the eternal sweep of time. The shrine—and its surrounding garden, which has some 100,000 shrubs, many of which were donated by the Japanese people—is one of the most popular with the Japanese. At New Year's, about 2½ million people come to pay their ancestral respects. *1-1 Kamizonocho, Yoyogi, Shibuya-ku. Admission free. Open sunrise–sunset.*

Before you reach the shrine, on the left when you walk from Harajuku Station, is the **Iris Garden.** In late June the garden is worth visiting, when the flowers are in bloom. Beyond the shrine is the **Treasure House,** a repository for the personal effects and clothes of Emperor and Empress Meiji—perhaps of less interest to the foreign visitor than to the Japanese. *1-1 Kamizonocho, Yoyogi, Shibuya-ku, tel. 03/3379–5511. Admission: ¥200. Open 9–4:30 Mar. 1–Oct. 30 (9–4 in winter). Closed 3rd Fri. of each month.*

If you have walked as far as the Treasure House, consider exiting the Inner Garden on the northeast side, and walk beyond Sangubashi Subway Station to the **Japanese Sword Museum,** which exhibits the works of noted swordsmiths, both ancient and modern. Sword making is a complex and intricate art in Japan and was perfected during the shogun period. Swords still hold an aura of dignity and honor. Only a few swordsmiths are left in modern Japan; many live and work in the small town of Seti, north of Nagoya. *4-25-10, Yoyogi, Shibuya-ku, tel. 03/ 3379–1386. Admission: ¥500. Open 9–4. Closed Mon.*

From the Sword Museum, if you retrace your steps to Sangubashi Subway Station, it is two stops on the Odayku Line to Shinjuku, the antithesis of the serenity of the Meiji Jingu Shrine. If you did not make it to either the Treasure House or the Sword Museum, then walk back to Harajuku Station and take the JR Yamanote Line two stops north to Shinjuku.

Shinjuku

Numbers in the margin correspond with points of interest on the Shinjuku map.

To experience **Shinjuku,** one should arrive by subway, though we would not recommend using the subway during the morning or evening rush hour. More than 2 million commuters pass through Shinjuku Station twice a day. Nine trains and subway lines converge in Shinjuku to transport human cargo. Broad-shouldered men in white gloves ease commuters into packed trains with a determined shove. The sight of the endless ebb and flow of humanity is worth seeing, but not experiencing.

Shinjuku is a microcosm of Japan, where the ultramodern confronts the past: high-tech industries work alongside the oldest professions; modern, slick, deluxe hotels look down on pink motels, where rooms rent by the hour; and 50-story buildings, complete with plazas and underground parking, tower over one- or two-level buildings crammed into twisting alleys. Shinjuku is a fascinating nightmare, which is alternately off-putting and exciting.

When Ieyasu Tokugawa became shogun and made Edo his capital, Shinjuku was at the junction of two important arteries leading into the city from the west. Here, travelers could rest their horses and freshen up or dally with ladies of pleasure before entering Edo. When the Tokugawa Dynasty collapsed in 1868, the 16-year-old Emperor Meiji moved his capital to Edo, renaming it Tokyo (Eastern Capital). Shinjuku in this modern age was destined to become the connecting railhead to Japan's western provinces. As a playground, its reputation was maintained with its artists, writers, and students, and it became the bohemian section of Tokyo in the 1930s. After the war, Tokyo spread west rather than east; Shinjuku has now developed into Tokyo's high-tech center. By the 1970s, the property values of the district were the nation's most expensive, far outstripping the Ginza area.

The heart of Shinjuku is still a commuting junction. In the maze of passageways leading to the trains, a vast underground shopping center of more than 130 shops is located. The large department stores near Shinjuku Station offer everything from bargain basements to museums to restaurants on their upper floors, while the station itself is a bewildering city. One week in the station would not be sufficient time to know half of it, especially with 60 exits from which to choose.

Shinjuku is divided by its train station into its two very different areas, western Shinjuku and eastern Shinjuku.

Western Shinjuku The New Metropolitan Center is on the west side (Nishi-Shinjuku) of Shinjuku Station. This is Tokyo's 21st-century model city, with modern high rises separated by concrete plazas. All of Tokyo is subject to serious earthquakes, except, apparently, Shinjuku. In the 1923 quake that virtually paralyzed Japan's capital, Shinjuku was the only suburb left vertical. On that basis, and because of some sounder scientific evidence, 13 skyscrapers have been built in the last 16 years in the area, and another in Tokyo houses the municipal government.

❶ ❷ ❸ Three of the skyscrapers here are hotels. The first to be built was the **Keio Plaza Inter-Continental Hotel** (2-2-1 Nishi-Shinjuku, Shinjuku-ku). The **Century Hyatt** (2-7-2 Nishi-Shinjuku, Shinjuku-ku) and the **Tokyo Hilton** (6-6-2 Nishi-Shinjuku, Shinjuku-ku) followed. The other skyscrapers contain banks, government offices, and showrooms for Japanese computer, optical, and electronics companies.

❹ The skyscraper closest to the railway tracks is the **Yasuda Kasai Kaijo Building** (Yasuda Fire and Marine Insurance Building). On the 42nd floor is the **Togo Seiji Museum**. Seiji Togo was a master of putting to canvas the grace and charm of young maidens; more than a hundred of his works are on display at any time. This is also the museum that bought the painting *Sunflowers* by Vincent van Gogh for more than ¥5 billion. The museum's gallery has an obstructed view of the old part of Shinjuku, where clubs and pink hotels abound. *1-26-1 Nishi-Shinjuku, Shinjuku-ku, tel. 03/3349–3081. Admission: ¥500 adults, ¥200 children under 12. Open 9:30–5. Closed Mon.*

❺ A few blocks from the Yasuda Building, the **Shinjuku Sumitomo Building** (2-6-1 Nishi-Shinjuku, Shinjuku-ku) stands across from the Century Hyatt. Notable for its futuristic architecture, this is actually a 52-story, six-side building, but because three of its sides are wider, it appears triangular. The center of the building is a long hollow well, and from the ground floor you can look up to see light reflected in by its glass roof. If you are hungry, ride up to the top three floors, where you'll find several restaurants catering to the people who work in the building. Most of the restaurants open at 10 AM and stay open through the evening.

❻ If you walk two blocks west of the Sumitomo Building, you'll reach the **Shinjuku NS Building** (2-4-1 Nishi-Shinjuku, Shinjuku-ku), a little dwarfed by the other skyscrapers with only 30 floors; it, too, has a hollow core that allows one's atten-

157

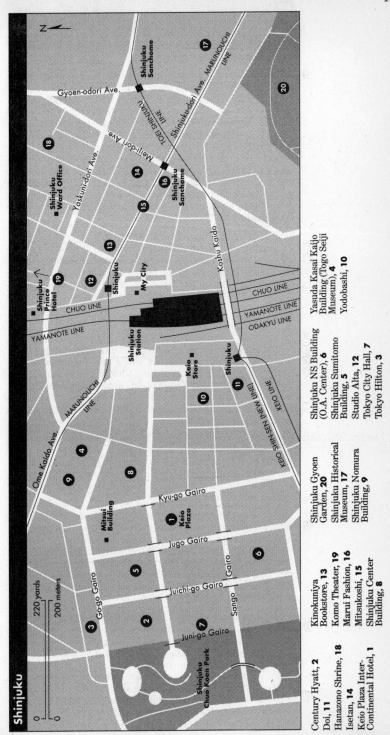

Shinjuku

Century Hyatt, **2**
Doi, **11**
Hanazono Shrine, **18**
Isetan, **14**
Keio Plaza Inter-
Continental Hotel, **1**

Kinokuniya
Bookstore, **13**
Komo Theater, **19**
Marui Fashion, **16**
Mitsukoshi, **15**
Shinjuku Center
Building, **8**

Shinjuku Gyoen
Garden, **20**
Shinjuku Historical
Museum, **17**
Shinjuku Nomura
Building, **9**

Shinjuku NS Building
(O.A. Center), **6**
Shinjuku Sumitomo
Building, **5**
Studio Alta, **12**
Tokyo City Hall, **7**
Tokyo Hilton, **3**

Yasuda Kasai Kaijo
Building (Togo Seiji
Museum), **4**
Yodobashi, **10**

tion to be directed to the 24-foot clock standing in the lobby.
Most visitors to this building head directly to the fifth floor,
where the **O.A. Center** is located. Here, around 20 computer
companies display their latest wares.

7 Architect Kenzo Tange's grandiose **City Hall complex,** which
now dominates this whole area, opened in March 1991. Built at
a cost of ¥157 billion, it was clearly meant to celebrate the fact
that Tokyo's annual budget is bigger than that of the entire
People's Republic of China. Is the intricate lattice facade supposed to invoke a Gothic cathedral or a microchip? Tokyoites either love it or hate it; it's been called everything from "a fitting
tribute" to a "forbidding castle." The main building, now the
tallest in Tokyo, soars 48 stories, splitting on the 33rd floor into
two towers; from the observation decks on the 45th floor of both
towers (open 9–8; admission free) you can see—on a clear
day—all the way from Mt. Fuji to the Boso Peninsula in Chiba
Prefecture.

Several other buildings in the area have free observation floors:
8 the **Shinjuku Center Building** (across from the Yasuda Build-
9 ing), on the 53rd floor; the **Shinjuku Nomura Building** (next to
the Yasuda Building), on the 50th floor; and the **Shinjuku Sumitomo Building,** on the 51st floor. However, a more comfortable way of inspecting the horizon is on the Keio Plaza Hotel's
47th floor; take in the view with some refreshment at the Pole
Star Lounge.

As you walk back toward the Shinjuku Station, you may want
to stop at a few of Tokyo's leading discount camera stores in the
10 area. Two well-known camera shops are **Yodobashi** (1-11-1
11 Nishi-Shinjuku, Shinjuku-ku, near Chuo-dori Ave.) and **Doi** (1-
18-27 Nishi-Shinjuku, Shinjuku-ku, near Kokusai-dori Ave.);
both shops are about a block from Keio Mall near the station.
Even if you have no intention of buying, the array of goods on
display is a vision in itself.

Eastern Shinjuku   While the west side of Shinjuku is a sterile wasteland of modern
high rises, the east side is a labyrinth of streets and alleys
packed with department stores, shops, bars, restaurants, theaters, strip shows, and hotels for temporary stays. It starts out
as a jumbled mass of shopping stores; as one walks north, the
sights become more and more tawdry.

As you leave the station by the east exit (*higashi-guchi*), a huge
12 video screen marks **Studio Alta** (3-24-3 Shinjuku, Shinjuku-ku).
It's a well-known landmark, with a crowd usually gathered to
look at its flickering images. The building houses a television
studio, and beneath it is the largest subterranean plaza in Japan. Full of shops and restaurants, this is a good place to come
during the winter months for something to eat and to watch the
melee of people walking around.

Studio Alta is on one end of **Shinjuku-dori Avenue,** a street full
13 of shops. Here you'll find **Kinokuniya Bookstore** (3-17-7 Shinjuku, Shinjuku-ku), with its sixth floor devoted to foreign-
language books, including 40,000 English titles. Right near
Kinokuniya is **Camera no Sakuraya** (3-26-10 Shinjuku,
Shinjuku-ku), a discount store for cameras and electronics
goods. Farther up on the same side of the street as Kinokuniya
14 is **Isetan** (3-14-1 Shinjuku, Shinjuku-ku), the trendiest of the
fashion stores in the neighborhood, with a foreign customer-
service counter on the fifth floor. On the opposite side of the

15
16 street are the two big stores, **Mitsukoshi** (3-29-1 Shinjuku, Shinjuku-ku) and **Marui Fashion** (3-30-16 Shinjuku, Shinjuku-ku). On Sundays, Shinjuku-dori Avenue and its side streets are closed to traffic; the area becomes a sea of shoppers.

17 You may want to visit the **Shinjuku Historical Museum,** which opened in March 1989. It displays, through historical documents, artifacts, and models, Shinjuku's growth during the Edo and Showa periods. Shinjuku was virtually leveled during the firebombing of Tokyo at the end of World War II. The museum offers a glimpse of city life in old traditional Japan. *22 Sen-ei-cho, Shinjuku-ku, tel. 03/3359–2131. Admission: ¥200 adults, ¥100 children under 18. Open 9–5. Closed Mon.*

18 If you retrace your steps, a few blocks north of Isetan department store and Yasukuni-dori is **Hanazono Shrine.** It is far from being one of Tokyo's major shrines, but in the hub of bacchanalian pleasure palaces, this is a tranquil oasis tucked between shops and tall office buildings. The shrine, constructed before the Edojo Castle, is believed to aid a businessman's commercial prosperity. *Admission free. Open sunrise–sunset.*

To the north of Yasukuni-dori Avenue and west of Hanazono Shrine is **Kabukicho.** After the courtesans were liberated in 1872 and the formalities governing geisha entertainment were dissolved, this area became Japan's largest center of prostitution until laws against the practice became more strict. In an attempt to change the neighborhood's image after World War II, plans were made to replace the fire-gutted Ginza Kabukiza theater with a new one in Shinjuku. The plans never came to fruition (the old theater was resurrected), but the area got its
19 name. Today, however, Kabukicho has the **Koma Theater** (1-19-1 Kabuki-cho, Shinjuku-ku), which houses several discos and bars, as well as a theater with a revolving stage and more than 2,000 seats. The theater serves as a useful central landmark in the district.

Bewildering as it is, Kabukicho is a maze of bars, discos, strip joints, and theaters. It is unrefined nightlife at its best, and raunchy seediness at its worst. Neon signs flash the world of various pleasures, and, at the places not to visit, touts try to lure their customers into bars where the ¥18,000 bottle of beer has been made famous. However, if you do not follow these touts, and instead choose a place that looks respectable, there is rarely any problem. Perhaps stay away from the cheap *nomiya* (bars) under the railway tracks in Shomben-yokocho. For the Ni-chome area beyond the Koma Theater—where many of the bars are decidedly gay—you might want a knowledgeable guide. But do not be intimidated by the area. It is fun and one of the least expensive areas of Tokyo in which to engage in nighttime pleasures.

20 If one visits Shinjuku during the day and is anxious for some peace of mind, the **Shinjuku Gyoen Garden** is the place to head for. It's a stiff 20–30 minute walk from Shinjuku Station, so you may prefer to hop on the subway (the Marunouchi Line for one stop, to Shinjuku-Gyoenmae Station, which brings you close to the north end of the park). Shinjuku Gyoen was once the estate of the powerful *daimyo* (feudal lord) Naito, but became part of the imperial household after the Meiji Restoration; after World War II, it was opened to the public as a national park. A place for discovery, the park is perfect for leisurely walks; it has 150 acres of gardens, landscaped with artificial hills, ponds with bridges, and thoughtfully placed stone lanterns. The paths wind their way through more than 3,000 different kinds of plants, shrubs and trees and lead to Japanese-, French-, and English-style gardens, as well as a greenhouse filled with tropical plants. However, the most noted times to visit are during cherry blossom time (early April), when 1,900 trees of 65 different species flower, and in the fall, during the chrysanthemum exhibition. *11 Naitocho, Shinjuku-ku. Admission: ¥150. Open 9–4. Closed Mon.*

What to See and Do with Children

Amusement Centers

Korakuen. A small amusement center is situated near the Korakuen baseball stadium and Korakuen Garden. The major attraction is the giant roller coaster and the "circus train" that does a loop. *1-3-61 Koraku, Bunkyo-ku, tel. 03/3811–2111. Admission: ¥1,100 adults, ¥650 children under 12. Open 10–7.*

Tokyo Disneyland. Ever since Tokyo Disneyland opened in April 1983, some 10 million visitors a year have been coming to this amusement park, where Mickey-san and his coterie of Disney characters entertain just the way they do in the California and Florida Disney parks.

The easiest way to reach Tokyo Disneyland is by the shuttle bus, which leaves Tokyo Station's Yaesu North exit every 30 minutes (cost: ¥600; ¥300 children under 18). You may also go by subway; from Nihombashi, take the Tozai Line to Urayasu Station and walk over to the Tokyo Disneyland Bus Terminal for the 15-minute ride (cost: ¥200 adults, ¥100 children). *1-1 Maihama, Urayasu-shi, tel. 0473/54–0001 or 03/3366–5600. There are several types of admission tickets. For example, one can purchase the entrance admission for ¥3,000 (¥2,700 juniors, ¥2,000 children), then buy individual tickets. However, if you plan to see most of the attractions, the Tokyo Disneyland Passport at ¥4,400 (¥4,000 juniors, ¥3,000 children) is the most economical buy. Tickets can be purchased in advance in Tokyo Station, near the Yaesu-guchi exit (you'll notice red-jacketed attendants standing outside the booth), or from any travel agent, such as the Japan Travel Bureau. Tokyo Disneyland is open every day 9–7 (Fri. 9–8), except for 6 days in Dec., 6 days in Jan., and 3 days in Feb.*

Toshima-en Amusement Park. This is a large, well-equipped amusement park located in the northwest corner of Tokyo. There are four roller coasters, a German carousel, haunted houses, and seven swimming pools. To reach it, take a subway from Tokyo Station to Ikebukuro and change to a special train that runs frequently from Seibu-Ikebukuro Station to Toshima-en. *3-25-1 Kouyamacho, Nerima-ku, tel. 03/3990–3131. Admission: ¥1,600 adults, ¥800 children under 12. Admission plus amusement tickets are ¥4,000 adults, ¥3,300 children. Open 9–5.*

Museums

Goto Planetarium. This planetarium, located on Aoyama-dori Avenue, near Shibuya Station, has daily shows displaying the seasonal movements of the constellations, the moons of the universe, and other heavenly bodies projected onto a dome 65 feet in diameter. A special Saturday evening show adds music to the stars. Be warned that the narrative is only in Japanese. *Tokyo Bunkakaikan, 2-21-12 Shibuya, Shibuya-ku, tel. 03/3407-7409. Admission: ¥700 adults, ¥400 children 6-15, ¥300 children under 6. Open 10-6. Closed Mon.*

NHK Broadcasting Center (Nippon Hoso Kyokai). The Japanese National Public Television offers tours around the broadcasting complex where techniques for sound effects and film are displayed. Explanations are given only in Japanese, although there is a pamphlet available in English. Perhaps the most exciting part of the tour is when one is permitted to watch an actual filming of a scene and some of the stage sets. An Edo mansion fit for a samurai, for example, seems more authentic than the real thing. *2-2-1 Jinnan, Shibuya-ku, tel. 03/3465-1111. Admission free. Open 10-5. Closed 4th Mon. of each month.*

Transportation Museum. This is a fun place to take children. Displays include the early development of the railway system and a miniature layout of the rail services, as well as Japan's first airplane, which lifted off in 1903. *1-25 Kanda Sudacho, Chiyoda-ku, tel. 03/3251-8481. Admission: ¥260 adults, ¥150 children 4-15. Open 9:30-5. Closed Mon.*

Shops

Kiddyland. All the toys and playthings here will surely keep children and teenagers busy. *6-1-9 Jingu-mae, Shibuya-ku, tel. 03/3409-3431. Open 10-8. Closed 3rd Tues. of each month.*

Toy Park. This is reputedly the largest toy shop in Japan. *Hakuhinkan 2F-4F, 8-8-11 Ginza, Chuo-ku, tel. 03/3571-8008. Open 11-8.*

Zoos

Tama Dobutsu Koen. At least here animals have space to roam, usually with moats to keep them separated from the visitors. In the Lions Park, visitors ride through in a minibus. To reach this zoo, take the Keio Line from Shinjuku and transfer at Takata Fudo Station for the train going to Dobutsu Koen Station. *300 Hodokubo, Hino-shi, tel. 0425/91-1611. Admission: ¥400 adults, ¥100 children 12-15. Open 9:30-4. Closed Mon.*

Ueno Dobutsuen. The Ueno Zoo's major attraction is the pair of pandas and their child. However, the zoo is terribly crowded on weekends, and the animals are penned in such small cages it is almost criminal. *9 Ueno-koen, Taito-ku, tel. 03/3828-5171. Admission: ¥400 adults, ¥100 children 12-15. Open 9:30-4:30 (enter by 4). Closed Mon.*

Off the Beaten Track

The Arakawa Line. Feeling nostalgic? Take the JR Yamanote Line to Otsuka, cross the street in front of the station, and change to the Arakawa Line—Tokyo's last surviving trolley. West, the line goes to Higashi-Ikebukuro (site of the Sunshine City skyscraper complex, billed as a "complete city within a city" and remarkable only as a complete flop) and Zoshigaya, before turning south to the terminus at Waseda, not far from Waseda University. East, the trolley takes you through the back gardens of old neighborhoods to Oji—once the site of Japan's first Western-style paper mill, built in 1875 by the Oji Paper Manufacturing Company. The mill is long gone, but the memory lingers on at the **Oji Paper Museum,** the only one of its kind in Japan. Some of the exhibits here show the process of milling paper from pulp; others illustrate the astonishing variety of things that can be made from paper itself. *1-1-8 Horifune, Kita-ku, tel. 03/3914–9151. Walk south from the trolley stop about 100 yards; the museum is between the Arakawa tracks and those of the JR. Admission: ¥200 adults, ¥100 children under 12. Open 9:30–4:30. Closed Mon. and national holidays.*

Asakura Sculpture Gallery. In the past two or three years, tourists have begun to "discover" the Nezu and Yanaka areas of Shitamachi (downtown)—much to the dismay of the handful of foreigners who have lived for years in this inexpensive, charming part of the city. To some, the appeal lies in its narrow streets, with their old shops and houses; others are drawn to the fact that many of the greatest figures in the world of modern Japanese culture lived and died in this same area, including novelists Ogai Mori, Soseki Natsume, and Ryunosuke Akutagawa; scholar Tenshin Okakura, who founded the Japan Art Institute; painter Taikan Yokoyama; and sculptors Koun Takamura and Fumio Asakura. If there's one single attraction here, it is probably Asakura's home and studio, converted into a gallery after his death in 1964.

Asakura's work was deeply influenced by Confucian thought—an influence reflected in the extraordinary little pond and rock garden in the central courtyard of the house. The arrangement of the stones makes a symbolic statement of Confucian ethics—that all its virtues must be tempered with humility. The stone of Benevolence, for example, broad and flat, is worn smooth by the flow of water from the fountain; the tall stones of Wisdom and Righteousness are softened with coverings of ferns and foliage; the stone of Propriety is made to support a bridge; and the stone of Sincerity barely rises above the surface of the pond. The studio is filled with Asakura's works, among them many of his most famous pieces; the tearoom on the opposite side of the courtyard is a haven of quietness from which to contemplate his garden. *7-8-10 Yanaka, Taito-ku, tel. 03/3821–4549. From the south end of the JR Nippori Station, walk west (the Tennoji Temple will be on the left side of the street) until you reach a police box. Turn right, then right again at the end of the street; the museum is a 3-story black building on the right, a few hundred yards down. Admission: ¥300 adults, ¥150 children 6–15. Open 9:30–4:30. Closed Mon. and Fri.*

Asakusabashi and Ryogoku. Sumo, the centuries-old national sport of Japan, is not to be taken lightly—as anyone who has ever seen a sumo wrestler will testify. Indeed, sheer weight is almost a prerequisite to success; one of the current champions tips the scales at a touch under 550 pounds. There are various techniques of pushing, grappling, and throwing in sumo, but the basic rules are exquisitely simple: except for hitting below the belt (which is all a sumo wrestler wears) and striking with the closed fist, almost anything goes. The contestants square off in a dirt ring about 15 feet in diameter and charge; the first one to step out of the ring, or touch the ground with anything but the soles of his feet, loses.

There are no free agents in sumo. To compete, you must belong to a *heya* (stable) run by a retired wrestler who has purchased that right from the Sumo Association. Sumo is very much a closed world, hierarchical and formal. Youngsters recruited into the sport live in the stable dormitory, doing all the community chores and waiting on their seniors while they learn; when they rise high enough in the tournament rankings, they acquire servant-apprentices of their own.

While tournaments and exhibitions are held in different parts of the country at different times, all the stables in the Sumo Association—now some 30 in number—are in Tokyo. Most of them are clustered on both sides of the Sumida River near the new Kokugikan (National Sumo Arena), with its distinctive green roof, in the areas called Asakusabashi and Ryogoku. One of the easiest to find is the Tatsunami Stable (3-26 Ryogoku), only a few steps from the west end of the JR Ryogoku Station building; another is the Takasago Stable (1-22-5 Yanagibashi), on a narrow side street one block west of the JR Asakusabashi Station. Wander this area when the wrestlers are in town (Jan., May, and Sept. are best bets), and you are more than likely to see some of them on the streets, cleaving the air like leviathans in their wood clogs and kimonos; come 7–11 AM, and you can peer through the doors and windows of the stable to watch them in practice sessions.

Sengakuji Temple. One day in the year 1701, a young provincial baron named Asano Takumi no kami, serving an official term of duty at the shogun's court, attacked and seriously wounded a courtier named Kira Yoshinaka. Kira had demanded the usual tokens of esteem that someone in his high position would expect for his goodwill; Asano refused, and Kira had humiliated him in public to the point where he could no longer contain his rage.

Kira survived the attack. Asano, for daring to draw his sword in the confines of Edojo Castle, was ordered to commit suicide; his family line was abolished and his fief confiscated. Headed by Oishi Kuranosuke, the clan steward, 47 of Asano's loyal retainers vowed revenge. Kira was rich and well protected; Asano's retainers were *ronin*—masterless samurai. It took them almost two years of planning, subterfuge, and hardship, but on the night of December 14, 1702, they stormed Kira's villa in Edo, cut off his head, and brought it in triumph to Asano's tomb at Sengakuji, the family temple. Oishi and his followers were also sentenced to commit suicide—which they accepted as the reward not the price, of their honorable vendetta—and were buried in the temple graveyard with their lord.

The event captured the imagination of the Japanese like nothing else in their history; through the centuries it has become the national epic, the last word on the subject of loyalty and sacrifice, celebrated in every medium from Kabuki to film. The temple still stands; the graves are still there, the air around them filled with the smoke from bundles of incense that visitors still lay reverently on the tombstones.

The story gets even better. There's a small museum on the temple grounds with a collection of weapons and other memorabilia of the event; one of these items dispels forever the myth of Japanese vagueness and indirection in the matter of contracts and formal documents. Kira's family, naturally, also wanted to give him a proper burial, but the law insisted that this could not be done without his head. They asked for it back, and Oishi—mirror of chivalry that he was—agreed. He entrusted it to the temple, and the priests wrote him a receipt, which survives even now in the corner of a dusty glass case. "Item," it begins, "One head." *2-11-1 Takanawa, Minato-ku, tel. 03/3441–2208. Take the Toei Asakusa subway line to the Sengakuji stop, turn right, and walk up the hill. The entrance to the temple is just past the first traffic light, on the left. Admission to the museum: ¥200 adults, ¥100 children under 12. Open 9–4.*

Shopping

by Kiko Itasaka

You have all heard horror stories about prices in Japan. Many of them are true. Yes, a cup of coffee can cost U.S. $10, a melon can cost U.S. $100, and a taxi ride from the airport to central Tokyo costs about U.S. $200. The yen has appreciated drastically over the past few years, making the U.S. dollar in Japan seem to have the power of a peso. This does not mean that potential shoppers should get discouraged; shopping in Japan isn't always impossibly expensive, and bargains can still be found. If you need gifts and souvenirs you will still be able to find them, though shopping in Tokyo requires a certain amount of ingenuity and effort.

Some items are better bought at home, such as European designer clothing or imported fruit, but why would anyone go all the way to Tokyo to buy these items? The best shoppers in Japan know that they should concentrate on Japanese goods that are hard to find in America, such as crafts, toys, and kimonos. These are all items that can be found in areas that are easy to reach by public transportation. Try to avoid taxis and instead use Tokyo's convenient subways and trains. Traffic and the Byzantine mazes of streets make travel by taxi time-consuming and inordinately expensive. The shopper with only limited time should stick to hotel arcades, department stores, and stores that specifically cater to foreigners. For those with a little more time and a sense of adventure, Tokyo shopping can be fascinating.

Remember that in some cases, prices in smaller stores and markets might be listed with *Kanji* (Japanese pictographs derived from Chinese written characters) instead of Arabic numbers. In such cases, just ask, "How much?" It's a phrase that all Japanese will recognize, because it is the name of a popular TV game show in Japan, and someone will either tell you or write down the price for you.

Shopping in Tokyo is generally an extremely pleasant experience, because salespeople are often helpful and polite. In major stores, many people speak at least enough English for you to complete your transactions. There is a saying in Japan that the customer equals God. Upon entering a store, you will be greeted with a bow and the word *Iraasyaimase* (welcome). The salespeople are definitely there to serve you.

On April 1, 1989, Japan instituted an across-the-board 3% value added tax (VAT) in place of past taxes imposed on luxury goods, as well as on restaurant and hotel bills. This tax can be avoided at the duty-free airport shops and at **Amita** in the Tokyo Hilton Hotel (6–6–2 Nishi-Shinjuku, Shinjuku-ku, tel. 03/3348–3887; open 10–8). However, because these places tend to have higher profit margins, any tax savings is often offset by the higher cost of goods.

Stores in Tokyo generally open around 10–11 and close around 7–8. The stores mentioned in this section are open daily, except where noted.

Other shopping options may be found in the Exploring section earlier in this chapter.

Shopping Districts

Ginza Ginza was the first entertainment and shopping district in Tokyo, dating back to the Edo period (1603–1868). Tokyo's first department store, Mitsukoshi, was founded in this area, which once consisted of long, willow-lined avenues. The willows have long since gone, and the streets are now lined with department stores and boutiques. The exclusive stores in this area feature quality and selective merchandise at higher prices. Here it is not unusual to see a well-turned out Japanese woman in a kimono on a shopping spree, accompanied by her daughter, who is exquisitely dressed in a Chanel suit. *Nearest train: Yurakucho (Yamanote Line); nearest subway stations: Ginza (Marunouchi, Ginza, and Hibiya lines), Ginza Itchome (Yurakucho Line).*

Shibuya This area is primarily an entertainment district filled with movie theaters, restaurants, and bars, mostly geared toward teenagers and young adults. The shopping is also catered toward these groups, with many reasonably priced smaller shops, and a few department stores that are casual yet chic. *Nearest train station: Harajuku (Yamanote Line); nearest subway station: Hanzomon (Ginza Line).*

Shinjuku Amid the honky-tonk atmosphere of this bustling area, which includes the red-light and gay districts of Tokyo, are some of the city's most fashionable department stores. Shinjuku's merchandise reflects the crowds—young, stylish, and slightly flashy. In addition to clothing, this area features a cluster of electronic goods stores. *Nearest train station: Shinjuku (Yamanote Line); nearest subway stations: Shinjuku (Marunouchi Line), Shinjuku 3-Chome (Toei Shinjuku Line).*

Harajuku Teenagers all seem to congregate in Harajuku, particularly on the main avenue known as Takeshita-dori. A wild sense of fashion prevails, from '50s greaser looks to '60s mod styles to a variety of assorted looks that are perhaps indicative of what will be the rage in the year 2000. The average age on this street is clearly under 20, and maybe even under 16. Teens all over the world are strapped for cash, so, not surprisingly, everything in this area is moderately priced. The multitude of tiny stores offer not only clothing and accessories but also a lot of kitsch.

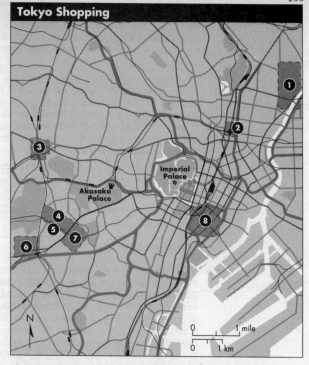

Tokyo Shopping

Nearest train station: Harajuku (Yamanote Line); nearest subway station: Meiji Jingumae (Chiyoda Line).

Omotesando Known as the Champs-Elysées of Tokyo, this long, wide avenue is lined with cafés and designer boutiques. Paradoxically, it is nearly parallel to the neighboring Takeshita-dori of Harajuku, but it couldn't be more different in atmosphere. Boutiques and cafés, however, are not the only attractions. You'll find a number of antiques and print shops, as well as one of the best toy shops in Tokyo—Kiddyland. Closed to traffic on Sundays, this is a street for browsers, strollers, and those who like to languish over café au lait before sauntering into the next store. *Nearest subway station: Omotesando (Chiyoda and Hanzomon lines).*

Aoyama Shopping in Aoyama is an aesthetically pleasing experience, but it can potentially empty your wallet in no time. For those interested in fashion, this is where many of the leading Japanese and Western designers have boutiques. Although the prices of most European and American designers will be high, Japanese designer clothes are 30%–40% lower than they are in the United States. Because many of them are unique and timeless designs, purchases might be worth the investment. Even if you do not want to buy anything, you'll have fun simply observing the artfully executed clothing. In fact, shopping here is similar to walking through an art gallery—enjoying the masterpieces, reveling in the atmosphere, and not bothering with the price tags. *Nearest subway station: Omotesando (Chiyoda and Hanzomon lines).*

Akihabara For the camera and electronic-goods buff who wants to see everything available on the market, Akihabara is high-tech heaven, with its endless multistory buildings. Walkman and portable CD players were on sale here long before they made it across the ocean. The best deals in Japan may be found here, but in general, prices are lower in the United States. *Nearest train station: Akihabara (Yamanote Line); nearest subway station: Akihabara (Hibiya Line).*

Asakusa While sightseeing in this area, take the time to stroll through its arcades. Much of the wares are the kind of souvenirs that you would expect to find on sale at any tourist stop, but if you look a little harder, you will find shops that have tortoiseshell accessories, beautiful wood combs, delicate fans, and other gift items. Venture to some of the back streets, where the small shops have been in business for many generations and offer fine traditional goods. *Nearest subway station: Asakusa (Toei Asakusa and Ginza lines).*

Gifts

The best presents and gifts from Japan are those that are uniquely Japanese. Obviously you do not want to buy a Gucci bag that would cost far less at home. For reasonable prices, you can find a wide range of interesting things, from traditional crafts to kitsch examples of popular culture in Japan.

Ceramics Ceramics and pottery in Japan are fragile and cumbersome, but they make wonderful gifts if you are willing to take the trouble of bringing the packages home. In the 16th century, the art of making pottery flourished with the popularity and demand for tea-ceremony utensils. Feudal lords from all over Japan competed to have the finest wares, and as a result, distinctive styles of pottery developed in various regions. Some of the more prominent pottery centers are Arita in Kyushu, where the ceramic ware often features patterns with flowers and birds; Mashiko, outside of Tokyo in the Tochigi Prefecture, with pottery having a simple and rough dark-brown glaze; and Kasama, in Ibaraki Prefecture, with its unique pottery glaze made from ash and ground rocks.

Those who cannot take the time to travel all over Japan can try Tokyo's specialty shops or department stores, which tend to have fairly complete selections of wares.

Tachikichi. This shop has a selection of pottery from different localities. *5-5-8 Ningyocho, Nihonbashi, Chuo-ku, tel. 03/ 3571-2924. Open 11–6:30. Closed Sun.*
Kisso. This store offers an excellent variety of ceramics in modern design, using traditional glazes, as well as a restaurant and a gift shop. *Axis Bldg., 5-17-1 Roppongi, Minato-ku, tel. 03/ 3582-4191. Open 11:30–2 and 5:30–9. Closed Sun.*

Dolls Many types of traditional dolls are available in Japan, each with its own charm. **Kokeshi** dolls are long, cylindrical, painted, and made of wood, with no arms or legs. Fine examples of Japanese folk art, they date back to the Edo period (1603–1868). **Daruma** are papier-mâché dolls, having rounded bottoms and faces that are often painted with amusing expressions. They are constructed so that no matter how you push them, they roll and remain upright. Legend has it that they are modeled after a Buddhist priest who maintained his seated lotus position for long periods of time. **Hakata** dolls, made in Hakata City of Kyushu, are clay dolls of traditional Japanese figures, such as geisha or samurai.

Kyugetsu. This shop has been in business for over a century and offers every kind of doll imaginable. *1-20-4 Yanagibashi, Taito-ku, tel. 03/3861-5511. Open 9-6. Closed Sun.*

Electronics Goods The best bargains for electronics goods are found at home and not in Japan. If you are curious to see what is available you should go to the area surrounding Akihabara Station, where you will find over 200 stores full of stereos, refrigerators, CD players, and anything else you can plug in.

Raijo Kaikan. Because many of the Akihabara shops are represented in this arcade, you'll get a quick idea of what is available. *1-15-16 Soto-Kanda, Chiyoda-ku. Open 10-7.*

In the Shinjuku district, **Doi** (1-18-27 Nishi-Shinjuku, Shinjuku-ku, tel. 03/3344-2310) and **Yodobashi** (1-11-1 Nishi-Shinjuku, tel. 03/3346-1010) have a vast camera selection. As long as you negotiate, prices can be extremely competitive (depending on the current exchange rate) with those found overseas in places such as Hong Kong and New York. Both camera stores are two short blocks west of the Shinjuku train station, close to the Keio department store. Both stores are open 10-8.

Folk Crafts Japanese folk crafts, called *mingei*, are simple and sturdy, yet imbued with Japanese aesthetics. They are unique, durable, and reasonably priced. While folk crafts may lack the sophistication of a delicately painted scroll, they do have a basic beauty that speaks for itself. Many objects fall into this category, such as bamboo wares, fabrics, paper boxes, dolls, and toys.

Bingo-ya. A complete selection of crafts from all over Japan can be found here. *10-6 Wakamatsucho, Shinjuku, tel. 03/3202-8778. Open 10-7. Closed Mon.*

Japan Traditional Craft Center. This gallery is a good place to familiarize yourself with the wonders of Japanese folk crafts. Their creation is demonstrated in videos, and many of the folk-craft items are for sale. *3-1-1 Minami Aoyama, Minato-ku, tel. 03/3403-2460. Open 10-6. Closed Thurs.*

Kimonos Kimonos in Japan are usually only worn on special occasions, such as weddings or graduations, and, like tuxedos in the United States, are often rented instead of purchased. They are extremely expensive and difficult to maintain. A wedding kimono, for example, can cost as much as ¥1 million.

In general, most foreigners, who are unwilling to pay this much for a garment that they probably want to use as a bathrobe, settle for a secondhand or antique silk kimono. These vary in price and quality. You can get one for as low as ¥1,000, but to find one in decent condition, you should expect to pay about ¥5,000. If you are willing to forgo silk, new cotton kimonos, known as *yukata*, with attractive geometric blue-and-white designs, are about ¥5,000. Department stores usually have good selections of new silk kimonos, but some smaller stores feature less expensive or secondhand goods.

Hayashi. International Arcade. *1-7 Uchisaiwaicho, Chiyoda-ku, tel. 03/3591-9826. Open Mon.-Sat. 9:30-7, Sun. 9:30-6.*
Oriental Bazaar. *5-9-13 Jingu-mae, Shibuya-ku, tel. 03/3400-3933. Open 9:30-6:30. Closed Thurs.*

Pearls Japan remains one of the best places in the world to buy pearls. They will not be inexpensive, but pearls of the same quality cost considerably more in the United States. It is best to go to a reputable dealer where you know that you will be guaranteed the best in pearls and will not be misled.

Mikimoto. Kokichi Mikimoto created his technique for cultured pearls in 1893. Since then, the name Mikimoto has become associated with the highest quality in pearls. Although the prices at Mikimoto are high, you would pay more for pearls of this quality in the United States. *4-5-5 Ginza, Chuo-ku, tel. 03/3535–4611. Open 10:30–6. Closed Wed.*

Tasaki Pearl Gallery. Tasaki offers pearls at slightly lower prices than does Mikimoto. The store has several showrooms and offers tours that demonstrate the technique of culturing pearls and explain the maintenance and care of these gems. *3-3 Akasaka, Minato-ku, tel. 03/5561–8881. Open 9–6:30.*

Arcades and Shopping Centers

For shoppers who do not have the time or energy to dash about Tokyo in search of the perfect gifts, there are arcades and shopping centers that carry a wide selection of merchandise. Many of these establishments are used to dealing with foreigners, and they have a good sense of what sort of items will please the folks back home.

Axis. This attractive building has many small selective shops with unique merchandise. On the first floor is **Living Motif,** a home-furnishings shop with high-tech foreign and Japanese goods of exquisite design. Those with a penchant for paper should look at the stationery section, with mass-produced paper that looks as though it is handmade. The other floors in Axis include lighting-fixture stores, design studios, and antique and furniture shops, all worth seeing. Do not ignore the basement floor, which houses **Nuno,** a fabric shop that sells traditional Japanese materials with modern touches. The fabrics are all creations of Junichi Arai, who once designed fabrics for such famous Japanese designers as Issey Miyake and Rei Kawakubo of Comme des Garçons. Be sure to look at **Kisso.** Although this is a restaurant, in the front and back, along with lacquered chopsticks and fine baskets, is an extraordinary selection of unique modern handmade ceramics with traditional Japanese glazes of contemporary designs, shapes, and colors. *5-17-1 Roppongi, Minato-ku, tel. 03/3582–4191.*

International Arcade. This selection of shops has a range of goods (including cameras, electronics goods, pearls, and kimonos) all sold by sales help using excellent English. Not only is the arcade conveniently located near the Imperial Hotel and TIC (Tourist Information Center), but the shops are all tax-free. Particularly recommended is **Hayashi Kimono,** which offers a good selection of reasonably priced new and used kimonos, all in excellent condition. *1-7 Uchisaiwaicho, Chiyodaku, tel. 03/3591–9826. Open 9:30–7.*

Boutiques

Japanese boutiques can often make you forget you are shopping. Of course, the function of these boutiques is to sell clothes, but in many cases you will not be aware that crass materialism is at work. As much attention is paid to the interior decoration and the lighting as to the clothing, so you have a sense that you are viewing works of art. Although many Japanese designers are represented in department stores for convenient shopping, you'll get a sense of Japanese aesthetics by visiting the simple and elegant boutiques in Aoyama and Omotesando; the stores are conveniently located within walking distance of one another. Even if you don't buy anything, you will be sure to enjoy yourself.

From 1st Building (3-6-1 Kita-Aoyama, Minato-ku). This building houses the boutiques of several of Japan's leading designers, including **Issey Miyake** (tel. 03/3499–6476; open 11–8), named after the well-known designer of loose, asymmetrical, and elegant clothing, and **Comme des Garçons** (tel. 03/3499–4370; open 11–8; closed Mon.), featuring the line of the controversial Rei Kawakubo, who brought new meaning to the word *black*.

Hanae Mori Building. In this glass-mirrored structure, designed by the famous Japanese architect Kenzo Tange, you can see the designs of the doyenne of Japanese fashion, Hanae Mori. Mori's clothing has a classic look with a European influence. On the first floor, there is a café where you can observe Japan's beautiful people walking along the street or sitting next to you. *3-6-1 Kita-Aoyama, Minato–ku, tel. 03/3400–3301. Open 10:30–7.*

Jurgen Lehl. As his name indicates, Lehl is not of Japanese origin, but his fashions and textiles fit well into the Japanese design world. *1-13-18 Jingumae, Shibuya, tel. 03/3498–6723. Open 11–8.*

Madame Nicole. Matsuda, Nicole's designer, combines a traditional Western fashion sense with the Japanese sensibility. *3-1-25 Jingumae, Shibuya-ku, tel. 03/3478–0998. Open 11–8.*

Department Stores

Today, most Japanese department stores are part of conglomerates that own railways, real estate, and even baseball teams. These stores often include travel agencies, theaters, and art galleries. A shopper can easily spend an afternoon or even an entire day shopping, especially because a cluster of reasonably priced restaurants is usually located on the top or basement floor. Many floors have coffee shops for lighter meals.

Major department stores accept credit cards and provide shipping services. Some staff will speak English. If you are having communication difficulties, someone will eventually come to the rescue. On the first floor of most stores is a general-information booth that has maps of the store in English. Because many of the stores are confusing, these guides are useful.

A trip to a Japanese department store is not merely a shopping excursion; it will also provide insights into Japanese culture.

Arrive just before opening hours, and you will witness a ceremony with all of the pomp of the changing of the guard at Buckingham Palace. At 10 AM sharp, two immaculately groomed young women will face the customers from behind the doors and bow ceremoniously, after which they open the doors. As you walk through the store, you will find that everyone is standing at attention, bowing and welcoming you. Notice the uniformity of the angle of the bows—many stores have training sessions in which new employees are taught this art.

For yet another look at Japanese culture, head for the basement floor, which usually houses food halls. Here you will see more clearly than anywhere else just what the average Japanese person eats. Needless to say, the fish section is large, and the meat prices are exorbitant. Many counters have small samples of food for the customers' benefit. If you can be discreet, or give the impression that you are planning on making a purchase, you can try some of these samples.

Ginza/Nihombashi **Matsuya.** In contrast to all the refined shopping in the Ginza/Nihombashi area, this slightly disorganized department store is a welcome change. The merchandise here is geared toward a younger crowd. The shopper with the patience to comb through the offerings will be rewarded with many good finds, particularly in the sections for young women's clothing. *3-6-1 Ginza, Chuo-ku, tel. 03/3567–1211. Open 10–7. Closed Tues.*

Matsuzakaya. Not quite as old as the nearby Mitsukoshi, this store is a mere 350 years old. It offers both Western and Japanese traditional goods. *6-10-1 Ginza, Chuo-ku, tel. 03/3572–1111. Open 10–7. Closed Wed.*

Mitsukoshi was founded in 1673 as a dry-goods store. In later years, it became one of the first stores to introduce Western merchandise to Japan. Through the years it has retained its image of quality and excellence, with a particularly strong representation of Western fashion designers, such as Chanel, Lanvin, and Givenchy. Mitsukoshi also has a fine selection of traditional Japanese goods. Catering to a distinguished clientele, it is one of Japan's most prestigious department stores. *1-7-4 Muromachi, Nihombashi, Chuo-ku, tel. 03/3241–3311. Open 10–6:30. Closed Mon.; 4-6-16 Ginza, Chuo-ku, tel. 03/3562–1111. Open 10–7.*

Takashimaya. This store has a broad and upscale appeal, with both Japanese and Western designer goods. This is where many brides-to-be shop for their weddings, because the kimono department is one of the best in Tokyo. This store also features a complete selection of traditional crafts, antiques, and curios. *4-4-1 Nihombashi, Chuo-ku, tel. 03/3211–4111. Open 10–6:30. Closed Wed.*

Wako. This is a specialty store that borders on being a department store. With a reputation for quality at high prices, Wako is particularly known for its glassware. It is also known for its very pretty saleswomen, who tend to marry well-to-do customers. *4-5-11 Ginza, Chuo-ku, tel. 03/3562–2111. Open weekdays 10–5:30, Sat. 10–6. Closed Sun.*

Shibuya **Parco.** This is actually not one store but three, all located near one another. Not surprisingly, they are owned by Seibu *(see* below). Actually, more than being department stores, Parco Part 1, Part 2, Part 3, and Part 4, as they are called, are malls that extend upward—filled with small retail stores and boutiques. Parts 1 and 4 are for a very young crowd, Part 2 is mainly designer fashions, and Part 3 is a mixture of men's and women's fashions and household goods. *14 Udagawacho, Shibuya-ku, tel. 03/3464–5111.*

Seibu. The main branch of this store is rather out of the main shopping course, in Ikebukuro. The Shibuya branch, while smaller, is more manageable than the Ikebukuro branch, where even many Japanese customers get lost. The department store is a leading member of a group of stores that owns a railway line and even a baseball team, the Seibu Lions. If you follow Japanese baseball, when the Lions win the pennant, prepare to go shopping—all of the Seibu stores have major sales on all merchandise the following day. This store has an excellent selection of household goods, from furniture to chinaware and lacquer. *21-1 Udagawa-cho, Shibuya-ku, tel. 03/3462-0111. Open 10-7. Closed Wed.*

Tokyu. This standard department store offers a good selection of imported clothing, accessories, and home furnishings. *2-24-1 Dogenzaka, Shibuya-ku, tel. 03/3477-3111. Open 10-7. Closed Tues.*

Tokyu Hands. Known commonly as just "Hands," this special-ty-hobby store is crowded any day, any time. It offers an excellent selection of carpentry tools, sewing accessories, kitchen goods, plants, and an impressive assortment of other related do-it-yourself merchandise. The toys department is chock-full of kitsch, such as plastic foods, and the stationery department has a very complete selection of Japanese papers. *12-18 Udagawa-cho, Shibuya-ku, tel. 03/5489-5111. Open 10-8. Closed 2nd and 3rd Wed. of each month.*

Shinjuku **Isetan.** Often called the "Bloomingdale's of Japan," a description that does not quite do this store justice, Isetan has become a favorite with shoppers of all ages. It features one of the most complete selections of Japanese designers in one place. For those who want distinctive designer looks but not the high prices, the store includes many spin-offs. In addition to European designers, a number of Americans are represented, such as Calvin Klein and Norma Kamali. Don't be surprised if the fit is a little different from that in America—these clothes are made specifically for the Japanese. Chinaware, stationery, furniture, you name it—all reflect the general tone of Isetan: high quality and interesting design. Look at the folk-crafts department for a small but good selection of fans, table mats, and other gifts. *3-14-1 Shinjuku-ku, tel. 03/3352-1111. Open weekdays 10-7. Closed Wed.*

Keio. This no-nonsense department store has a standard but complete selection of merchandise. *1-1-4 Nishi-Shinjuku, Shinjuku-ku, tel. 03/3342-2111. Open 10-7. Closed Thurs.*

Marui. More than a department store, Marui is a group of specialty stores that seem to be spawning all over Shinjuku. Of the most interest are the fashion stores—Young Fashion and Men's. Marui has been wildly successful for its easy credit policies. Many young people shop here simply because it is the only place where they can get credit. The merchandise is for the young and carefree. Twice a year, in February and July, prices are slashed dramatically in major clearance sales. At these times, incredible bargains can be found. If you are in the neighborhood, you will know exactly when the sales are taking place: The lines will extend into the street and around the block. (Let it not be said that Japanese men do not care about fashion. The most enthusiastic customers line up from 6AM for the men's sales.) *3-30-16 Shinjuku, Shinjuku-ku, tel. 03/3354-0101. Open 10:30-7:30. Closed Wed.*

Odakyu. Slightly snazzier than its neighboring Keio, this is a very family-oriented store. It is particularly good for children's clothing. Across the street from the main building is Odakyu Halc, which has a varied selection of home furnishings and interior goods on its upper floors. *1-1-3 Nishi-Shinjuku, Shinjuku-ku, tel. 03/3342-1111. Open 10-7. Closed Tues.*

Fitness Centers

The only health club in the city that offers short-term temporary memberships is the **Clark Hatch Fitness Center** (Azabu Towers, 2–1–3 Azabudai, Minato-ku, tel. 03/3584–4092). Tokyo does have, however, an abundance of good hotels with fine fitness facilities, important for a traveler in a city with limited greenery, much traffic, and a difficult language. These are some of the hotels:

Century Hyatt (2-7-2 Nishi-Shinjuku, Shinjuku-ku, tel. 03/ 3349–0111), on the edge of Shinjuku Chuo Koen (Shinjuku Central Park), has exercise rooms for men and women, provides jogging maps in each room, and has an Olympic-size pool on the hotel's 28th floor.

Hotel New Otani and Tower (4-1 Kioi-cho, Chiyoda-ku, tel. 03/ 3265–1111), not far from the Imperial Gardens, provides jogging route maps in each room. It also boasts four tennis courts, an outdoor Olympic-size pool, and a golf driving range. Its private health club is open to hotel guests when not being used by members.

Hotel Okura (10-4 Toranomon 2-chome Minato-ku, tel. 03/3582– 0111) is across from the U.S. Embassy and is where U.S. presidents stay. It has both indoor and outdoor six-lane 25-meter pools, a modern fitness room with an instructor, and a health-food restaurant prepares special meals. The hotel is a 15-minute jog from the Imperial Gardens.

Imperial Hotel (1-1-1 Uchisaiwaicho, Chiyoda-ku, tel. 03/3504– 1111) overlooks the Imperial Gardens and provides complimentary jogging gear to guests. It also has a glass-enclosed pool, sauna, and massage room.

Miyako Hotel Tokyo (1-1-50 Shiroganedai, Minato-ku, tel. 03/ 3447–3111) has a 25-meter four-lane indoor pool and, for a fee, fitness rooms for men and women.

Tokyo Hilton International (6-2 Nishi-Shinjuku 6-chome, Shinjuku-ku, tel. 03/3344–5111) has tennis courts, a large indoor pool, and modern exercise equipment.

Dining

by Jared Lubarsky

A resident of Tokyo, Jared Lubarsky has reviewed restaurants for the Mainichi Daily News.

At last count, there were over 187,000 bars and restaurants in Tokyo; wining and dining is a major component in the local way of life. Japanese companies nationwide spend about $65 million a day (that, at least, is what they report to the tax authorities) on business entertainment, and a good slice of that is spent in Tokyo.

That gives you your first caveat: all that spending on company tabs tends to drive up the bill, and dining out can be hideously expensive. The other side of that coin, of course, is that Tokyo's 187,000 choices also include a fair number of bargains—good cooking of all sorts, at prices the traveler on a budget can handle. The options, in fact, go all the way down to street food and yakitori joints under railroad trestles, where the Japanese go when they have to spend their own money. Food and drink, incidentally, are safe wherever you go.

Tokyo is not really an international city yet; in many ways, it is still stubbornly provincial. Whatever the rest of the world has pronounced good, however, eventually makes its way here—

sometimes in astonishing variety. (The Highlander Bar in the Hotel Okura, for example, stocks 224 different brands of Scotch whisky, 48 of them single malts.) French, Italian, Chinese, Indian, Middle Eastern, Latin, East European: it's hard to think of a national cuisine of any prominence that goes unrepresented, as Japanese chefs by the thousands go abroad, learn their craft at great restaurants, and bring it home to this city.

Restaurants in Japan naturally expect most of their clients to be Japanese, and the Japanese are the world's champion modifiers. Only the most serious restaurateurs refrain from editing out some of the authenticity of foreign cuisines; in areas like Shibuya, Harajuku, and Shinjuku, all too many of the foreign restaurants cater to students and young office workers, who come for the *fuinki* (the atmosphere) but can't make much of an informed judgment about the food. Choose your bistro or trattoria carefully, and expect to pay dearly for the real thing—but count also on the fact that Tokyo's best is world-class.

Here are a few general hints and observations. Tokyo's finest hotels also have some of the city's first-rate places to eat and drink. (Alas, this is not always the case elsewhere.) A good number of France's two- and three-star restaurants have established branches and joint ventures in Tokyo, and they regularly send their chefs over to supervise. Some of them stay, find backers, and open restaurants of their own. The style almost everywhere is *nouvelle:* small portions, with lots of kiwi fruit and raspberry sauces. More and more, you find interesting fusions of French and Japanese culinary traditions. Meals are served in poetically beautiful presentations, in bowls and dishes of different shapes and patterns; fresh Japanese ingredients, like *shimeji* mushrooms and local wild vegetables, are often used.

Tokyoites know and like French food. They have less of a chance, unfortunately, to experience the real range and virtuosity of Italian cuisine; only a small handful of the city's Italian restaurants would measure up to Italian standards. Indian food here, however, is consistently good and relatively inexpensive. Chinese food is the most consistently modified; it can be quite appetizing, but for repertoire and richness of taste, travelers coming here through Hong Kong will be disappointed. Significantly, Tokyo has no Chinatown.

A few pointers are in order on the geography of food and drink. The farther "downtown" you go—into Shitamachi, for example—the less likely you are to find the real thing in foreign cuisines. There is superb Japanese food all over the city, but aficionados of sushi swear (with excellent reason) by Tsukiji; the sushi bars in the area around the central fish market tend to have the best ingredients, serve the biggest portions, and charge the most reasonable prices. Asakusa takes pride in its tempura restaurants, but tempura is reliable almost everywhere, especially at branches of the well-established, citywide chains. Every department store and skyscraper office building in Tokyo has at least one whole floor devoted to restaurants; none of them have any great distinction, but they are all inexpensive and are quite passable places for lunch.

The quintessential Japanese restaurant is the *ryotei,* a large, villalike establishment, usually walled off from the bustle of the outside world and containing a number of small, private dining rooms. The rooms are all in traditional style, with tatami-mat floors, low tables, and a hanging scroll or a flower arrangement in the alcove. One or more of the staff is assigned to each room to serve the many dishes that comprise the meal, pour your sake, and provide light conversation. ("Waitress" is the wrong word; "attendant" is closer, but there really isn't a suitable term in English.) A ryotei is an adventure; an encounter with foods you've never seen before, and with a graceful, almost ritualized style of service that is unique to Japan and centuries old. Many parts of the city are proverbial for their ryotei; the top houses tend to be in Akasaka, Tsukiji, Asakusa and nearby Yanagibashi, and Shimbashi.

Price-category estimates for the restaurants below are based on the cost of an average meal (three courses, if Western style) per person, exclusive of drinks, taxes, and service charges; thus, a restaurant listed as **Moderate** can easily slide up a category to **Expensive** when it comes time to pay the bill.

A 3% national consumer tax is added to all restaurant bills. Another 3% local tax is added to the bill if it exceeds ¥5,000. At more expensive restaurants, a 10%–15% service charge is also added to the bill. Tipping is not necessary.

Note that business hours indicate when the last order of the evening is accepted, not when the restaurant actually closes.

The most highly recommended restaurants are indicated by a star ★.

Category	Cost*
Very Expensive	over ¥8,000
Expensive	¥5,000–¥8,000
Moderate	¥3,000–¥5,000
Inexpensive	under ¥3,000

Cost is per person without tax, service, or drinks

Credit Cards The following credit card abbreviations are used; AE, American Express; D, Discover; DC, Diners Club; MC, MasterCard; V, Visa.

Japanese

Asakusa **Tatsumiya.** This is a *ryotei* (a traditional Japanese restaurant) with at least two delightfully untraditional features: It is neither inaccessible nor outrageously expensive. Most ryotei tend to oppress the first-time visitor a little with the weight of their antiquity and the ceremonious formality of their service. Tatsumiya opened in 1980, and it takes a different attitude to the past: The rooms are almost cluttered—with antique chests, braziers, clocks, lanterns, bowls, utensils, and craftwork (some of which are even for sale). The cuisine itself follows the *kaiseki* repertoire, derived from the tradition of the tea-ceremony meal. Seven courses are offered: something raw, something boiled, something vinegared, something grilled. The atmosphere is relaxed and friendly, in the *Shitamachi* (downtown) style. *1–33–5 Asakusa, Taito-ku (nearest subway station: Asakusa), tel. 03/3842–7373. Reservations advised. Jacket*

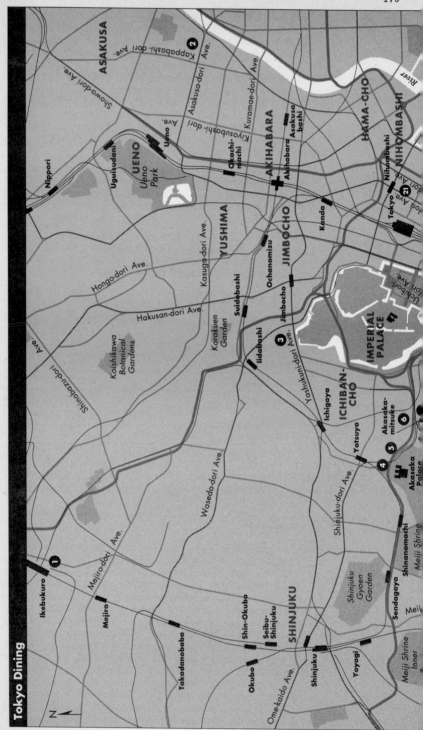

Tokyo Dining

N

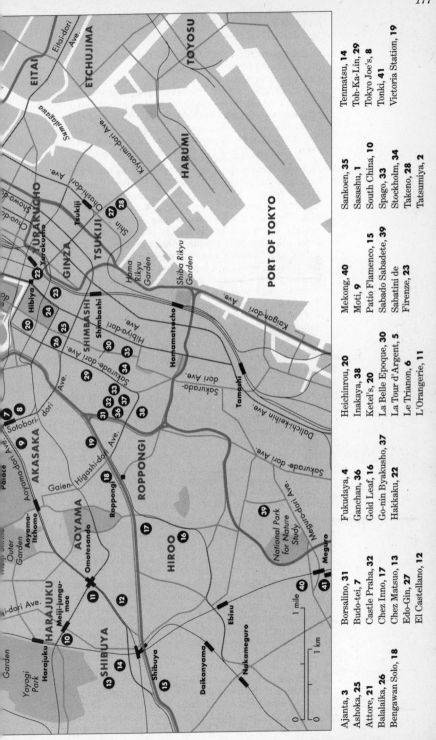

Ajanta, **3**
Ashoka, **25**
Attore, **21**
Balalaika, **26**
Bengawan Solo, **18**

Borsalino, **31**
Budo-tei, **7**
Castle Praha, **32**
Chez Inno, **17**
Chez Matsuo, **13**
Edo-Gin, **27**
El Castellano, **12**

Fukudaya, **4**
Ganchan, **36**
Gold Leaf, **16**
Go-nin Byakusho, **37**
Hakkaku, **22**

Heichinrou, **20**
Inakaya, **38**
Ketel's, **20**
La Belle Epoque, **30**
La Tour d'Argent, **5**
Le Trianon, **6**
L'Orangerie, **11**

Mekong, **40**
Moti, **9**
Patio Flamenco, **15**
Sabado Sabadete, **39**
Sabatini de
Firenze, **23**

Sankoen, **35**
Sasashu, **1**
South China, **10**
Spago, **33**
Stockholm, **34**
Takeno, **28**
Tatsumiya, **2**

Tenmatsu, **14**
Toh-Ka-Lin, **29**
Tokyo Joe's, **8**
Tonki, **41**
Victoria Station, **19**

and tie advised. No credit cards. Open noon–2 and 5–10 (enter by 8:30). Closed Mon. Expensive.

Ginza **Hakkaku.** On the second floor of the Yuraku Food Center building, crammed between other restaurants, this small bar can easily be recognized by its big red lantern hanging outside. At lunchtime, good tempura dishes are offered at very reasonable prices. There is table seating or a counter/bar; you'll be rubbing elbows with local businessmen. *Yuraku Food Center, 2–2 Nishi-Ginza, Chuo-ku (nearest subway station: Yurakucho), tel. 03/3561–0539. No reservations. Dress: casual. AE, V. Open 11–2 and 5:50–9:30. Closed Sun. Moderate.*

Ikebukuro **Sasashu.** Strictly speaking, Sasashu is not a restaurant but an
★ *izakaya*—a drinkery that specializes in sake. It's included here for two reasons. First, it stocks only the finest and rarest, the Latours and Mouton-Rothschilds, of sake: these are wines that take gold medals in the annual sake concours year after year. Second, the restaurant serves the best food of any izakaya in town—the Japanese wouldn't dream of drinking well without eating well. Sasashu is a rambling, two-story building in traditional style, with thick beams and step-up tatami floors. The specialty of the house is salmon steak, brushed with sake and soy sauce and broiled over a charcoal hibachi. *2–2 Ikebukuro, Toshima-ku (nearest subway station: Ikebukuro), tel. 03/ 3971–6796. Reservations advised, especially Jan.–Feb. Dress: informal. AE, MC, V. Open 5–9:30. Closed Sun. and holidays. Expensive.*

Meguro **Tonki.** Meguro, distinguished for almost nothing else culinary,
★ has the numero uno *tonkatsu* (deep-fried pork cutlet) restaurant in Tokyo. It's a family joint, with Formica-top tables and a fellow who comes around to take your order ahead while you're waiting in line. And people do wait in line, every night. Tonki is one of those successful places that never went conglomerate; it kept getting more popular and never got around to putting frills on what it does best: pork cutlets, soup, raw cabbage salad, rice, pickles, and tea. That's the standard course, and almost everybody orders it, with good reason. *1–1–2 Shimo-Meguro, Meguro-ku (nearest JR station: Meguro), tel. 03/ 3491–9928. No reservations; expect a 10-min. wait. Dress: informal. MC, V. Open 4–10:45. Closed Tues. Inexpensive.*

Roppongi **Inakaya.** The style here is *robatayaki* (charcoal grill cookery),
★ while the ambience is pure theater. The centerpiece is a large U-shape counter; inside, two cooks in traditional garb sit on cushions behind the grill, with a wonderful cornucopia of food spread out in front of them: fresh vegetables, fish and seafood, skewers of beef and chicken. Point to what you want, or tell your waiter (they all speak a little English); the cook will bring it up out of the pit, prepare it, and hand it across on an eight-food wooden paddle. *Reine Bldg. 1F, 5–3–4 Roppongi, Minato-ku (nearest subway station: Roppongi), tel. 03/3408–5040. No reservations; expect a ½-hour wait any evening after 7. Dress: informal. AE, DC, MC, V. Open 5 PM–5 AM. Closed New Year's Day. Very Expensive.*

Ganchan. While the Japanese prefer their sushi bars to be immaculately clean and light, they expect yakitori joints to be smoky, noisy, and cluttered—like Ganchan. There's counter seating only, for about 15; you have to squeeze to get to the chairs in back by the kitchen. The walls are festooned with festival masks, paper kites and lanterns, gimcracks of all sorts, handwritten menus, and greeting cards from celebrity patrons. Behind the counter, the cooks yell at each other, fan the grill, and serve up enormous schooners of beer. Try the *tsukune* (balls of minced chicken) and the fresh asparagus wrapped in bacon. *6–8–23 Roppongi, Minato-ku (nearest subway station: Roppongi), tel. 03/3478–0092. No reservations. Dress: informal. V. Open 6 PM–3 AM, Sun. and holidays 6–midnight. Moderate–Expensive.*

★ **Go-nin Byakusho (Five Farmers).** The specialty here is Tohoku cooking, from the northeastern part of Japan: hearty food, strong on boiled vegetables and grilled fish, served in a wonderful variety of folk-craft dishes, bowls, and baskets. The floor under the tables and counter spaces is on two levels, so you can stretch your legs. Five Farmers has a particularly fine collection of lacquer chests and other antiques from Tohoku farmhouses. Try the *oden*, a bubbling assortment of fish cakes and vegetables served in a hibachi. *Roppongi Sq. Bldg. 4F, 3–10–3 Roppongi, Minato (nearest subway station: Roppongi), tel. 03/3470–1675. No reservations. Dress: informal. AE, MC, V. Open Mon.–Sat. 11:30–2, 5–10. Closed Sun. Moderate–Expensive.*

Shibuya **Tenmatsu.** You don't really have to spend a lot of money to enjoy a first-rate tempura restaurant, and Tenmatsu proves the point. The best seats in the house, as in any *tempura-ya*, are at the immaculate wooden counter, where your tidbits of choice are taken straight from the oil and served up immediately. You also get to watch the chef in action. Tenmatsu's brand of good-natured professional hospitality just adds to your enjoyment of the meal. Here you can rely on a set menu or order à la carte from delicacies like lotus root, shrimp, *unagi* (eel), and *kisu* (a small white freshwater fish). *1–6–1 Dogenzaka, Shibuya-ku (nearest JR/subway station: Shibuya), tel. 03/3462–2815. Reservations advised for counter seating. Dress: informal. MC, V. Open 11–2:30 and 5–9. Closed Thurs. Moderate–Expensive.*

Tsukiji **Edo-Gin.** In an area that teems with sushi bars, Edo-Gin maintains its reputation as one of the best. Portions have shrunk a bit lately, but you would have to visit once every few years to notice. Edo-Gin still serves up generous slabs of fish that drape over the vinegared rice rather than perch demurely on top. The centerpiece of the main room is a huge tank, in which the day's ingredients swim about until they are required; you can't get any fresher than that! *4–5–1 Tsukiji, Chuo-ku (nearest subway station: Tsukiji), tel. 03/3543–4405. No reservations. Dress: informal. AE, MC, V. Open 11–9:30. Closed Sun. and some national holidays. Moderate–Expensive.*

★ **Takeno.** Just a stone's throw from the Tokyo central fish market, Takeno is a rough-cut neighborhood restaurant that tends to fill up at noon with the market's wholesalers and auctioneers and office personnel from the nearby Dentsu ad agency and Asahi Shimbun newspaper company. Nothing here but the freshest and the best—big portions of it, at very small tariffs. Sushi, sashimi, and tempura are the staple fare; prices are not posted because they vary with the costs that morning in the market. *6–21–2 Tsukiji, Chuo-ku (nearest subway station: Tsukiji), tel. 03/3541–8698. No reservations. Dress: informal. No credit cards. Open 11–9. Closed Sun. and holidays. Moderate–Expensive.*

Yotsuya **Fukudaya.** This is not a restaurant you decide to just try on
★ your own, even if you could: ryotei of this caliber are reluctant
to take reservations from people they don't already know. In
any case, it's far better to experience Fukudaya as somebody's
guest. That's exactly why it exists: for the Japanese, who seldom entertain at home, to host people they want to impress.
And Fukudaya *is* impressive. The atmosphere includes graceful attendants in exquisite kimonos, seats with silk cushions
and lacquered armrests, and private gardens, manicured to
perfection, with flagstone walks. A seemingly endless series of
courses is offered, with small portions of fish, seafood, and vegetables arranged like works of art. Sake is served in Imari porcelain cups—yours to take home as a parting gift. *6 Kioicho,
Chiyodu-ku (nearest subway station: Yotsuya), tel. 03/3261–
8577. Reservations required. Jacket and tie required. No credit
cards. Open Noon–10. Closed Sun. and holidays. Very Expensive.*

American

Akasaka-mitsuke **Tokyo Joe's.** The very first foreign branch of famed Miami Joe's
was in Osaka, a city where volume-for-value really counts in
the reputation of a restaurant. The Tokyo branch opened about
five years ago and upholds its reputation the same way—by
serving enormous quantities of stone crab, with melted butter
and mustard mayonnaise. The turnover here is fierce; waiters
in long red aprons scurry to keep up with it, but the service is
remarkably smooth. The crabs are flown in fresh from the Florida Keys, their one and only habitat; there are other choices on
the menu, but it's midnight madness to order anything else.
Top it all off—if you have room—with Key lime pie. *Akasaka
Eight-One Bldg. B1, 2–13–5 Nagata-cho, Chiyoda-ku (nearest
subway station: Akasaka-mitsuke), tel. 03/3508–0325. Reservations advised. Dress: informal. AE, MC, V. Open 11 AM–
11:30 PM. Very Expensive.*

Roppongi **Spago.** So far, this is the only venture overseas by trendsetting
Spago of Los Angeles. Owner-chef-celebrity Wolfgang Puck
comes periodically to Tokyo to oversee the authenticity of his
California cuisine: Will duck sausage pizza with boursin cheese
and pearl onions ever be as American as apple pie? Maybe.
Meanwhile, Spago is a clean, well-lighted place, painted pink
and white and adorned with potted palms. The service is
smooth, and the tables on the glassed-in veranda attract a fair
sample of Tokyo's Gilded Youth. *5–7–8 Roppongi, Minato-ku
(nearest subway station: Roppongi), tel. 03/3423–4025. Reservations advised. Dress: informal. AE, DC, MC, V. Open 5:30–
10:30. Closed Dec. 31 and Jan. 1. Very Expensive.*

Victoria Station. The basic elements of an American restaurant
chain are instantly recognizable and infinitely exportable: a
certain kind of packaging, a style of management, and a penchant for themes. Victoria Station's theme is the British railway system, executed with platform signs on the walls,
railroad prints, old posters, brass fittings—and even a trun-
cated caboose. The space is huge and is well laid out in "compartments," with a much-appreciated no-smoking section. The
specialty of the house is roast prime rib; the salad bar is one of
the best in town. *6–3–14 Roppongi, Minato-ku (nearest subway station: Roppongi), tel. 03/3479–4601. Dress: informal.*

AE, MC, V. Open 11 AM–midnight, Sun. and holidays 11 AM–10 PM. Moderate–Expensive.

Chinese

Harajuku **South China.** A Chinese restaurant for everybody—or at least for everybody you know, and most of their friends. South China occupies the three basement floors of a building near the main entrance to the Meiji Shrine; it can host a reception for a thousand people or a banquet for a hundred, and it boasts 13 smaller rooms for private parties. How many tons of red lacquer have gone into the decor is anybody's guess. The menu is on a commensurate scale—over 20 entries, about half of them Cantonese. South China's 35 cooks can also handle the fiery Szechuan cuisine, as well as the Peking and Shanghai styles. Specialties of the house include shark's fin with crab meat and Peking duck. *Co-op Olympia Bldg. B1-3, 6–35 Jingu-mae, Shibuya-ku (nearest JR station: Harajuku), tel. 03/3400–0031. Dress: informal. AE, MC, V. Open 11:30–9. Moderate–Expensive.*

Toranomon **Toh-Ka-Lin.** Year after year, the Hotel Okura is rated by business travelers as one of the three best hotels in the world. That judgment has relatively little to do with its architecture, which is rather understated. It has to do instead with its polish, its impeccable standards of service—and, to judge by the Toh-Ka-Lin, the quality of its restaurants. The style of the cuisine here is eclectic; two stellar examples are the Peking duck and the sautéed quail wrapped in lettuce leaf. Some people would find it a little bizarre to drink fine French wines with Chinese food, but in case you don't, the Toh-Ka-Lin also has one of the most extensive wine lists in town. *Hotel Okura, 2–04–4 Toranomon, Minato-ku (nearest subway stations: Kamiya-cho and Toranomon), tel. 03/3505–6068. Dress: informal. AE, DC, MC, V. Open 11:30–4:30 and 6–10. Expensive–Very Expensive.*

Uchisaiwai-cho ★ **Heichinrou.** A branch of one of the oldest and best restaurants in Yokohama's Chinatown. On the top floor of a prestigious office building about five minutes' walk from the Imperial Hotel, Heichinrou commands a spectacular view of Hibiya-Koen Park and the Imperial Palace grounds; much of the clientele comes from the law offices, securities firms, and foreign banks on the floors below. The decor is rich but subdued; the lighting is soft; the linen is impeccable. Heichinrou boasts a banquet room that will seat a hundred, and a "VIP Room," with separate telephone service, for power lunches. The cuisine is Cantonese, and it's first-rate. *Fukoku Seimei Bldg. 28F, 2-2-2 Uchisaiwai-cho, Chiyoda-ku (nearest subway station: Uchisaiwai-cho), tel. 03/3508–0555. Reservations advised, especially for a table by the window. Jacket and tie required. AE, DC, MC, V. Open 11–9. Closed Sun. and holidays. Very Expensive.*

Czech

Roppongi **Castle Praha.** Czechoslovakian cooking is an interesting style that tends to include elements of German cuisine: veal and pork dishes, sausages of many kinds, potatoes, and dumplings. Castle Praha is spacious and comfortable by Tokyo standards, with seating for 160 in the main section, and two rooms for private parties. The high ceilings are set off by fixtures of Czechoslovakian crystal; at night, the view of Roppongi—from 17 stories up—is superb. A violinist and accordion player stroll from table to table every evening playing a repertoire of romantic Bohemian melodies. Try the pork cutlet "Bratislava Castle," stuffed with mild sausage, grilled, and served with a paprika and sour cream sauce. *Tonichi Bldg. 17, 6–2–31 Roppongi, Minato-ku (nearest subway station: Roppongi), tel. 03/3405–2831. Reservations advised for a table by the window. Dress: informal. AE, DC, MC, V. Open 11:30–2:30 and 5–10. Expensive.*

French

Akasaka-mitsuke **La Tour d'Argent.** Pride of the New Otani Hotel since 1984, La Tour d'Argent is a worthy scion of its ritzy Parisian parent. This is a place of grand centerpieces. One of them is in the foyer, enclosed in a glass case—the entire table setting at the Café Anglais (forerunner of the original Tour d'Argent) on June 7, 1867, when Bismarck hosted a dinner for Czar Alexander II of Russia and Emperor William I of Prussia. The other, in the main dining room, is the enormous drapery-sculpted marble carving table, with its silver duck press. The specialty of the house, naturally, is *caneton:* as in Paris, you receive a card recording the number of the duck you were served. In 1921 when Crown Prince Hirohito dined at the Tour d'Argent in Paris, he had duck number 53,210; the numbers here in Tokyo began with 53,211 when the restaurant opened. *4–1 Kioi-cho, Chiyoda-ku (nearest subway station: Akasaka-mitsuke), tel. 03/3239–3111. Reservations required. Jacket and tie required. AE, DC, MC, V. Open 5:30–10:30 (enter by 9). Very Expensive.*

Le Trianon. Chef Sadao Hotta came over in 1976 from the Tokyo branch of Maxim's to open Le Trianon in the old guest house of the Akasaka Prince Hotel. The house was built for the king of Korea in the style of a French country estate, with parquet floors, lofty wooden beams, and stained-glass windows. The restaurant, which takes up the whole second floor, has seven private dining rooms; the largest will hold a party of 12. Many of the regular clientele work in the nearby centers of power: the National Diet, the Liberal-Democratic party headquarters, and the Supreme Court. *1–2 Kioi-cho, Chiyoda-ku (nearest subway station: Akasaka-mitsuke), tel. 03/3234–1111. Reservations required. Jacket and tie required. AE, DC, MC, V. Open 11:00–3 and 5–9:30. Very Expensive.*

★ **Budo-tei.** The word *budo-tei* in Japanese means "grape arbor"; this is a restaurant that prides itself on its thoughtfully chosen selection of wines. (There's one bottle on the list for about U.S. $1,400. Nobody's ordered it yet, but you never know when that sort of customer will drop in.) In fact, the Budo-tei is not as formidable as all that; it's the kind of quiet, friendly place where they remember your name when you come back a few months later and save you a piece of your favorite dessert. The decor is modest: hardwood floors, ceiling beams, and a few good pieces of sculpture and pottery highlighted in niches along the bare white walls. The three-course gourmet lunch is probably the best bargain in town. *Akasaka Tokyu Plaza 1F, 2–14–3 Nagata-cho, Chiyoda-ku (nearest subway station: Akasaka-mitsuke), tel. 03/3593–0123. AE, MC, V. Open noon–2 and 5–9. Closed Sun. and holidays. Expensive.*

Kyobashi **Chez Inno.** Chef Noboru Inoue studied his craft at Maxim's in Paris and Les Frères Troisgros in Roanne; the result is a brilliant, innovative French food. The main dining room, with seating for 28, has velvet banquettes, white stucco walls, and stained-glass windows; there's also a smaller room for private parties. Across the street is the elegant Seiyo Hotel—making this block the locus of the very best Tokyo has to offer the upscale traveler. Try the fresh lamb in wine sauce with truffles and *fines herbes*, or the lobster with caviar. *3-2-11 Kyobashi (nearest subway station: Kyobashi), tel. 03/3274-2020. AE, DC, V. Open 11:30-2 and 6-9. Sun. 6-9. Very Expensive.*

Omotesando **L'Orangerie.** This very fashion-minded restaurant is on the fifth floor of the Hanae Mori Building, just a minute's walk from the Omotesando subway station on Aoyama-dori; it's a joint venture of the original L'Orangerie in Paris and Mme. Mori's formidable empire in couture. A muted elegance marks the decor, with cream walls, deep brown carpets, and a few good paintings. Mirrors add depth to a room that actually seats only 40. The menu, an ambitious one to begin with, changes every two weeks; the salad of sautéed sweetbreads, when they have it, is excellent. The lunch and dinner menus are nouvelle and very pricey; L'Orangerie is best approached on a warm Sunday between 11 and 2:30, for the buffet brunch, when for ¥3,000 you can sit out in the courtyard, amid the grape arbors and orange trees. *Hanae Mori Bldg. 5F, 3-6-1 Kita-Aoyama, Minato-ku (nearest subway station: Omotesando), tel. 03/ 3407-7461. Reservations required. Jacket and tie required at dinner. AE, DC, MC, V. Open 11:30-2:30 and 5:30-9:30, Sun. 11 AM-2:30 PM. Lunch: Moderate–Expensive. Dinner: Very Expensive.*

Shoto **Chez Matsuo.** Shoto is the kind of area you don't expect Tokyo to have—at least not so close to Shibuya Station. It's a neighborhood of stately homes (the governor of Tokyo's, among them) with walls half a block long, a sort of sedate Beverly Hills. Chez Matsuo occupies the first floor of a lovely old two-story house in Western style. The two dining rooms look out on the garden, where you can dine by candlelight on summer evenings. Owner-chef Matsuo studied his craft in Paris, and in London as a sommelier. His food is nouvelle; the specialty of the house is Supreme of Duck. *1-23-15 Shoto, Shibuya-ku (nearest subway/JR station: Shibuya), tel. 03/3465-0610. Reservations advised. Jacket and tie required. AE, DC, MC, V. Open noon-2:30 (last order at 1) and 6-8. Closed Mon. Very Expensive.*

Toranomon **La Belle Epoque.** The flagship restaurant of the Hotel Okura, across the street from the American embassy, La Belle Epoque is a monument to the Japanese passion for art nouveau, curvilinear and graceful à la Aubrey Beardsley and Gustav Klimt, with panels of stained glass separating the tables into flowered alcoves. A chanson singer holds forth every evening to the strains of a harp and a piano. From the north dining room there's a fine view of the city, with the Eiffel-inspired Tokyo Tower in the foreground. The cuisine is French classique; chef Philippe Mouchel has three-star credentials, having trained at both the Restaurant Paul Bocuse near Lyons and the Moulin de Mougins on the French Riviera. *2-10-4 Toranomon, Minatoku (nearest subway station: Kamiyacho), tel. 03/3505-6073. Reservations required. Jacket and tie required. AE, DC, MC, V. Open 11:30-2:30 and 5:30-10. Very Expensive.*

German

Ginza   **Ketel's.** Helmut Ketel came to Tokyo and went into the food business just after World War I; the same family, by now in the third generation, has been running the business ever since. The first floor of present-day Ketel's (which opened in 1930) is a restaurant-pub with seating for about 40; the main dining room, one flight down, seats 70 in quiet comfort. Ketel's does not go overboard on atmospheric effects; the emphasis instead is on good, solid food and plenty of it. Try the sausage salad and the sauerbraten with potato dumplings. *5–5–15 Ginza, Chuo-ku (nearest subway station: Ginza), tel. 03/3571–5056. Reservations advised weekends. Dress: informal. AE, DC, MC, V. Open 11:30–2:30 and 5–9:45, Sun. and holidays 11:30–8:45. Very Expensive.*

Indian

Asakusa   **Moti.** This is the second of three Motis, at last count; the first is in Akasaka-mitsuke, and the most recent is in Roppongi. They all serve the same good Indian cooking; the Asakusa branch, right by the Chiyoda Line subway station, is the easiest to get into and the most comfortable. Moti has the inevitable Indian friezes, copper bowls, and white elephants, but the owners have not gone overboard on decor: the drawing card here is the food. They recruit their cooks in India through a member of the family who runs a restaurant in Delhi. The vegetarian dishes here, including lentils, eggplant, and cauliflower, are very good; so is the chicken *masala* style, cooked in butter and spices. *Kinpa Bldg. 3F, 2–14–31 Akasaka, Minato-ku (nearest subway station: Akasaka), tel. 03/3584–6640. Reservations advised. Dress: informal. AE, MC. Open Mon.–Sat. 11:30–10, Sun. and holidays noon–10. Inexpensive.*

Ginza   **Ashoka.** The owners of the Ashoka set out to take the high ground—to provide a decor commensurate with its fashionable address. The room is hushed and spacious; incense perfumes the air; the lighting is recessed, and the carpets thick; floor-to-ceiling windows overlook Chuo-dori, the main street of the Ginza. The waiters have spiffy uniforms; the *thali* (a selection of curries and other specialties of the house) is served up on a figured brass tray. All in all, a good show for the raj. The *khandari nan*, a flat bread with nuts and raisins, is excellent; so is the chicken tikka, boneless chunks marinated and cooked in the tandoor (clay oven). *Pearl Bldg. 2F, 7–9–18 Ginza, Chuo-ku (nearest subway station: Ginza), tel. 03/3572–2377. Reservations advised. Dress: informal. AE, DC, MC, V. Open 11:30–9, Sun. noon–7:30. Moderate–Expensive.*

Nibancho   **Ajanta.** The owner of Ajanta came to Tokyo to study electrical engineering, and he opened a small coffee shop near the Indian embassy; that was about 30 years ago. He used to cook a little for his friends; the coffee shop is now one of the oldest and best Indian restaurants in town. There's no decor to speak of; the emphasis instead is on the variety and intricacy of Indian cooking—and none of its dressier rivals can match Ajanta's menu for sheer depth. The curries are hot to begin with, but you can order them hotter. In one corner, there's a small boutique, where saris and imported Indian foodstuffs are for sale. *3–11 Nibancho, Chiyoda-ku, (nearest subway station: Kojimachi),* *tel. 03/3264–6955. Reservations advised. Dress: informal. Open 24 hrs. AE, MC, V. Inexpensive–Moderate.*

Indochinese

Meguro **Mekong.** The owner of Mekong fled Cambodia and came to Japan almost two decades ago, and he went to work for a trading company. Later, with the help of some friends, he opened a hole-in-the-wall restaurant near Ebisu, with an eclectic menu of Cambodian, Thai, and Vietnamese cooking. Mekong prospered, and in 1987 it moved to larger quarters in Meguro—but it has remained very much a plastic-tablecloth operation. The selections are few, and the service can be a little disorganized, but at these prices, nobody complains. A menu in English attests to Mekong's popularity with the local foreign community. Try the fried spring rolls and the beef with mustard-leaf pickles. *Koyo Bldg. 2F, 2–16–4 Kamiosaki, Shinagawa-ku (nearest JR station: Meguro), tel. 03/3442–6664. Reservations advised weekends. Dress: informal. V. Open noon–3 and 5–11. Inexpensive.*

Indonesian

Roppongi **Bengawan Solo.** The Japanese, whose native aesthetic demands a separate dish and vessel for everything they eat, have to overcome a certain resistance to the idea of *rijsttafel*—a kind of Indonesian smorgasbord of curries, salad, and grilled tidbits that tends to get mixed up on a serving platter. Nevertheless, Bengawan Solo has maintained its popularity with Tokyo residents for about 30 years; this is one of the oldest and most durable restaurants in the city. The parent organization, in Jakarta, supplies the periodic infusion of new staff, as needed; the company also has a thriving import business in Indonesian foodstuffs. Bengawan Solo added a back room some years ago without appreciably reducing the amiable clutter of batik pictures, shadow puppets, carvings, and pennants that make up the decor. The eight-course rijsttafel is spicy-hot and ample; if it doesn't quite stretch for two, order an extra Gado-Gado salad with peanut sauce. *7–18–13 Roppongi, Minato-ku (nearest subway station: Roppongi), tel. 03/3408–5698. Reservations advised. Dress: informal. AE, MC, V. Open Mon.–Sat. 11:30–2:30 and 5–11, holidays 11:30–2:30 and 5–10. Moderate–Expensive.*

Italian

Kyobashi **Attore.** The Italian restaurant of the elegant Seiyo Hotel
★ Attore is divided into two sections. The "casual" side, with seating for 60, has a bar counter, banquettes, and a see-through glass wall to the kitchen; the comfortable decor is achieved with track lighting, potted plants, marble floors, and Indian-looking print tablecloths. The "formal" side, with seating for 40, has mauve wall panels and carpets, armchairs, and soft, recessed lighting. On either side of the room, you get what is hands-down the best Italian cuisine in Tokyo; chef Katsuyuki Muroi trained for six years in Tuscany and northern Italy and acquired a wonderful repertoire. Try the pâté of pheasant and porcini mushrooms with white truffle cheese sauce, or the walnut-smoked lamb chops with sun-dried tomatoes. *1–11–2 Ginza Chuo-ku (nearest subway station: Ginza), tel. 03/3535–*

1111. Reservations advised. Jacket and tie suggested. AE, D, MC, V. Open 11–11. Very Expensive.

Ginza **Sabatini di Firenze.** The owner and the chef at the original Ristorante Sabatini in Florence spend half the year in Tokyo, looking after their joint venture on the seventh floor of the Sony Building, at the Sukiya-bashi intersection in the heart of the Ginza. The setting, naturally, is *très* Florentine: marble floors and sculpted paneling, beams and pilasters, sconces and chandeliers. Phalanxes of mahogany and brass service carts glide hither and yon. The antipasto of chicken livers *alla Fiorentina* and the *pennette* in cream sauce are good here. *5–3–1 Ginza, Chuo-ku (nearest subway station: Ginza), tel. 03/3573–0013. Reservations advised. Jacket and tie required. AE, DC, MC, V. Open noon–2:30 and 5:30–10. Expensive.*

Roppongi **Borsalino.** The accent at Borsalino, a five-minute walk from the Roppongi subway station, is Milanese. The decor is all right angles and designer concepts, in black and white; softened with a few tall plants and a buffet, the effect is comfortable and elegant. The buffet is the best part, holding as it does Borsalino's admirable selection of antipasti: scallops and green beans in sauce Marsala; ratatouille of diced eggplant, tomatoes, and zucchini; omelet *aux fines herbes*—a changeable feast. The *fritto misto* (mixed fry) of shrimp and squid is another must. *6–8–21 Roppongi, Minato-ku (nearest subway station: Roppongi), tel. 03/3401–7751. Reservations advised. Dress: informal. AE, DC, MC. V. Open Tues.–Sat. noon–2 and 6–10:30, Sun. 6–10:30. Closed Mon. Expensive–Very Expensive.*

Korean

Azabu Ju-ban **Sankoen.** With the embassy of the Republic of Korea a few blocks away, Sankoen is in a neighborhood thick with barbecue joints; not much seems to distinguish one from another. About seven or eight years ago, however, Sankoen suddenly caught on, and people started coming in droves. Not just the neighborhood families showed up, but also customers who worked in the media industry. The Sankoen opened a branch, then moved the main operation across the street to new, two-story quarters; late into the night, people are still waiting in line to get in. Korean barbecue is a smoky affair; you cook your own dinner—thin slices of beef and special cuts of meat—on a gas grill at your table. Sankoen also makes a great salad to go with its brisket. *1–8–7 Azabu Ju-ban, Minato-ku (nearest subway station: Roppongi), tel. 03/3585–6306. No reservations. Dress: casual. AE, V. Open 11:30 AM–1:30 AM, Sun. 11:30 AM–Midnight. Closed Wed. Expensive.*

Russian

Ginza **Balalaika.** With all the astonishing, radical changes taking
★ place these days in the Soviet Union, someone may come up with a nouvelle version of Russian cooking; until then, this is the place to go when you are truly seriously hungry. The Balalaika is by no means cheap, but it serves an excellent sort of ballast, if you have the room to stow it away. For example: *blinchiki*, small, sweet pancakes with garnishes of red and black caviar; *solyanka*, a savory broth with sausages and vegetables, which is just the thing to sop up with the Balalaika's excellent black bread; chicken Kiev; and *walenicki*, crescent-

shaped pastries filled with cheese and topped with sour cream. What atmosphere there is here is provided by the Balalaika Trio, which holds forth every evening from 6 PM. Off the main dining room, simply furnished and softly lighted, are three small banquet rooms for private parties. *5–9–9 Ginza, Chuo-ku (nearest subway station: Ginza), tel. 03/3572–8387. Reservations advised weekends. Dress: informal. AE, MC. V. Open 11–2 and 5–10.* Expensive.

Spanish

Aoyama   **El Castellano.** Owner Vicente, a native of Toledo who opened El Castellano in the late 1980s, doesn't believe in advertising; he relies instead on word of mouth. He runs a warm, friendly, cluttered place where Tokyo's Spanish residents come to eat. There's room here for perhaps 30 (elbow to elbow), and the word of mouth has gotten around well enough to pack it almost every night. No pretensions to elegance here: the once-white-washed walls are covered with messages of appreciation scrawled with felt-tip pens, accented here and there with the inevitable bullfight posters, painted crockery, and photographs of Spanish soccer teams. Try the paella and a salad, with a jug of Spanish wine: a no-frills, eminently satisfying meal. *Marusan Aoyama Bldg. 2F, 2–9–12 Shibuya, Shibuya-ku (nearest subway station: Omotesando), tel. 03/3407–7197. Reservations advised. Dress: informal. No credit cards. Open 6–10. Closed Sun. and holidays. Moderate–Expensive.*

Shibuya   **Patio Flamenco.** This establishment rates less for its cuisine (good but not memorable) than for its dinner show. Owner Yoko Komatsubara, for many years Japan's leading professional flamenco dancer, travels regularly to Spain to find the talented singers, dancers, and guitarists who hold forth here nightly. A small room with seating for perhaps 30, the Patio Flamenco makes you feel as if you have the show to yourself. The specialty of the house is the paella Valenciana, with shrimp, squid, and mussels. Performances begin at 7, 8:30, and 10; expect a separate cover charge of ¥2,500 per person for the entertainment. *2–10–12 Dogenzaka, Shibuya-ku (nearest subway/JR station: Shibuya), tel. 03/3496–2753. Reservations advised. Dress: informal. AE, MC, V. Open 5:30–11:30. Expensive–Very Expensive.*

Shiroganedai   **Sabado Sabadete.** Catalonia-born jewelry designer Mañuel Benito loves to cook. For a while, he indulged this passion by renting out a bar on Saturday nights and making an enormous *paella* for his friends; to keep them happy while they were waiting, he added a few *tapas* (Spanish-style hors d'oeuvres). Word got around: by 8 it was standing room only, and by 9 there wasn't room in the bar to lift a fork. Inspired by this success, Benito found a trendy location and opened his Sabado Sabadete full-time in 1991. The highlight of every evening is still the moment when the chef, in his bright-red Catalan cap, shouts out the Japanese equivalent of "soup's on!" and dishes out his bubbling-hot *paella.* Don't miss the *empañadas* (3-cornered pastries stuffed with minced beef and vegetables) or the *escalivada* (a Spanish ratatouille with red peppers, onions, and eggplant). *Genteel Shiroganedai Bldg. 2F, 5–3–2 Shiroganedai, Minato-ku (nearest subway Hiroo), tel. 03/3445–9353. Reservaitons advised. No credit cards. Open 6–11. Closed Sun. and holidays. Moderate–Expensive.*

Swedish

Azabu **Stockholm.** The claim to fame here, of course, is the smorgasbord—which, being unpronounceable in Japanese, is usually called a "Viking." At Stockholm, the groaning board is very good indeed: deviled eggs with caviar, herring in sour cream, shrimp, salmon, smoked hams, pâtés, roast chicken, steak tartare, salads of every description, cheeses, fruits, and pastries. You can also pass up the smorgasbord and order from an extensive dinner and à la carte menu; the specialty of the house is loin of reindeer steak. Elegance is the keynote here: deep leather chairs in the bar, brick archways, royal-blue carpeting, and tapestries on the walls. *Sweden Center Bldg. B1, 6–11–9 Roppongi, Minato-ku (nearest subway station: Roppongi), tel. 03/3403–9046. Reservations advised. Jacket and tie required. AE, DC, MC. V. Open 11–2 and 5–10. Very Expensive.*

Thai

Hiroo **Gold Leaf.** The hottest gastronomic fad in Tokyo now-a-days, literally and figuratively, is "ethnic"; in effect, that's meant a welcome profusion of good new Thai restaurants—among which the Gold Leaf (as the name implies) is probably the most elegant. Gleaming hardwood floors, black-laquered furniture, and fine linen complete the decor. The two chefs, trained in the cooking school of the famed Oriental Hotel in Bangkok, prepare a decidedly upscale version of this spicy yet subtle traditional cuisine. Try the prawn soup and the green curry with chicken. *Taisei-Koki Bldg. B1, 5–4–12 Hiroo, Shibuya-ku (nearest subway: Hiroo), tel. 03/3448–1521. Reservations advised. AE, D, MC, V. Open noon–2:30 and 6–11. Expensive.*

Lodging

When you select a hotel in Tokyo, you should focus on three factors: the hotel's location, the size of its rooms, and the costliness of the capital city. Three factors of minimal concern are cleanliness, safety, and helpful service, because these attributes may be found at practically all Japanese hotels.

The general location of the hotel has a considerable effect on the price charged for a room. Real estate throughout Tokyo is horrendously expensive, and the more central the location, the more outrageous is the cost of a square yard. Consequently, hotel prices in the central Imperial Palace and Ginza districts (in Chiyoda-ku ward) reflect the area's super-expensive real estate. On a business trip to Tokyo, it may be easier to select a hotel close to where one's business partners are located, but for the visitor, the hotel's location may be only marginally important. Bear in mind that, except for rush hour, Tokyo's subway and train system is comfortable and always rapid, inexpensive, safe, and efficient. The only drawback is that trains stop running at midnight.

As a working estimate, expect to pay about ¥350 for each square foot of your hotel guest room, with this price decreasing as you move away from central Tokyo. Because anything less than 65 square feet is small for a double room, expect around ¥23,000 for what one may consider an average room. Less expensive hotels offer fewer services but more basic furniture than do expensive hotels. This affects the cost of the guest room (on a square-foot basis) less than one might imagine. The larger hotels make more of their profits from the banquet and dining facilities than from the guest rooms. The cost of the extra services is not part of the room rate. Consequently, even though the deluxe hotels do charge a high price for the guest rooms, in one sense they give more for the yen than do the less expensive hotels. Of course, that's all very well, but one must be willing to pay ¥26,000 and more to enjoy the bargain!

In other words, rather than selecting an inexpensive hotel in a central location, consider choosing a better hotel in the suburban downtown areas of Roppongi, Shinjuku, or even Ikebukuro.

In Tokyo, hotels may be divided into six categories: first-class (full-service) hotel, business hotel, *ryokan*, capsule hotel, youth hostel, and pink hotel.

First-class (full-service) **hotels** are exactly what you would expect; most of these hotels in Tokyo tend also to be priced in the Expensive and Very Expensive categories. Virtually all of these full-service hotels have several restaurants offering different national cuisines, room service, direct-dial telephone and another phone in the bathroom, minibars, a *yakuta* (cotton bedroom kimono), concierge service, and porters. Most of the larger full-service hotels are now equipped with a business center and a physical fitness center. A few also have swimming pools. At least 90% of the guest rooms are Western style. Usually a few token Japanese rooms (tatami mats and futons) are available, and these are offered at a higher price than the other rooms.

Business hotels are found throughout Japan; Tokyo has an ample supply of them. Business hotels are designed primarily for the traveler who needs a room in which to leave his luggage, sleep, and take a quick shower or bath. Guest rooms are never large; some are tiny. A single traveler will often take a small double room rather than suffer claustrophobia in a single room. Each room has a telephone, a small writing desk, a television (sometimes the pay-as-you-watch variety), slippers, a yakuta, and a private bathroom. These bathrooms are small, plastic, prefabricated units with tub, shower, and washbasin; they are invariably scrupulously clean. The hotel's facilities are limited usually to one restaurant and a 24-hour receptionist, with no room service or porters. Since the definition of a business hotel is relative, the listing below has not separated them into a special category. However, most of those hotels listed in the Moderate price category could be classified as business hotels.

Ryokans have lost their strict meaning as a more personal hotel where guests are served dinner and breakfast in their rooms. Some are still like that, but often they mean any hostelry that offers rooms with tatami mats on the floors and futons. They may or may not serve meals in the room. Those listed in the Tokyo section do not. All are of the frugal variety, often family-run. Many of them have rooms with and without bath, and service stems from goodwill, not from professionalism. Because they have few rooms and the owners are usually on hand to answer their guests' questions, these small, relatively inexpensive ryokans are very hospitable places to stay.

Capsule hotels are literally plastic cubicles stacked on top of each other. They are used by very junior business travelers or commuters who have missed their last train home. Guests crawl into their capsule, which has a small bed, an intercom, and a radio. Washing and toilet facilities are shared. (Women are not allowed at capsule hotels.) One such place is **Green Plaza Shinjuku** (1-29-3 Kabukicho, Shinjuku-ku, tel. 03/3207–5411), two minutes from Shinjuku Station. It is the largest of its kind, with 660 sleeping slots. Checking out in the morning is pandemonium. A rush of bleary-eyed businessmen clamor to settle their accounts and scurry sheepishly to their offices. A night's stay in a capsule is about ¥4,100 a night.

Pink hotels are "love" hotels, where rooms are rented by the hour. However, after the peak time (around 9 PM), one can sometimes rent (very inexpensively, about ¥4,000–¥5,000, depending on your negotiation) a room for the entire night. Be aware, though, that if you do not leave by the agreed-upon time in the morning, your extra time will be charged at the hourly rate! They are, by the way, spotlessly clean. These pink hotels are easily recognized by their garish facades and are usually located near the entertainment quarters—several may be found in Kabukicho (Shinjuku), Roppongi, and along the suburban highways. In Shinjuku, one such hotel, the **Hotel Perrier** (2-7-12 Kabukicho, Shinjuku-ku, tel. 03/3207–5921), has rooms with saunas and various scintillating decors—one room, the Galaxy Room, has lights that turn on and off with the sound of your voice.

Separate categories are provided in this section for (1) hotels near Narita Airport and (2) youth hostels and dormitory accommodations. All rooms at the hotels listed below have private baths, unless otherwise specified.

A 3% federal consumer tax is added to all hotel bills. Another 3% local tax is added to the bill if it exceeds ¥10,000. At most hotels, a 10%–15% service charge is added to the total bill. Tipping is not necessary.

The most highly recommended accommodations are indicated by a star ★.

Category	Cost*
Very Expensive	over ¥26,000
Expensive	¥19,000–¥26,000
Moderate	¥10,000–¥19,000
Inexpensive	under ¥10,000

Cost is for a double room, without tax or service

Credit Cards The following credit card abbreviations are used: AE, American Express; DC, Diners Club; MC, MasterCard; V, Visa.

Very Expensive

Akasaka Prince Hotel. This 40-story building on top of a small hill has an eye-catching design. The architect is the well-known Kenzo Tange, who completed this ultramodern building in 1983. It may be considered either coldly sterile or classical in the simplicity of its half-moon shape; all the guest rooms (the higher up, the better) have wide, sweeping views of Tokyo. The decor of white and pastel grays in the guest rooms accentuates the light from the wide windows that run the length of the room. The result is a feeling of spaciousness, though the rooms are no larger in size than those in other deluxe hotels. A welcome feature is the dressing mirror and sink in an alcove before the bathroom. The marble and off-white reception areas on the ground floor are pristine. The hotel's whole atmosphere is crisp, but a little impersonal; it's ideal for the clusters of people at large weddings and convention parties. The Grand Ballroom can accommodate up to 2,500 guests. *1-2 Kioi-cho, Chiyoda-ku, Tokyo 102 (nearest subway: Akasaka-mitsuke), tel. 03/ 3234-1111. 761 rooms, most Western style. Facilities: 12 restaurants, including the Blue Gardenia on the 40th floor, which serves Continental food; the Top of Akasaka for cocktails, with spectacular views of Tokyo's skyline; and a French restaurant, Le Trianon, in the old gatehouse to the side of the hotel. Also massage service, dry cleaning, 30 meeting rooms, travel desk, banquet facilities. AE, DC, MC, V.*

ANA Hotel Tokyo. In the proximity of the U.S. Embassy, the ANA Hotel arrived on the Tokyo scene in 1986. The first-floor marble lobby clamors for glitter and fashion; it covers a large area split by a coffee shop, dining lounge, escalator, and reception desks, with a central fountain as its focal point. Guest rooms are bright and airy; the 34th floor serves as the concierge floor, with a separate breakfast room and evening cocktail lounge for its guests. Throughout the hotel, tasteful vases and artwork help to offset some of the coldness of the marble interior. *12-33 Akasaka 1-chome, Minato-ku, Tokyo 107 (nearest subways: Kamiyacho and Toranomon), tel. 03/3505-1111. 900 rooms. Facilities: gym, outdoor pool, men's sauna, business center, shopping arcade, travel desk, beauty salon, Chinese, French, and Japanese restaurants, 3 bar lounges, and the Astral lounge on the top (37th) floor for superb views over the city. AE, DC, MC, V.*

Asakusa View Hotel. If you want an elegant place to stay in the heart of Tokyo's old Asakusa area—actually resurrected after the World War II fire bombings—then this hotel is the only choice. A smart marble lobby features a harpist in the tea lounge, and expensive boutiques line the second floor. The standard pastel guest rooms are similar to what you find in all modern Tokyo hotels, but you also have access to communal *hinoki* (Japanese cypress) bathtubs that look onto a sixth-floor Japanese garden. *3-17-1 Nishi-Asakusa, Taito-ku, Tokyo 111 (nearest subway: Tawaramachi), tel. 03/3847-1111. 350 rooms, mostly Western style. Concierge floor. Facilities: Chinese, French, Italian, and Japanese restaurants, coffee lounge, outdoor pool, a bar that keeps your personal bottle, gym and fitness center, banquet rooms. AE, DC, MC, V.*

★ **Capitol Tokyu Hotel.** The Capitol Tokyu was once the Hilton, before the latter moved to its new location in Shinjuku in 1984; the lease reverted to the Tokyu chain. It is now Tokyu's flagship hotel. Though it is only 26 years old, it has a feeling of being a grand hotel of a past era, which can be a welcome change to the glitter of Tokyo's newer hotels. The hotel is also relatively small by Tokyo's standards, and, with close to two permanent staff members to every guest, service is excellent. Perhaps that is why the hotel has such a repeat trade among foreign businessmen. Guest-room furnishings (dark wood furniture) have a tra-

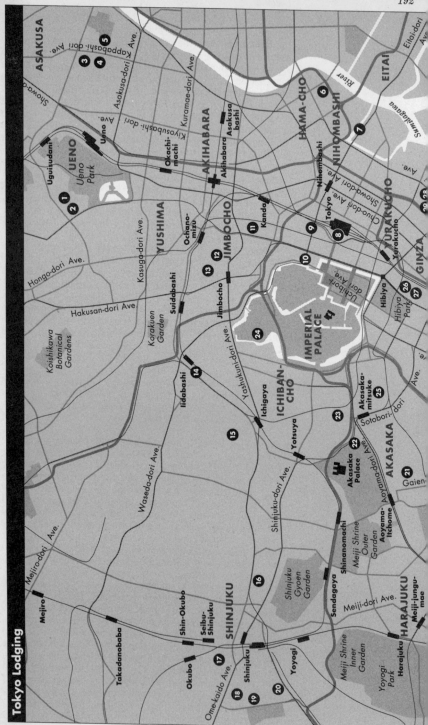

193

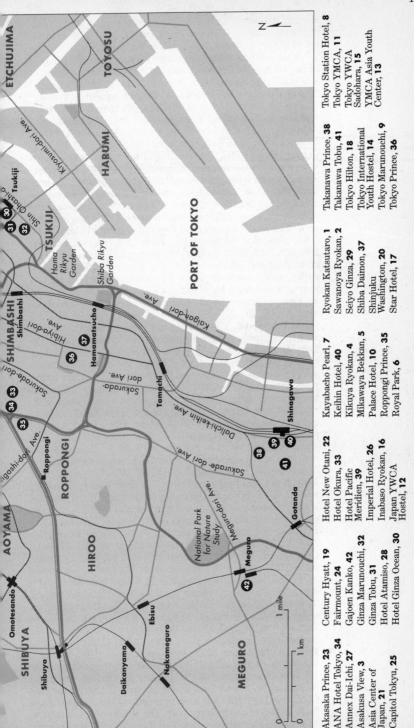

Akasaka Prince, 23
ANA Hotel Tokyo, 34
Annex Dai-Ichi, 27
Asakusa View, 3
Asia Center of
Japan, 21
Capitol Tokyu, 25

Century Hyatt, 19
Fairmount, 24
Gajoen Kanko, 42
Ginza Marunouchi, 32
Ginza Tobu, 31
Hotel Atamiso, 28
Hotel Ginza Ocean, 30

Hotel New Otani, 22
Hotel Okura, 33
Hotel Pacific
Meridien, 39
Imperial Hotel, 26
Inabaso Ryokan, 16
Japan YWCA
Hostel, 12

Kayabacho Pearl, 7
Keihin Hotel, 40
Kikuya Ryokan, 4
Mikawaya Bekkan, 5
Palace Hotel, 10
Roppongi Prince, 35
Royal Park, 6

Ryokan Katsutaro, 1
Sawanoya Ryokan, 2
Seiyo Ginza, 29
Shiba Daimon, 37
Shinjuku
Washington, 20
Star Hotel, 17

Takanawa Prince, 38
Takanawa Tobu, 41
Tokyo Hilton, 18
Tokyo International
Youth Hostel, 14
Tokyo Marunouchi, 9
Tokyo Prince, 36

Tokyo Station Hotel, 8
Tokyo YMCA, 11
Tokyo YWCA
Sadohara, 15
YMCA Asia Youth
Center, 13

ditional Western feel, but the shoji screens add a warm lightness to the ambience. As an extra benefit, some of the rooms, no. 1039, for example, look onto the Hie Jinja Shrine. To the left of the lobby is a small garden with a pond; two of the hotel's dining rooms (the Origami breakfast café and the Tea Lounge) look onto it (a pleasant sight to start the day at breakfast). *10-3 Nagatacho 2-chome, Chiyoda-ku, Tokyo 100 (nearest subway: Kokkai-gijidomae), tel. 03/3581–4511. 490 rooms. Facilities: 8 restaurants (including Chinese, Continental, French, and Japanese), bars, business center, steam bath, massage in one's room, outdoor pool, small shopping arcade. AE, DC, MC, V.*

Century Hyatt Hotel. This member of the Hyatt international hotel chain has the trademark atrium-style lobby—seven stories high, with open-glass elevators soaring upward and three huge chandeliers suspended from above. The larger rooms are arranged to offer the semblance of a separate sitting area, and all rooms are decorated in modern pastels. The single rooms tend to be small and lack good views from their windows. *2-7-2 Nishi-Shinjuku, Shinjuku-ku, Tokyo 160 (nearest subway: Shinjuku), tel. 03/3349–0111. 762 rooms, including a few luxurious Japanese-style rooms, 1- and 2-bedroom Western-style suites, and 2 concierge floors. Facilities: indoor pool, 12 restaurants and bars; the Hyatt places emphasis on its cuisine, with special gourmet weeks supervised by visiting international chefs. AE, DC, MC, V.*

Ginza Tobu Hotel. This shining new (opened late 1987) hotel, with its relatively reasonable prices, friendly service, and comfortably sized rooms, makes it worth considering as a deluxe hotel in the high-rent district of Ginza. The extra ¥3,000 for a guest room on the concierge floors provides a much larger room; breakfast, afternoon tea, and complimentary cocktails in the concierge lounge; and extras, such as a terry-cloth bathrobe and hair dryers. Especially useful is the hotel's 24-hour coffeehouse restaurant. *6-13-10 Ginza, Chuo-ku, Tokyo 104 (nearest subway: Higashi-Ginza), tel. 03/3546–0111. 106 rooms, all Western style. 2 concierge floors. Facilities: 24-hour coffeehouse, French restaurant, excellent Japanese restaurant (The Muraki), business center. AE, DC, MC, V.*

Hotel New Otani Tokyo and Tower. The New Otani is virtually a town in itself. When all the rooms (almost 2,100) are occupied and all the banquet facilities are in use, the traffic flow in and out of the restaurants, lounges, and shopping arcades is like rush hour at a busy railway station. The hotel's redeeming feature is its peaceful, 10-acre manicured garden. *4-1 Kioi-cho, Chiyoda-ku, Tokyo 102 (nearest subway: Akasaka-mitsuke), tel. 03/3265–1111. 2,051 rooms, 30 on the 21st fl. for women only. Facilities: outdoor pool, spa facilities (includes a sports and beauty complex), rooms for the physically handicapped, 24-hour child-care facilities, Christian chapel, shopping arcades, banking facilities, numerous restaurants (including Japan's first Trader Vic's and the revolving Sky Lounge, which completes one revolution every hour). AE, DC, MC, V.*

★ **Hotel Okura.** As one of the most prestigious of Tokyo hotels, the Okura is continually striving to maintain the position at the top. The Okura is understated in its sophistication, except for its vast lobby. Ever since it was completed just before the 1964 Olympics, the Okura has been a favorite of the diplomatic and knowledgeable business traveler. The atmosphere is traditional, even old-fashioned to some, and the emphasis is on exemplary service. The spacious guest rooms are tastefully furnished, including sliding frosted shoji screens in front of the windows, which permits a relaxing light to fill the room. Remote-control draperies, hair dryers, and terry-cloth bathrobes are but a few of the extras that come with the room. The odd-numbered rooms, 871–889 inclusive, look onto a small Japanese landscaped garden. On the hotel grounds is the Okura Art Museum, in a traditional Japanese building, with exhibits of antique porcelain, mother-of-pearl, and ceramics. A tea ceremony is held every day 11 AM–noon and 1 PM–5 PM. In recent years, the Okura has added the South Wing, which is slightly detached from most of the hotel's facilities; the main building is preferable. *10-4 Toranomon 2-chome, Minato-ku, Tokyo 105 (nearest subways: Kamiyacho and Toranomon), tel. 03/3582–0111. 980 rooms (including 83 suites and 11 superb Japanese-style rooms). Facilities: gym, indoor (heated) and outdoor pools, steam bath, masseur, business center, 8 restaurants (French, Chinese, Japanese, etc.), extensive banquet facilities. AE, DC, MC, V.*

Hotel Pacific Meridien. Located on grounds that were once part of the imperial family's estate, the Pacific Meridien is across from the Shinagawa Station and glitters with glass and marble. The hotel markets itself to convention groups and to business travelers who wish to be in this area of Tokyo. Decor is pastel and lilac all the way to the Sky Lounge on the 30th floor, which has views over Tokyo Bay. The coffee lounge on the ground floor offers a tranquil view of the gardens. *3-13-3 Takanawa, Minato-ku, Tokyo 108 (nearest JR station: Shinagawa), tel. 03/3445–6711. 954 rooms. Facilities: 9 restaurants and bars, outdoor pool, shopping arcade (good bookstore with English-language books), business center, banquet halls, parking garage, large Japanese garden. AE, DC, MC, V.*

Imperial Hotel. The location of this prestigious establishment could not be better—in the heart of central Tokyo, between the Imperial Palace and Ginza. You can exit from the rear of the hotel and be in the center of the city's shopping and restaurant district. If you exit from the front of the hotel and walk five minutes, you can begin jogging around the grounds of the Imperial Palace. Guest rooms are newly furnished with the choicest rooms high up (on the 30th floor) in the New Tower; these afford views of the Imperial Palace. The lobby has a vast lounge area for watching Tokyo's beautiful people. The shopping arcade has prestigious boutiques, while the restaurants are some of Tokyo's finest and most sophisticated. A particularly memorable place to meet acquaintances before dinner is the Old Imperial Bar, with artifacts from the former Imperial building, designed by Frank Lloyd Wright. From its outset (the Imperial opened its doors in 1891), the hotel has been justly proud of its Western-style facilities and Japanese service. Now, with its new tower addition, the hotel is a vast complex, but it still retains its personalized service. *1-1 Uchisaiwaicho 1-chome, Chiyoda-ku, Tokyo 100 (nearest subways: Hibiya and Yurakucho), tel. 03/3504–1111. 1,135 rooms, which range from standard twin size to suites that are larger than many homes. Facilities: indoor pool, fitness center, and masseur on the 20th floor; 64 boutiques in the shopping arcade; business center; limousine service, 21 restaurants and bars, though none stays open 24 hours a day. AE, DC, MC, V.*

★ **Palace Hotel.** This is a less expensive alternative to the Imperial Hotel for anyone wanting a deluxe hotel near the Imperial

Palace. Service is extremely helpful and professional; half the staff has been with the hotel for more than 10 years. The location is as close to the Imperial Palace as one could be; only a water-filled moat separates the hotel from the palace grounds. On the other hand, it is a taxi or subway ride to the bright lights of Ginza, or anywhere else, for that matter. The sedate, calm atmosphere of the hotel reflects its over 50 years as a leading Tokyo accommodation. The guest rooms are reasonably spacious; those on the upper floors facing the Imperial Palace are definitely preferred. The hotel's public areas are rectangular and uninspiring. Nevertheless, the hotel's location and good value make it particularly attractive to businessmen who want to be close to downtown. *1-1-1 Marunouchi, Chiyoda-ku, Tokyo 100 (nearest subway: Tokyo), tel. 03/3211–5211. 404 rooms. Facilities: business center, shopping arcade, 7 restaurants (including French, Japanese, and Chinese), 3 bars, 2 lounges. AE, DC, MC, V.*

★ **Seiyo Ginza.** Tokyo's most expensive hotel has set out to challenge the elite Imperial and Okura. However, instead of competing on the basis of traditional elegance, the Seiyo is sophisticated, modern, and international. It is designed for the generous expense account and for those who care less about being in Japan and more about Western pampering and the latest technology. With only 80 rooms and a staff of 240, the emphasis is on personal service. There is no lobby with registration and cashier desks; instead, all that is done in a personal reception room with your private secretary. Each guest is assigned a "personal secretary," who checks you in and will make all your arrangements during your stay in Tokyo. Separate telephones in the bedrooms have a direct line to the secretary. Laser discs are available for use in the bedroom, and television sets have VCRs with access to a 200-title film library. It's shockingly expensive, between ¥45,000 and ¥100,000 for a double room. *1 Ginza, Chuo-ku, Tokyo 104, (nearest subway station: Ginza), tel. 03/3535–1111. 80 rooms. Facilities: 4 restaurants (including the Pastorale, which may rank as one of Tokyo's best and most expensive—about ¥60,000 for two—French restaurants), business services, bathrooms with steam baths, fitness center. AE, DC, MC, V.*

Takanawa Prince Hotel. This hotel is separated from its big brother, the New Takanawa Prince, by a beautiful garden that is part Western and part Japanese. This Prince establishment is more geared to the individual traveler than to large groups, though the lobby's design is the large, open plan so favored by the Japanese. Guest rooms are fairly compact, and those overlooking the garden are the best. *13-1 Takanawa 3-chome, Minato-ku, Tokyo 108 (nearest JR station: Shinagawa), tel. 03/3447–1111. 416 rooms, each with a balcony, and 18 tatami suites. Facilities: 2 pools, 6 restaurants and bars, shopping arcade. AE, DC, MC, V.*

Tokyo Hilton Hotel. Built in 1984, the Hilton is the newest of the three deluxe Shinjuku skyscraper hotels and is the largest Hilton in Asia. The Hilton is frequented by Western businessmen. The atmosphere of its public areas is one of impersonal efficiency. However, the guest rooms offer good views of the other Shinjuku skyscrapers and benefit from using shoji screens instead of curtains. The Imari Room, with its displays of museum-quality traditional pottery, is one of Tokyo's more elegant places to dine. *6-2 Nishi-Shinjuku 6-chome, Shinjuku-ku, Tokyo 160 (nearest subway: Shinjuku), tel. 03/3344–5111. 839* *rooms, including the concierge floor. Facilities: sauna, indoor and outdoor pools, business center, small shopping arcade, beauty salon, 8 restaurants (including American, Mediterranean, Chinese, Continental, and Japanese), disco, nightclub cabaret. AE, DC, MC, V.*

Tokyo Prince Hotel. This square, squat building, which overlooks the garden of Shiba-Koen Park and the famed Zojoji Temple, appears larger than it is, with a wide-open lobby and unappealing furniture that accentuates the hotel's lack of warmth and personality. You may want to leave this member of the Prince chain to the tour groups that tend to patronize the hotel. *3-1 Shiba-koen 3-chome, Minato-ku, Tokyo 105 (nearest subway: Onarimon), tel. 03/3432–1111. 484 rooms. Facilities: pool; shopping arcade; French, Chinese, and Japanese restaurants; American snack-café; 4 cocktail lounges. AE, DC, MC, V.*

Expensive

Annex Dai-Ichi Hotel. This hotel is not, in fact, an annex at all. The old Shimbashi Dai-Ichi Hotel next door has been slated for demolition; the 20-story Annex, built in 1989, is the first of three new hotels planned for this strategic location and operated separately. The lobby is in the geometric black and white of current fashion. The rooms are designed in coordinated pastels, grays, and beige—with a sense of luxury provided by touches like marble washstands, full-length double wardrobe mirrors, and (on the Hibiya side of the building) extra-large desks of walnut and brass, running the length of the window. *1-5-2 Uchisaiwai-cho, Chiyoda-ku, Tokyo 100 (nearest JR station: Shimbashi), tel. 03/3503–5611. 160 double rooms, 10 suites. Facilities: exclusive guest lounge. AE, DC, MC, V.*

Ginza Marunouchi Hotel. This establishment opened in 1976 and immediately became popular with foreign visitors because of its price and its location to the side of Ginza's high-rent district. Recent redecorating has improved this small hotel. Guest rooms are small, compact, and clean. Except when a large tour group arrives, the lobby/lounge area invites a shared fellowship among the guests. *1-12 Tsukiji 4-chome, Chuo-ku, Tokyo 104 (nearest subway: Higashi-Ginza), tel. 03/3543–5431. 110 rooms. Facilities: Western restaurant. AE, DC, MC, V.*

★ **Hotel Atamiso.** This hotel is not well known to many Westerners; its location, however, is convenient (near Ginza area), and the staff's friendliness (marginal English is spoken) makes this place a real find. Formerly a ryokan, the Atamiso was transformed into a Western hotel in 1984 but has kept its Japanese appreciation of hospitality. A recent change of ownership has not affected this lodging's personal approach. For the size of the rooms, the hotel is an extremely good value. The hotel is too small to computerize its guests' names, so the receptionist remembers names of guests instead of consulting a computer screen. *4-14-3 Ginza, Chuo-ku, Tokyo 104 (nearest subway: Higashi-Ginza), tel. 03/3541–3621. 76 rooms (singles, doubles, and Japanese-style rooms). Facilities: Swiss and Japanese restaurants. AE, DC, MC, V.*

Roppongi Prince Hotel. The most memorable feature of the Roppongi Prince is a swimming pool in its open central courtyard. A solar mirror directs sunshine into the courtyard, and the pool's surrounding decks have their floors heated. The sides of the pool are made of transparent Plexiglas. The swimmer, above and below water, becomes the visual entertainment for voyeurs sitting around the pool or in one of the two café/restaurants off to the side. The remaining facilities, including the rooms, are functional rather than memorable. However, for the price, the rooms are relatively spacious. In a good location, the hotel is in walking distance of either the IBM building (for business) or Roppongi (for partying). *2-7 Roppongi 3-chome, Minato-ku, Tokyo 106 (nearest subway: Roppongi), tel. 03/ 3587-1111. 221 rooms. Facilities: Italian, Western, and Japanese restaurants; discounted tickets to Roppongi's discos; pool. AE, DC, MC, V.*

Royal Park Hotel. This hotel would recommend itself if only for the connecting passageway to the Tokyo City Air Terminal where you can complete all your check-in procedures before you climb on the bus for Narita Airport. There's no luxury—especially at the end of an intensive business trip—like being able to pack, ring for the bellhop, and not have to touch your baggage again until it comes off the conveyor belt back home. Built in 1989, the 20-story Royal Park is well-designed: The large, open lobby has perhaps a bit more marble than it needs, and the inevitable space-age chandelier, but this is offset by wood-paneled columns, brass trim, and lots of comfortable lounge space. Guest rooms, done in coordinated neutral grays and browns, have good proportions; deluxe twins have handsome writing tables instead of built-in desktops. Ask for a room on one of the Executive Floors (16F-18F) with a northeast view of the Sumida River; another good option would be a room lower down (6F-8F) on the opposite side, overlooking the hotel's delightful 5th-floor Japanese garden. *2-1-1 Nihonbashi-Kakigaracho, Chuo-ku, Tokyo 103 (nearest subway: Suitengumae), tel.03/3667-1111. 441 rooms, 9 suites. Facilities: 3 restaurants, shops. AE, DC, MC, V.*

Tokyo Marunouchi Hotel. In business since 1924, the Tokyo Marunouchi has rooms that were last refurbished in 1987; these have seen a lot of traffic since then. This hotel is very popular with Westerners, and the staff have come to anticipate their needs. Within two blocks of Tokyo Station, three blocks from the Imperial Palace, and two subway stops from Ginza, the lodging is in the prime-rent district. The guest rooms tend to be a little drab but are (for Tokyo) of reasonable size; they have more individuality than the boxlike rooms in other modern Tokyo hotels. *1-6-3 Marunouchi, Chiyoda-ku, Tokyo 100 (nearest subway: Tokyo), tel. 03/3215-2151. 210 rooms. Facilities: bar, coffeehouse, Western restaurant. AE, DC, MC, V.*

Tokyo Station Hotel. Above Tokyo Station, this building is part of Tokyo's heritage. It was recently saved from the wrecker's ball by preservationists and is currently undergoing renovation. For the moment, this hotel should only be recommended for an overnight stay between trains, though it can be a useful place for breakfast before setting out on a journey. *1-9-1 Marunouchi, Chiyoda-ku, Tokyo 100 (nearest subway: Tokyo), tel. 03/3231-2511. 170 rooms, not all with bath. AE, DC, MC, V.*

Moderate

★ **Fairmount Hotel.** Nostalgia buffs will love the Fairmount; here's a place that underwent a major renovation in 1988 and the water pipes are still exposed. Neatly wrapped and painted, of course, but exposed just the same. In relentlessly high-tech

Tokyo, you'd have to look long for a hotel with pull-chain venti-
lators and real tile in the bathrooms; the Fairmount has all that
and furniture (a little chipped) that Sears & Roebuck must have
phased out of the catalog in 1955. The hotel isn't seedy, mind
you, just old (it was built in 1951) and a bit set in its ways. The
best thing about the seven-story Fairmount is its frontage on
the park that runs along the east side of the Imperial Palace
grounds; rooms facing the park have a wonderful view of the
moat and Chidoriga-fuchi pond, where Tokyo couples take
rented rowboats out on summer Sunday afternoons. *2-1-17
Kudan-Minami, Chiyoda-ku Tokyo 102 (nearest subway:
Kudanshita), tel. 03/3262–1151. 205 rooms, 3 suites. Facilities:
restaurant, bar. AE, DC, MC, V.*

Gajoen Kanko Hotel. After a major renovation in 1986, this
pre–World War II hotel has made a comeback and offers good
value in a residential area, away from the noise and bustle of
Tokyo's traffic. The Gajoen Kanko is full of old prints, scrolls,
and decor that is oriental rococo. The hotel has grown since its
days as an occupation-era accommodation by the addition of an
annex. This place may not appeal to all, but it is one of the very
few Tokyo accommodations that have character and individuality. *1-8-1 Shimo-Meguro, Meguro-ku, Tokyo 153 (nearest JR
station: Meguro), tel. 03/3491–0111. 104 rooms. Facilities:
Chinese and Western restaurants. AE, DC, MC, V.*

★ **Hotel Ginza Ocean.** This delightful small hotel is around the
corner from the Kabuki-za Theater in the Ginza section. The
rooms, though not large, are comfortable. Virtually no English
is spoken here, but sign language serves to communicate basic
needs. *7-18-15 Ginza, Chuo-ku, Tokyo 104 (nearest subway:
Higashi-Ginza), tel. 03/3545–1221. 32 Western-style rooms.
Facilities: excellent Japanese restaurant, Matsuryu. AE, MC,
V.*

Shiba Daimon Hotel. For a moderately priced hotel that is popular with in-the-know Japanese, try this small establishment
located close to the Zenoji Temple. The smart, clean rooms are
no smaller than what you usually find in Tokyo hotels. Service
is politely Japanese—speak a couple of words of the native
tongue, and the staff is even friendlier. Shiba Daimon does not
cater to the foreign tourist, and there are no English-language
brochures available, but the staff is willing to help when they
can. A good restaurant situated on the ground floor serves
breakfast and then Chinese cuisine in the evening. *2-3-6 Shiba-
nole, Minato-ku, Tokyo 105 (nearest subways: Daimon and
Hamamatsu-cho), tel. 03/3431–3716. 70 rooms. Facilities: restaurant. AE, DC, MC, V.*

Shinjuku Washington Hotel. This is truly a business hotel,
where service is computerized as much as possible. On the
third-floor lobby, automated check-in and check-out systems
are available; you are assigned a room and provided with a plastic card that allows entry to your small room and access to the
minibar. A few staff members in the lobby explain the process,
but after that you are on your own. *3-2-9 Nishi-Shinjuku,
Shinjuku-ku, Tokyo 160 (nearest subway: Shinjuku), tel. 03/
3343–3111. 1,300 rooms. Facilities: refrigerator, minibar, TV,
in rooms. AE, DC, MC, V.*

★ **Star Hotel.** This small, friendly hotel has rates more reasonable
than many in the area. The staff speak only Japanese but are
sympathetic to sign language. The rooms are clean, though not
spacious; a small, pleasant restaurant serves Japanese and
Western food. It lacks the amenities of doormen, bellhops,

telex machines, and the countless bars of the larger hotels, but the size of the hotel allows the front-desk manager to remember your name without the help of a computer. *7-10-5 Nishi-Shinjuku, Shinjuku-ku, Tokyo 160 (nearest subway: Shinjuku), tel. 03/3361–1111. 80 Western-style rooms. Facilities: Japanese–Western restaurant. AE, DC, MC, V.*

Takanawa Tobu Hotel. Across the street from the monolithic New Takanawa Prince and a five-minute walk from the Shinagawa Station, the hotel offers good value. The guest rooms are on the small side, and no proper lobby sitting area is available, but the virtues are a welcoming staff (who speak modest English) and a friendly bar lounge. *7-6 Takanawa 4-chome, Minato-ku, Tokyo 108 (nearest JR station: Shinagawa), tel. 03/3447–0111. 201 rooms. Facilities: bar; small Western restaurant, the Boulogne. AE, DC, MC, V.*

Inexpensive

Asia Center of Japan. This hotel seems to host more foreign guests than many other establishments. It is popular for its central location, only a 15-minute walk to Roppongi for a cosmopolitan night of entertainment. The rooms are basic, clean, small, and not too well soundproofed, but you get a good value for what you pay. *10-32 Akasaka 2-chome, Minato-ku, Tokyo 107 (nearest subways: Roppongi and Aoyama Itchome; turn left out of the subway up Aoyama-dori and right at the Akasaka Post Office. The hotel is just down the first left-hand side street), tel. 03/3402–6111. 173 Western-style rooms; some with private bath. Facilities: cafeteria-style dining room, bar, garden patio. No credit cards.*

Inabaso Ryokan. Close to all the action offered by Shinjuku, this inn has become a popular rest stop for foreigners, in part because all the rooms have a private bath and a refrigerator. *5-6-13 Shinjuku, Shinjuku-ku, Tokyo 160 (nearest subway: Shinjuku Sanchome; a 10-minute walk from the station, on the left-hand side of Yasukuni-dori Ave., behind a gas station), tel. 03/3341–9581. 11 tatami rooms and 2 Western style. Facilities: refrigerator, television, air-conditioning. Continental and Japanese breakfasts. AE, V.*

Kayabacho Pearl Hotel. The rooms are strictly utilitarian, but the price is low, unless you sleep late; the staff adds a ¥2,000 charge for late check-out (after 10 AM). The hotel is located just across the bridge from Tokyo City Air Terminal, a five-minute walk from exit number 3 or 4 of Kayabacho Station on the Hibiya or Tozai Line. *1-2-5 Shinkawa, Chuo-ku, Tokyo 104 (nearest subway: Kayabacho), tel. 03/3553–2211. 270 rooms, all with phone and television. Facilities: restaurant, open 7–midnight. AE, MC, V.*

Keihin Hotel. Directly across the street from Shinagawa Station, the Keshin is best described as a business hotel. The building is small, as are the rooms, but the staff are personable, and the manager speaks English enthusiastically and enjoys having Westerners stay. For a modest hotel, the Keshin is a good value, due to its location in the low-rent district of Shinagawa. *4-10-20 Takanawa, Minato-ku, Tokyo 108 (nearest JR station: Shinagawa), tel. 03/3449–5711. 65 Western-style rooms. Facilities: Japanese restaurant; many other cafés (Western and Japanese) nearby. AE, MC, V.*

Kikuya Ryokan. This small inn in the Asakusa district is a 10-minute walk from the Sensoji Temple. Be warned, the inn locks its doors at midnight, and everything here is midget-sized. *2-18-9 Nishi-Asakusa, Taito-ku, Tokyo 111 (nearest subway: Tawaramachi; then walk 2 blocks up Kokusai-dori Ave., take a left, and just before Kappabashi-dori Ave., the ryokan is on the left-hand side), tel. 03/3841–6404. 8 tatami rooms, 4 with private bath. Facilities: air-conditioning, Continental breakfast only. AE, MC, V.*

Mikawaya Bekkan. This small ryokan resembles a boarding house; its tiny tatami-mat rooms have noisy kerosene heaters during the winter and cranky air-conditioning units during the summer. The shared washing facilities are compact, and the communal bath has hot water between 4 and 8 PM. Doors to the inn close at 11 PM. The owners are not very helpful, so don't expect much in the way of hospitality. Still, the rooms are clean, the price is inexpensive for Tokyo, and the location—right by Asakusa's Sensoji Temple—is ideal for exploring the area. Japanese-style dinner is optional, though you are expected to take either a Western or Japanese breakfast. *1-31-11 Asakusa, Taito-ku, Tokyo 111 (nearest subway: Asakusa on the Ginza Line; walk to the Kaminarimon Gate and take a right up the stall-covered Nakamise toward the Sensoji Shrine. The inn will be down the fourth alley on the left), tel. 03/3843–2345. 12 rooms. Facilities: restaurant for breakfast and dinner, air-conditioning. AE, MC, V.*

Ryokan Katsutaro. This is a simple, economical Japanese hotel that is a five-minute walk from Ueno Park and a 10-minute walk from the National Museum. The lodging is small, with the quietest rooms in the back, away from the main street. *4-16-8 Ikenohata, Taito-ku, Tokyo 110 (nearest subway: Nezu; leave by the Ikenohata exit, cross the road, take the street running northeast, go right at the "T" junction, and the ryokan is 25 yards on the left-hand side of Dobutsu-en-Uramon-dori Ave.), tel. 03/3821–9808. 7 rooms, 4 with private bath. Facilities: coin-operated TV. Continental breakfast. AE, MC, V.*

★ **Sawanoya Ryokan.** Sawanoya is situated in a quiet area to the northwest of Ueno Park; the residential locale and the hospitality of the ryokan make you feel at home in traditional Tokyo. The owners truly welcome travelers; they help them plan trips and arrange future accommodations. No dinner is offered, but breakfast (Continental or Japanese) is available at an extra charge. *2-3-11 Yanaka, Taito-ku, Tokyo 110 (nearest subway: Nezu; walk 275 yards north along Shinobazu-dori Ave., take the street on the right, and the Sawanoya is 165 yards on the right), tel. 03/3822–2251. 12 rooms, only 2 with private bath. Facilities: breakfast, pay TV, air-conditioning. AE.*

Hostels and Dormitory Accommodations

Japan YWCA Hostel. All rooms are for women only, without private bath. *4-8-8 Kudan Minami, Chiyoda-ku, Tokyo 102, tel. 03/3264–0661. 11 rooms. Inexpensive.*

Tokyo International Youth Hostel. All residents here are required off the premises 10 AM–3 PM. The hostel is very close to Iidabashi Station on the JR, Tozai, and Yurakucho lines. *18F Central Plaza Bldg., 21-1 Kagura-kashi, Shinjuku-ku, Tokyo, tel. 03/3235–1107. 138 bunk beds. Inexpensive.*

Tokyo YMCA. Rooms are with and without bath. Both men and women can stay at the hostel, which is a three-minute walk from Awajicho Station on the Marunouchi Line or seven minutes from Kanda Station on the Ginza Line. *7 Kanda-*

Mitoshirocho, Chiyoda-ku, Tokyo 101. 86 rooms, tel. 03/3293–1919. Inexpensive.

Tokyo YWCA Sadohara. Rooms are available here with bath; also rooms for married couples. The hostel is located close (3-minute walk) to the Ichigaya Station. *1-1 Ichigaya-Sada-haracho, Shinjuku-ku, Tokyo, tel. 03/3268–7313. 20 rooms. Inexpensive.*

YMCA Asia Youth Center. Both men and women can stay here; all rooms have private baths. The hostel is an eight-minute walk from Suidobashi Station on the JR Mita Line. *5-5 Sara-gakucho 2-chome, Chiyoda-ku, Tokyo, tel. 03/3233–0611. 55 rooms. Inexpensive.*

Near Narita Airport

Narita Prince Hotel. A shuttle bus (at Terminal bus stop #3) is offered, which makes a regular 10-minute trip to the hotel. The modern and efficient Narita Prince is an all-purpose hotel, with banquet rooms and meeting facilities. *560 Tokko, Narita-shi, Chiba 286-01, tel. 0476/33–1111. 321 soundproof rooms. Facilities: outdoor pool, sauna, tennis courts, shopping arcade, 5 restaurants. AE, DC, MC, V. Expensive.*

Holiday Inn Tobu Narita. An eight-minute taxi ride from the airport, this establishment offers Western-style accommodations with a full range of amenities. *320-1 Tokko, Narita-shi, Chiba 286-01, tel. 0476/32–1234. 254 soundproof rooms that can also be rented for daytime-only use (¥12,826 for 2 beds). Facilities: outdoor pool, steam bath, massage, barber and beauty salons. French, Chinese, Japanese, and steak restaurants, bar. AE, DC, MC, V. Expensive.*

Narita International Hotel. This accommodation resembles a resort hotel with spacious grounds. It is new and modern, but it has some greenery on its 72 acres of land. A shuttle bus runs between the hotel and the airport in 20 minutes. *650-35 Nanaei, Tomisato-machi, Inba-gun, Chiba 288-02, tel. 0476/93–1234. 212 rooms, with individually controlled air-conditioning. Facilities: outdoor pool (the largest in Narita), tennis courts, jogging trail, duty-free shop, Japanese and Western restaurants. AE, DC, MC, V. Expensive.*

The Arts

Few cities have as much to offer as Tokyo does in the performing arts. It has Japan's own great stage traditions: Kabuki, Noh, Bunraku puppet drama, music, and dance. It has an astonishing variety of music, classical and popular; Tokyo is a proving ground for local talent and a magnet for orchestras and concert soloists from all over the world. The Rolling Stones, Jean Pierre Rampal, the Berlin Philharmonic, Oscar Peterson: Whenever you visit, the headliners will be here. It has modern theater—in somewhat limited choices, to be sure, unless you can follow dialogue in Japanese, but Western repertory companies can always find receptive audiences here for plays in English. In recent years musicals have found enormous popularity here; it doesn't take long for a hit show in New York or London to open in Tokyo. Film, too, presents a much broader range of possibilities than it used to. The major commercial distributors bring in the movies they expect to draw the biggest receipts—horror films and Oscar nominees—but there are now dozens of small theaters in Tokyo catering to more sophisticated audiences. Japan has yet to develop any serious strength of its own in opera or ballet, but for that reason touring companies like the Metropolitan and the Bolshoi, Sadler's Wells, and the Bayerische Staatsoper find Tokyo a very compelling venue—as well they might, when ¥20,000 seats are sold out even before the box office opens.

Information and Tickets The best comprehensive guide in English to performance schedules in Tokyo is the "Cityscope" insert in the monthly *Tokyo Journal* magazine. You can probably pick up the *Journal* at one of the newsstands at Narita Airport on your way into the city; if not, it's on sale in the bookstores at all the major international hotels. "Cityscope" has reviews and recommendations; in addition to films, plays, and concerts, it also covers museums and art galleries, television, festivals, and special events. Another source, rather less complete, is the *Tour Companion,* a tabloid visitor's guide published every two weeks that is available free of charge at hotels and at Japan National Tourist Organization offices. For a weekly update, the Monday edition of the English-language *Mainichi Daily News* also carries information on performances.

If your hotel cannot help you with bookings, two of the city's major ticket agencies have numbers to call for assistance in English: **Ticket Pia** (tel. 03/5237–9999) and **Ticket Saison** (tel. 03/3286–5482). A third possibility is the **Playguide** agency, which has outlets in most of the department stores and in other locations all over the city; you can stop in at the main office (Playguide Bldg., 2-6-4 Ginza, Chuo-ku, tel. 03/3561–8821) and ask for the nearest counter. Note that agencies normally do not have tickets for same-day performances but only for advanced booking.

Traditional Theater

Kabuki emerged as a popular form of entertainment in the early 17th century; before long, it had been banned by the authorities as a threat to public order. Eventually it cleaned up its act, and by the latter half of the 18th century, it had become Everyman's Theater par excellence—especially among the townspeople of bustling, hustling Edo. Kabuki had music, dancing, and spectacle; it had acrobatics and sword fights; it had pathos and tragedy and historical romance and social satire. It didn't have beautiful girls—women have been banned from the Kabuki stage since 1629—but in recompense it developed a professional role for female impersonators, who train for years to project a seductive, dazzling femininity that few real women ever achieve. It had superstars and quick-change artists and legions of fans, who brought their lunch to the theater, stayed all day, and shouted out the names of their favorite actors at the stirring moments in their favorite plays. Edo is now Tokyo, but Kabuki is still here, just as it has been for centuries. The traditions are passed down from generation to generation in a small group of families; the roles and great stage names are hereditary. The Kabuki repertoire does not really grow or change, but stars like Ennosuke Ichikawa and Tamasaburo Bando have put exciting, personal stamps on their performances that continue to draw audiences young and old.

Certainly the best place to see Kabuki is at the **Kabuki-za** (4-12-15 Ginza, Chuo-ku, tel. 03/3541–8597), built especially for this purpose in 1925, with its *hanamichi* (runway) passing diagonally through the audience to the revolving stage. The Kabuki-za was rebuilt after the war. The facade of the building recalls the castle architecture of the 16th century; the lanterns and banners and huge theater posters outside identify it unmistakably. Matinees usually begin at 11 AM and end at 3:30 PM; evening performances, at 4:30 PM, end around 9 PM. Reserved seats are expensive and hard to come by on short notice; for a mere ¥400, however, you can buy an unreserved ticket that allows you to see one act of a play from the topmost gallery. The gallery is cleared after each act, but there's nothing to prevent you from buying another ticket: the price is low for an hour or so of this fascinating spectacle. Bring binoculars: the gallery is *very* far from the stage. You might also want to rent an earphone set (¥600) to follow the play in English, but this is really more of an intrusion than a help—and you can't use the set in the upmost gallery, anyway.

Two other theaters in Tokyo specialize in traditional performances and offer Kabuki at various times during the year. The **Shimbashi Embujo** (6-18-2 Ginza, Chuo-ku, tel. 03/5565–6000), which dates back to 1925, was built originally for the geisha of the Shimbashi quarter to present their spring and autumn performances of traditional music and dance. It's a bigger house than the Kabuki-za, and it still presents a lot of traditional dance as well as conventional drama (in Japanese), but there is no gallery; reserved seats commonly run ¥3,000–¥12,000. The **National Theater of Japan** (4-1 Hayabusa, Chiyoda-ku, tel. 03/3265–7411), mentioned in our exploring tour of the Imperial Palace area, plays host to Kabuki companies based elsewhere; it also has a training program for young people who may not have one of the hereditary family connections but want to break into this closely guarded profession. Debut performances, called *kao-mise*, are worth watching to catch the stars of the next generation. *Admission: ¥1,300–¥7,800.*

Noh is a dramatic tradition far older than Kabuki; it reached a point of formal perfection in the 14th century and survives virtually unchanged from that period. Where Kabuki was Everyman's Theater, Noh developed for the most part under the patronage of the warrior class. It is dignified and solemn, ritualized and symbolic; many of the plays in the repertoire are drawn from classical literature or tales of the supernatural, and the texts are richly poetic. Where the Kabuki actor is usually in brightly colored makeup derived from the Chinese opera, the principal character in a Noh play wears a carved wooden mask; such is the skill of the actor, and the mysterious effect of the play, that the mask seems to express a whole range of emotions. As in Kabuki, the various roles of the Noh repertoire all have specific costumes—robes of silk brocade with intricate patterns that are works of art in themselves. Noh is not a very *accessible* kind of theater: its language is archaic; its conventions are obscure; and its measured, stately pace can put even Japanese audiences to sleep. More than anything else you will see in Tokyo, however, Noh will provide an experience of Japan as an *ancient* culture.

Somewhat like Kabuki, Noh is divided into a number of schools, the traditions of which developed as the exclusive property of hereditary families. It is occasionally performed in public halls, like the **National Noh Theater** (4-18-1 Sendagaya, Shibuya-ku, tel. 03/3423–1331), but primarily in the theaters of these schools—which also teach their dance and recitation styles to amateurs. The most important of these are the **Kanze Noh-gakudo** (1-1-6 Shoto, Shibuya-ku, tel. 03/3469–5241), the **Kita Noh-gakudo** (4-6-9 Kami-Osaki, Shinagawa-ku, tel. 03/3491–7773), the **Hosho Noh-gakudo** (1-5-9 Hongo, Bunkyo-ku, tel. 03/3811–4843), and the **Umewaka Noh-gakuin** (2-6-14 Higashi-Nakano, Nakano-ku, tel. 03/3363–7748). The very best way to see Noh, however, is in the open air, at torchlight performances called Takigi Noh, held in the courtyards of temples; the setting and the aesthetics of the drama combine in an eerie theatrical experience. These performances are given at various times during the year; consult the "Cityscope" or *Tour Companion* listings. Tickets are normally available only through the temples and are sold out very quickly.

The third major form of traditional Japanese drama is **Bunraku,** or puppet theater. Itinerant puppeteers were plying their trade in Japan as early as the 10th century; sometime in the late 16th century, a form of narrative ballad called *joruri,* performed to the accompaniment of a three-string banjolike instrument called the *shamisen,* was grafted onto their art, and Bunraku was born. The golden age of Bunraku came some 200 years later, when most of the great Bunraku plays were written and the puppets themselves evolved to their present form—so expressive and intricate in their movements that they require three people at one time to manipulate them. Puppeteers and narrators (who deliver their lines in a kind of high-pitch croak, deep in the throat) train for many years to master this difficult and unusual genre of popular entertainment.

The spiritual center of Bunraku today is Osaka, rather than Tokyo, but performances are given here with some frequency in the Small Hall of the National Theater. In recent years, it has also begun to enjoy a minor vogue with younger audiences, and Bunraku troupes will occasionally get booked into trendier locations. Consult the "Cityscope" listings, or check with one of the English-speaking ticket agencies.

Modern Theater

The **Shingeki** (Modern Theater) movement began in Japan at about the turn of the century; the first problem its earnest young actors and directors encountered was the fact that they had no native repertoire. The "conservative" faction at first tended to approach the problem with translations of Shakespeare; the "radicals," with Ibsen, Gorki, and Shaw. It wasn't until around 1915 that Japanese playwrights began writing for the Shingeki stage. Japan of the 1930s and 1940s, in any case, was none too hospitable an environment for modern drama; the movement did not develop any real vitality until after World War II.

The watershed years came around 1965, when experimental theater companies—unable to find commercial space—began taking their work to young audiences in various unusual ways: street plays and "happenings"; dramatic readings in underground malls and rented lofts; tents put up on vacant lots for unannounced performances (miraculously filled to capacity by word of mouth) and taken down the next day. It was in this period that surrealist playwright Kobo Abe found his stride, and director Tadashi Suzuki developed the unique system of training that now draws aspiring actors from all over the world to his "theater community" in the mountains of Toyama Prefecture. Japanese drama today is a lively art indeed; theaters small and large, in unexpected pockets all over Tokyo, attest to its vitality.

The great majority of these performances, however, are in Japanese, for Japanese audiences; you're unlikely to find one with program notes in English to help you follow it. Unless it's a play you already know well, and you're curious to see how it translates (*Fiddler on the Roof*, for example, has been running in Japanese for over 20 years), you might do well to think of some other way to spend your evenings out.

There is one exception: the **Takarazuka**—the wonderfully goofy all-girl review. The troupe was founded in the Osaka suburb of Takarazuka in 1913 and has been going strong ever since; today it has not one but five companies, one of them with a permanent home in Tokyo, right across the street from the Imperial Hotel (1-1-3 Yuraku-cho, Chiyoda-ku, tel. 03/3591– 1711). A Takarazuka chorine never gives her parents a moment's anxiety about her chosen career; this is show business with a difference—a life chaste and chaperoned, where the yearning admirers waiting with roses by the stage door are mostly teenage girls. Everybody sings; everybody dances; the sets are breathtaking; the costumes are swell. Where else but at the Takarazuka could you see a musical version of *Gone With the Wind*, sung in Japanese, with a girl in a mustache and a frock coat playing Rhett Butler?

Music

The live music scene in Tokyo keeps getting better and better. Every year, a host of new promoters and booking agencies gets into the act; major corporations, anxious to polish their images as cultural institutions, are building concert halls and unusual performance spaces all over the city, adding to what was already an excellent roster of public auditoriums. It would be impossible to list them all; here are only a few of the most important:

The biggest acts from abroad in **rock** and **popular music** tend to appear at the 56,000-seat **Tokyo Dome sports arena,** which opened in 1988 on the site of the old Korakuen Stadium (1-3-61 Koraku, Bunkyo-Ku, tel. 03/3811–2111), and at **Nakano Sun Plaza** (4-1-1 Nakano, Nakano-ku, tel. 03/3388–1151). For **Western classical music,** including **opera,** the major venues are **NHK Hall,** home base for the Japan Broadcasting Corporation's NHK Symphony Orchestra (2-2-1 Jinnan, Shibuya-ku, tel. 03/ 3465–1111); **Tokyo Bunka Kaikan** (5-45 Ueno Koen, Taito-ku, tel. 03/3828–2111), which we've mentioned in our exploring tour of Ueno; and **Suntory Hall,** in the new Ark Hills complex (1-13-1 Akasaka, Minato-ku, tel. 03/3505–1001). To these should be added three fine places designed especially for **chamber music: Iino Hall** (2-1-1 Uchisaiwai-cho, Chiyoda-ku, tel. 03/ 3506–3251), **Ishibashi Memorial Hall** (4-24-24 Higashi Ueno, Taito-ku, tel. 03/3843–3043), and the very recent **Casals Hall** (1-6 Kanda Surugadai, Chiyoda-ku, tel. 03/3294–1229), de-

signed by architect Arata Isozaki, who also did, among other
things, the Museum of Contemporary Art in Los Angeles.

Dance

Traditional Japanese Dance, like flower arranging and the tea
ceremony, is divided into dozens of styles, ancient of lineage
and fiercely proud of their differences from each other; in fact,
only the aficionado can really tell them apart. They survive, not
so much as performing arts but as schools, offering dance as a
cultured accomplishment to interested amateurs; at least once
a year, teachers and their students in each of these schools will
hold a recital, so that on any given evening there's very likely to
be one somewhere in Tokyo. Truly professional performances
are given, as we've mentioned, at the National Theater and the
Shimbashi Embujo; the most important of the classical schools,
however, developed as an aspect of Kabuki, and if you attend a
play at the Kabuki-za you are almost guaranteed to see a representative example.

Ballet began to attract a Japanese following in 1920, when
Anna Pavlova danced *The Dying Swan* at the old Imperial Theater; the well-known companies that come to Tokyo from
abroad perform to full houses, usually at the Tokyo Bunka
Kaikan in Ueno. There are now about 15 professional Japanese
ballet companies, several of which have toured abroad, but this
has yet to become an art form on which Japan has had much of
an impact. **Modern Dance** is a different story—a story that begins with a visit in 1955 by the Martha Graham Dance Company. The decade that followed was one of great turmoil in Japan;
it was a period of dissatisfaction—political, intellectual, artistic—with old forms and conventions. The work of pioneers like
Graham inspired a great number of talented dancers and chore-
ographers to explore new avenues of self-expression; one of the
fruits of that exploration was **Butoh,** a movement that was at
once uniquely Japanese and a major contribution to the world
of modern dance.

The father of Butoh was the dancer Tatsumi Hijikata (1928–
1986); the watershed work was his *Revolt of the Flesh,* which
premiered in 1968. Others soon followed: Kazuo Ohno, Min
Tanaka, Akaji Maro and the Dai Rakuda Kan troupe, Ushio
Amagatsu and the Sankai Juku. To most Japanese, their work
was inexplicably grotesque. Dancers performed with shaved
heads, dressed in rags or with naked bodies painted completely
white, their movements agonized and contorted. The images
were dark and demonic, violent and explicitly sexual. Butoh
was an exploration of the unconscious: its gods were the gods of
the Japanese village and the gods of prehistory; its literary
inspirations came from Mishima, Genet, Artaud. Like many
other modern Japanese artists, the Butoh dancers and chore-
ographers were largely ignored by the mainstream until they
began to appear abroad—to thunderous critical acclaim; now
they are equally honored at home. Butoh does not lend itself to
conventional spaces (about three years ago, for example, the
Dai Rakuda Kan premiered one of its new works in a limestone
cave in Gumma Prefecture), but if there's a performance in Tokyo, "Cityscope" will have the schedule. Don't miss it.

Film

One of the positive things about the business of foreign film distribution in Japan is that it is extremely profitable—so much so that the distributors can afford to add Japanese subtitles rather than dub their offerings, the way it's done so often elsewhere. The original soundtrack, of course, may not be all that helpful to you if the film is Polish or Italian, but the vast majority of first-run foreign films here are made in the United States. There are, however, other disincentives: the choices are limited; the good films take so long to open in Tokyo that you've probably seen them all already at home; and the tickets are expensive—around ¥1,200 for general admission, and ¥1,500–¥2,000 for a reserved seat, called a *shiteiseki*.

The native Japanese film industry has been in a slump for over 20 years, and it shows no signs of recovery; it yields, at best, one or two films a year worth seeing, and these are invariably by independent producer/directors. A very small number of theaters will offer one showing a week, with English subtitles, of films that seem to have some international appeal; "Cityscope" will have the listings. The **Japan Foundation**, a government-funded cultural exchange organization (3-6 Kioi-cho, Chiyoda-ku, tel. 03/3263–4507), periodically has showings of older films with English subtitles; these begin at 4 PM, however, and the auditorium seats only 60. Call directly, or check the "Cityscope" for dates and titles.

First-run theaters that feature new releases, both Japanese and foreign, are clustered for the most part in three areas: Shinjuku, Shibuya, and Yurakucho/Hibiya/Ginza. The most astonishing thing about them is how early they shut down; in most cases, the last showing of the evening starts at around 7. This is not the case, however, with the best news on the Tokyo film scene: the growing number of small theaters that take a special interest in classics, revivals, and serious imports. Many of them are in the "vertical boutique" buildings that represent the latest Japanese thinking in urban architecture and upscale marketing; somewhere on the premises will also be a chrome-and-marble coffee shop, a fashionable little bar, or even a decent restaurant. Most of them have a midnight show—at least on the weekends. One such is the **Cine Vivant** (Wave Building, 6-2-27 Roppongi, Minato-ku, tel. 03/3403–6061); another is the **Cine Saison Shibuya** (Prime Building, 2-29-5 Dogen-zaka, Shibuya-ku, tel. 03/3770–1721); still others are the **Haiyu-za Cinema Ten** (4-9-2 Roppongi, Minato-ku, tel. 03/3401–4073), and the **Hibiya Chanter Cinema** (1-2-2 Yuraku-cho, Chiyoda-ku, tel. 03/3591–1511).

Nightlife

Tokyo has more entertainment choices and a greater diversity of nightlife than any other Japanese city. For the tourist to Japan, the structure of Japan's nightlife may be confusing. The neon lights of bars and clubs excite with their glitter, but these places are forbidding to enter for several reasons: an indication of the prices charged for a drink is rarely offered (the charge could be a mere ¥1,000 a drink, or a ¥20,000 cover and another ¥15,000 for a bottle of whiskey); it is often unclear whether the bar has hostesses, and, if it does, whether there is a hostess charge and whether she is there for conversation only; and, finally, one never knows whether foreigners will be welcome, let alone whether a word of English will be spoken.

In this section, the establishments listed make foreigners welcome; often, someone will be around who speaks a few words of English. Most of the bars listed are more of the international variety, rather than being bars with hostesses. Hostess bars become like personal clubs, and your appreciation of them depends on how well you enjoy the conversations of the particular hostesses. You are unlikely to appreciate them unless you speak Japanese, especially when the tab will be about ¥20,000 to ¥30,000 a person. Some bars, called "karaoke bars," have music videos. Patrons request a piece of music and accompany it by singing the song into a microphone while reading the words to the song from the bottom of the video screen.

There are five major districts in Tokyo that have an extensive nightlife. While each area offers similar entertainment, the areas have different characters and different price ranges:

Akasaka has an area of two main streets, Tamachi-dori and Hitotsugi-dori, with small alleys connecting them. Cabarets, wine bars, nightclubs, coffee shops, eating and drinking places, as well as a couple of expensive ryotei with geisha entertainment, are all here. It is a sophisticated neighborhood that is not quite as expensive as Ginza and not as trendy as Roppongi. Also, the area's compactness makes it a comfortable locale for the foreigner to test the waters of Japanese nightlife.

Ginza is probably the city's most well-known entertainment district. However, its heyday is over as an attractive place for foreign visitors to visit at night. The exorbitant price of Ginza's real estate has made its nightlife one of the most, if not the most, expensive in the world. Not even foreign businessmen on expense accounts take their Japanese clients there. Only Japanese corporate expense accounts can afford the prices. However, some affordable places to visit in the evening are available here—not nightclubs as such, but bars and eating and drinking places.

Roppongi, spreading out toward Shibuya, has become Tokyo's main entertainment area for the cosmopolitan, trendy, and fashionable. It is the district where Westerners feel most comfortable; the prices are considerably better here than in Ginza, or even in Akasaka. During the day Roppongi is a quiet, residential area, but after 9 PM it seems that every Tokyo reveler is here making the rounds. More discos and bars of the variety you usually find in any major world capital are located here than in anyplace else in Japan. While Akasaka and Ginza virtually close down by midnight, some of the Roppongi bars stay open until the subways start running in the morning, so, if you have the stamina, this is the area to come for an all-nighter.

Shibuya has recently developed a nightlife. Less expensive than Roppongi and not raunchy like Shinjuku, it attracts students and young professionals to its numerous *nomiya* (inexpensive bars). Not many of the establishments speak English, but if you know a little Japanese, this is a pleasant and inexpensive area for a night's entertainment.

Shinjuku's Kabukicho is the wildest of areas in Tokyo for evening revelry, offering a wide range of places, from the sleazy to the respectable. Bars, nightclubs, cabarets, discos, restaurants, and love hotels are all here. Just stay clear of touts speaking English to lure you to their dive, and you'll be fine. We do, however, recommend that unescorted women stay out of Kabukicho after 9 PM because by then there are bound to be a few drunken males who will make irritating advances.

Bars

Charleston. This has been for years the schmoozing-and-hunting bar for Tokyo's single (or putatively single) foreign community, and the young Japanese who want to meet them. Noisy and packed until the wee small hours. *3-8-11 Roppongi: minato-ku, tel. 03/3402–0372. Drinks are ¥750 and up. Open daily 6PM–5AM.*

Fleur. Owned by the Palace Hotel, this lounge/bar/restaurant has a Mediterranean feel to its decor. The establishment is a comfortable place for a leisurely evening of conversation and drinks interspersed with food. Drinks may be purchased either by the glass or by the bottle. *2-2-2 Ginza, Chuo-ku, tel. 03/3561– 2650. Drinks start at ¥700, a bottle of domestic whiskey at ¥4,800. Open Mon.–Fri. 11:30–11; Sat. 11:30–8:30.*

Garbus Cine Café. Young sophisticates, especially those with latent screen ambitions, come to this smart café for exotic coffees, as well as cocktails. The large plate-glass windows of the café overlook a small square, where palms of famous movie actors are imprinted in stone. The square also flickers with a digital clock flashing the time from under a water fountain. *Hibiya Chanter 1F, 1-2-2 Yurakucho, Chiyoda-ku, tel. 03/3501–3185. Coffees start at ¥515, whiskies at ¥600. Open daily 11–11.*

Hard Rock Cafe. Akin to the London establishment of the same name, the bar reopened a couple of years ago with a new decor, similar to that of an American midwestern saloon and offering the same kind of fare for snacks. The building is easy to spot, with a huge sculpted gorilla hanging from the outside wall. *5-4-20 Roppongi, Minato-ku, tel. 03/3408–7018. Drinks start at ¥900. No cover, unless there is a special group playing. Open weekdays 4 PM–2 AM, Fri. and Sat. 11:30 AM–4 AM.*

Henry Africa. Both Japanese and expatriates frequent this Akasaka bar, where the decor is like a movie set used to film an African safari, including the elephant tusks. (There is a similar bar with the same name in Roppongi.) *Akasaka Ishida Bldg., 2F, 3-13-14 Akasaka, Minato-ku, tel. 03/3585–0149. Drinks begin at ¥550. Snacks are available. Open daily 11:30–11:30, Sun. 5:30–11:30.*

Highlander. Should you become tired of Japanese whiskey and want some real Scotch, the Highlander at the Hotel Okura has a selection of more than 200 brands from which to choose. This is a smart place to meet business acquaintances or to have a civilized drink. *Hotel Okura, 2-10-4 Toranomon, Minato-ku, tel. 03/3505–6077. Drinks are ¥700 and up. Open daily 11:30 AM–1 AM.*

Ikka. If you want a small personal Japanese bar in Ginza where there are conversational waitresses, then Mama-san Shino Suzuki has promised to make you feel welcome. You will probably be the only Westerner there, unless there is another carrying this guide. Neither Mama-san nor her young assistants speak English, so you may want to learn a few Japanese words before you visit. We recommend this bar because the prices are a third less than those at many other bars in the Ginza neighborhood. *Koike Bldg., 3F, 6-3-5 Ginza, Chuo-ku, tel. 03/3574–1819. Cost: ¥10,000; a bottle of whiskey is also ¥10,000. Open nightly 5 PM–2 AM.*

Maggie's Revenge. An Australian woman runs this popular expatriate's bar and has established a loyal following among both the Japanese and the foreign communities. The music is live (piano and/or guitar) and the atmosphere is congenial to mixing and talking with others. *Takano Bldg., 3-8-12 Roppongi, Minato-ku, tel. 03/3479–1096. Cover charge: ¥700. Drinks start at ¥600. Open Mon.–Thurs. 6:30 PM–3 AM, Fri.–Sat. 6 PM–4 AM.*

The Old Imperial Bar. If you want a place to meet someone for evening drinks, this hotel bar has a comfortable old-world charm with mementos taken from the original Imperial Hotel designed by Frank Lloyd Wright. *Imperial Hotel, 1-1-1 Uchisaiwaicho, Chiyoda-ku, tel. 03/3504–1111. Drinks ¥700 and up. Open daily 11–11.*

Paradiso. Underground, and with exposed black stone for its decor, this large bar, in the building next to the Lexington Queen disco, attracts a trendy and fashionable crowd. Along one wall is the bar, well-stocked by numerous female bartenders. For that reason the cover is more expensive at the bar than at the tables. *3-13-12 Roppongi, Minato-ku, Tokyo, tel. 03/3478–4212. Cover: at the bar, ¥2,000; at a table, ¥1,000. Most drinks are ¥1,200. Open 7 PM–4 AM, Sun. and holidays 7–11:30 PM.*

Suishin. This is one of many sake bars that you can find under the railway trestles south of Yurakucho Subway Station and near the JNTO's Tourist Information Office. This particular sake bar is small, barren except for a counter and chairs, but it is reputed to have some of the best Hiroshima sake. To find it, go down the alley under the railway between Tokyu Kotsu Kaikan and the Seibu Department Store; the pub is on the west side of the alley. *7-2-15 Ginza, tel. 03/3214–8046. Sake begins at ¥700. Open 11:30 AM–2 PM and 4–11:30 PM.*

Wine Bar. Similar to a European wine bar, the cellarlike atmosphere appeals to Japanese and foreigners alike. It is a good place to take a date before hopping on to the Roppongi discos. *3-21-3 Akasaka, Minato-ku, tel. 3586–7186. Drinks start at ¥380. Open Mon.–Fri. 5 PM–1 AM, Sat. 5 PM–midnight.*

Yuraku Food Center (2-2 Nishi-Ginza, Chuo-ku). Inside this building and one floor up is a collection of places to eat and drink at reasonable prices. It is where the people who work in the neighborhood go after work. One popular place for drinks, as well as for snacks, is the **Americana** (tel. 03/3564–1971). Drinks start at ¥600. Farther along the hallway is the **Music Pub** (tel. 03/3563–3757), which has live bands playing swing jazz. The cover varies but is usually about ¥2,200, and drinks start at ¥700. There are also restaurants in the food center that, along with the bars, start closing at 11 PM. Yuraku Food Center is situated to the east of Yurakucho Subway Station and is the next building east of the Kotsu Kaikan Building (where JNTO has its administrative offices). The Kotsu Kaikan Building can be recognized by the circular sky lounge on its rooftop.

Beer Halls

Kirin City. This beer hall is a newer entry and has less of the glass-thumping atmosphere of other brewery-sponsored drinking establishments. (There are also Kirin beer halls in Roppongi, just south of the Roppongi Crossing, tel. 03/3479–2573; and in Shinjuku, on the west side of the station and opposite the Yodobashi Camera store, tel. 03/3344–6234.) *Izumo Bldg., 8-8 Ginza, Chuo-ko, tel. 03/3571–7739. Beer is ¥430. Open noon–11.*

Levante Beer Hall. This is a favorite spot for the Japanese male to stop in and have some drinks and down a half dozen raw oysters. Over the years, this old-fashioned beer hall has become a well-known landmark and an anachronism in an area that is modern with its marble and flashing lights. Located in the Ginza district, Levante is behind the Imperial Hotel and opposite the Tokyu Kotsu Kakan store. *2-8-7 Yurakucho, Chiyoda-ku, tel. 03/3201–2661. Beer starts at ¥530, oysters (Oct.–Mar.) at ¥2,500. Open Mon.–Sat. 5–10.*

Sapporo Lion. For a casual evening spent drinking beer and eating snacks—anything from yakitori to spaghetti—the Sapporo Lion offers an inexpensive night out. The beer hall's entrance is off Chuo-dori Avenue, near the Matsuzakaya Department Store. *6-10-12 Ginza, Chuo-ku, tel. 03/3571–2590. Beer is ¥790. Open daily 11:30–11.*

Discos

Cleo Paradiso. This is where you come if you have missed the last subway and want to live it up all night long. The black-marble decor makes this disco/bar a sleek, chic establishment where, in the early morning hours, the clientele let their hair down and start dancing on the tables when the small dance floor becomes too congested. *Shadai Bldg., BI, 3-18-2 Roppongi, Minato-ku, tel. 03/3586–8494. Cost: ¥3,000, including 3 tickets for either food or drink. Open nightly 8 PM–5 AM.*

Lexington Queen. From the day it opened in 1980, the Lexington Queen has been patronized by celebrities—from sumo wrestlers to rock stars to media celebrities, such as Sylvester Stallone and Rod Stewart. And they still keep coming. Why? Because the owner is Bill Hersey, society writer for *Tokyo Weekender*, a weekly newspaper. A lot of attractive people show up here, from foreign models to those working in the movie industry. *Daisan Goto Bldg., B1, 3-13-14 Roppongi, Minato-ku, tel. 03/3401–1661. Cost: ¥4,000 men, ¥3,000 women, which includes a free drink and a meal ticket to be used at the sushi bar. Many waiters speak some English. Open nightly 6 PM–4 AM.*

Neo Japanesque. Located through the courtyard of the Forum building, this disco has an enthusiastic staff (many of whom speak English) who usher guests to the tier-type seating to the side of the flashing neon-lit stage, where laser beams dance patterns on the walls. Don't expect too much from the name; it is more an international, intimate disco than anything else, and it appeals to people in their mid-30s and 40s. *Roppongi Forum Bldg. B2, 5-16-5 Roppongi, Minato-ku, tel. 03/3586–0050. Cost: ¥4,500 men, ¥3,500 women, which includes 3 drinks; no unescorted men permitted. Open nightly 7 PM–4 AM.*

The Square Building Discos. (Roppongi Square Bldg., 3-10-3 Roppongi, Minato-ku). Ten floors of mostly discos, ephemeral ventures that tend to fold in a year or two, only to open again with a new name and a new decor. Only the money behind them remains the same. The most durable of the lot is **Giza**, with its Egyptian motif (tel. 03/3403–6538; cost: ¥4,000 for men,

¥3,000 for women; open 5 PM–4 AM); another that's been around for a while, and also trades on exotic chic, is **Nepenta** (tel. 03/3407–0751; cost: ¥4,000 for men, ¥3,000 for women; open 6 PM–5 AM). Three of the more recent to appear are **Bio**, which bills itself as a "Fitness Discotheque" and draws a predictably athletic crowd (tel. 03/3423–0050; cost: ¥4,000 for men, ¥3,000 for women; open 6 PM–5 AM); **Buzz-zz**, which boasts the latest music videos from "Rock America" (tel. 03/3405–7900); cost ¥4,000 for men, ¥3,000 for women; open 6 PM–midnight); and **The Circus**, a self-declared "Funky Oasis" that features rap music (tel. 03/5474–4570; cost: ¥4,500 for men, ¥3,500 for women; open 6 PM–6 *AM*).

Live Music

Blue Note Tokyo. Young entrepreneur Tosuke Ito acquired the Tokyo franchise for this famed New York night spot in 1988 and set about making it the premier jazz club in town. In the first year of operation, he had booked international headliners such as Chuck Mangione, Nancy Wilson, and Oscar Peterson, and the club's still going strong. *5-13-3 Minami-Aoyama, Minato-ku, tel. 03/3407–5781. Cover charge varies from ¥5,000 for relative unknowns to as high as ¥17,000 for superstars. Two sets a night, at 7:30 and 10. AE, MC, V.*

Body and Soul. Owner Kyoko Seki has been a jazz fan and an impresario for more than 15 years; her tiny third-floor walk-up club in Roppongi is where the professional musicians drop in after work, to drink and hang out and maybe sit in for a set with the featured performer. Nothing fancy about this place; just good, serious jazz. *7-14-12 Roppongi, Minato-ku, tel. 03/3408–2094. Cover charge ¥2,000 (sometimes ¥2,300); drinks from ¥700. Open 7 PM–2 AM. Closed Sun. AE.*

Pit Inn. The shows change nightly, but the emphasis is on Japanese and Western light jazz, attracting performers such as the late Sarah Vaughan. The atmosphere is friendly, with seating shaped in a half-moon facing the stage. It is by no means elegant, more like a well-worn theater than a nightclub. The audience is mostly in their early 20s. *3-16-4 Shinjuku, Shinjuku-ku, tel. 03/3354–2024. Cost: ¥2,500, 1 drink included.*

Satin Doll. Japanese jazz singers perform here every night in a comfortable, relaxing setting. This is a more elegant place than, for example, the Pit Inn. *Haiyuza Bldg. 3F, 4-9-2 Roppongi, Minato-ku, tel. 03/3401–3080. Cost: table charge varies according to who is playing, but it is usually about ¥1,300; drinks start at ¥750. Open 5:30 PM–midnight.*

Nightclubs and Cabarets

Cordon Bleu. A full-course meal is served in this dinner theater, with seats to accommodate about 150 people. However, it is more intimate than its size suggests and attracts well-known names. Muhammad Ali's name is in the guest book. There are three shows a night (7:30, 9:30, and 11:30), with singers and topless dancers bobbing up and down onstage. It is possible to just eat hors d'oeuvres and watch the show. *6-6-4 Akasaka, Minato-ku, tel. 03/582–7800. Reservations advised. Cost: ¥21,600 for full-course dinner and one drink; ¥14,400 for hors d'oeuvres and 1 drink. Open nightly 6:30 PM–2:30 AM.*

Showboat. Downstairs at the Hilton is this small, cheerful club with international cabaret acts, which attract both hotel guests and nonresidents for their leg-kicking dancers and warbling singers. *Tokyo Hilton Hotel, 6-6-2 Nishi-Shinjuku, Shinjuku-ku, tel. 03/3344–0510. Cover charge ¥3,500; table charge ¥1,000. Open nightly 6 PM–1 AM; showtimes 7, 9, 11.*

Skyline Lounges

Pole Star Lounge. For a view of old and new Shinjuku flickering beneath you, this lounge bar on the penthouse floor of the Keio Plaza is hard to beat. *Keio Plaza Inter-Continental, 2-2-1 Nishi-Shinjuku, Shinjuku-ku, tel. 03/3344–0111. Drinks start at ¥1,500. Open Mon.–Sat. 4–11:30, Sun. 3–11:30.*

Top of Akasaka. On the 40th floor of the Akasaka Prince Hotel, you can enjoy some of the finest views of Tokyo. If you can time your visit for dusk, the price of one drink gets you two views— the daylight sprawl of buildings and the twinkling lights of evening. *Akasaka Prince, 1-2 Kioi-cho, Chiyoda-ku, tel. 03/3234– 1111. Drinks start at ¥1,100. Open 11 AM–2 AM.*

4 Tokyo Excursions

Nikko

by Jared Lubarsky At Nikko, a few hours' journey to the north of Tokyo, is the monument to a warlord so splendid and powerful that he became a god. In the year 1600, Ieyasu Tokugawa won a battle at a place called Sekigahara, in the mountains of south-central Japan, that left him the undisputed ruler of all Japan. He died in 1616, but the Tokugawa Shogunate would last about another 252 years, holding in its sway a peaceful, prosperous, and united country.

A fit resting place would have to be made for the founder of such a dynasty. Ieyasu had provided for one in his will: a mausoleum at Nikko, in a forest of tall cedars, where a religious center had been founded more than eight centuries earlier. The year after his death, in accordance with Buddhist custom, he was given a *kaimyo*—an honorific name to bear in the afterlife; thenceforth, he was Tosho-Daigongen: The Great Incarnation Who Illuminates the East. The Imperial Court at Kyoto declared him a god, and his remains were taken in a procession of great pomp and ceremony to be enshrined at Nikko.

The dynasty he left behind was enormously rich. Ieyasu's personal fief, on the Kanto Plain, was worth 2.5 million *koku* of rice; one koku, in monetary terms, was equivalent to the cost of keeping one retainer in the necessities of life for a year. The shogunate itself, however, was still an uncertainty; it had only recently taken control after more than a century of civil war. The founder's tomb had a political purpose: It was meant to inspire awe and to make manifest the wealth and power of the Tokugawas. It was Ieyasu's legacy, a statement of his family's right to rule.

Toshogu Shrine was built by his grandson, the third shogun, Iemitsu. (It was Iemitsu who established the policy of national isolation, which closed the doors of Japan to the outside world for more than 200 years.) The mausoleum and shrine required the labor of 15,000 people for two years (1634–1636); craftsmen and artists of the first rank were assembled from all over the country. Every surface was carved and painted and lacquered in the most intricate imaginable detail; Toshogu shimmers in the reflections from 2,489,000 sheets of gold leaf. Roof beams and rafter ends with dragon heads, lions, and elephants in bas-relief; friezes of phoenixes, wild ducks, and monkeys; inlaid pillars and red-lacquer corridors—the Toshogu is everything a 17th-century warlord would consider gorgeous, and the inspiration is very Chinese.

Foreign visitors have differed about the effect Iemitsu achieved. Victorian-era traveler Isabella Bird, who came to Nikko in 1878, was unrestrained in her enthusiasm: "To pass from court to court," she writes in her *Unbeaten Tracks in Japan*, "is to pass from splendour to splendour; one is almost glad to feel that this is the last, and that the strain on one's capacity for admiration is nearly over." Fosco Mariani, a more recent visitor, felt somewhat differently: "You are taken aback," he observes in his *Meeting with Japan* (1959). "You ask yourself whether it is a joke, or a nightmare, or a huge wedding cake, a masterpiece of sugar icing made for some extravagant prince with a perverse, rococo taste, who wished to alarm and entertain his guests." Clearly, it is impossible to feel indifferent about Toshogu; perhaps, in the end, that is all Ieyasu could ever really have expected.

Nikko (which means "sunlight") is not simply the site of the Tokugawa shrine, however; it is also a national park of great beauty, about which opinion has never been divided. From above Toshogu, the Irohazaka Driveway coils its way up through maple forests to the park plateau and Chuzenji, a deep lake some 13 miles around. To the north, there are hot springs; at the west end of the lake, the spectacular Kegon Falls tumble more than 300 feet to the Daiya River. Towering above this landscape, at 1,312 feet, is the extinct volcanic cone of Mt. Nantai. "Think nothing splendid," asserts an old Japanese proverb, "until you have seen Nikko." Whoever said it first may not even have been thinking of the mausoleum down below.

Arriving and Departing

It's possible, but unwise, to go by car from Tokyo to Nikko. The trip will take at least three hours; getting from central Tokyo to the Tohoku Expressway—an hour of the trip or more—is a nightmare. Coming back, especially on a Saturday or Sunday evening, is even worse. If you must drive, take the expressway north to exit 10 (marked in English), and follow the green tollroad signs from there into Nikko.

Far easier and more comfortable are the Limited Express trains of the Tobu Railway, with six direct connections every morning, starting at 7:20 AM (additional trains on weekends and holidays) from the Tobu Asakusa Station, a minute's walk from the last stop on the Ginza subway line in Tokyo. The one-way fare is ¥2,280. All seats are reserved. Bookings are not accepted over the phone; consult your hotel or a travel agent. From Asakusa to the Tobu Nikko Station is one hour and 40 minutes. If you are making a day trip, the last return trains are at 7:38 (express) and 8:45 (local).

If you have a JR Rail Pass, we suggest you use JR service, which connects Tokyo and Nikko, from Ueno. Take the Tohoku Line limited express to Utsunomiya (1 hr, 25 min) or the faster Shinkansen (45 min) to Utsunomiya and transfer to the train (45 minutes) for JR Nikko Station. The earliest departure from Ueno is at 6:06 AM; the last train back leaves Nikko at 9:24 and arrives in Tokyo at 11:49, or 11:18 if you ride the Shinkansen.

Getting Around

In Nikko itself, you won't need much in the way of transportation but your own two feet; nothing is terribly far from anything else. Local buses leave the railway station for Lake Chuzenji, stopping just above the entrance to the Toshogu Shrine, approximately every 30 minutes from 6:20 AM. The fare to Chuzenji is ¥980 for adults, ¥490 for children under 12; the ride takes about 50 minutes. The last return bus from the lake leaves at 7:24 PM. Cabs are readily available; the one-way fare from the Tobu Nikko Station to Chuzenji is about ¥4,650.

Guided Tours

From Tokyo, two companies offer guided tours to Nikko. **Japan Amenity Travel** (tel. 03/3573–1011) operates a one-day motor-coach tour (lunch included) daily March 20–November 30. The tour includes the Toshogu Shrine and Lake Chuzenji. Pickup from major hotels begins at 8 AM. Cost: ¥16,200 adults, ¥12,100 children under 12 (lunch included).

Tobu Travel Co., Ltd. (tel. 03/3281–6622). All-Day Nikko Tour departs at 9 AM; it includes Lake Chuzenji and returns at 7:30 PM. Cost (breakfast and lunch included): ¥18,500 adults, ¥14,000 children under 12.

Exploring

Numbers in the margin correspond with points of interest on the Nikko map.

Toshogu Shrine Area The town of Nikko is essentially one long avenue (Cryptomeria Avenue), about a mile from the railway stations to Toshogu, that is lined with tourist inns and shops. If you have time, you might want to make this a leisurely walk; the antiques shops along the way may turn up interesting—but expensive—pieces (armor fittings, hibachi [charcoal braziers], pottery, dolls), and the souvenir shops will have ample selections of the local wood carvings. Alternatively, you can save yourself the hike up through town by taking the bus from either railway station (fare: ¥170) to Shinkyo (the Sacred Bridge).

1 At the top of the hill, on the left, is the entrance to the **Kanaya Hotel,** owned and operated by the same family for over 100 years; the main building is a delightful, rambling Victorian survival that has played host to royalty and other important personages—as the guest book attests—from all over the world. The road curves to the left and crosses the Daiya River; on the

2 left is the red-lacquer wood **Shinkyo,** built in 1636 for shoguns and imperial messengers on their visits to the shrine. It is still used for ceremonial occasions. (The original structure was destroyed in a flood; the present version dates to 1907.) Once, ordinary mortals were not permitted on the bridge. Now, you may pay ¥300 for the privilege of walking over it.

The main entrances to the Toshogu Shrine area are opposite the bridge, on the right, where there is also a **Monument to Masatane Matsudaira,** one of the two feudal lords charged with the actual construction of the Toshogu. Matsudaira's great contribution was the planting of the wonderful cryptomerias (Japanese cedars) around the shrine and along the 23-mile avenue that leads to it from the other side of the town; some 1,300 of these trees still stand—a setting of solemn majesty the buildings themselves could never have achieved.

Take either the ramp or the stone stairway to the grounds of the Toshogu Shrine (The buildings on the grounds are open 8–5 [enter by 4:30] Apr. 1–Oct. 31; 8–4 [enter by 3:30] Nov. 1–Mar. 31.) At the top of the stairway, in the corner of the car park, you can purchase a multiple entry ticket (¥750 adults, ¥350 children under 12) for the Rinnoji Temple, the Daiyuin (the mausoleum of the third shogun, Iemitsu Tokugawa), the Toshugu Shrine, and the Futaarasan Shrine; separate fees are charged for admission to other areas.

3 Turn left from the ticket area to enter the grounds of the **Rinnoji Temple** (open 8–4; enter by 3:30). The Rinnoji belongs to the Tendai sect of Buddhism, the head temple of which is Enryakuji, on Mt. Hiei near Kyoto. Behind the Hondo—the

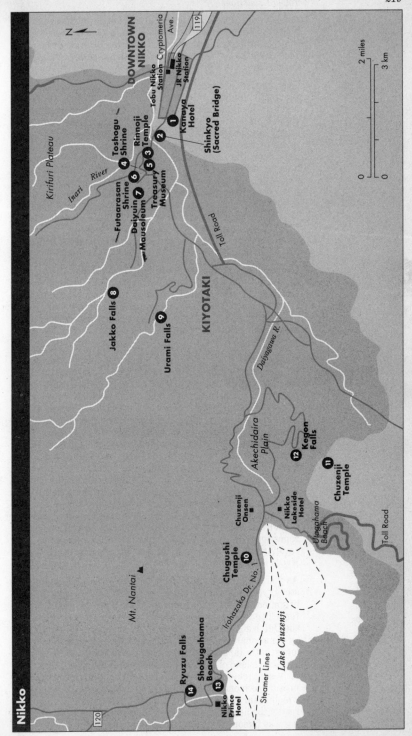

Nikko

abbot's quarters—is an especially fine little Japanese garden, made in 1815, and a museum, which has a good collection of lacquer, paintings, and Buddhist sculpture. *Museum admission, including the gardens: ¥300 adults, ¥100 children under 12. Open 8–4.*

The main hall of the temple, called the **Sambutsudo,** is the largest single building at Toshogu; it enshrines an image of Amida Nyorai, the Buddha of the Western Paradise, flanked on the right by a Senju (Thousand-Armed) Kannon, the goddess of mercy, and on the left by a Bato-Kannon, regarded as the protector of animals. These three images are lacquered in gold and date from the early part of the 17th century. The original Sambutsudo is said to have been built in 848 by the priest Ennin (794–864), also known as Jikaku-Daishi; the present building dates from 1648. Opposite, on the north side of the compound, is the **Gohotendo,** a hall that enshrines three of the Seven Gods of Good Fortune; these three are Buddhist deities derived from Chinese folk mythology: Daikoku and Bishamon, who bring wealth and good harvests, and Benten, patroness of music and the arts.

4 Leave Rinnoji by the west gate, turn right, and walk up the cedar-lined avenue to the stone *torii* arch of the **Toshogu Shrine.** On the left is the five-story **Pagoda** of the shrine—a reconstruction dating to 1818 but recently repaired. The first story is decorated with the 12 signs of the zodiac; the black-lacquer doors above each bear the three hollyhock leaves of the Tokugawa family crest.

Walk up the stone steps, and enter the shrine through the Omotemon (Front Gate) or the Niomon—Gate of the Deva Kings—with its two red-painted guardian gods. From here the path turns to the left; in the first group of buildings you reach on the left is the **Stable,** decorated with carved panels of pine trees and monkeys. The second panel from the left is the famous group of three monkeys—"Hear no evil, see no evil, speak no evil"—that has become almost the symbol of Nikko, reproduced endlessly on plaques, bags, and souvenirs of every sort. The Stable houses a white horse; this animal, either real or represented in a painting or carving, is traditionally found in Shinto shrines. A few steps farther, where the path turns to the right, is a granite font where visitors purify themselves by washing their hands and rinsing their mouths before entering the shrine; behind it is the **Kyozo** (Sutra Library), which is a repository for some 7,000 Buddhist scriptures, kept in a huge revolving bookcase nearly 20 feet high. Unfortunately, the Kyozo is not open to the public.

As you pass under the second (bronze) torii arch and up the steps, you see on the right a belfry and a tall bronze candelabrum; on the left is a drum tower and a bronze revolving lantern. The two works in bronze were presented to the shrine by the Dutch government in the mid-17th century. Under the policy of national seclusion, only the Dutch retained trading privileges with Japan, and even then were confined to the tiny artificial island of Deshima, in the port of Nagasaki; they regularly sent tokens of their esteem to the shogunate to keep their precarious monopoly. Behind the drum tower is the **Yakushido,** which enshrines a manifestation of the Buddha (Yakushi Nyorai) as the healer of illnesses. The original 17th-century building was famous for a huge India-ink painting on the ceiling of the nave, *The Roaring Dragon*, by Yasunobu Kano (1607–1685); the work was so named because when visitors clapped their hands beneath it, the echoes made it seem as though the dragon had roared. The Yakushido was destroyed by fire in 1961, and rebuilt; the dragon on the ceiling is by Nampu Katayama.

At the top of the steps is the **Yomeimon,** the Gate of Sunlight, which is the centerpiece of the shrine and is designated a National Treasure. It is also called the Higurashimon (Twilight Gate), implying that one could spend all day until sunset looking at its richness of detail. Rich the gate certainly is; dazzling white and two stories (36 feet) high, it has 12 columns, beams, and roof brackets that are carved with dragons, lions, clouds, peonies, Chinese sages, and immortals. The gate has numerous carvings that are painted red, gold, blue, and green. On one of the central columns, there are two carved tigers; the natural grain of the wood is used to bring out the "fur." To the right and left of the Yomeimon as you enter are galleries running east and west for some 700 feet, their paneled fences also carved and painted with a profusion of motifs from nature: pine and plum branches, pheasants, cranes, and wild ducks.

Inside the gate to the left is the **Mikoshigura,** a storeroom where the portable shrines that appear in the annual Toshogu Festival on May 17–18 are kept; the paintings on the ceiling, of *tennin* (Buddhist angels) playing harps, are by Ryokaku Kano. To the right is the **Kaguraden,** a hall where ceremonial dances are performed to honor the gods. Directly ahead, across the courtyard, is the **Karamon** (Chinese Gate), the official entrance to the inner shrine—also a National Treasure, and, like the Yomeimon, carved and painted in elaborate detail with dragons and other auspicious figures. Extending right and left from the gate is a wall, which encloses the **Honden** (Main Hall) of the shrine.

The entrance is to the right; here you remove your shoes (lockers are provided) and pass into the outer part of the hall, called the **Haiden** (Oratory), with its lacquered pillars, carved friezes, and coffered ceilings painted with dragons. Over the lintels are paintings of the 36 great poets of the Heian period, by Mitsuoki Tosa (1617–1691), with their poems in the calligraphy of Emperor Gomizuno-o. The Haiden is divided into three chambers: At the back of the central chamber is the Sacred Mirror, believed to represent the spirit of the deity enshrined; the room on the right was reserved for visiting shoguns and members of the three principal branches of the Tokugawa family; and the room on the left for the chief abbot of Rinnoji—who was always a prince of the imperial line.

Beyond the Haiden is a passage called the Ishi-no-Ma (Stone Room); this connects in turn with the sanctum, which is divided into three parts: the Haiden (Sanctuary), the Naijin (Inner Chamber), and the Nai-Naijin (Innermost Chamber). No visitors come this far; here, in the very heart of Toshogu, is the gold-lacquered shrine where the spirit of Ieyasu resides—along with two other deities, whom the Tokugawas later decided were fit companions. One was Hideyoshi Toyotomi, Ieyasu's mentor and liege lord in the long wars of unification at the end of the 16th century; the other was Yoritomo Minamoto, brilliant military tactician and founder of the earlier (12th-century) Kamakura Shogunate. (Ieyasu, born Takechiyo

Matsudaira, son of a lesser baron in what is today Aichi Prefecture, claimed Yoritomo for an ancestor.)

Return to the courtyard between the Karamon and Yomeimon gates, turn left, walk down the long passage painted in red cinnabar, and then left into an open corridor. Just above the gateway here is another famous symbol of the Toshogu, the **Sleeping Cat**—a small panel said to have been carved by the sculptor Jingoro Hidari. A separate admission charge (¥430 adults, ¥300 children under 12) is levied to go beyond this point to the **Sakashitamon** (The Gate at the Foot of the Hill) and to the flight of 200 stone steps, up through the cryptomeria trees to **Ieyasu's Tomb.** The climb is worth making, if only for the view of the Yomeimon and Karamon from above.

5 Retrace your steps (it's a lot easier coming down), return to the arch in front of the shrine, and turn right. A few minutes' walk will bring you to the **Treasury Museum,** on the left, which houses a collection of antiquities from the various shrines and temples. *Admission: ¥300 adults, ¥100 children under 12. Open Apr.–Oct. 8:30–5, Nov.–Mar. 8:30–4.*

6 At the end of the avenue, bear right for the **Futaarasan Shrine.** To the gods enshrined here, Ieyasu must seem but a callow newcomer: Futaarasan was founded in the 8th century to honor the Shinto deity Okuni-nushi-no-Mikoto (god of the rice fields, bestower of prosperity), his consort Tagorihime-no-Mikoto, and their son Ajisukitaka-hikone-no-Mikoto. The shrine is actually in three parts: the Honsha, or main shrine, at Toshogu; the Chugushi, or middle shrine, on Lake Chuzenji; and the Okumiya, or inner shrine, on top of Mt. Nantai.

Walk through the bronze torii arch to the Karamon (Chinese Gate) and the Honden (sanctum)—the present version of which dates to 1619. To the left, in the corner of the enclosure, is an antique bronze lantern, some seven feet high, under a canopy. Legend has it that the lantern would assume the shape of a goblin at night; the deep nicks in the bronze were inflicted by swordsmen of the Edo period—on guard duty, perhaps, startled into action by a flickering shape in the dark. This proves, if not the existence of goblins, then the incredible cutting power of the Japanese blade. *Admission free. Open Apr.–Oct., 8–5; Nov.–Mar., 9–4.*

Retrace your steps and turn right. The first two buildings you come to, on the left, are the Jogyodo and Hokkedo (popularly called the Futatsudo, or **Twin Halls**) of the Rinnoji Temple, founded in 848. Between them, a path leads to the compound of the **Jigendo Hall,** built in honor of Tenkai (1536–1643), the first abbot of the Nikko temples. The Jigendo is at the north end of the compound, to the right. At the west end is the **Go-oden,** shrine to Prince Kitashirakawa (1847–1895), last of the imperial princes to serve as abbot; behind it is his tomb and the tombs of his 13 predecessors.

7 Return to the Twin Halls and turn left for the **Daiyuin Mausoleum.** (Admission is included in multiple entry ticket to Toshogu Shrine area mentioned earlier. Open Apr.–Oct., 8–4:30; Nov.–Mar., 8–3:30.) Iemitsu (1603–1651), one suspects, had it in mind to upstage his illustrious grandfather; he marked the approach to his own tomb with no fewer than six different decorative gates. The first is another Niomon—a Gate of the Deva Kings—like the one at the Toshogu Shrine; the dragon painted on the ceiling is by Yasunobu Kano (1613–1685). A flight of stone steps leads from here to the second gate, the Nitenmon, a two-story structure protected front and back by carved and painted images of guardian gods. Beyond it, you climb two more flights of steps to the middle courtyard; there is a bell tower on the right and a drum tower on the left, and directly ahead is the third gate, the Yashamon, so named for the figures of Yasha (a demon) in the four niches. This structure is also called the Botanmon (Peony Gate) for the carvings that decorate it.

On the other side of the courtyard is the Karamon (Chinese Gate), gilded and elaborately carved; beyond it is the Haiden: the oratory of the shrine. The Haiden, too, is richly carved and decorated, with the ceiling covered with dragons; the Chinese lions on the panels at the rear are by two distinguished painters of the Kano school. Behind the Haiden is the Ai-no-Ma (anteroom or Connecting Chamber); a separate fee (¥430 adults, ¥300 children under 12) is charged for admission. From here you can see the sanctum (Honden). Designated a National Treasure, it houses a gilded and lacquered Buddhist altar some nine feet high, decorated with paintings of animals, birds, and flowers, in which resides the object of all this veneration: a seated wooden figure of Iemitsu.

Return to the Karamon Gate, turn left and left again; at the far west end of the wall, on the right, is the fifth gate: the Kokamon, built in the Chinese style of the late Ming Dynasty. From here, another flight of stone steps leads to a small, white-painted oratory. There is one last climb, to the sixth and last gate—the bronze Inukimon—and Iemitsu's tomb.

If you return to the torii arch in front of the Futaarasan Shrine and take the path to the right (south) down Nishisando, you will soon come to an exit from the Toshogu Shrine area on the main road. At this point, you may have given Nikko all the time you had to spare; if so, turn left, and a short walk will bring you back to the Sacred Bridge. If not, turn right, and in a minute or so you will come to the Nishisando bus stop, where you can take the local bus to Lake Chuzenji.

To Lake Chuzenji About ½-mile farther (Tamozawa bus stop), there is a narrow
8 road to the right that leads to the **Jakko Falls**—an uphill walk of some 2 miles. The falls descend in a series of seven terraced stages, forming a sheet of water about 100 feet high. Another turn to the right off the Chuzenji road, by the Arasawa bus
9 stop, leads to the **Urami Falls.** "The water," wrote the great 17th-century poet Basho, "seemed to take a flying leap and drop a hundred feet from the top of a cave into a green pool surrounded by a thousand rocks. One was supposed to inch one's way into the cave and enjoy the falls from behind." It's a steep climb to the cave; the falls and the gorge are striking, but only the visitor with good hiking shoes and a willingness to get wet should try this particular view.

The real climb to Chuzenji Lake begins at **Umagaeshi** (literally: Horse-Return), about 6 miles from the Tobu Station. Here, in the old days, the road became too rough for riding; the traveler on horseback had to alight and proceed on foot. The lake is 1,270 meters (4,165 feet) above sea level. From Umagaeshi, the bus climbs a new one-way toll road up the pass; the old road has been widened and is used for the traffic coming down. The two

roads are full of steep hairpin turns, and on a clear day the view
up and down the valley is magnificent—especially from the
halfway point at **Akechidaira,** from which you can see the summit of **Mt. Nantai,** reaching 2,484 meters (8,149 ft.). From May
5 to October 15, you'll often see energetic climbers making the
ascent in about four hours.

⑩ The bus trip ends at Chuzenji village, which was named after
the temple established here in 784. The temple was renamed
Chugushi in the 19th century and incorporated into the Futaarasan Shrine; it lies just outside the village, on the road along
the north side of the lake. The treasure house (admission: ¥300
adults, ¥150 children under 12) has an interesting historical
collection, including swords, lacquer ware and medieval-period
shrine palanquins. *Temple open Apr.–Oct., 8–5; Nov.–Mar.,
8:40–3:30.*

⑪ Chugushi is not to be confused with the present-day **Chuzenji
Temple** (Tashikikannon), which you reach by turning left as you
leave the village and walking about a mile along the eastern
shore of the lake. The temple is part of the Rinnoji, at Toshogu;
the principal object of worship is a statue of Kannon, the goddess of mercy, over 17 feet high, said to have been carved over
1,000 years ago by the priest Shodo from the living trunk of a
single Judas tree. *Admission: ¥300 adults, ¥150 ages 12–18,
¥100 elementary school children. Open Apr.–Oct., 8–5; Nov.,
8–4; Dec.–Feb., 8:30–3:30; Mar., 8–4.*

In front of the temple was the Utagahama (Singing Beach), so
named because an angel was said to have descended from heav-
en here to sing and dance for Shodo; unfortunately, the "beach"
is now a parking lot and a pier.

Just by the bus stop at Chuzenji village is a ropeway (round-
trip fare: ¥720 adults, ¥360 children under 12) to Chanokidaira
Hill; about 1,000 feet above the lake, it commands a wonderful
view of the whole surrounding area. Just below the ropeway,
⑫ on the outskirts of the village, is the top of **Kegon Falls.** Farther
on, as the road starts to descend into the valley, you'll find an
elevator (fare: ¥520 adults, ¥310 children under 12) that will
take you to an observation platform at the bottom of the gorge.
The flow of water over the falls is carefully regulated, but it is
especially impressive after a summer rain or a typhoon; in the
winter, the falls do not freeze completely, but form a beautiful
cascade of icicles.

If you have budgeted an extra day for Nikko, you might want to
consider a walk around the lake. A paved road along the north
shore extends for about 5 miles (⅛ of the whole distance), as far
⑬ as **Shobugahama Beach;** a "nature trail" parallels the road, but
it's not very attractive, especially in summer when there are
hordes of visitors. It is better to come this far by boat or bus.
From here the road branches off, for Senjogahara Plain and
Yunoko Lake. Just above the Nikko Prince Hotel at Shobu-
⑭ gahama are the **Ryuzu** (Dragon's Head) **Falls;** to the left is a
steep footpath that continues around the lake to Senjugahama,
and thence to a campsite at Asegata. The path is well marked
but can be rough going in places. From Asegata, it's less than
an hour's walk back to Chuzenji Temple.

Dining

Nikko has no shortage of popular restaurants geared to the tourist trade, though there is nothing special to distinguish one from another. Because they all have display cases outside, with price-tagged plastic models of the food they serve, you at least know what you're letting yourself in for. Noodle shops are always safe for lunch; the dishes called *soba* and *udon* are inexpensive, filling and tasty. In recent years Nikko has also come in to its share of Western-style fast-food restaurants.

For a meal in somewhat more upscale surroundings, try the dining room at one of the hotels listed below. Lunch will cost about ¥3,500 per person. Lunch at the Kanaya, with its air of old-fashioned gentility, is especially pleasant; the Boat House, at the hotel's branch hotel on the shore of Chuzenji, often has fresh trout from the lake.

Lodging

Kanko (tourist) hotels everywhere in Japan do most of their business with tour groups and large private parties; at Nikko and Chuzenji, especially, hotels seem almost relentless in the way they organize their schedules to move these groups in and out. At 7 or 7:30 AM, someone will knock on your door, demanding to remove the bedding; by 8:30, in most cases, no more breakfast service is available. Nothing is leisurely about kanko hotels; they tend to be noisy and relatively expensive for what they provide.

Four Western-style hotels in the area provide a welcome alternative. They fall into two price categories, Very Expensive and Expensive. Be warned that these hotels may add a surcharge to the basic rate at various times: weekends, nights before local festivals, July–August, October—in other words, whenever you are likely to want a room. Call ahead, or check with your travel agent for the prevailing rate at the time.

A 3% federal consumer tax is added to all hotel bills. Another 3% local tax is added to the bill if it exceeds ¥10,000. At most hotels, a 10%–15% service charge is added to the total bill. Tipping is not necessary.

The most highly recommended accommodations are indicated by a star ★.

Category	Cost*
Very Expensive	over ¥20,000
Expensive	¥15,000–¥20,000
Moderate	¥10,000–¥15,000
Inexpensive	under ¥10,000

Cost is for double room, without tax or service

Credit Cards The following credit card abbreviations are used: AE, American Express; DC, Diners Club; MC, MasterCard; V, Visa.

Nikko **Nikko Kanaya Hotel.** A little worn around the edges after a
★ century of operation, the Kanaya still has the best location in town—literally across the street from the Toshogu Shrine

area. The hotel is very touristy—daytime visitors, especially Westerners, come to browse through the old building and its gift shops. The staff is very helpful and is better at giving information on the area than the city information office. Rooms vary a great deal, as do their prices—up to ¥25,000 per person on weekends. The more expensive are all spacious and comfortable, with wonderful high ceilings; in the annex, you fall asleep to the sound of the Daiya River murmuring below by the Sacred Bridge. *1300 KamiHatsuishi-cho, Nikko 321-14, tel. 0288/54-0001 or (Tokyo office) 03/271-5215. 78 rooms, 59 with bath. Facilities: pool, nearby golf. AE, MC, V. Moderate–Very Expensive.*

Pension Turtle. This member of the Japanese Inn Group offers friendly, modest, and cost-conscious accommodations with or without private bath. Located 15 minutes by foot from the Shinkyo in the direction of Lake Chuzenji (take the Chuzenji bus from either railway station and get off at the Sogo Kaiken-mae bus stop), the inn is conveniently located near the Toshogu Shrine. *2-16 Takumi-cho, Nikko 321-14, tel. 0288/53-3168. 7 Western- and 5 Japanese-style rooms. Facilities: Japanese and Western breakfasts and dinners. AE. Inexpensive.*

Chuzenji **Nikko Lakeside Hotel.** This is a recently built hotel in the village of Chuzenji, at the foot of the lake. The accommodation has no particular character, but the views are good, and the transportation connections (to buses and excursion boats) are ideal. *2482 Chugishi, Nikko 321-16, tel. 0288/55-0321. 100 rooms, all with bath. AE, MC, V. Expensive–Very Expensive.*

Chuzenji Kanaya. On the road from the village to Shobugahama, this branch of the Nikko Kanaya has its own boat house and restaurant on the lake. The atmosphere here is something like that of a private club. The hotel is temporarily closed due to renovations and is due to reopen in Spring 1992. *2482 Chugushi, Nikko 321-16, tel. 0288/55-0356. 31 rooms, 5 with bath. Facilities: boating, fishing, waterskiing. AE, MC, V. Expensive.*

Shobugahama **Nikko Prince Hotel.** This is a new luxury hotel, within walking distance of the Ryuzu Falls. The Prince chain is one of Japan's largest and most successful leisure conglomerates, with hotels in most major cities and resorts. Minor differences in architecture aside, they are all pretty much the same experience: modern creature comforts and professionalism. *Shobugahama Chugushi, Nikko 321-16, tel. 0288/55-0661. 44 twin rooms and 16 split-level maisonettes, all with bath. Facilities: pool, 2 tennis courts, water sports. AE, DC, MC, V. Very Expensive.*

Kamakura

by Nigel Fisher

Visitors are attracted to Kamakura by its cultural souvenirs of the 141-year period when the city was the seat of Japan's first shoguns. The attraction is even greater because, after the 14th century, the ravages of history occurred elsewhere, and Kamakura's glorious past was unsullied; its history became a romantic blend of fact and fiction. During the 12th century, the Taira and the Minamoto clans were at each other's throats battling for supremacy. The Taira family won a major battle that should have secured their absolute control over Japan, but they made a serious mistake. They killed the Minamoto chief but spared his son, Yoritomo, and sent him to live in a monastery.

But Yoritomo Minamoto was not destined for a monk's life; instead he sought to avenge his father. Gathering support against the Taira clan, he chose Kamakura as his base of operations. Surrounded on three sides by hills and with the fourth side guarded by the sea, Kamakura was a natural location for defense against enemy attacks. The battle between the Minamoto and the Taira clans revived. By 1192, under the leadership of Yoritomo's skillful half-brother, Yoshitsune, the Taira were defeated, and the Kamakura era (1192–1333) began; Yoritomo established a shogunate government. The emperor was left as a figurehead in Kyoto, and, for the first time in Japan's history, the seat of power was structurally and geographically removed from Kyoto. The little fishing village of Kamakura became Japan's power center.

Yoritomo kept his antagonists at bay during his lifetime, but his successors were less than successful. His first son was assassinated, even though he had abdicated his position as shogun to become a monk, and the second son had his head sliced off by a disgruntled nephew. Because neither of Yoritomo's two sons had children, the Minamoto Dynasty ended. Yoritomo's wife, Masako, who had followed tradition by shaving her head and becoming a nun when her husband died, filled the power vacuum. On the murder of her second son, her family, the Hojos, took power. This family remained in control, often acting as regents for nominal child shoguns, for the next hundred years.

The demise of the Kamakura era began as the Hojo resources were drained in the support of armies warding off two Mongolian invasions (1274 and 1281) from China's Yuan Dynasty. Though the fortuitous typhoons—the *kamikaze* (divine wind)—may have saved the day against the Mongols, Kamakura still had to pay the various clans who fought alongside the Kamakura army and who had to remain on the alert for further invasions. Displeased with what they received, these clans grew dissatisfied with the Kamakura Shogunate. Emperor Godaigo saw his opportunity and rallied the discontented nobles to successfully defeat the shogunate. Thus ended the Kamakura era. The nation's authority, brought back to Kyoto, was shortly to be wrested away from Emperor Godaigo by the Ashikaga clan.

Kamakura reverted back to being a sleepy backwater on the edge of the sea. The town remained an isolated temple town until the Yokosuka railway line was built in 1889, and not until after World War II did Kamakura develop rapidly as a wealthy residential district for Yokohama and Tokyo.

Arriving and Departing

By far the best way to reach Kamakura is by train. From Tokyo, trains run from Tokyo Station (and Shimbashi Station) every 10–15 minutes during the day. The trip takes 56 minutes to Kita-Kamakura (North Kamakura) and one hour to Kamakura. Take the JR Yokosuka Line from track no. 1 downstairs in Tokyo Station. (Track no. 1 upstairs is on a different line and does not go to Kamakura.) The cost is ¥760 to Kita-Kamakura, and ¥880 to Kamakura (or use your JR Rail Pass).

Guided Tours

Unfortunately, no English-speaking tours may be booked in Kamakura. However, you can take one of the Japanese-speaking tours, which depart from Kamakura Station at 9:40 AM. Purchase tickets at the bus office to the right of the station. Take with you the book *Exploring Kamakura: A Guide for the Curious Traveler*, written in English by Michael Cooper, and you'll have more information at your fingertips than your fellow Japanese tourists on the bus.

On Saturdays and Sundays, a free guide service is offered by the Kanagawa Student Guide Federation. In exchange for the chance to practice their English, students show you the city. Arrangements need to be made in advance through the Japan National Tourist Office in Tokyo (tel. 03/3502–1461). Be at Kamakura Station by 10 AM.

Tours from Tokyo are available every day, often combined with Hakone. All major hotels in Tokyo can make the bookings, and, in most instances, a free pickup service is available from the major hotels. However, before you select a tour, make sure that it covers all of the Kamakura that you wish to see. Many do nothing much more than offer a fleeting glance of the Daibutsu (Great Buddha) in Hase. Our advice is to see Kamakura on your own. It is one of the easiest sightseeing trips to enjoy out of Tokyo.

Exploring

Numbers in the margin correspond with points of interest on the Kamakura map.

A tour of Kamakura is a walk through Japan's feudal era that brings back the personalities who lived and fought in the city's glorious age. The city has 65 Buddhist temples and 19 Shinto shrines. This chapter can include only a small percentage of them, but, hopefully, we can induce you to spend a little longer in Kamakura than the guided tours from Tokyo permit. Furthermore, Kamakura is accustomed to tourists, and most of the sights are either within walking distance of each other or a short hop on the bus or train.

For the purpose of seeing Kamakura's major temples and shrines, the following exploring section is divided into three separate areas. Traveling between each area is easily accomplished by short train rides. You could also walk everywhere, but there is certainly enough walking around the shrines and temples to satisfy most visitors.

The first tour explores the Tokyo side of Kamakura. Referred to as Kita-Kamakura (*kita* means north), it features the Engakuji Temple. The second tour covers Kamakura, one station stop south of Kita-Kamakura. This is downtown Kamakura, with a multitude of shops, restaurants, and Kamakura's venerated Tsurugaoka Hachimangu Shrine. The third tour visits Hase, to the southwest of Kamakura. It is reached by a 10-minute train ride on the Enoden Line. Hase's main attractions are the Daibutsu (Great Buddha) in Kotokuin Temple and the Hasedera Temple. These four sights (Engakuji, Tsurugaoka Hachimangu, Daibutsu, and Hasedera) are Kamakura's most important. It is easy to cover all four in a day and still leave time for lunch, shopping, and even a few more temples. However, a single day would be insufficient to cover all the places discussed in the following excursion, so judicious pruning may be required, and with only one day, you should not take the time to visit Enoshima Island, described at the end of this excursion.

Kita-Kamakura is the first train station to be reached from Tokyo on this excursion. For geographical simplicity, this excursion works its way south through Kamakura and Hase to Enoshima Island, a resort area along the coast. From there, rather than return through Kamakura, we take a train, using the Odakyu Line, back to Tokyo's Shinjuku. However, most visitors only have the time to go as far south as Hase before returning to Kamakura and Tokyo.

Kita-Kamakura

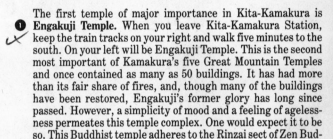

The first temple of major importance in Kita-Kamakura is **Engakuji Temple.** When you leave Kita-Kamakura Station, keep the train tracks on your right and walk five minutes to the south. On your left will be Engakuji Temple. This is the second most important of Kamakura's five Great Mountain Temples and once contained as many as 50 buildings. It has had more than its fair share of fires, and, though many of the buildings have been restored, Engakuji's former glory has long since passed. However, a simplicity of mood and a feeling of agelessness permeates this temple complex. One would expect it to be so. This Buddhist temple adheres to the Rinzai sect of Zen Buddhism.

Introduced into Japan from China at the beginning of the Kamakura period (1192–1333), Zen Buddhism was quickly accepted by the samurai class. The samurai were initially military louts and had none of the gentility of the Kyoto court; they despised the soft living of Kyoto and were especially attracted to Zen Buddhism, particularly the Rinzai sect, with its asceticism and its spontaneous moments of enlightenment. Rinzai sees the path to enlightenment through the ability to get beyond the immediate reality by understanding, for example, what is meant by the sound of one hand clapping. To reach this understanding is to have reached a spiritual level where mortal feeling is transcended. Searching for the spiritual among the old Japanese cedars and stone-paved walkways of Engakuji seems natural.

Among the National Treasures within the temple complex is the Shariden (Hall of the Holy Relics of Buddha). It has survived the many fires that have raged through the complex these last seven centuries and is the only temple to have kept its original form since it was built, in 1282. You cannot go beyond its gate, but you can peer through the gate for a fairly good look. The other famous National Treasure at Engakuji is the great belfry standing on the hilltop. Cast in 1301, Kamakura's most celebrated bell stands eight feet tall. Recently, though, visitors were no longer allowed to ring the bell. Only on rare occasions is it used, such as New Year's. Should one be so fortunate as to hear its deep resonant tone, one will be one step closer to understanding the sound of one hand clapping. The two structures open to the public are Butsunichian, which has a long tearoom where visitors can enjoy the Japanese tea ceremony, and the Obai-in. The latter is the mausoleum of Hojo Tokimune, his

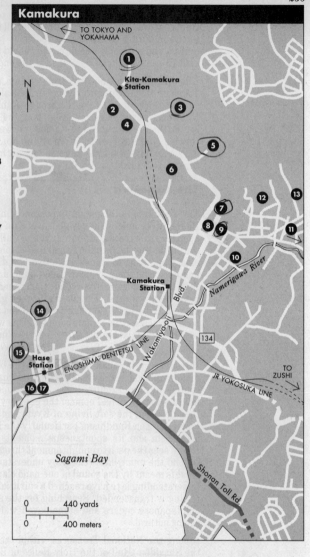

son, and his grandson, the last three regents before Kamakura fell. Off to the side of the mausoleum is a quiet garden with <u>apricot trees</u> (they bloom in February), where you can contemplate Kamakura's demise. *Admission: ¥200 adults, ¥100 children under 12. Open 8–5; 8–5:30 in summer.*

Ten minutes away from Engakuji, on the other side of the railway line, is **Tokeiji Temple**, founded in 1285. Its fame, or notoriety, is indicated by its more common name, the "Divorce Temple." In feudal Japan, the husband could obtain a divorce by simply sending his wife packing. Not so for the wife; no matter what cruel and unusual punishments her husband meted out, she had no grounds for securing a divorce. However, in the 13th century, Hojo Tokimune (whose mausoleum you saw at

Engakuji) decreed that if a woman ran away and made it to Tokeiji before being caught by her husband, she could receive sanctuary at the temple and stay there as a nun. After three years (later reduced to two), she was officially declared divorced. The temple remained a convent until the end of the Meiji Restoration. The last abbess died in 1902; her headstone is in the cemetery at the back of the temple. The cemetery has the peace of a Japanese garden. The headstones, scattered among the plum trees (they blossom in Feb.), are the symbols of refuge from a male-dominated society. *Admission: ¥200. Open 8:30–5.*

If you have limited time in Kamakura, then return from Tokeiji Temple to Kita-Kamakura Station for the train (one stop) to Kamakura. If, however, you have the energy and the time, you can walk to visit four temples en route to the Tsurugaoka Hachimangu Shrine, the next major place of interest.

❸ Meigetsu-in Temple requires a small detour from the direct route to Tsurugaoka Hachimangu Shrine, but if you are in Kamakura in June, the detour may be worthwhile to see the hydrangeas in bloom—a wafting sea of pink, white, and blue. To reach the Meigetsu-in Temple from Tokeiji, you must cross back over the railway line, walk down the main road a hundred yards or so, and then turn left. A word of warning, though: This normally quiet and peaceful temple, which is usually so conducive to reflection, becomes a rush of humanity when the hydrangeas bloom in June. *Admission: ¥100 adults. Open 9–4:30, hydrangea season 7–6.*

❹ The next temple to visit is **Jochiji,** located on the same side of the railway lines as Tokeiji. Jochiji Temple's entrance is on the right and over a small bridge. The temple is at the top of a series of moss-covered steps. The buildings are new replacements (about 50 years old) for the originals, which, like so many other temples in Japan, were destroyed by fire. But rather than Jochiji's buildings, it is the garden that makes the temple complex so appealing—standing in the northern sector are statues of the Seven Gods of Fortune. *Admission: ¥100. Open 9–5.*

❺ The next temple on the way to Tsurugaoka Hachimangu Shrine is **Kenchoji,** the most important of Kamakura's five main temples. One has only an inkling of how magnificent this temple was when it was completed in 1253. Successive fires destroyed the buildings and, though many of the buildings have been authentically reconstructed, the complex is half its original size. Near the Sanmon Gate is a bronze bell cast in 1255. It is the most revered treasure of the temple. The other key structures are the Main Hall and its Ceremonial Gate, a huge structure held together by wood wedges, yet having a light and delicate appearance. Both Kenchoji and Engakuji (the temple we visited first) are still active temples of the Rinzai sect of Zen Buddhism, where novitiates are trained and laymen come to take sessions in zazen meditation. You will often see groups of laymen sitting on the grounds while the master, who carries a wooden staff, stands among them ensuring that their concentration is not wandering. *Admission: ¥200. Open 8:30–4:30.*

❻ Across the road from Kenchoji is **Ennoji Temple.** While it may not have great aesthetic value, this structure is a macabre change from the others. During the feudal period, a belief was held that souls en route to the afterlife would be judged by the

Ten Kings of Heaven. Ennoji houses statues of these judges, and, far from looking compassionate, the judges display the most merciless countenances. To see them is enough to place you on your best behavior until their images fade from your memory. *Admission: ¥100. Open 10–4.*

If you walk another 200 yards south from Ennoji Temple, you arrive at the **Tsurugaoka Hachimangu Shrine.** However, for the benefit of those who took the train from Kita-Kamakura to Kamakura, we will begin our visit to Tsurugaoka Hachimangu Shrine from the station.

Kamakura

From the east side of Kamakura Station, walk across the plaza and go left on the main broad avenue, Wakamiya Oji. You'll easily recognize it. The golden arch of McDonald's is on the left and straight ahead is the first of three torii arches leading to the Tsurugaoka Hachimangu Shrine (often abbreviated to "Hachiman Shrine"). This is Kamakura's most important Shinto shrine and the best place to remember the Minamoto family.

When Yoritomo Minamoto became a father-to-be, he decreed that a stately avenue should be built through the center of Kamakura from the sea to the shrine. Such an avenue was to be fitting for a young prince's procession to the shrine. The avenue was completed and a son, Yoriie, was born, and a magnificent procession advanced up the avenue to the shrine for the prince to be blessed. Yoriie's future, though, was limited. At the age of 18, he became shogun. Weak in popularity and unable to master intrigue, Yoriie soon abdicated to become a monk. A year later he was assassinated. Although Yoriie never completed great deeds, his memory lives on with Wakamiya Oji, which translates as "Young Prince Avenue."

At the far end of Wakamiya Oji and at the entrance to the shrine, a small steeply arched vermilion bridge (Drum Bridge) crosses over a small stream that links two lotus ponds. Yoritomo had requested the creation of these ponds, and his wife, Masako, suggested placing islands in each. In the large pond to the right, filled with white lotus flowers, she placed three islands to represent the Minamoto clan (the Genji Pond); in the smaller pond to the left, she had four islands symbolizing the defeated Taira clan (the Heike Pond). The symbolism is significant. Three is considered a lucky number; four is unlucky.

Once you go over the Drum Bridge, the first structure you see is the Maiden Hall. The hall is the setting for the story so often retold in Noh and Kabuki theater, and it bears telling here. Though Yoritomo was the political force in defeating the Taira and establishing Kamakura Shogunate, it was his dashing half brother, Yoshitsune, who militarily defeated the Taira. In so doing, he won the admiration of many, and Kyoto used this to promote rumors that Yoshitsune had plans to become shogun. Yoritomo started to believe these rumors about his half brother and, despite Yoshitsune's declaration of allegiance, Yoritomo had him exiled and sent assassins to have him killed. Yoshitsune spent his life fleeing from one place to another until, in his 30th year, his enemies surrounded him and he was left with two options, suicide or capture. He chose the former.

Meanwhile his lover, Shizuka Gozen, a former dancer, was left behind in Kamakura. Yoritomo and his wife, Masako, commanded Shizuka to perform a dance, expecting her to do penitence. Instead, she danced to the joy of her love for Yoshitune and her concern for him in exile. Yoritomo was furious, and only Masako's influence kept him from ordering her death. However, when he found out that she was with child by his half brother, he ordered that, if it was a boy, the child was to be killed. Tension built up as Shizuka came closer to motherhood. A boy was born. Some historians tell how the child was brutally slaughtered down by the sea, while others say the child was placed in a cradle and cast adrift in the reeds, Moses-style. The tear-rendering drama is enacted once a year during the Spring Festival on the stage at Maiden Hall.

Behind the Maiden Hall is a flight of steps leading to the shrine's Main Hall. To the left of these steps is a ginkgo tree that was witness to a dastardly deed 700 years ago. From behind this tree, Priest Kugyo lurched out and lopped off the head of his uncle, the 26-year-old Minamoto-no-Sanetomo, the second and last son of Yoritomo. The priest was quickly apprehended, but the head of the second son was never found.

Like all Shinto shrines, the Main Hall is relatively bare and not particularly noteworthy. It was originally built in 1191, but the current version dates back to 1828. Within the shrine's precincts are two museums. The **Municipal Museum of Modern Art** (tel. 0467/22–500) the ferro-concrete complex near the Heike Pond, contains Japanese oil and watercolor paintings, wood blocks, and sculptures. *Admission: ¥200. Open 10–4:30. Closed Mon. and the day following national holidays.*

The other museum, the **Kamakura Museum** (tel. 0467/22–0753) exhibits a fine collection of objects pertaining to the Kamakura period and a display of ukiyo-e (wood-block prints). Of the two exhibitions, the latter is more interesting and has more relevance to Japan's early shogunate. *Admission: ¥200. Open 9–4. Closed Mon. and national holidays.*

While crowds may gather at the Tsurugaoka Hachimangu Shrine, peace is often found at the **Hokokuji Temple,** a little Zen temple of the Rinzai sect, which was built in 1334. Over the years, it fell into disrepair and neglect until, recently, an enterprising priest took over. He has since cleaned up the gardens and successfully promotes the temple for sessions in zazen and for calligraphy exhibitions. While some criticize the temple's commercial endeavors, on a quiet day the gardens offer rest and, at the back of the temple, a thick bamboo grove, with a small teahouse. Relaxing here an hour or so makes for a delightful interlude from the endless trail from statue to altar. To reach Hokokuji, take the street that leads off to the right from Tsurugaoka Hachimangu Shrine and Wakamiya Oji. After a mile, there will be a sign on the right-hand side, which leads you to Hokokuji. *Admission: ¥100. Open 9–4.*

Several other temples are in the vicinity of Hokokuji. **Jomyoji Temple,** which was founded in 1188, is across the street and 100 yards to the right. Some 300 yards back on the road to Kamakura and then up the street to the right is **Yoritomo's Tomb.** It is surprisingly plain, but you may want to pay tribute to the man who placed Kamakura on the map. To the right of Yoritomo's Tomb (you must retrace your steps for 100 yards and make virtually a U-turn at the first street on the left) is the **Kamakuragu Shrine.** This Shinto shrine was built after the Meiji Restoration as a tribute to Prince Morinaga and as propaganda for the revived imperial regime. Prince Morinaga was the third son of Godaigo. After Godaigo's successful defeat of the Kamakura Shogunate, the imperial family soon came under pressure from the Ashikaga clan. Morinaga was an effective champion of the imperial cause. Naturally, this did not suit the Ashikaga clan's plans for takeover, so they denounced Morinaga as a traitor to the throne of Godaigo. Morinaga was held captive in the cave behind the present site of the Kamakuragu Shrine, and, before the truth finally dawned on Godaigo, Morinaga was beheaded.

A bus to and from Kamakura Station (bus stop #5) travels the street on which all these temples have their access roads. We recommend walking out from Kamakura and returning by the bus, because it is easier to recognize the stop for downtown Kamakura than the stops for each of the shrines. Downtown Kamakura is a good place to stop for lunch and shop. Restaurants and shops selling locally made products abound on Wakamiya Oji Avenue, and its parallel street, Komachi-dori Avenue.

Hase

Hase is the next area to explore for reliving Kamakura's past. Here you'll find the **Daibutsu** (Great Buddha) in the **Kotokuin Temple,** and also the Hasedera Temple. To reach Hase, take the train (the Enoden Line located on the western side of the JR Kamakura Station) three stops to Hase Station. Off to the left of the station is the main street, and this leads, after a 10-minute walk, to the Kotukuin Temple.

Kotokuin Temple is totally dominated by the 37-foot-tall bronze statue of the Great Buddha. Sitting cross-legged, robed with drapes flowing in the classical lines reminiscent of ancient Greece, the compassionate Amida Buddha serenely smiles down on its audience. The bronze statue was cast in 1292, three centuries before Europeans reached Japan; the concept of the classical Greek lines used in the Buddha's robe must have been transmitted down the Silk Route through China during the time of Alexander the Great. The Daibutsu was probably first conceived, though not completed, in 1180 by Yoritomo Minamoto, who wanted a statue to outshine the enormous Daibutsu in Nara. Until 1495, the statue was housed in a wooden temple, which was washed away in a great tidal wave. Since then, the loving Buddha has stood exposed, facing the cold winters and hot summers for the last five centuries.

To some of us, it seems sacrilegious to walk inside the Great Buddha and inspect the statue's innards. But not to the Japanese. For an extra ¥20, one can enter Buddha's right side into his stomach. Not particularly interesting, but it is something that is done by many visitors. *Admission to the Kotokuin Temple: ¥150. Open 8–5:45.*

If you retrace your steps from Kotokuin for about three-quarters of the way along the main street (toward Hase Station) and then take a right turn, **Hasedera Temple** will be before you. Hasedera is one of the most enchanting, sad, and beautiful temples in Japan. First, as you enter, is the garden with a small pond formation that inspires serenity despite the many visitors. Then, as you climb the flights of steep stone steps up to the Amida and Kannon Hall, you are flabbergasted by the innumerable small stone images of Jizobosatsu. Jizobosatsu is one manifestation of the bodhisattva who stands on the border of this life and the next to guide souls to salvation. In its Japanese version, Jizobosatsu has many representations. Here at Hasedera, the Jizobosatsu is the bodhisattva who guides the souls of stillborn children. Mothers who have experienced the misfortunes of losing their unborn children dedicate small images of this god as a means of praying for the souls of their children. Included in the term "stillborn" are aborted children. The sight of the stone statues is strangely touching and melancholic.

Walking farther up the steps, one reaches the temple's main building; visitors are allowed in the **Amida Hall** (Amida-do) and the **Kannon Hall** (Kannon-do). The Kannon Hall is Hasedera's main attraction. In the center of the hall is Juichimen (11-faced Kannon); standing 30 feet tall, it is the largest carved wood statue in Japan. The merciful Kannon has 10 smaller faces on top of his head symbolizing his ability to see and search out in all directions those in need of help. No one knows for sure when Juichimen was carved. Certainly it was before the 12th century. According to the temple records, a monk, Tokudo Shonin, carved two images of the 11-faced Kannon from a huge laurel tree in 721. The image from the main trunk was installed in Hase, located in what is known today as the Nara Prefecture. The other image was thrown into the sea to go wherever the sea decided that there were sentient souls in need of the benevolence of Kannon. The statue washed up near Kamakura. (It was not until much later, in 1342, that the statue was covered with gold leaf by Takauji Ashikaga, the first of the 15 Ashikaga shoguns who followed the Kamakura era.)

Amida Hall, the other major building of Hasedera Temple, has the image of a seated Amida. Yoritomo Minamoto ordered the sculpting of this statue in an effort to ward off the dangers of reaching the ripe old age of 42. (This age was considered to be unlucky.) The statue did the trick. Yoritomo made it until he was 52, when he was thrown from a horse and died soon after. Hence, the popular name for this Buddha is the *yakuyoke* (good-luck) Amida, and many visitors take the opportunity to make a special prayer here, especially before graduation exams. To the left of Amida Hall is a small restaurant where you can buy good-luck candy and admire the view over Kamakura Beach and Sagami Bay. Hasedera is the only Kamakura temple looking onto the sea, and this view, accompanied by the benevolent spirit of Hasedera, makes an appropriate end to a day of Kamakura sightseeing. *Admission: ¥200. Open Mar.– Nov., daily 7–5:40; Dec.–Feb. 28, daily 7–4:40.*

Enoshima

The Kamakura story would not be complete without Nichiren, the monk who created the only native Japanese sect of Buddhism. Nichiren spent several years advocating his beliefs and criticizing the Hojo regents, who held power after the Minamoto shoguns. Exasperated, the authorities sent him to exile on the Izu Peninsula, then allowed him to return. But Nichiren still kept on criticizing and, in 1271, the Hojo rulers condemned him to death. Execution was to take place on a hill to the south of Hase. As the executioner swung his sword, a lightening bolt struck the blade and snapped it in two. A little taken aback, the executioner sat down to collect his wits. Meanwhile, a messenger ran back to tell the Hojo regents of the event. On his way, he met another messenger, who was carrying a writ from the Hojo regents commuting Nichiren's sentence to exile on Sado Island.

16 Followers of Nichiren built a temple in 1337 to mark this event on the hill where he was to be executed. The temple is **Ryukoji** and is reached by continuing south on the Edoden Line from Hase. The train cuts through Kamakura's defensive hills to the shoreline en route to Enoshima. Get off the train at the last station, Koshigoe, and walk in the direction of Enoshima. The temple is on the right.

While there are other Nichiren temples closer to Kamakura, Myohonji and Ankokuronji, for example, Ryukoji not only has the typical Nichiren-style main hall with gold tassels hanging from its roof but also a beautiful pagoda (1904), built as if to embrace the surrounding trees.

The shoreline in this vicinity, by the way, has some of the beaches closest to Tokyo, and, during the hot, humid summer months, it seems that all of the city's teeming millions pour onto these beaches in search of a vacant patch of rather dirty gray sand. It is not a beach resort to be recommended.

17 A more enjoyable place to feel the sea breezes is to cross over the causeway from Enoshima Station to **Enoshima Island.** The island is only 2½ miles in circumference and peaks with a hill at its center. At the top of the hill is the shrine at which fishermen would pray for a bountiful catch—before it became a tourist attraction. It used to be quite a hike up to the shrine, but now there is a series of moving escalators to the top with an array of souvenir stalls. Spaced around the island are several cafés and restaurants. On a clear, warm day you can have lunch at one of these restaurants with a balcony facing the bay.

The way back to Tokyo from Enoshima is by train to Shinjuku on the Odakyu Railways. The train runs every 30 minutes and takes 75 minutes to make the trip. The cost is ¥770. Alternatively, one can retrace one's steps to Kamakura and take the JR Yokosuka Line to Tokyo Station.

Dining

Kamakura has a multitude of restaurants from which to choose, with places to eat near every sightseeing area. One can literally drop into a restaurant whenever the appetite strikes or a rest is needed. However, should you be in the vicinity of those mentioned below and the urge for a good meal comes over you, they are recommended.

A 3% federal consumer tax is added to all restaurant bills. Another 3% local tax is added to the bill if it exceeds ¥5,000. At more expensive restaurants, a 10%–15% service charge is also added to the bill. Tipping is not necessary.

The most highly recommended restaurants are indicated by a star ★.

Category	Cost*
Very Expensive	over ¥6,000
Expensive	¥4,000–¥6,000
Moderate	¥2,000–¥4,000
Inexpensive	under ¥2,000

*Cost is per person without tax, service, or drinks

Credit Cards The following credit card abbreviations are used: AE, American Express; DC, Diners Club; MC, MasterCard; V, Visa.

★ **Tori-ichi.** This elegant restaurant serves traditional Japanese fare (*keiseki*) in tranquil surroundings. In an old country-style building, kimono-dressed waitresses serve sumptuous multi-course meals, including one or more subtle-tasting soups, sushi, tempura, grilled fish, and other delicacies. *7-13 Onarimachi, Kamakura, tel. 0467/22–1818. Reservations advised. Dress: informal. DC. Open noon–9 (last order at 8). Very Expensive.*

Kaseiro. On the street that leads toward Daibutsu at the Kotokuin Temple, this establishment offers the best Chinese food in the city. The restaurant is located in an old Japanese house, where the dining room windows look onto a small, restful garden. *3-1-14 Hase Kamakura-shi, Kamakura, tel. 0467/ 22–0280. Dress: informal. AE, DC, V. Open 11–8. Moderate.*

Tonkatsu Komachi. This restaurant is a useful place for lunch when you are shopping on Komachi-dori Avenue or going to (and from) Tsurugaoka Hachimangu Shrine. A range of Japanese food is offered (visual menu in the window); however, the tasty *tonkatsu* (pork cutlet) is its specialty. *1-6-11 Komachi, Kamakura 248, tel. 0467/22–2025. Dress: informal. No credit cards. Open 11:30–8. Moderate.*

Yokohama

by Nigel Fisher

For more than 200 years, Japan had closed its doors to virtually all foreign contact. Then, in 1853, Commodore Perry's Black Ships entered the port city of Uraga and forced the Tokugawa Shogunate to reluctantly open Japan to the West. Three years later, Townsend Harris became America's first diplomatic representative to Japan. Once the commercial treaty with the United States was signed, Harris lost no time in setting up his residence in the Hangakuji Temple in Kanagawa. However, Kanagawa was one of the 53 relay stations on the Tokaido Highway, and the presence of unclean, long-haired barbarians caused offense to the traditional Japanese. Moreover, many samurai wanted Japan to remain in isolation and would be willing to give their lives to rid Japan of the foreign pestilence. Unable to protect the foreigners in Kanagawa, the shogunate required that Harris and all foreigners move from Kanagawa and establish a foreign trading port at nearby Yokohama.

At the time, Yokohama was a small fishing village surrounded by ugly mud flats. Foreigners, diplomats, and traders were confined to a compound, guarded with checkpoints. Harris considered, probably correctly, that he and every other Westerner were being placed in isolation. But changes were happening very fast in Japan. Within 30 years, seven centuries of shogunate rule would come to an end, and the period known as the Meiji Restoration would begin, in which, under the authority of Emperor Meiji, Japan sought Western advice and ideas. By the early 1900s, Yokohama was to become one of the world's busiest ports and Japan's major export and import center.

Yokohama's growth has been as dramatic as the crippling blows it has suffered. As soon as it became a designated international port in 1869, it started to grow rapidly. Most of the foreign traders who came to Japan set up business in Yokohama; the city's port became the main center from which Japan's foreign trade flowed. As the port grew, so did the international community. An especially large community of British citizens developed from whom the Japanese frequently sought advice, on the grounds that Great Britain was also an island nation. Reminders of their presence can still be seen by an occasional game of cricket at the Yokohama Country and Athletic Club, which, while now open to all nations, used to be the domain where British expatriates would drink their gin and enjoy their refined activities.

Then Yokohama came tumbling down. On September 1, 1923, the Great Kanto Earthquake struck both Tokyo and Yokohama. It destroyed much of Yokohama. Some 60,000 homes made of wood and paper were razed, and 20,000 lives were lost. After such devastation, Yokohama could not retain its exclusiveness as Japan's international city and chief trading port. During the six years that it took to restore the city, many foreign businesses took up quarters elsewhere, primarily in Kobe and Osaka, and did not return to Yokohama.

Nevertheless, over the next 20 years, Yokohama mushroomed once more; a large industrial zone was built along its shoreline. Then everything came tumbling down again. On May 29, 1945, in a span of four hours, 700 American B-29 bombers leveled 42% of the city. Destruction was more extensive than that caused by the earthquake. Even so, Yokohama rose once more from the debris, and, boosted by Japan's postwar economic miracle, extended its urban sprawl all the way to Tokyo to the north and to Kamakura in the south.

With the advent of air travel and increased competition from other ports (Nagoya and Kobe, for example), Yokohama's decline as Japan's seaport continued. The glamour of great liners docked at Yokohama's piers has become only a memory, kept alive by a museum ship and the occasional visit by Cunard's *Queen Elizabeth II* while cruising the Pacific. The only regularly scheduled passenger service is by a Soviet vessel, which makes weekly runs to Nakhodka at the extremity of the Trans-Siberian Railway, and then only from May to October. To replace its emphasis on being a port city, Yokahama has concentrated on its industries—shipbuilding, automobiles, and petrochemicals are three of its largest—and its service to Tokyo as a satellite city. Yokohama has always been politically and culturally overshadowed by Tokyo, and that is no more apparent than today, as commuters swarm into Tokyo every morning from their homes in Yokohama.

Is Yokohama worth a visit? Certainly, it should not get top priority. The city has perhaps more interest to the Japanese than to Westerners. Up to World War II, people from Tokyo would come to Yokohama to see the strange *gaijin* (foreigners), their alien ways, and their European-style buildings. That image still persists, despite the destruction of most of the city's late-19th- and early-20th-century buildings. After all, Yokohama had Japan's first bakery (in 1860), operated by an enterprising Japanese, Noda Hyogo, who catered to Westerners. It was also the first city to have public toilets. Eighty-three of them were built in 1871! A year later, Japan's first railway, linking Yokohama and Shimbashi in Tokyo, was completed. So Yokohama does have memories of Japan's first encounters with the West; a notable building in the center of the city is the Port Memorial Hall, which commemorates Yokohama's position as the front-runner in opening Japan to the West. Yet, as fun as this trivia may be, Yokohama has less to see than one would expect. Indeed, a visit to Yokohama should only be made if one has an extra day to spare while in Tokyo, or when returning to Tokyo from an excursion to Kamakura, 20 minutes on the train south of Yokohama.

Arriving and Departing

Between the Airport and Center City From Narita Airport, a direct limousine-bus service departs two or three times an hour between 7 AM and 11 PM for Yokohama City Air Terminal (YCAT). Alternatively, you can take the limousine-bus service from Narita to Tokyo Station and continue on to Yokohama by train. With either method, the total journey will take more than two hours, more likely three if the traffic is heavy. From Haneda Airport, buses depart every 15 minutes for YCAT, taking 30 minutes to make the trip. YCAT is a five-minute taxi ride from Yokohama Station.

By Train *From Tokyo* JR trains from Tokyo Station leave approximately every 10 minutes, depending on the time of day. Take the Yokosuka, the Tokaido, or Keihin Tohoku lines to Yokohama Station. (The Yokosuka and Tokaido lines take 30 min, and the Keihin Tohoku Line takes 40 min.) From there, the Keihin Tohoku Line (platform 3) goes on to Kannai and Ishikawa-cho, Yokohama's business and downtown areas. If one is going directly to downtown Yokohama from Tokyo, the blue-colored commuter trains of the Keihin Tohoku Line are best. From Shibuya Station in Tokyo, the Tokyu Toyoko Line, a private line, connects directly with Yokohama Station and, hence, is an alternative if you leave from the western part of Tokyo.

From Nagoya and Points South The Shinkansen Kodama trains stop at Shin-Yokohama Station, 5 miles from the city center. It is then necessary to take the local train for the seven-minute ride into town.

Getting Around

By Train Yokohama Station is the city transport center, where all train lines link together and connect with the city's subway and bus service. However, Kannai and Ishikawa-cho are the two train stations for the downtown areas. Use the Keihin Tohoku Line from Yokohama Station to reach these areas. Trains leave every two to five minutes from platform 3. Once you are at Kannai or Ishikawa-cho, most of Yokohama's points of interest are within easy walking distance of each other. The one notable exception is the Sankeien Garden, which requires a short train and bus ride from downtown.

By Taxi During the day, ample taxis are available. Taxi stands are outside the train stations, and cabs may also be flagged in the streets. However, often the congested traffic makes walking a faster means of traveling. The basic fare is ¥480 for the first 2 kilometers, then ¥90 for every additional 395 meters. Vacant taxis show a red light in the windshield.

By Subway One line connects Shin-Yokohama, Yokohama, and Totsuka.

By Bus Buses exist, but their routes confuse even the locals.

By Car Rental cars are available from Yokohama Station, but the congested traffic and lack of street signs make driving difficult.

Important Addresses and Numbers

Tourist Information The **Yokohama Tourist Office** (tel. 045/441–7300; open 10–6; closed Dec. 28–Jan. 3) is in the central passageway of the Yokohama Station. A similar office with the same closing times is located at Shin-Yokohama Station (tel. 045/441–7300). The head office of the **Yokohama International Tourist Association** (tel. 045/641–5824; open 9–5 weekdays, 9–noon Sat.; closed national holidays) is on the first floor of the Silk Center Building, a 15-minute walk from Kannai Station.

Emergencies **Ambulance** or **Fire,** tel. 119; **Police,** tel. 110. **The Yokohama Police Station** has a Foreign Affairs Department (tel. 045/623–0110).

Doctors **Washinzaka Hospital,** (169 Yamate-cho, Naka-ku, tel. 045/623–7688).

English Bookstore **Maruzen,** (Yokohama Bridge, 2-34 Bentendori, Naka-ku, tel. 045/212–2031).

Guided Tours

Double-decker buses of the **Blue Line** depart every 30 minutes from the east exit of Yokohama Station, circle the major tourist route—Osanbashi Pier, Chinatown, Motomachi, Harbor View Park, Yamashita Pier, Osanbashi Pier, Bashamichi—and return to the station. These tours operate weekdays 10–4:40, weekends and national holidays 10–5.

The Teiki Yuran Bus is a seven-hour sightseeing bus tour that covers the major sights and includes lunch at a Chinese restaurant in Chinatown. The tour is in Japanese only, though pamphlets written in English are available at most sightseeing stops. Tickets are sold at the bus offices at Yokohama Station (east side) and at Kannai, and the tour departs from bus stop no. 14 on the east side of Yokohama Station. Cost: ¥5,160 adults, ¥3,420 children under 12.

A shuttle boat, the *Sea Bass,* connects Yokohama Station and Yamashita Park in 15 minutes. The boat leaves every 20 minutes 10–7 from the east side of Yokohama Station and offers another view of Yokohama.

Sightseeing boats (tel. 045/651–2697) named the *Marine Shuttle* and the *Akai-Kutsu* make 40-, 60-, and 90-minute tours of the harbor and bay for ¥750, ¥1,200, and ¥2,000, respectively. Boarding is at the pier at Yamashita Park; boat departures are approximately every hour 10:30–6:30.

Home Visit System

The Yokohama International Tourist Association arranges visits to the homes of English-speaking Japanese families. These visits are usually for a few hours and are designed to give foreigners a glimpse into the Japanese way of life. To arrange a visit or for more information, call the Yokohama International Tourist Association (tel. 045/641–5824).

Exploring

Numbers in the margin correspond with points of interest on the Yokohama map.

As large as Yokohama is, its central area is quite self-contained. Because Yokohama developed as a port city, much of its activity has always been around its waterfront (the Bund) on the west side of Tokyo Bay. Kannai (literally: "within the checkpoint") is downtown, where the international community was originally confined by the shogunate. Though downtown has expanded to include the waterfront and Ishikawa-cho, Kannai has always been Yokohama's heart.

Downtown may be viewed as consisting of two adjacent rectangular areas. One area is the old district of Kannai, bounded by Bashamichi Street to the north and Nippon-odori Avenue to the south, with Kannai Station on the western side and the waterfront on the eastern. This area contains the business offices of modern Yokohama. South of Nippon-odori is another main area. Its northern boundary is Nippon-odori, and the southern boundary runs along the Motomachi Shopping Street and the International Cemetery. This rectangle is flanked by the Ishikawa-cho Station to the west, and Yashamita-Koen Park and the waterfront to the east. The middle of this part of the city is dominated by Chinatown.

Notwithstanding the lure of Bashamichi's shops and its reconstructed 19th-century appearance, the southern area holds the most interest if you are short of time. That is where the following walking tour of Yokohama begins.

Whether one is coming from Tokyo, Nagoya, or Kamakura, the best place to begin a tour of Yokohama is from the **Ishikawa-cho Station.** Take the south exit from the station and head in the direction of the waterfront. Within a block of the station is the

1 beginning of the **Motomachi Shopping Street,** which follows the Nakamura River toward the harbor. This is where the Japanese set up shop 100 years ago to serve the strange foreigners living within Kannai. Now the same street is lined with smart boutiques, jewelry stores, and coffee shops, and it attracts a fashionable younger crowd.

At the far end of Motomachi and up to the right is a small hill.

2 Here is the **International Cemetery,** a Yokohama landmark as a preserve for foreigners and a reminder of the port city's heritage. The cemetery started in 1854 when an American sailor chose this spot for his final resting place. Since then the burial ground has been restricted to non-Japanese. About 4,000 graves are on this hillside, and the inscriptions on the crosses and headstones attest to some 40 different nationalities who lived and died in Yokohama.

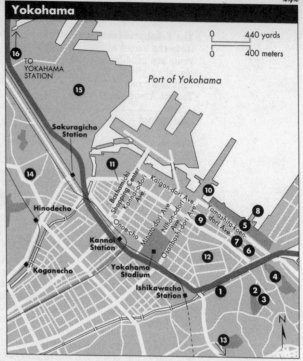

❸ Behind the cemetery is the **Yamate Museum,** which preserves
mementoes of the late-19th-century lifestyle of Westerners
who lived in Yokohama. It is perhaps more interesting to the
Japanese than it is to foreigners. *247 Yamate, Naka-ku, tel.
045/622–1188. Admission: ¥200. Open 11–4, Sun. and holidays 11–5. Closed Dec. 30–Jan. 1.*

❹ One hundred yards beyond the museum is **Minato-No-Mieru-
Oka Park** (Harbor View Park). Once the barracks of the British
forces in Yokohama, the hilltop park offers a fine view overlook-
❺ ing **Yamashita-Koen Park** and the harbor beyond. Should you
ever find yourself staying the night in Yokohama, come to this
park for the splendid sight of the harbor lights and floodlit gardens of Yamashita below.

Yamashita-Koen Park, just down from Minoto-No-Mieru-Oka,
parallels the waterfront. It is a park for strolling or a place to
rest, if one can find an empty bench free of dating Japanese cou-
❻ ples. Near the park is the **Yokohama Doll Museum,** which
houses 4,000 dolls from Japan and the rest of the world. The
fairy-tale quality of the museum is a pleasant diversion from
Yokohama's rather mundane sights with or without the presence of a child in tow. *18 Yamashita-cho, Naka-ku, tel. 045/
671–9361. Admission: ¥300. Open 10–5, July–Aug. 10–7.
Closed Mon. (Tues. after a national holiday), Dec. 29–Jan. 1.*

Yamashita-Koen Park is a green urban oasis. Its existence is
perhaps the only redeeming factor of the Great Kanto Earthquake in 1923. The debris of collapsed buildings left by the
earthquake were swept away, and the area was made into a 17-

acre park with lawns, trees, and flowers. The park's fountain, by the way, is a statue of the Guardian of the Water, presented to Yokohama by San Diego, one of Yokohama's sister cities.

At the entrance to Yamashita-Koen Park is the rather ugly **Marine Tower** (tel. 045/641-7838), a decagonal building standing 348 feet high. It has a navigational beacon at the 338-foot mark and purports to be the tallest lighthouse in the world. At the 100-meter (328-foot) level, an observation gallery offers 360-degree views of the harbor and city. It is the best place to acquire an aerial appreciation of the area and, on clear days, preferably in the autumn, it is possible to see Mt. Fuji in the distance. Also contained within the Marine Tower is a bird museum (Birdpia) and the Yokohama Science Museum. *The Marine Tower Observation Room admission: ¥700 adults, ¥350 children 6–15, ¥250 children 3–6. Open spring and autumn 10–7, summer 10–9, winter 10–6. (If sunny on holidays, open until 8:30.)*

On the waterfront and halfway down the park is where the *Hikawa-maru* is moored. For 30 years, the ship shuttled passengers between Yokohama and Seattle, making a total of 238 trips. It recalls the time when Yokohama was a great passenger port of oceangoing liners. It is not worth touring the ship, as brochures suggest, but the *Hikawa-maru* does have a public restaurant. A visit is best in the summer, when the ship's upper deck becomes a beer garden.

At the northern end of the park is the Silk Center Building; on its second floor is the **Silk Museum.** At the turn of the century, all of the Japanese silk for export was shipped out of Yokohama, and the museum pays tribute to those days. As well as a display of a variety of silk fabrics, the museum has an informative exhibit on the silk-making process. The attendants are very happy to answer questions. Also in the Silk Center Building, on the first floor, is the head office of the Yokohama International Tourist Association and the Kanagawa Prefecture Tourist Information Office. *1 Yamashita-cho, Naka-ku, tel. 045/641–0841. Admission: ¥300. Open 9–4:30. Closed Mon., on the day after a national holiday, and Dec. 29–Jan. 1.*

Across the street from the Silk Building is the **Yokohama Archives of History.** The building was once the British Consulate and now houses some 140,000 items recording the history of Yokohama since the port's opening. On the other side of the street is the monument to the U.S.–Japanese Friendship Treaty. *3 Nihon Odori, Naka-ku, tel. 045/201–2100. Admission: ¥200 adults, ¥100 children under 15. Open 9:30–4:30. Closed Mon., on the day after a national holiday, and Dec. 29–Jan. 1.*

If one continues along the street running parallel to the waterfront, one reaches **Bashamichi,** the street that runs between Kannai Station and Shinko Pier. Literally, Bashamichi means "horse-carriage street," so named after it was widened to allow Westerners' carriages to pass. Now this redbrick road has become a nostalgic symbol of the city's 19th-century international past with antique-looking telephone booths and imitation gas lamps. Halfway up the street is the **Kanagawa Prefectural Museum.** This Western-style structure with a domed roof was built in 1904 and is one of the few buildings in Yokohama to have survived both the Great Kanto Earthquake and World War II. The exhibits inside the museum—archaeological and natural-history artifacts from the region—have only marginal interest for the tourist. *5-60 Minami Naka-dori, Naka-ku, tel. 045/ 201-0926. Admission: ¥200. Open 9-4. Closed Mon. and the last Fri. of each month.*

12 At the top end (away from the waterfront) of Bashamichi is **Kannai Station.** One of Yokohama's unique neighborhoods, **Chinatown** is a 10-minute walk from there. From the station, just before you reach Yokohama Stadium, turn left to cut through Yokohama-Koen Park to reach the top of Nippon-odori Avenue. Then take a right, and you'll enter Chinatown through the North Gate leading to the 15-meter-high vermilion Hairomon Gate. If you have decided not to walk as far as Bashimichi, take the left from the Silk Building up Nippon-odori, past the monument to the U.S.–Japanese Friendship Treaty, and then left, through the North Gate.

Yokohama's Chinatown is the largest settlement of Chinese in Japan. Not only are its small alleys full of shops selling Chinese goods, biscuits, and medicines, but also wonderful exotic aromas exude from the shops selling spices. The area offers a good opportunity to dine on authentic Chinese food and is the choice place for lunch in Yokohama. You'll find more than a hundred restaurants from which to choose. If you prefer a good Western meal, continue walking along the main street through Chinatown; you'll exit at the East Gate leading to Yamashita-Koen Park and the New Grand Hotel.

Additional Attractions

What has been left out of this walking tour through Yokohama are Sankeien Garden, Iseyama Shrine, Nippon Memorial Park, and Sojiji Temple. Let's first go to the Sankeien Garden, of which the *hamakko* (the name the locals give each other) are justly proud.

13 **Sankeien Garden** was once the garden of Tomitaro Hara, one of Yokohama's wealthiest men, who made his money as a silk merchant before becoming a patron of the arts. His garden was opened to the public in 1906. Amid its rolling hills, valleys, and ponds are traditional Japanese buildings, some of which have been transported from Kamakura and the Kansai area of Western Honshu. Especially noteworthy is the Rinshunkaku building, a villa built for the Tokugawa clan in 1649. There is also a tea-ceremony house, Choshukaku, built by the third Tokugawa shogun, Iemitsu Tokugawa. The other noteworthy buildings are the small temple transported from Kyoto's famed Daitokuji Temple and the farmhouse brought from the Gifu district in the Japan Alps.

Walks through Sankeien are especially rewarding for its flowering trees in the spring: plum blossoms in February, and cherry blossoms in early April. Then, in June, come the irises, followed by the water lilies. With the coming of autumn, the trees come back into their own with their tinted golden leaves. To reach Sankeien Garden, use the JR Keihin Tohoku Line to Negishi Station, where you can take a 10-minute bus ride to the garden. *293 Honmoku Sannotani, Naka-ku, tel. 045/621-0635. General admission: ¥300 adults, ¥60 children. The inner garden with the old traditional buildings has a separate admission of ¥300 adults, ¥120 children; it is open 9-4. The outer garden is open 9-4:30. Both gardens closed Dec. 29-31.*

⓮ Iseyama Shrine, a branch of the nation's revered Grand Shrines of Ise, is the most important shrine in Yokohama (admission free; open dawn–dusk). Its location requires a 10-minute walk from the Sakuragicho Station and is, for the tourist, perhaps only worth the time if one has seen most of everything else in Yokohama. The **⓯ Nippon Memorial Park,** also 10 minutes by foot from the Sakuragicho Station but in the direction of the bay, is now the resting place of the *Nippon-maru.* This 1930 sailing vessel was used as a training ship and, in its time, made 46 voyages around the world. She was a beautiful sight under sail, but now she resides in permanent dry dock alongside the recently constructed (1989) maritime museum.

The last notable sight to visit before totally leaving Yokohama is the **⓰ Sojiji Temple.** This is a worthwhile stop en route back to Tokyo. Take the JR Keihin Tohoku Line two stops to Tsurumi Station. Upon exiting the station, walk five minutes south (back toward Yokohama), passing Tsurumi University on your right. You'll soon reach the temple complex, which you may enter at the stone lanterns.

The Soto Buddhist sect, founded in 1321, was headquartered at Ishikawa on the Noto Peninsula (on the north coast of Japan, near Kanazawa). However, when the complex at Ishikawa was destroyed by fire in the 19th century, the sect erected its Yokohama temple complex. (Another Sojiji Temple is located at Eiheiji in Fukui Prefecture.) The Yokohama Sojiji is, therefore, relatively new, but it is a good example of Zen architecture; it is a very busy temple, with more than 200 monks and novitiates living in the complex. Visitors are not allowed to enter Emperor Godaigo's mausoleum (he was the emperor who defeated the Kamakura Shogunate), but one can visit the Buddha Hall and Main Hall. Both are large concrete structures. The Treasure House contains a wide variety of Buddhas. *Admission: ¥300. Open 9–3.*

Dining

Yokohama is a large, international city. The number and variety of restaurants are great, including more than 100 Chinese restaurants in Chinatown. The number of Japanese restaurants is uncountable; in the Mitsukoshi Department Store alone there are at least 32 tearooms and restaurants. The following are thus a small selection of what Yokohama offers and are restaurants familiar with the needs of foreign guests.

A 3% federal consumer tax is added to all restaurant bills. Another 3% local tax is added to the bill if it exceeds ¥5,000. At more expensive restaurants, a 10%–15% service charge is also added to the bill. Tipping is not necessary.

The most highly recommended restaurants are indicated by a star ★.

Category	Cost
Very Expensive	over ¥6,000
Expensive	¥4,000–¥6,000

Moderate	¥2,000–¥4,000
Inexpensive	under ¥2,000

Cost is per person without tax, service, or drinks

Credit Cards The following credit card abbreviations are used: AE, American Express; DC, Diners Club; MC, MasterCard; V, Visa.

Kaseiro. A smart Chinese restaurant with red carpets and gold-tone walls, Kaseiro serves Beijing cuisine and is the best of its kind in the city. *186 Yamashita-cho, Naka-ku, tel. 045/681–2918. Jacket and tie suggested in the evening. AE, MC, V. Open 11:30–8. Expensive.*

★ **Janomeya.** Janomeya is the best place in the city for sukiyaki. *5-126 Isezaki-cho, Naka-ku, tel. 045/251–0832. (Located south of Kannai Station toward the pedestrian street, Iseki-cho.) Dress: informal. AE, MC, V. Open 11:30–9:30. Expensive.*

Rinka-en. If you visit the Sankeien Garden, drop in at this traditional country restaurant serving kaiseki-style cuisine. The owner, by the way, is the granddaughter of Mr. Hara, the founder of the Sankeien Garden. *Honmoku Sannotani, Naka-ku, tel. 045/621–0318. Jacket and tie suggested. No credit cards. Open noon–5. Closed Wed. and midsummer. Expensive.*

Scandia. Known for its smorgasbord, Scandia is located near ness lunches as well as for dinner. It also stays open later (midnight) than many other restaurants. *1-1 Kaigan-dori, Naka-ku, Yokohama 231, tel. 045/201–2262. Dress: informal. No credit cards. Open 11 AM–midnight; Sun. 5–midnight. Expensive.*

★ **Seryna.** This establishment is famous for its Ishiyaki steak, which is fried on a hot stone, as well as for its shabu-shabu. *Shin-Kannai Bldg., 1 floor down, Sumiyoshi-cho, Naka-ku, tel. 045/681–2727. Dress: informal. AE, DC, MC, V. Open 11:30–10. Expensive.*

★ **Starlight Grill.** On the rooftop at the New Grand Hotel, the ambience of this restaurant brings back the days when Europeans arrived by majestic ocean liners—tasseled draperies and old-fashioned service, with great views over the harbor. The cuisine is classical French. *Hotel New Grand, 10 Yamashira-cho, Naka-ku, tel. 045/681–1841. Jacket and tie required. AE, DC, MC, V. Open 11:30–9:30. Expensive.*

★ **Aichiya.** Should you wish to try fugu (blowfish), the only chef in Yokohama licensed to prepare this delicacy is at this seafood restaurant. The crabs here—as expensive as the fugu—are also a treat. *7-156-1 Sezaki-cho, Naka-ku, tel. 045/251–4163. Jacket and tie suggested. No credit cards. Open 3–10. Closed Mon. Moderate.*

Chongking. This is the city's best restaurant for Szechuan cooking. Although there has been a recent refurbishing, the focus of attention here is purely on the food. *164 Yamashita-cho, Naka-ku, tel. 045/641–8288. Dress: informal. AE, DC, MC, V. Open noon–9. Moderate.*

Rome Station. Located between Chinatown and Yamashita-Koen Park (just down from the Holiday Inn), this restaurant is popular for Italian food. *26 Yamashita-cho, Naka-ku, tel. 045/681–1818. Dress: informal. No credit cards. Open 11:30–10:30, holidays noon–9. Moderate.*

Fuji-Hakone-Izu National Park

by Nigel Fisher

The Fuji-Hakone-Izu National Park is one of Japan's most popular resort areas. The park's proximity to Tokyo has encouraged several tour operators to promote the region to foreign visitors. However, while the area offers certain pleasures, perhaps other excursions from Tokyo, for example to Nikko and Kamakura, should take precedence for those with limited time in Japan.

The park's chief attraction is, of course, Mt. Fuji. This dormant volcano (last erupted in 1707) is undoubtedly beautiful and, in changing light and from different perspectives, spellbinding. Mt. Fuji rises to an altitude of 12,388 feet (3,776 meters), and its perfect symmetry has challenged poets and artists to immortalize its supreme majesty. It is no wonder the mountain's serenity has caused mortals to assign it spiritual qualities and to admire its conical perfection. Unfortunately, during spring and summer, Mt. Fuji often hides behind a blanket of clouds, to the disappointment of the crowds of tourists who travel to Hakone or the Fuji Five Lakes for a glimpse of Japan's most revered mountain.

Aside from Mt. Fuji, the Fuji-Hakone-Izu National Park offers an escape from the urban pace and congestion of Tokyo. Each of the three areas of the park—the Izu Peninsula, Hakone, and the Fuji Five Lakes—has its own special attractions. The Izu Peninsula has a craggy coastline with beaches and numerous hot-spring resorts, both along the shore and among the mountains. The Hakone region has aerial cable cars traversing the mountains, boiling hot springs, and lake cruises. The Fuji Five Lakes is a recreational area with some of the best views of Mt. Fuji's cone. In each of these areas are monuments to Japan's past.

Though it is possible to make a grand tour of all three areas at one time, most travelers make each of them a separate excursion from Tokyo. For those interested in climbing Mt. Fuji, a popular activity in July and August, *see* Mt. Fuji section, below.

Routes to reach the different areas of the national park are given at the beginning of each section. Because these are tourist attractions accustomed to foreign visitors, there is always someone to help out in English should you want to explore off the beaten track.

Guided Tours

Several different tours from Tokyo cover Hakone and the Fuji Five Lakes, either as separate tours or combined with other destinations. For example, the Imperial Coachman Tour, managed through the **Japan Amenity Travel** (tel. 03/3573–1011), offers the following full-day excursion: first to the Fuji Lakes district, then to Hakone with a ride on the gondola over Owakudani Valley, a cruise on Lake Ashino to Hakone-machi and the Hakone Barrier, and then the Shinkansen back to Tokyo. (Cost: ¥18,500 with lunch; ¥13,900 children under 12.) Another option is to combine Kamakura and Hakone in one day.

Operated by **Hankyu Express International** (tel. 03/3459–4439), the tour does short shrift to Kamakura, with a quick stop at Daibutsu (the Great Buddha), before going to Hakone, crossing Lake Ashino on the cruise boat, and traveling the ropeway over Owakudani Valley. (Cost: ¥18,500, including lunch.) These tours, and others of longer duration, may be arranged through your Tokyo hotel. They depart daily and have pickup services at most of Tokyo's major hotels.

You may also consider including Hakone on a tour that continues on to Kyoto. For example, through **Japan Amenity Travel,** you may take a three-day tour that includes the Fuji Lakes area, Hakone, Kyoto, and Nara. For two nights and no meals, the cost is ¥63,700, or ¥80,000 including most meals. However, read the print carefully. This tour, billed as three days, is only 2½ days, and it ends in Kyoto, which means a ¥12,600 fare back on the Shinkansen to Tokyo.

There are no tours of the Izu Peninsula, though the Japan Travel Bureau can make arrangements for all your hotel and travel needs.

Izu Peninsula

South of Mt. Fuji, the Izu Peninsula projects out into the Pacific. The central part consists of the Amagi Highlands, a continuation of the Hakone Mountains. The shores are a combination of rugged headlands and beautiful bays. The whole area is covered with woods and some 2,300 hot springs (*izu* means "springs"). In fact, the Izu Peninsula has ⅕ of all the hot-spring baths in Japan, and, with its mild climate, the region is a favorite resort area for the Japanese, especially for honeymooners.

Arriving and Departing
By Train
The best way to start a tour of the Izu Peninsula is to take the Kodama Shinkansen from Tokyo to Atami (48 min). Atami is also served by the Odoriko Super Express (not the Shinkansen), which continues beyond Atami to Ito. The Odoriko from Tokyo to Ito takes one hour, 52 minutes. South of Atami, the railway line is privately owned by Izu Railways. Hence, the JR Rail Pass is not valid after Atami. The journey between Tokyo and Shimoda by the Odoriko takes two hours, 44 minutes.

To continue around the Izu Peninsula from Shimoda or up through its center, one must use buses, which run frequently during the day. However, you should always check the time of the last bus to make sure that you are not left stranded.

Shuzenji, the spa resort in the northern central part of the Izu Peninsula, can be reached from Tokyo via Mishima on the Izu-Hakone Railway Line. Mishima is on the JR Tokaido Line, with direct train service to Tokyo. The train ride between Shuzenji and Tokyo takes approximately two hours, 20 minutes.

By Car
It is approximately a four-hour drive from Tokyo to Atami on the express highway. It will take a further three hours to drive down the east coast of the Izu Peninsula to Shimoda. Driving back up the peninsula, it is 40 minutes from Kawazu on the coast to Yugashima and another 30 minutes to the Shuzenji hot-spring resort. While a car is not recommended for traveling from Tokyo to the Izu Peninsula, once there, a car does make exploring easier than it would be by public transportation.

Exploring *Numbers in the margin correspond with points of interest on the Fuji-Hakone-Izu National Park map.*

❶ The gateway to the Izu Peninsula is **Atami.** Often, honeymooners make it no farther into the peninsula, so Atami has numerous hotels, ryokans, and souvenir shops. When you arrive, collect a map from the Atami Tourist Information Office (tel. 0557/81–6002) located at the train station.

The most worthwhile attraction in the area is the **MOA Art Museum,** named after its founder, Mokichi Okada. While establishing one of Japan's new religions, the Church of Messianity, Okada was able to collect more than 3,000 works of art, dating from the Asuka period (6th and 7th centuries) to the present day, including a most notable exhibit of *ukiyo-e* (wood-block prints) and ceramics. Located on a hill above the station and set in a garden full of old plum trees and azaleas, the museum also offers a sweeping view over Atami and the bay. *To find out about special exhibitions, call 0557/84–2511. Admission: ¥1,500. Open 9:30–3:30. Closed Thurs.*

Fifteen minutes by bus from Atami, or an eight-minute walk from Kinomiya Station (the next stop south of Atami and serviced only by local trains), is **Atami Baien Plum Garden.** The time to visit here is in late January or early February, when the 850 trees come into bloom. At other times, it is simply a pleasant, relaxed garden. If you do come here, also stop by the small shrine, dedicated to the God of Temperance, to see the huge and ancient camphor tree on its grounds. The tree has been designated a national monument.

Another excursion from Atami, but only if you have the time and the inclination for a beach picnic, is to take the 40-minute high-speed ferry from the pier over to **Hatsushima Island.** The island, only 2.5 miles (4 km) in circumference, can easily be walked around in less than two hours. Another sight in Atami that has low priority and is barely worth the 15-minute walk from the Atami Station is the **Oya Geyser.** It used to gush at a fixed time every 24 hours, but it stopped after the Great Kanto Earthquake. Not happy with this, the local chamber of commerce now makes it gush for four minutes every five minutes and gives it top billing in the tourist brochures.

❷ Ten miles to the south of Atami is **Ito,** a full-fledged spa resort town that can trace its history with the West to 1604, with the arrival of William Adams (1564–1620), the Englishman whose adventures served as the basis for James Clavell's novel *Shogun.*

Four years earlier, Adams beached his Dutch vessel, *De Liefde,* on the shores of Kyushu and became the first Englishman to set foot on Japan. He was first taken to Osakajo Castle for interrogation by Shogun Ieyasu Tokugawa and was temporarily imprisoned on the basis of the rumor that he and his men were Portuguese pirates. However, Ieyasu was won over by Adams's personality and, as shogun, provided him with a house in Nihombashi, Edo (present-day Tokyo), and appointed him adviser on foreign affairs and teacher of mathematics, geography, gunnery, and navigation to shogunate officials. In 1604, Adams was ordered to build an 80-ton Western-style vessel. Pleased with this venture, the shogun ordered the construction of a larger oceangoing vessel. These two ships were built at Ito, and Adams lived there 1605–1610. All this history was

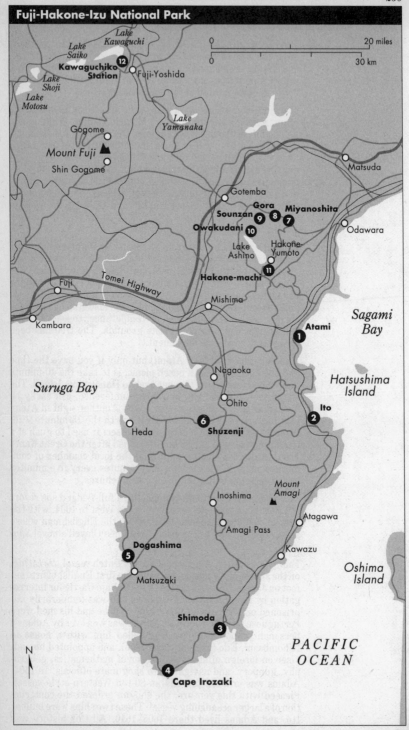

Fuji-Hakone-Izu National Park

0 — 20 miles
0 — 30 km

Lake Kawaguchi

Lake Saiko

Lake Shoji

Lake Motosu

Kawaguchiko Station ⑫

Fuji-Yoshida

Gogome

Lake Yamanaka

Mount Fuji ▲

Shin Gogome

Matsuda

Gotemba

Gora ⑧

Sounzan ⑨

Miyanoshita ⑦

Owakudani ⑩

Odawara

Lake Ashino

Hakone-Yumoto ⑪

Fuji

Tomei Highway

Hakone-machi

Mishima

Kambara

Atami ①

Sagami Bay

Hatsushima Island

Nagaoka

Suruga Bay

Ohito

Ito ②

Heda

Shuzenji ⑥

Mount Amagi ▲

Inoshima

Amagi Pass

Atagawa

Dogashima

Kawazu

Oshima Island

Matsuzaki

Shimoda ③

PACIFIC OCEAN

N

Cape Irozaki ④

temporarily forgotten until the British Commonwealth occupation forces used Ito as a health resort after World War II. Adams's memory was revived, and since then, the Anjin Festival has been held every August. A monument to the Englishman stands at the mouth of the river.

One reason that the British Commonwealth occupation forces chose Ito is that there are 800 thermal springs in the area. That has been and still is Ito's major attraction as a resort, plus the fact that it is situated on a beautiful indented rocky coastline. Some 150 hotels and inns are situated within the area. Aside from the hot springs, there are a number of other attractions. The **Izu Cactus Garden** (tel. 0557/51–1111) consists of a series of pyramidal greenhouses set up at the base of Mt. Omuro. The greenhouses contain 5,000 kinds of cacti from around the world. The park is 20 minutes by bus from Ito Station. *Admission: ¥1,500. Open 8:40–5, Dec. 16–Mar. 15 8:40–4:30. Closed Dec. 28–30.*

Five minutes by bus, or a 15-minute walk beyond the Izu Cactus Park, is the **Ikeda Art Museum** (tel. 0557/45–2211) at Lake Ippeki, which has works by Picasso, Dali, Chagall, and Matisse and a number of wood-block prints. *Admission: ¥800. Open 10–4:30; July–Aug. 10–5:30*

Then there is **Mount Omura Park,** which has, on its east side, 3,000 cherry trees of 35 different varieties. They bloom at various times throughout the year. The park is reached by a 20-minute bus ride from Ito Station. *Admission free.*

South of Ito, the coastal scenery is more of the same—each sweep around a headland gives another picturesque sight of a rocky indented shoreline. There are several spa towns en route to Shimoda. Higashi-Izu is a collection of hot-spring towns, of which **Atagawa** is the most fashionable. Farther south is **Kawazu,** which offers quiet solitude, with pools in the forested mountainside and waterfalls plunging through lush greenery. However, for history, none of these resort towns has the distinction of **Shimoda.**

Shimoda's meeting with the West occurred when Commodore Perry anchored his ships off the coast in 1854. To commemorate the event, the Kurofune Matsuri (Black Ship Festival) is held annually May 16–18. It was here, too, that the first American Consulate was located before being transferred to Yokohama in 1857. Townsend Harris was the consul, and Tojin Okichi was his consort. There are several versions about the Harris-Okichi relationship. With the Japanese penchant for sad romance, the heroine is Okichi. One version has Okichi being ordered by the authorities to leave her lover and comfort Harris so that he may feel at home. Another version suggests that Harris picked Okichi out of a line of prostitutes. In either case, when Harris returned to America, he abandoned her. (Harris's version is that he forthrightly declined her advances.) Whatever is the truth, apparently when Harris left poor Okichi, she tried for a reconciliation with her old lover. When that failed, she opened a restaurant, took to drink, and eventually took a final plunge into the river.

The easiest itinerary in English to follow is the one given by the **Shimoda Tourist Office** (tel. 05582/2–1531), located in front of the station. The 1½-mile itinerary covers most of the major sites, and all of those concerning Okichi. Also, on request, the tourist office will find travelers accommodations in Shimoda.

The **Hofukuji Temple** was the family temple of Tojin Okichi and serves as her memorial museum. The adjoining annex displays a life-size image of the woman. Just behind the temple is her grave; you'll notice that incense is still kept burning in her memory. (The grave of her lover, Tsurumatsu, is at the Todenji Temple.) *Admission: ¥300. Open 8–5.*

The major site on this Shimoda walk is **Ryosenji,** the temple at which the talks were concluded on the Japan–U.S. Friendship Treaty that forced the Tokugawa Shogunate to open Japan to the West. The temple's treasury hall also contains personal artifacts of Tojin Okichi. In the adjoining temple, **Chorakuji,** the U.S.–Japan treaty was actually signed, as well as the trading agreement with the Russians. *Admission: Ryosenji, ¥300; Chorakuji ¥200. Open 9–5.*

Slightly farther down the road is a monument to Perry and to Harris, built to celebrate the establishment of U.S.–Japanese relations. Still farther along, overlooking Shimoda Harbor, is another monument to Perry. Finally, one comes across the Sushikane Restaurant. It is said to be the same restaurant as the one opened by Tojin Okichi a few years before she committed suicide. Part of the restaurant's display are Okichi's belongings.

④ Shimoda is not quite at the southernmost point of the Izu Peninsula. That point is **Cape Irozaki,** reached either by bus from Shimoda Station or by a sightseeing boat from Shimoda. If you visit Cape Irozaki in January, you are in for a special treat: a blanket of yellow daffodils to greet you. To reach the cape, whatever the season, the best plan is to take the boat one way and the bus the other. Both take about 40 minutes. The bus travels past Yumigahama Beach, one of the best sandy beaches on the whole peninsula, and then continues on to Cape Irozaki, the last stop on the route. From where the bus stops, there is a walk past the **Irozaki Jungle Park** (tel. 0558/65–0050), with huge hothouses containing 3,000 varied and colorful tropical plants, to the lighthouse at the edge of the cliff facing the breadth of the Pacific Ocean. *Park admission: ¥700. Open 8–5.*

Just as Shimoda is the end of the line for the trains, so it is for visitors. Most take the two-hour, 45-minute express train ride back to Tokyo.

⑤ However, for the more adventurous, a bus from Shimoda continues around the Izu Peninsula to the seaside town of **Dogashima.** There is little to do here but walk the sandy beaches and watch the fishermen at work. The tourist office (tel. 05585/2–1268) is in the small building behind the bus station and near the pier.

Dogashima is famous for its sedimentary rock formations jutting out from the coast into the sea. The best way to see them is on the sightseeing boat that leaves from the pier. Erosion has shaped the rocks into different forms. If you understand Japanese you'll hear the names of the rocks being called out from the loudspeaker on the cruise boat, which makes 20-minute runs to see the rock formations (cost: ¥700). If you don't understand Japanese, close your ears to the incessant loudspeaker and take the boat anyway. It is the best (virtually only) way to appreciate the varied shapes of these rocks.

❻ From Dogashima, another bus travels up the coast as far as Heta and then turns inland to **Shuzenji**, a traditional spa town in the center of the peninsula. A more relaxing return trip is to take the boat from Dogashima to Numazu and catch the train back to Tokyo from there.

An alternative, and easier, way of reaching Shuzenji is to take one of the five daily buses from Shimoda and go by way of the Amagi Mountains. The scenery is attractive and the trip only takes about two hours (cost: approximately ¥1,900). However, you may wish to stretch your legs at **Inoshishi-mura,** where trained boars and badgers put on a show. The show is not particularly worthwhile, but there is a pleasant 15-minute walk to **Joren-no-taki Waterfall,** from which you can rejoin the bus. By the way, the specialty dish at the local ryokans is roasted boar meat.

Shuzenji is a lavish inland spa town along the valley of the Katsuragawa River. Don't judge the town by the area around the station. Most of the hotels and springs are a mile to the west of the station. Though Shuzenji has the notoriety of being the place where the second Kamakura shogun was assassinated (though he had abdicated his office) early in the 13th century, there is little to interest the foreign visitor. However, we recommend making this return trip through the center of the Izu Peninsula, because it offers a mountainous contrast to the route along the coast. There are numerous hotels in Shuzenji, and 15 miles farther north is **Izu-Nagaoka,** with several deluxe ryokans.

Time Out If you are just changing from bus to train at Shuzenji and need refreshment, across the station plaza on the right is a very pleasant and modest upstairs café called **Aguri** (tel. 0558/72–2628), which serves tasty noodle dishes.

From Shuzenji, you can catch the private railway line (cost: ¥470) to Mishima and change for the Shinkansen to Tokyo or Kyoto. There are also frequent buses that leave from Mishima Station to make the 40-minute ride to Hakone–machi (cost: ¥900).

Hakone

Hakone is a popular day trip from Tokyo and a good place for a close-up view of Mt. Fuji. A word of caution, though, before you dash off to Hakone with plans to see Mt. Fuji: It is often cloud covered, especially during the summer months. Also, the excursion to Hakone has become so popular that sometimes it seems that all of Tokyo has come with you. You can expect to stand in line at the cable cars and be stuck in traffic on the roads.

Arriving and Departing
By Train
The privately owned Odakyu Line has trains departing from Tokyo's Shinjuku Station to Odawara. Odakyu's commuter trains leave every half hour. However, Odakyu also has a special train, the "Romance Car," which offers comfortable seating and large viewing windows. These Romance Cars go one stop beyond Odawara to Hakone-Yumoto. Reservations on the Romance Car are required, and tickets can be purchased from

any Odakyu railway station or Odakyu Travel Service agency (cost: ¥1,440). Beyond Odawara and Hakone-Yumoto, travel is either on the privately owned Hakone Tozan Tetsudo Line or by bus.

If you are using a JR Rail Pass, it is more economical to take the Kodama Shinkansen from Tokyo Station to Odawara. (The faster Hikari does not stop at Odawara.) From Odawara, change to the private railway.

The most economical way of traveling to and within Hakone is to purchase the Hakone Free Pass. Sold by the Odakyu Railways, this coupon ticket allows you to use any mode of transportation in the Hakone area, such as the Hakone Tozan Railway, the Hakone Tozan Bus, the Hakone Ropeway, the Hakone Cruise Boat, the Sounzan Cable Car, and so on (cost: ¥4,520 from Shinjuku, with an additional surcharge of ¥620 to travel on the Romance Car). If you hold a JR Rail Pass, then purchase the Hakone Free Pass just for the travel within the Hakone region and use JR Railways to reach Odawara (cost: ¥3,500). The coupon is valid for four days and is sold at any station serving the Odakyu Railways. With the exception of a detour up the east side of Lake Ashino to the Prince Hotel, all of the itinerary described below is covered by the Hakone Free Pass. On this itinerary, the savings from the Hakone Free Pass amount to ¥1,070 from Shinjuku. With a JR Pass and the coupon bought in Odawara, the savings are ¥300.

Getting Around   Hakone has a network of public transportation from cable cars to buses and from railways to cruise boats. Because traffic on the narrow mountain roads is a slow-moving jam, rental cars are not advised. Indeed, part of the pleasure of exploring Hakone is traveling one way on the cruise boats and ropeways, which you would miss when driving your own car.

Exploring   The following itinerary covers the best of Hakone in a one-day trip out of Tokyo. If you want to enjoy the curative powers of the thermal waters or do some hiking, then an overnight stay will be necessary. The two areas we recommend are around Miyanoshita, an old-fashioned spa town, and the new Prince Hotel resort area, on the slopes of Mt. Komagatake facing Lake Ashino.

Though the itinerary described below sounds complex, it is not. In fact, though many companies offer guided tours of the region, this is one excursion from Tokyo that is so well defined that there is no risk of becoming lost. Indeed, except in the coldest winter months, thousands of Japanese visitors take this same itinerary. The route is a procession of tourists. However, if you wish to take a guided tour, see the beginning of this chapter.

From Odawara or Hakone-Yumoto, you will travel to Togendai on the shore of Lake Ashino. The way we recommend is over the mountains (described below). However, the easiest way is simply to catch a bus from Odawara Station. To do so, though, misses half the reason for coming to Hakone in the first place. Still, if any members of your group cannot stand heights, we recommend putting them on the bus at Hakone-Yumoto or Miyanoshita for Togendai and joining them on the pier at Togendai in about 2½ hours. The bus is scheduled to do the journey in 60 minutes, though traffic usually increases travel time to 90 minutes. Your trip over the mountains will take about two hours.

To go over the mountains, either from Odawara or Hakone-Yumato, take the Hakone Tozan Tetsudo Line for Gora. The train may be accused and excused for being possibly the slowest train you've ever taken. It takes 50 minutes to travel the 10 miles from Odawara to Gora (35 min from Hakone-Yumoto). How the train climbs the mountain is a wonder. But, by using three switchbacks, it steps up the cliff side, and the views become grander as the plunges down the mountain grow steeper.

The train makes several stops on the way. The first of note is **Miyanoshita.** True, Hakone-Yumoto is a bigger resort center, with some 60 inns, but Miyanoshita has a more sophisticated air and elegant approach. There is one old Western-style hotel, the **Fujiya,** that is full of 19th-century charm. But, if you're not staying there, drop in for a morning coffee on the first floor overlooking the garden and, on the way out, take a peek at the library for its vintage collection of old books and magazines. (*See* Lodging, below.)

The next stop of note is **Chokoku-no-mori.** Within a minute's walk of the station is the **Hakone Open-Air Museum.** This is one of Japan's more attractive museums, in which the building is designed to work with the environment. Outside are displayed numerous statues by such masters as Rodin and Moore; inside, there are works by Picasso, Leger, and Kotaro Takamura, among others. Perhaps the collection of art exhibits may have more novelty interest to the Japanese, but the setting of the sculpture gardens set into the cliff side has universal appeal. *To find out about special exhibitions, call 0460/21161. Admission: ¥1,500 adults, ¥800 children under 12. Open daily 9–5:30 (9–4 in winter).*

The final stop on the line is **Gora.** Gora is a small town that services both the visitor who has chosen the village as a base for hiking and exploring, and those passing through on their way up to Sounzan. Shops and small restaurants abound. However, if you can be first out of the train, forget the souvenir stands and make a dash for the cable car located in the same building as the train station. If you let the rest of the passengers arrive there before you, and perhaps a tour bus or two, you may stand 45 minutes in line.

The cable car travels up to **Sounzan.** It departs every 15 minutes and takes nine minutes to make the journey to the top (cost: ¥290; free with the Hakone Free Pass). There are four stops en route, and one may get off and reboard the cable car if one has purchased the full fare up to the top. The one stop in particular where you may consider disembarking is **Koenkami,** the second stop up, to visit the **Hakone Art Museum** for its collection of porcelain and ceramics from China, Korea, and Japan. *Admission: ¥800. Open 9–5. Closed Thurs.*

At Sounzan, the ropeway begins a 33-minute journey down to **Togendai.** The ropeway is in the same building as the cable-car terminus. With your ticket (cost: ¥1,180) or your Hakone Free Pass, stand in line to get a boarding-pass number. This will determine when you can stand in the line for clambering into a gondola. The gondola seats about eight adults and departs every minute. Try to make sure your fellow passengers are of little weight. You'll feel safer when crossing the valley.

Less than 10 minutes out of Sounzan, the gondola swings over a ridge and crosses over **Owakudani Valley**. Suspended hundreds of feet above the "boiling valley," you may still observe volcanic activity on the ground below, with sulfurous steam escaping through holes from some inferno deep within the earth.

10 Having swung safely over the valley, at the top of the far ridge you'll reach **Owakudani**, one of the two stations on the ropeway route. If you want to disembark here, signal to the station conductor, and he will open the gondola's door. One word of caution, though: When you want to reembark, you, and the others in front of you, must wait for someone to disembark. It can be at least a 15-minute wait.

Below Owakudani Station is a restaurant. The reputation for its food is terrible, but, on a clear day, the view of Mt. Fuji is perfect, and that view should tempt you to suffer the food. Next to the station is the **Owakudani Natural Science Museum**, which has exhibits relating to the ecosystems and volcanic history of the area. *Admission: ¥300. Open 9–5.*

There is also a ½-mile-long walking course which passes by some "hellholes" with steam pouring out. You may see someone who boils eggs in the holes and sells them at exorbitant prices.

From Owakudani, the descent to Togendai on the shore of **Lake Ashino** takes 25 minutes. There is no reason to linger at Togendai. It is an arrival and departure point. Buses leave from here back to Hakone-Yumoto and Odawara, as well as the resort villages in the northern area of Hakone. For us, it is the
11 departure point for the cruise boat to **Hakone-machi**. The boat is free with your Hakone Free Pass; otherwise you must purchase your ticket (cost: ¥870) at the office in the terminus. The pier is 100 yards away, and, if the boat is in, you'll recognize it by its gawdy design. (One boat is made to look like a 17th-century warship.) Boats depart every 30 minutes, and the cruise to Hakone-machi takes about 35 minutes, giving you the opportunity to appreciate the bow-shape Lake Ashino. Because the mountains plunge to the lake, one of the attractions of the boat ride is the reflection of the mountains in the lake's waters.

The key sight in Hakone-machi is **Hakone Sekisho** (Hakone Barrier), located a few minutes' walk from the pier in the direction of Moto-Hakone, if you keep as close to the lake shore as is possible. Hakone was on the main Tokaido Highway between the imperial capital of Kyoto and the administrative center of the shogunate at Edo (present-day Tokyo). Because of the steep mountains, travelers could scarcely avoid passing through Hakone. It was, thus, a strategic checkpoint where travelers to and from Edo could be stopped. The Tokugawa Shogunate erected a barrier in 1618 and required travelers to be rigorously searched. Especially important for the security of the shogunate was the examination of each *daimyo* (feudal lord) and his retainers, making their required visit to Edo. Every procession was checked for its number of warriors and their weaponry.

To fully understand the significance of the Hakone Sekisho, remember that the Tokugawa Shogunate required that each daimyo make a visit to Edo once every two years. This served two purposes. It reaffirmed the shogun's authority and diminished the authority of the daimyo, who had to be absent from his lands for a considerable time in order to make the trip. Second, because the daimyo had to travel with a large number of retainers, the expense to the daimyo was great and kept him poor. The less trustworthy daimyo were given lands far from Edo, so their expenses and their time away from their power base were even more crippling. One other method to control the obeisance of the daimyo was used: The wives of the daimyo were required to live in Edo all the time. They were, in fact, hostages; if a daimyo stepped out of line, he did so at the risk of his wife's head. The Hakone Sekisho was, therefore, also a barrier to prevent wives from returning to their husbands.

For two and a half centuries, travelers were stopped at the Hakone Barrier. Then, in 1869, with the Meiji Restoration, it was demolished. However, for the delight of tourists, an exact replica, including an exhibition hall displaying costumes and arms used during Japan's feudal period, was rebuilt in 1965. *Admission:¥200. Open 9–4:30.*

From Hakone-machi and the Hakone Sekisho, buses run every 15–30 minutes to Hakone-Yumoto (50 min) and Odawara (1 hr) for either the Romance Car back to Shinjuku Station or the JR Shinkansen to Tokyo Station. The bus is free with the Hakone Free Pass.

Fuji Five Lakes

Whereas Hakone is the region south of Mt. Fuji, Fuji-Goko (literally, "Fuji-five-lakes") is the area to the north of Mt. Fuji. Needless to say, the star attractions of this area are the view of the mountain and the base from which one can climb to its summit. However, the area also has five lakes that add to the scenic beauty and offer the chance to see Mt. Fuji reflected in the waters. The Fuji Lakes are a popular resort for families and business seminars. Numerous outdoor activities, ranging from skating and fishing in the winter to boating and hiking in the summer, are organized to accommodate the increasing numbers who visit here each year.

Of the five lakes, Lake Kawaguchi and Lake Yamanaka are the two most developed resort areas. Lake Yamanaka, to the east of Lake Kawaguchi, is the largest lake, but Lake Kawaguchi is considered the focus of Fuji-Goko. The area can be visited in a day trip from Tokyo, but because the main reason for coming to this region is relaxation, more than one day is really necessary unless you want to spend most of the day on buses or trains. Though there are plenty of others who would disagree with us, for the foreign visitor we rank this region as the third most interesting in this chapter, unless you plan to climb Mt. Fuji.

Arriving and Departing The transportation hub, as well as being one of the major resort areas in Fuji-Goko, is Kawaguchiko. Getting there from Tokyo requires a change of trains at Otsuki. The JR Chuo Line departs from Shinjuku Station to Otsuki on the hour, every hour, in the morning (less frequently in the afternoon) and takes approximately one hour. (It is the same train that goes to Matsumoto.) At Otsuki, change to the private Fujikyuko Line for Kawaguchiko, which takes another 50 minutes. The total traveling time is about two hours, and one can use one's JR Pass as far as Otsuki. The fare from Otsuki to Kawaguchiko is ¥1,070. Because there are about seven trains a day (more in the summer) from Shinjuku that make convenient connections at Otsuki, we suggest you arrange a schedule with Japan Travel

Bureau or the JR information office the day before you leave Tokyo. There are also one or two trains on Sundays in the summer months that operate directly between Shinjuku and Kawaguchiko Station. From July 12 to August 31, a daily express train departs from Shinjuku at mid-afternoon and arrives at Kawaguchiko in the late afternoon; a train making the return trip departs Kawaguchiko in the late afternoon and arrives at Shinjuku in the early evening. (Times should be verified before your departure; only coaches 1, 2, and 3 make the through run.)

There is also a direct bus service from Shinjuku to Kawaguchiko that operates about 24 trips a day between 7:30 AM and 6 PM (cost: ¥1,520).

For a different route back to Tokyo, you may want to consider taking the bus from Kawaguchiko to Mishima. It is a two-hour bus ride, with approximately six buses a day (cost: ¥1,970), and it skirts the western lakes and circles Mt. Fuji before descending the mountains to Mishima. At Mishima, transfer to the JR Shinkansen Line for Tokyo or Kyoto. A shorter bus ride (70 min, cost: ¥1,340) is from Kawaguchiko to Gotemba with a transfer to the JR local line.

Should one want to go to Hakone rather than Tokyo from Fuji-Goko, take the bus from Kawaguchiko first to Gotemba, then change to another bus to Sengoku. From Sengoku, there are frequent buses to Hakone-Yumoto, Togendai, and elsewhere in the Hakone region. If you want to go to the Izu Peninsula, then take the bus to Mishima and, from there, go by train either to Shuzenji or Atami.

Buses depart from Kawaguchiko Station to all parts of the area and to all five lakes. On a single day's visit, you will probably only have the time to visit Lake Kawaguchi and, if you don't rest up, possibly one other lake.

Exploring ⑫ Arriving from Tokyo at **Kawaguchiko Station,** you'll have a five to 10-minute walk to the lake shore. If you take a left along the shore, another five minutes will bring you to the ropeway for a quick ride up to **Mt. Tenjo.** At the top of Mt. Tenjo (3,622 feet), there is an observatory from where one can get a look at the lay of the land. Lake Kawaguchi is laid out before you, and beyond the lake is a classic view of Mt. Fuji. Back down the ropeway and across the road is the pier for the Kawaguchi's cruise boat. The boat offers 30-minute tours of the lake. The promise, not always fulfilled, is to have two views of Mt. Fuji: one in its natural form, and another inverted in the reflection from the water.

On the north shore of the lake next to the Fuji Lake Hotel is **Fuji-Hakubutsukan** (Fuji Museum; tel. 0555/73–2266), where on the first floor there are displays related to the geology and history of the area. The kids view these academic exhibits while adults (only those aged 18 and older are permitted) visit the second floor. Here are exhibits of erotic paraphernalia used, apparently, by Japanese families until relatively recently. *Admission: ¥350. Open 8:30–4.*

Kawaguchi is the most developed of the five lakes; all around its shores are villas owned by companies and universities, where weekend retreats are held. There are also a number of recreational facilities, the largest of which is the **Fuji-kyu Highland.**

It is not particularly recommended for the day visitor, but it does have everything to amuse children, from a scream-engendering loop-the-loop to a more genteel carousel. The amusement park stays open all year and in the winter offers superb skating, with Mt. Fuji for its backdrop. To reach Fuji-kyu Highland, take the train back (in the direction of Odawara) one stop, or walk the 15 minutes from Lake Kawaguchi.

Buses from Kawaguchiko Station go to all the other lakes. The lake that is the farthest away is **Motosu**. It takes about 50 minutes to reach the lake by bus. Motosu is the deepest lake of the Fuji-Goko and has the clearest waters. **Shoji** is the smallest of the lakes and is regarded by many to be the prettiest. It has the added pleasure of not being built up with vacation homes. The Shoji Trail leads from the lake to Mt. Fuji through Aokigahara (Sea of Trees), a forest under which is a magnetic lava field that makes compasses go haywire. For that reason, people planning to climb Mt. Fuji are advised to take this route with a guide.

Between Shoji and Kawaguchi is **Saiko,** the third largest lake of the region and only modestly developed. From its western side, there is a good view of Mt. Fuji. The largest of the five lakes is **Yamanaka,** 35 minutes by bus to the east of Kawaguchi. Lake Yamanaka has a 30-minute cruise-boat ride circling the lake and several hotels on its shore. Because this lake is the closest to the popular trail up Mt. Fuji that starts at Gogome, many climbers use this lake resort for their base.

Mt. Fuji

There are six possible routes to the summit of Mt. Fuji, but two are recommended: Gogome (fifth station) on the north side, and Shin Gogome (new fifth station) on the south side. From Gogome, it is a five-hour climb to the summit, and a three-hour descent if you return the same way. From Shin Gogome, the ascent to the summit is slightly longer and stonier than from Gogome, but the descent is faster. Hence, we recommend climbing Mt. Fuji from Gogome and descending to the Shin Gogome, via the Sunabashiri—more about that in a moment.

Arriving and Departing Buses take about one hour from Kawaguchiko Station to Gogome, and there are three to 15 runs a day, depending on the season (cost: ¥1,620). There also three buses from Tokyo (Hamamatsucho or Shinjuku stations) that go directly to Gogome, departing from Hamamatsucho at 8:15 AM and 7 PM, and from Shinjuku at 7:45 AM, 8:45 AM, and 7:30 PM. The last bus allows sufficient time for the tireless to make it to Mt. Fuji's summit before sunrise. The journey takes about three hours from Hamamatsucho and two hours, 30 minutes from Shinjuku (cost: ¥2,340 from Hamamatsucho, ¥2,160 from Shinjuku). Reservations are required, through the Fuji Kyuko Railway (tel. 03/3455–2211), the Japan Travel Bureau (tel. 03/3284–7026), or other major travel agents.

To return from Shin Gogome, there is a bus that takes 35 minutes to Gotemba (cost: ¥1,300). Then take the JR Tokaido and Gotemba lines to Tokyo Station, or the JR Line to Matsuda and change to the Odakyu Line for Shinjuku (cost: ¥1,700).

The Climb It has become increasingly popular to make the climb at night in order to reach the summit just before sunrise. Sunrises, wherever you are, are beautiful, but the sunrise from the top of

Mt. Fuji is exceptional. *Goraiko*, as the sunrise is named, takes on a mystical quality as the reflection of the light shimmers across the sky just before the sun itself appears over the horizon. Mind you, there is no guarantee of seeing it: Mt. Fuji attracts clouds, especially in the early morning.

The climb is taxing, but not as arduous as one would imagine it is climbing to Japan's highest mountain, 12,388 feet above sea level. However, it is humiliating to struggle to find the oxygen for another step ahead when 83-year-old grandmothers stride past you; on occasion, they do. Have no fear in getting off the trail on either of the two main routes. Some 30,000 people make the climb during the official season, July 1–August 31, and en route there are vendors selling food and drinks. (Consider taking your own nourishment and some water rather than paying their high prices.) In all, there are 10 stations to the top—you start at the fifth. However, the stations are located at unequal distances. Also, along the route at each station are huts where, dormitory-style, you can catch some sleep. A popular one is at the Hachigome (eighth station), from which it is about a 90-minute climb to the top. However, these huts are often overcrowded and are none too clean, so more and more people leave Gogome (the fifth station) at midnight and plan to be at the summit 4½ hours later for sunrise. The mountain huts are open July 1–Aug. 31. Lodging costs approximately ¥4,800 with two meals, ¥3,800 without food. Camping on the mountain is prohibited.

Coming back down is easy. Instead of returning to Gogome, descend to Shin Gogome, using the volcanic sand slide called Sunabashiri—you take a giant step and slide. It's fun, but not so much fun that you will want to climb Mt. Fuji again.

Be prepared for fickle weather around and up Mt. Fuji. Summer days can be warm (very hot when climbing), and nights can be freezing cold. Wear strong hiking shoes. The sun really burns at high altitude, so take protective clothing and a hat. Gloves are a good idea; they protect the hands while climbing and when sliding down the volcanic sand during the descent. Use a backpack so that your hands are free.

Lodging

Because the region covered in this chapter is a resort area, most hotels quote prices on a per-person basis with two meals, exclusive of service and tax. If you do not want dinner at your hotel, it is usually possible to renegotiate the price. Stipulate, too, whether you wish to have Japanese or Western breakfasts, if any. For the purposes here, the categories assigned to all hotels reflect the cost of a double room with private bath and no meals. However, if you make reservations at any of the noncity hotels, you will be expected to take breakfast and dinner at the hotel—that will be the rate quoted to you, unless you specify otherwise. During the peak season, July 15–Aug. 31, prices can increase by 40%.

A 3% federal consumer tax is added to all hotel bills. Another 3% local tax is added to the bill if it exceeds ¥10,000. At most hotels, a 10%–15% service charge is added to the total bill. Tipping is not necessary.

The most highly recommended accommodations are indicated by a star ★.

Category	Cost*
Very Expensive	over ¥20,000
Expensive	¥15,000–¥20,000
Moderate	¥10,000–¥15,000
Inexpensive	under ¥10,000

Cost is for double room, without tax or service

Credit Cards The following credit card abbreviations are used: AE, American Express; DC, Diners Club; MC, MasterCard; V, Visa.

The Izu Peninsula
Atami
★ **Taikanso Ryokan.** A Japanese inn of the old style with beautiful furnishings and individualized service, the villa was once owned by the Japanese artist, Taikan. The views over the sea must have been his inspiration. *7-1 Hayashigaokacho, Atami, Shizuoka 413, tel. 0557/81–8137. A 10-minute walk from the station. 43 Japanese-style rooms. Breakfast and dinner served in your room. AE, V. Very Expensive.*

New Fujiya Hotel. A modern resort hotel with large public areas, it is a useful hotel to use simply as a base for sightseeing. It is located inland, and only the top rooms have a view of the sea. The impersonal, but professional, service only gets flustered when a group arrives. *1-16 Ginzacho, Atami, Shizuoka 413, tel. 0557/81–0111. Five minutes by taxi from the station. 316 rooms, half are Western-style. Facilities: indoor pool, hot-spring baths, sauna, Japanese and Western restaurants. AE, MC, V. Moderate.*

Dogashima **Ginsuiso.** This is the smartest luxury resort on Izu's west coast. Service is first class, despite its popularity with tour groups. The location along the top of the cliff with every room overlooking the sea is superb. *2977-1 Nishina, Nishi-Izucho, Dogashima, tel. 05585/2–1211. 90 Japanese-style rooms. Facilities: outdoor pool, nightclub with cabaret, shops. MC, V. Very Expensive.*

Ito **Ryokan Nagoya.** This small, very personable establishment
★ with understated elegance and sophistication has antiques furnishings placed around the inn with simplicity and harmony. English is not spoken, but smiles and a few words in Japanese seem to go a long way. *1-1-18 Sakuragaoka, Ito, Shizuoka, tel. 0557/37–4316. 13 rooms. Breakfast and dinner served in your room. No credit cards. Very Expensive.*

Izu-Nagaoka **Ryokan Sanyoso.** Elegant and beautiful, the Sanyoso is deco-
★ rated with antiques and luxurious furniture, as one would expect from the former villa of the Iwasaki family of the Mitsubishi conglomerate. *270 Domanoue, Izu-Nagaoka, Tagata-gun, Shizuoka 410, tel. 05594/8–0123. Five minutes by taxi from the station. 20 rooms. AE, MC, V. Very Expensive.*

★ **Izu Hotel.** Actually a small Japanese inn, the Izu has a classic Japanese garden upon which to gaze from your tatami room. Not as elegant as the Ryokan Sanyoso (*see* above), but also not quite as expensive. *1356 Nagoaka, Izu-Nagaoka-cho, Tagata-gun, Shizuoka 410-22, tel. 05594/8–0678. 9 Japanese rooms. Facilities: outdoor pool. AE, V. Expensive.*

★ **Matsushiro-kan.** This small ryokan is nothing fancy, yet because it is a family operation, it feels like a friendly home. Some English is spoken. Japanese meals are served in a common dining room. *55 Kona, Izu-Nagaoka, Tagata-gun, Shizuoka 410-22, tel. 05594/8–0072. Five minutes by bus or taxi from the station. 18 rooms. AE, V. Moderate.*

Shimoda **Shimoda Prince Hotel.** This V-shape modern resort hotel faces the Pacific, only steps away from a white sandy beach. The building and rooms are more functional than aesthetic in design and are geared to those seeking a holiday by the sea. However, the broad expanse of picture windows from the dining room, offering a panorama of the Pacific Ocean, does make this establishment the best in town. *1547-1 Shirahama, Shimoda, Shizuoka 415, tel. 05582/2–7575. Located just out of Shimoda, 10 min by taxi from the station. 134 rooms, mostly Western-style. Facilities: Continental main dining room, Japanese restaurant, terrace lounge, bar, nightclub, outdoor pool, sauna, tennis courts. AE, DC, MC, V. Very Expensive.*

Shimoda Tokyu Hotel. Perched just above the bay, the Shimoda Tokyu has impressive views of the Pacific from one side and mountains from the other. The public areas are large and lack character and warmth, but that is typical of Japanese resort hotels. *5-12-1 Shimoda, Shimoda, Shizuoka 415, tel. 05582/2–2411. 117 rooms, mostly Western-style. Facilities: outdoor pool, hot-spring baths, Western dining room, Japanese restaurant, sushi bar, summer garden restaurant, tennis courts, shops. AE, MC, V. Expensive.*

Hakone **Hakone Prince Hotel.** This is a completely self-contained resort
Lake Ashino complex on the edge of the lake at Hakone-en. The hotel attracts tours, the individual traveler, and business meetings.
★ The location is superb, with the lake on one side and Mt. Komagatake on the other. One can escape the largeness of the hotel by staying in one of two Japanese-style annexes, Request the *ryuguden,* which overlooks the lake and has its own hot-spring bath; it is absolutely superb, despite having the most expensive rooms in the hotel. *144 Moto-Hakone, Hakone-machi, Ashigarashimo-gun, Kanagawa 250-05, tel. 0460/3–7111. 373 rooms; the main building has 96 rooms; the chalet has 12 rooms; the lakeside lodge has 50 rooms; the 2 annexes have a total of 73 rooms. Facilities: formal Western dining room, steak and seafood restaurant, Chinese restaurant, Japanese restaurants, coffeehouse, bar/lounge, tennis courts, outdoor pools, shops. AE, DC, MC, V. Expensive–Very Expensive.*

Miyanoshita **Ryokan Naraya.** A traditional inn, the Naraya retains a simple,
★ even mystical, understated elegance and an exquisite formal hospitality. The same family has owned the inn for generations and has earned the right to choose their guests. The main building has more atmosphere than does the annex. *162 Miyanoshita, Hakone-machi, Kanagawa 250-04, tel. 0460/2–2411. 19 rooms, not all with private bath. You are expected to have breakfast and dinner, which are served in your room. AE, MC, V. Very Expensive.*

★ **Fujiya Hotel.** Though the Western building is showing signs of age (built in 1878, but with modern additions), that simply increases the hotel's charm, which is especially felt in the library, with its stacks of old books. In the delightful gardens in the back is an old imperial villa used for dining. With the exceptional service and hospitality of a fine Japanese inn, this is the best traditional Western hotel in town. *359 Miyanoshita, Hakone-machi, Kanagawa 250-04, tel. 0460/2-2211. 149 Western-style rooms. Facilities: Western and Japanese restaurants, indoor and outdoor pools, thermal pool, golf. AE, MC, V. Expensive.*

Hotel Kowakien. This hotel attracts busloads of tourists. It's far from ideal, but its prices are reasonable for the fair-size rooms. Thus, the hotel is worth knowing about, and one can usually get a reservation. (The hotel also owns the adjacent **Hakone Kowakien,** which is equally large and with little character, but has Japanese-style rooms.) *1297 Ninotaira, Hakone-machi, Kanagawa 250-04, tel. 0460/2-4111. 250 Western-style rooms. Facilities: Western and Japanese restaurants, indoor and outdoor pools, thermal pool, sauna, golf, tennis, gym. AE, DC, MC, V. Moderate–Expensive.*

Sengoku **Fuji-Hakone Guest House.** A small, family-run Japanese inn, this guest house has simple tatami rooms with the bare essentials. The owners speak English and are a great help in planning off-the-beaten-path excursions. *912 Sengokuhara, Hakone, Kanagawa 250-06, tel. 0460/4-6577. Located between Odawara Stn. and Togendai. Take bus at Odawara St. terminal (bus lane #4), get off at the Senkyoro-mae bus stop, and walk back 1 block. 12 Japanese-style rooms, none with private bath. Facilities: hot spring. AE, MC, V. Inexpensive.*

Fuji Five Lakes **Fuji View Hotel.** Conveniently located on Lake Kawaguchi, the
Lake Kawaguchi Fuji View is a little threadbare, but it does provide comfort. Its terraced lounge offers fine views of the lake and of Mt. Fuji beyond. The staff also speak English and are helpful in planning your excursions. *511 Katsuyama-mura, Minami-Tsuru-gun, Yamanashi 401-04, tel. 05558/3-2211. 62 rooms, mostly Western-style. Facilities: Western restaurant; hotel will arrange golf, boating, tennis. AE, DC, MC, V. Expensive.*

Hotel Ashiwada. This new Japanese-style hotel on Lake Kawaguchi has been designed as a utilitarian base for those interested in seeking the recreational facilities in the area rather than sitting around the hotel. The staff are helpful and, though Japanese food is served in the small dining room, they will make English breakfasts. *395 Nagahama, Ashiwada-mura, Minami-Tsuru-gun, Yamanashi 401-04, tel. 05558/2-2321. 42 Japanese-style rooms, not all with private bath. Facilities: Japanese dining room, laundry room. AE, MC, V. Moderate.*

Lake Yamanaka **Hotel Mount Fuji.** The best resort hotel on Lake Yamanaka, the Mount Fuji offers all the facilities needed for a recreational holiday, and its guest rooms are larger than those at the other hotels on the lake. The lounges are spacious, rather like waiting rooms, but they do offer fine views of the lake and mountain. *Yamanaka, Yamanakako-mura, Yamanashi 401-05, tel. 0555/62-2111. 88 Western-style rooms, 20 Japanese-style. Facilities: Western and Japanese restaurants, outdoor pool, tennis, golf, skating. AE, MC, V. Moderate.*

New Yamanakako Hotel. This is a less expensive accommodation on the lake. Though the rooms are slightly smaller than those at Hotel Mount Fuji, the New Yamanakako has its own thermal pool, especially pleasant after summer hiking or winter skating. *Yamanaka, Yamanakako-mura, Yamanashi 401-05, tel. 05556/2-2311. 66 rooms, mostly Western-style. Facilities: Western and Japanese restaurants, thermal pool, tennis. AE, DC, V. Moderate.*

5 Nagoya, Ise-Shima, and the Kii Peninsula

by Nigel Fisher

As you travel on the Shinkansen down the industrial corridor of Honshu from Tokyo to Hiroshima, the sight from the train window is one long strip of factories and concrete office blocks. Although this strip may be an economic miracle, one town blends into the next. Indeed, if you had not heard of places like Kyoto, the inclination would be to stay on the train in the vain hope of reaching greenery and the Japan of tourist brochures. To the north and south of this industrial corridor, however, a traveler will find countryside, small towns, and an area still rich in traditional culture. Consider, then, disembarking the Tokyo–Hiroshima train (the Tokaido Line) at Nagoya, the fourth largest industrial center of Japan, to explore the country to the city's north and southwest.

Nagoya has only a few major national treasures. The two most important are the Nagoyajo Castle and the Atsuta Jingu Shrine. Even in the most favorable terms, the city is very limited in its architectural attractiveness, but it is a convenient base from which to set out into the countryside. After visiting the major sights of Nagoya, the first recommended excursion takes you on a trip of one or two days to the north of the city to see cormorant fishing, sword making, fertility shrines, and much more. Heading south from Nagoya, the second and longer excursion covers the Grand Shrines of Ise, the Shima Peninsula and its pearl industry, and proceeds to the Kii Peninsula, including Mt. Koya and Yoshino. This second excursion ends at Nara.

Nagoya

A visit to Nagoya today gives little indication of the city's role in the Tokugawa period (1603–1868). Then, Nagoya was an important stop between Kyoto and Edo (Tokyo). In 1612, Ieyasu Tokugawa established Nagoya town by permitting his ninth son to build a castle. In the shadow of this magnificent castle congregated craft industries and also pleasure quarters for the samurai. A town was born and quickly grew in strategic importance. Supported by taxing the rich harvests of the vast surrounding Nobi plain, the Tokugawa family used the castle as their power center for the next 250 years. By the early 1800s, Nagoya's population had grown to around 100,000. Although it was smaller than Edo, where the million-plus population surpassed even Paris, Nagoya had become as large as the more established cities of Kanazawa and Sendai.

Only with the Meiji Restoration in 1868, however, when Japan embraced Western ideas and technology, did Nagoya develop as a port city. Once its harbor was open to international shipping (1907), Nagoya's industrial growth accelerated, so that by the 1930s it was supporting Japanese expansionism in China with munitions and aircraft. That choice of industry caused Nagoya's ruin. American bombers virtually razed the city to the ground during World War II. Very little was left standing (and nothing belonging to the Tokugawa period) by the time the Japanese surrendered unconditionally, on August 14, 1945.

Nagoya has been born again as an industrial metropolis. Except for the fact that every building is of recent vintage, there is no evidence of its war-blitzed past. Now the fourth largest city in Japan, Nagoya bustles with 2.2 million people living in its 126.5-square-mile area. Industry is booming, with shipbuilding, ceramics, railway rolling stock, automobiles, textiles, machine tools, food processing, and even aircraft. Nagoya has become prosperous: a comfortable cosmopolitan town for its 36,000 foreign residents, but with only a few sites to interest the visitor.

In rebuilding this city, urban planners created the new Nagoya on the grid system, with wide avenues intersecting at right angles. Hisaya-odori, a broad avenue with a park in its meridian, is 328 feet wide and bisects the town. At its center is Nagoya's symbol of modernity, an imposing 590-foot-high television tower; it is ugly to look at but useful for visitors to establish their bearings. To the north of the tower is Nagoyajo Castle, to the west are the botanical gardens and zoo, to the south is Atsuta Jingu Shrine, and to the east is the Japan Railways (JR) station. The main downtown commercial area (subway stop: Sakae) favors the blocks east of Hisaya-odori Avenue, and a secondary commercial area has developed next to the JR station.

Arriving and Departing

By Plane   There are direct overseas flights to Nagoya on Japan Airlines (JAL) from Honolulu, Hong Kong, and Seoul. The major airlines that have routes to Japan have offices in downtown Nagoya. For domestic travel, All Nippon Airways (ANA) and Japan Air System offer flights between Nagoya and most major Japanese cities.

Between the   The Meitetsu bus makes the 50-minute run between the airport
Airport and   and the Meitetsu Bus Center, near the Nagoya Railway Sta-
Center City   tion.

By Train   Nagoya is on the Shinkansen Line, with frequent bullet trains between Nagoya and Tokyo (1 hour, 52 minutes on the fast Hikari; 2½ hours on the slower Kodama); Nagoya and Kyoto (43 minutes); and Nagoya and Shin-Osaka (1 hour). You can also take the less expensive Limited Express trains. Limited Express trains proceed from Nagoya into and across the Japan Alps (to Takayama and Toyama, and to Matsumoto and Nagano).

By Bus   Buses connect Nagoya with Tokyo and Kyoto. However, while the bus fare is half that of the Shinkansen trains, the journey by bus takes three times as long.

By Car   The journey on the expressway to Nagoya from Tokyo takes about five hours; from Kyoto, allow two hours.

Getting Around

By Subway   Several main subway lines run under the major avenues. The Higashiyama Line runs from the north down to the JR station and then due east, cutting through the city center at Sakae. The Meijo Line runs north–south, passing through the city center at downtown Sakae. The Tsurumai Line also runs north–south through the city, but between the JR station and Sakae, at the city center. A fourth subway line, the Sakura-dori, opened in 1990, cuts through the city center from the JR Station, paralleling the Higashiyama Line.

By Bus   Buses crisscross the city, running either in a north to south or an east to west direction.

By Taxi Metered taxis are plentiful, with an initial fare of ¥480.

Important Addresses and Numbers

Tourist Information **Nagoya International Center** (1–47 Nakono, 1-chome, Naka-mura-ku, Nagoya, tel. 052/531–3313). The center also provides an English language telephone hot-line service, tel. 052/581–0100) manned from 9–8:30. **City Tourist Information Office** (1-4 Meieki 1-chome, Nakamura-ku, Nagoya, tel. 052/541–4301). A branch of the Tourist Office is also in the center of the Nagoya Railway Station (tel. 052/541–4301, open 9–5).

The Japan Travel-Phone This toll-free service will answer travel-related questions and help with communication, daily 9-5. Dial 0120/444–800 for information on western Japan.

Travel Agencies **Japan Travel Bureau** (tel. 0521/563–1501) has several locations, including the JR station and in the Matsuzakaya Department Store downtown. The major domestic airlines (JAL, tel. 052/563–4141; JAS, tel. 052/201–8111; and ANA, tel. 052/962–6211) have offices in Nagoya, as do major international carriers.

Emergencies **Police** (dial 110); **Ambulance** (dial 119).
Doctors **National Nagoya Hospital** (tel. 0521/951–1111); **Kokusai Central Clinic** (Nagoya International Center Building, tel. 0521/201–5311).

English Bookstore **Maruzen** (tel. 0521/261–2251) is located downtown behind the International Hotel Nagoya. 3-23-3 Nishiki, Naka-ku, Nagoya.

Guided Tours

Five different sightseeing bus tours of the city are operated daily by the **Nagoya Yuran Bus Company** (tel. 052/561–4036). The three-hour "panoramic course" tour (¥1,970) includes Nagoyajo Castle and Atsuta Jingu Shrine and has scheduled morning and afternoon departures. A full-day tour (¥4,850) takes travelers out of Nagoya to visit the Meiji Village and the Tagata Shrine.

Exploring

Numbers in the margin correspond with points of interest on the Nagoya map.

With its rectangular layout, Nagoya is simple to navigate. Under the main avenues run four subway lines—two running north to south and two running east to west—from the **Nagoya Railway Station,** where this tour of the city begins. First, stop at the Visitor's Information Office in the middle of the station's central mall, identified by a big red question mark. Even if the tourist section, with its English-speaking attendant, is closed, you can collect an English-language map from the other officials behind the counter. In Japanese or sign language, they will also give directions and obtain hotel reservations for you.

To get to the first attraction on this tour, the Nagoyajo Castle, take the subway from the railway station to the center of town (walking takes about 15 minutes) or take bus #8 directly to Nagoyajo. The subway is easy to take, because all subway signs are written in both Japanese and English; a subway stop is located right in front of the railway station. Take the Higashiyama subway line for two stops to Sakae; it lets you off

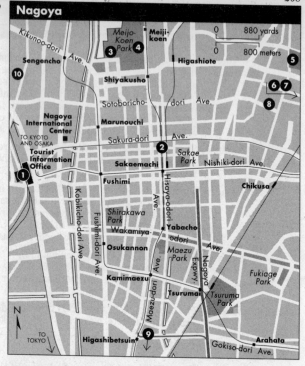

in the middle of downtown Nagoya on Hisaya-odori Avenue.
You can either change here for the Meijo subway line to ride
one stop to the Shiyakusho Station, or exit and walk up Hisaya-
odori Avenue past the 590-foot-tall **TV tower** to Nagoyajo Castle.

Your Nagoya tourist brochure will suggest taking the elevator
up the TV tower to its observation platform for the view. Certainly, if there is no smog, haze, or clouds, you will get a wide
panorama that reaches the Japan Alps to the north and Ise Bay
to the south. However, what one mostly sees is the city, and, if
you have seen urban sprawls before, the view will simply add to
that tiresome list.

Continuing up Hisaya-odori Avenue, past the Prefectural Government Office and Shiyakusho subway station, one catches a
first glimpse of **Nagoyajo Castle,** standing as a memory of times
long past. The castle was originally built in 1612, severely damaged in 1945, and rebuilt with ferro-concrete in 1959. Its fame
has been its impressive size and the pair of golden dolphins,
male and female, mounted on the roof of the *donjon* (stronghold). The donjon and the dolphins are replicas, but they are
faithful to their originals. In contrast to the castle's exterior,
however, the interior makes no attempt to replicate the original residential quarters of the Tokugawa family. Instead, you'll
find a museum containing artifacts—toys, armor, swords and
so forth—from the original castle. Completely incongruous to
this re-created 17th-century castle is an elevator that takes visitors between floors; yet perhaps without it, one would miss the

fourth floor of the castle. Here is a collection of paper dolls representing the people who take part in the city's Chrysanthemum Exhibition, held in October—the best time to appreciate Nagoyajo Castle.

To the east of the castle, but within the castle complex, are the
❹ **Ninomaru Gardens.** The refined simplicity of these gardens makes them a place to restore one's inner harmony, which Nagoya's traffic does its best to undermine. However, during the October festival, the display of chrysanthemum bushes can be disconcerting. Each bush has been shaped so that its flowers form faces and hands. Then, the bush is dressed in costumes and arranged to represent a legend or historic event. The effect is extremely surrealistic, resembling a fantasy filled with flower children. *Admission to the castle and gardens: ¥400. Open 9:30–4:30. Closed Dec. 29–Jan. 1.*

After the castle, the next Nagoya attraction worth visiting is
❺ the **Tokugawa Museum.** Walk back to Shiyakusho Station for the Meijo subway to Ozone Station, or take bus #16 from "Stop 6" to Shindekamachi. Because the museum is on a back street, you may need to ask directions for Tokugawa Bijutsukan (Tokugawa Museum).

Some 7,000 historical treasures are stored in Tokugawa Museum, but even after its 1987 rebuilding, only a fraction of the collection is displayed at any one time. All that you can be sure of seeing are ancient armor, swords, paintings, and assorted artifacts from the Tokugawa family. For many, the main reason for visiting the museum is the various picture scrolls, including one illustrating the *Tale of Genji.* If you'd like to see the scrolls, ask your hotel to telephone the museum to make sure they are on display. *Tel. 052/935–6262. Admission: ¥1,000. Open 10–4:30. Closed Mon.*

From the Tokugawa Museum, it is a 15-minute brisk walk east along Chayagasaka-dori Avenue. After passing the Nagoya Women's College, take a right down Tenma-dori Avenue and
❻ that will lead to the **Nittaiji Temple,** which was given to Japan by the king of Siam in 1904. Supposedly, its function is to serve as a repository for Buddha's ashes, but all one can see is a magnificent gilded Buddha. The actual temple, though, is less note-
❼ worthy than the nearby **Gohyaku Rakan Hall** (Hall of the 500 Rakan), with rows of Buddha's 500 disciples carved in wood, each statue in a slightly different pose from the others. Slightly closer to the Tokugawa Museum (in a southwest direction) is
❽ **Kenchuji Temple.** Its fame is its original two-story gate (1651), one of the few Nagoya structures to survive the bombing of World War II.

If the Nagoyajo Castle is the number one tourist attraction in
❾ Nagoya, the **Atsuta Jingu Shrine,** in the southern part of the city, is number two. To get there from either the Tokugawa Museum or the castle and downtown, take the Meijo subway line south to Jingunishi Station. From there, it is a short walk to the Atsuta Jingu Shrine.

For 1,700 years, a shrine has been at the site of the Atsuta Jingu. The current one is, like Nagoyajo Castle, a concrete replica of the one destroyed in World War II. That diminishes neither its importance nor the reverence in which it is held by the Japanese. The Atsuta Jingu Shrine remains one of the three most important shrines in the country and has the distinction of serving as the repository of one of the emperor's three imperial regalia, the Kusanagi-no-Tsurugi (Grass Mowing Sword). The shrine is located on thickly wooded grounds, with a 15th-century bridge (Nijugo-cho-bashi). The attraction is an oasis of tradition in the midst of bustling, modern industrialism. Especially when witnessing Shinto priests blessing newborn children held in the arms of their kimono-clad mothers, one can easily recognize the reverence with which the Atsuta Jingu Shrine is still accorded. *Admission free. Open sunrise–sunset.*

A little farther to the south of the shrine is **Nagoyako Port,** now Japan's third largest port, outranked only by Kobe and Tokyo. From here, Honda, whose plants are in Nagoya's suburbs, ships its automobiles around the world.

⑩ The last place of major interest in Nagoya is the **Noritake China Factory,** a 15-minute walk north of Nagoya Railway Station or five minutes from the Kamejime subway station. Noritake is the world's largest manufacturer of porcelain. A free, one-hour tour of the factory is offered, with an English-speaking guide and a short film. *Tel. 052/562–5072. Admission free. Open weekdays 10–4. 1-hr. factory tours at 10 and 1. Reservations for the tour are required.*

Rather than making purchases at the factory, you may want to browse through the downtown shops. To return downtown, use the Higashiyama subway, which travels via the JR station to the Sakae stop. Sakae is not only Nagoya's shopping center but also the entertainment center, with hundreds of bars and small restaurants. Many of these restaurants display their dishes with prices in the windows, so you may decide what you want and how much it will cost before you enter. Furthermore, because Nagoya prides itself on being an international city, Westerners are usually welcomed without the fluster of embarrassment that sometimes greets them in less cosmopolitan areas.

Excursions from Nagoya

While Nagoya is modern Japan hurtling into the 21st century, traditional Japan is still visible to the north and south of the city. The two excursions described below take in most of these sights. The first makes a circular excursion to the north of Nagoya. The second excursion goes southwest to the Ise Peninsula. From there, one can either return to Nagoya or, better yet, continue on to Nara and Kyoto either directly or, as we have done in this excursion, via the Kii Peninsula to Nara.

Gifu and North of Nagoya

Numbers in the margin correspond with the numbers on the Nagoya Excursions map.

To the north of Nagoya, and not more than an hour or so by train, are several places of interest whose origins for the most part are centuries old. The general area is the southern part of the Gifu Prefecture, an area that also includes the mountains of the Japan Alps around Takayama. However, this tour does not go that far north and instead keeps within the foothills of the mountains.

❶ Begin this excursion at its northernmost point, **Gifu,** and work
your way back down to Nagoya. Gifu is ½-hour's journey on a
JR train from Nagoya. It is not far and travel can easily be done
in a day. However, during the summer, in order to watch the
evening event of cormorants fishing in the rivers, you may want
to make this an overnight excursion.

Bombing during World War II destroyed the attractiveness of
Gifu. However, the city is still worth visiting for several reasons. Gifu is famous for making paper lanterns and umbrellas,
for ukai fishing, and for its bathhouses, which have been described as "sex spas." The latter may not interest most foreigners, but they do seem to raise the local hotel prices. Gifu is also
a major manufacturer of apparel, and you'll see some 2,000
wholesale shops crammed on a couple of city blocks as you leave
the station. Gifu has a city tourist office at the train station (tel.
0582/62–4415).

Umbrellas are made by certain families in small shops. Though
these umbrellas are available in Gifu's downtown stores, there
are one or two umbrella-making shops a 15-minute walk to the
southeast of the JR station. If you speak a little Japanese, the
shop owner may invite you back to watch the process. The easiest store to visit is **Sakaida's** (tel. 0582/63–0111).

Lantern making is easier to see. The major factory, **Ozeki** (tel.
0582/63–0111), welcomes visitors. To reach Ozeki, take the
tram toward downtown Gifu and disembark at the junction of
the main road, which leads to the Kinkazan Tunnel. The factory
is up this road on the left. Visitors are led through the process
of winding bamboo or wire around several pieces of wood to
give the lantern shape. The tour then progresses to where the
paper is pasted onto the bamboo. Once the paste has dried, the
pieces of wood that have given the lantern its shape are removed from one end of the lantern. The actual design on the
lantern may either be stenciled on the paper at the beginning of
the process or painted on by hand after the lantern has been
made. To arrange to see the lantern-making process, consult
the infor-mation desk at your hotel.

Ukai fishing is the major summer (May 11–Oct. 15) evening
pastime for locals and visitors. It is an organized spectator attraction and an occasion for frolicking while watching a centuries-old way of catching fish. Fishermen, dressed in the
traditional costume of reed skirts, glide down the river in their
boats. Suspended in front of each boat is a wood brazier burning bright to attract *ayu* (river smelt or sweet fish) to the surface. Cormorants, several to a boat, are slipped overboard on
their leashes to use their long beaks to snap up the fish. Because of a small ring around each of the birds' necks, the fish
never quite reach the cormorants' stomachs. Instead, their
long necks expand to hold five wiggling fish. When a bird can't
take in another fish, the fisherman hauls the bird back to the
boat, where it is made to regurgitate its neckful. The actual
performance lasts less than ½-hour, but the frolicking takes
much longer.

Approximately 130 boats, carrying 10 to 30 spectators in each,
heave-to in the Nagara River about two hours before the fishing commences. This is party time, consumed by eating and
drinking. A boat, full of singing and dancing maidens dressed
as geisha, drifts through the spectator boats. Other boats ply

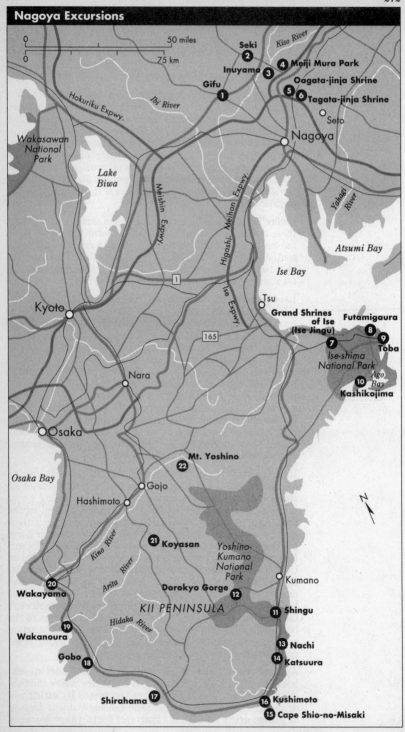

the river, selling food and drink. Since the ayu are attracted by the light from a boat's wood-burning braziers, no fishing occurs when the river is muddy from heavy rains or on nights when there is a full moon. Tickets for the spectator boats are sold in most of Gifu's hotels and also at the main ticket office downstream from the Nagarabashi Bridge. *Cost: about ¥2,600. The ticket office opens at 6, but you may order advance reservations through the Gifu City Spectators Office, tel. 0582/62–0104, or at the Gifu City Tourist Agency at the station, tel. 0582/62–4415.*

Architectural sights in Gifu are worth visiting only if you have the spare time to wander around waiting for the ukai fishing. An unusual statue of Buddha (45 feet tall), with a six-foot-long ear as a symbol of omnipotent wisdom, is housed in an orange-and-white building, **Shoji.** This building is easy to recognize from the street as you ride the bus from the train station into downtown Gifu and toward the river. It is about a five-minute walk from its entrance to the cable car that takes you to Mt. Kinka. The statue, one of the three largest Buddhas in Japan, was completed in 1747 after 38 years of pasting together 2,000 pounds of paper *sutra* (prayers); this was then coated with clay and stucco before being lacquered and gilded.

The other major feature of Gifu is the **Gifujo Castle** which houses a museum and stands before Mt. Kinka (Gold). The castle serves as a picturesque backdrop to the city. It is relatively new (1951), replacing a 16th-century structure that was destroyed by an earthquake in 1891. You can either climb up the mountainside or take the cable car (ropeway), but the castle really looks its best at night from down below, when it is all lit up. *Admission: ¥300. Open spring and fall, 9–6; summer, 9–7; winter, 9–4:30.*

❷ **Seki,** which is north of Gifu, is an easy excursion of 15 kilometers (9 miles) on a tramcar/train. It is one of the most famous traditional centers of sword production. Seki is a must to visit, but only if you can time your trip to coincide with a demonstration showing the traditional method of sword production. This show will help you understand the artistry and mystique of the traditional Japanese sword, which may cost around ¥6 million. *The demonstration occurs at the Sangyo Shinko Center (Industry Promotion Center), tel. 05752/2–3131. Admission free. The show is given 5 times a day on the 1st Sun. of the month; in Oct. the show is held on the 2nd Sun.; in Jan. it is held on Jan. 2.*

❸ The next stop is **Inuyama.** Though the JR line can be used from Gifu, the privately operated Meitetsu Line is more convenient. However, if you are using a JR Rail Pass, take the JR train to Unuma and change to the Meitetsu Line for a three-minute ride to Inuyama. If you are coming straight from Seki, the JR line goes to Inuyama. Coming to Inuyama directly from Nagoya, take the Meitetsu Line, which continues on to Gifu.

Inuyama is known for having Japan's oldest existing castle, **Inuyamajo,** built in 1440. It is not a grand structure, but it is a pleasant change to see the real thing rather than another concrete replica. The top floor of this quaint three–story castle is a lookout room that offers a commanding view of the river below. *Admission: ¥300. Open 9–5. Closed Dec. 29–Jan. 1.*

Even better is Inuyamajo's location on a cliff above the **Kiso River,** which makes the castle romantically picturesque. This part of the Kiso River is attractive; it has been dubbed "Nihon Rhine" (the Japanese Rhine); with its mysterious rock that looms up out of the water, it's a fine place for water nymphs to congregate. A pleasant way to see the river is by raft (completely safe). To take this 8-mile river trip, take the train on the Meitetsu Hirome Line from Inuyama to Nihon-Rhine-Imawatri. Once there, check out several companies before selecting the type of boat you prefer. The trip downstream takes about one hour and costs ¥2,700.

Inuyama also offers another opportunity to watch cormorant fishing, and, as in Gifu, tickets are available from the major hotels. Because there is no difference between cormorant fishing in Gifu and Inuyama, the choice is best decided by where you will be at nightfall.

In the Urakuen Garden of the Meitetsu Inuyama Hotel and 350 yards from the castle is the **Jo-an Teahouse.** Registered as a national treasure, the building was constructed by Grand Master Urakusai Oda during the early development of the tea-making ceremony and moved to its present site only recently. *Admission: ¥800 for teahouse and gardens; additional ¥500 for tea. Open daily 9–5.*

④ A short distance to the east and south of Inuyama on the Meitetsu-Komaki Line is **Meiji Mura Park.** (Get off at the Meiji-mura-guchi Station and take a bus for 3 mi to the park.) More than 50 buildings from the Meiji Restoration (1868–1912) have been transplanted here. Emperor Meiji, who regained his imperial power from the Tokugawa Shogun dynasty, opened the doors of Japan to the west and began Japan's rapid transformation into a modern economy. This transformation is illustrated by Meiji Mura's exhibits. Traditional buildings, such as a Kabuki theater and a bathhouse, exist alongside Christian places of worship and Western-style mansions. The 19th-century buildings and Western architecture make this park more appealing to the Japanese than to Westerners. An exception may be the lobby taken from the old Imperial Hotel, which was designed by Frank Lloyd Wright. *Admission: ¥1,300. Open 10–5 Mar.– Oct., 10–4 Nov.–Feb.*

⑤⑥ More fascinating for the foreign tourist are two of Japan's most accessible fertility shrines, **Oagata-jinja Shrine** (the first stop southeast of Meiji Mura) and **Tagata-jinja Shrine** (two stops southeast of Meiji Mura). Both stops are on the Komaki Line. Oagata-jinja is the female shrine. It attracts women who are about to marry and wives who want children. Most of the objects in the shrine are symbols to that end, such as a cleft rock resembling female genitalia. Tagata-jinja is the male shrine, with a bewildering collection of phalluses, ranging in size from a few inches to six feet, left as offerings by thankful mothers.

The big event at Tagata-jinja is on March 15. Every year at this time, a splendid festival is held; sake flows liberally from morning to night. The festival's focal point is a nine-foot phallus, carried by a woman who is accompanied by a Shinto priest (with an elongated nose) and by several other women carrying more modest-size male accoutrements. The procession, which starts from a minor shrine on the other side of town, makes frequent stops to imbibe from sake casks set up at the side of the road.

The participants become progressively drunker; when they finally reach Tagata-jinja in the late afternoon, the entire village is seeing double. *Admission free. Open sunrise to sunset.*

Time Out   If you have to wait for a train, drop into **Terukumni** (tel. 0508/77–9647), a small nomiya located on the main street not far from the station. There is sushi if you are hungry, but you can also order just a beer.

From Tagata-jinja, one can hop on board a train at the Tagata Station and be back in Nagoya in 30 minutes, but you will need to transfer to the Miejo subway at Kamijida. It may be easier to return to Inuyama and take the direct train to Nagoya.

Ise-Shima National Park and the Kii Peninsula

Southwest of Nagoya are the Shima and Kii Peninsulas. On the Shima Peninsula are the most venerated shrines in Japan, the Grand Shrines of Ise. The shrines are part of Ise-Shima National Park, which extends farther south to Toba, the center of the pearl industry, and Kashikojima, with its indented coastline studded with pine-clad islands. From there, the Kii Peninsula extends south and west of the Shima Peninsula. Here the attractions are magnificent marine scenery, coastal fishing villages and resorts, and Yoshino-Kumano National Park. The latter features pristine gorges, holy mountains, and two large, ancient Buddhist community complexes, one of which, Mt. Yoshino, has perhaps the finest display of cherry blossoms in Japan.

A traveler may visit the Grand Shrines of Ise in a day or all of the Shima Peninsula in two. To cover both the Shima Peninsula and the Kii Peninsula requires a minimum of five days. Also, one has the option of returning to Nagoya from anywhere on these peninsulas, or heading directly for Nara, Kyoto, and Osaka.

❼ **The Grand Shrines of Ise** (also called the Ise Jingu Shrines) in Ise-shi are the first recommended attractions to visit outside Nagoya. You may travel to the shrines from Nagoya on a JR train, but the trip requires a train change, usually at Taki, and each train is a local. The fastest and most direct route is the privately owned Kintetsu Line. Fare: ¥1,800 (taking the Kintetsu train all the way to Kashikojima costs ¥2,800). Even if you have a JR Rail Pass, the time saved on the Kintetsu may be worth the extra cost.

The journey out of Nagoya takes you through depressing industrial suburbs, but don't despair. Thirty minutes before Ise-shi, the polluting factories end and the farmlands begin. Ise-shi is a small town whose major business comes from the pilgrims who pay respects to the Outer Shrine (Geku) and the Inner Shrine (Naiku). From either the Kintetsu or the JR train station it is only a 10-minute walk through town to the Outer Shrine. A frequent shuttle bus makes the 4-mile trip between the Outer and Inner Shrines; a bus also goes directly from the Inner Shrine to Ise-shi Station. The most crowded times to visit the shrines are during the Grand Festival held October 15–17 every year, when thousands come to see the pageantry, and on New Year's Eve and Day when Shinto believers pray for a good new year.

Astounding as it may be, the main halls at both the Outer and Inner Shrines are, in accord with Shinto tradition, torn down every 20 years. New constructions are then built, as exact replicas of the previous halls, using the same centuries-old method, on adjacent sites. The main halls you see now were erected in 1973 and are due to be replaced in 1993. Whether they will be (at a cost of at least ¥4.5 billion, which was the price in 1973) is uncertain.

The Outer Shrine is dedicated to Toyouke-Omikami, goddess of grain and agriculture. Its buildings are all in a traditional style, predating the surge of Chinese influence that swept through the country in the 6th century. Located deep in a park full of ancient cedars, Geku dates from AD 478. Its plain design makes it seem part of the magnificent grounds; it is made from unpainted *hinoki* (cypress) wood, with a fine, closely shaven thatch roof. Unfortunately, the visitor can see very little of the exterior of the Geku and none of its interior. Four fences surround the shrine, and only the imperial family and its envoys may enter it.

The same is true for the other even more venerated shrine, the Inner Shrine, located to the southwest of Geku. Naiku is where the Yata-no-Kagami (Sacred Mirror) is kept, one of the three sacred treasures of the imperial regalia. This shrine is also the home to Amaterasu, the sun goddess and the highest deity in the Shinto pantheon. (The name "Japan" in Japanese is *Nihon*, meaning "the origin of the sun.") Amaterasu, born of the left eye of Izanagi, was the great-great-grandmother of the first mortal emperor of Japan, Jimmu Tenno. Seventy generations later, Hirohito, who led Japan through World War II and into prosperous peacetime, became the 123rd divine emperor. Hirohito, however, renounced his divine relationship at the insistence of the U.S. occupation forces.

The Grand Shrines both have more of a natural harmony with nature than the more controlled, even contrived, buildings in later Japanese architecture. The Inner Shrine's architecture is simple. If one did not know its origin, one would term it classically modern. Again, the use of unpainted cedar causes the shrine to blend into the ancient forest that circles it and covers the grounds of the 63-acre park. As with Geku, the visitor can see very little through the wooden fences surrounding the shrine. Although the sightseeing is limited at the Grand Shrines, one's reward is in feeling the sanctity surrounding both sights. This experience is totally Japanese, one that Westerners can only begin to understand. *Admission to grounds of both shrines free. Grounds open sunrise–sunset.*

Two routes may be followed onward to Toba, the resort town made famous by Mikimoto pearls. You can take a 45-minute bus ride from near the Inner Shrine for ¥910. There is one bus every hour, with the last bus at 3:56 PM. The bus goes along the **Ise-Shima Skyline Drive,** which offers fine mountainous and wooded scenery. The other alternative, and perhaps the more memorable, is to take the JR train (it follows the coast road, #137) from Ise-shi to Toba with a stop at **Futamigaura,** a popular spot for Japanese lovers. Two rocks, one said to be male and the other female, rise out of the water. Because they are of the opposite sex, the Japanese married them, linking the two together with a straw rope (replaced every Jan. 5 as part of a cheerful festival). These rocks, known as the **Meoto-Iwa** (wedded rocks), represent Izanagi and Izanami, Japan's Adam and Eve. Imagine the striking view with the sun rising behind them.

❾ Back on the train, it is less than 10 minutes to **Toba.** Toba is where the cultivation of pearls was perfected. Before Kokichi Mikimoto completed his technique for harvesting pearl-bearing oysters at the turn of the century, pearls were a rare freak of nature. *Ama* (women divers—women because it was believed they had bigger lungs) could dive all day long; even after bringing up a thousand oysters, they might not find one with a valuable pearl. Thanks to Mikimoto, the odds have changed. Nevertheless, even after the considerable effort of injecting an irritating substance—muscarine, from Iowa—into two-year-old oysters, only one in two bears pearls, and no more than 5% are of gem quality. Because the two-year-old oyster takes three more years to secrete layer after layer of nacre over his irritating implant to form the pearl, these gems remain expensive.

On **Pearl Island,** 500 yards from Toba Station, **Mikimoto's Museum** (he died in 1954) gives a fascinating, if a little long-winded, account of pearl cultivation. A demonstration is also given by female pearl divers. *Admission: ¥850. Open 8:30–5 (9–4 in winter).*

Before pearl-oyster farming, women dove for pearls with more frequency than now. Such a hit-or-miss operation can no longer support them in face of the larger quantities (and cheaper prices) possible through Mikimoto's research and farming. However, on the outlying islands, women do still dive for abalone, octopus, and edible seaweed. These women are not lithe, scantily clad nymphs of the water, but mature ladies who wear diving suits and make peculiar whistling sounds.

Toba is a resort town with resort hotels and activities. An aquarium displays native and exotic marine life, such as rare Alaskan sea otters and Baikal seals (admission: ¥1,200; open 8–5). The ship *Brazil Maru,* which transported many Japanese rice farmers to Brazil, is now a floating entertainment center with restaurants and souvenir shops. (admission: ¥1,050; open daily 8:30–4:30). Cruise boats make 50-minute tours of Toba Bay (cost: ¥1,350), and ferries go to the outer islands. Because the town has a couple of reasonable hotels (Toba International offers the best views; *see* Dining and Lodging, below), Toba makes a possible overnight stop. Alternatively, Kashikojima is 40 minutes away by rail.

❿ The Kintetsu Line continues from Toba to **Kashikojima,** in the center of Ago Bay, but the tracks cut inland. (There are also two buses a day at 9:40 and 2:25, fare is ¥1,300.) To appreciate the spectacular coastline, disembark the train at Ugata and take the bus to Nakiri. Then change buses for the one going along the headland to Goza, a small fishing village that faces Kashikojima from across Ago Bay. From Goza, frequent ferries navigate past hundreds of rafts, from which pearl-bearing oysters are suspended, to Kashikojima. Ago Bay has a wonderfully indented coastline and is a fitting climax to the Ise Peninsula. The town of Kashikojima is now the pearl center and has a few reasonable hotels for an overnight stay; the most sophisticated is the Shima Kanko Hotel (*see* Dining and Lodging, below). Consider however, one of the smaller guest houses, such as the Asanaro, where you will have the opportunity to explore and meet the local community. Be sure to visit Daio, the fishing village tucked behind a promontory. Standing above the village is a grand lighthouse. To reach this towering structure, walk up the narrow street lined with fish stalls at the back of the harbor (admission ¥80; open daily 9–5). From this lighthouse, you can see another, 7 miles to the east. That's Anori, the third oldest in Japan. Between the two lighthouses on the curving bay are small fishing villages, coffee shops, and restaurants. And there are three golf courses, of which Hamajima Country Club (Hamajima 517–04, tel. 05995/2–1141; greens fees ¥8,000 weekdays, ¥18,000 weekend, caddy ¥3,500) has especially fine views of Ago Bay, dotted with numerous small islands and oyster beds.

It is possible to follow the coast from Kashikojima to the Kii Peninsula. However, one indentation following another begins to become tedious. Certainly the journey seems to take forever. One is far better off retracing one's steps. For the Kii Peninsula, take the train back from Kashikojima past Toba and Iseshi to Taki and change there for the JR line; for Nara and Kyoto, continue on to Matsusaka and change there for the JR or Kintetsu Line; for Nagoya, you will not need to change trains unless you want to transfer to the JR in order to use your Rail Pass.

Because we are going to the Kii Peninsula, transfer at Taki to the JR Kisei main line for Shingu and Kushimoto. Take your nap at the beginning of the train ride, for within hours the scenery becomes more and more picturesque as the train runs along the coastline. The first major town is Kumano. The town itself is not particularly attractive, but it is often used by hikers as a gateway to the Yoshino-Kumano National Park. However, with **⑪** limited time it is better to continue on the train to **Shingu.**

Shingu has an important shrine, Kumano-Hayatama Taisha, but the thrill for the adventurous is to take a four-hour trip up the Kumano River on flat-bottom, air propeller-driven boats to **⑫** **Dorokyo Gorge.** The trip up the valley is gently attractive, with hills rising on either side of emerald-green water. In late May–early June, with azaleas and rhododendrons lining the banks, the valley is a beautiful introduction to the gorge that lies farther upstream. That's the reason for the trip. Dorokyo is considered by many to be Japan's finest gorge. Sheer, 150-foot cliffs tower above the Kumano River, which alternates between gushing rapids and calm waters. The bus ride between Shingu and Dorokyo takes 45 minutes.)

The boat trip ends at **Doro-hatcho,** the first of the three gorges and rapids that extend for several miles upstream. Long, fiberglass boats continue up the gorge for a two-hour round-trip (cost is ¥3,280). A less expensive alternative is a bus up to Kitayamakyo, where there are good glimpses of the Doro-hatcho Gorge.

From Doro-hatcho, you can take a bus back to Shingu. If you do not want to continue around the Kii Peninsula, an alternative is to backtrack by bus as far as Shiko and take the Shingu-Nara bus. The bus takes seven hours from Shingu (6 hrs from Shiko) to reach Nara and passes through the heart of Yoshino-Kumano National Park. (The bus stops at Gojo, where you can make your way to Mt. Koya and Yoshino.)

Back in Shingu, if you have the time, take a quick look at Kumano-Hayatama Taisha Shrine, one of the three main shrines of Kii Peninsula. Though it is a bright and cheerful place, it is not worth missing your train, unless you are there on October 15 for its festival. The other two main shrines are at Hongu, near Doro-hatcho, and at Nachi, the next stop around the Kii Peninsula.

The next major attraction to visit is **Nachi-no-taki,** the highest waterfall in Japan, with a drop of 430 feet. To get there, take the local JR train 9 miles to **Nachi,** then take a 20-minute bus ride (the bus leaves from the Nachi train station). Where the bus stops at the falls, you'll see a *torii* arch at the top of several stone steps, which lead down to a paved clearing near the foot of the falls. For a view from the top, climb up the path from the bus stop to **Nachi-Taisha,** which, aside from being one of the three great shrines of the Kii area (founded in the 4th century), offers a close-up view above the waterfall. Next to the shrine is the Buddhist Seigantoji Temple, a popular stop for pilgrims.

A couple of miles farther down the coast from Nachi, and the halfway point (6 hours either way by rail) between Osaka and Nagoya, is **Katsuura,** located on a pleasant bay surrounding pine-covered islands. Sightseeing boats cruise the bay (cost: ¥1,550), promoting it as Kii-no-Matsushima. The bay is named after one of the three big scenic draws in Japan, Matsushima Bay near Sendai, and if you've seen that, taking the cruise is not worth the money.

Another 30 miles down the coast at the bottom of the Kii Peninsula is **Cape Shio-no-misaki,** Honshu's most southerly point, marked by a white lighthouse high above its rocky cliffs. Nearby is the resort town of **Kushimoto,** which, with its direct flights to Nagoya and Osaka, has become popular with residents from those cities. Stretching out to sea toward Oshima (the island a mile offshore) is a notable and odd formation of 30 large rocks, spaced evenly as they jut out to sea. They resemble what their name suggests, Hashi-kui-iwa (rock pillars), though more imaginative authors describe them as a procession of hooded monks trying to reach Oshima.

Rounding the peninsula, 34 miles to the north, is **Shirahama,** rated (by the Japanese) as one of the three best hot-spring resorts in the country. (The other two are Beppu on Kyushu and Atami on the Izu Peninsula. We would add Noboribetsu Onsen in Hokkaido to these.) Unfortunately, the Japanese have a penchant for building mammoth, drab hotels around their spa waters, and this town fits that mold. But it does have some attractive coastal scenery, so Shirahama can be a pleasant place for an overnight stay. Be warned, though, that the town itself is a 17-minute bus ride from the train station.

Between Shirahama and Wakanoura is the famous **Dojoji Temple** in **Gobo.** According to legend, Kiyohime, a farmer's daughter, became enamored of a young priest, Anchin, who often passed by her house. One day she blurted out her feelings to him. He, in turn, promised to return that night and take advantage of her feelings. However, during the course of the day, the priest had second thoughts and returned to the Dojoji Temple. Spurned, Kiyohime became enraged. She turned herself into a dragon and set in pursuit of Anchin, who, scared out of his wits, hid under the temple bell that had not yet been suspended.

Kiyohime sensed his presence and wrapped her dragon body around the bell. Her fiery breath heated the bell until it became red-hot. The next morning, only the charred remains of Anchin's body were found under the bell.

Equally as good as Shirahama for an overnight stay is **Wakanoura,** 30 miles farther north. It is another resort, one that makes the rather ambitious claim of having the most beautiful coastal scenery in Japan. A few miles north of Wakanoura is **Wakayama.** This is the largest town one reaches since leaving Nagoya. Ferries (from Wakayama-ko Port) depart for Komatsushima on the island of Shikoku. As a city, Wakayama has little of interest for the visitor other than its being a source for replenishing camera film, yen, and other needs before traveling inland to visit sacred Koyasan (Mt. Koya) and Mt. Yoshino before ending this itinerary in Nara.

To get to Koyasan, take the JR line to Hashimoto and change onto the Nankai Line for the final 12 miles to Gokuraku-bashi Station. From there, a cable car runs up to the top of sacred Mt. Koya. (If one has cut across the Yoshino-Kumano National Park by bus from Shingu or Hongu on Rte. 168, instead of circling the Kii Peninsula, get off the bus at Gojo and backtrack one station on the JR line to Hashimoto for the Nankai Line.)

To reach Koyasan directly from Tokyo or Kyoto, go first to Osaka and take the private Nankai Line that departs for Koyasan every 30 minutes from Namba Station. (To reach Namba Station from Shin-Osaka Shinkansen Station, use the Midosuji subway.) The Osaka-Koyasan journey takes just under two hours, including the five-minute cable car ride up to the Koyasan Station.

On a mesa amid the mountains is **Koyasan,** a great complex of 120 temples, monasteries, schools, and graves. It is the seat of the Shingon sect of Buddhism founded by Kobo Daishi in 816. Every year about a million visitors pass through the Daimon Gate, a huge wooden structure typical of many entrances to Japanese temples.

After you arrive at Koyasan Station at the top of Mt. Koya, you will need to take a bus (fare: ¥300) into the center of town. Koyasan's key attractions are on either side (east and west) of the main street. En route from the station, you will pass the mausoleums of the first and second Tokugawa shoguns. You may want to walk back and visit these two gilted structures later. (Open 9–5.) The bus will reach a "T" junction. This is where the tourist office (600 Koyasan, Koya-cho, Ito-gun, Wakayama-ken, tel. 07365/6–2616) is located; you may want to get out here and collect a map.

The eastern part of Koyasan has the **Okunoin Cemetery** and the southwestern part has many of the major temples. To reach the eastern sector, take the bus that turns left at this "T" junction and disembark at the Ukunoin-mae bus stop. Here is an entrance to Okunoin Cemetery. Many of your fellow visitors will be Japanese, who are either making a pilgrimmage to the mausoleum of Kobo Daishi or paying their respects to their ancestors buried here. Among magnificent cedar trees and on either side of a mile-long avenue are the permanent homes of some of Japan's most illustrious families, who lie under the moss-covered pagodas. You'll see monuments to virtually every historical figure in Japanese history (or at least 100,000 of them). At the end of the avenue stands the **Lantern Hall,** named after its 11,000 lanterns. Two fires burn in this hall: one has been alight since 1016, the other since 1088. At the rear of the hall is the mausoleum of Kobo Daishi (774–835). *Lantern Hall admission free. Open 8–5 Apr.–Oct.; 8:30–4:30 Nov.–Mar.*

Walk back through the cemetery, but instead of taking the left-hand fork in the avenue, continue straight ahead. This will lead back to the tourist office and to the southwestern side of Mt. Koya and **Kongobuji Temple** (Temple of the Diamond Seat). This is the chief temple of Shingon Buddhism, a sect that is closest to that practiced in Tibet. Kongobuji was built in 1592 as the family temple of Hideyoshi Toyotomi. Since then, however, it has been rebuilt (1861) and is now the main temple of the community. *Admission: ¥350. Open 8–5; in winter 8–4:30.*

Two hundred yards to the southwest from Kongobuji is **Danjogaran,** a complex consisting of many halls and the Daito (Great Central Pagoda), a red pagoda with an interior of brilliantly colored beams that is home to five sacred images of Buddha. This two-story pagoda, built in 1937, stands out in part because of its unusual style, but also because of its rich vermilion color. *Admission to buildings: ¥100 each. Open Apr.–Oct. 8–5; Nov.–Mar. 8:30–4:30.*

South and across a small path from the Danjogaran is the **Reihokan Museum,** with a total of 5,000 art treasures. The exhibits are continually changing, but at least some of the 180 pieces that have been designated as national treasures are always on display. *Admission: ¥500. Open 9–5 (9–4 in winter).* Spread over an area of 3.4 miles by 1.4 miles at an altitude of 3,000 feet, Koyasan can easily require an overnight stay. However, if one is making only a day trip to Koyasan from Kyoto or Osaka, most of the major sights—the Danjogaran, the Kongobuji, the Lantern Hall, and the avenue of mausoleums—can be visited in an afternoon. If you only spend a day in Koyasan, though, you will miss the mystical atmosphere of a night on the revered mountain and the experience of witnessing one of the early-morning temple services.

Koyasan has no hotels. Instead, 53 temples have a monopoly on the accommodations business, and prices are higher than at any other temple in Japan. Each is run autonomously by its abbot, and in this, and only this, Buddhist sect, wealth is necessary for advancement in the religious hierarchy *(see* Dining and Lodging, below).

㉒ The next and final stop before Nara is **Mt. Yoshino,** the other major religious and historical site of the region. To get to Yoshino from Koyasan, rejoin the train at Hashimoto for Yoshino-guchi, and change to the Kintetsu Line for Yoshino. (This Kintetsu Line is the Osaka–Yoshino route, which departs from Abeno-bashi Station in Osaka. Yoshino may also be reached directly from Kashikojima on the Kintetsu Line.)

Though the community of temples at Mt. Yoshino is less impressive than that of Koyasan, Mt. Yoshino is one of the most beautiful places in Japan to visit during cherry-blossom season. The Cherry Blossom Festival, which attracts thousands of visitors each year, is April 11–12. Because of its 100,000 trees in four groves that are staggered down the mountainside, and because of the differing temperatures, the wafting sea of pink petals lasts at least two weeks. When you look upon this vision of color, thank En-no-Ozunu, the 7th-century Buddhist priest who planted the trees and put a curse on anyone who tampered with them.

In the middle of the cherry groves is **Kimpusenji Temple,** the main temple of the area. Make a point of seeing the main hall, Zaodo, which is not only the second largest wooden structure in Japan, but also has two superb sculptures of Deva kings at the main gate. The other important temple is **Nyoirinji,** founded in the 10th century and located just to the south of Kimpusenji. Here the last remaining 143 warriors prayed before going into their final battle for the imperial cause in the 14th century. Behind the temple is the mausoleum of Emperor Godaigo (1288–1339), who brought down the Kamakura Shogunate. *Admission:* ¥*300. Open 9–5.*

Built into the surrounding mountains, Yoshino is a quaint town where the shops—and there are many to serve the thousands of visitors—are on the third floor of the house, the first and second floors being below the road. All around Yoshino are superb mountain vistas and isolated temples. For the hiker (and pilgrim) Mt. Sanjo is considered the holiest mountain, with two temples at the summit, one of which is dedicated to En-no-Ozunu, the cherry-tree priest. Lodgings are available at both temples May 8–September 27. The Tourist Office (Yoshinoyama, Yoshino-machi, Yoshino-gun, Nara ken, tel. 07463/2–3014) can arrange accommodations at local minshukus. From Yoshino, **Nara** is an hour away (on the Kintetsu Line, with a change either at Kashihara-jingu Station or to the JR line at Yoshino-guchi), and **Kyoto** is 50 minutes farther north.

Dining and Lodging

Dining

Nagoya is known for only a few special dishes. **Kishimen** are white, flat noodles of the *udon* variety; they have a velvety smoothness against the palate. **Moriguchi-zuke** (Japanese pickle) is made from a special radish, pickled either with or without sweet sake. **Uiro** is a sweet cake made of rice powder and sugar, most often eaten during the tea ceremony.

Other than these items, Nagoya's cuisine is mostly Kyoto-style *(see* Dining in Chapter 7), but every type of Japanese and international food may be found in this cosmopolitan city. For Western cuisine, the best choices in the city are the French restaurants at Hotel Nagoya Castle, the Nagoya Kanko Hotel, and the International Hotel Nagoya. The one good Western restaurant outside the hotels is the Okura Restaurant.

On the Ise Peninsula, the **lobster** is especially fine. On the Kii Peninsula, farmers raise cattle for **Matsuzaka beef** (the town of Matsuzaka is 90 minutes by train from Nagoya). However, the best beef is typically shipped to Tokyo, Kyoto, and Osaka.

Outside Nagoya, if you want to eat Western food, you should eat Western cuisine in the dining rooms of the larger hotels. However, we strongly recommend that you eat out at local Japanese restaurants. Most reasonably priced restaurants have a visual display of their menu in the window. On this basis, you can decide what you want before you enter. If you cannot order in Japanese, and no English is spoken, after securing a table, lead the waiter to the window display and point.

Unless the establishment is a *ryotei* (high-class, traditional Japanese restaurant), reservations are usually not required at restaurants, unless they are the formal restaurants at a hotel or a ryokan. Whenever reservations are recommended or required at any of the restaurants listed, this is indicated.

A 3% federal consumer tax is added to all restaurant bills. Another 3% is added to the bill if it exceeds ¥5,000. At more expensive restaurants, a 10%–15% service charge is also added to the bill. Tipping is not the custom.

Category	Cost*
Very Expensive	over ¥6,000
Expensive	¥4,000–¥6,000
Moderate	¥2,000–¥4,000
Inexpensive	under ¥2,000

Cost is per person without tax, service, or drinks

Lodging

The cosmopolitan city of Nagoya offers a range of lodging, from clean, efficient business hotels offering the basics to large luxury hotels with additional amenities. Nagoya has three major areas in which to stay: the district around the Nagoya JR Station, the downtown area, and Nagoya Castle area. Though ryokans are listed below, international-style hotels are often more convenient for the Nagoya visitor who may want to dine at flexible hours.

Outside Nagoya, most hotels quote prices on a per-person basis with two meals, exclusive of service and tax. If you do not want dinner at your hotel, it is usually possible to renegotiate the price. Stipulate, too, whether you wish to have Japanese or Western breakfast, if any. The categories assigned to all hotels below reflect the cost of a double room with private bath but no meals. However, if you make reservations at any of the noncity hotels, you will be expected to take breakfast and dinner at the hotel; the rate quoted to you will include these meals unless you specify otherwise.

A 3% federal consumer tax is added to all hotel bills. Another 3% is added to the bill if it exceeds ¥10,000. At most hotels, a 10%–15% service charge is added to the total bill. Tipping is not the custom.

Category	Cost*
Very Expensive	over ¥20,000
Expensive	¥15,000–¥20,000
Moderate	¥10,000–¥15,000
Inexpensive	under ¥10,000

Cost is for double room, without tax or service

The most highly recommended restaurants and accommodations for each city or area are indicated by a star ★.

Credit Cards The following credit card abbreviations are used: AE, American Express; DC, Diners Club; MC, MasterCard; V, Visa.

Nagoya

Dining **Koraku.** One of the most exclusive restaurants in Nagoya,
★ Koraku serves some of the best chicken dishes in all of Japan. The restaurant is in an old samurai mansion, with formal service by women dressed in beautiful kimonos. *3-3 Chikaramachi, Higashi-ku, Nagoya, tel. 052/931–3472. Dress: formal. Reservations essential, preferably with an introduction. AE. No lunch. Very Expensive.*

Kamone. The innovative Japanese menu here adds Chinese and/or French touches to the dishes and, as if to enhance the foreign culinary influences on the Japanese dishes, the decor is more Western than Japanese—window drapes instead of shoji screens, for example. Since the restaurant is on the 15th floor of the Meiji Seimei Building, try for a table by the window in order to enjoy the view. *1-1 Shin-Sakaemachi, Naka-ku, Nagoya (located across from the Sakaecho subway station exit), tel. 052/951–7787. Reservations advised. Jacket and tie required. DC, MC, V. Open noon–3 and 5–9. Closed Mon. Expensive.*

★ **Okura Restaurant.** The Okura has the best French cuisine in Nagoya, outside of the hotels. This is the place where Western businessmen often entertain their Japanese partners. Some recommended dishes include the veal slices with mushrooms in madeira sauce and the steamed salmon. Another good choice is Matsuzaka beef (a Nagoya specialty) served with béarnaise sauce. *Tokyo Kaijo Bldg., 23rd floor, Naka-ku, Nagoya, tel. 052/201–3201. Reservations required. Dress: formal. AE, DC, V. Expensive.*

Torikyu. This traditionally decorated restaurant in a Meiji-period building specializes in chicken dishes—raw, grilled, in a casserole, or as a very formal meal. The restaurant is next to a river, and in the old days, patrons used to arrive by boat. *1-15 Naiyacho, Nakamura-ku, Nagoya, tel. 052/541–1888. Reservations advised. Jacket and tie required. AE. Open 11–9:30. Closed Sun. Expensive.*

★ **Yaegaki.** This is the best tempura restaurant in town; the fish and vegetables are cooked before you, and you eat them immediately after the chef decides they're done to perfection. The restaurant building is one of the few wood structures among a sea of concrete, and it has its own small garden. An English-language menu is offered. *3-7 Nishiki, Naka-ku, Nagoya, tel. 052/951–3250. Reservations advised. Jacket and tie required. AE, V. Open noon–9. Closed Sun. Expensive.*

Kami Doraku. The specialty here is crab, either boiled or steamed, elegantly served by waitresses dressed in kimonos. The restaurant, which is located opposite the Nagoya Tokyu Hotel's entrance, may be identified by its small sign of a crab. *4-chome, Sakae, Naka-ku, Nagoya, tel. 052/242–1234. Reservations advised. Jacket and tie required. AE, V. Moderate.*

Kisoji. Located not far from the International Hotel Nagoya, Kisoji has a reasonably priced (¥4,000) *shabu-shabu* beef dinner, but if you take the shabu-shabu special with tempura and sashimi, the price jumps up. The decor is rustic, but the kimono-clad waitresses give it a touch of tradition and smartness.

Nishiki 3-chome, Naka-ku, Nagoya, tel. 052/951–3755. Dress: informal. Open 11–10. V. Moderate.

Usquebaugh. This new bar/restaurant with a polished wood decor takes its name from the Gaelic word for "water of life"— whiskey. Nautical paintings and gear hang on the walls, and there are some inpressive glass-enclosed wine racks. Modern *kaiseki* cuisine is served at reasonable prices; you can also have a light meal at the bar. The restaurant is located on Hirokuji-dori Avenue, one block east of the Rich Hotel. *2-4-1 Sakae, Naka-ku, Nagoya, tel. 052/201–5811. Jacket and tie required. AE, DC, MC, V. Moderate.*

Yamamotoya. For Nagoya's local dish, *misonikomi* (noodles in broth), you can't beat this no-frills eatery, which serves a steaming bowl of *udon* for ¥1,500. The superb misonikomi is especially welcome during the colder months. The restaurant is located one block east of the Rich Hotel. *2-4-5 Sakae, Naka-ku, Nagoya, tel. 052/471–5547. Dress: casual. No credit cards. Inexpensive.*

Lodging **Nagoya Hilton.** The newest of the city's leading hotels, this 28-
★ story building delivers all the modern creature comforts of an international deluxe accommodation. Rooms on the upper floors have a panoramic view of Nagoya. The light-pastel furnishings and the *shoji* window screens add to the bright, airy feel of the rooms. The plastic polyurethane covering on the tables and chairs should be eliminated, but the king-size beds are a pleasure. Single travelers do especially well because the hotel has none of the closet-size rooms found in most Japanese hotels. You'll appreciate the attentive, enthusiastic staff. Be sure to browse the designer boutiques in the Hilton Plaza. The collection of high-price and -status merchandise symbolizes Japan's new-found riches and the importance attached to image. *1-3-3 Sakae, Naka–ku, Nagoya 460, tel. 052/212–1111. 453 rooms, including 26 suites, and 2 concierge floors. Facilities: 3 specialty restaurants (Chinese, Continental, and Japanese), coffee shop, Clark Hatch fitness center, sauna, indoor pool, massage service in room, tennis court, extensive business center, wedding and conference facilities, and shopping plaza with elegant boutiques. AE, DC, MC, V. Very Expensive.*

Nagoya Castle Hotel. Its location next to Nagoyajo Castle makes this the choice hotel in Nagoya. A room with a view onto the castle shows Nagoya at its best—especially at night, when the castle is floodlit. The bedrooms are spacious and attractively furnished, including original oil paintings. Even the lobby is attractively and hospitably decorated, with plenty of wood paneling. The establishment is efficiently run, with a range of restaurants and bars; at the Rosen Bar, Western and Japanese businessmen meet for a drink after work. The hotel has a new, vast annex of 6,400 square feet of convention halls. *3-19 Hinokuchi-cho, Nishi-ku, Nagoya 451 (Castle Area), tel. 052/ 521–2121. 274 rooms, including 5 suites. Facilities: Western, Chinese, and Japanese restaurants, indoor pool, health club, business center, shops, beauty salon, and an hourly shuttle bus to the JR station. AE, DC, MC, V. Expensive–Very Expensive.*

The International Hotel Nagoya. With the best location in the city, the International Hotel has been a longtime favorite with business travelers. While not the newest accommodation in town, it has maintained a high standard; the lobby reminds you of Europe, with its gold and dark-brown tones and its antique furnishings. Rooms were renovated in 1988, and though some are small, they are comfortably furnished with paintings on the walls—a pleasant change from the uniformity of many other hotels. Still, the rooms should be larger, considering the price. *3-23-3 Nishiki, Naka-ku, Nagoya 460 (downtown), tel. 052/ 961–3111. 265 Western-style rooms. Facilities: Western, Chinese, and Japanese restaurants, penthouse bar with live music, business center. AE, DC, MC, V. Expensive.*

Ryokan Suihoen. A large concrete city, Nagoya is not the ideal setting for old-style ryokans, but this one is the most traditional, luxurious, and expensive of its kind in Nagoya. The tatami rooms are furnished with good reproductions of traditional furniture. Meals may be served in your room. *1-19-20 Sakae, Naka-ku, Nagoya 460 (downtown), tel. 052/241–3521. 25 rooms, most with bath. AE. Expensive.*

The Castle Plaza Hotel. A five-minute walk from the main railway station, the Castle Plaza is an efficient and top-notch business person's hotel, with more amenities than most. The few Japanese rooms are larger in size than the others. *4-3-25 Meieki, Nakamura-ku, Nagoya 450, tel. 052/582–2121. 258 Western-style rooms, 4 Japanese-style rooms. Facilities: gym, indoor pool, sauna, Western and Japanese restaurant. AE, V. Moderate.*

Nagoya Plaza Hotel. This downtown basic business hotel is the best low-price hotel in the area. The rooms are furnished with the bare essentials, a little threadbare, perhaps, but the guest rooms are slightly larger than similarly priced hotels. *3-8-21 Nishiki, Naka-ku, Nagoya 460 (downtown, close to the Sakae subway station), tel. 052/951–6311. 176 Western-style rooms. Facilities: Only breakfast, Japanese or Western, is available. AE, MC. Inexpensive–Moderate.*

★ **Nagoya Terminal Hotel.** Since its recent redecoration, this has now become the best choice for a less-expensive business hotel close to the station. Of course, the rooms are small, as one must expect in Japan, but they are not as depressing as most. Even the public rooms are pleasant. At the Kurumaya restaurant the creative chef imports French ideas for his Japanese cooking. The Playmates lounge bar offers a 20th-floor panorama view, and the Bagpiper is a friendly bar. *1–2 Mei-Eki 1-chome, Nakamura-ku, Nagoya 450, tel. 052/561–3751. 246 rooms. Facilities: Japanese/French restaurant, coffee shop, bar, banquet facilities. AE, DC, V. Inexpensive–Moderate.*

Oyone Ryokan. In a small modern building, Oyone is a friendly inn resembling a small B&B with its small, sparsely furnished rooms. *2-2-12 Aoi, Higashi-ku, Nagoya (downtown—take the Higashiyama subway line, exit at Chikusa, 2 stops after Sakae), tel. 052/936–8788. 18 rooms, all without bath, but with air-conditioning. AE, MC, V. Inexpensive.*

Ryokan Meiryu. This inn has no particular charm except its low price for a small tatami room, which has nothing more than a table and a futon. Meals (optional) are served in a small dining room. *2-24-21 Kamimaezu, Naka-ku, Nagoya 460 (downtown—the hotel is located opposite the YMCA, 2 stops Kamimimaezu Station on the Meijo subway south of Sakae), tel. 052/331–8686. 23 rooms, all without bath. AE. Inexpensive.*

Outside Nagoya

Futaminoura
Lodging

Ryokan Futamikan. This traditional Japanese inn is located on the coast near the wedded rocks off the Ise Peninsula, about 10 miles north of Toba. *569-1 Futamimachi, Mie Prefecture (3-minute taxi ride away from Futaminoura Station), tel. 05964/3–2003. 43 rooms. AE. Expensive.*

Gifu
Lodging

Ryokan Sugiyama. Close to the Nagara River, Sugiyama is Gifu's best Japanese inn. The presence of the river adds to the mood of peace and quiet. Very good food, including *ayu* (river smelt), is usually served in the rooms. *73-1 Nagara, Gifu 502, tel. 0582/31–0161. 49 Japanese-style rooms. AE. Expensive.*

Gifu Grand Hotel. This large resort hotel is efficiently run and slightly impersonal, but it is popular with the Japanese who come for its thermal baths. *648 Nagara, Gifu 502, tel. 0582/33–1111. 147 rooms, about half Western-style. Facilities: pool, hot springs, sauna, Western and Japanese restaurants. AE, V. Moderate.*

Inuyama
Lodging

Mietetsu Inuyama Hotel. This resort hotel's location on the Kiso River makes it a good base for shooting the rapids. *107 Kita-Koken, Inuyama, Aichi Prefecture 484, tel. 0568/61–2211. 99 rooms, mostly Western-style, but Japanese-style rooms in the annex. Facilities: Western and Japanese restaurants, outdoor pool. AE, V. Moderate.*

Ise-shi
Lodging

Hoshide Ryokan. A small Japanese inn in a traditional-style wood building, the Hoshide is bare and simple, but it has clean tatami rooms and congenial hosts. The food served follows a macrobiotic diet, though instant coffee is available at breakfast! *2-15-2 Kawasaki, Ise-shi, Mie Prefecture 516 (a 7-min walk from the Kintetsu Station or the Ise Outer Shrine), tel. 0596/28–2377. 13 Japanese-style rooms, without private bath. Facilities: laundry room, Japanese bath. AE, V. Moderate.*

Kashikojima
Lodging
★

Shima Kanko Hotel. This large and established resort hotel has grand views over Ago Bay, especially at sunset. Certainly for its location, it's a choice hotel; the staff are friendly and efficient, willing to help advise you in your travel and touring, even making arrangements for golf. Some English is spoken. The hotel's smart French restaurant offers the best Western cuisine on the Shima Peninsula, creatively using local lobster (a succulent specialty of the region) to its best advantage. Guest rooms are spacious and smartly furnished, though in a rather dreary pale yellow/beige color. All rooms have views of the bay. *731 Shimmei Ago-cho, Shima-gun, Mie Prefecture 517 (a shuttle bus runs to and from Kashikojima Station), tel. 05994/3–1211. 147 Western-style rooms, 51 Japanese-style rooms. Facilities: pool, arrangements for golf, boating, and fishing, beauty parlors, shops, French and Japanese restaurants. AE, DC, V. Moderate–Expensive.*

★ **Asanaro Minshuku.** Owner Yuzoo Matsmura is boisterously friendly. In broken English, he welcomes his guests with enthusiastic abandon. The inn is located in a small fishing village facing the Pacific between Daio and Anori lighthouses. Rooms are large, spotlessly clean, and come with air-conditioning and heating. Bathrooms, also spotless, are just down the hall. Breakfast and dinner are served in your room. Dinner is absolutely superb—fresh broiled lobsters, sashimi, fried oysters, fish cooked in soy sauce or grilled, and fresh fruit. Matsmura-san will insist you use his bicycles to explore and will take you in his car to all the places you missed. He also owns a snack bar (pub), similarly called Asanaro (tel. 05994/3–4197) in Ugata, where he will no doubt take you after dinner. *3578 Kooka Ago-chiyo, Shima Gun, Mie 517–05, tel. 05994/5–3963. 8 rooms. 2 meals included. Owner will meet guests at Ugata Station; telephone on arrival. No credit cards. Inexpensive.*

★ **Ryokan Ishiyama-So.** On tiny Yokoyama-jima Island in Ago Bay, this small inn is just a two-minute ferry ride from Kashikojima. Phone ahead, and your hosts will meet you at the quay. The inn is nothing fancy, but it has warmth and hospitality. The meals are good, too, but don't let the hosts try pleasing you with Western-style food. *Yokoyama-jima, Kashikojima, Ago-cho, Shima-gun, Mie Prefecture 517-05, tel. 05995/2–1527. 12 Japanese-style rooms, 3 with private bath. AE, MC. Inexpensive.*

Koyasan (Mt. Koya) Lodging
Mt. Koya has no actual hotels. Fifty-three of the temples offer Japanese-style accommodations—tatami floors and futon mattresses. The temples do not have private baths, and the two meals served are vegetarian, the same as those eaten by the priests. The price is either side of ¥10,000 per person, including the two meals. If possible, reservations should be made in advance through **Koya-san Kanko Kyokai,** Koya-san, Koya-machi, Itsu-gun, Wakayama Prefecture, tel. 07365/6–2616. Reservations can also be booked through the Nankai Railway Company office in Osaka. The Japan Travel Bureau in most Japanese cities can also make reservations.

Matsuzaka Dining ★
Restaurant Wadakin. This establishment claims to be the originator of Matsuzaka beef; it raises cattle with loving care on its farm. Sukiyaki or the chef's steak dinner will satisfy both your taste buds and any craving for red meat. *1878 Nakamachi, Matsuzaka 515, Mie Prefecture (located 10 min on foot directly away from the railway station, opposite a parking garage), tel. 0598/21–3291. Jacket and tie required. Open 10:30–9. Closed 4th Tues. of each month. No credit cards. Expensive.*

Shirahama Lodging
Shirasso Grand Hotel. This resort-spa hotel seems to be more appealing to the Japanese than to Westerners. Though it has little architectural merit as a modern, rectangular cement block structure, it does have thermal baths for adults. *Shirahama, Wakayama Prefecture 649, tel. 0739/42–2566. 125 Western-style rooms. Facilities: shopping arcade, electronic games for children, thermal baths, Western and Japanese restaurants. AE, DC, V. Expensive.*

Toba Lodging
Toba International Hotel. Toba's chief resort hotel sits up on a bluff overlooking the town and bay. Take a room facing the sea, and be sure to be up for the marvelous sunrises. The hotel has all the amenities for the entire family. *1-23-1 Toba, Mie Prefecture 517, tel. 0599/25–3121. 147 rooms, mostly Western, but Japanese-style rooms in the annex. Facilities: golf, fishing, pool, boating. AE, DC, V. Moderate.*

6 The Japan Alps

by Nigel Fisher

Although 80% of all of Japan is categorized as mountainous, it took a Briton, the Reverend Walter Weston, to call the north–south mountain ranges of Honshu's central region the Japan Alps. Through his writings, the Reverend Weston helped to change the Japanese attitudes to the mountains from one of reverence and superstition—a place where gods alight from the heavens—to one of physical appreciation. Mountain climbing is now a popular national sport, and the Japan Alps are a training ground for the Japanese. Another Englishman, Archdeacon A. C. Shaw, who served as his church's prelate in Tokyo, gave prestige to the mountains by building his summer villa on the lower slopes of Mt. Asama to escape the muggy summers of the capital. Since then, and over the course of the past hundred years, the Japan Alps have been "discovered" by the Japanese, not only for their grandeur but also for the rural traditional culture, architecture, and folkcraft, which have been bulldozed away by the industrial progress sweeping the coastal plains. Of all the regions of Japan, the Alps have the perhaps the most to offer the first-time visitor: forested mountains, snowy peaks, rushing rivers, fortified castles, temples, folklore, festivals, and food.

In the winter, the Japan Alps attract skiers to their northern slopes, where the snow is deepest. The southern slopes, those facing the Pacific, get very little snow. In spring, the trees start blossoming, and, by summer, the alpine flowers are out. The temperatures are warm and crisp compared with the hot humidity of the lowland areas of the Chubu region (middle or central part). In autumn, the changing colors of the trees turn the Japan Alps into a kaleidoscope of hues. Then winter comes again, with the sweetest shrimps to be plucked from the cold waters of the Sea of Japan. In other words, the Japan Alps offer particular seasonal delights, but it is in the summer that they are the most crowded with both Japanese and foreign tourists.

The Japan Alps are only the ranges within the Chubu region of Honshu. Chubu is the relatively fat section of Japan's main island, bracketed by Tokyo and Niigata to the north and east and Kyoto and Fukui on the south and west. This chapter focuses on the mountains of Chubu, the so-called Japan Alps, and includes the north coast of Chubu, along with Japan's fifth largest island, Sado, which is situated in the Sea of Japan slightly north of Niigata.

Essential Information

Arriving and Departing

Several major access routes are available into the Japan Alps, and which one you take depends on where you are coming from and which places you want to visit. Below are several routes into the Japan Alps by train, arranged by destination. For Kanazawa, flight information is also given.

By Train   **Kanazawa.** From Osaka, the JR Hokuriku to Kanazawa takes just under three hours; the same train from Kyoto takes two hours and 20 minutes. From Niigata, the JR Hokuriku takes four hours. From Tokyo, take the Tokaido Shinkansen to Maibara, then the Hokuriku Honsen Express to Kanazawa for a journey that takes four hours and 40 minutes.

Karuizawa. From Tokyo's Ueno Station on the JR Shinetsu Line, the train to Karuizawa takes two hours. From Niigata, use the Shinkansen to Takasaki and change to the JR Shinetsu Line to Karuizawa. The total traveling time is approximately two hours.

Matsumoto. From Tokyo's Shinjuku Station on the JR Chuo Line, the journey to Matsumoto takes three hours. From Nagoya, the JR Chuo Line takes two hours and 15 minutes.

Nagano. From Tokyo's Ueno Station on the JR Shinetsu Line, the same train that goes to Karuizawa continues on to Nagano. The total journey takes just under three hours. From Nagoya, the JR Chuo Line to Nagano takes just over three hours. It is the same train that stops in Matsumoto.

Niigata. From Tokyo's Ueno Station the Joetsu Shinkansen to Niigata makes the journey in two hours, seven minutes.

Takayama. From Nagoya, the JR Takayama Line takes three to 3½ hours, depending on the train. From Toyama, the JR Takayama Line takes just under two hours. There are only four trains a day.

Toyama. From Nagoya, the JR Takayama to Toyama takes five hours; there are only three trains a day in each direction.

By Plane **Kanazawa.** From Tokyo's Haneda to Komatsu Airport is a one-hour flight on Japan Airlines (JAL) or All Nippon Airlines (ANA), plus 55 minutes for the airport bus connection.

Getting Around

Because of the mountains, travel through the Japan Alps is well defined by the valleys, which permit the building of roads and railways. Hence, these valleys tend to determine one's itinerary through the Japan Alps. Remember, too, that the last train or bus in the evening can be quite early.

All major stations have someone who speaks sufficient English to plan your schedule. Each major town described in the following excursion section has a tourist office at the railway station to supply free maps and, if necessary, to find you accommodations.

Rental cars are available at the major stations. However, it is best to make arrangements to collect the car before you leave Tokyo, Nagoya, or Kyoto for the Japan Alps. The Nippon-Hertz company has the greatest number of locations in this region.

During the winter months, certain roads through the central Japan Alps are closed. In particular, the direct route between Matsumoto and Takayama via Kamikochi cannot be taken between November and April.

Important Addresses and Numbers

Tourist Information **JR Travel Information Centers and Japan Travel Bureau** are available at all the train stations at the major cities and towns.

Kanazawa **Kanazawa Tourist Information Service** is in front of the JR station (tel. 0762/31–6311).

Karuizawa **Karuizawa Station Tourist Office** is at the JR station (tel. 0267/
42–2491).

Kiso Valley **The Magome Tourist Information Office** (tel. 0264/59–2336).
Open 8:30–5; closed Sunday December–March. Reservations
at the local inns are made from here. **Tsumago Tourist Information Office** (tel. 0264/57–3123). Open 9–5; closed January 1–3.
Reservations at the local inns are made from here.

Matsumoto **Matsumoto City Tourist Information Office** is on the street level
at the front of the JR station (tel. 0263/32–2814).

Niigata **Niigata City Tourist Information Center** is in front of the JR station (tel. 0252/41–7914).

Takayama **Hida Tourist Information Office** is in front of the JR station (tel.
0577/32–5328). Open April–October, 8:30–6:30; November 1–
March, 8:30–5.

**The Japan
Travel-Phone** The nationwide service for English language assistance or
travel information is available 9–5 daily. Dial toll-free 0120/
444-800 for information on western Japan. When using a yellow, blue, or green public phone (do not use the red phones),
insert a ¥10 coin, which will be returned.

Emergencies **Police,** dial 110; **ambulance,** dial 119.

Guided Tours

The Japan Travel Bureau has offices at every JR station in each
major city and town and can assist in local tours, hotel reservations, and travel ticketing. Though one should not assume that
any English will be spoken, usually someone is available whose
knowledge is sufficient for one's basic needs. Most of the traveling through this region is very straightforward, using public
transport. On the two occasions where public transportation is
infrequent—the Noto Peninsula and Sado Island—local tours
are available, though the guide will be speaking Japanese.

Noto Peninsula We recommend using the tours to the Noto Peninsula from Kanazawa. The Hokuriku-Tetsudo Co., for example, has a tour
that in 6½ hours covers much of the peninsula for ¥5,500. It operates year-round and departs from Kanazawa Station.

Sado Island The Sado Island tour is useful only because it covers the Skyline Drive, which public buses do not travel. The price for this
tour, which departs from Ryotsu, May–November, is ¥3,600.

Regional Tour The Japan Travel Bureau operates a five-day tour from Tokyo
departing every Tuesday, April 1–October 26. The tour goes
via Lake Shirakaba to Matsumoto (overnight), to Tsumago and
Takayama (overnight), to Kanazawa (overnight), to Awara Spa
(overnight), and ends in Kyoto. Cost: ¥150,000, including four
breakfasts and two dinners.

Exploring

Although several routes, by train and road, are available into
the Japan Alps from either the Sea of Japan or the Pacific
coastal regions, this chapter begins its itinerary from Tokyo
and enters the eastern edge of the Japan Alps at Karuizawa.
From there it stays up in the mountains to work its way first to
Nagano, then west to Matsumoto. A tour has been included
from Matsumoto that visits the old post towns, Tsumago and

Magome, along the Kiso Valley, where the trunk road between Kyoto and Tokyo used to pass during the Edo period (1603–1868). (This excursion may also be managed from Nagoya.) From Matsumoto the itinerary crosses over the mountains via Kamikochi to one of Japan's most attractive and preserved towns, Takayama. Then the tour descends to the Sea of Japan to Kanazawa and the Noto Peninsula. Many travelers may want to end their journey through this part of Japan and take the train from Kanazawa to Kyoto. However, we make the final leg of our journey north along the Sea of Japan to Niigata, where we take a short ferry ride to Japan's fifth largest island, Sado.

To cover and enjoy the whole itinerary would take a week, or five days if one did not go up to Niigata and over to Sado Island. However, there is no need to cover all the destinations in the itinerary. For example, if one was returning to Kyoto from Tokyo, one could go up to Kanazawa and cross the Japan Alps via Takayama en route to Nagoya, where one could rejoin the Shinkansen for Tokyo. Such a trip could easily be managed in 48 hours.

Numbers in the margin correspond with points of interest on the Japan Alps map.

Karuizawa

❶ **Karuizawa,** two hours on the JR Shinetsu Line from Tokyo's Ueno Station, is a fashionable entrance to the Japan Alps from Tokyo. For traveling around Karuizawa, the best way is by bicycle. Plenty of bicycles are available for hire (about ¥500 an hour, ¥1,500 a day) at the Karuizawa train station, which is a mile south of the main town.

Karuizawa's popularity began when Archdeacon A. C. Shaw, the English prelate who made the mountain air respectable, built his villa in 1888 as a retreat from the summer mugginess of Tokyo. His example was soon followed by other foreigners living in Tokyo, and Karuizawa's popularity continues today among affluent Tokyoites who transfer their urban lifestyle in the summer to this small town located 3,000 feet above sea level. The camp followers come as well; in the summer, branches of more than 500 trendy boutiques open their doors to sell the same goods as their main stores in Tokyo. Karuizawa becomes a little Ginza.

Nature, though, still prevails over Karuizawa. **Mt. Asama,** a triple-cratered active volcano, soars 8,399 feet above and to the northwest of town. Lately, Mt. Asama has been making grumbling sounds, possibly threatening to erupt; these noises certainly provide a sufficient reason to prohibit climbing up to the volcano's crater. For the time being, one must be satisfied with a panoramic view of Mt. Asama and its neighbor, **Mt. Myogi,** as well as the whole **Yatsugatake Mountain Range,** from the observation platform at **Usui Pass.** The view justifies the 90-minute uphill walk from Nite Bridge, located at the end of Karuizawa Ginza, the boutique-filled street.

Outside Karuizawa are the **Shiraito Falls,** whose height is only about 10 feet, but whose width is 220 feet. The falls is at its best in the autumn, when the maples are crimson and the sun glints in the streaks of white water that tumble over the rocks. It can be reached by a 30-minute bus ride from Karuizawa Station.

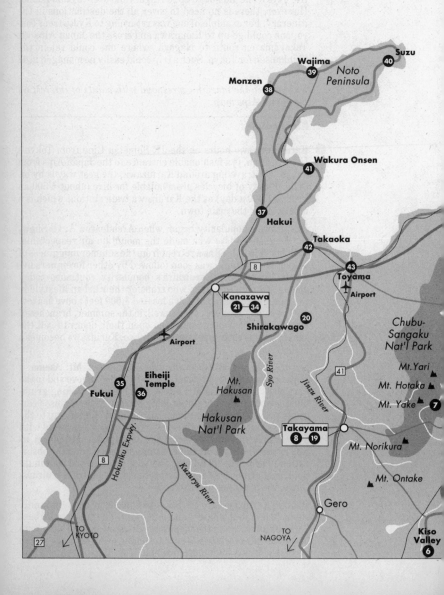

0   50 miles

0   75 km

SEA OF JAPAN

Suzu 40

Wajima 39   *Noto Peninsula*

Monzen 38

Wakura Onsen 41

Hakui 37

Takaoka 42

Toyama 43
Airport

Kanazawa 21 34

20

Shirakawago

Airport

Eiheiji Temple 36

Fukui 35

Mt. Hakusan

Syo River

Jinzu River

Chubu-Sangaku Nat'l Park

Mt. Yari

Mt. Hotaka

Mt. Yake 7

Hakusan Nat'l Park

Takayama 8 19

Mt. Norikura

Mt. Ontake

Hokuriku Expwy.

Kuzuryu River

8

27

TO KYOTO

Gero

TO NAGOYA

Kiso Valley 6

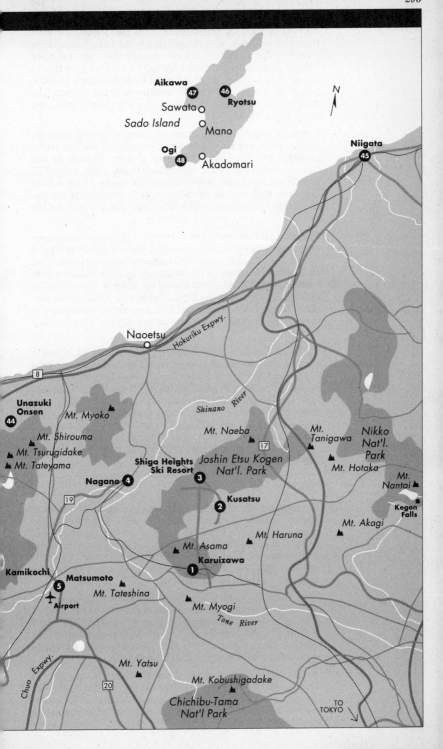

However, you can also take the 25-minute bus ride to Mine-no-chaya (mountain-top teahouse) and then hike for an hour down through the forests of birch and larch to the falls. You can then return to Karuizawa by bus or continue the walk, via more falls, at **Ryugaeshi** and return through **Kose Onsen,** a spa, to the old **Mikasa Hotel,** the oldest wood Western-style hotel in Japan. From the Mikasa it is a 30-minute walk back to town. The total course from Mine-no-chaya to town is about 7 miles and takes 4½ hours.

Karuizawa has other amusements, such as archery in summer, skating rinks, tennis, and horseback riding, all of which can be arranged through your hotel. Also, a short distance by bus from Karuizawa and close to **Hoshino Onsen,** a spa, is the **Wild Bird Wood Sanctuary,** where about 120 species of birds have taken up residence. Along the 1½-mile forestal course are two observation huts from which the birds' habitat may be observed.

The same JR train continues on from Karuizawa to climb steeply through the mountains to reach a plateau before making a quick descent into Nagano. This is the easiest route to take, but an alternative is through the mountains by road (bus or car) via ❷ **Kusatsu,** one of Japan's best-known spa resorts. More than 130 ryokan cluster around the Yuba (Hot Spring Field) which supplies the gushing, boiling, sulfur-laden water. Netsunoyu is the main public bath; its water is unbearably hot, even for some Japanese.

The Shiga-Kusatsu-kogen Ridge Highway (a toll road, closed in winter), continues across the Kusatsu Pass and at times climbs as high as 6,550 feet to Yudanaka, the base from which skiers ❸ set out to the **Shiga Heights Ski Resort.** This is Nagano's largest ski area, with 22 ski grounds and a combination of 81 lifts, gondolas, and ropeways. Nearby **Yudanaka Onsen,** by the way, is a hot-spring resort made famous by photographs of monkeys covered with snow sitting in open-air pools to keep warm. From here, both the road and train line descend for the 15-mile run to Nagano.

Nagano

❹ Thousands of pilgrims each year come to **Nagano's** attraction, **Zenkoji Temple.** Founded in the 7th century by Yoshimitsu Honda, this temple is unique to Japan for two reasons: it belongs to no particular Buddhist sect, and it has never closed its doors to women. Zenkoji's most venerated statue, a bronze dating from 552, is displayed only once every seven years—the next time will be in spring 1994.

From the train station, a frequent bus service makes the 10-minute journey through the center of Nagano to the temple. After getting off at the temple bus stop, you will find a 200-yard pedestrian avenue lined with food, souvenir shops, and smaller temples. Then, up two flights of steps and through a magnificent roofed gate, Zenkoji is laid out before you.

In the courtyard before the Main Hall are six magnificent Buddhas, which represent various aspects of life. To the left and right are several small shrines; in the center of the courtyard each pilgrim deposits a smoldering stick of incense into a giant brass burner. The temple has burned to the ground many times; each time it has been resurrected with donations from all over Japan. The most recent version was finished in 1707, and the gigantic Main Hall is the largest thatch-roof building in Japan. If you wonder why the fishnets cover the inside of the roof, it's because their presence dissuades pigeons from resting and dropping "good fortune" on the pilgrims' heads or on the scribe who sits on the temple floor writing short inscriptions in the small books carried by the pilgrims.

The main attraction for the pilgrims is beneath the altar. Under the Inner Sanctuary is a tunnel; you'll notice the entrance by the line waiting to enter. The goal of each pilgrim is to walk through the pitch-dark tunnel and touch the lock, a specific stone in the wall known as the "Key to Paradise," and thus be assured of an easy path to salvation. *Inner Sanctuary open daily 5:30 AM–4:30 PM.*

Even though Nagano is the prefectural capital and has a population of 300,000, the actual city has little but Zenkoji to interest the visitor. Behind the temple is an amusement park for small kids, and at Mt. Jizuki there is a zoo, but, aside from that, Nagano remains a pilgrims' town and a gateway into the surrounding mountains. However, should one find oneself staying overnight in Nagano, there is an ancient traditional ryokan, the Hotel Fujiya, just before the pedestrian avenue to Zenkoji. The ryokan's pride is its *daimyo* (feudal lord) suite; for ¥20,000 per person, one can enjoy the suite's several rooms decorated with ancient scrolls and look into a garden that is magnetic in its contrasting complexity and simplicity (*see* Nagano Lodging, below).

Matsumoto

From Nagano, the JR Shinonoi climbs steeply into the mountains and, at one spot, Shinonoi, uses switchbacks in order to make the grade up to the high plateau on which **Matsumoto** is situated. In a basin surrounded by the high peaks of the mountain ranges, the town of Matsumoto has one of Japan's finest castles, set in grounds of cherry trees and open spaces, about a 20-minute walk to the north and east from the train station (pick up a map from the tourist office at the front of the station). En route you will pass through the old section, with many stone Kura houses, typical of the early Meiji period, which are unusual in their use of irregular stones held in place by mortar.

Known as **Karasujo** (Crow Castle) for its unusual black protective walls, the castle was built in 1504 during the turbulence of civil wars. The moats and walls remain, and the imposing five-tier, six-story *donjon* (keep) is the oldest of its kind to have survived. While it is an exercise in agility to climb and walk through all six stories, the effort adds to the feeling of what life as a samurai was like during feudal Japan. The views from the sixth story of the donjon are inspiring, with a broad panorama of the surrounding alpine peaks.

In front of Karasujo Castle is the **Japan Folklore Museum,** whose 70,000 artifacts display the folklore, history, and everyday life of preshogun days and of the Edo period. *Admission: ¥500, covering castle and museum. Castle and museum open 8:30–4:30. Closed Dec. 29–Jan. 3.*

The other points of interest in town are minor in comparison
with the castle. Directly across town to the east of the JR station is the **Matsumoto Folkcraft Museum,** which displays some
600 local home utensils of wood, bamboo, and glass. To get
there, either take a taxi or a 15-minute bus ride and get out at
the Shimoganai Mingeikan Guchi bus stop. *Admission: ¥200.*
Open 9–5. Closed Mon. and Dec. 29–Jan. 3.

More worthwhile is the **Japan Ukiyo-e Museum,** west of the JR
station. Unfortunately it is too far to walk, and there is no bus,
so one must invest in a ¥1,000 taxi ride. Located next to the
Japan Judicature Museum, the oldest Japanese palatial court
building still existing, the Ukiyo-e Museum every month rotates its collection of 100,000 ukiyo-e wood-block prints from
the Edo period. The collection not only has some of Japan's finest prints, but it is also the largest of its kind in the world. *Ad-*
mission: ¥600. Open 10–4:30. Closed Mon.

One stop from Matsumoto Station on the Oito Line is **Hotaka.**
From the station, it is a 10-minute walk to the **Rokuzan Art Mu-**
seum. Rokuzan Ogiwara, who died at the age of 32, was a master sculptor and is often referred to as the "Rodin of the
Orient." His works are displayed here. Aside from the appeal of
Rokuzan's works, the gallery is in a beautiful setting of greenery against a backdrop of the Northern Alps. *Admission:*
¥500. Open 9–5 (9–4 Nov.–Mar.). Closed Mon. and days fol-
lowing national holidays.

Also near Hotaka is the **Gohoden Wasabi-en,** the largest farm
growing *wasabi* (Japanese horseradish). To reach it you must
rent a bike or take a 40-minute walk along a path from the train
station. (The station attendant will give you directions.) Wasabi is cultivated in the clean water beds built in a shallow,
curving valley. The Gohoden farm scenery is pastoral Japan.
Surrounded by rows of acacia and poplar trees on the embankments, the fields of fresh green wasabi leaves bloom with white
flowers in the late spring.

Kiso Valley

❻ Another trip from Matsumoto is to the **Kiso Valley,** located halfway between Matsumoto and Nagoya. Called Kisoji by the Japanese, this deep valley is formed by the Kiso River and is surrounded by the Central Alps to the east and the North Alps to
the west. It was through this valley that the old Nakasendo
Highway connected Kyoto and Edo (present-day Tokyo) between 1603 and 1867. This part of the highway was the most difficult section for travelers. The valley's thick forests and steep
slopes required three days to pass through, while today the
new road allows the same trip to be done in a few hours.

With the building of the new Tokaido route from Kyoto to Tokyo
along the Pacific coast, and with the Chuo train line from Nagoya to Niigata, the 11 old post villages where travelers could re-
fresh themselves became deserted backwaters (sometimes
referred to as Minami-Kiso). Two of the villages, **Tsumago** and
Magome, are easy to reach. Take the JR train from Matsumoto
to Nagiso, about 60 minutes away, and then take a 10-minute
bus ride (fare: ¥240) from the Nagiso JR station to Tsumago.
Buses from the JR station leave every hour for the 30-minute
trip. From Tsumago you can take either the footpath to
Magome or another bus. Still another bus travels from Magome

to Nakatsugawa on the JR line. Then, it is back to Matsumoto or on to Nagoya by train, or over the mountains to Takayama (*see* below).

Both Tsumago and Magome have retained much of their old characters. Indeed, more than in most places in Japan, walking along the main street of Tsumago is like stepping back in time to the shogun era (except for the souvenir shops). If you have time, it's a pleasant three-hour walk along the old post trail between Tsumago and Magome. Since both are served by buses from Nakatsugawa Station and Nagiso, you can bus to one village and return from the other. There are ryokans and minshukus throughout the valley should you wish to stay overnight, and both Tsumago and Magome have tourist information offices that will help find accommodations and provide free maps.

This trip to Kiso Valley could with equal ease be accomplished as a day trip from Nagoya, because getting there requires taking the JR Chuo Line, which runs between Nagoya and Matsumoto to Nakatsugawa Station and Nagiso.

Takayama

Getting There   There are two routes to **Takayama.** One is by JR trains all the way, but this requires descending to the coastal plain and, just to the north of Nagoya at Gero, changing trains for the journey up the Hida River Valley to Takayama. This is the least interesting route and can take up to four hours' traveling time, but it is the only way in the winter. If you wish to go straight from Kiso valley to Takayama, take a 1-hour, 50-minute bus ride from Magome to Gero and transfer to the JR train for a 45-minute run to Takayama. Buses leave three times daily (7:21 AM and 12:05 with a change at Sakashita, and a direct bus at 4 PM; cost: ¥1,950.

❼   The other route is straight over the mountains via **Kamikochi.** It is one of the most scenic routes through the Japan Alps and should not be missed, and one should perhaps consider spending the night at Kamikochi to fully enjoy the scenery. It does require a bus/train combination, but it is straightforward and poses no problem whatsoever. However, it can only be accomplished in the summer, May–October, because winter snows close the road. Coming from either Tokyo or Kyoto take the Shinkansen to Nagoya and change for the JR Limited Express to Takayama. The train leaves every hour during the day and takes two hours and 20 minutes.

First take the Matsumoto Electric Railway from Matsumoto Station to Shin-Shimashima. The journey takes 30 minutes (fare: ¥590). Do not make the mistake of getting off the train at Shimojima, three stops before Shin-Shimashima. Once off the train, cross over the road at Shin-Shimashima Station for the bus going to Nakanoyu and Kamikochi. The total bus journey takes about one hour and 20 minutes (fare: ¥1,750). The most scenic part is the 20 minutes from Nakanoyu to Kamikochi, and you'll quickly understand why the road is closed by the winter snows. Just before reaching Kamikochi, the valley opens onto a plain with a backdrop of mountains. **Mt. Oku-Hotaka** is the highest at 10,466 feet. To the left is **Mt. Mae-Hotaka,** 10,138 feet, and to the right is the smaller **Mt. Nishi-Hotaka.** Through the narrow basin flow the icy waters of the Azusagawa River to form a small lake, **Taisho Pond,** at the entrance to the basin, where lodges and inns are located. The bus terminal is a few hundred yards beyond.

There are trails throughout Kamikochi to please every level of hiker and climber. One easy three-hour walk is along the river past the rock sculpture of the Reverend Walter Weston, the Briton who was the first to explore and climb these mountains. Then comes the Kappabashi Bridge, a small suspension bridge over the crystal-clear waters of the Azusagawa. Continuing on the south side of the river, the trail cuts through the pasture to rejoin the river at Myoshin Bridge. The Hodaka Shrine is on the other side at the edge of Myoshin Pond. Here is another bridge that leads to the trail back on the opposite side of the river to the Kappabashi Bridge.

From Kamikochi, buses (six a day) take an hour and 15 minutes to **Hirayu Onsen,** (fare: ¥1,250), where one must change to another bus for the 70-minute ride to Takayama (fare: ¥1,200).

Exploring
⑧ One of the most attractive towns in the Japan Alps, **Takayama,** is often left off foreign tourists' itineraries; it is their loss. In the heart of the Hida Mountains, this tranquil town has retained its old-fashioned charm. No wonder so many artists have made their homes here. The city is laid out in a grid pattern; it's compact and easy to explore on foot or by rented bicycle. A rental shop is to the right of the station building (cost: ¥250 per hour). An exotic option is a 2½-hour ricksha tour of town for ¥6,000.

Make a point of collecting maps and information from the tourist office just in front of the JR station. The staff is very helpful. *Open 8:30–6:30 (8:30–5 Nov.–Mar.)*

Numbers in the margin for this exploring section correspond with points of interest on the Takayama map.

Walking (or riding) down Hirokoji-dori Street for a few blocks, one reaches the old section of town with its small shops, houses, and tearooms. Before the bridge, which crosses the small Miyagawa River, go right, past another bridge, and the
⑨ **Takayama Jinya** will be on your right. Though perhaps not worth the admission charge to enter, this imposing structure was the manor house of the governor, with samurai barracks and a garden behind the house. In front of the manor house, 7 AM–noon each morning, a market sells vegetables, fruits, and local handicrafts. *Admission to house: ¥300. Open daily 8:45–4:30.*

Across the river from the market area and up the hill, a small
⑩ street leads to **Shiroyama Park** and **Shorenji Temple.** The Main Hall of this temple was built in 1504 and was moved in 1961 from its original site in Shirakawago before the area was flooded by the Miboro Dam. Now, positioned on the hill looking down on Takayama, the sweep of its curved roof, its superb drum tower, and the surrounding gardens give an earthy tranquillity that symbolizes the atmosphere of all of Takayama. *Admission: ¥ 200. Open daily 8–4:30. (Shiroyama Park is always open; no admission charge.)*

Down from Shiroyama Park, the main street leads to a junc-
⑪ tion. To the right is the **Tenshoji Temple** and youth hostel. This is a magnificent building and a delightful place for a youth hostel, though the rooms are sure to be bitterly cold in the winter.

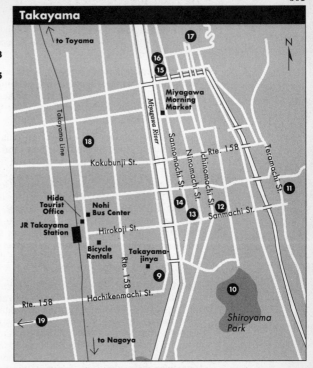

Takayama

⑫ To the left of the temple is the folk toy museum and the **Takayama-shi Kyodo-kan** (History Museum), which exhibits various antiques and folklore materials of the Hida people. *Admission: ¥300. Open 8:30–5. Closed Mon. and Dec. 29–31.*

⑬ Just down the street from the Provincial Hall is the **Hida Minzoku Koko-kan (Archaeology Museum)** in an old house that once belonged to a physician who served the local lord. The unique structure of the mansion, with its hanging ceilings, secret windows, and hidden passages, hints of spies, so prevalent in the Edo period. Now the house displays wall hangings, weaving machines, and sundry items, both archaeological and folkloric, collected from the Hida region. *Admission: ¥300. Open daily 7–7 (8–5 Dec.–Feb.).*

⑭ Turning right from the Archaeology Museum and following the streets parallel to the Miyagawa River, one enters the **Sanmachi-Suji** section. It includes Ichinomachi, Ninomachi, and Sannomachi streets. This was the merchant area during the feudal days. Most of the old teahouses, inns, dye houses, and sake breweries with latticed windows and doors are preserved in their original state, making Sanmachi-Suji a rare vestige of old Japan before the Meiji Restoration. Down along the river is another section of the daily morning markets, Miyagawa, that sell flowers and vegetables until noon each day.

⑮ Across a small tributary of the Miyagawa and on the left side of Ninomachi Street is the **Kusakabe Mingeikan Folkcraft Museum.** The building is the old Kusakabe (wealthy merchant) family home of the 1880s. Inside, the heavy beams of polished wood emphasize the refined taste of that period, and it is an appropriate setting for a display of Hida folkcrafts. *Admission: ¥309. Open daily 9–5 (9–4:30 and closed Fri. Dec.–Feb.). Closed Dec. 27–Jan. 4.*

On the next corner is another elegant merchant house, the **⑯ Yoshijima-ke Family House.** It was rebuilt in 1908, but it retains the distinctive characteristics of the Hida architectural style. *Admission: ¥250. Open daily 9–5 (9–4:30 and closed Tues. Dec.–Feb.). Closed Dec. 28–Jan. 1.*

Up the street to the right of the Yoshijima House and next to **⑰** the Hachiman Shrine is the **Takayama Yatai Kaikan Hall,** which displays four of the 11 Takayama festival floats *(yatai)*, which are used in Takayama's famous Spring Sanno Matsuri (Apr. 14–15) and Autumn Yahata Matsuri (Oct. 9–10) festivals. (Some 160,000 visitors come each year for the festivals, nearly tripling Takayama's population of 68,000. Hotels are booked solid, so if you plan to visit during this time, make your reservation months in advance.) These floats have many figurines representing people in the parade, as well as elaborately carved wooden lion heads used for dances in the parade. *Admission: ¥460. Open 8:30–5 (9–4:30 Dec.–Feb.).*

More than two centuries ago, when the country was ravaged by the plague, the building of yatai and parading them through the streets was a way of appeasing the gods. Because these actions seemed to work in Takayama, they continued building bigger and more elaborate yatai as preventive medicine. The yatai are gigantic (the cost to build one today would exceed ¥1 million), and the embellishments of wood-carved panels and tapestries are works of art. Technical wizardry is also involved. Each yatai has puppets, controlled by rods and wires, that perform amazing feats, including gymnastics that you would expect only Olympians to perform.

Walking in the direction of the train station, just off to the right **⑱** side of the main modern shopping street is **Kokubunji,** the oldest temple in the city. Founded in 1588, it preserves many objects of art, including the precious sword used by the Heike clan. In the Main Hall (built in 1615) there is a seated figure of Yakushinyorai (Healing Buddha), and before the three-story pagoda is a statue of Kannon. The ginkgo tree standing beside the pagoda is said to be more than 1,200 years old. *Admission to Main Hall: ¥200. Open 9–4. Closed Dec. 31 and Jan. 1.*

The delight of Takayama is that the entire town resembles a museum piece; there is also a "Folk Village," less than 2 miles away, that is a real museum, though it's so well done that it looks like a working village one would expect to have found in **⑲** medieval Japan. To get to this village, **Hida Minzoku-mura,** either walk the 15 minutes or take the bus at platform #2 from the bus terminal located in a bay on the left side (same side as the tourist information booth) of the JR station.

Set against a mountain backdrop, Hida Minzoku-mura (Hida Folk Village) is a collection of traditional farmhouses moved to a park from several areas within the Hida region. Since the traditional Hida farmhouse is held together by ropes rather than nails, the dismantling and reassembling of the buildings posed few problems. Many of them have high-pitch thatch roofs, called *gassho-zukuri* (hands in prayer); others are shingle-roofed. Twelve of the houses are "private houses" that display such folk materials as tableware and spinning and weaving tools. Another five houses are folkcraft workshops, with demonstrations of ichii ittobori wood carving, Hidanuri lacquering, and other traditional arts of the region. *Admission: ¥500. Open daily 8:30–5 (8:30–4:30 Nov.–Mar.). Closed Dec. 30–Jan. 2.*

Numbers in the margin correspond with points of interest on the Japan Alps map.

From Takayama there are frequent trains out of the mountains to Toyama and on to Kanazawa (an absolute must to visit) and the Noto Peninsula. Kanazawa, with a change of trains at Toyama is about a two-hour trip from Takayama. However, before heading directly for Kanazawa, there is a possible side trip to visit a traditional village that is still inhabited, **Shirakawago Gassho-mura,** on the banks of the Shokawa River opposite Ogimachi Town.

Shirakawago Gassho-mura is actually a transplant, made up of gassho-zukuri–style houses rescued from four villages that fell prey to progress—the building of the Miboro Dam 20 years ago. Eight houses were saved. With their roofs shaped as hands in prayer, each gassho-zukuri house is 60 feet long, 33 feet wide, and four stories high. They are, in fact, a version of the modern condo; each house is home to several families, though today the village survives from its tourist income.

To reach the village from Takayama, take the Nohi bus to Makido for an hour and 35 minutes and then the JR bus to Ogimachi for one hour. It is possible to stay overnight at a gasshozukuri–style minshuku by making reservations at the tourist office near the Gassho-shuraku bus stop. There are only six buses a day (four a day Dec.–Mar.) from Takayama, so before leaving Takayama, plan your schedule with the help of the tourist office in front of Takayama Station. *Admission: ¥500. Village open daily 8:30–5.*

From Shirakawago, instead of returning to Takayama, you may want to take a bus that leaves Ogimachi for Kanazawa; the trip takes just under three hours (departs Ogimachi 2:40 PM; arrives Kanazawa 5:27 PM). The advantage of this route is the opportunity to see more of the Hida Mountains, as the views from the JR train from Takayama are limited by tunnels and narrow valleys.

It you are not arriving from Takayama, Kanazawa can easily be reached by JR limited express trains from Kyoto (2 hours, 30 minutes) and Nagoya (3 hours). There is a small tourist information booth (look for a question-mark sign) just in front of the Kanazawa Station exit. The bus terminal will be in front, slightly to the left.

Kanazawa

Numbers in the margin for this exploring section correspond with points of interest on the Kanazawa map.

Many sizable Japanese cities were destroyed by the bombs of World War II; **Kanazawa** is an exception. Many of its old neighborhoods have remained intact for the past two or three centuries, despite modern Japan's tendency to bulldoze the old and replace it with concrete. **Kanazawajo Castle,** though, has fallen

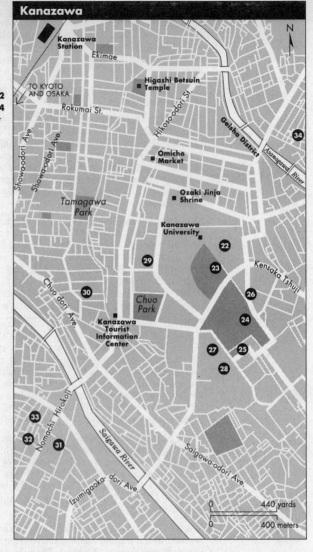

❷❸ victim to seven fires in all, and only the **Ishikawa Gate** remains intact (rebuilt in 1788). Note the gate's lead tiles. The *daimyos* (feudal lords) never knew when they might be under siege and require more munitions, which could be made from the lead tiles.

Because Kanazawa was a fortress town, and its whole reason for being centered on the castle, this is the best point from which to start appreciating Kanazawa and its past. To reach the castle from the train station, take any bus (fare: ¥160) from gate 11 at the bus terminal outside the JR station. One can also purchase, for ¥650, an intracity "Free Pass" from the Hokutetsu Bus Ticket Office, in front of the JR station. The pass permits unlimited day travel on the city's buses. At press time, the Kanazawa JR station was being rebuilt. Beneath the station there will be arcades with numerous restaurants and shops. A station branch of the Kanazawa Information Office (tel. 0762/31–6311, open Mon.–Sat., 9–5) will be adjacent to the JR Reserved Seat Ticketing office. To reach the station plaza, you must walk through the underground passage.

Should you want to go directly downtown, for example to the City Information Center (tel. 0762/22–1500; open 10–6; closed Wed.) on the ground floor of the Kohrinbo 190 Building, take bus #30, #31, or #32 from gate 8, or bus #20 or #21 from gate 9.

During the Tokugawa period (1603–1868), the fertile region around Kanazawa (Kaga region) was dominated by the Maeda daimyo. Their wealth was tremendous, based on the 1 million koku rice harvests of the region. With this wealth came power and distrust. They distrusted the shogun in Edo, and the shogun distrusted them. The manifestation of this distrust was a mighty castle that had not only the protection of high walls and moats but also the intentionally winding, narrow town streets around the castle, which made attacks more difficult. Two other security measures were taken. A Buddhist temple complex was set up on the road to Edo as a delaying tactic; it also supplied an underground escape route back to the castle. Then, at another two approaches to the city, entertainment quarters were established so that invaders might be waylaid by amorous pursuits rather than by fighting.

These security measures appear to have been successful. Kanazawa maintained its independence and prospered for three centuries. Moreover, throughout its dynasty, the Maeda clan encouraged education and cultural pursuits. It seems fitting, therefore, that the castle grounds are now the site of Kanazawa University.

❷❹ The best-known tourist attraction in Kanazawa is **Kenrokuen Garden,** across from Kanazawajo Castle's Ishikawa Gate. For many Japanese, Kenrokuen is one of the three finest landscaped gardens in Japan. (The other two are Mito's Kairakuen and Okayama's Korakuen.) Kenrokuen began as the outer garden of Kanazawajo in 1676 under the fifth daimyo. Two hundred years and eight generations of daimyos later, Kenrokuen reached its final form. It received its name because it possessed the six superior qualities required for the perfect garden: extensiveness, factitiousness, antiquity, abundant water, wide prospect, and quiet seclusion. Today, the last quality seems in question. The gardens are near bedlam in the holiday season, with Japanese tourists being told the names of the trees through their group leader's megaphone. Either arrive at the garden first thing in the morning or risk losing its intended solemnity. *Admission: ¥300. Open daily 6:30–6 (8–4:30 Oct. 16–Mar. 15).*

❷❺ In the southeast of Kenrokuen is the **Seisonkaku Villa,** a two-story residence built in 1863 by one of the Maeda lords for his mother's retirement. Now it houses the family heirlooms and a collection of art objects that have been handed down through the generations of the Maeda clan. *Admission: ¥500. Open 8:30–4:30. Closed Wed.*

❷❻ A much quieter garden, and one preferred by those who desire tranquillity, is **Gyokusenen Garden.** (Admission: ¥400. Open daily 9–4; closed mid-Dec.–mid-Mar.) This garden has an intimacy created by an owner (a wealthy merchant) seeking calm and contemplative peace rather than grand accolades for his green thumb. The moss, maple trees, and small steppingstones by the pond are more serene than the bold strokes of Kenrokuen. The garden is located to the northeast of Kenrokuen Garden and before the **Kanko Bussankan,** a building that demonstrates Yuzan dyeing, pottery, and lacquerware production.

㉗ Walking southwest for five minutes takes you to the **Ishikawa Prefectural Art Museum,** which displays the best permanent collection of Kutani pottery, dyed fabrics, old Japanese paintings, and various other art objects. *Admission:* ¥*350. Open 9:30–4:30.*

㉘ A narrow path at the back of the museum leads to the **Honda Museum.** The Honda family members were the key political advisers to the Maeda daimyos, and the museum contains 700 art objects, armor, and household utensils used by the Honda family during its tenure. Don't miss the uniforms of the Honda family's personal firefighters and the trousseau of the Maeda brides marrying into the Honda family. *Admission:* ¥*500. Open 9–5. Closed Thurs. Nov.–Feb. and Dec. 29–Jan. 1.*

㉙ Retracing your steps and keeping south of Kanazawajo, you find the **Ōyama Jinja Shrine.** Built in 1599, the shrine is dedicated to Lord Toshiie Maeda, the founder of the Maeda clan. However, architecturally, the shrine is noted for its three-story Shimmon Gate, designed in 1875 with the assistance of two Dutch instructors. At the top of the gate's squared arch is a stained-glass window that originally beamed a light to guide ships in from the Sea of Japan to the Kanaiwa port, 4 miles to the northwest. *Admission free.*

㉚ A few blocks southwest of the Oyama Jinja is the **Nagamachi Samurai District,** where the Maeda clan's samurai lived. Narrow, crooked streets are lined with tile-roof mud walls designed to protect the quarters from curious eyes. One of the houses has been carefully restored and turned into a museum, Buke Yaskiki. Another old house has become the Saihitsuan Yuzen Silk Center, which demonstrates the art of painting intricate designs on yuzen silk used for kimonos. *Admission:* ¥*500. Open 9–12 and 1–4:30. Closed Thurs. and Dec. 28–Jan. 4.*

Time Out While in this area of samurai houses, you can take green tea and Japanese cookies at **Nikore** (tel. 0762/61–0056). Mrs. Mori and her son converted a samurai house in order to serve tea on a veranda facing a small garden. To find Nikore, walk straight ahead from Saihitsuan Yuzen Silk Center and cross the street. It's on your right, marked by three Japanese *Kanji* characters in yellow. Open 10–5.

After your green tea, go left from Nikore to the corner and take another left. On the next corner across the street is the **Nomura House.** Though most of the samurai houses were demolished with the Meiji Restoration, this abode was rebuilt by an industrialist at the turn of the century and furnished in that period's traditional style. Visit the Jyodan-no-ma drawing room made of cypress wood, with elaborate designs in rosewood and ebony. Each of the sliding (paper) doors has a great landscape drawn by Sasaki Senkai of the Kano school. Facing the living room is a small garden with a winding stream and a bridge made of cherry granite. *Tel. 0762/21–3553. Admission: ¥400. Open 10–5.*

③① Crossing over to the south side of the Saigawa River and a five-minute walk beyond is the **Myoryuji Temple,** famous for its complicated structure. Its popular name, the **Ninjadera** (Temple of the Ninja—ninja are warriors and experts in the art of concealment), tells all. The innocent-looking temple is a complex of labyrinthine corridors, trapdoors, hidden chambers, secret tunnels, and 29 staircases to 22 of its 23 rooms. An exaggerated case of paranoia, perhaps, but it was designed to hold off invaders until the daimyo could make good his escape. In high tourist season, there is a line of visitors waiting for a tour. Reservations are essential, though late in the afternoon one may be able to slip in with a small group. *Tel. 0762/41–2877. Admission: ¥500. Open 9–4:30 (Dec.–Feb., 9–4).*

The small housed *jizo* figure (representations of bodhisattva, an altruist Buddhist deity) in the temple grounds is not on the tour, but he does have a story to tell. His facial features are almost rubbed away. In days before penicillin, syphilitics would rub the little jizo's nose in the hope that their disease would go away. Today Japanese come to ritually scrub him with a nail brush and take photographs of themselves with the little figure. Why the little jizo is here at the temple is a mystery, but it is also said that the daimyo used the secret passages of the Ninjadera as a way of reaching the Western Pleasure Quarter undetected.

③② One street over and one block to the south from the Myoryuji is the **Kosen Kutani Pottery Kiln,** where you can watch the entire process of making local Kutani pottery. *Admission free. Open 8:30–12 and 1–5. Closed Sun. afternoon.*

③③ From the Kosen Kutani Pottery Kiln you can catch a bus or make a brisk walk back along Hirokoji-dori Avenue and over the Seigawa Ohashi Bridge to the downtown shopping center and Kanazawajo. If you are walking, pass through **Nishi-no-Kurawa (Western Pleasure Quarter)** en route. No longer are the geishas walled in, though the checkpoint, which kept the ladies from escaping, has been preserved, and the area lacks the bustle of intrigue that existed 200 years ago. In the maze of narrow, crooked streets, perhaps you'll see a geisha or two. They are said to be younger and more beautiful in this **③④** quarter than those in **Higashi-no-Kurawa (Eastern Pleasure Quarter),** on the other side of town and across the Asanogawa, Kanazawa's other river.

The Eastern Pleasure Quarter was set aside as a high-class area of entertainment. Now, the pleasures of visiting here are the old buildings with wood-slat facades in the narrow, winding streets. Most of the old geisha houses have been turned into tearooms or minshukus, but occasionally one sees a scurrying geisha traveling to her appointment. One elegant former geisha house, **Shima-ke,** is open to the public and gives us a chance to see the inside and its relaxing garden. *Admission: ¥200. Open 8:30–4:30. Closed Mon.*

The easiest way to reach the Eastern Pleasure Quarter, is to take the JR bus from the JR station using a Japan Rail Pass. The bus stops at Hachira-cho, just before the Asonagawa Ohasi Bridge. You can also take this bus to get to the **Omicho Market** and, if you don't mind a 10-minute walk, you can take it to the site of Kanazawa's Castle and the Kenrokuen Gardens.

From here one can return to the JR station on bus #11, #12, or #80 from the Hashibo bus stop across Asanogawa Ohashi Bridge.

Only Kanazawa's major sights have been touched upon here. It is a city full of little surprises, such as a small temple that does an amazing business reading *sutra* (Buddhist precepts) and dispensing herbs to cure hemorrhoids. Anyone staying for more than a day should obtain a copy of Ruth Stevens's detailed English-language guide, *Kanazawa*. It's a book written with a love for the city and leads the visitor to all the discoveries Ms. Stevens has made during her 10 years of living there. The book can be purchased in English-language bookstores in Tokyo; sometimes it is available in the lobby book stand of the Holiday Inn Hotel across from the Kanazawa JR station.

Numbers in the margin correspond with points of interest on the Japan Alps map.

35 **36** From Kanazawa you can take a train west to **Fukui.** The town is not very interesting, but 12 miles southwest of Fukui is **Eiheiji Temple,** one of the two main temples of the Soto sect of Zen Buddhism. Founded in 1244, the complex of 70 temple buildings is built on a hillside surrounded by trees, some of which are as old as the original temple buildings. The temple is still very active, and there are 200 novitiates in training at any given time. Visitors are welcome, and an English pamphlet is given at the gate to mark out the key buildings, once visitors have had a long-winded introductory lesson to the Soto sect. Foreigners are also welcome to stay at the temple, though arrangements should be made in advance. *Admission: ¥300. Open 5–5.*

Eiheiji Temple is most easily reached by train from Fukui. If you do not want to return to Fukui and reboard the train for Kyoto and Osaka, there is a bus that runs down to the JR line that allows you to travel up to Ohno and the two gorges, Kuzuryu and Managawa, both noted for their scenic beauty.

Noto Peninsula

The **Noto Peninsula** is rolling countryside with paddies, divided by steep hills, and a coastline that is mild and peaceful. On the eastern side there are many indentations and sea-bathing opportunities on the inner (*uchi*) shore, while the western outer (*soto*) coast is rugged and rock-strewn. Working one's way around the peninsula is best by car or, because it is relatively flat, by bicycle. However, the peninsula can also be explored through a combination of train and bus. There are also daylong bus tours of the peninsula that set out every day from Kanazawa (*see* Guided Tours, above).

Wajima is the terminal for the JR line from Kanazawa and is reached in a two-hour, 15-minute train ride; however, the line turns inland and misses some of Noto Peninsula's best sights. Hence, the best itinerary is to take the 40-minute train ride **37** from Kanazawa as far as **Hakui.** The Chirihama beach is a 20-minute walk from the station. This stretch of coast is good for taking in the summer sun and for swimming, as well as being one of the noted scenic spots along the Noto coast. The Japanese like this area because they can drive their cars along the sand and bring *bento* picnic lunches.

A few miles north by bus from Hakui (buses leave outside the train station) is the 17th-century **Myojoji Temple,** a five-story pagoda that stands out from the surrounding plain. It was originally built in the 13th century, though the present structure dates to the 1600s.

Although it's a longer journey, rather than take the inland bus route north to Monzen, take the bus that runs along the coast to Monzen, which includes the 8-mile stretch of coastline known as Noto-Kongo. The coastline is noted for its oceanic beauty, marked by fantastic formations of eroded rock. The journey will take about 70 minutes. **Monzen** is where the Zen temple **Sojiji** stands. Sojiji was once the headquarters of the Soto sect, but a fire destroyed most of the buildings in 1818 and the sect moved its headquarters to Yokohama. (The Eiheiji Temple near Fukui, mentioned earlier in this chapter, is, in fact, as important to the Soto sect as is the one in Yokohama.)

The next stop on the bus, only 10 miles up the road, is **Wajima,** a fishing town that is known not for its fish but for its lacquer ware. Every shop in town seems to sell this craft, though before you buy, first visit the **Wajima Shikki Kaikan** (Lacquer Ware Hall). It's easy to find; ask the ticket-booth conductor at the bus station for directions. Here the patient process of its creativity is shown: It involves about 18 different steps, from wood preparation to coating of numerous layers of lacquer, with careful polishing in between each coat. *Admission: ¥300. Open 8:30–5:30.*

Once familiar with the product, walk to the *asaichi* (morning market), held every day between 8 and 11:30, except the 10th and 25th of each month. Here, among the fruit, vegetables, and seafood, the local crafts and lacquer ware are sold to tourists. There is also *yuichi* (evening market), a smaller version of asaichi, which starts around 3:30 PM.

From Wajima, a bus travels 20 minutes farther north up to Sosogi, a small village, passing terraced rice fields that descend from the hills to the edge of the sea. At Sosogi the road forks inland. Soon after the fork (five minutes) are two traditional farm manor houses. The **Shimo-Tokikuni House** is more than 300 years old and is furnished with antiques. Rent the tape recorder at the entrance for an English explanation of each room. Close by is **Kami-Tokikuni House,** which took 28 years to rebuild in the last century and remains in near-perfect condition. Each room has a special purpose, and, by following the English leaflet, one becomes very conscious of the strict adherence to the class ranking system of medieval Japan. *Both houses charge a small admission. Open 9–4:30.*

The same bus route (hourly service) continues to **Suzu,** on the *uchi* coast (inner, or eastern, shore), serviced by the Noto Railway Line. It is, in fact, possible to travel around the northern tip of the Noto Peninsula by bus (continue on from Sosogi to **Cape Rokko** Rokkozaki and down to the northern terminus of the Noto Railway Line at Tako-jima), but the views and scenery do not justify the infrequency of public transport.

From Suzu, take the train line south to **Tsukumo-wan** (Noto Ogi Station). Tsukumo-wan means "a bay with 99 indentations." To help appreciate this part of the rocky coastline, there are glass-bottom boats which circle the bay. Farther south and on the train line is **Wakura Onsen.** This is the Noto Peninsula's smart resort town, with many hotels and ryokans. It is especially popular among Japanese families, who take their children across the bridge to Notojima Island, where there is an elaborate new marine park. Wakura Onsen is on the train line linked directly with Kanazawa, approximately a two-hour ride away. However, one can take a bus south and east along the coastal road (Rte. 160) to the city of **Takaoka.**

Takaoka is the southern gateway to the Noto Peninsula and is not worth lingering in, but if there is time, the city does claim to have Japan's third largest *Daibutsu* (statue of Buddha), after those at Nara and Kamakura. It is made of bronze and stands 16 meters high. There is also the **Zuiryuji Temple,** a 10-minute walk from the station, which is a delightful Zen temple of the Soto sect and doubles as the local youth hostel. However, the city is mostly known for its craft traditions of copper, lacquer ware, and ironware, especially its cast-iron bells.

Southeast of Takaoka is **Toyama,** a busy industrial center. Its only redeeming virtue is the Toyamajoshi (castle park), which is a spread of greenery with a reconstructed version of the original (1532) castle in the center of town. Forty minutes to Toyama's northeast, one stop after Kurobe on the Toyama Chiho Tesudo Line, is **Unazuki Onsen,** located at the mouth of a mountain valley. There is a tramcarlike train (the Kurobe Kyokoku Railway—operates May–mid-Nov.) that runs through this valley for 12 picturesque miles, past gushing springs and plunging waterfalls and through the Kurobe Gorge to Keyakidaira (cost: ¥1,260).

From Toyama (or Kurobe, if you have visited Unazuki Onsen), this itinerary takes the express train up to **Niigata** to board the ferry to Sado Island. Niigata is Japan's major port and industrial city on the Japan Sea coast and is linked to Tokyo's Ueno Station by a two-hour trip on the Joetsu Shinkansen. Niigata is a good place for replenishing supplies and changing money; however, the city has limited attractions for the sightseer. The tourist information office to the left of the station can help you find a hotel as well as supply city maps and ferry schedules for Sado Island.

Sado Island

Sado has always been a melancholy island. Its role in history has been as a place where antigovernment intellectuals, such as the Buddhist monk Nichiren, were banished to endure the harshest exile. Then, when gold was discovered during the Edo period (1603–1868), the homeless, especially those from Edo (now Tokyo), were sent to Sado to work as forced laborers in the gold mines. This heritage of hardship has left behind a tradition of soulful ballads and folk dances. Even the bamboo grown on the island is said to be the best for making *takohochi*, the plaintive flutes that accompany the ballads.

May through September is the best time to visit Sado. During the other months the weather can prevent sea and air crossings, and in January and February Sado is also bitterly cold. Though the island is Japan's fifth largest, it is comparatively small (331 sq mi). Two parallel mountain chains, running along the north and south coasts, are split by an extensive plain containing small rice farms and the island's principal cities. Despite the fact that more than a million tourists visit the island each year (more than 10 times the number of island inhabitants), the pace of life is slow, even preindustrial. That is Sado's attraction.

Getting There **By Boat.** There are four ferry routes across to Sado Island. The bus from bay #6 at the terminal in front of the Niigata JR station takes 15 minutes to reach the dock for the Sado Kinsen ferries (tel. 025/245–1234) sailing to Ryotsu. The same company has ferries going to Ogi, leaving from Naoetsu (tel. 0225/43–3791), south of Niigata. From Niigata to Ryotsu the ferry crossing takes 2½ hours, with six or seven crossings a day (cost: ¥1,780 for ordinary second class, ¥2,600 for a seat reservation, ¥3,560 for first class, and ¥5,340 for special class). The hydrofoil takes one hour, with seven to 10 crossings in the summer, two in the winter, and anywhere between three and eight at other seasons depending on the weather. In Febru ary, the hydrofoil service is down to one crossing per day (cost: ¥5,460 one way, ¥10,590 round trip). To Ogi from Naoetsu the hydrofoil cost is the same as the Niigata–Ryotsu crossing, while the regular ferry is ¥1,960 for ordinary second class, ¥2,780 for a seat reservation, ¥3,930 for first class, and ¥5,890 for special class). The ferry terminal is a ¥130 bus ride or ¥660 taxi ride from the Naoetsu JR station.

There is one ferry a day from Niigata to Akadomari in winter; two more are added in summer. The route takes two hours (cost: ¥1,550). Depending on the season, one to three ferries sail between Teradomari (near Okutsu on Honshu) and Akadomari, taking two hours (cost: ¥1,220 for second class and ¥2,450 for first class).

By Plane. The small plane takes 25 minutes from Niigata; there are six flights in the summer and three in the winter (cost: ¥7,360).

Getting Around Frequent bus service is available between the major towns, making travel around the island simple. There are also four- and eight-hour tours of the island that depart from both Ryotsu and Ogi. However, these tour buses do tend to patronize the souvenir shops. The best combination is to use the tour bus for the mountain skyline drive (¥3,700) or the two-day Skyline and Historic Site combined tour (¥5,150) and then rent a bike to explore on one's own.

Exploring Sado's usual port of entry is **Ryotsu,** the island's largest
46 township. The center of town is the strip of land that runs between Lake Kamo and the Sea of Japan, with most of the hotels and ryokans on the shore of the lake. Lake Kamo is actually connected to the Sea of Japan by a small inlet running through the middle of town. The Ebisu quarter has the island's concentration of restaurants and bars. Every evening (8:30–9:30) April–early November, the Ryotsu Kaikan Hall stages a performance of *Okesa*, melancholic folk dances and songs performed by women, and the *Ondeko*, a lion dance to drum beats. *Admission: ¥600 (¥100 discount if the ticket is bought at any ryokan in Ryotsu)*. Similar performances during the summer season are given elsewhere on Sado: the Sado Kaikan in Aikowa; the Niigata Kotsu, 2nd floor, in Ogi; and the Sado Chuo Kaikan in Sawata.

The simplest way to begin exploring Sado is to take the bus from Ryotsu to **Aikawa**. Buses leave every 30 minutes and take about 90 minutes to make the trip (fare: ¥630). Once Aikawa was a small town of 10,000 people. Then, in 1601, gold was discovered, and the rush was on. The population swelled to 100,000 until the ore was exhausted. Now it is back to 10,000 inhabitants, and the tourists coming to see the old gold mine are a major source of the town's income.

Though some 10,000 tons of silver and gold ore are still mined annually, Aikawa's **Sado Kinzan Mine** is more of a tourist attraction than anything else. There are some 250 miles of underground tunnels, some running as deep as 1,969 feet beneath sea level, and some of this extensive digging is open to the public. Instead of the slave labor that was used throughout the Edo period, there are now robots serving in its place. These robots are, in fact, quite lifelike, and they demonstrate the appalling conditions that were endured by the miners. Sound effects of shovels and pick axes add to the sickening reality. *Admission: ¥500. Open 8–5:30 (until sunset in autumn and winter).*

To reach the mine from the bus terminus, it is a tough 40-minute uphill walk or a five-minute taxi ride (about ¥800). On the way back from Sado Kinzan, walking is easier.

North of Aikawa is **Senkakuwan** (Senkaku Bay), the most dramatic stretch of coastline and a must-see on Sado Island. To reach the bay, take a 15-minute bus ride from Aikawa to Tassha and then the 40-minute sightseeing cruise boat (Apr.–Oct.) to see rugged beauty accented by fantastic, sea-eroded rock formations and cliffs rising 60 feet out of the water. The boat disembarks at the Senkakuwan Yuen, a park where one can picnic, stroll, and gaze upon the varied rock formations offshore. From the park, you can return by bus to Aikawa. *One-way cruise-boat fare: ¥550; includes admission to the park.*

The most scenic drive on Sado is the **Osado Skyline**. However, no public buses take this route. You must either take a tour bus from Ryotsu or a taxi from Aikawa across the skyline drive to Chikuse (cost: ¥3,700), where one connects with a public bus either to Ryotsu or back to Aikawa.

To reach the southwestern tip of Sado, first make your way on a bus to Sawata either from Aikawa or Ryotsu, then transfer to the bus for Ogi. En route you may want to stop at **Mano**, where the emperor Juntoku (1197–1242) is buried. There is a sadness to this mausoleum built for a man who at 24 was exiled for life to Sado by the Kamakura shogunate. At Mano, incidentally, the *tsuburosashi* dance is given nightly at the Sado New Hotel. The unique dance is performed by a man holding a *tsuburo* (phallic symbol) with the goddesses Shagri and Zeni Daiko. The trip from Sawata to Ogi takes 50 minutes, with the journey's highlight being the beautiful Benteniwa rock formations, just past Tazawaki. Be sure to take a window seat on the right-hand side of the bus.

Ogi can be used as a port for returning to Honshu by the ferry, which takes 2½ hours to reach Naoetsu or on the jetfoil, which takes an hour. Other than that, Ogi's chief attraction is the *taraibune*, round, tublike boats used in the past for fishing. They are now available to tourists for rent (¥450). They accommodate up to three people, and with a single oar you wend your way around the harbor. The taraibune can also be rented at

Shukunegi; it's a more attractive town on the Sawasaki Coast, where the water is dotted with rocky islets and the shore is covered with rock lilies in summer. It has become a sleepy backwater since it stopped building small wood ships to ply the waters between Sado and Honshu, and has retained its traditional atmosphere and buildings. One can reach Shukunegi from Ogi by a sightseeing boat or by bus; both take about 20 minutes, so consider using the boat one way to have the view of the cliffs, which were created by an earthquake 250 years ago.

Rather than return to Ryotsu for the ferry to Niigata, it's nice to take the bus along the coast from Ogi to Akadomari and catch the ferry for Niigata from there.

Dining and Lodging

Dining

Virtually all regions in Japan have their own way of cooking, and none more so than the regions within the Japan Alps and the coastal areas of the Sea of Japan. In the area called Hokuriku, which consists of the Ishikawa, Fukui, and Toyama prefectures, fish from the cold, salty waters of the Sea of Japan is superb.

Toyama has **beni-zuwaigani,** a long-leg red crab that is a special delicacy during the November–March season. **Amaebi,** a sweet prawn that, when eaten raw with **wasabi** (Japanese horseradish) literally melts in the mouth, is available from Toyama Bay. Another local treat is **masu-zushi,** salmon trout pressed onto shallow, round cakes of vinegared rice.

In Ishikawa, the cuisine is called **Kaga,** in which the harvest from the sea is prepared with Kyoto-style elegance. **Tai** (bream), cooked in a style called **karamushi,** is certainly one dish to try. The **kaga-ryori** is a kind of cooking in which the mountain vegetables of mushrooms and ferns are used. Fish and shellfish are frequently included in regional dishes. **Miso soup,** for example, often contains tiny clams still in their shells; sweet crab legs are a mouth-watering delicacy.

In Fukui, the **echizen-gani** crabs stretch 28 inches on the average. These crabs are pure heaven when boiled with a little salt and eaten with the fingers after being dipped in a little rice vinegar. **Wakasa-karei** is a fresh sole that is dried briefly before being lightly grilled. In both Fukui and Ishikawa, there is **echizen-soba,** buckwheat noodles, handmade and served with mountain vegetables. Echizen-soba is also served with dips of sesame oil and bean paste, a reflection of the Buddhist vegetarian tradition.

In the Niigata Prefecture, try **noppei. Sato imo** (a kind of sweet potato) is its base, and mushrooms, salmon, and other local ingredients are added to make a cold soup that goes with hot rice and grilled fish. **Wappameshi** is a hot dish of steamed rice garnished with local ingredients. In the autumn, try **kiku-no-ohitashi,** a side dish of chrysanthemum petals marinated in vinegar. Like other prefectures on the Sea of Japan coast, Niigata has outstanding fish in winter—yellowtail, flatfish, sole, oysters, abalone, and shrimp. A local specialty is **nanban ebi,** raw shrimp dipped in soy sauce and wasabi. It is especially sweet and butter-tender on Sado island. Also on Sado Island, take advantage of the excellent Wakame (seaweed) dishes and Sazae-no-Tsuboyaki (wreath shellfish) broiled in their shells with soy or miso sauce.

In the landlocked Hida Prefecture around Takayama, the cuisine looks to the mountains and rivers for its produce. The typical cuisine of the district is called **san-sai,** in which mountain vegetables, such as edible ferns and wild plants, are cooked with the rich local miso or bean paste. **San-sai ryori** includes fresh river fish, such as the **ayu,** which are grilled with salt or soy sauce. The local specialty is **hoba-miso,** where miso, mixed with vegetables, is roasted on a magnolia leaf. Other local foods are **mitarashi-dango,** grilled rice balls flavored with soy sauce, and **shio-senbei,** salty rice crackers.

The Nagano Prefecture is famous for its handmade buckwheat noodles; more esoteric dishes in the area include raw horsemeat and sweet-boiled baby bees. Matsumoto is known for its wasabi.

In most of Japan outside the large cities, one is usually advised to eat Western-style food in the dining rooms of the larger hotels. However, we strongly recommend that you eat out whenever possible at local Japanese restaurants. Most reasonably priced Japanese restaurants will have a visual display of their menu in the window. On this basis, you can decide what you want before you enter. If you cannot order in Japanese and no English is spoken, after securing a table, lead the waiter to the window display and point.

A 3% federal consumer tax is added to all restaurant bills. Another 3% local tax is added to the bill if it exceeds ¥5,000. At more expensive restaurants, a 10%–15% service charge is also added to the bill. Tipping is not the custom.

Category	Cost*
Very Expensive	over ¥6,000
Expensive	¥4,000–¥6,000
Moderate	¥2,000–¥4,000
Inexpensive	under ¥2,000

Cost is per person without tax, service, or drinks

Lodging

Accommodations cover the wide spectrum from Japanese-style inns to modern, large resort hotels that have little character but offer all the facilities of an international hotel. All of the large city and resort hotels offer Western and Japanese dining. During the summer season, hotel reservations are advised.

Youth hostels have not been listed. However, there are youth hostels in all the major areas. Their names and addresses can easily be obtained by requesting the Japan National Tourist Organization's free booklet *Youth Hostels in Japan.*

Outside the cities or major towns, most hotels quote prices on a per-person basis with two meals, exclusive of service and tax. If you do not want dinner at your hotel, it is usually possible to renegotiate the price. Stipulate, too, whether you wish to have Japanese or Western breakfasts, if any. The categories assigned below to all hotels reflect the cost of a double room with private bath and no meals. However, if you make reservations at any of the noncity hotels, you will be expected to take breakfast and dinner at the hotel—that will be the rate quoted to you unless you specify otherwise.

A 3% federal consumer tax is added to all hotel bills. Another 3% local tax is added to the bill if it exceeds ¥10,000. At most hotels, a 10%–15% service charge is added to the total bill. Tipping is not the custom.

Category	Cost*
Very Expensive	over ¥20,000
Expensive	¥15,000–¥20,000
Moderate	¥10,000–¥15,000
Inexpensive	under ¥10,000

Cost is for double room, without tax or service

The most highly recommended restaurants and accommodations in each city or area are indicated by a star ★.

Credit Cards The following credit-card abbreviations are used: AE, American Express; DC, Diners Club; MC, MasterCard; V, Visa.

Kamikochi

All hotels and ryokans close down mid-November–late April.

Lodging **Imperial Hotel.** This is the best place to stay in Kamikochi. It
★ may have no particular charm, but it's modern and well maintained. It is owned by Tokyo's Imperial Hotel, whose staff, on a monthly rotating basis, operates this establishment in the summer. You'll see the hotel right near the bus terminal. *Kamikochi, Azumimura, tel. 0263/95–2006. 75 rooms. Facilities: Western and Japanese cuisine. AE, V. Expensive.*

Gosenjuku Ryokan. A standard Japanese inn that is reasonably priced and located just beyond the bus terminal en route to the Kappabashi Bridge. *4468 Kamikochi, Azumimura, tel. 0263/95–2131. 31 Japanese-style rooms. AE, V. Moderate.*

Kanazawa

Dining **Goriya.** The specialty is river fish, including *gori*. One of Kanazawa's oldest restaurants (over 200 years old), Goriya is justly famous, with its lovely garden on the banks of the Asano River. The dining areas consist of several small rooms, and the setting is unusual, even if the cooking may not be Kanazawa's finest. *60 Tokiwa-cho, Kanazawa, tel. 0762/52–5596. Reservations advised. Jacket and tie required. AE, V, MC. Open 11–9:30. Very Expensive.*

★ **Tsubajin.** One of Kanazawa's best restaurants for Kaga cooking, Tsubajin is actually part of a small, traditional, and expensive ryokan. Try the crab, and also the house specialty, a chicken stew called *jibuni*. Be forewarned that dinner for two will exceed ¥20,000. *5-1-8 Teramachi, Kanazawa, Ishikawa 920, tel. 0762/41–2181. Reservations required. Dress: formal.*

AE. Open 11–9. Lunch is less elaborate and less expensive than dinner. Very Expensive.

★ **Kincharyo.** This restaurant, associated with the famous Kincharyo ryokan, recently moved to the Tokyu Hotel and is now that establishment's showpiece. The private dining room's Gotenyo ceiling is an impressive piece of delicate craftsmanship. Equally compelling is the lacquered, curved countertop of the sushi bar. The main dining room's decor is less noteworthy but the chef's culinary skill is superb. The menu here features seasonal specialties. In the spring, for example, your seven or eight dishes may include *hotaru-ika* (baby squid that by law may be taken from Toyama Bay only in the spring) and *i-doko* (baby octopus) no larger than a thumbnail. *3F, Kanazawa Tokyu Hotel, 1-1 Korimbo, 2-chome, Kanazawa, tel. 0762/31–2411. Jacket and tie. Reservations advised. AE, DC, MC, V. Open 11–2 and 5–10. Expensive.*

★ **Miyoshian.** Excellent *bento* (box lunches) and fish and vegetable dinners have been served here for about 100 years in the renowned Kenrokuen Garden. *11-Kenroku-cho, Kanazawa, tel. 0762/21–0127. Reservations advised. Jacket and tie required at dinner. AE, V. Open 11:30–9:30. Closed Tues. Moderate.*

Sennin. For a restaurant near the station, the Sennin is a lively, friendly izakaya with counter service or tatami-mat seating (you sit on the floor, but there is a well for your feet). An array of Kaga cooking is offered from succulent sweet shrimp to *kami* (crab) and vegetables served in steaming broth. The restaurant is located beyond the right side of Miyako Hotel in the basement of the Live One building—look for a plaque above the stairs reading "Kirin," because the restaurant's name is written in kanji. *2-13-4 Katamachi, Kanazawa, tel. 0762/21–1700. No reservations. Dress: casual. No credit cards. Open noon–2:30 and 5–10. Moderate.*

Lodging **ANA Kanazawa.** After opening in early summer 1990, this new member of the ANA chain is contending for the No. 1 ranking in Kanazawa. It certainly is the swankiest hotel. The building has a moon-shaped tower, an expansive lobby, and the hotel has more than its share of marble glitter. It is within a block of the JR station and a 10-minute taxi ride from Kanazawa's center. Guest rooms are remarkably soothing. Soft beige wallpaper, fabrics, and furnishings give a restful ambience and the L-shape rooms are a pleasant change from the usual box-like shape of most Japanese hotel rooms. The staff, most of whom speak English, go out of their way to help foreign guests. Of the several restaurants, the penthouse Teppanyaki offers succulent grills with a panoramic view of the city, while the Unkai restaurant offers kaiseki dinners with excellent sashimi and a view of a miniature version of Kanazawa's renowned Kenrokuen garden. *16-3, Showa-cho, Kanazawa 920, tel. 0762/24–6111, fax 0762/24–6100. 255 rooms. Facilities: Chinese, Japanese, and Western restaurants; coffee shop, shopping arcade, fitness center, parking. AE, DC, MC, V. Expensive.*

★ **Ryokan Asadaya.** This new, small, luxury ryokan is designed in a grand style that combines the luxury of modernity with classical simplicity. The antique furnishings and the carefully positioned scrolls and paintings establish a pleasing harmony. There is no ferro-concrete or plastic here. *23 Jukken-machi, Kanazawa, Ishikawa 920, tel. 0762/32–2228. 5 rooms. Facilities: superb regional cuisine served in the room or in the restaurant. AE. Very Expensive.*

★ **Ryokan Kincharyo.** This small picture-postcard Japanese inn with six small houses on an incline overlooks the Saigawa River. Prime ministers and princes have slept here, and guests need references in order to stay here. The Kaga cooking is superb, featuring regional fresh fish and vegetables. *1 Teramachi, Kanazawa, Ishikawa 920, tel. 0762/43–2121. AE. Very Expensive.*

Holiday Inn Kanazawa. This modern facility lacks the character of the city, as do most of the contemporary hotels. On the other hand, it has a fresh, smart lobby with a book stand, and the guest rooms have good–size American beds, a rare find, especially in single rooms. The Holiday Inn gets our vote for best hotel near the station. As an added benefit, coffee refills are free in the coffee lounge, instead of the usual ¥400 plus per cup. *1-10 Horikawacho, Kanazawa, Ishikawa 920. Located a 3-minute walk to the left of the station, tel. 0762/23–1111, fax 0792/23–1110. 169 Western-style rooms. Facilities: shops, coffee shop, Japanese and Western restaurant, lounge on 12th floor. AE, DC, MC, V. Expensive.*

★ **Kanazawa New Grand Hotel.** English is spoken at this large, established international hotel in the center of the city. The service is excellent, and its location across from the Oyama Shrine is another plus. Watching the sunset is especially pleasant from the hotel's sky lounge or from the adjacent Sky Restaurant Roi, which features French nouvelle cuisine, possibly the best of its kind in Kanazawa. Guest rooms use soft colors and are reasonably spacious. *1-50, Takaokamachi, Kanazawa, Ishikawa 920, tel. 0762/33–1311, fax 0782/33–1581. 109 rooms, mostly Western style. Facilities: Continental, Japanese, and Chinese restaurants; coffee shop, sky lounge shops. AE, DC, MC, V. Expensive.*

Kanazawa Tokyu Hotel. Conveniently located in the heart of town, this modern four-year-old hotel has a spacious lobby on the second floor and a pleasant coffee shop. Guest rooms are standard and efficient, with pale cream walls. Kincharyo is a superb Japanese restaurant. The Schloss Restaurant on the 16th floor serves French cuisine and offers a skyline view. *1-1 Korimbo 2-chome, Kanazawa 920, tel. 0762/31–2411. 120 rooms. Facilities: 3 restaurants, shops, meeting rooms. AE, DC, MC, V. Expensive.*

Ryokan Miyabo. A traditional Japanese inn, where the rooms open onto beautiful gardens. Once the teahouse of Kanazawa's first mayor, the ryokan is peaceful, authentic, and charming, though it could use a slight sprucing up. *3 Shimo-Kakinokibatake, Kanazawa, Ishikawa 920, tel. 0762/31–4228. 39 Japanese-style rooms. Meals usually included. AE, V. Expensive.*

Garden Hotel Kanazawa. Across from the station, this is a good alternative business hotel to the Kanazawa Station Hotel. Recently spruced up, and with a cheerful, polite staff, the hotel is equally good, though with higher prices (¥5,800 for a single and ¥10,000 for a small double). The hotel also has a small, but comfortable and friendly lounge for breakfast or light snacks. *2-16-16, Hon-machi, Kanazawa 920, tel. 0762/63–3333, fax 0762/63–7761. 54 rooms. Facilities: restaurant, coffee shop. AE, V. Inexpensive–Moderate.*

Kanazawa Station Hotel. The rooms are not as coffin-like as they often are at inexpensive business hotels; hence, we rate it Kanazawa's best in this category. A three-minute walk from the station and across from the Holiday Inn, it is also convenient for the bus stop to downtown. There is a small comfortable lounge for tea, coffee, and drinks, and a room for breakfast. *18-8 Horikawacho, Kanazawa, Ishikawa 920, tel. 0762/23–2600, fax 0762/23–2607. 62 rooms. Facilities: Japanese restaurant, coffee lounge. AE, DC, MC, V. Inexpensive.*

Minshuku Toyo. This very small private house is just across the wooden pedestrian bridge, Ume-no-hashi, in the Eastern Pleasure Quarter (Higashiyama). Rooms are small, but the price is only ¥3,800 for a single and ¥4,800 for a double, and guests are not required to take their meals at the inn. There is a small restaurant next door and an excellent traditional Japanese restaurant, the Seifuso, across the street, but a kaiseki dinner there will exceed ¥10,000 per person. *1–18–19, Higashiyama, Kanazawa 920, tel. 0762/52–9020. 5 rooms, none with private bath. Take the JR bus from the station to Higashi-hashi Bridge. No credit cards. Inexpensive.*

Yogetsu. A small minshuku in a 100-year-old geisha house in the Eastern Pleasure Quarter. With aged wood and beams, it's a delightful home. The guest rooms are small, but the hosts are very welcoming. *1-13-22 Higashiyama, Kanazawa, Ishikawa 920, tel. 0762/52–0497. 5 rooms. Facilities: Japanese breakfast and dinner usually included. Inexpensive.*

Karuizawa

Lodging **Hotel Kayu Kajima-no-Mori.** An exclusive resort, this hotel is tastefully furnished with Japanese handicrafts and antiques. The buildings are surrounded by forest, which heightens the mood of tranquillity. *Hanareyama, Karuizawa-machi, Nagano Prefecture 389–01, tel. 0267/42–3535. 50 rooms. Facilities: golf course, tennis courts, Western/Japanese restaurant. AE, DC, V. Very Expensive.*

★ **Karuizawa Prince Hotel.** Though the Prince is a large resort hotel, it is quiet and relaxing. Because of its popularity, reservations need to be made well in advance for the summer season. In winter, the neighboring mountain serves as a modest ski-slope for the hotel. *1016-75 Karuizawa, Nagano Prefecture 389–01, tel. 0267/42–8111, fax 0267/42–7139. 240 rooms, mostly Western style. Facilities: golf, pool, horseback riding. Western and Japanese restaurants. AE, MC, V. Expensive; Very Expensive during July and Aug.*

Pensione Grasshopper. Among the guest houses in the area, the Grasshopper has friendly hospitality, western beds, (great views of Mount Asama from room 208) and a mix of Japanese and Western fare. Kayo Iwasaki speaks English. The house is in the suburbs, and the management will transport you to and from the station. *5410 Karyada, Karuizawa, Kitasaku-gun, Nagano 389-01, tel. 0267/46–1333. 10 rooms, none with private bath. Facilities: dining room. MC, V. Inexpensive.*

Kiso Valley

Lodging Many small Japanese inns are located in the area, though reservations are strongly advised, especially during weekends. The **Magome Tourist Information Office** (tel. 0264/59–2336) and the **Tsumago Tourist Information Office** (tel. 0264/57–3123) will make these reservations for you. Telephone between 9 and 5. Magome's office is closed Sundays December–March; Tsumago's office closes January 1–3.

One particularly good minshuku is the **Onyado Daikichi,** Tsumago, Minamo Kisomachi, (Kiso-gun 399–54, tel. 0264/57–2595, fax 0274/57–2209). All six tatami rooms face the valley, the wooden bath is shared, the dinners, making good use of the local exotic specialties (horse sashimi, fried grasshoppers, and mountain vegetables), are excellent, and Nobaka-san (the lady of the house) in her limited English makes foreigners feel very welcome.

Matsumoto

Dining **Kura.** For an informal evening dining on feathery tempura or sushi from the sea of Japan, Kura is well priced. In an old moated house—the moat smells a bit—in the center of town, husband and wife run the cashier's desk while the two waitresses bring trays of food from the kitchen to a high ceilinged, tavernlike dining room. There are tables and counter service and shabu shabu for those who like to cook their food. *Ko Kudesai (behind the Parco department store), tel. 0263/33–6444. No reservations. Dress: casual. No credit cards. Moderate.*

Hachinen. Named after a local resistance hero of the Shogunate era, this bar is for the young or young at heart. Diners sit on stools at three counter areas, eating, talking, and drinking. Most of the Japanese food is grilled, but noodles and a hotpot are offered as well. It is in the central shopping area, down a small alley that has a Dunkin' Donuts on the corner. *Ise-machidori, tel. 0263/35–3832. No reservations. Dress: casual. No credit cards. Inexpensive.*

Lodging **Matsumoto Tokyu.** The convenience of this hotel across from the JR train station makes it a good choice as a functional base in Matsumoto. The rooms are not much larger than those of a typical business hotel, so you may want to upgrade yours. But beware, while the small doubles fall in the moderate price range, the deluxe twin-bed rooms with a separate mirror and sink outside the bathroom climb to the Very Expensive category. *1-2-37 Fukashi, Matsumoto 920, tel. 0263/36–0109. 99 Western-style rooms. Facilities: dining rooms serving Japanese and Western food. AE, V. Moderate–Expensive.*

Hotel New Station. Like all business-class hotels, the single rooms are tiny, but the furniture that can fit into the rooms is worn wood rather than plastic. The hotel offers good value and has at least some character. The deluxe twin for ¥12,000 is actually a full-sized room. The staff is friendly and cheerful. The location is a minute from the station in the direction of the castle and close to many restaurants, but you should be sure to have one meal in the hotel. In the rock pool just inside the door are iwana, a freshwater fish special to the region with a taste akin to smoked salmon, which quicky become sashimi or are grilled or boiled in sake. (If this hotel is fully booked, the Mount Hotel is an adequate, slightly more expensive hotel at the back of the JR station, tel. 0263/35-6480.) *1-1-11 Chuo, Matsumoto City 390, tel. 0263/35–3850. 103 rooms. Facilities: Japanese restaurant, conference rooms. AE, V. Inexpensive–Moderate.*

Enjyo Bekkan. This small inn is just outside Matsumoto in the spa village of Utsukushigahara Onsen reached by a 20-minute bus ride from the Matsumoto JR station to the Utsukushigahara bus terminal. The tatami rooms don't leave much room after your futon is laid out, but the inn is neat and clean. Some English is spoken. Only a few rooms have private bath. *110 Utsukushigahara Onsen, Satoyamabe-ku, Matsumoto City, Nagano 390–02, tel. 0263/33–7233. Facilities: only Japanese food served in a small dining room. AE, MC, V. Inexpensive.*

Nagano

Lodging ★ **Hotel Fujiya.** This establishment appears the same today as it was 300 years ago. The age-darkened wood and creaking floors transport guests back to the day when feudal lords stayed here while making pilgrimages to Zenkoji. The tatami guest rooms vary from small (¥15,000 for two, including meals) to large. Consider the royal suite (¥30,000 for two, including meals); it has three rooms with sliding doors onto an old, slightly overgrown garden. The furnishings are priceless antiques and scrolls. The hotel also has a deep, indulgent Japanese bath. This inn is not smart or sophisticated, but it is wonderfully old-fashioned. No English is spoken, but the management loves its inn and will respect foreigners who show their appreciation. *Central Avenue, Nagano City 380, tel. 0262/32–1241. 30 rooms. AE. Moderate–Very Expensive.*

Niigata

Lodging ★ **Onaya Ryokan.** This is a classic ryokan, a joy to stay in, with excellent food and service. The guest rooms look over a tranquil Japanese garden. All rooms have a private toilet, but the Japanese bath is separate and prepared for guests individually. No English is spoken, and guests should know a few words of Japanese. *981 Furamachi-dori, Niigata 951, tel. 0252/29–2951. 24 Japanese-style rooms. AE. Expensive.*

★ **Okura Hotel Niigata.** A modern, sparkling hotel on the Shinano River, across the bridge from the station, the Okura is the newest addition to Niigata's international hotels. The service is first-class, and the rooms are tastefully decorated, with rich-colored bedspreads contrasting with the pastel walls. For those who like to read or work at the hotel, the Okura is one of few places that has ample lighting in its rooms. Because of the view, rooms overlooking the Shinano River are the best. The formal French restaurant in the penthouse looks down on the city lights, and over the Japan Sea to Sado Island. The Japanese restaurant has superb kaiseki dinners, while the Chinese restaurant is nothing special. Breakfast and lighter meals are served in the Grill Room. (If you cannot get reservations here, the next choice is the Hotel Niigata, tel. 0252/45–3331, a 15-min walk from the station.) *6-53 Kawabata-cho, Niigata 951, tel. 0252/24–6111, fax 025/225–7060. 300 rooms, mostly Western style. Facilities: 4 restaurants (2 European, 1 Japanese, 1 Chinese), business center, shopping arcade. AE, DC, MC, V. Moderate–Expensive.*

Niigata Toei Hotel. For an inexpensive business hotel conveniently located near the station, this ranks the best. The 9th floor has two restaurants and a bar for evening entertainment. *1-6, 2 Benten, Niigata 950, tel. 025/244–7101. 90 rooms. Facilities: 2 restaurants, banquet/conference rooms. AE, D, MC, V. Moderate–Expensive.*

Sado Island

Lodging Hotel reservations can be made at the information counters of Sado Kisen ship company at Niigata Port or Ryotsu Port.

Sado Royal Hotel Mancho. This is the best hotel on Sado's west coast. The establishment caters mostly to Japanese tourists, but the staff makes the few Westerners who come by feel welcome; however, English is not spoken. *58 Shimoto, Aikawa, tel. 0259/74–3221. 87 rooms. Facilities: Japanese dining, but a few Western dishes are offered. DC, V. Expensive.*

★ **Sado Seaside Hotel.** Located 20 minutes by foot from the Ryotsu Port, this is more a friendly inn than a hotel. If you telephone before you catch the ferry from Niigata, the owner will meet you at the dock. He'll be carrying a green Seaside Hotel flag. *Ryotsu, tel. 0259/27–7211. 14 Japanese-style rooms, not all with private bath. Facilities: Japanese meals available, laundry room, Japanese baths. AE. Inexpensive.*

Takayama

Dining **Suzaki.** This is Takayama's number one restaurant for *kaiseki*
★ cuisine served in traditional style with kimono-clad waitresses. Make a point of including in your dinner *sansai-ryori*, a dish prepared from wild plants. Each dish is exquisitively presented on delicate chinaware. *4-14 Sinmei, tel. 0577/32–0023. Reservations advised. Jacket and tie required. AE, V. Open lunch and dinner. Expensive.*

Kukushu. The most established restaurant for Takayama's wellknown *shojin-ryori*, a vegetarian meal that consists of various individual items made from mountain plants, Kukushu is located on the far side of the Miyagawa River from the railway station and near the Tenshoji Temple. *2 Babacho Rd., Yakayama, tel. 0577/32–0174. Reservations advised. Jacket and tie required. AE, V. Open lunch and dinner. Moderate–Expensive.*

Susuya. Across Kokobunji-dori from the Sogo Palace hotel is this delightful small Japanese restaurant in a traditional Hida-style house. Owned by the same family for generations, the timbered restaurant is small and intimate. The traditional specialty is *sansai-ryori*, with mountain plants and freshly caught river fish, such as ayu, grilled with soy sauce. It's superb. *24 Hanakawa, tel. 0577/32–2484. Reservations advised. Dress: casual. AE, V. Open lunch and dinner. Moderate.*

Lodging The **Hida Tourist Information Office** (tel. 0577/32–5328), just in front of the train station, will help you find accommodations, both in town and in the surrounding mountains. This is one of the most helpful information offices in Japan.

★ **Ryokan Kinkikan.** This splendid traditional Japanese inn is Takayama's top place to stay. It is also very small, and reservations are essential. Antique Hida furniture is used throughout the inn and makes classic Japan come alive. *48 Asahicho, Takayama 506 (located in the center of town, left off Kokobunji-dori and two blocks from the river), tel. 0577/32–3131. 9 Japanese-style rooms. AE. Very Expensive.*

★ **Ryokan Hishuya.** For the genuine atmosphere of a Japanese inn, with delicately served meals and refined furnishings, stay at this ryokan. Quiet and contemplative, it is away from Takayama and close to Hida-no-sato Village. *2581 Kami-*

Okamotocho, Takayama 506, tel. 0577/33–4001. 16 Japanese-style rooms. AE, MC. Expensive.

★ **Hida Plaza Hotel.** The best international-style hotel in town is the Hida. While the additional modern building (adjacent to the older structure) is not attractive, the rooms in this newer part of the hotel are larger, but in terms of value, all the rooms are a cut above most Japanese hotels. In the older structure, the traditional Hida ambience is present, particularly in the old, exposed beams and wide-plank floors of the Japanese restaurant. The Hida plaza is a three-minute walk from the train station and a 10-minute walk from downtown. *2-60 Hanaokacho, Takayama 506, tel. 0577/33–4600. Fax 0577/33–4602. 152 western-style rooms. Facilities: Japanese and Continental restaurants, coffee shop, disco, karaoke bar, indoor pool, health center, sauna, mineral baths, shopping arcade. AE, DC, MC, V. Moderate.*

Honjin Hiranoya. There are two parts to this hotel, Honkan (old) Hiranoya and Shinkan (new) Hiranoya, in two buildings on the same street, across from one another. Though both have the same name and ownership, they were built three centuries apart. Years ago the old structure was a samurai house; now it is a friendly ryokan with lots of aged charm, though short on elegance. The rooms vary from Western-style to tatami-style. The Shinkan Hiranoya has modern tatami rooms and a superb multiperson bath on the seventh floor with huge windows overlooking the Hida Mountains. Downstairs is a lounge/bar that often has live entertainment. Both buildings have the Hida drum—Teiko—that used to be thumped as a welcome greeting. Meals are included. *1-chome, Honmachi Takayama, tel. 0577/34–1234. 19 rooms in the old building, 27 rooms in the new. Facilities: restaurant. AE, DC, MC, V. Moderate.*

The Sogo Palace. Conveniently located in the center of Takayama, this is a fairly modern Japanese inn. It may not have the charm of the older, traditional inns, but it caters to and understands the international traveler. Service is extremely friendly and helpful, which adds to the pleasure of this hotel. *54 Suehirocho, Takayama 506, tel. 0577/33–5000. 20 Japanese-style and 7 Western-style rooms. V. Moderate.*

★ **Yamaku.** This inn offers one of the best values in town. Though listed as a minshuku, Yanaku is more like a small, privately run Japanese-style hotel. The building is old, and cosy nooks in the lobby with chairs and coffee tables serve as small lounges. The tatami guest rooms are typically small, but the ample closets help add space. Room #33 is the quietest. The public baths are large and are given the kind of social importance found in an onsen—in the men's bath, a water wheel slowly turns to hypnotize you as you soak. Dinner hours—from 5:30 to 7:30—are more flexible than those at the typical minshuku: The food is good, though not extraordinary. The location of the inn is on the other side of town from the Takayama JR station (a 20-min walk), where most of the sightseeing attractions are. *58, Tenshojimachi, Takayama City, tel. 0577/32–3756. 22 rooms, none with private bath. Facilities: Japanese meals served in dining room, souvenir shop. Inexpensive.*

7 Kyoto

Introduction

by Nigel Fisher

Kyoto's history is full of contradictions: famine and prosperity, war and peace, calamity and tranquillity. Although the city was Japan's capital for more than 10 centuries, the real center of political power was often somewhere else, such as in Kamakura (1192–1333) and in Edo (1603–1868). Such was Kyoto's decline in the 17th and 18th centuries that, when the power of the government was returned from the shoguns to the emperor, he moved his capital and imperial court to Edo, renaming it Tokyo. Though that move may have pained the Kyoto residents, it actually saved the city from destruction. While most major cities in Japan were flattened by World War II bombs, Kyoto survived; it is now the sixth largest city in Japan.

Until 710, Japan's capital was moved to a new location with the succession of each new emperor. This continuous movement started to become rather expensive as the size of the court and the number of administrators grew, so Nara was chosen as the permanent capital. It did not last long as the capital. Buddhists rallied for, and achieved, tremendous political power. In the effort to thwart them, Emperor Kammu moved the capital in 784 to Nagaoka; the Buddhists were left behind in their elaborate temples. Within 10 years, however, Kammu decided that Kyoto (then called Uda) was better suited for his capital. Poets were asked to compose verse about Uda and invariably they included the phrase Heian-kyo, meaning "Capital of Peace," which no doubt reflected the hope and desire of the time.

For 1,074 years, Kyoto remained the capital, though at times only in name. From 794 to the end of the 12th century, the city flourished under imperial rule. One might say that this was the time when Japan's culture started to become independent of Chinese influences and began to develop its unique characteristics. Unfortunately, the use of wood for construction, coupled with Japan's two primordial enemies, fire and earthquakes, have destroyed all the buildings from this era, except the Byodoin Temple in Uji. The short life span of a building in the 11th century is exemplified by the Imperial Palace, which burned down 14 times in a 122-year period. As if natural disasters were not enough, imperial power waned in the 12th century. Then came a period of rule by the shoguns, but each shogun's rule was tenuous; by the 15th century, civil wars tore the country apart. Many of Kyoto's buildings were destroyed or looted, especially during the Onin Civil War.

The decade of the Onin Civil War (1467–1477) was a dispute between two feudal lords, Yamana and Hosokawa, over who should be the shogun's successor. The dispute was devastating for Kyoto. Yamana camped in the western part of the city with 90,000 troops, and Hosokawa settled in the eastern part with 100,000 troops; central Kyoto was the battlefield.

Not until the end of the 16th century, when Japan was welded by the might of Nobunaga Oda and Hideyoshi Toyotomi, did Japan settle down. This period was soon followed by the usurpation of power by Ieyasu Tokugawa, who began the dynasty of the Tokugawa Shogunate that lasted for the next 264 years, during which time the government's power was in Edo. However, Kyoto did remain the imperial capital, and the first three Tokugawa shoguns paid homage to it. Old temples were restored, and new villas were built. Much of what one sees in

Kyoto was built or rebuilt at this time (the first half of the 17th century) to legitimize the rule of the Tokugawa Shogunate.

Steeped in history and tradition, Kyoto has in many ways been the cradle of Japanese culture, especially with its courtly aesthetic pastimes, such as moon-viewing parties, and tea ceremonies. A stroll through Kyoto today is a walk through 11 centuries of Japanese history. Yet this city has been swept into the modern industrialized world with the rest of Japan. Glass-plate windows, held in place by girders and ferro-concrete, dominate central Kyoto. Elderly women, however, continue to wear kimonos as they make their way slowly along the canal walkways. Geishas still entertain, albeit at prices out of reach for most of us. Sixteen hundred temples and several hundred shrines surround central Kyoto. Rather a lot to see, to say the least. Our exploration of Kyoto will be selective.

Essential Information

Festivals and Seasonal Events

Many of the special celebrations of Kyoto are associated with the changing of the seasons. Most are free of charge and attract thousands of visitors as well as locals. Double-check with your hotel concierge or the Kyoto Tourist Information Center for current dates and times. For the big three festivals of Kyoto, the Gion, Jidai, and Aoi festivals, hotel bookings should be made well in advance.

May 15. The **Aoi Festival,** also known as the Hollyhock Festival, is the first of Kyoto's three most popular celebrations. Dating back to the 6th century, an "imperial" procession of 300 courtiers starts from the Imperial Palace and makes its way to Shimogamo Shrine to pray for the prosperity of the city. Today's participants are local Kyotoites.

July 16–17. The **Gion Festival,** which dates back to the 9th century, is perhaps Kyoto's most popular festival. Twenty-nine huge floats sail along downtown streets and make their way to the Yasaka Jinja Shrine to thank the gods for protection from a pestilence that once ravaged the city.

Aug. 16. Daimonji Gozan Okuribi features huge bonfires that form Chinese characters on five of the mountains that surround Kyoto. The most famous is the "Dai," meaning big, on the side of Mt. Daimonji in the eastern district of Kyoto. Dress in a cool yukata (cotton robe) and walk down to the banks of the Kamogawa River to view this spectacular summer sight, or catch all five fires from the rooftop of your hotel downtown.

Oct. 22. Jidai Festival, the Festival of Eras, features a colorful costume procession of fashions from the 8th through 19th centuries. The procession begins at the Imperial Palace and winds up at Heian Jingu Shrine. More than 2,000 Kyotoites voluntarily participate in this festival, which dates back to 1895.

Oct. 22. For the **Kurama Fire Festival** at the Kurama Shrine, a roaring bonfire and rowdy portable shrine procession makes its way through the narrow streets of the small village in the northern suburbs of Kyoto. If you catch a spark, it is believed to bring good luck.

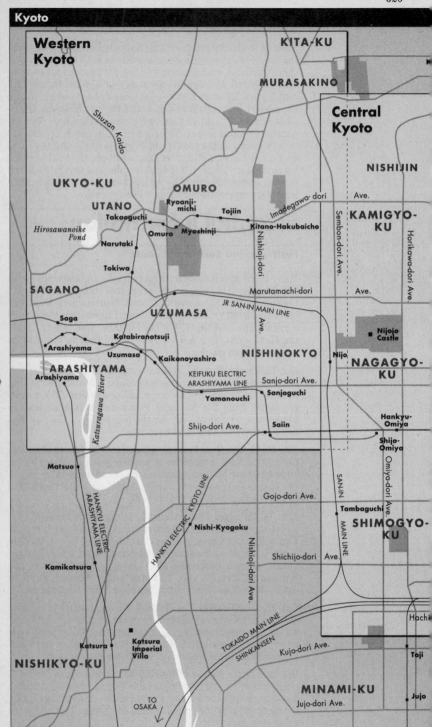

Western Kyoto

KITA-KU

MURASAKINO

H

Central Kyoto

NISHIJIN

Shuzan Kaido

UKYO-KU

UTANO

OMURO

Ryoanji-michi

Tojiin

Imadegawa- dori

Ave.

KAMIGYO-KU

Takaoguchi

Kitano-Hakubaicho

Semban-dori Ave.

Horikawa-dori Ave.

Hirosawanoike Pond

Omuro

Myoshinji

Nishioji-dori

Narutaki

Tokiwa

SAGANO

Marutamachi-dori

Ave.

JR SAN-IN MAIN LINE

UZUMASA

Saga

Ave.

Nijojo Castle

Katabiranotsuji

Arashiyama

Uzumasa

NISHINOKYO

Nijo

NAGAGYO-KU

Kaikonoyashiro

ARASHIYAMA

Arashiyama

KEIFUKU ELECTRIC ARASHIYAMA LINE

Sanjo-dori Ave.

Sanjoguchi

Katsuragawa River

Yamanouchi

Shijo-dori Ave.

Saiin

Hankyu-Omiya

Shijo-Omiya

Matsuo

Omiya-dori Ave.

HANKYU ELECTRIC ARASHIYAMA LINE

Gojo-dori Ave.

Tambaguchi

SAN-IN MAIN LINE

SHIMOGYO-KU

HANKYU ELECTRIC KYOTO LINE

Nishi-Kyogoku

Nishioji-dori Ave.

Shichijo-dori Ave.

Kamikatsura

Hachi

TOKAIDO MAIN LINE

SHINKANSEN

Katsura

Katsura Imperial Villa

Kujo-dori Ave.

Toji

NISHIKYO-KU

TO OSAKA

MINAMI-KU

Jujo-dori Ave.

Jujo

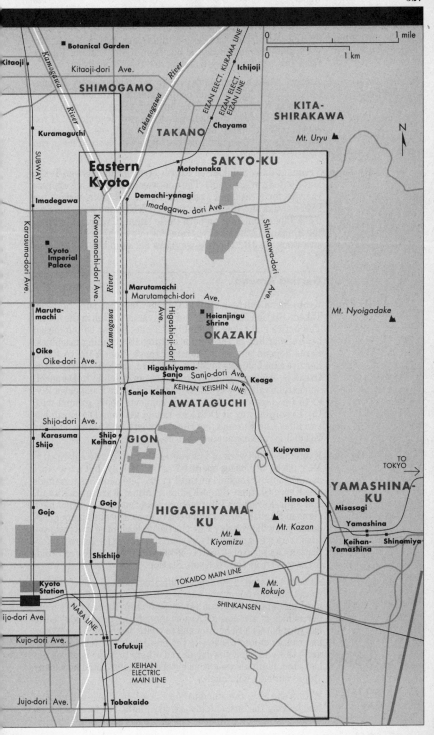

Eastern Kyoto

Arriving and Departing

By Plane The closest airport to Kyoto is the Osaka International Airport, about an hour away by bus from Kyoto Station. Flights from Tokyo to Osaka are frequent and take 70 minutes.

Between the Airport and Center City Airport buses depart for Kyoto approximately every 20 minutes, 7:55 AM–9:30 PM, and drop passengers at nine hotels, as well as at Kyoto Station. The bus trip takes 75 minutes and costs ¥830 or ¥900, depending on the Kyoto destination. If you consider the distance involved and the high cost, it does not make sense to take a taxi from the airport to Kyoto as it can run well over ¥10,000.

By Train Frequent daily Shinkansen express trains run between Tokyo and Kyoto (2 hrs, 40 min). The one-way fare, including express charges for a reserved seat, is ¥12,970. JR train service between Osaka and Kyoto (30 min) costs ¥530, one way. You may use a Japan Rail Pass on both these trains. Two private lines, the Keihan and the Hankyu trains (40 min each), are less expensive than the JR. The one-way fare between the two cities is ¥330.

Getting Around

By Train Kyoto has a thirteen-station subway line that runs between Takeda Station in the south and Kitayama Station in the north. The entire run takes 15 minutes. Tickets must be purchased before boarding at the station's automatic vending machines. Fares depend on destination and range from ¥160 to ¥320. Service runs 5:30 AM–11:30 PM. In Kyoto, the Keihan train from Osaka is now partly underground (from Shichijo to Demachi) and extends all the way up the east bank of the Kamogawa River to Imadegawa. From there it connects above ground with the Eizan Railway at Demachi-Yanagi station. The Eizan has two lines, the Kurama line running north to Kurama, and the Eizan line running northeast to Yase.

By Bus Kyoto has a network of bus routes that cover the entire city. Most of the city buses operate 7 AM–9 PM daily, but a few start as early as 5:30 AM and run until 11 PM. The main bus terminals are Kyoto Station, Sanjo-Keihan Station, Karasuma-Kitaoji, and Shijo-Karasuma Intersection. Many city buses do not have signs in English, so you will need to know the bus number. Because you will probably ride the bus at least once in Kyoto, try to pick up a bus map early in your stay from the Tourist Information Center (tel. 075/371–5649) at the Kyoto Tower Building, across from the JR Kyoto Station.

At each bus stop, a guidepost indicates the stop name, the bus route, and the bus-route number. Because the information at most guideposts is only in Japanese (except for the route number, which is given as an Arabic numeral), you are advised to ask your hotel clerk beforehand to write down your destination and route number to show to the bus driver and fellow passengers; this will allow the driver and others to help you if you get lost. You might also ask your hotel clerk beforehand how many stops your ride will take.

Within the city, the standard fare is ¥180, which you pay before leaving the bus; outside the city limits, the fare varies according to distance. Special one-day passes are available that are valid for unlimited rides on the subway, city buses, and private Kyoto bus lines, with restrictions on some routes. The passes cost ¥1,050 for adults and ¥530 for children under 12.

By Taxi Taxis are readily available in Kyoto. Fares for smaller-size cabs start at ¥470 for the first 2 km, with a cost of ¥90 for each additional 540 meters. Medium-size cabs have room for one more person and start at ¥500. The average fare range from Kyoto Station to various hotels is ¥900–¥1,300.

Important Addresses and Numbers

Tourist The Japan National Tourist Organization (JNTO) **Tourist Infor-**
Information **mation Center** (TIC) is located in the Kyoto Tower Building (in front of the JR Kyoto Station). *Karasuma-dori Higashi-Shiokojicho, Shimogyo-ku, tel. 075/371–5649. Open 9–5 weekdays; 9–noon Sat. Closed Sun. and national holidays.*

The **JNTO Teletourist Service** (tel. 075/361–2911) offers taped information on events in and around the city.

The **Kyoto City Government** operates a tourist information office. *Kyoto Kaikan, Okazaki, Sakyo-ku, tel. 075/752–0215. Open 8:30–5 weekdays, 8:30–noon Sat. Closed Sun. and national holidays.*

The **Japan Travel-Phone,** a nationwide telephone information system in English for visitors, is available 9–5 daily, year-round. It is run out of the same office as the TIC (*see* above). In Kyoto, tel. 075/371–5649. The call costs ¥10 for three minutes.

Consulates The nearest U.S., Canadian, and British consulates are located in Osaka (*see* Chapter 9).

Emergencies **Police,** tel. 110; **Ambulance,** tel. 119.

Doctors **Japan Baptist Hospital,** Kitashirakawa, Yamamoto-cho, Sakyo-ku, tel. 075/781–5191.
Daini Sekijuji Byoin (2nd Red Cross Hospital) at Kamanza-dori, Marutamachi-agaru, Kamigyo-ku, tel. 075/231–5171; and Daiichi Sekijuji (Red Cross Hospital) at Higashiyama Hommachi, Higashiyama-ku, tel. 075/561–1121.
Sakabe Clinic (435 Yamamoto-cho, Gokomachi, Nijo Sagaru, Nakagyo-ku, tel. 075/231–1624), has 24-hour emergency facilities.

English Bookstores **Maruzen Kyoto** (3F, Kawaramachi-Takoyakushi Intersection, Nakagyo-ku, tel. 075/241–2161).
Izumiya Book Center (Avanti Bldg., 6F, south of Kyoto Station, Minami-ku, tel. 075/682–5031).
Kyoto Shoin (3F Kawaramachi, north of Shijo, Nakagyo-ku, tel. 075/221–1062).

Travel Agencies **Japan Travel Bureau** (Kyoto Eki-mae, Shiokoji Karasuma Higashi-iru, Shimogyo-ku, tel. 075/361–7241).
Fujita Travel Service (International Hotel Kyoto lobby, tel. 075/222–0121).
Kintetsu Gray Line Tours Reservation Center (New Miyako Hotel, Minami-ku, tel. 075/691–0903).
Joe Okada Travel Service (Masugata Bldg., Teramachi-agaru Imadegawa, Kamigyo-ku, tel. 075/241–3716).

Guided Tours

Orientation Tours	Half-day morning and afternoon deluxe motor-coach tours featuring different city highlights are offered daily by the **Japan Travel Bureau** (Kyoto Eki-mae, Shiokoji Karasuma Higashi-iru, Shimogyo-ku, tel. 075/361–7241). Tours are also given daily March–November by **Kintetsu Gray Line Tours** (New Miyako Hotel, Minami-ku, tel. 075/691–0903) and **Fujita Travel Service** (International Hotel Kyoto lobby, tel. 075/222–0121, or the Kyoto Grand Hotel lobby, tel. 075/343–2304). Pickup service is provided at major hotels, and reservations can be made through travel agents or by calling the numbers above.
Special-Interest Tours	**Joe Okada Travel Service** (Masugata Bldg., Teramachi-agaru Imadegawa, Kamigyo-ku, tel. 075/241–3716) features morning and afternoon Industrial Tours with different itineraries Tuesday–Friday, March–November. Among the tour stops are Nissan Automobile, bamboo, tea, drum, and tofu factories. The morning tour includes a visit to a Zen meditation garden. Morning pickup is made at several Kyoto hotels. The tour terminates at the Kyoto Handicraft Center, where afternoon tours begin. The center operates an hourly bus that will drop you back at your hotel. Joe Okada Travel Service and Japan Travel Bureau (*see* above) also offer evening tours that feature cultural ceremonies and samurai fighting arts. Home visits also are arranged by the **Tourist Section, Department of Cultural Affairs and Tourism** (Kyoto City Government, Kyoto Kaikan, Okazaki, Sakyo-ku, Kyoto, tel. 075/752–0215).
Walking Tours	The Japan National Tourist Organization publishes suggested walking routes, which offer maps and brief descriptions for five tours (ranging in length from about 40 min to 80 min). The walking-tour brochures are available from the JNTO's Tourist Information Center office at the Kyoto Tower Building in front of the Kyoto Station (tel. 075/371–5649). For its guests, the Kyoto Grand Hotel suggests three jogging and walking courses around the famous temples near that hotel.
Excursions	Full- and half-day tours to Nara are offered by **Japan Travel Bureau** (tel. 075/361–7241), **Fujita Travel Service** (tel. 075/222–0121), and **Kintetsu Gray Line Tours** (tel. 075/691–0903). Pickup service is available at principal hotels.
Personal Guides	Contact **Fujita Travel Service** (tel. 075/222–1111), **Joe Okada Travel Service** (tel. 075/241–3716), and **Inter Kyoto** (tel. 075/256–3685). **Volunteer Guides** are available free of charge through the Tourist Information Center (TIC), but arrangements must be made by visiting the TIC in person one day in advance (*see* Important Addresses and Numbers, above).

Exploring

Most of what interests the visitor is on the north side of Kyoto Railway Station. Let's think of this northern sector as three rectangular areas abutting each other, with their short south sides running along the north side of the railway tracks. The middle rectangular area fronts the exit of Kyoto Railway Station. This is central Kyoto. Here are the hotels, the business district, Pontocho, a geisha district, and the Kiyamachi entertainment district. Central Kyoto also contains one of the oldest city temples (Toji Temple), the rebuilt Imperial Palace, and Nijojo Castle, former Kyoto abode of the Tokugawa shoguns.

The rectangular area to the east of central Kyoto is appropriately named the eastern district (Higashiyama). This area includes Gion, which serves as a traditional shopping neighborhood by day and a geisha entertainment locale by night. Many of Kyoto's renowned tourist attractions are to be found in the eastern district; it can easily take two full days to cover them. Some of the famous sights here are the Ginkakuji Temple (Silver Pavilion), the Heian Jingu Shrine, and the Kiyomizudera Temple.

The rectangular area to the west of central Kyoto is the western district. Here are more reflections of Kyoto's past, including the Ryoanji Temple and the Kinkakuji Temple (Golden Pavilion).

An exploration of these three areas will take up most of a three-day visit to Kyoto. However, two other areas have major sights to see and experience. Farther to the west of the western district is Arashiyama, which is home to Tenryuji Temple. To the north of central Kyoto is the northern district of Mt. Hiei and Kyoto's suburb, Ohara, where the poignant story of Kenreimon-in takes place at Jakko-in Temple.

Kyoto's attractions do cover a wide area. However, many of the sights are clustered together, so one may walk from one to another. Where they are not near each other, Kyoto's bus system, which works on a grid pattern, is easy to follow. Maps of the bus routes are supplied by the JNTO office. The following exploring sections keep to the divisions described above so as to allow walking from one sight to another. However, notwithstanding the traffic, if armed with a bus-route map, one could cross and recross Kyoto with not too much difficulty should one wish to choose sights to suit one's special interests.

Rather than start with central Kyoto, our exploration begins in eastern district (Higashiyama); if you have time to visit only one district, this is the one we would recommend. This area has a lot to see, more than one could cover comfortably in one day, so you may want to judiciously prune some of the following itinerary according to your interests.

Eastern Kyoto (Higashiyama)

Numbers in the margin correspond with points of interest on the Eastern Kyoto map.

Let's start at the northernmost landmark in eastern Kyoto, **Ginkakuji Temple.** One of Kyoto's most famous sights, it is a wonderful villa turned temple. To reach Ginkakuji, take the #5 bus from Kyoto Station to Ginkakuji-michi bus stop. Walk on the street along the canal, going east. Just after the street crosses another canal flowing north–south, there will be the **Hakusasonso Garden,** the quiet villa of the late painter Hashimoto Kansetsu, with an exquisite garden and tea house open to the public. *Admission: ¥600; with tea and sweets, an extra ¥350. Open 10–5.*

Ginkakuji means Silver Pavilion, but it's not silver. It was only intended to be. Shogun Yoshimasa Ashikaga (1435–1490) had this villa built for his retirement. He started building it as early

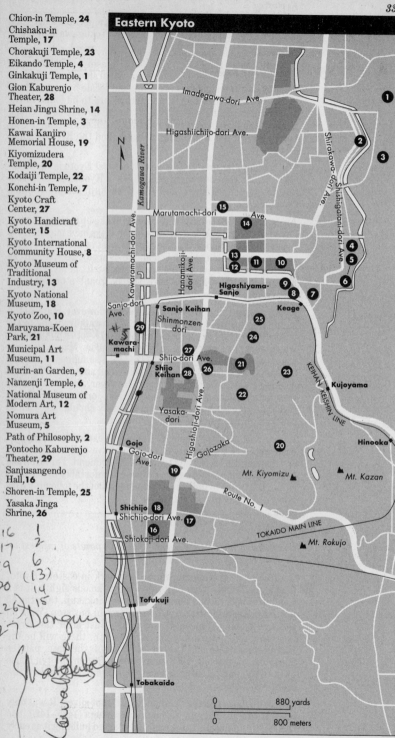

Eastern Kyoto

as the 1460s, but it was not until 1474 that, disillusioned with politics, he gave his full attention to the important matters of constructing his villa and devoting his time to the aesthetic arts of women, moon gazing, and the tea ceremony, which he helped develop into a high art. Though he never had time to complete the coating of the pavilion with silver foil, he had constructed a dozen or so buildings. Many of them were designed for cultural pursuits such as incense sniffing and tea tasting. On his death, the villa was converted into a Buddhist temple, as was often the custom during the feudal era. However, with the decline of the Ashikaga family, Ginkakuji fell into decline, and many buildings were destroyed.

What we see today are the two remaining original buildings, **Togudo** (East Request Hall) and the Silver Pavilion. The four other structures on the grounds were built in the 17th and 19th centuries. The front room of Togudo is where Yoshimasa is thought to have lived, and the statue of the priest is probably of Yoshimasa himself. The back room is called Dojinsai (Comradely Abstinence), it is noteworthy because it became the prototype for the traditional tea-ceremony room that is still used today.

Ginkakuji is a simple and unadorned two-story building. On the upper floor, it contains a gilt image of Kannon (the Goddess of Mercy) said to have been carved by Unkei, a famous Kamakura-period sculptor, though it is not ordinarily open to public view. Mostly it is the exterior shape of the structure that is so appealing and restful, as it combines Chinese elements with the developing Japanese Muromachi (1333–1568) architecture. Ginkakuji overlooks the complex gardens attributed to architect and artist Soami. They are in two sections and serve to contrast each other to establish a balance. Adjacent to the pavilion is the pond, with a composition of rocks and plants designed to offer different perspectives from each viewpoint; the other garden has two sculptured mounds of sand, with the higher one perhaps symbolizing Mt. Fuji. The garden sparkles in the moonlight and has been aptly named "Sea of Silver Sand." *Ginkakuji-machi, Sakyo-ku. Admission: ¥400 adults, ¥200 children 6–15. Open 8:30–5 Mar. 15–Nov. 30, 9–4:30 winter.*

If you can tear yourself away from Ginkakuji, retrace your steps on the entrance road until you reach, on your left, the ② **Path of Philosophy** or, as the Japanese say, "Tetsugaku-no-michi." This walkway along the canal is lined with cherry trees and has been a place for contemplative strolls since a famous scholar, Ikutaro Nishida, took his constitutional along the shaded paths. Now professors and students have to push their way through tourists who take the same stroll and whose interest lies mainly with the path's specialty shops.

Time Out The Path of Philosophy has several coffee shops and small restaurants at which to stop and relax along the way. **Omen** restaurant, one block west of the Path of Philosophy, is an inexpensive, popular place, known for its homemade white noodles. If you are desperate for Western food, you can try **Bobby Soxer** for pizza.

③ At the first bridge off the path, cross over the canal and take the road east to **Honen-in Temple,** a modest structure with a thatched roof. Not too many people come here, and the walk through the trees leading to the temple is mercifully quiet and comforting. The temple was built in 1680, on a site that in the 13th century simply consisted of an open-air Amida statue. Honen-in honors a man, Priest Honen (1133–1212), who brought Buddhism down from its lofty peak to the common folk. He made the radical claim that all were equal in the eyes of Buddha. Honen focused on faith in the Amida Buddha; he believed that *nembutsu* ("Namu Amida Butsu," the invocation of Amida Buddha), which he is said to have repeated up to 60,000 times a day, and reliance on Amida, the All-Merciful, were the path of salvation. Because his ideas threatened other sects, especially the Tendai sect, Honen's teachings of "Jodo-shu, the the Pure Land Sect," were accused of advocating that the masses seduce the ladies of noble classes. At the insistence of the established Buddhist powers, Emperor Gotoba had several of Honen's followers executed and Honen sent to exile. Eventually, in 1211, Honen was pardoned and permitted to return to Kyoto, where a year later, at Chion-in Temple, he fasted to death at the age of 79. *Admission free. Open 7–4.*

From Honen-in Temple, walk back to the Path of Philosophy and continue in a southerly direction. After a short walk, you'll reach **Eikando Temple** on your left.

Eikando is the temple's popular name. Officially it is Zenrinji Temple, founded in 856 by Priest Shinsho, but it honors the memory of an 11th-century priest, Priest Eikan, which explains the popular name. He was a man of the people and would lead them in a dance in celebration of Amida Buddha. On one such occasion, the Amida statue came to life and stepped down from his pedastal to join the dancers. Taken aback, Eikan slowed his dancing feet. Amida looked back over his shoulder to reprimand Eikan for slowing his pace. This is the legend that explains why the unusal statue in the Amidado Hall has its face turned to the side, as if glancing backward. For the energetic, a climb to the top of the pagoda offers superb views of the grounds below and Kyoto beyond. In autumn, the grounds are especially magnificent with the turning leaves of the maple trees. The buildings are 16th-century reconstructions made after the originals were destroyed in the Onin War (1467–1477). *Admission: ¥400. Open 9–5 (enter by 4:30).*

If you cross the street from Eikando Temple, and continue south, you'll see the **Nomura Art Museum** on the right. Instead of bequeathing their villas to Buddhist sects, the modern wealthy Japanese tend to donate their art collections to museums. Such is the case here. Founder of the Daiwa Bank and a host of other companies, Tokushichi Nomura gave his collection of scrolls, paintings, tea-ceremony utensils, ceramics, and other art objects to establish his namesake museum. *61 Shimogawara-cho, Nanzen-ji, Sakyo-ku, tel. 075/751–0374. Admission: ¥500. Open 10–4:30 mid-Mar.–mid-June and mid-Sept.–Dec. Closed Mon.*

If the day is close to an end, you may be tempted to walk from the Nomura Art Museum to the Heian Jingu Shrine, and the Kyoto Handicraft Center on Marutamachi-dori behind it. If not, continue this tour, which will come back shortly to the Heian Jingu Shrine.

 Next, walk south from the Nomura Art Museum and follow the main path; on your left you'll reach **Nanzenji Temple,** which is another one of those retirement villas turned into a temple on the death of its owner. This donor was Emperor Kameyama (1249–1305). The Onin Civil War (1467–1477) demolished the buildings, but some were resurrected during the 16th century, and Nanzenji has become one of Kyoto's most important temples, in part because it is the headquarters of the Rinzai sect of Zen Buddhism. As you enter the temple, you'll pass through the **Sanmon** (Triple Gate), built in 1628. This is the classic "gateless" gate of Zen Buddhism serving as a symbol of entrance into the most sacred part of the temple precincts. From the top floor of the gate there is a view of Kyoto spread out below. The steps are pretty steep, and you might decide to forgo the pleasure, but give a moment to Goemon Ishikawa, a Robin Hood–style outlaw of Japan who hid in this gate until his eventual capture.

On through the gate is the **Hojo Hall,** a National Treasure. Inside, the chambers are divided by screens with impressive 16th-century paintings. These wall panels of the *Twenty-four Paragons of Filial Piety and Hermits* are by Eitoku Kano (1543–1590) of the Kano school (really the Kano family, because the school consists of eight generations—Eitoku being from the fifth—of one bloodline). The Zen-style garden attached to the Hojo Hall has stones amid the sculpted trees and sand. This garden has been assigned several names, but the one that stands out is "Leaping Tiger Garden."

Within Nanzenji's 27 pine-tree–covered acres are several other temples, known more for their gardens than for their buildings. Two are worth visiting if you have time: **Nanzen-in Temple,** once the temporary abode of the Kameyama (1249–1305), who founded the temple, holds a mausoleum and has a garden that dates to the 14th century and has a small creek that passes through it. Only recently open to the public, Nanzen-in is not as famous as other temples, making it a peaceful place to visit. *Admission: ¥350. Open 8:30–5:30 (4:30 in winter).*

Outside the main gate of Nanzenji on a side street to the left as you go out is **Konchi-in Temple,** with its pair of gardens, one with a pond in the shape of the Chinese character *kokoro*, or heart, and the other a dry garden with a "sea of sand" and a backdrop of greenery borrowed from the mountains behind. The garden was designed by the famous tea master and landscape designer, Kobori Enshu, in 1632. The two rock groupings in front of a plant-filled mound are in the crane-and-tortoise style. Since ancient times these creatures have been associated with longevity, beauty, and eternal youth. In the feudal eras, the symbolism of the crane and the tortoise became very popular with the samurai class, whose profession often left them with only the hope of immortality. *86 Fukuchi- cho, Nanzenji, Sakyo-ku. Admission: ¥400 adults, ¥300 high school students, ¥200 for children under 12. Open 8:30–5 (8:30–4:30 in winter).*

At the intersection at the foot of the road to Nanzenji, you'll see the expansive grounds of the brand-new **Kyoto International Community House** across the street to the left. The center, constructed to promote Kyoto's image as an international city, offers library and information facilities and rental halls for public performances. The book *Easy Living in Kyoto* (available free) gives helpful information for a lengthy stay. *2-1 Torii-cho, Awata-guchi, Sakyo-ku, tel. 075/752–3010. Admission free.*

Open 9 AM–9 PM. Closed Mon. (when Mon. is a national holiday, the House closes the following day instead).

9 Walk back to the main road to Nanzenji and turn left. Cross at the traffic light to **Murin-an Garden,** whose entrance is on a side road half a block east. The property was once part of Nanzenji Temple, but it was sold to Prince Yamagata, a former prime minister and advocate of the reforms which followed the Meiji Restoration (1868). The garden incorporates new ideas into Japanese thinking, just as the Meiji Restoration did. There is more freedom of movement in this garden than in the rigid, perfected harmony of more traditional gardens. *Admission: ¥200. Open 9–4:30. Closed Dec. 29–Jan. 3.*

10 Walk back toward the canal and turn left. If you were to cross the canal at the first right, you would be at the **Kyoto Zoo.** There is no pressing reason to visit it, unless you have children in tow. The zoo has a Children's Corner, where your youngsters can feed the farm animals. *Hoshoji-cho, Okazaki, Sakyo-ku, tel. 075/771–0210. Admission: ¥300 adults, free for elementary school children and younger. Open 9–5, 9–4:30 Dec.–Feb. Closed Mon.*

Unless you turn off for the zoo, continue to the next right and cross the bridge over the canal. You'll see an immense vermilion *torii* gate, because this is the road that leads to the Heian Jingu **11** Shrine. Immediately after the torii gate, the **Municipal Art 12 Museum** will be on your right, and the **National Museum of Modern Art** will be on your left.

The Municipal Art Museum is primarily an exhibition hall for traveling shows and those of local art societies. It owns a collection of Japanese paintings of the Kyoto school, a selection of which goes on exhibit once a year. *Enshoji-cho, Okazaki, Sakyo-ku, tel. 075/771–4107. Admission: depends on exhibition, but usually around ¥600. Open 9–5. Closed Mon.*

The National Museum of Modern Art, established in 1903, reopened in 1986 in a new building designed by Fumihiko Maki, one of the top contemporary architects in Japan. The museum is known for its collection of 20th-century Japanese paintings, as well as for its ceramic treasures by Kanjiro Kawai, Rosanji Kitaoji, Shoji Hamada, and others. *Enshoji-cho, Okazaki, Sakyo-ku, tel. 075/761–4111. Admission: ¥360 (more for special exhibitions). Open 9:30–5. Closed Mon.*

13 If you are interested in fine arts and crafts, visit the **Kyoto Museum of Traditional Industry** (Dento Sangyo Kaikan). Walk north from the Museum of Modern Art to the next traffic light, turn left, and continue down the avenue to the bridge. The museum will be on your left. The first floor has fine displays of every major Kyoto craft, and the basement has a reconstructed Kyoto house, a craft demonstration room, and a gift shop. *9-2 Seishoji-cho, Okazaki, Sakyo-ku, tel. 075/761–3421. Admission free. Open 9–5 (enter by 4:30). Closed Mon.*

14 The street between the Municipal Art Museum and the National Museum of Modern Art leads directly to the **Heian Jingu Shrine.** This shrine is one of Kyoto's newest historical sites. It was built in 1895 to mark the 1,100th anniversary of the founding of Kyoto. The shrine is dedicated to two emperors: Kammu (737–806), who founded the city in 794, and Komei (1831–1866), the last emperor to live out his reign in Kyoto. The new buildings are for the most part replicas of the old Imperial Palace, but only two-thirds the original size. In fact, because the original palace (rebuilt many times) was finally destroyed in 1227, and only scattered pieces of information are available relating to its construction, the Heian Jingu Shrine should be taken as a Meiji interpretation of the old palace. Still, the dignity and the relative spacing of the **East Honden, West Honden** (Main Halls), and the **Daigokuden** (Great Hall of State), where the Heian emperor would issue decrees, conjure up an image of the magnificence that the Heian court must have presented.

During New Year, the imposing gravel forecourt leading to Daigokuden is trampled by kimono-clad and gray-suited Japanese who come to pay homage; the most wonderful time to visit is in the spring, during cherry blossom time. The gardens are also a modern interpretation of a Heian garden, but they follow the Heian aesthetic of focusing on a large pond whose shores are gracefully linked by the arched Taibei-kaku Chinese-style bridge. An even better time to visit the shrine is during Jidai Festival, held on October 22. The festival celebrates the founding of Kyoto. The pageant features a procession of 2,000 people, attired in costumes from every period of Kyoto history. It winds its way from the original site of the Imperial Palace and ends at the Heian Jingu Shrine. *Okazakinishi Tenno-cho, Sakyo-ku. Admission to the garden: ¥500 adults, ¥400 teenagers 15–18, ¥250 children 6–14, ¥50 children under 6. Open 8:30–5:30 Mar. 15–Aug. 31, 8:30–5 Sept.–Oct. and Mar. 1–Mar. 14, 8:30–4:30 Nov.–Feb.*

Another choice time to be at the shrine is on June 1–2 for Takigi-noh performances. This form of Noh is so-called because it is performed at night in the open air and the lighting is provided by burning firewood *(takigi);* the performances are presented on a stage built before the shrine's Daigokuden Hall. Admission for Takigi-noh ¥3,000 at the gate; ¥2,000 in advance. Call the TIC for advance ticket outlets. (*see* Important Addresses and Numbers, above).

If the urge comes on to do some shopping, on the north side of the Heian Jingu Shrine and slightly to the left, across Marutamachi-dori Avenue, is the **Kyoto Handicraft Center,** where there are seven floors of everything Japanese, from dolls to cassette recorders. The center caters to tourists. (*See* Shopping, below.) *Kumano Jinja Higashi, Sakyo-ku, tel. 075/761–5080. Open 9:30–6 (9:30–5:30 in winter). Closed Dec. 31–Jan. 3.*

At the crossroads of Marutamachi-dori Avenue and Higashioji-dori Avenue (west of the Kyoto Handicraft Center) is the Kumano Jinjya-mae bus stop. If you've had enough sightseeing for one day, just five stops south on Higashioji-dori Avenue, using bus #202 or bus #206, is the Gion bus stop; here, the world of restaurants and bars is at your disposal. Gion will be discussed later. If you are going to continue sightseeing, stay on the #202 bus for five more stops (Higashiyama-Shichijo) to explore the southern part of Higashiyama. If you have taken the #206, stay on it for one more stop (it makes a right turn onto Shichijo-dori Ave. and heads for the station) and get off at the Sanjusangendo-mae bus stop. You may want to join this tour here tomorrow. If that is the case, you may also reach Sanjusangendo-mae bus stop by taking the #206 or the #208 bus from Kyoto Station.

If you disembarked from the bus at Sanjusangendo-mae bus stop, Sanjusangendo Hall will be to the south, just beyond the Kyoto Park Hotel. If you disembarked from bus #202 at Higashiyama-Shichijo bus stop, you need to walk down Shichijo-dori Avenue and take the first major street to the left. However, you may want to visit Chishaku-in Temple first; that will allow you to avoid doubling back.

16 **Sanjusangendo Hall** is the popular name for Rengeo-in Temple. Sanjusan means "33"; that is the number of spaces between the 35 pillars that lead down the narrow, 394-foot-long hall. Enthroned in the middle of the hall is the six-foot-tall, 1,000-handed Kannon (National Treasure), carved by Tankei, a sculptor of the Kamakura period (1192–1333). Surrounding the statue are 1,000 smaller statues of Kannon, and in the corridor behind are 28 guardian deities who are protectors of the Buddhist universe. Notice the frivolous-faced Garuda, a bird that feeds on dragons. If you are wondering about the 33 spaces mentioned earlier, Kannon can assume 33 different shapes on her missions of mercy. Because there are 1,001 statues of Kannon in the hall, 33,033 shapes are possible. People come to the hall to see if they can find the likeness of a loved one (a deceased relative) among the 1,001 statues. *657 Sanjusangendo-Mawari-cho, Higashiyama-ku. Admission: ¥400 adults, ¥350 high school students, ¥200 junior high school students and younger. Open 8–4:30 (9–3:30 in winter).*

From Sanjusangendo, you need to retrace your steps back to Shichijo-dori Avenue and take a right. Chishaku-in Temple will be facing you on the other side of Higashioji-dori Avenue.

17 The major reason for visiting **Chishaku-in Temple** is for its famous paintings. They were executed by Tohaku Hasegawa and his son Kyuzo (known as the Hasegawa school, rivals of the Kano school), and are some of the best examples of Momoyama art. These paintings were originally created for the sliding screens at Shoun-in Temple, a temple built in 1591 on the same site but no longer in existence. Shoun-in was commissioned by Hideyoshi Toyotomi. When his concubine, Yodogimi, bore him an heir in 1589, Hideyoshi named his son Tsurumatsu (Crane-pine), two symbols of longevity. Ironically, the child died when he was two, and Shoun-in was built for Tsurumatsu's enshrinement. The Hasegawas were then commissioned to do the paintings. Saved from the fires that destroyed Shoun-in, the paintings are now on display in the Exhibition Hall of Chishaku-in. These paintings, rich in detail and using strong colors on a gold ground, splendidly display the seasons by using the symbols of cherry, maple, pine, and plum trees and autumn grasses.

You may also want to take a few moments in the pond-viewing garden. It is only a vestige of its former glory, but from the temple's veranda, you'll have a pleasing view of the pond and garden. *Admission: ¥350. Open 9–4:30.*

18 Back across Higashioji-dori Avenue is the prestigious **Kyoto National Museum.** It has a collection of more than 8,000 works of art housed in two buildings. Exhibitions are continually changing, but you can count on an excellent display of paintings, sculpture, textiles, calligraphy, ceramics, lacquer ware, metalwork, and archaeological artifacts from its permanent collection. *Yamato-oji-dori, Higashiyama-ku, tel. 075/541–*

1151. *Admission:* ¥*360 (more for special exhibitions). Open 9–4:30. Closed Mon.*

⑲ Just north, less than a five-minute walk along Higashioji-dori Avenue from the Kyoto National Museum, is **Kawai Kanjiro Memorial House.** Now a museum, this was the home and studio of one of Japan's most renowned potters. The house was designed by Kanjiro Kawai, who took for his inspiration a traditional rural Japanese cottage. He was one of the leaders of the *Mingei* (Folk Art) Movement, which sought to promote a revival of interest in traditional folk arts during the 1920s and '30s, when all things Western were in vogue in Japan. On display are some of the artist's personal memorabilia and, of more interest, some of his exquisite works. An admirer of Western, Chinese, and Korean ceramic techniques, Kawai won many awards, including the Grand Prix at the 1937 Paris World Exposition. *Gojozaka, Higashiyama, tel. 075/561–3585. Admission:* ¥*700 adults,* ¥*500 college and high school students,* ¥*300 junior high students and younger. Open 10–5. Closed Mon., Aug. 10–20, Dec. 24–Jan. 7. (When Mon. is a national holiday, museum closes following day instead.)*

⑳ The next place to visit is a very special temple, **Kiyomizudera Temple,** which may be reached by crossing the major avenue Gojo-dori and walking up Higashioji-dori Avenue. The street to the right, Gojozaka, leads into Kiyomizuzaka, which is the street you take to the temple.

Kiyomizuzaka is lined with shops selling souvenirs, religious articles, and ceramics. There are also tea shops where you can sample *yatsuhashi,* a doughy triangular sweet filled with cinnamon-flavored bean paste—a Kyoto specialty. Because of the immense popularity of the temple above it on the hill, this narrow slope is often crowded with sightseers and bus tour groups, but the magnificent temple is worth the struggle.

Kiyomizudera Temple is a 1633 reconstruction of the temple that was built here in 798, four years after Kyoto was founded. It is a unique temple in more ways than one. It does not belong to one of the local Kyoto Buddhist sects but rather to the Hosso sect that developed in Nara. Kiyomizudera is one of the most visited temples in Kyoto and is closely associated with the city's skyline. In the past, people would come here to escape the open political intrigue of Kyoto and to scheme in secrecy. Visually, Kiyomizudera is unique because it is built on a steep hillside. Part of its Main Hall is held up by 139 giant pillars. Finally, it is one of the few temples where you can walk around the veranda without taking your shoes off.

The temple's location is marvelous. Indeed, one reason for coming here is the view. From the wood veranda you have both a fine view of the city and a breathtaking look at the valley below. "Have you the courage to jump from the veranda of Kiyomizu?" is a saying asked when someone sets out on a daring new venture.

The temple is dedicated to the popular 11-faced Kannon (Goddess of Mercy), who can bring about easy childbirth. Over time, Kiyomizudera has become "everyone's temple"; you'll see evidence of this throughout the grounds, from the little *jizo bosatsu* statues (representing the god of travel and children) stacked in rows to the many *koma-inu* (mythical guard dogs) marking the pathways, which have been given by the temple's grateful patrons. *Kiyomizu, 1-chome, Higashiyama-ku. Admission: ¥300 adults, ¥200 junior high school students and younger. Open: 8–6 (8–6:30 Sat. and holidays).*

From Kiyomizudera, we need to work our way north to **㉑ Maruyama-Koen Park.** If you take a right halfway down the road leading up to Kiyomizudera, you can walk along the Sannenzaka and Ninenzaka slopes. These two lovely winding streets are an example of old Kyoto with their cobbled paths and delightful wooden buildings. This area is one of four historic preservation districts in Kyoto, and the shops along the way offer local crafts such as *Kiyomizu-yaki* (Kiyomizu-style pottery), Kyoto dolls, bamboo basketry, rice crackers, and antiques.

Take a left after Ninenzaka Slope and then an immediate right, as you keep going in a northerly direction. A further five-min-**㉒** ute walk on the right is **Kodaiji Temple,** a quiet nunnery established in the early 17th century and only recently opened to the public. The temple was built as a memorial to Hideyoshi Toyotomi by his wife Kita no Mandokoro, who lived out her remaining days in the nunnery there. Kodaiji has gardens designed by Kobori Enshu, and the Kaisando (Founder's Hall) has ceilings decorated in raised lacquer and paintings by artists of the Tosa school. The teahouse above on the hill was designed by tea master Sen no Rikyu. It has a unique umbrella-shape bamboo ceiling and a thatched roof. *Admission: ¥500. Open 9–4:30 (9–4 in winter).*

Continuing northward: by doing a right–left zigzag at the Maruyama Music Hall, you reach Maruyama-Koen Park. The **㉓** road to the right (east) leads to **Chorakuji Temple.** Chorakuji Temple is famous today for the stone lanterns that lead to the temple. It is a hard climb up the mountainside. It's a pleasant temple, but perhaps not worth the climb.

Proceed north through Maruyama-Koen Park and you'll find **㉔ Chion-in Temple,** headquarters of the Jodo sect of Buddhism, the second largest Buddhist sect in Japan. The entrance here is through a 79-foot, two-story Sanmon Gate (recently under reconstruction). In many people's minds, this is the most daunting temple gate in all of Japan, and it leads to one of Japan's largest temples. On the site of Chion-in, Honen, the founder of the Jodo sect, fasted and died in 1212. The temple was built in 1234; because of fires and earthquakes, the oldest standing buildings are the Main Hall (1633) and the Daihojo Hall (1639). The temple's belfry houses the largest bell in Japan, which was cast in 1633 and requires 17 monks to ring. The corridor behind the Main Hall, which leads to the Assembly Hall, is called *uguisu bari* (nightingale floor). It was constructed to "sing" at every footstep to warn the monks of intruders. Walk underneath the corridor to examine the way the boards and nails are placed to create this inventive burglar alarm. *400 Hayashi-shita-cho, 3-chome, Yamato Oji, Higashi-Hairu, Shinbashi-dori, Higashiyama-ku. Admission: ¥300. Open 9–4:30 (9–4 in winter). Not all buildings are open to the public.*

㉕ More paintings by the Kano school are on view at the **Shoren-in Temple,** a five-minute walk to the north of Chion-in. Though the temple's present building dates only from 1895, the sliding screens of the Main Hall have the works of Motonobu Kano, second-generation Kano, and Mitsunobu Kano of the sixth generation. The gardens of this temple are pleasant—a pond motif with a balanced grouping of rocks and plants. It was no doubt more grandiose when Soami designed it in the 16th century, but with the addition of paths through the garden, it invites a stroll. Another garden on the east side of the temple is sometimes attributed, probably incorrectly, to Kobori Enshu. Occasionally, koto concerts are held in the evening in the Soami garden. (Check with a Japan Travel Bureau office for concert schedules.) *Admission: ¥400. Open 9–5. Closed Nov. 12.*

Should you have missed visiting the Heian Jingu Shrine, the National Museum of Modern Art, and the Municipal Museum of Art described earlier, these are just 10 minutes by foot north of Shoren-in, on the other side of Sanjo-dori Avenue. If you take a right (east) from Shoren-in on Sanjo-dori Avenue, you'll eventually reach the Miyako Hotel; left (west) on Sanjo-dori Avenue leads across Higashioji-dori Avenue to the downtown area and covered mall. If you turn left on Higashioji-dori Avenue, you will reach Shijo-dori Avenue and the Gion district.

At the Gion bus stop, Shijo-dori Avenue goes off to the right (west). Before going down this street, consider taking a short **26** walk east (into Maruyama-Koen Park) to **Yasaka Jinja Shrine.** Because its location is close to the shopping districts, worshipers drop by for some quick salvation. This is a good shrine to come to if you have business or health problems; you'll want to come here to leave a message for the God of Prosperity and Good Health, to whom the shrine is dedicated. Especially at New Year, Kyoto residents flock here to ask for good fortune for the coming year. *625 Gion-machi, Kitagawa, Higa-shiyama-ku. Admission free. Open 24 hours.*

Walk back from Yasaka Jinja, cross Higashioji-dori Avenue, and you are in Kyoto's Gion district. This is Shijo-dori Avenue. **27** On the corner is the **Kyoto Craft Center,** where Kyoto residents shop for fine contemporary and traditional crafts—ceramics, lacquerware, prints, and textiles. You can also find moderately priced souvenirs, such as dolls, coasters, bookmarks, and paper products. *Higashi-Kitagawa, Hanami-koji, Gion-Shijo, Higashiyama-ku, tel. 075/561–9660. Open 10–6. Closed Wed.*

Parallel to Shijo-dori Avenue and to the north is Shinmonzen Street. This street is famous for its antiques shops and art galleries. Here you'll find collectors' items—at collectors' prices, too—but there is no harm in just browsing. The shops on Shijo-dori Avenue have slightly more affordable products, from handcrafted hair ornaments to incense to parasols—all articles that are part of the geisha world.

Off Shijo-dori Avenue (halfway between Higashioji-dori and the Kamogawa) is Hanamikoji-dori Avenue, which runs off to the south (on the right, if you are walking back from the river). This avenue will bring you into the heart of the Gion district. Here is where the top geisha live and work; they can be seen scurrying in the evening en route to their assignments, trailed by young apprentice geisha (*maiko*), who can be distinguished from their mistresses by the longer sleeve lengths of their kimonos. Because Westerners have little opportunity to enjoy a geisha's performance in a private party setting, a popular entertainment during the month of April is the Miyako-Odori **28** (Cherry Blossom Dance) held at the **Gion Kaburenjo Theater** (Gion Hanamikoji, Higashiyama-ku, tel. 075/561–1115). Miyako-Odori features musical presentations by geisha, who are dressed in their elaborate traditional kimonos and makeup. Next door to the theater is Gion Corner, where demonstrations of traditional performing arts are held nightly from March through November (*see* The Arts and Nightlife, below).

If you continue along Shijo-dori Avenue, you'll cross over the Kamogawa River and be on Pontocho-dori Avenue. Like Gion, this area is known for its nightlife and geisha entertainment. At the top (north) end of Pontocho-dori Avenue, the **Pontocho Kaburenjo Theater** presents geisha song-and-dance performances in the spring (May 1–May 24) and autumn (Oct. 15–Nov. 7). *Pontocho, Sanjo Sagaru, Nakagyo-ku, tel. 075/221–2025.*

Western Kyoto

Numbers in the margin correspond with points of interest on the Western Kyoto map.

This exploration starts at the northern part of western Kyoto, where the major attractions are located. Then, if you become tired or run out of time, you can cut short the tour and return to your hotel. We have chosen to begin this exploration at the Kitano Temmangu Shrine because it is a Kyoto landmark, but if you are short of time, you may want to begin at Daitokuji Temple.

To reach the Kitano Temmangu Shrine from downtown, take either bus #50 or bus #52 from downtown Kyoto and Kyoto Station. The rides take a little more than ½ hour. The **Kitano Temmangu Shrine** made history in about 942 when Michizane Sugawara was enshrined there. Previously the shrine had been dedicated to Tenjin, the god of thunder. Michizane had been a noted poet and politician, but when Emperor Godaigo ascended to the throne, Michizane was accused of treason and sent to exile on Kyushu, where he died. For decades afterward, Kyoto suffered inexplicable calamities. Then the answer came in a dream. The problem was Michizane's spirit; he would not rest until he had been pardoned. Because the dream identified Michizane with the god of thunder, Kitano Temmangu Shrine was dedicated to him. Furthermore, Michizane's rank as minister of the right was posthumously restored. When that was not enough, he was promoted to the higher position of minister of the left, and later to prime minister. The shrine was also the place where Hideyoshi Toyotomi held an elaborate tea party, inviting the whole of Kyoto to join him. Apart from unifying the warring clans of Japan and attempting to conquer Korea, Toyotomi is remembered in Kyoto as the man responsible for restoring many of the city's temples and shrines during the late 16th century. The shrine's present structure, by the way, dates from 1607. A large flea market is held on the shrine's grounds on the 25th of each month that has food stalls and an array of antiques, old kimonos, and other collectibles. *Bakurocho, Kamigyo-ku. Admission free. The plum garden is open in Feb. and Mar. Admission: ¥400 (includes powdered green tea). Open 5:30 AM–6 PM.*

About a five-minute walk north of Kitano is the **Hirano Shrine,** which actually consists of four shrine buildings dating from the 17th century. However, the shrine has a much older history. It was brought from Nagaoka (the previous capital) as one of the many shrines used to protect Kyoto (Heian-kyo) during its for-

Western Kyoto

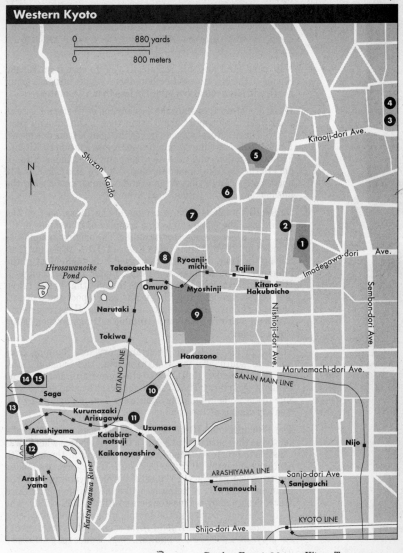

0   880 yards

0   800 meters

N

Shuzan Kaido

Kitaoji-dori Ave.

Hirosawanoike Pond

Takaoguchi

Ryoanji-michi

Tojiin

Kitano-Hakubaicho

Imadegawa-dori

Ave.

Sembon-dori Ave.

Omuro

Myoshinji

Narutaki

Tokiwa

Nishioji-dori Ave.

KITANO LINE

Hanazono

Marutamachi-dori Ave.

SAN-IN MAIN LINE

Saga

Kurumazaki
Arisugawa

Uzumasa

Katabira-
notsuji

Kaikonoyashiro

Nijo

Arashi-
yama

Katsuragawa River

ARASHIYAMA LINE

Sanjo-dori Ave.

Sanjoguchi

Yamanouchi

KYOTO LINE

Shijo-dori Ave.

mative days. The buildings are less the reason to visit here than the gardens, with their 80 varieties of cherry trees. *Miyamoto-cho 1, Hirano, Kita-ku. Admission free. Open 5 AM–5:30 PM June–Oct., 6 AM–5 PM Nov.–May.*

Now head for Daitokuji Temple. If you go east from Hirano Shrine to the bus stop on Sembon-dori Avenue, bus #206 going north will have you at Daitokuji in less than 10 minutes.

If you do not want to start the exploration of Western Kyoto at the Kitano Temmangu Shrine but instead with Daitokuji Temple, you have several ways to get to the temple from downtown Kyoto. Take the subway north from Kyoto Station to Kitaoji-Eki-mae Station, and take any bus going west along Kitaoji-dori to the Daitokuji-mae bus stop. You can also take bus #12 north up Horikawa-dori Avenue and disembark soon after the bus makes a left on Kitaoji-dori Avenue.

③ Daitokuji Temple is a large temple of the Rinzai sect of Zen Buddhism. The name refers to a complex of 24 temples in all, several of which are open to the public. The original temple was founded in 1319 by Priest Daito Kokushi (1282–1337), but fires during the Onin Civil Wars destroyed it in 1468. Most of the buildings you see today were built under the patronage of Hideyoshi Toyotomi. However, it is thought that Priest Ikkyu oversaw its development. Ikkyu was both a poet and a priest, and he certainly caused a few tongues to wag. He is reported to have said, "Brothels are more suitable settings for meditation than temples."

The layout of the temple is straightforward. Running from north to south are the Chokushi-mon, the Sanmon Gate, Butsuden (Buddha Hall), Hatto (Lecture Hall), and the Hojo (Abbots' Quarters). The 23 subtemples are located on the west side of these main buildings and were donated mainly by the wealthy vassals of Toyotomi.

The **Chokushi-mon** (Gate of Imperial Messengers) originally served as the south gate of Kyoto's Imperial Palace when it was constructed in 1590. Then, Empress Meisho in the mid-17th century bequeathed it to the Daitokuji. It is appreciated today for its curved-gable style, typical of the Momoyama period. The Sanmon triple gate is noteworthy for the addition of its third story, designed by tea master Sen-no-Rikyu (1521–1591), who is, by the way, buried in the temple grounds. *Daitokuji-cho, Murasakino, Kita-ku, Kyoto. Admission to different temples ranges from ¥300 to ¥400 adults. Temple hours vary between 8 and 5.*

④ Of all the sub-temples at this complex, **Daisen-in** is perhaps the most well known, especially for its excellent landscape paintings by the renowned Soami (1465–1523) and for its *karesansui* (dry-style) garden that some attribute to Soami and others to Kogaku Soko (1465–1548). The sand and stone represent the eternal aspects of nature, while the streams suggest the course of life. The single rock, once owned by Shogun Yoshimasa Ashikaga, may be seen as a ship. Be aware, though, that Daisen-in has become commercialized. *Admission: ¥400 adults, ¥300 students under 15. Open 9–5 (9–4:30 in winter).*

Another sub-temple open to the public is **Koto-in,** famous for its long, maple tree–lined approach and the single stone lantern that is central to the main garden. Not as popular as Daisen-in, it is often quiet and peaceful, as in **Ryogen-in,** still another sub-temple. Ryogen-in has five small gardens of moss and stone, one of which (on the north side) is the oldest in the Daitoku-ji. *Admission to each: ¥300. Open 9–5, 9–4:30 in winter (enter by 4).*

⑤ The best way to our next stop, **Kinkakuji Temple,** is to hop on bus #12 going west on Kitaoji-dori Avenue for a 10-minute ride to the Kinkakuji-mae bus stop.

For a retirement home, Kinkakuji Temple (Golden Pavilion) is pretty magnificent. Shogun Yoshimitsu Ashikaga (1358–1409) had it constructed in 1393 for the time when he quit politics (in 1394) to manage the affairs of state through the new shogun, his 10-year-old son. On Yoshimitsu's death, his son followed his father's wishes and converted the villa into a temple named Rokuonji. The structure is positioned, following the Shinden style of the Heian period, at the edge of the lake. The three-story pavilion is supported on pillars, extends over the pond, and is reflected in the calm waters. It is a beautiful sight, but it also was designed to convey its existence somewhere between heaven and earth. The pavilion was the shogun's political state-ment of his prestige and power. To underscore that statement, he had the ceiling of the third floor of the pavilion covered in gold leaf. Hence, not only the harmony and balance of the pavil-ion and its reflection, but also the richness of color shimmering in the light and in the water make Kinkakuji one of Kyoto's most powerful visions.

In 1950, a student-monk with metaphysical aspirations torched Kinkakuji and razed it to the ground. It was rebuilt in 1955 fol-lowing the original design, except that all three stories were covered with gold leaf (as had been the shogun's intention) in-stead of only the third-floor ceiling. Marveling at this pavilion, one finds it difficult to imagine the historical perspective of the time when Shogun Yoshimitsu Ashikaga lived out his golden years. The country was in turmoil, and Kyoto residents suf-fered severe famines and plagues that sometimes reached death tolls of 1,000 souls a day. *1-Kinkakuji-cho, Kita-ku. Ad-mission: ¥300 adults and older students, ¥200 junior high school students and younger. Open 9–5:30 (9–5 Oct.–Mar.).*

From Kinkakuji, walk back to the Kinkakuji-mae bus stop and take bus #12 or #59 south to the Ritsumeikan-Daigaku-mae bus **⑥** stop for the **Domoto Art Museum,** which exhibits paintings and sculpture by Insho Domoto, the 20th-century abstract artist. *Kami-yanagi-cho, Hirano, Kita-ku, tel. 075/463–2348. Admis-sion: ¥500 adults, ¥400 high school students, ¥200 junior high and younger students. Open 10–5. Closed Mon. and Dec. 29–Jan. 3.*

When you leave the Domoto Art Museum, either hop on the #12 or #59 bus, or walk for about 10 minutes going south; the **⑦** **Ryoanji Temple** will be on your right.

The garden at Ryoanji, rather than the temple, attracts visi-tors from all over the world. Knowing that the temple belongs to the Rinzai sect of Zen Buddhism helps one to appreciate the austere aesthetics of the garden. It is a dry (*kare sansui*) gar-den: just 15 rocks arranged in three groupings of seven, five, and three in gravel. From the temple's veranda, the proper viewing place, only 14 rocks can be seen at one time. Move slightly and another rock appears and one of the original 14 disappears. That's significant. In the Buddhist world, 15 is a number which denotes completeness. You must have a total view of the garden to make it a whole and meaningful experience.

Ideally, one would make a special trip out to Ryoanji in the morning before the crowds come, disturbing the contemplative scene. If you do need a moment or two to yourself, there is a small restaurant on the temple grounds near an ancient pond, where you can rest awhile with an expensive beer. *13 Goryoshita-machi, Ryoanji, Ukyo-ku. Admission: ¥350 adults, ¥200 junior high school students. Open 8–5 (8:30–4:30 Dec.–Feb.)*

From Ryoanji, it is about a mile farther south to Myoshinji Temple. En route there will be the **Ninnaji Temple** on the right. The temple was once the palace of Emperor Omuro, who started the building's construction in 896. Needless to say, nothing of that remains. The complex of buildings that stands today was rebuilt in the 17th century. There is an attractive five-story pagoda (built 1637), and the Main Hall, which was moved from the Imperial Palace, is also worth noting as a National Treasure, with its focus of worship, the Amida Buddha. *Admission: ¥350. Open 9–5.*

At Ninnaji, take the street veering to the left (southwest direction); within ½-mile you'll reach Myoshinji. Another option from Ryoanji is to take the #12 bus or #59 three stops south to Ninnaji and then change to bus #8 or bus #10.

Should you wish to see Japan's oldest bell (cast in 698), it hangs in the belfry near the South Gate of **Myoshinji Temple.** The temple complex is large; in all, it has some 40 structures, though only four are open to the public. Myoshinji was founded in the 14th century. When Emperor Hanazono died and his villa was converted into a temple, the work required so many laborers that a complex of buildings was built to house them. Thus, the temple complex began. Beware of the dragon on the ceiling of Myoshinji's Hatto (Lecture Hall). Known as the "Dragon Glaring in Eight Directions," it will be looking at you wherever you stand. *Admission: ¥400. Open 9–4.*

The other temple to visit is **Taizoin,** which was built in 1404; like the rest of the Myoshinji Temple complex, it suffered in the Onin War and had to be rebuilt. Taizoin has a famous painting by Sanraku Kano called *Four Sages of Mt. Shang,* recalling the four wise men who lived in isolation on a mountain to avoid the reign of destruction. The garden of Taizoin is gentle and quiet—a good place to rest. *Admission: ¥400. Open 9–5.*

Leave the temple complex by the south side and you can pick up the #61 or #62 bus; both go southwest to the Uzumasa Eigamura Movie Village. If, however, you have no interest in stopping off here—a visit will take at least two or three hours—continue on the bus to Koryuji Temple.

Uzumasa Eigamura Movie Village is Japan's equivalent of the United States' Hollywood. Had Kyoto been severely damaged in World War II, this would have been the place to see old Japan. Traditional country villages, ancient temples, and old-fashioned houses make up the stage sets, and if you are lucky, a couple of actors dressed as samurai will be snarling at each other, ready to draw their swords. It is a fine place to bring children. For adults, whether it is worth the time touring the facilities and visiting the museum depends on your interest in Japanese movies. *10 Hachigaoka-cho, Uzumasa-higashi, Ukyo-ku, tel. 075/881-7716. Admission: ¥1,800. Open 9–5 (9:30–4 in winter). Closed July 24–26, Dec. 21–Jan. 1.*

⑪ Koryuji Temple is a short walk south of Uzumasa Eigamura Movie Village. One of Kyoto's oldest temples, it was founded in 622 by Kawakatsu Hata in memory of Prince Shotoku (572–621). Shotoku, known for issuing the Seventeen-Article Constitution, was the first powerful advocate of Buddhism after it was introduced to Japan in 552. In the Hatto (Lecture) Hall of the main temple stand three statues, each a National Treasure. The center of worship is the seated figure of Buddha, flanked by the figures of the Thousand-Handed Kannon and Fukukenjaku-Kannon. In the rear hall (Taishido) is a wood statue of Prince Shotoku, which is thought to have been carved by him personally. Another statue of Shotoku in this hall was probably made when he was 16 years old.

In the temple's Treasure House (Reihoden), you'll find numerous works of art, many of which are National Treasures, including the most famous of all, the Miroku-Bosatsu. The statue has been declared Japan's number one National Treasure. This image of Buddha is the epitome of serene calmness, and of all the Buddhas that you see in Kyoto, this is likely to be the one that will most captivate your heart. No one knows when it was made, but it is thought to be from the 6th or 7th century, perhaps even carved by Shotoku himself. *Hachigaoka-cho, Uzumasa, Ukyo-ku. Admission: ¥500. Open 9–5 Mar.–Nov., 9–4:30 Dec.–Feb.*

From Koryuji, it is easy to head back into downtown Kyoto. Either take the bus back past the Movie Village to Hanazono JR Station, where the San-in Line will take you into Kyoto Station, or take the privately owned railway, the Keifuku Electric Railway Arashiyama Line, and go east to its last stop at Shijo Omiya. This stop is on Shijo-dori Avenue, where buses #201 or #203 will take you to Gion, or bus #26 will take you to Kyoto Station.

However, because we are so close to the area known as Arashiyama, we are going to take the Keifuku Electric Railway Arashiyama Line going west to Tenryuji Temple and the bamboo forests just to the north. This visit is a pleasant end to the day. You may get the chance to watch some cormorant fishing. If you decide to postpone this excursion until tomorrow, use the JR San-in Line from Kyoto Station to Saga Station, or use the Keifuku Electric Railway Arashiyama Station.

Arashiyama

The pleasure of Arashiyama, the westernmost part of Kyoto, is the same as it was a millennium ago. The gentle foothills of the mountains, covered with cherry and maple trees, are splendid, but it is the bamboo forests that really create the atmosphere of untroubled peace. It is no wonder that the aristocracy of feudal Japan liked to come here and leave behind the famine, riots, and political intrigue that plagued Kyoto with the decline of the Ashikaga Shogunate.

To the south of Arashiyama Station is the Oigawa River and the **⑫ Togetsukyo Bridge.** During the evening in July and August you can watch Ukai fishing from this bridge. Fishermen use cormorants to scoop up small sweetfish, which are attracted to the light from the flaming torches hung over the fisherman's boats. The cormorants would love to swallow the fish, but small rings around their necks prevent their appetites from being assuaged. After about five fish, the cormorant has more than his gullet can hold. Then the fisherman pulls the bird back on a string, makes the bird regurgitate his catch, and sends him back for more. The best way to watch this spectacle is to join one of the charter passenger boats. *Cost: ¥1,400 adults, ¥800 children. Reservations: Arashiyama Tausen, 14-4 Nakao-shita-cho, Arashiyama, Nishikyo-ku, tel. 075/861–1627. You may also contact Japan Travel Bureau (075/361–7241) or your hotel information desk.*

The temple to head for is Tenryuji. If you have arrived at Arashiyama Station, then walk north; if you have arrived on the JR line at Saga Station, then walk west.

⓭ Tenryuji Temple is for good reason known as the Temple of the Heavenly Dragon. Emperor Godaigo, who had successfully brought an end to the Kamakura Shogunate, was unable to hold on to his power. He was forced from his throne by Takauji Ashikaga. After Godaigo died, Takauji had twinges of conscience. That is when Priest Muso Kokushi had a dream in which a golden dragon rose from the nearby Oigawa River. He told the shogun about his dream and interpreted it to mean the spirit of Godaigo was not at peace. Worried that this was an ill omen, Takauji built Tenryuji in 1339 on the same spot where Godaigo had his favorite villa. Apparently that appeased the spirit of the late emperor. In the Hatto (Lecture) Hall, where today's monks meditate, a huge "Cloud Dragon" is painted on the ceiling. Now for the bad news. The temple was often ravaged by fire, and the current buildings are as recent as 1900; the painting of the dragon was rendered by 20th-century artist Shonen Suzuki. The garden of Tenryuji dates to the 14th century. It is noted for the arrangement of vertical stones in the large pond and for being one of the first to use "borrowed scenery," incorporating the mountains in the distance into the design of the garden. *68 Susukino-Baba-cho, Saga-Tenryu-ji, Ukyo-ku. Admission: ¥500 adults, ¥300 junior high school students and younger. Open 8:30–5:30 Apr.–Oct., 8:30–5 Nov.–Mar.*

One of the best ways to enjoy some contemplative peace is to walk the estate grounds of one of Japan's new elite—Denjiro Okochi, a renowned silent movie actor of samurai films. To reach his estate, leave the Tenryuji Temple and walk north on a **⓮** narrow street through a **bamboo forest**, one of the best you'll see in the Kyoto region. Bamboo forests offer a unique compo-**⓯** sure and tranquillity. The **Okochi Sanso Villa** will soon be in front of you, with its superb location. The views of Arashiyama and Kyoto are splendid, and on the grounds you are offered tea and cake while you absorb nature's pleasures. *8 Tabuchiyama-cho, Ogurayama, Saga Ukyo-ku, tel. 075/872–2233. Admission: ¥800. Open 9–5.*

Central Kyoto

Numbers in the margin correspond with points of interest on the central Kyoto map.

Exploration of central Kyoto follows tours of eastern and western Kyoto, because the sights here are likely to be convenient to your hotel and you can visit each sight individually rather than combining them into a single itinerary.

The two major places in this area to see are Nijo Castle and the Imperial Palace. Let's go to the Imperial Palace first, because that is one of the sights that requires permission. The easiest ways to reach the **Imperial Palace** are to take the subway to Imadegawa or to take the bus to the Karasuma-Imadegawa stop. You will join the tour at the Seishomon Gate entrance.

The palace was rebuilt on a smaller scale in 1855, and, in fact, was home only to two emperors, including the young Emperor Meiji before he moved his Imperial Household to Tokyo. On the 30-minute tour, you will only have a chance for a brief glimpse of the Shishinden Hall (where the inauguration of emperors and other important imperial ceremonies take place) and a visit to the gardens. Though a trip to the Imperial Palace is on most people's agenda, and despite the space it fills in downtown Kyoto, it perhaps holds less interest than do some of the older historic buildings in the city. *Admission free. To visit the Imperial Palace, arrive before 9:40 AM for the 10 AM guided tour in English. Present yourself, along with your passport, at the office of the Imperial Household Agency in the palace grounds. For the 2 PM guided tour in English, arrive by 1:40 PM. Sat. afternoon tours only on 1st and 3rd Sat. of the month; no tours Sun. Imperial Household Agency, Gyoen-nai, Kamigyo-ku, Kyoto, tel. 075/211–1211. Office open 9 AM–noon and 1 PM–4 PM weekdays, 9–noon Sat.*

If you have chosen to visit the Imperial Palace, **Nijojo Castle** is easily combined on the same trip. Take the bus going west along Marutamachi-dori Avenue for a couple of stops to Horikawa-dori Avenue, and then walk two blocks south along Horikawa-dori Avenue to Nijojo Castle.

Nijojo Castle was the local Kyoto address for the Tokugawa Shogunate. While it dominates central Kyoto, it is an intrusion, both politically and artistically. The man who built the castle in 1603, Ieyasu Tokugawa, did so to emphasize that political power had been completely removed from the emperor and that he alone determined the destiny of Japan. As if to make that statement stronger, he built and decorated his castle with blatant ostentation in order to cower the populace with his wealth and power. Such overt displays were antithetical to the refined restraint of Kyoto's aristocracy.

Ieyasu Tokugawa had risen to power through skillful politics and treachery. His military might was unassailable, and that is probably why his Kyoto castle had relatively modest exterior defenses. However, as he well knew, defense against treachery is never certain. The interior of the castle was built with that in mind. Each building had concealed rooms where bodyguards could maintain a watchful eye for potential assassins, and the corridors had a built-in squeaking system, so no one could walk in the building without announcing his presence. Rooms were locked only from the inside, so no one from the outer rooms could gain access to the inner rooms without admittance. The outer rooms were kept for visitors of low rank and were adorned with garish paintings that would impress them. The inner rooms were for the important lords, whom the shogun

○ –shopping
streets

Bet. Sanjo-dori
Ave & Shijo-
dori

Bet. Higashio-
ji-dout
Karasuma
Station

Shenmojen-
dori: antiques

Porta-
Under-
ground
Shopping

Central Kyoto

0   440 yards

0   400 meters

N

Kuramaguchi

Kamogawa River

Imadegawa-dori Ave.

Imadegawa

Kawaramachi-dori Ave.

Sembon-dori Ave.

Horikawa-dori Ave.

Karasuma-dori Ave.

Marutamachi-dori Ave.

Marutamachi

Oike

Oike-dori Ave.

Nijo

SAN-IN MAIN LINE

Sanjo-dori Ave.

Hankyu-Omiya

Karasuma

Shijo-dori Ave.

Shijo-Omiya   Shijo

Omiya-dori Ave.

Horikawa-dori Ave.

Karasuma-dori Ave.

Kawaramachi-dori Ave.

Kamogawa River

Gojo-dori Ave.

Tambaguchi

Gojo

Shichijo-dori Ave.

TOKAIDO   MAIN LINE

SHINKANSEN   Hachijo-dori Ave.   **Kyoto
Station**

would impress with the refined, tasteful paintings of the Kano school.

The opulence and grandeur of the castle was, in many ways, a snub to the emperor. It relegated the emperor and his palace to insignificance, and the Tokugawa family even appointed a governor to manage the emperor and the imperial family. The Tokugawa shoguns were rarely in Kyoto. Ieyasu stayed in the castle three times, the second shogun twice, including the time in 1626 when the emperor, Emperor Gomizuno-o, was granted an audience. After that, for the next 224 years, no Tokugawa shogun came to Kyoto. The castle started to fall into disrepair and neglect. Only when the Tokugawa Shogunate was under pressure from a failing economy, and international pressure developed to open Japan to trade, did the 14th shogun, Iemochi Tokugawa (1846–1866), come to Kyoto to confer with the emperor. The emperor told the shogun to rid Japan of foreigners, but Iemochi did not have the strength. As the shogun's power continued to wane, the 15th and last shogun, Keiki Tokugawa (1837–1913), spent most of his time in Nijojo Castle. Here he resigned, and the imperial decree was issued that abolished the shogunate after 264 years of rule.

After the Meiji Restoration (1868), Nijojo Castle became the Kyoto Prefectural Office until 1884; during that time, it suffered from acts of vandalism. Since 1939, the castle has belonged to the city of Kyoto, and considerable restoration work has been completed.

Entrance to the castle is through the impressive **Karamon** (Chinese) **Gate.** Notice that one must turn right and left at sharp angles to make this entrance—a common attribute of Japanese castles designed to slow the advance of any attacker. From the Karamon Gate, the carriageway leads to the **Ninomaru** (Second Inner) **Palace.** The five buildings of the palace are divided into many chambers. The outer buildings were for visits by men of lowly rank, the inner ones for higher ranks. The most notable room, the **Ohiroma Hall,** is easy to recognize. In the room, figures in costume reconstruct the occasion when Keiki Tokugawa returned the power of government to the emperor. This spacious hall was where, in the early 17th century, the shogun would sit on a raised throne to greet important visitors seated below him. The sliding screens of this room have magnificent paintings of forest scenes.

As impressive as the Ninomaru Palace is the garden designed by the landscaper Kobori Enshu shortly before Emperor Gomizuno-o's visit in 1626. Notice the crane and tortoise islands flanking the center island (the land of paradise). The symbolic meaning is clear: strength and longevity. The garden was originally designed with no deciduous, for the shogun did not wish to be reminded of the transitory nature of life by autumn's falling leaves.

The other major building on the grounds is the **Honmaru Palace** but, because it is a replacement for the original that burned down in the 18th century, Honmaru holds less interest than Ninomaru. *Horikawa Nishi-iru, Nijo-dori, Nakagyo-ku, tel. 075/841–0096. Admission: ¥500 adults, ¥190 children under 12. Open: 8:45–5 (enter by 4). Closed Dec. 26–Jan. 4.*

If, after the overt opulence and blatant use of wealth demonstrated by Nijojo Castle, you feel in need of some refinement,

❸ the **Urasenke Center** offers an introduction to the tea ceremony. To get there requires taking bus #9 north along Horikawa-dori Avenue. The Chado Tea Ceremony is a demonstration on preparing and serving tea; in this demonstration, one recognizes that *chado*, which may be loosely translated as "the way of tea," means more than just serving tea: It is an aesthetic experience designed to help achieve a profound understanding of life's basic tenets through serenity and harmony. *Urasenke Center, Horikawa-dori, Teranouchi-agaru, Kamikyo-ku, tel. 075/431–3111 (main office). Admission: ¥1,000. Demonstrations at 1:30 and 3 Thurs. Requests to attend the demonstration should be made before midday by calling Urasenke's foreign affairs division, tel. 075/451–8516. You may also request a short course in the preparation and serving of tea. These are given Thurs. 10–11:30, except Jan., Aug., Dec., and on national holidays. Reservations are made by calling the foreign affairs division at the number above. Course: ¥1,500.*

For another change of pace, if you have interest in traditional Japanese silk weaving, visit the Nishijin silk weaving district south from the Urasenke Center on Horikawa-dori Avenue at the corner of Imadegawa-dori Avenue. To get to this district,
❹ take the #9 bus. At the **Nishijin Textile Center** here, demonstrations are given of age-old weaving techniques, and fashion shows and special exhibitions are presented. On the mezzanine, you can buy kimonos and gift items, such as *happi* (workmen's) coats, and silk purses. *Horikawa-dori, Imadegawa-minami-iru, Kamigyo-ku, tel. 075/451–9231. Admission free. Open 9–5.*

From the Urasenke Center, the Nishijin Textile Center, or Nijojo Castle, use the #9 bus down (south) Horikawa-dori Avenue. Disembark at the Kyoto Tokyu Hotel. Across from the
❺ Tokyu Hotel is the **Kyoto Costume Museum.** It is on the fifth floor of the Izutsu Building, at the intersection of Horikawa and Shinhanayacho. You may want to pop in here to see the range of fashion that starts in the pre-Nara era and works up through the historical eras to the Meiji period. It is one of the best of its kind and, in its own way, gives an account of the history of Japan. Exhibitions change twice a year, with each exhibition highlighting a specific period in Japanese history. *Izutsu Building, Shimogyo-ku, tel. 075/351–6750. Admission: ¥300. Open 9–5. Closed Sun.*

❻
❼ The last major attractions in central Kyoto are the **Nishi-Honganji Temple** and the **Higashi-Honganji Temple.** They were originally just one temple, until the early 17th century. Then Ieyasu Tokugawa took advantage of a rift among the Jodo-shinshu sect of Buddhism and, to diminish its power, split them apart into two different factions. The original faction has the west temple, Nishi-Honganji, and the latter faction the eastern temple, Higashi-Honganji. To reach the two temples, walk south on Horikawa-dori Avenue from the Kyoto Costume Museum and cross the street.

While the rebuilt (1895) structure of Higashi-Honganji is the largest wood structure in Japan, it contains fewer historical objects of interest than does its rival temple, Nishi-Honganji, where many of the buildings were brought from Hideyoshi Toyotomi's Jurakudai Palace in Kyoto and from Fushimijo Castle, which Ieyasu Tokugawa had dismantled outside of Kyoto in the attempt to erase the memory of his predecessor.

Hideyoshi Toyotomi was quite a man. Though most of the work in unifying Japan was accomplished by the warrior Nobunaga Oda (he was ambushed a year after defeating the monks on Mt. Hiei), it was Hideyoshi who completed the job. Not only did he stop civil strife, but he also restored the arts. For a brief period (1582–1598), Japan entered one of the most colorful (and short-est) periods of its history. How Hideyoshi achieved his feats is not exactly known. One legend relates that he was the son of the emperor's concubine. She had been much admired by a man to whom the emperor owed a favor, so the emperor gave the concubine to him. Unknown to either of the men, she was soon with child, namely, Hideyoshi. In fact, Hideyoshi was brought up as a farmer's son. His nickname was Saru-san (Mr. Monkey), because he was small and ugly. Whatever his origins (he changed his names frequently), he brought peace to Japan.

Because much of what was dear to Hideyoshi Toyotomi was de-stroyed by the Tokugawas, it is only at Nishi-Honganji that one can see the artistic works closely associated with his personal life, including the great Karamon (Chinese) Gate brought from Fushimijo Castle, the Dashoin Hall (also from Fushimijo), and the Noh stage from Jurakudai Palace.

Nishi-Honganji Temple. Visits to some of the buildings are per-mitted four times a day on application from the temple office. Prior to leaving home, write to the temple (enclosing a self-ad-dressed envelope and an international reply coupon) at Shichijo-Agaru, Horikawa-dori, Shimogyo-ku, Kyoto. Give your name, the number of people in your party, and the day and time you would like to visit. You can also phone for an ap-pointment after you arrive in Kyoto: tel. 075/371–5181; be-cause you'll probably experience language problems, ask your hotel to make the arrangements for you.

Tours of Daishoin Hall (in Japanese) are given weekdays at 10, 11, 1:30, and 2:30, and on Sat. at 10 and 11. However, check in advance to be sure your visit doesn't coincide with a holiday ceremony, when tours are automatically canceled. Shichijo-agaru, Horikawa-dori, Shimogyo-ku. Admission free. Open 5:30 AM–5:30 PM Mar., Apr., Sept., Oct.; 5:30 AM–6 PM May, June, July, Aug.; 6 AM–5 PM Nov., Dec., Jan., Feb. Closed Sat. afternoon, Sun., and national holidays.

Higashi-Honganji Temple: Shichijo-agaru, Karasuma-dori, Shimogyo-ku. Admission free. Open daily 9–4.

8 From Nishi-Honganji it is a 10-minute walk southeast to Kyoto Station. However, if you have the time, visit the **Toji Temple,** one of Kyoto's oldest temples. Leave Nishi-Honganji by the west exit and take bus #207 south on Omiya-dori. Get off at the Toji-higashimon-mae bus stop, and Toji Temple will be across the street.

Toji Temple was established by imperial edict in 796. It was called Kyo-o-gokokuji and was built to guard the city. It was one of the two temples that Emperor Kammu permitted to be built in the city. He had had enough of the powerful Buddhists during his days in Nara. The temple was later given to Priest Kukai (Kobo Daishi), who began the Shingon sect of Buddhism; Toji became one of Kyoto's most important temples.

Fires and battles during the 16th century destroyed the tem-ple's buildings, but many were rebuilt, including the Kondo

(Main Hall) in 1603. However, the Kodo (Lecture) Hall has managed to survive the ravages of war since it was built in 1491. Inside this hall are 15 original statues of Buddhist gods that were carved in the 8th and 9th centuries. The eye-catching building here is the 180-foot, five-story pagoda, reconstructed in 1695.

An interesting time to visit the temple is on the 21st of each month, when a flea market, known locally as Kobo-san, is held. Antique kimonos, fans, and other memorabilia can sometimes be found at bargain prices, if you know your way around the savvy dealers. Many elderly people flock to the temple on this day to pray to Kobo Daishi, the temple's founder, and to shop. *1 Kujo-cho. Admission (to the main buildings): ¥400 adults, ¥350 high school students, ¥250 children under 15. Open 9–4:30.*

This concludes the exploration of central Kyoto. From Toji Temple, it is about a 10-minute walk east to the central exit of JR Kyoto Station; one can also take the Kinki Nippon Electric train at Toji Station for the one-stop ride to Kyoto Station.

Northern Kyoto

In the northern suburbs of Kyoto are Mt. Hiei and Ohara. Our first destination is Ohara, for several centuries a sleepy Kyoto backwater surrounded by mountains. Although it is now catching up with modernity, it still has a feeling of old Japan, with several temples that deserve visiting. To reach this area, take either the #17 or the #18 Kyoto bus (not city bus) from Kyoto Station and get out at Ohara bus stop. This is a long bus ride, about 90 minutes, that costs ¥480.

From the bus station, the road heading northeast leads to **Sanzen-in Temple,** a small temple of the Tendai sect. It was founded by a renowned priest, Dengyo-Daishi (767–822). The Main Hall was built by Priest Eshin (942–1017), who probably carved the temple's Amida Buddha (though some say it was carved 100 years after Eshin's death). Flanked by the two disciples, Daiseishi and Kannon, the statue is a remarkable piece of work because, rather than being the bountiful Amida, it displays much more the omnipotence of Amida. Although Eshin was not really a master sculptor, this statue possibly reflects Eshin's belief that, contrary to the prevailing belief of the Heian aristocracy that salvation could be achieved through one's own actions, salvation could be achieved only through Amida's limitless mercy. The statue is in the Hondo (Main Hall), itself an ancient building from the 12th century. Unusual for a Buddhist temple, it faces east and not south. Note its ceiling. The painting depicts the descent of Amida accompanied by 25 bodhisattvas to welcome the believer.

Not only is the temple worth visiting, but the grounds are also delightful. Full of maple trees, the gardens are serene in any season. During autumn, the colors are magnificent, and the approach to the temple up a gentle slope enhances the anticipation for the burned gold trees guarding the old, weathered temple. *Ragoin-cho, Ohara, Sakyo-ku. Admission: ¥500 adults, ¥300 senior and junior high school students. Open 8:30–5 (8:30–4:30 in winter).*

Two hundred yards from Sanzen-in is the small, little-fre-
quented **Jikko-in Temple,** where one can sit, relax, and drink
powdered green tea. To enter, ring the gong on the outside of
the gate, and then wander through the carefully cultivated garden. *Admission: ¥500. Open 9–5.*

On the other side of Ohara and the Takanogawa River is **Jakko-
in,** a temple to touch the heart. To reach there, walk back to the
Ohara bus stop and take the road leading to the northwest. In
April 1185, the Taira clan met its end in a naval battle against
the Minamoto clan. For two years, Yoshitsune Minamoto had
been gaining the upper hand in the battles, and this battle was
final. The Minamotos slaughtered the clan, making the Inland
Sea run red with Taira blood. Recognizing that all was lost, the
Taira women drowned themselves, taking with them the young
infant Emperor Antoku. His mother, Kenreimonin, too, leapt
into the sea, but Minamoto soldiers snagged her hair with a
grappling hook and hauled her back on board their ship. She
was the sole surviving member of the Taira clan. At 29, she was
beautiful.

Taken back to Kyoto, Kenreimonin shaved her beautiful head
and became a nun. First, she had a small hut at Chorakuji (*see*
Exploring Western Kyoto, above), and when that collapsed in
an earthquake, she was accepted at Jakko-in Temple. She was
given a 10-foot-square cell made of brushwood and thatch, and
she was left with images of her drowning son and her massacred relatives. Here she lived in solitude and sadness until, 27
years later, death ended her memories and took away the last
of the Taira. Her mausoleum is in the temple grounds.

When Kenreimonin came to Jakko-in, it was far removed from
Kyoto. Now Kyoto's sprawl reaches this far out, but the temple, hidden in trees, is still a place of solitude and peace, and a
sanctuary for nuns. It is easy to relive the experience eight centuries ago, when Kenreimonin walked up the tree-shrouded
path to the temple with the autumn drizzle falling and reflecting her tears. *Admission: ¥500. Open 9–5 (10–4:30 in winter).*

The next stop is Mt. Hiei. Take the Kyoto bus (#16, #17, or #18)
down the main highway, Route 367, to the Yase-Yuenchi bus
stop, next to the Yaseyuen Train Station. You'll see the entrance to the cable car on your left. It departs every 30 minutes,
and you can transfer to the ropeway at Hiei for the remaining
distance to the top. At the summit is an observatory offering
panoramic views of the mountains and of Lake Biwa. *Admission: ¥300. Open 9–6; 9–5 Oct.–Mar. (During midsummer,
observatory stays open until 9.)*

From the observatory, a serpentine mountain path leads to the
Enryakuji Temple. It was, and still is, a most important center
of Buddhism. At one time, it consisted of 3,000 buildings and
had its own standing army. That was its downfall. Enryakuji
really began in 788. Emperor Kammu, the founding father of
Kyoto, requested Priest Saicho (767–822) to establish a temple
on Mt. Hiei to protect the area (including Nagaoka, which was
the current capital) from the evil spirits. Demons and evil spirits were thought to come from the northeast, and Mt. Hiei was
a natural barrier between the fledgling city and the northeastern Kimmon (Devil's Gate), where devils would pass. The tem-

ple's monks were to serve as lookouts and, through their faith, keep evil at bay.

The temple grew, and, because neither women nor police were allowed on its mountaintop sanctuary, criminals also flocked there, ostensibly to seek salvation. By the 11th century, the temple had formed its own army to secure order on its estate. In time, this army grew and became stronger than that of most feudal lords. The power of the Enryakuji threatened Kyoto. No imperial army could manage a war without the support of Enryakuji, and when there was no war, Enryakuji's armies would burn and slaughter monks of rival Buddhist sects. Not until the 16th century was there a force strong enough to assault the temple, though many had tried. With the accusations that the monks had concubines and never read the sutras, Nobunaga Oda (1534–1582), the general who unified Japan by ending the Onin Wars, attacked the monastery in 1571 to rid it of its evil. In the battle, not only were monks killed, but also most of the buildings were destroyed. What structures we see today were built in the 17th century.

Enryakuji is divided into three precincts: the Eastern Precinct, where the main building in the complex, the Konponchudo, stands; the Western Precinct, with the oldest building, the Shakado; and the Yokawa district, a few miles north. The Konponchudo dates to 1642, and its dark, cavernous interior quickly conveys the sense of mysticism for which the esoteric Tendai sect is known. Giant pillars and a coffered ceiling give shelter to the central altar, surrounded with religious images and sacred objects. The ornate lanterns that hang before the altar are said to have been lit by Saicho himself and have never been extinguished throughout the centuries.

The Western precinct is where Saicho founded his temple and where he is buried. An incense burner wafts smoke before his tomb, which lies in a small hollow. The peaceful atmosphere of the cedar trees surrounding the main structures (Jodoin Temple, Ninaido Hall, and Shakado Hall) offers an imitation of the essence of the life of a Tendai Buddhist monk, who has devoted his life to the esoteric. Enryakuji is still an important training ground for Buddhism, on a par with the temples at Koyasan. One comes to visit here because of the feeling of profound religious significance, rather than for the particular buildings. It is experiential, and, though it's only a twentieth of its original size, one is awed by the magnitude of the temple complex and the commitment to esoteric pursuits. *4220 Sakamoto Honhachi, Otsu-shi. Admission: ¥400 adults, ¥250 12–18-year-olds. Open 8:30–4:30, 9–4 Dec.–Mar.*

Additional Attractions

Historical Buildings and Sights

The following lists include additional places of interest in Kyoto that were not covered in the preceding exploring tours:**Katsura Detached Villa.** Katsura Detached Villa is considered the epitome of cultivated Shoin architecture and garden design. Built in the 17th century for Prince Toshihito, brother of Emperor Goyozei, it is charmingly located on the banks of the Katsuragawa River, with peaceful views of Arashiyama and the Kameyama Hills. Perhaps more than anywhere else in the area, the setting is the most perfect example of Japanese integration of nature and architecture. The villa is fairly remote from other historical sites. You should allow an entire morning for your visit.

Although the villa was built over several decades, beginning in 1620, with new additions over time, the overall architectural effect is one of elegant harmony, thanks to the faultless craftsmanship and the meticulous structural details. The main building includes the Nakashoin, with three apartments containing nature paintings by the Kano family of artists, and the Hall for Imperial Visits, with decorations made from different kinds of rare wood, including sandalwood and ebony.

The garden has several rustic teahouses alongside a central pond. The names of these teahouses—such as the Tower of Moonlit Waves and the Hut of Smiling Thoughts—conjure up the physical control and delicate aesthetics of the tea ceremony.

Katsura Detached Villa requires special permission for a visit. To obtain this permission, applications must be made by mail or telephone at least a week in advance. Application forms are available at JNTO offices throughout the world. You will need to enclose a self-addressed envelope and an international reply coupon. Send the application to the Imperial Household Agency (Kyoto Gyoen Nai, Kamigyo-ku, Kyoto, tel. 075/211-1211). After you have received permission, you must pick up the permit the day before your scheduled visit from the Imperial Palace. The office is open 9–noon and 1–4 in the afternoon on weekdays; 9–noon on Saturdays. You will need your passport to pick up your permit, and you must be at least 20 years of age. The time of your tour will be stated, and you must not be late. The tour is in Japanese only, although a videotape introducing various aspects of the garden in English is shown in the waiting room before each tour begins. *Katsura Shimizu-cho, Ukyo-ku, tel. 075/381-2029. Admission free. Tours weekdays at 10 and 2, Sat. at 10. Closed Sun., national holidays, and Dec. 25–Jan. 5.*

Getting There To reach the villa, take the Hankyu Railway Line from Kyoto's Hankyu Kawara-machi Station to Katsura Station, and then walk 10 minutes to the villa.

Shugakuin Imperial Villa. Located in northeastern Kyoto, this villa consists of a complex of three palaces. The Upper and Lower Villa were built in the 17th century by the Tokugawa family to entertain the emperor. The Middle Villa was added later as a palace home for Princess Ake, daughter of the emperor. When she decided that a nun's life was her calling, the villa was transformed into a temple. The most pleasant aspects of a visit here are the grounds and the panoramic views from the Upper Villa.

Special permission is required to visit the villa. Follow the same instructions for permission as for the Katsura Detached Villa (*see* above.) *Shugakuin Muromachi, Sakyo-ku. Admission free. Tours (in Japanese only) at 9, 10, 11; extra tours 1 and 3 Sat. Closed Sun., national holidays, and Dec. 25– Jan. 5.*

This villa may be visited on the way back from Mt. Hiei by taking the Eizan Railway from Yase Yuen Station to Shugakuin Station; the villa is a 15-minute walk from the station. If you come from downtown Kyoto, the trip takes an hour on bus #5 from Kyoto Station, or 20 minutes by Keifuku Eizan train from Demachi-Yanagi station, north of Imadegawa beside the Kamogawa River.

Temples and Shrines

Byodo-in Temple. Located to the south of Kyoto in Uji City, the temple was originally the private villa of a 10th-century "prime minister" who was a member of the influential Fujiwara family. The Amida-do, also known as the Phoenix Hall, was built in the 11th century by the Fujiwaras and is still considered one of Japan's most beautiful religious buildings, where heaven is brought close to earth. There is also a magnificent statue of a seated Buddha by one of Japan's most famous 11th-century sculptors, Jocho. To reach the temple, take the JR train to Uji Station; from there, the temple is a 12-minute walk. Uji is a famous tea-producing district, and the slope up the temple is lined with tea shops where you can sample the finest green tea and perhaps pick up a small package to take home. *Ujirenge, Uji-shi, tel. 0774/21–2861. Admission: ¥400 adults, ¥200 children 12–15, ¥150 children 6–12. Open 8:30–5 Mar.–Nov. (9–4 in winter).*

Daigoji Temple. Located in Yamashina, a suburb southeast of Kyoto, Daigoji was founded in 874. Over the succeeding centuries, other buildings were added, and its gardens expanded. Its five-story pagoda, whose origin dates from 951, is reputed to be the oldest existing structure in Kyoto. By the late-16th century, the temple had begun to decline in importance and showed signs of neglect. Then Hideyoshi Toyotomi paid a visit one April, when the temple's famous cherry trees were in blossom. Hideyoshi ordered the temple restored. Be sure also to see the paintings by the Kano school in the smaller Samboin Temple. To reach Daigoji, take the Kyoto City Bus Higashi 9 or the Keihan Bus #12 from Sanjo Keihan, and disembark at the Daigo-Samboin stop. The ride takes about 40 minutes. *22 Higashi Uji-cho, Fushimi-ku. Admission: ¥500 adults, ¥250 children under 12 years. Open 9–5 (9–4 in winter).*

Fushimi-Inari Taisha Shrine. This is one of Kyoto's oldest and most revered shrines. The Fushimi-Inari is dedicated to the goddesses of agriculture (rice and rice wine) and prosperity. It also serves as the headquarters for all the 40,000 shrines representing Inari. The shrine is noted for its bronze foxes and for some 10,000 small torii arches, donated by the thankful, which stand on the hill behind the structure. To reach the shrine, use the JR train on the Nara Line. If you are coming from Tofukuji, join the JR train at Tofukuji Station and journey for one stop to the south (toward Nara). *68 Fukakusa Yabunouchi-cho, Fushimi-ku. Admission free. Open sunrise–sunset.*

Kamigamo Jinja Shrine. Along with its sister shrine, the Shimogamo Jinja Shrine (further south on the Kamogawa River), Kamigamo was built by a legendary warrior named Kamo. Such is Kamo's fame that even the river that flows by the shrine and through the center of Kyoto bears his name. However, Kamigamo has always been associated with Wakeikazuchi, a god of thunder, rain, and fertility. Indeed, until 1212, a virgin from the imperial household was always in residence at the shrine. Now the shrine is famous for its Aoi (Hollyhock) Festival, which started in the 6th century when people thought that the Kamigamo deities were angry at being neglected. Now held every May 15, the festival consists of 500 people wearing Heian-period costumes riding on horseback or in ox-drawn carriages from the Imperial Palace to Shimogamo and then to Kamigamo. *339 Motoyama. Admission free. Open 9–4:30.*

Tofukuji Temple. Located southeast of Kyoto Station, this Zen temple of the Rinzai sect was established in 1236. In all, two dozen subtemples and the main temple comprise the temple complex, which ranks as one of the most important Zen temples in Kyoto, along with the Myoshinji and Daitokuji temples. The autumn is an especially fine time for visiting, when the burnished colors of the maple trees add to the pleasure of the gardens. To reach Tofukuji, either take bus #208 from Kyoto Station to the temple or take either the JR train on the Nara Line or the Keihan train to Tofukuji Station; from either it is a 15-minute walk to the temple. You may want to combine a visit here with the Fushimi-Inari Taisha Shrine situated farther south. *Honmachi, 15-chome, Higashiyama-ku. Admission: ¥300 adults, ¥200 junior high and elementary school students. Open 9–4.*

Shopping

Temples, shrines, gardens, and the quintessential elements of Japanese culture are all part of Kyoto's attractions, but none of these can be brought home, except in photographs. What can be taken back, however, are mementos (*omiyage*)—tangible gifts for which this city is famous. The ancient craftsmen of Kyoto served the imperial court for more than 1,000 years. In Japan, the prefix *kyo-* before a craft is synonymous with fine craftsmanship. The crafts of Kyoto are known throughout the world for their superb artistry and refinement.

Kyo-ningyo are the exquisite display dolls that have been made in Kyoto since the 9th century. Constructed of wood coated with white shell paste and clothed in elaborate miniature patterned silk brocades, Kyoto dolls are considered the finest in Japan. Kyoto is also known for fine ceramic dolls.

Kyo-shikki refers to Kyoto lacquer ware, which also has its roots in the 9th century. The making of lacquer ware, adopted from the Chinese, is a delicate process requiring patience and skill. Finished lacquer-ware products range from furniture to spoons and bowls, which are carved from cypress, cedar, or horse-chestnut wood. These products have a brilliant luster, and some designs are decorated with gold leaf and inlaid mother-of-pearl.

Kyo-sensu are embellished folding fans used as accoutrements in the Noh play, the tea ceremony, and Japanese dance. They also have a practical use—to ward off heat. Unlike other Japanese crafts, which have their origin in Tang Dynasty China, the folding fan originated in Kyoto.

Kyo-yaki is the general term used for ceramics made in local kilns; the most popular ware is from Kyoto's Kiyomizu district. Often colorfully hand-painted in blue, red, and green on white, these elegantly shaped teacups, bowls, and vases are thrown on potters' wheels located in the Kiyomizu district and in Kiyomizu-danchi in Yamashina. Streets leading up to

Kiyomizudera Temple—Chawanzaka, Sannenzaka, and Nin-nenzaka—are sprinkled with kyo-yaki shops.

Kyo-yuzen is a paste-resistant silk-dyeing technique developed by 17th-century dyer Yuzen Miyazaki. Fantastic designs are created on plain white silk pieces through the process of either *tegaki yuzen* (hand-painting) or *kata yuzen* (stencil).

Nishijin-ori is the weaving of silk. Nishijin refers to a Kyoto district producing the best silk textiles in all of Japan, used to make kimonos. Walk along the narrow backstreets of Nishijin and hear the persistently rhythmic sound of looms.

Keep in mind that most shops slide their doors open at 10. Most shopkeepers partake of the morning ritual of sweeping and watering the entrance to welcome the morning's first customers. Shops lock up at 6 or 7 in the evening. Usually, once a week shops remain closed. As Sunday is a big shopping day for the Japanese, most stores remain open on this day.

The traditional greeting of a shopkeeper to a customer is *oideyasu*, voiced in a lilting Kyoto dialect with the required bowing of the head. When a customer makes a purchase, the shopkeeper will respond with *ookini*, a smile, and a bow. Take notice of the careful effort and adroitness with which purchases are wrapped; it is an art in itself. Also, the clicking of the abacus rather than the clanging of a cash register can still be heard in many Kyoto shops.

American Express, MasterCard, and Visa are widely accepted, as are traveler's checks.

Kyoto attracts more than 40 million visitors a year, so residents are used to strangers among them. But they are not jaded or nonchalant, and they make every effort to make the visitor from abroad feel comfortable. Taxi drivers and shopkeepers alike often make an effort to converse in English, with varying degrees of competence.

Begin your shopping spree by visiting the **Museum of Traditional Industry**, in Okazaki Park (*see above*), to get an idea of the variety and quality of crafts available in Kyoto. The **Kyoto Craft Center** on Shijo in Gion offers two floors of both contemporary and traditional crafts for sale in a modern setting. *Shijo-dori, Gion-machi, Higashiyama-ku, tel. 075/561–9660. Open 10–6. Closed Wed.*

The **Kyoto Handicraft Center** is a seven-story shopping emporium offering everything from tape decks and pearl necklaces to porcelains and lacquer, most of which are designed to appeal to tourists. It's a good place to compare prices and grab last-minute souvenirs. *Kumano Jinja Higashi, Sakyo-ku, tel. 075/761–5080. Open 9:30–6, 9:30–5:30 Dec.–Feb. Closed Dec. 31–Jan. 3.*

Shopping Districts

Compared with sprawling Tokyo, Kyoto is compact and relatively easy to find your way around in. Major shops for tourists and natives alike line both sides of **Shijo-dori Avenue,** which runs east–west, and **Kawaramachi-dori Avenue,** running north–south. Concentrate on Shijo-dori Avenue, between Yasaka Jinja Shrine and Karasuma Station, and Kawaramachi-dori Avenue between Sanjo-dori Avenue and Shijo-dori Avenue.

Shin-Kyogoku, a covered arcade running parallel to Kawaramachi-dori Avenue, is another general-purpose shopping area with many souvenir shops.

Roads leading to Kiyomizudera Temple are steep inclines, yet the steepness is hardly noticed because of the alluring shops that line the entire way to the temple. Be sure to peek into these shops for unique gifts. Food shops offer sample morsels, and tea shops offer complimentary cups of tea.

Whereas the shopping districts above are traditional in atmosphere, Kyoto's latest shopping "district" is the modern underground arcade, **Porta,** at Kyoto Station. More than 200 shops and restaurants can be found in this sprawling, subterranean arcade.

Gift Ideas

Art and Antiques **Shinmonzen-dori** holds the key to shopping for art and antiques in Kyoto. It is an unpretentious little street of two-story wood buildings that is lined with telephone and electricity poles between Higashioji-dori Avenue and Hanamikoji-dori Avenue, just north of Gion. What gives the street away as a treasure trove are the large credit-card signs jutting out from the shops. There are no fewer than 17 shops specializing in scrolls, *netsuke* (small carved figures attached to Japanese clothing), lacquer, bronze, wood-block prints, paintings, and antiques. Shop with confidence, because shopkeepers are trustworthy and goods are authentic. Pick up a copy of the pamphlet *Shinmonzen Street Shopping Guide* from your hotel or from the Tourist Information Center.

Nawate-dori, between Shijo-dori and Sanjo-dori, is noted for fine antique textiles, ceramics, and paintings.

Teramachi-dori, between Oike-dori and Marutamachi, is known for antiques of all kinds, and tea-ceremony utensils.

Bamboo The Japanese hope for their sons and daughters to be as strong and flexible as bamboo. Around many Japanese homes are small bamboo groves, for the deep-rooted plant has the ability to withstand earthquakes. On the other hand, bamboo is so flexible that it bends into innumerable shapes. The entire city of Kyoto is surrounded by vast bamboo groves. Bamboo is carefully cut and dried for several months before being stripped and woven into baskets and vases.

Kagoshin is a historic shop that has made bamboo baskets since 1862. Only the best varieties of bamboo are used in this fiercely proud little shop. *Ohashi-higashi, Sanjo-dori, Higashiyamaku, tel. 075/771–0209. Open 9–6. Closed Sun. and holidays.*

Ceramics **Tachikichi,** on Shijo-dori west of Kawaramachi, has four floors of contemporary and traditional ceramics and the best reputation in town. *Shijo-Tominokoji, Nakagyo-ku, tel. 075/211–3143. Open 10–7. Closed Wed.*

Asahi-do, located in the heart of the pottery district near Kiyomizudera Temple, specializes in Kyoto-style hand-painted porcelains, and a variety of other ceramics. *1–280 Kiyomizu,*

*Higashiyama-ku, tel. 075/531–2181. Open 8:30–6 Mon.–Sat.,
Sun. 9–6.*

Dolls Dolls were first used in Japan in the purification rites associated with the Doll Festival, an annual family oriented event that falls on March 3. Kyoto *ningyo* (dolls) are made with fine detail and embellishment.

Nakanishi Toku Shoten has old museum-quality dolls. The owner, Mr. Nakanishi, turned his extensive doll collection into the shop nearly two decades ago and has since been educating customers with his vast knowledge of the doll trade. *359 Moto-cho, Yamatooji Higashi-iru, Furumonzen-dori, Higashiyama-ku, tel. 075/561–7309. Open 10–6.*

Folk Crafts **Yamato Mingei-ten,** next to Maruzen Book Store downtown, has the best selection of Japanese folk crafts, including ceramics, metal work, paper, lacquer ware, and textiles. *Kawaramachi, Takoyakushi-agaru, Nakagyo-ku. tel. 221–2641. Open 10 AM–8:30 PM; closed Fri.*

Kimonos and Shimmering new silk kimonos can cost more than U.S. $10,000,
Accessories while equally stunning old silk kimonos can cost less than U.S. $30. Unless you have a lot of money to spend, it is wiser to look upon new silk kimonos as art objects.

First visit the **Nishijin Textile Center,** in Central Kyoto, for an orientation on silk-weaving techniques. *Horikawa-dori, Imadegawa-minamiiru, Kamigyo-ku, tel. 075/451–9231. Admission free. Open 9–5.*

Then proceed two blocks east on Imadegawa-dori and a block south to **Aizen Kobo,** which specializes in the finest hand-woven indigo-dyed textiles. The shop is in a traditional weaving family's home, and the friendly owners will show you a wide variety of dyed and woven goods, including garments designed by Hisako Utsuki, the owner's wife. *Omiya Nishi-iru, Nakasuji-dori, Kamigyo-ku, tel. 075/441–0355. Open 9–5:30.*

Authentic silk kimonos are very heavy; this factor may dissuade some of you from making that special purchase. If smaller objects are your fancy, try a fan or comb. The most famous fan shop in all of Kyoto is **Miyawaki Baisen-an.** The store has been in business since 1823. It delights customers not only with its fine collection of lacquered, scented, painted, and paper fans but also with the old-world atmosphere that emanates from the building that houses the shop. *Tominokoji Nishiiru, Rokkaku-dori, Nakagyo-ku, tel. 075/221–0181. Open 9–5.*

Umbrellas are used to protect kimonos from the scorching sun or pelting rain. Head for **Kasagen** to purchase authentic oiled paper umbrellas. The shop has been in existence since 1861, and its umbrellas are guaranteed to last years. *284 Gionmachi Kitagawa, Higashiyama-ku, tel. 075/561–2832. Open 9:30–9.*

Department Stores

Kyoto department stores are small by comparison with their mammoth counterparts in Tokyo and Osaka. One department store looks just like the other, as they have similar floor plans. Scarves, shoes, jewelry, and handbags can be always found on the ground floor. The basement floor is devoted to foodstuffs, and the top floor is reserved for pets and pet-care goods, gardening, and restaurants.

Daimaru is the most conveniently located of these one-stop shopping emporiums. It is along the main Shijo-dori shopping avenue and, according to its advertisement, boasts a 270-year history. *Shijo Karasuma, Shimogyo-ku, tel. 075/211–8111. Open 10–7; closed Wed.*

Hankyu is directly across from Takashimaya. It has two restaurant floors. Window displays show the type of food served and prices are clearly marked. *Shijo Kawaramachi, Shimogyo-ku, tel. 075/223–2288. Open 10–7; closed Thurs.*

Kintetsu is located on the main avenue leading north from Kyoto Station. *Karasuma-dori, Shimogyo-ku, tel. 075/361–1111. Open 10–7; closed Thurs.*

Takashimaya has a well-trained English-speaking staff at its information desk, as well as a convenient money-exchange counter on its premises. *Shijo Kawaramachi, Shimogyo-ku, tel. 075/221–8811. Open 10–7; closed Wed.*

Food and Flea Markets

The common bond between food and flea markets is the atmosphere of excitement that stems from the harried shouts of eager merchants trying to attract customers.

Kyoto has a wonderful food market, **Nishiki-koji,** which branches off from the Shin-Kyogoku covered arcade. Try to avoid the market in late afternoon, for this is the time housewives come to do their daily shopping. The market is long and narrow; when a sizable crowd is present, there is always the possibility of being pushed into the delicious display of fresh fish.

Two renowned flea markets take place monthly in Kyoto. Reserve the 21st of the month for the famous **Toji Temple market** and the 25th of the month for the **Kitano Temmangu Shrine market.** Both are open from dawn to dusk. Among the old kimonos, antiques, and bric-a-brac may be an unusual souvenir item.

Unusual Shopping

Shops dedicated to incense, wood tubs, and casks, Buddhist objects, and chopsticks indeed offer unusual experiences. But the prized souvenir of a visit to Kyoto should be the **shuenshu,** a booklet usually no larger than four-by-six inches. It is most often covered with brocade, and the blank sheets of heavyweight paper inside continuously fold out. The booklet can be purchased at stationery stores or at temples for as little as ¥1,000 and serves as a "passport" to collect ink stamps from places visited while in Japan. Stamps and stamp pads are ubiquitous in Japan; they may be found at attractions, train stations, and some restaurants. Most ink stamping can be done for free, but at temples you can ask a monk to write calligraphy over the stamp for a small fee.

Dining

by Diane Durston

A resident of Kyoto for over 10 years, Diane Durston is the author of Old Kyoto: A Guide to Traditional Shops, Restaurants, and Inns *and* Kyoto: Seven Paths to the Heart of the City.

"Paris East" is a difficult epithet to live up to, but in many ways the elegant sister cities do seem to be of the same flesh and blood—both are the homes of their nation's haute cuisine.

Although Tokyo has been the capital since 1868, Kyoto—which wore the crown for the 10 centuries before—is still the classic Japanese city. The traditional arts, crafts, customs, language, and literature were all born, raised, and refined here. Kyoto has the matchless villas, the incomparable gardens, the magnificent temples and shrines—2,000 of them. And it is to Kyoto that you travel for the most artful Japanese cuisine.

The presence of the imperial court was the original inspiration for Kyoto's exclusive *yusoku ryori*. Once served on lacquered pedestals to the emperor himself, it is now offered at but one restaurant in the city, Mankamero.

The dining experience not to be missed in Kyoto, however, is *kaiseki ryori*, the elegant full-course meal that was originally intended to be served with the tea ceremony. All the senses are involved in this culinary event: the scent and flavor of the freshest ingredients at the peak of season; the visual delight of a continuous procession of porcelain dishes and lacquered bowls (each a different shape and size) gracefully adorned with an appropriately shaped morsel of fish or vegetable to match; the textures of foods unknown and exotic, presented in sequence to banish boredom; the sound of water in a stone basin outside in the garden; and finally, that other necessity—the atmosphere of the room itself, complete with a hanging scroll displayed in the alcove and a flower arrangement, both to evoke the season and to accent the restrained appointments of the tatami room. Kaiseki ryori is often costly, yet always unforgettable.

For those seeking initiation (or a reasonably priced sample), the *kaiseki bento* (box lunch) offered by many *ryotei* (as high-class Japanese restaurants are known) is a good place to start; box lunches are so popular in Kyoto that the restaurants that serve them compete to make their bento unique, exquisite, and delicious.

Located a two-day journey from the sea, Kyoto is historically more famous for ingenious ways of serving preserved fish— dried, salted, or pickled—than for its raw fish dishes (though with modern transportation, there are now several decent sushi shops in town). Compared with the style of cooking elsewhere in Japan, *Kyo-ryori* (Kyoto cuisine) is lighter and more delicate than most. The natural flavor of the ingredients is stressed over the enhancement of heavy sauces and broths. Pickled vegetables (*tsukemono*) and traditional sweets (*wagashi*) are two other specialties of Kyoto; they make excellent souvenirs. The food shops are often kept just as they were a century ago—well worth the trip just to browse.

Kyoto is also the home of *shojin ryori*, the Zen vegetarian-style cooking, best sampled right on the grounds of one of the city's Zen temples. Local delicacies like *fu* (glutinous wheat cakes) and *yuba* (soy milk skimmings) have found their way into the mainstream of Kyoto-style cuisine but were originally devised as protein substitutes in the traditional Buddhist diet.

A few practical notes on dining in Kyoto need to be mentioned. Many of the city's finest traditional restaurants have done business in the old style for generations and do not believe in modern nuisances like credit cards. Though several establishments are changing their ways, it's wise to check in advance. Also, people generally dine early in Kyoto (7–8 PM), so most places (apart from hotel restaurants and drinking places) close relatively early. Make sure to check the listings below before you go. Concerning appropriate attire, the average Japanese businessman wears a suit and tie to dinner—anywhere. Young people, though, tend to dress more informally. Although many Kyoto restaurants do have someone who speaks English, call the Kyoto Tourist Information Center (TIC) at 075/371–5649 if you need assistance in making reservations.

Famous throughout Japan for the best in traditional Japanese cuisine, Kyoto, unfortunately, has never been the place to go for Western food. Recently, however, some fine French, American, Indian, and Chinese restaurants have opened in the city—a welcome surprise to foreign residents (and visitors who've had enough of raw fish and squiggly foods). Apart from the restaurants listed below, Kyoto does have its share of the sort of budget quasi-Western–style chain restaurants found all over Japan, serving things like sandwiches and salads, gratins, curried rice, and spaghetti. These are easy to locate along Kawaramachi-dori downtown, and they usually come complete with plastic models in the window to which you can point if other methods of communication fail.

Kyoto is not without an impressive (depending on how you look at it) array of American fast-food chains, including McDonald's, Kentucky Fried Chicken, Mr. Donut, Tony Roma's, and both Shakey's and Chicago Pizza in case you get homesick. Many have branches in the downtown area, as well as throughout the city. For specific locations, call the TIC. An additional source of information is the *Kyoto Visitors' Guide*, available free at most hotels.

A 3% federal consumer tax is added to all restaurant bills. Another 3% local tax is added to the bill if it exceeds ¥5,000. At more expensive restaurants, a 10%–15% service charge is also added to the bill. Tipping is not necessary.

The most highly recommended restaurants are indicated by a star ★.

Category	Cost*
Very Expensive	over ¥15,000
Expensive	¥7,000–¥15,000
Moderate	¥3,000–¥7,000
Inexpensive	under ¥3,000

Cost is per person without tax, service, or drinks

Credit Cards The following credit card abbreviations are used: AE, American Express; DC, Diners Club; MC, MasterCard; V, Visa.

Kyoto Dining

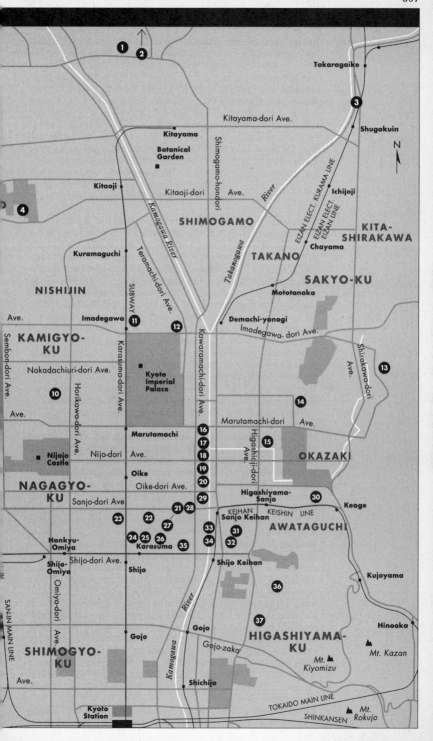

Eastern District

Japanese **Ashiya Steak House.** Located a short walk from the Gion district, famous for its teahouses and geisha, there is no better place in Kyoto to enjoy "a good steak . . . a real martini . . . and the essence of traditional Japan," in the words of 30-year-resident and owner, Bob Strickland, and his wife, Tokiko. While you are seated at a *kotatsu* (recessed hearth), your *teppan-yaki* dinner of the finest Omi beefsteak, grilled and sliced in style, will be prepared as you watch. Cocktails, domestic and imported wines, and beer are available, as well as the best Japanese sake. Cocktails can be had in the art gallery upstairs, which has a display of traditional and contemporary arts and crafts. *172-13 Yon-chome, Matsubara-cho, Higashiyama-ku, tel. 075/541-7961. Dress: informal. Reservations required. AE, DC, MC, V. Open 5:30–11:30 (last order at 10). Closed Mon. Expensive.*

★ **Yagenbori.** North of Shijo-dori in the heart of Kyoto's still-thriving geisha district, this restaurant is in a teahouse just a few steps down a cobbled path from the romantic Shirakawa River in Gion. The *omakase* full-course meal is an elegant sampler of Kyoto's finest kaiseki cuisine, with local delicacies beautifully presented on fine handmade ceramics. The *shabu-shabu* (thinly sliced beef, dipped briefly into hot stock) and *suppon* (turtle dishes) are excellent. Don't miss the *hoba miso* (bean paste with *kinoko* mushrooms and green onions, which are wrapped in a giant oak leaf and grilled at your table over a charcoal hibachi) on the à la carte menu. *Sueyoshi-cho, Kiridoshi-kado, Gion, Higashiyama-ku, tel. 075/551-3331. Dress: informal. Reservations advised. AE, DC, MC, V. Lunch noon–2, dinner 4–11. Moderate–Expensive.*

★ **Minokichi.** One of Kyoto's largest and best restaurants, Minokichi attracts locals and novices alike. The extensive menu (in English) offers *Kyo-ryori* (Kyoto cuisine) and includes tempura, sukiyaki, sushi, and kaiseki, all served elegantly beneath an immense country-farmhouse tiled roof. Whether you prefer tables and chairs or *zabuton* cushions on tatami, all rooms overlook a lush central courtyard garden and pond. Established during the Edo period in 1735, Minokichi has a comfortable folk-style atmosphere with heavy wood beams and folk ceramics, many by famous potters like Kanjiro Kawai and Shoji Hamada. *Dobutsuen-mae-dori, Sanjo-agaru, Sakyo-ku, tel. 075/771-4185. Dress: informal. Dinner reservations advised. AE, DC, MC, V. Open 11:30–9. Moderate.*

Rokusei Nishimise. Few restaurants in Kyoto have matched Rokusei Nishimise's magical combination of traditional cuisine served in a contemporary setting. Polished marble floors and manicured interior garden niches offset the popular *te-oke bento* lunch, a collage of flavors and colors presented in a handmade cypress-wood bucket/serving tray. With an 80-year history as caterers of formal kaiseki cuisine, Rokusei also offers an exquisitely different full-course meal each month at reasonable prices. A three-minute walk west of the turn-of-the-century gardens of Heian Shrine, the restaurant itself overlooks a tree-lined canal and is famous for its colorful azaleas in May. *71 Nishitenno-cho, Okazaki, Sakyo-ku, tel. 075/751-6171. Dress: informal. Dinner reservations advised. DC, V. Open 11:30–9. Closed Mon. Moderate.*

Kappa Nawate. Lively (noisy to some ears) and fun, Kappa Nawate has all the boisterous local atmosphere, grilled goodies, and *nama* (draft) beer a dozen people crammed around a counter could possibly ever hope for. The head cook vacillates between edgy and jovial—he has fish to grill and little patience with the indecisive eater. The English menu helps, but the choices are next to limitless: *oden* (vegetables and other foods simmered in broth), yakitori, sashimi, you name it. A favorite after-work watering hole in the middle of the Gion entertainment district, Kappa stays open later than most such grills in Kyoto. *Sueyoshi-cho, Higashi-kita-kado, Nawate-dori, Shoji 2-sujime-agaru, Higashiyama-ku, tel. 075/531–4048. Dress: casual. No reservations. No credit cards. Open 6 PM–2 AM. Closed twice a month (call first). Inexpensive–Moderate.*

★ **Omen.** Just south of Ginkakuji (Temple of the Silver Pavilion), this is one of the best places to stop for an inexpensive homestyle lunch before proceeding down the old canal (a walkway beneath the cherry trees known as the Path of Philosophy) on the way to Nanzenji Temple. Omen is not only the name of the shop but also the name of the house specialty: thick white noodles brought to your table in a basket with a bowl of hot broth and a platter of seven different vegetables. The noodles are added to the broth a little at a time, along with the vegetables (spinach, cabbage, green onions, mushrooms, burdock, eggplant, radishes, and others, depending on the season). Sprinkle the top with roasted sesame seeds and you have a dish so popular that you can expect a few minutes' wait before you're seated. Like the food, the restaurant itself is country-style, with a choice of counter stools, tables and chairs, or tatami mat seating. The waiters dress in *happi* (workmen's) coats and headbands; the atmosphere is lively and comfortable. *74 Ishibashi-cho, Jodo-ji, Sakyo-ku, tel. 075/771–8994. Dress: casual. No reservations. No credit cards. Open 11–11. Closed Thurs. Inexpensive.*

★ **Rakusho.** Along the path between Maruyama-Koen Park and Kiyomizudera Temple, this tea shop in a former villa is a pleasant place to stop for morning coffee or afternoon tea. A table beside the sliding glass doors looks out on an elaborately landscaped garden that features a pond in which the owner's colorful array of prize-winning *koi* carp, hoping it's feeding time again, lurk just beneath the surface. Flowering plum trees, azaleas, irises, camellias, and maple trees take turns anointing the four seasons while you sip your bowl of *matcha* (frothy tea-ceremony tea) or freshly brewed coffee. Just minutes on foot from Sannenzaka, one of Kyoto's historic preservation districts—a cobblestone path lined with shops dealing in ceramics, antiques, and souvenirs on the way to Kiyomizudera Temple at the top of the slope. *Kodai-ji Kitamon-mae-dori, Washio-cho, Higashiyama-ku, tel. 075/561–6892. Dress: casual. No reservations. No credit cards. Open daily 9:30–6. Inexpensive.*

American **Time Paradox.** The Japanese owner-chef here learned most of the great things he knows in California. The tantalizing menu offers homemade *gratins*, thick-crust pizza, spinach omelets, scallops in garlic wine sauce, bread sticks baked fresh while you wait, and crispy spinach, bacon, and avocado salads. Beer and wine are also served. Located a few blocks south of Kyoto University (just north of Heian Jingu Shrine), it is a popular student haunt, heavy on the foreign element. *Yoshida-hondori, Marutamachi-agaru, Sakyo-ku, tel. 075/751–6903. Dress: casual. Reservations advised weekends. No credit* cards. *Open 5 PM–1 AM (last order at midnight). Closed Thurs. Inexpensive.*

Western District

Japanese **Kitcho.** What Maxim's is to Paris, Kitcho is to Kyoto—classic cuisine, unparalleled traditional atmosphere, exclusive elegance. Lunches start at ¥45,000, dinners are ¥50,000 and up, making this perhaps the world's most expensive restaurant. Although the original restaurant is in Osaka, the Kyoto branch has the advantage of a stunning location beside the Oi River, nestled at the foot of the hills of Arashiyama. Here you can experience the full sensory delight of formal kaiseki cuisine. Only the finest ingredients are used, prepared by master chefs and served on priceless lacquered trays in exquisite antique porcelain ware—all in an elegant private room sparsely decorated with a hanging scroll painted by a famous master, whose message sets the seasonal theme for the evening. The ability to identify the vessels used, an appreciation of the literary allusions made in the combination of objects and foods served, and knowledge of the arts of Japan all add depth to the experience. Expect to spend a minimum of two hours. *58 Susuki-no-banbacho, Tenryu-ji, Saga, Ukyo-ku, tel. 075/881–1101. Jacket and tie. Reservations required. AE. Lunch 11–1, dinner 4–7. Closed 1st, 3rd Wed. Very Expensive.*

★ **Nishiki.** Tucked inside a rustic bamboo fence, Nishiki sits on an island in the middle of the Oi River, surrounded by the densely forested Arashiyama mountains. The *oshukuzen-bento* lunch is the best sampler of formal, Kyoto-style kaiseki cuisine available at such a reasonable price. Unlike most bento lunches, it is served in seven courses and is so beautifully presented in a tiered lacquer box, with meticulous attention to the finest foods in season, that it rivals meals at three times the price. A summer lunch might include a course of *kamo-nasu*, the prized Kyoto eggplant, served *dengaku*-style, smothered in sweet miso sauce in a silver serving dish the shape of an eggplant itself. The top layer of the lacquered box might be covered with a miniature bamboo trellis in which are nestled tiny porcelain cups the shape of morning glories, a favorite summer flower in Kyoto, each one filled with a different appetizer—a touch of sea urchin or a few sprigs of spinach in sesame sauce. *Nakanoshima Koen-uchi, Arashiyama, Ukyo-ku, tel. 075/871–8888. Dress: informal. Call for reservations, or expect a 30-minute wait. AE, DC, MC, V. Open 11–9 (last order at 7). Closed Tues. Moderate.*

★ **Sagano.** Amid the lush green bamboo forests of the Arashiyama district, this quiet retreat serves one of the finest *yudofu* meals (cubes of bean curd simmered in a broth at your table) in Kyoto. The full course includes such local delicacies as tempura and *aburage* (deep-fried tofu) with black sesame seeds and a gingko-nut center garnished with a sprig of *kinome* leaves from the Japanese pepper tree. Take a seat at the sunken counter, and waitresses in kimonos will prepare the meal in front of you—with a backdrop of antique wood-block prints on folding screens, surrounded by walls lined with delicately hand-painted antique porcelain bowls—or walk out through the garden to private, Japanese-style rooms in the back. If weather permits, dine on low tables in the courtyard garden beneath the towering bamboo. It's reasonably priced for this superb combination of atmosphere and good food. Reservations are a good idea year-round, particularly during the fall tourist season when the maple trees of Arashiyama are at their brilliant-red best. *45 Susuki-no-banba-cho, Saga, Tenryu-ji, Ukyo-ku, tel. 075/871–6947. Dress: informal. No credit cards. Open 11–8. Moderate.*

Spanish **Bodegon.** A white-walled, tile-floored, wrought-iron and blown-glass Spanish restaurant in Arashiyama is about as rare (and as welcome) as decent paella in a neighborhood famous for its tofu. Bodegon sits unobtrusively along the main street that runs through the center of this scenic district, offering guests Spanish wines and Kyoto hospitality. A wildly popular tourist area in daylight, Arashiyama rolls up its sidewalks after dark, so Bodegon is a good place to escape the crowds downtown in the evening. *Susuki-no-banba-cho, Tenryu-ji, Saga, tel. 075/ 872–9652. Dress: informal. Reservations suggested on weekends. No credit cards. Lunch noon–2, dinner 5–10. Closed Thurs. Moderate.*

Central District

Japanese **Daimonjiya.** One of Kyoto's many famous *ryori-ryokan* (restaurant/inns), Daimonjiya is noted for its superb formal kaiseki cuisine. Located on the Sanjo Arcade in the downtown shopping district, its inconspicuous traditional entrance is easy to miss among the boutiques and record shops that now line the street. A narrow stone path leads down a bamboo-fence corridor to the doorway of this classic 80-year-old inn, a popular haunt of literary men such as the late Eiji Yoshikawa, author of *Musashi*. The evening kaiseki meal is exquisitely presented; the *kaiseki bento* (box lunch) offered at lunchtime is one of Kyoto's finest and is moderately priced. *19 Ishibashi-cho, Sanjo-Teramachi Higashi-iru, Nakagyo-ku, tel. 075/221– 0603. Jacket and tie. Dinner reservations required. AE, DC, MC, V. Lunch 11:30–1, dinner 5–7 (last seating). Very Expensive.*

Mankamero. Established in 1716, Mankamero is the only restaurant in Kyoto that serves formal *yusoku ryori*, the type of cuisine once served to members of the imperial court. The preparation of foods is carried out by a specially appointed imperial chef, using unique utensils made only for the preparation of this type of cuisine. Dressed in ceremonial robes, the chef "dismembers" the fish into elaborately arranged sections brought to the guest on pedestal trays. Prices are also quite elaborate, though in recent years an incomparable *take-kago bento* lunch (served in a bamboo basket) is offered at prices within reach of the rest of us commoners. *Inokuma-dori, Demizu-agaru, Kamigyo-ku, tel. 075/441–5020. Jacket and tie. Reservations required. AE, DC, MC, V. Open noon–8. Closed once a month. Very Expensive.*

Omi Steak House. Located behind the Fujita Hotel in the Meiji-period villa of former industrialist Baron Fujita, this is the place to sample the beer-fed, pampered, melt-in-your-mouth Omi beef. (Though not as famous internationally perhaps as Kobe beef, it is preferred by many connoisseurs.) The full-course steak and/or seafood dinner is prepared by a chef on a grill before you at a sunken counter, which overlooks a small bamboo garden. A drink in the basement bar of the Fujita Hotel, overlooking a beautifully landscaped duck pond and waterfall, is the right place to begin the evening—or end it. *Fujita*

Hotel, Nijo-dori, Kiyamachi-kado, Nakagyo-ku, tel. 075/222–1511. Jacket and tie. Reservations advised weekends. AE, DC, MC, V. Open 4–9:30. Expensive.

★ **Chidori.** Next door to Omi Steak House (*see* above) in the same villa, the less expensive Chidori opens for lunch and dinner with sunken, counter-style seating in a room that overlooks the main garden. Both American and Japanese beefsteak are served at Chidori, so state your preference. *Fujita Hotel, Nijo-dori, Kiyamachi-kado, Nakagyo-ku, tel. 075/222–1511. Dress: informal. Reservations advised. AE, DC, MC, V. Open noon–9:30. Moderate–Expensive.*

★ **Mishima-tei.** There is really only one choice for sukiyaki in Kyoto, and that is Mishima-tei. Located conveniently in the heart of the downtown shopping district, it is also one of the best restaurants in the area. Kyoto housewives line up out front to pay premium prices for Mishima-tei's famous high-quality beef, sold by the 100-gram over the counter at the meat shop downstairs. Mishima-tei was established in 1904, and climbing the staircase of this three-story, traditional wood-frame restaurant is like journeying into the past. Down the long, dark corridors, with polished wood floors, maids in kimonos bustle about with trays of beef and refills of sake to dozens of private tatami-mat rooms. Ask for a room that faces the central courtyard garden for the best view, and enjoy your meal in privacy. Mishima-tei has not yet undergone any massive remodeling, and it retains an authentic turn-of-the-century atmosphere. The floors creak nostalgically, the beef is excellent, and history beckons. *Teramachi, Sanjo-sagaru, Higashi-iru, Nakagyo-ku, tel. 075/221–0003. Dress: informal. Reservations advised. AE, DC, MC, V. Open 11:30–10. Moderate–Expensive.*

Yoshikawa. This quiet, traditional inn with its beautiful landscape gardens is within walking distance of the downtown shopping area. The specialty of the house is tempura, either a full-course kaiseki dinner served in a tatami room or a lunch at the counter in its cozy "tempura corner," where the chef fries each vegetable and shrimp in front of you while you wait. Tempura should be light and crisp—best right from the pot—and for this Yoshikawa is famous. English is spoken. *Tominokoji, Oike-sagaru, Nakagyo-ku, tel. 075/221–5544 or 075/221–0052. Dress: casual at lunch, jacket and tie at dinner. AE, DC, MC, V. Reservations advised. Lunch 11–2, dinner 5–9. Closed Sun. Moderate–Expensive.*

Agatha. This restaurant offers a "mystery" twist on the Japanese *robatayaki* (charcoal grill). The decor is period Agatha Christie—'40s book covers and movie posters, chic polished marble walls, potted palms, decent jazz, black-and-white checkerboard floors, and counter or table seating. Watch the chef grill interesting variations of traditional Japanese delicacies, such as long-stem white *enoki* mushrooms wrapped in strips of thinly sliced beef, scallops in bacon, or pork in *shiso* (a red or green mintlike herb). Both the A-course and the B-course combine these treats with unadorned standards such as *tebasaki* (grilled chicken wings). Salad and appetizers are included, and a wide selection of drinks are available—everything from sake to a gin fizz. Popular with the *juppie* (Japanese yuppie) crowd, this restaurant has two other branches in Kyoto, and one each in Osaka, Tokyo, and . . . Boston. *2nd floor, Yurika Bldg., Kiyamachi-dori, Sanjo-agaru, Nakagyo-ku, tel. 075/223–2379. Dress: informal. Reservations advised weekends. AE, DC, MC, V. Open 5–midnight. Moderate.*

Oiwa. At the head of the Takasegawa Canal, south of the Fujita Hotel, Oiwa serves *kushikatsu*, which are skewered meats and vegetables battered, deep-fried, and then dipped in a variety of sauces. The building itself is actually a *kura* (treasure house) that belongs to a kimono merchant family, and it is one of the first to have been turned into a restaurant in Kyoto, where restorations of this type are still a new idea. The Japanese chef was trained in one of the finest French restaurants in Tokyo, and his version of kushikatsu (usually considered a working man's snack with beer) might be called unpretentiously elegant. Order by the skewer or ask for the *omakase* course. Oiwa is a fine place to spend a relaxing evening. *Kiyamachi-dori, Nijo-sagaru, Nakagyo-ku, tel. 075/231-7667. Dress: informal. Reservations advised weekends. No credit cards. Open 5-10, Sun. 4-10. Closed Wed. Moderate.*

Yamatomi. The geisha district that runs along the west bank of the Kamogawa River is known as Pontocho. Many of the places along the narrow street are teahouses, and you must be formally introduced by a regular patron to enter. There are a few reasonably priced restaurants on Pontocho, and Yamatomi is among the best. The specialty of the house is called *teppin-age*, a tempura-style meal of battered vegetables, seafood, and meat that you cook yourself in a small iron kettle at your table. In the winter, the feature item is *oden*, a combination of vegetables and local specialties simmered in copper vats behind the counter from which you choose. But it's really the hot, humid summers that make Kyoto-ites flock to Yamatomi. Summer is the season when all the restaurants and teahouses along Pontocho set up temporary verandas out over the river bank so their guests can enjoy both their meals and the cool river breeze under the stars. You may catch sight of guests being entertained by geisha on the veranda of the teahouse next door—paying 10 times the price you'll pay at Yamatomi. *Pontocho, Shijo-agaru, Nakagyo-ku, tel. 075/221-3268. Dress: informal. No credit cards. Open noon-11. Closed Tues. Inexpensive-Moderate.*

Tagoto. One of the best noodle shops in which to stop for lunch in the downtown area, Tagoto is located on the north side of the covered Sanjo Arcade, ½-block west of the avenue Kawaramachi-dori. Tagoto has been serving homemade *soba* (buckwheat) noodle soup for over a hundred years in the same location on a shopping street that is now almost completely modernized. Tagoto, too, has remodeled, and the result is a pleasant surprise—modern, yet in traditional Japanese style. Natural woods, *shoji* paper windows, tatami mats, and an interior garden combine with slate floors, tables and chairs, and air-conditioned comfort. Tagoto serves both thin soba and thick white *udon* noodle dishes with a variety of toppings (such as shrimp tempura), hot or cold to suit the season. *Sanjo-dori, Teramachi Higashi-iru, Nakagyo-ku, tel. 075/221-3030. Dress: casual. No reservations. No credit cards. Open 11-9. Closed Tues. Inexpensive.*

Chinese **Mr. Chow's.** You have to know about Mr. Chow's fantastic new Kyoto hideaway to find it, tucked away as it is in the basement of Karasuma Plaza 21 in the middle of the banking district downtown. With first-class restaurants in Beverly Hills, London, and New York, restaurateur Michael Chow has brought his own brand of chic, elegance, and superb Chinese cuisine to Kyoto at last. The interior is white on white, the mirrored bar fully stocked, and the food fabulous. The full-course lunch is excellent and reasonably priced. *Basement of the Karasuma Plaza 21, Karasuma-dori, Rokkaku-sagaru, Nakagyo-ku, tel. 075/241–6039. Jacket and tie. Reservations advised. AE, DC, MC, V. Lunch 11:30–2, dinner 5–10. Closed Wed. Expensive.*

Coffee Shop   **Inoda.** Hidden down a side street in the center of town, this 100-year-old establishment is one of Kyoto's oldest and best-loved coffee shops. The turn-of-the-century Western-style brick buildings along the street Sanjo-dori nearby are part of a historic preservation district, and Inoda's original old shop blends well with its surroundings. Floor-to-ceiling glass windows overlook an interior garden; a spacious room seats nearly 100 people. And the coffee is excellent: for breakfast, toast and coffee; for lunch, sandwiches and coffee; for a break from sightseeing, coffee and coffee. It even has some stained-glass windows and a pair of witty parrots. *Sakaimachi-dori, Sanjo-sagaru, Nakagyo-ku, tel. 075/221–0505. Dress: casual. No reservations. No credit cards. Open daily 7–6. Inexpensive.*

Continental   **Carnival Times.** Since its opening in 1991, this seafood palace has proved to be one of Kyoto's most popular new restaurants. Located in the 60-year-old Kyoto Electric Co. Building, it has been restored to its original art deco design and then some. When the piano player and saxophonist are on break, a splendid vintage "Symphonion" music box takes over. The food—lobster, shellfish, and four varieties of crab (including Alaskan King)—is marvelous, the wine is Californian, and the service is, if anything, overly attentive. *561–1 Komano-cho, Marutamachi Sagaru, Nakasuji-dori, Kamigyo-ku, Kyoto, tel. 075/223–0606. Dress: informal. Dinner reservations advised. AE, DC. Open 11:30–11:30. Moderate.*

French   **★ Ogawa.** Down a narrow passageway across from the Takasegawa Canal, this is the place to sample the best in Kyoto-style nouvelle cuisine. Finding a seat at the counter of this intimate French restaurant is like getting tickets for opening night at the opera—one you've never seen. With particularly Japanese sensitivity to the best ingredients only in the peak of the season, proprietor Ogawa promises never to bore his guests by serving them the same meal twice. *Ayu* (a popular local river fish) is offered in the summer (or perhaps abalone), salmon in the fall, crab in the winter, shrimp in the spring. Ogawa features marvelous sauces, puddings, and, yes, even fresh papaya sherbet and mango mousse with mint sauce. The full-course meal at lunch and dinner is spectacular, but some prefer to order hors d'oeuvres with wine over which to languish ecstatically for hours. Counter seating is available only for 16. *Kiyamachi Oike-agaru Higashi-iru, Nakagyo-ku, tel. 075/256–2203. Jacket and tie suggested. Reservations required. AE, DC, MC, V. Lunch 11:30–2, dinner 5–10 (last order at 9:30). Closed Tues. Moderate–Expensive.*

★ Natsuka. This fine French restaurant overlooks the Kamogawa River. The Japanese couple who manage the place lived and learned their trade in Paris for several years. Natsuka has the most reasonably priced French lunch menu in town (¥1,500 fixed menu). The dessert tray here is sumptuous, with a choice of two freshly baked delights from about eight possibilities. *Pontocho, Shijo-agaru, Higashigawa, Nakagyo-ku, tel. 075/255–2105. Dress: informal. Dinner reservations advised. AE,*

DC, MC. Lunch 11:30–2, dinner 5–10. Last order at 9 (at 8 on Sun.). Closed Wed. Moderate.

Indian **Ashoka.** Unlike cosmopolitan Tokyo, Kyoto, with all its fine Japanese restaurants, suffers from a serious lack of international options—particularly when it comes to cuisine. That was true until the owners of Ashoka brought their tandoori chicken (and their wonderful Indian chefs) to town. Marinated for hours and baked on long skewers in a clay oven while you watch, this chicken dish is the closest you'll get to downright spiciness in the capital of the culinary dainty. Ashoka's atmosphere includes red carpets, carved screens, brass lanterns, and tuxedoed waiters, though the dress code for guests ranges from denim to silk. The dazzling *Thali* course dinner offers half a dozen curries in little bowls on a brass tray with rice and tandoori—if you're sure you're that hungry. *Kikusui Bldg., 3rd floor, Teramachi-dori, Shijo-agaru, Nakagyo-ku, tel. 075/ 241–1318. Dress: informal. Reservations advised weekends. AE, DC, MC, V. Lunch 11:30–2:30, dinner 5–9. Closed 2nd Tues. of each month. Inexpensive–Moderate.*

Italian **divo-diva.** Authentic Italian food prepared by chefs trained in
★ Italy but with a Japanese flair for color and design. The long narrow room has a counter, three small tables, and one elegant long table for parties and large groups. In the short time divo-diva has been in business, it has become one of the most popular restaurants in Kyoto. The contemporary interior has tasteful lighting. The wine list is interesting (and not prohibitively expensive). The pasta and breads are homemade. The entire staff spent time last year in Italy practicing their Italian. *Nishi-kikoji, Takakura-nishi-iru, Nakagyo-ku, tel. 075/256–1326. Dress: informal. Reservations advised. AE, MC, V. Open lunch 11–2, dinner 5–10. Closed Wed. Inexpensive–Moderate.*

Mixed Menu **Tinguely.** Located in the same basement as the Chinese restaurant Mr. Chow's (*see* above), Tinguely overlooks a mini-terrace and has a black interior. This dining spot may be described as ethnic (the menu covers a lot of bases—East and West), eclectic (not the place you'd think the local banking district would frequent—but it does), and kinetic (the flashing, jangling work of artist Jean Tinguely hangs from every rafter). It's a bizarre place for breakfast; a topic of conversation at lunch; and a "mysterious space for city adults" in the evening, as the restaurant's slogan says. *Basement of the Karasuma Plaza 21, Karasuma-dori, Rokkaku-sagaru, Nakagyo-ku, tel. 075/255–6810. Dress: informal. Reservations advised weekends. AE, DC, MC, V. Open weekdays 7:30 AM–11 PM, Sat. 11–11. Closed Sun. Inexpensive.*

Northern District

Japanese **Heihachi-Jaya.** A bit off the beaten path in the northeastern
★ corner of Kyoto, along the old road to the Sea of Japan, this roadside inn has offered comfort to many a weary traveler in its 400-year history. Heihachi-Jaya hugs the levee of the Takano River and is surrounded by maple trees in a quiet landscape garden with a stream. Apart from the excellent bento lunch and full-course kaiseki dinner, what makes this restaurant special is its clay sauna, the *kamaburo*, a mound-shaped clay steam bath heated from beneath the floor by a pinewood fire. Have a bath and sauna, change into a cotton kimono if you wish, and

retire to the dining room (or to a private room) for a *very* relaxing meal—an experience not to be missed. *8-1 Kawagishi-cho, Yamabana, Sakyo-ku, tel. 075/781–5008. Dress: informal. Credit cards at lunch: DC, MC, V. Reservations advised. Open 11–9. Closed 4th Thurs. of each month. Moderate–Expensive.*

Izusen. In the garden of Daiji-in, a sub-temple of Daitokuji, a revered center of Zen Buddhism in Japan, this restaurant specializes in *shojin ryori* (Zen vegetarian cuisine). Lunches are presented in sets of red-lacquer bowls of diminishing sizes, each one fitting inside the next when the meal is completed. Two Kyoto specialties, *fu* (glutinous wheat cake) and *yuba* (skimmed from steaming soy milk), are served in a multitude of inventive forms—in soups and sauces that prove vegetarianism to be as exciting a culinary experience as any "carnal" dish can hope to be. Meals are served in tatami-mat rooms, Japanese-style, and in warm weather on low tables outside beneath the trees in the temple garden. *4 Daitoku-ji-cho, Murasakino, Kita-ku, tel. 075/491–6665. Dress: informal. Reservations advised in spring and fall. No credit cards. Open 11–5. Moderate.*

★ **Sagenta.** Discovering Kibune is one of the best parts of summer in Kyoto. A short, bump'n'rumble train ride into the mountains north of Kyoto on the nostalgic little Keifuku train lets you off on a mountain path that leads farther up into the forest beside a cool stream. The path is lined on both sides with restaurants that place tables near the stream during the summer months; you can dine beneath a canopy of trees, with the water flowing at your feet. Most of the restaurants along the river are excellent, but some are quite expensive. Sagenta is the last restaurant, at the very top of the slope, serving kaiseki lunches year-round, as well as one-pot *nabe* dishes in fall and winter. It is reasonably priced, particularly for its popular summertime specialty *nagashi-somen*, chilled noodles that flow down a bamboo spout from the kitchen to a boat-shape trough; you catch the noodles from the trough as they float past, dip them in a sauce, and eat them with mushrooms, seasonal green vegetables, and shrimp. *76 Kibune-cho, Kurama, Sakyo-ku, tel. 075/ 741–2244. Dress: informal. Reservations advised in summer. AE, DC, MC, V. Open 10–10. Closed periodically during winter. Inexpensive–Moderate.*

★ **Azekura.** On the northern outskirts of Kyoto, not far from Kamigamo Shrine, Azekura serves home-style buckwheat noodles under the giant wood beams of a 300-year-old sake warehouse. Originally built in Nara, the warehouse was moved here 20 years ago by a kimono merchant named Mikio Ichida, who also maintains a textile exhibition hall, a small museum, and a weavers' workshop within the walls of this former samurai estate. Have lunch on low stools around a small charcoal brazier or on tatami next to a window overlooking the garden and waterwheel outside. The soba (buckwheat noodles) at Azekura have a heartier country flavor than you'll find in most of the other noodle shops in town. A perfect place to stop while exploring the *shake-machi* district around the shrine, an area in which shrine priests and farmers have lived for over 10 centuries. *30 Okamoto-cho, Kamigamo, Kita-ku, tel. 075/701–0161. Dress: casual. No reservations. No credit cards. Open 9–5. Closed Mon. Inexpensive.*

Papa Jon's. Just north of Doshisha University is a new American-owned café that serves the finest homemade cakes and espresso in town. Owner-chef Charles Roche features the work of local artists on the walls of his elegant little shop. This, plus the antique European decor and sunlit coziness, provides a welcome place to rest after a visit to the nearby Imperial Palace. *642–2 Shokoku-ji Monzen, Karasuma Kamidachiuri Higashi-iru, Kamigyo-ku, tel. 075/415–2655. Dress: informal. No reservations. No credit cards. Open 11:30–10. Closed Mon. Inexpensive.*

American
★

Knuckle's. Explaining the concept of the "knuckle sandwich" to his Kyoto customers is one of owner (and New Yorker) Charles Roche's favorite tasks—that, and introducing them to home-style American cooking: fresh-baked cheesecake, lasagna, nachos, Reuben sandwiches, and, of course, the deluxe Knuckle Sandwich, washed down with a Corona beer (with a twist of lime), a real margarita, or a cup of the best espresso in town. Roche, a long-time resident of Kyoto, got tired of his stomach always feeling homesick, and he opened this easy-going eatery in northern Kyoto about four years ago. It is now home-away-from-home for a menagerie of expatriates, local Yankee sympathizers, and anyone not in the mood for raw fish. A good place to find out what gives in the ancient capital. *Kitaoji-dori, Sembon Higashi-iru, Kita-ku, tel. 075/441–5849. Dress: casual. No reservations. No credit cards. Open noon–10. Closed Mon. Inexpensive.*

Coffee Shop
★

Honyarado. Kyoto has always been a university town, and Doshisha University, on the north side of the old Imperial Palace, is one of the oldest and most respected in the city. Honyarado is a "home-away-from-dormitory" for many of its students. During the student movement of the '60s and '70s, Kyoto had its share of "incidents." What's left of the spirit of the peace movement—the environmentalists, the poets, and the musicians of that era—eat their lunches at Honyarado. The notices on the bulletin are of a less incendiary nature these days (rooms for rent, poetry readings, used stereos for sale), but the sandwiches are still on homemade wheat bread, the stew is still good, and the company still real. Take along a good book (this guide, perhaps?), order lunch, and relax. *Imadegawa-dori, Teramachi Nishi-iru, Kamigyo-ku, tel. 075/222–1574. Dress: casual. No reservations. No credit cards. Open 9 AM–10 PM. Closed 1st Wed. of each month. Inexpensive.*

Lodging

Kyoto is a tourist city, and its hotel rooms are often designed merely as places to rest at night. Most rooms are small by international standards, but they are adequate for relaxing after a busy day of sightseeing. As throughout Japan, service in this city is impeccable; the information desks are well stocked with maps and pamphlets about the sights. The assistant manager, concierge, or guest-relations manager is always available in the lobby to respond to guests' needs.

Each room in expensively and moderately priced lodgings comes equipped with a hot-water thermos and tea bags or instant coffee. Stocked refrigerators, television featuring English-language CNN news, and radio are standard, as are *yukata* (cotton kimonos), intended for use in the rooms.

Kyoto offers a nice choice of both Western- and Japanese-style accommodations. *Ryokans*, as traditional Japanese inns are called, have been in existence for hundreds of years. Most inns were originally roadside establishments that housed pilgrims and nobility alike.

A ryokan stay can be almost spiritual in nature. The removal of your shoes is the first prerequisite upon entering. A pair of slippers will be provided for you to walk down the corridors. A personal attendant will lead you to a sparsely decorated tatami-mat room. Remove your slippers before stepping on the matted floor. As most ryokans are small two-story wood buildings, usually not more than 20 or 30 rooms are available at any time; minimizing the number of guests maximizes tranquillity.

Once in the room, take notice of the artistic flower arrangement and/or scroll in the *tokonoma* alcove. Sit on a *zabuton* (cushion) at the low table. An attendant will pour a cup of tea and bring in a morsel of sweets to revive your energy. If you are lucky enough to have a room facing the inner garden, the attendant will open the *shoji* (screen) leading into the garden. In the summer, be aware of the continuous music of cicadas. At night, be on the lookout for fireflies. In the autumn, hear the poignant cry of crickets. A ryokan stay is intended to bring you in harmony with nature.

The attendant is responsible for carrying in the multicourse meals; breakfast and dinner are part of the room rate unless you specify that you want to eat out. The attendant will transform the versatile tatami room at night into a bedroom by laying down thick and oh-so-comfortable *futon* mattresses. The traditional grain-filled pillows, however, may need some getting used to; if you find them annoying, ask if alternative pillows are available.

The attendant will also guide the guest to the bath. As a foreigner, you may be instructed on how to bathe in the Japanese way. Remember to lather outside the tub, rinse off, then soak in the tub. Japanese like their water extremely hot. It is permissible to dilute the water with cold water from the tap. At the end of the bath, don't drain the tub.

Not all ryokans offer private toilets and baths, so check in advance if you don't like to share facilities.

When you visit the rest room, leave the slippers provided for walking the corridors outside. A separate pair of slippers await you for use in the rest room.

Obviously, higher priced inns offer the most personalized service. Be aware that they can be very, very expensive. Prices quoted are usually per person (including two meals) and not per room. Make sure to check carefully, as some ryokans cost as much as U.S. $1,000 per person per night.

Moderately and inexpensively priced inns offer only a fraction of the total ryokan experience. Tubs may be plastic rather than cedarwood. Meals may be served in the dining area rather than elaborately prepared and presented in your room. Rooms may overlook a street rather than a garden. The room, however, will have tatami straw mat floors, futon bedding, and a scroll and/or flower arrangement in its rightful place.

Most accommodations in the Very Expensive, Expensive, and Moderate categories have representation abroad, so ask at the nearest Japan National Tourist Organization (JNTO) office for information on booking. If there is no representation, bookings must be made by writing directly to the establishment. Book at least a month in advance, or as early as three months ahead, if you are traveling during peak spring and autumn seasons or around prime Japanese holidays and festivals.

For Japanese-style inns, cost is per person, including two meals. A 3% federal consumer tax is added to all hotel bills. Another 3% local tax is added to the bill if it exceeds ¥10,000. At most hotels, a 10%–15% service charge is added to the total bill. Tipping is not necessary.

Category	Cost*
Very Expensive	over ¥30,000
Expensive	¥20,000–¥30,000
Moderate	¥8,000–¥20,000
Inexpensive	under ¥8,000

Cost is for double room, without tax or service

The most highly recommended accommodations are indicated by a star ★.

Credit Cards The following credit card abbreviations are used: AE, American Express; DC, Diners Club; MC, MasterCard; V, Visa.

Very Expensive

Hiiragiya. Hiiragiya is on par with the Tawaraya (*see* below) as the preferred ryokan among dignitaries and celebrities. The inn was founded in 1818 to accommodate provincial lords and their parties who were visiting the capital. The founder himself was a metal smith whose artful sword guards were commissioned by powerful samurai. Luxurious elegance combined with strength is the pervasive style of this lodging place, which echoes with memories of the samurai visitors during the 19th century. Charlie Chaplin and Yukio Mishima have been among its noted past fans. As the motto of the inn implies, "A guest arrives . . . back home to comfort." Some baths feature stained-glass windows. *Fuyacho-Oike-kado, Nakagyo-ku, Kyoto, tel. 075/221–1136. 33 rooms; 28 with bath, 5 without. AE, DC, MC, V.*

★ **Takaragaike Prince Hotel.** Kyoto's only deluxe hotel is located on the northern outskirts of the city, across from the International Conference Hall and Takaragaike Pond. Its unusual doughnut-shape architectural design provides each room with a view of the surrounding mountains and forests. Corridors along the inside overlook the landscaped inner garden. Although it is about 30 minutes from the city center, the hotel provides the perfect respite after a hard day of sightseeing. The fine touches include the huge floral arrangements in the lobby, the impressive chandeliers all around the building, and the original Miró prints, which hang in every suite. The spacious rooms have beds that are probably the largest you'll find in Japan. All rooms are tastefully decorated in pastel colors which complement the natural green of the outside views. This is one of the only hotels in Kyoto with its own authentic teahouse, which overlooks the pond. Demonstrations of the tea ceremony can be arranged upon request. *Takaragaike, Sakyo-ku, Kyoto 606, tel. 075/712–1111. Adjacent to the Kyoto Inter-*

Kyoto Lodging

0   1 mile

0   1 km

KITA-KU

MURASAKIN

Kitaoji-dori Ave.

Shuzan Kaido

Kitsuji-dori Ave.

UKYO-KU

OMURO

UTANO

Ryoanji-michi

Tojiin

Imadegawa-dori

Takaoguchi

Hirosawanoike Pond

Omuro

Myoshinji

Kitano-Hakubaicho

Narutaki

Nishioji-dori

Tokiwa

Marutamachi-dori

SAGANO

JR SAN-IN MAIN LINE

Saga

UZUMASA

Ave.

Katabiranotsuji

Arashiyama

Uzumasa

Kaikonoyashiro

NISHINOKYO

ARASHIYAMA

Nijo

Arashiyama

Sanjo-dori Ave.

HANKYU ELECTRIC ARASHIYAMA LINE

Katsuragawa River

Yamanouchi

Sanjoguchi

Shijo-dori Ave.

Saiin

KEIFUKU ELECTR ARASHIYAMA LI

Matsuo

HANKYU ELECTRIC KYOTO LINE

Gojo-dori Ave.

Nishi-Kyogoku

Nishioji-dori

Tambaguch

Shichijo-dori

Kamikatsura

Ave.

Katsura Imperial Villa

TOKAIDO MAIN LINE

Katsura

SHINKANSEN

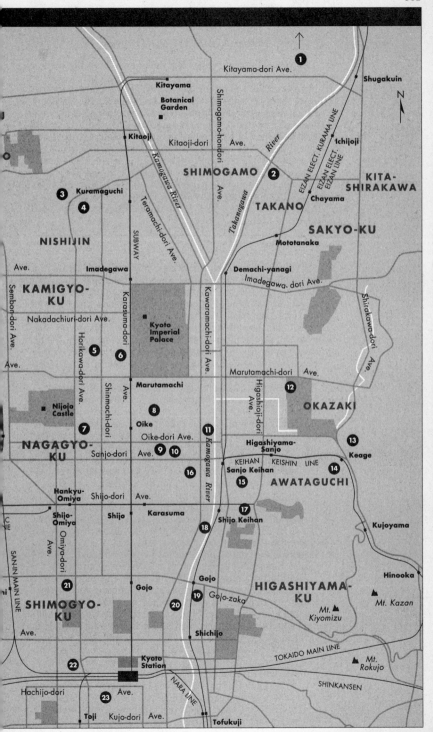

national Conference Hall. *322 rooms. Facilities: 6 restaurants (including French, Chinese, and Japanese), bars, souvenir shop, meeting and conference rooms, teahouse. AE, DC, MC, V.*

★ **Tawaraya.** The most famous of Kyoto's inns, this is the abode of kings and queens, princes and princesses, and presidents and dictators alike when they visit Kyoto. Tawaraya was founded more than 300 years ago and is currently run by the 11th generation of the Okazaki family. For all its subdued beauty and sense of tradition, the inn does have modern comforts such as heat and air-conditioning, but they are introduced so inconspicuously that they hardly detract from the venerable atmosphere of yesteryear. Rooms feature superb antiques from the Okazaki family collection. Because the inn is small, the service is first-rate, while the private gardens provide the beauty and peace you search for on a visit to Japan. *Fuyacho-Aneyakoji-agaru, Nakagyo-ku, Kyoto, tel. 075/211-5566. 19 rooms; 15 with bath, 4 without. AE, DC, V.*

Expensive

★ **ANA Hotel Kyoto.** The nearly three-year-old hotel, across from the Nijojo Castle, is part of the chain that belongs to All Nippon Airways (ANA), the airline with the largest domestic network in Japan. Its high-ceilinged lobby looks out to a picturesque courtyard waterfall. The background koto music that is played in the lobby is soothing to the senses and reminds you, at once, even among the ultra-Western decor, that you are in the ancient city of Kyoto. The rooms are long and narrow. *Nijo-jo-mae, Horikawa-dori, Nakagyo-ku, Kyoto 604, tel. 075/231-1155. 303 rooms. Directly across from Nijojo Castle. Facilities: 7 restaurants (including French, Chinese, and Japanese), bars, shopping arcade, health spa, indoor swimming pool. AE, DC, MC, V.*

Daimonjiya. Just off the busy shopping area of Sanjo-dori Avenue, this tiny inn is as famous for its guest rooms as for the food served. Each room, with fine wood interiors, overlooks a small garden. *Kaiseki* (formal Japanese meal with tea ceremony) is the specialty of the house; the chef was trained at the best Kyoto culinary establishment. You do not need to be a guest to use one of the rooms for a meal, but then you would be missing out on the quintessential ryokan experience. (A branch of the restaurant Daimonjiya is located in the Tokyo Hilton International Hotel.) *Nishi-iru, Kawaramachi-Sanjo, Nakagyo-ku, Kyoto, tel. 075/221-0603. 7 rooms. AE, DC.*

★ **Hotel Fujita Kyoto.** This pleasant hotel is situated along the famed Kamogawa River and is a 15-minute drive from the Kyoto Station. In the light of a full moon, the waterfall in its garden sparkles while waterfowl play. The lobby is narrow and long, with comfortable gray armchairs playing nicely against deep red carpeting. The Fujita features Japanese and Scandinavian decor throughout, and 18 rooms have Japanese-style furnishings. *Nishizume, Nijo-Ohashi, Kamogawa, Nakagyo-ku, Kyoto 604, tel. 075/222-1511. 195 rooms. Facilities: 6 bars and restaurants, beauty shop, souvenir shop. AE, DC, MC, V.*

Kyoto Brighton Hotel. The brand-new Brighton is unquestionably the best hotel in the city in this price range. The abundance of greenery in the central atrium and the soft colors give the Brighton an airy, spacious quality that most Kyoto hotels lack. Rooms are furnished in pastels and have separate sitting areas.

Nakadachiuri, Shinmachi-dori, Kamigyo-ku, tel. 075/441–4411. 183 rooms. Facilities: 3 banquet rooms, 4 restaurants, bar, pool, beauty salon. AE, DC, MC, V.

Kyoto Grand Hotel. The Grand's lobby can sometimes be crowded because the hotel is popular with tour groups. The green concrete building, which is on the drab side, has a circular attachment on the roof—a revolving restaurant. If your room faces the street, make sure to draw the curtains or slide the *shoji* screens before undressing, because office buildings are right across the way. The hotel is famous for its cheerful and friendly staff. The Grand's neighbors include the Nishi Honganji and Toji temples. *Shiokoji-Horikawa, Shimogyo-ku, Kyoto 600, tel. 075/341–2311. 600 rooms. Walking distance from Kyoto Station. Facilities: 13 restaurants (including Western, Japanese, and Chinese) and bars, indoor pool, sauna, bakery, shopping corner, barber shop, beauty parlor, travel agency. AE, DC, MC, V.*

★ **Kyoto Tokyu Hotel.** This seven-story hotel is part of Japan's largest hotel chain. The pillared main entrance, the entrance hall, and lobby are expansive and airy, while the courtyard, with its reflecting pool and waterfall, creates a dramatic atmosphere. The well-appointed rooms, predominantly decorated in off-white tones, are comfortable and spacious. *580 Kakimotocho, Gojo-sagaru, Horikawa-dori, Shimogyo-ku, Kyoto 600, tel. 075/341–2411. 437 rooms. Facilities: 7 restaurants (including French, Chinese, and Japanese) and bars, meeting and banquet rooms, outdoor pool, wedding hall, beauty parlor, photo studio, souvenir shop, flower shop, travel agency. AE, DC, MC, V.*

★ **Miyako Hotel.** The Miyako, the grand old dame of Kyoto's Western-style hotels, has been around for close to 100 years. The hotel sits dramatically on the western hills of Kyoto, near the temples and shrines of Higashiyama (Eastern Kyoto). The Miyako evokes the spirit of Europe rather than that of the Orient, but once you enter its Japanese wing, you know you are unmistakably in Japan. Every soundproof guest room offers beautiful panoramic views of the city and the surrounding hills. This hotel is popular with tour groups, so you may have to wait to have your bags picked up or to use the elevators. *Sanjo-keage, Higashiyama-ku, Kyoto 605, tel. 075/771–7111. 442 rooms, 27 Japanese-style. Facilities: numerous restaurants, lounges, bars, meeting and banquet facilities, shopping arcade, health facilities, outdoor pool. AE, DC, MC, V.*

★ **Seikoro.** This lovely inn is just a stone's throw away from busy Gojo Station, a convenience that makes it popular among both foreigners and Japanese. The 100-year-old ryokan is managed by a native resident who is fluent in English. Among the interesting decor are Western antiques that mysteriously blend in quite well with the otherwise traditional Japanese setting. *Toiyamachi-dori, Gojo-sagaru, Higashiyama-ku, Kyoto, tel. 075/561–0771. 24 rooms with bath. AE, MC, V.*

★ **Yachiyo.** The special entrance to Yachiyo has low-hanging tiled eaves and woodwork surrounded by carefully shaped bushes, pine trees, and rocks. The sidewalk from the gate to the ryokan curves snakelike into the doorway. Yachiyo is less expensive than its brethren in the deluxe category but nevertheless provides fine, attentive care. Perhaps the biggest draw in staying here is its proximity to Nanzenji, one of the most appealing temples in Kyoto. *34 Nanzenji-fukuchicho, Sakyo-ku, Kyoto,* *tel. 075/771–4148. 25 rooms, 20 with bath, 5 without. AE, DC, MC, V.*

Moderate

Gion Hotel. This hotel sits right in the heart of the Gion geisha district, just west of Yasaka Shrine. It is modest, clean, and the location is excellent—across from the Kyoto Craft Center and a five minute walk from downtown. *555 Gion machi, Minami-gawa, Higashiyama-ku, Kyoto, tel. 075/551–2111. Facilities: coffee shop, rooftop beer garden, bar. 130 rooms. AE, DC, MC, V.*

Holiday Inn Kyoto. This member of the famous American chain (a 15-minute taxi ride from Kyoto's downtown area) boasts the best sports facilities of any Kyoto hotel, including a bowling alley and ice-skating rink. The hotel is located in a residential area with small, modern houses, occasionally interrupted by large, traditional Japanese estates. Rooms for the handicapped are available. *36 Nishihirakicho, Takano, Sakyo-ku, Kyoto 606, tel. 075/721–3131. 270 rooms. Facilities: banquet and meeting rooms, 3 restaurants, bar, coffee shop, outdoor pool, indoor pool, gym, and sauna, bowling alley, ice-skating rink, tennis court, driving range, shopping mall. AE, DC, MC, V.*

Iwami. Amid the antique shops of Shinmonzen-dori Avenue is this priceless little inn, whose loyal clientele, including many foreigners, would like to keep its existence a secret. The inn has gained such a reputation, in fact, that rooms must be booked well in advance. When booking, be sure to ask for a room with a view of the garden or canal. *Higashioji, Nishi-iru, Shinmonzen-dori, Higashiyama-ku, Kyoto, tel. 075/561–7135. 7 rooms. No credit cards.*

Kyoto Palaceside Hotel. This six-story accommodation is across to slip out of bed for a quick jaunt around the imperial grounds. The white building's spacious and pillared lobby has leather sofas on one side and a souvenir shop on the other. The hotel is recommended for its location and its reasonable prices. *Shimo-dachiuri-agaru, Karasuma-dori, Kamigyo-ku, Kyoto 602, tel. 075/431–8171. 120 rooms. Facilities: souvenir shop, French restaurant, banquet rooms, bar. AE, DC, MC, V.*

New Miyako Hotel. This large hotel situated directly in front of Kyoto Station is under the same management as the Miyako Hotel (*see* above); it is used widely by groups and tours. The 10-story white edifice has two protruding wings with landscaping and street lamps reminiscent of a hotel in the United States. Its location makes it attractive for those planning train trips from the city. *17 Nishi-Kujoincho, Minami-ku, Kyoto 601, tel. 075/661–7111. 714 rooms: 4 Japanese-style. Facilities: Japanese, Chinese, and Continental restaurants, bar and tea lounge, shopping gallery, barber shop. AE, DC, MC, V.*

Three Sister's Inn Annex (*Rakutoso Bekkan*). A traditional inn popular with foreign guests for decades, the annex sits on the northeast edge of Heian Shrine, down a trellised path that hides it from the street. This is a quiet and friendly place, and a good introduction to inn customs because they are accustomed to foreign guests. The annex is nicer than the nearby main branch. *Heian Jingu, Higashi Kita Kado Sakyo-ku, Kyoto, tel. 075/761–6333. 12 rooms. AE, DC.*

Inexpensive

Hiraiwa. Imagine the ambience of a friendly, Western-style youth hostel with tatami-mat rooms, and you have the Hiraiwa ryokan, a member of the Hospitable and Economical Japanese Inn Group. To be a member, inns must have English-speaking staff and offer clean, comfortable accommodations. Hiraiwa is the most popular of these inns in Kyoto; it's a great place to meet fellow travelers from around the world. Rules and regulations during your stay are posted on the walls. Guests are welcome to eat with the family owners around the dining table in the small kitchen. No private facilities and no baths; only showers are available. *314 Hayao-cho, Kaminoguchiagaru, Ninomiyacho-dori, Shimogyo-ku, tel. 075/351–6748. 16 rooms. AE, V.*

Hirota Guest House. This hidden treasure of an inn, south of the Imperial Palace, is run by a professional English-speaking guide. A long passageway behind the family's accounting office leads to a lush garden that surrounds a beautifully restored sake storehouse. The Japanese-style rooms have a great view of the secluded, quiet garden. Make reservations well in advance. *665 Nijo-dori, Taminakaji Nishi-iru, Nakagyo-ku, tel. 075/221–2474. 3 rooms, 1 with bath and kitchen. No credit cards.*

★ **Myokenji.** This temple lodging is an alternative accommodation that affords the guest a firsthand look at the activities of monks. Be ready to share a room with several fellow travelers. If you are modest, write ahead for a private room. The reasonable room rate includes breakfast. *Teranouchi, Higashi-iru, Horikawa-dori, Kamigyo-ku, tel. 075/414–0808. 4 rooms— non-private with a capacity for 7 people. No credit cards.*

★ **Myorenji.** This is a 13th-century temple that has opened its amiable doors to weary travelers. Early to bed and early to rise is the motto here, so beware of the 8 PM curfew along with the optional 6 AM prayer sessions. You'll need to make reservations by mail in advance. *Teranouchi, Nishi-iru, Horikawa-dori, Kamigyo-ku, tel. 075/451–3527. 6 rooms—nonprivate with a capacity for 10 people. No credit cards.*

Ryokan Yuhara. Only a 15-minute walk from the old quarters of Gion and Pontocho, Yuhara is popular among repeat visitors wishing to save a few yen while exploring Kyoto. The friendliness of the staff more than compensates for the spartan amenities. Especially rewarding is a springtime stay when the cherry trees are in full bloom along the Takasegawa River, which the inn overlooks. *188 Kagiya-cho, Shomen-agaru, Kiyamachi-dori, tel. 075/371–9583. 8 rooms. No credit cards.*

The Arts and Nightlife

The Arts

Kyoto is quickly following Tokyo and Osaka as a must stop for both domestic and international artists. Kyoto has played host to the likes of Bruce Springsteen, but it is famous for the traditional arts—Kabuki, Noh, and traditional dances. All dialogue at theaters, however, is in Japanese; the infrequent visitor may find that time is better spent visiting shrines, temples, and gardens.

If you opt to take in a performance, information is available from a number of sources, the most convenient being from your hotel concierge or guest-relations manager. He or she may even have a few tickets on hand, so don't hesitate to ask.

Kyoto boasts a 24-hour recording of the week's tourist events, including festivals, sporting events, and performances. Call 075/361–2911 for a recording in English. Another good source of information is **JNTO's Tourist Information Center (TIC)**, which is located directly across from Kyoto Station. It is strongly suggested that you make a trip to TIC to pick up the latest information on Kyoto's arts scene and other tourist matters. At the TIC office you will find a monthly newspaper for tourists called *Kyoto Visitor's Guide*, which devotes a few pages to "This Month's Theater." If you don't have time to go to TIC, you can call 075/371–5649 for a helpful English-speaking information officer to answer questions.

Gion Corner
If there is one performance that should not be missed in Kyoto, it is the quick but comprehensive overview of Kyoto's performing arts at the Gion Corner. The one-hour show features court music and dance, ancient comic plays, Kyoto-style dancing performed by apprentice geisha called *maiko*, and puppet drama. Segments are also offered on the tea ceremony, flower arrangement, and koto music.

To obtain tickets, contact your hotel concierge or call **Gion Corner** (1st floor, Yasaka Hall, Gion, tel. 075/561–1119). The show is quite a bargain at ¥2,500. Two performances nightly are given at 7:40 and 8:40 March 1–November 29. No performances are offered August 16 and December–February.

Before attending the show, walk around the Gion and Pontocho areas. Most likely you will see beautifully adorned geisha and maiko making their way to work. It is permissible to take their picture, but as they have strict appointments, don't delay them.

Seasonal Dances
If you are in Kyoto in April, be sure to take in the **Miyako Odori;** or, in May and October, the **Kamogawa Odori.** These dances are performed by geisha and apprentices and pay tribute to the seasonal splendor of spring and fall. The stage setting is spectacular, with festive singing and dancing.

Performances are held at the **Gion Kaburenjo Theater** (Gion Hanamikoji, Higashiyama-ku, tel. 075/561–1115; tickets: ¥1,650, ¥3,300, and ¥3,800) and the **Pontocho Kaburenjo Theater** (Pontocho Sanjo-sagaru, Nakagyo-ku, tel. 075/221–2025; tickets: ¥1,650, ¥3,300, and ¥3,800).

Kabuki
Kabuki has found quite a following in the United States due to recent tours by Japan's Kabuki troupes in Washington, D.C., New York, and a few other cities. Kabuki is faster paced than Noh, but a single performance can easily take half a day. Devoted followers pack their box lunches and sit patiently through the entire performance, mesmerized by each movement of the performers.

For a first-timer, however, this all may be too exotic. Unless you are captured by the Kabuki spirit, don't spend more than an hour or two at Kyoto's famed **Minamiza Theater** (Shijo Kamogawa, Higashiyama-ku, tel. 075/561–1155), the oldest theater in Japan (under reconstruction, scheduled to re-open November 1991). December is the month to see Kabuki in

Kyoto when the annual *Kaomise* (Face Showing) Kabuki festival takes place. Top Kabuki stars from around the country make guest appearances during this month-long extravaganza. Performance and ticket information can be obtained through the Tourist Information Center (*see* Important Addresses and Numbers, above).

Noh Noh is another form of traditional theater, more ritualistic and sophisticated than Kabuki. Some understanding of the plot of each play is necessary to enjoy a performance, which is generally slow-moving and solemnly chanted. The major Noh theaters often provide synopses of the plays in English. The masks used by the main actors are carved to express a whole range of emotions, though the mask itself may appear expressionless until the actor "brings it to life." Particularly memorable are the outdoor performances of Noh, especially **Takigi Noh,** held outdoors by firelight on the nights of June 1–2 in the precincts of the Heian Jingu Shrine. With the stars twinkling, the moon beaming, and the cool evening breeze rustling the trees, the entire Noh performance takes on a different aura. The outdoor performance is a re-creation of what the original performances were like during the Heian period.

If you're going to be in Kyoto on days other than the two days specified for the outdoor performance and still want to see Noh, performances are given throughout the year at these two theaters: **Kanze Kaikan Noh Theater,** 44 Enshoji-cho, Okazaki, Sakyo-ku, tel. 075/771–6114; and **Kongo Noh Theater,** Muromachi, Shijo-agaru, Nakagyo-ku, tel. 075/221–3049.

Nightlife

Kyoto's nightlife is much more sedate than Tokyo's, but because it is a premier tourist city, visitors from around the world are greeted with a friendly "Hello," no matter where they venture in the evening. The Kiyamachi area along the small canal near Pontocho is as close to a consolidated nightlife area as you'll get in Kyoto. It is full of small drinking establishments with red lanterns (indicating inexpensive places) or small neon signs in front. It is also fun to walk around the Gion and Pontocho areas to try to catch a glimpse of a geisha or apprentice geisha going to or coming from work. Don't be afraid to walk around, because the streets and back alleys of Kyoto, like almost anywhere in Japan, are quite safe.

In the city center, check out the disco scene at **Gaia,** located in the Pleasure Dome Imagium Building (Nishikiyamachi Street north of Shijo, Nakagyo-ku, tel. 075/231–6600). This five-floor "labyrinth," as the owners call it, also has a bar, restaurant, club, and saloon. Don't underestimate bars in the hotels. They are often stylish and fun, with a loyal local clientele. Some hotels also feature dinner shows. Ask your hotel concierge for more suggestions on nightlife.

8 Nara

Introduction

by Kiko Itasaka

A freelance writer based in Tokyo and New York, Kiko Itasaka has contributed to Best of Japan *and* Mainichi Daily News.

The ancient city of Nara was founded in 710 by Emperor Kammu and predated Kyoto as the capital of Japan. Nara was the first capital to remain in one place over a long period of time. Until then, the capital had been established in a new location with each successive ruler. The founding of Nara, then known as Heijo-Kyo, occurred during a period when Japan's politics, arts, architecture, and religion had been heavily influenced by China. Even the Japanese writing system, which was developed at this time, utilized Chinese written characters.

Introduced by China beginning in the 6th century, Buddhism flourished in Nara and enjoyed the official favor of the rulers and aristocracy, as it coexisted with the indigenous religion of Shintoism. Many of Nara's Buddhist temples and monasteries were built by emperors and noble families, while other temples were transferred to Nara from former capitals. At its peak during the 8th century, Nara was said to have had as many as 50 pagodas. Emperor Shomu built the Todaiji, a grand temple complex that was to serve as a central monastery for other Buddhist monasteries constructed in each province of Japan. Todaiji's construction began in 745 and was completed in 752. It was established not only for spiritual purposes but also to serve as a symbol of a united Japan. Emperor Shomu, who emulated Chinese culture, astutely realized that religion could play a strong role in consolidating Japan.

In 784, the capital of Japan was transferred to Kyoto, and Nara was no longer a city of political consequence. As a result, the many buildings of Nara, including the Todaiji, remained essentially untouched by the ravages of war. Today in Nara, Japanese history and traditional culture are very much alive for the visitor. Kofukuji Temple, for example, recalls the power of the Fujiwara clan in the 7th century. Its close connection with Kasuga Taisha Shrine, the Fujiwara family shrine, demonstrates the peaceful coexistence between Buddhism and Shintoism. The Todaiji and Toshodaiji temples both reflect the pervasive influence of Buddhism on the Japanese way of life over the centuries.

For many years, Nara, a small and quiet city, has been a favorite with many travelers in Japan. Apart from many temples and historical sites of interest in Nara, the narrow backstreets of Naramachi, just south of Sarusawa Pond in Nara-Koen Park, have hidden treasures: old wooden shops, merchants' houses, and traditional restaurants. Here you'll find shops selling the crafts for which Nara is famous: handmade brushes (*fude*) and ink sticks (*sumi*) for calligraphy and ink painting, Nara dolls carved in wood, and *Nara-sarashi-jofu*, fine, handwoven, sun-bleached linen (*See* Exploring, below).

Most of Nara's sights are within walking distance of the centrally located and picturesque Nara-Koen Park, inhabited by approximately 1,000 very tame deer, which roam freely around the various temples and shrines. The deer are considered to be divine messengers; they are particularly friendly when you feed them deer crackers, which can be purchased at stalls in the park. It is a singular pleasure to wander around the lush green park, dotted with numerous ponds, as you stroll from temple to temple.

Most day-trippers tend to visit only Nara-Koen Park, but we recommend skipping some of its sights and taking the time to visit Horyuji, the oldest remaining temple in all of Japan. Horyuji is located in the outskirts of Nara.

It is impossible to see all of the temples and shrines of Nara in one day. The exploring section of this chapter has a two-day itinerary. If you have only one day to spend in Nara, you may prefer to visit Horyuji, and forgo the other temples near it; then you can proceed to explore more of the Nara-Koen Park district.

Essential Information

Arriving and Departing

By Plane The nearest airport is Osaka International, which is served by frequent flights from Tokyo.

Between the Airport and Center City There is no direct transportation from the airport to Nara. Bus service is available to central Osaka or Kyoto, from which you can take a train to Nara.

By Train From Kyoto, the Kinki Nippon (*Kintetsu*) Railway's Limited Express trains take 33 minutes to reach Nara. It leaves every half hour and costs ¥900. The Ordinary Express train to Nara leaves every hour, takes 45 minutes, and costs ¥490. The JR train from Kyoto to Nara takes 50 minutes and costs ¥680.

From Osaka's Kintetsu-Namba Station, Nara is a 30-minute ride on the Kinki Nippon Railway's Limited Express. Trains leave every hour, and the fare is ¥870. The Ordinary Express to Nara takes 40 minutes, leaves every 20 minutes, and costs ¥460. From Osaka, the JR train to Nara takes 50 minutes. The train leaves every 20 minutes and costs ¥760.

From Kobe, take the JR-Tokaido Line rapid train from the Sannomiya Station to Osaka and transfer to one of the trains described above.

Getting Around

By Train Because Nara's main attractions are concentrated in one area in the western part of the city, you will do much of your sightseeing on foot. However, the JR Kansai Main Line and the Kinki Nippon Railways' Nara Line slice through the city and bring you close to major attractions. Rates depend upon the distance you travel. From downtown to the Horyuji Temple, the ride costs about ¥250.

By Bus Two local bus routes circle the main sites (Todaiji, Kasuga Taisha, and Shin-Yakushiji) in the central and eastern parts of the city: the #1 bus runs counterclockwise and the #2 bus runs clockwise. This urban loop line costs ¥140 for a ride of any distance. The #52 bus westward to Horyuji (with stops at Toshodaiji and Yakushiji) takes about 50 minutes and costs ¥600. The #52 can be caught in front of either the Nara Kintetsu Station or the Nara JR Station.

By Taxi The rate is ¥480 for the first 1.5 km and ¥90 for each additional 360 meters. From Nara Kintetsu Station to Kasuga Taisha by taxi runs about ¥900 one-way; to Horyuji, about ¥5,000 one-way.

By Bicycle   Because Nara is a small city with relatively flat roads, it is a good place for cycling. Bicycles can be rented from **Kintetsu Sunflower** (tel. 0742/24–3528), located on Konishi-dori Avenue near the Kintetsu Station (cost: ¥720 for 4 hours; ¥1,030 for 8 hours). Ask the Nara City Tourist Information Office located on the first floor of the Kintetsu Station for further information or directions. Some hotels also have bicycles available for rental.

Important Addresses and Numbers

Tourist   **Nara City Tourist Information Office** is on the first floor of the
Information   Nara Kintetsu Station, tel. 0742/24–4858. Open daily 9–5.

A **City Information Window** (tel. 0742/22–9821) can be found at the JR Nara Station. Open daily 9–5.

Nara City Tourist Center is located at 23-4 Kami-Sanjo-Cho, Nara-Shi, tel. 0742/22–3900. Open 9–9, but the English-language staff is on duty only until 3. This center, a 10-minute walk from both Nara Kintetsu and Nara JR stations, has free maps, information on sightseeing in English, local crafts, a souvenir corner, and a lounge where you can rest and plan your day.

The **Japan Travel-Phone** (tel. 0120/444–800) will give you toll-free English-language tourist information.

Consulates   The nearest U.S., Canadian, and British consulates are located in Osaka (*see* Chapter 9).

Emergencies   **Police,** tel. 110; **Ambulance,** tel. 119.

English-Language   **Nanto Shorin Bookstore** (tel. 0742/223–6369) is located on San-
Bookstore   jo-dori Avenue.

Guided Tours

Orientation Tours   Tours of Nara in English must be arranged in advance through the Kyoto or Osaka offices of the **Kintetsu Gray Line Bus Company.** Arrangements can also be made at the travel office in the basement of the New Miyako Hotel in Kyoto (tel. 075/691–0903), or by calling 06/313–6868 in Osaka. The fare for the afternoon tour is ¥5,700 adults, ¥4,500 children 6–11, children under 6 free.

Walking Tours   The Japan National Tourist Organization (JNTO) publishes the leaflet *Walking Tour Courses in Nara*, which gives brief descriptions of highlights along the way. One two-hour tour includes Nara Park and several nearby temples and shrines; other tours start with a bus ride from the center of the city. Because Nara has no JNTO office, ask for the leaflet at JNTO offices in Tokyo (6-6 Yurakucho 1-chome, Chiyoda-ku, tel. 03/502–1461) or in Kyoto (Kyoto Tower Bldg., Higashi-Shiokojicho, Shimogyo-ku, tel. 075/371–5649).

Personal Guides   The **Student Guide Service** (4 Nobori Oji, Sarusawa Kanko Annai-sho, tel. 0742/26–4753) and the **YMCA Guide Service** (also at 4 Nobori Oji, tel. 0742/24–4858) are available for free at the JR Nara Station information center, and the Kintetsu Nara

Station. Because these services use volunteer guides, it is best to call in advance to determine availability.

Exploring

Numbers in the margin correspond with points of interest on the Nara map.

At its founding in the 8th century, Nara was planned as a rectangular city with checkerboard streets based on the model of the Chinese city of Ch'ang-an. The city still maintains this highly organized pattern, and it is therefore extremely easy to find one's way around, because the streets are mainly at right angles. Many sights are located within or near Nara-Koen Park. Other major temples, such as Horyuji, Yakushiji, and Toshodaiji, are located west and southwest of Nara, and all can be reached by the same bus.

1 Begin your tour of Nara at the resplendent **Todaiji Temple,** located in Nara-Koen Park. Get there by boarding bus #2, which departs from the front of the JR and Kintetsu stations, and get off at the Daibutsuden stop. Cross the street and you will be at the path that leads to the Todaiji Temple complex. Another alternative is to walk from Kintetsu Station to Todaiji in about 15 minutes. As you exit the station, turn right and walk along the main road. Cross one major intersection and take the next left, which will lead you to the gate of Todaiji. You may also walk from the JR station; however, because this route passes through the less attractive modern sections of town, and because you will be doing a lot of walking in Nara, this option seems a waste of time and energy.

As you walk along the path leading to the temple complex, you will pass through the impressive dark wood front gate known as **2** **Nandaimon** (Great Southern Gate). The original gate was destroyed in a typhoon in 962; it was rebuilt in 1199. The gate is supported by 18 large wood pillars, each 62 feet high and 39 inches in diameter. In the two outer niches on either side of the gate are wood figures of Deva Kings, who guard the great Buddha within. They are the work of master sculptor Unkei, of the Kamakura period (1185–1335). In the inner niches are a pair of stone *koma-inu* (Korean dogs); these creatures are mythical guardians placed beside the gates to ward off evil.

Continue straight along the path leading to the main buildings of the Todaiji complex. In front of you is the entrance of the Daibutsuden Hall, but before entering this building, first go to **3** the small temple on the left, the **Kaidan-in.** Inside are clay statues of the Four Heavenly Guardians. The images are depicted in full armor, wielding weapons and displaying fierce expressions. *Kaidan* is a Buddhist expression for the terrace on which priests are ordained. The Chinese Buddhist priest Ganjin (688–763) ordained many Japanese Buddhist priests here. The original temple was destroyed repeatedly by fire, and the current structure was built in 1731. *Admission: ¥400. Open daily 8–5 (8–4:30 in winter).*

4 From the Kaidan-in, return to the entrance of the **Daibutsuden** (Hall of the Great Buddha), purportedly the largest wooden structure in the world (157 feet high and 187 feet long). The elegant and austere white building, with its wood beams darkened with age, is an impressive sight. Note a pair of gilt ornaments

1, 2, 3   5, 6
4
8

11

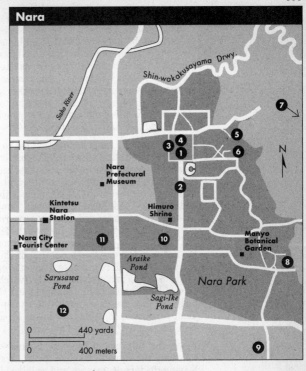

decorating the roof ridge. They are called *kutsugata* (shoe-shape) because they resemble footwear. In ancient times, these kutsugata not only were ornamental but also were believed to ward off fire. They unfortunately did not work, because the hall was repeatedly destroyed by fire. The current Daibutsuden was restored in 1709, at only two thirds the scale of the original structure. Inside the Daibutsuden is the Daibutsu, a 53-foot bronze statue of Buddha that is perhaps the most famous sight in all of Nara. The Daibutsu was originally commissioned by Emperor Shomu in 743. After numerous unsuccessful castings, the figure was finally made in 749. A statue of this scale had never before been built in Japan, and it was hoped that it would serve as a symbol to unite the country. The statue was dedicated in 752 in a grand ceremony attended by the then-retired Emperor Shomu, the imperial court members, and 10,000 priests and nuns.

Behind the Daibutsu to the right, you'll see a large wooden pillar with a hole at its base. You will also observe many Japanese tourists attempting to crawl through the opening, which is barely large enough for a petite adult. Local superstition has it that those who pass through the opening will eventually go to paradise. Children, in particular, love easing through and watching adults suffer the indignity of barely making it through the opening. In the back of the Daibutsu, to the left, is a model of the original Todaiji Temple. *Admission: ¥400. Open daily Jan.–Feb. 8–4:30, Mar. 8–5, Apr.–Sept. 7:30–5:30, Oct. 7:30–5, Nov.–Dec. 8–4:30.*

5:30

As you leave the exit of the Daibutsuden, turn left and walk up a winding path. Turn right, go up a stone staircase, and then veer left on the slope lined with stone lanterns. On your left, on

5 top of the slope, you will come to **Nigatsudo** (Second Month Temple), named because of a religious rite that used to be performed here every February. The temple was founded in 752 and houses some important images that are not on display to the public. However, because of the hilltop location, the temple's veranda offers a breathtaking, panoramic view of Nara-Koen Park. *Admission free. Open daily 8–5:30.*

6 Return along the same incline that led to Nigatsudo and turn left. The wood structure on your left is **Sangatsudo** (Third Month Temple), named after a rite that was performed annually in March. The entrance is on the right side as you face the building. Founded in 733, this temple is the original structure and the oldest building in the Todaiji Temple complex. As you enter, to your left are some benches covered with tatami straw mats. You can sit and absorb the wealth of 8th-century, National Treasure sculptures that crowd the small room. The principal image is the dry lacquer statue of Fukukenjaku Kannon, the Goddess of Mercy, whose diadem is encrusted with thousands of pearls and gemstones. The two clay statues on either side of her, the Gakko (Moonlight) and the Nikko (Sunlight) bodhisattvas, are considered fine examples of the Nara (or Tempyo) period, the height of classic Japanese sculpture. *Admission: ¥400. Open daily 7:30–5:30 (8–4:30 in winter).*

Leave the entrance of Sangatsudo, and walk straight ahead, following the signs in English for Mt. Wakakusa. You will be leaving the temple grounds and walking along a street. On the

7 left is the base of **Mt. Wakakusa,** which is actually more a hill covered with grass than a mountain. Once a year, on January 15, 15 priests set the hill's dry grass on fire. The blazes on the entire hill create a grand spectacle. On the right side of the street are many souvenir shops and small restaurants.

— Time Out Because there are very few areas to grab a bite in Nara-Koen Park, this is a good place to have a cup of coffee, a snack, or even lunch. Most of the restaurants on the street near Mt. Wakakusa are similar, but a few offer a better selection than the others. **Shiroganeya** (tel. 0742/22–2607) has noodles for ¥450–¥600 and lunches for ¥1,000–¥2,000. **Asahiken** (tel. 0742/22–2384) has a tasty tempura lunch for ¥1,200 and eel for ¥1,000. In both places, you pay when served.

8 If you continue past all of the restaurants and shops, at the end of the street you will see some stone steps. Cross a small bridge over a stream, and walk along on the path that leads into shady and peaceful woods. At the end of the path, turn left up the staircase before you, and you will be in front of the **Kasuga Taisha Shrine.** Kasuga was founded in 768 as a tutelary shrine for the Fujiwaras, a prominent feudal family. It is famous for the more than 2,000 stone laterns that line the major pathways to the shrine, all of which are lit three times a year on special festival days (Feb. 2, Aug. 14–15). For many years after its founding, the shrine was reconstructed, following the original design, exactly every 20 years according to Shinto custom, as is the case with the famous Ise Jingu Shrine in Mie Prefecture. (Kasuga, however, has not been rebuilt in many years.) The reason that many Shinto shrines are rebuilt is not only to renew the materials, but also to purify the site. It is said that Kasuga Taisha has been rebuilt over 50 times, the last time being in 1893. After you pass through the torii gate, the first wooden structure you'll see is the Haiden (Offering Hall), and to its left is the Naoraiden (Entertainment Hall). In back of the latter hall are the four Honden (Main Shrines). They are National Treasures, all built in the same Kasuga style, and painted bright vermilion and green—a striking contrast to the dark wooden exterior of most of the temples in Nara. The sacred deer of this shrine are protected, and they roam freely about the grounds. *Admission to Kasuga Shrine Museum: ¥350. Open 9–4. Admission to the shrine's outer courtyard free. For ¥500, you may enter the inner precincts to view the 4 Honden structures. Open Apr.–Oct. 8:30–5, Nov.–Mar. 9–4:30.*

Leaving Kasuga Taisha Shrine, walk down a path lined with stone lanterns past the Kasuga-Wakamiya Jinja Shrine. Continue down the woody path until you reach a road. Turn right and walk down the road. Take the first street on your left, and then your first right; you will be walking on another road parallel to the road you were on when you left the woods. This road is a residential street with many traditional Japanese houses. At the first left, turn, and walk approximately 100 yards. The road curves to the right and leads to the entrance of the **Shin-Yakushiji Temple.** This structure was founded in 747 by Empress Komyo (701–760) as a prayer requesting the recovery of her sick husband, Emperor Shomu. Most of the temple buildings were destroyed over the years. Only the Main Hall, which houses many fine objects of the Nara period, still exists. In the center of the hall is a wood statue of Yakushi Nyorai, the Physician of the Soul. Surrounding this statue are 12 clay images of the Twelve Divine Generals who protected Yakushi. Eleven of these figures are originals. The generals stand in threatening poses, bearing spears, swords, and other weapons, and display terrifying expressions. *Admission: ¥400. Open 8:30–6; (weekends 9–5:30).*

Leaving the Shin-Yakushiji Temple, retrace your steps and return along the street that leads to the temple. At the end of this street, turn left and walk straight until you get to the end of the road (approximately 650 yards). Across the street you will see a bus stop, where you can board the #1 bus back to the Daibutsuden stop. If time is limited and you want to skip Shin-Yakushiji Temple, take the path straight down from Kasuga Taisha to Nara-Koen Park, where you'll find the Nara National Museum and Kofukuji Temple. **Nara National Museum** specializes in Buddhist art. The East Wing, built in 1973, has many examples of calligraphy, paintings, and sculpture. The West Wing, built in 1895, features objects of archaeological interest. Each fall during the driest days of November, when the Shosoin Repository, located behind the Todaiji, opens its doors to air its magnificent collection, there is a special collection of part of its ancient treasures on display at the National Museum. For those who are in Nara at this time, it should not be missed. *10-6 Noborioji-cho, tel. 0742/22–7771. Admission: ¥360 (more for special exhibitions). Open 9–4:30. Closed Mon.*

Leaving the East Wing of the Museum, walk straight and you will find yourself at the **Kofukuji Temple** complex. This temple was originally founded in 669 in Kyoto by the Fujiwara family;

with the establishment of the new capital of Nara, it was transferred to its current location in 710. At its peak in the 8th century, Kofukuji (Happiness Producing Temple) was a powerful temple that had 175 buildings, of which fewer than a dozen remain. The history of this temple reflects the interesting relationship between Buddhism and Shintoism in Japan.

In 937, a Kofukuji monk had a dream in which the Shinto deity of Kasuga appeared in the form of a Buddha, asking to become a protector of the temple; in 947, some Kofukuji monks held a Buddhist ceremony at the Shinto Kasuga Taisha Shrine to mark the merging of the Buddhist temple with the Shinto shrine. Although you can enter many buildings in this temple complex, perhaps the most interesting is the *Kokuhokan* National Treasure House. This unattractive and modern concrete building holds a fabulous collection of National Treasure sculpture and other works of art from the Nara period. *Admission: ¥400. Open daily 9–5.*

Also of interest at the Kofukuji Temple complex are the two pagodas. The Five-Story Pagoda, at 164 feet, is the second tallest pagoda in all Japan. The original was built in 730 by Empress Komyo. Destroyed several times by fire, the current pagoda is an exact replica of the original and was built in 1426. The Three-Story Pagoda was built in 1114 and is renowned for its graceful lines and fine proportions.

There are several fine restaurants within minutes of the Kofukuji Pagoda (*See* Dining, below).

⓬ Before continuing on to the Western district and Horyuji Temple, take some time out from temple-viewing to walk along the quiet backstreets of **Naramachi.** Here, just south of Sarusawa Pond, is a maze of narrow residential streets lined with traditional houses and old shops, many of which deal in Nara's renowned arts and crafts. Gangoji Temple lies at the heart of this maze, and near it the little town museum known as the Naramachi Shiryokan (Historical Library). Maps to the area are available through the city's tourist information centers and the Shiryokan: a signboard map on the southwest edge of Sarusawa pond shows the way to all the important shops, museums, and galleries.

Look for **"Yu" Nakagawa** (tel. 0742/22–1322), which specializes in handwoven, sunbleached linen textiles, a Nara specialty known as *sarashi jofu.* Make an appointment to watch the making of ink sticks at **Kobaien** (tel. 0742/23–2965), for 400 years the makers of fine Nara ink sticks for calligraphy and ink painting. Visit the Silk Road folk-craft shop **Kikuoka** (0742/26–3889) near the Historical Library, On foot or by bicycle, Naramachi can offer a change of pace from ordinary sightseeing, and local residents are friendly and eager to help.

Numbers in the margin correspond with points of interest on the Western Nara Temples map.

From the JR Nara or Kintetsu Nara stations, it is quite simple to visit the four major temples located on the outskirts of Nara. From the Kintetsu and JR stations, take bus #52, which stops at Toshodaiji Temple, Yakushiji Temple, and Horyuji Temple, **❶** and returns along the same route. **Horyuji** is the most interesting of these temples, and it should be visited first. If time allows, go to the other temples as well. Get off the bus at the

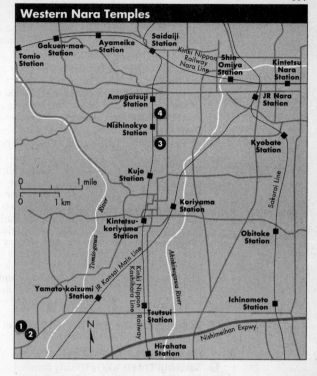

Horyuji-mae stop and walk down the path leading to the temple complex. Horyuji was founded in 607 by Prince Shotoku (573–621). Some of the temple buildings are among the oldest wood structures in the world. The first gate you pass through at Horyuji is the **Nandaimon,** rebuilt in 1438. The second gate is the **Chumon** (Middle Gate), which is the original gate, built in 607. Unlike most Japanese gates, which are supported by two pillars at the ends, this gate is supported by pillars in the center. Note the unusual shape of the pillars, which are entastic (curved outward in the center), an architectural technique used in ancient Greece that traveled as far as Japan. Entastic pillars in Japan exist only in the 7th-century structures of Nara.

As you pass through the gate you enter the western precincts of the temple. The first building you see on your right is the **Kondo** (Main Hall). On its left is a five-story pagoda. The entire pagoda was disassembled in World War II; after the war, it was reconstructed in its original form, using the same materials that were first used to build it in 607. In back of the pagoda is the **Daikodo** (Lecture Hall), which was destroyed by fire and rebuilt in 990. Inside the hall is an image of Yakushi Nyorai (Physician of the Soul).

From the Daikodo, walk back past the Kondo and continue on a straight path, exiting the western-precinct area. Turn left and walk past the pond on your right. You will come to two concrete buildings known as the **Daihozoden** (Great Treasure Hall). On display in these buildings are statues, sculptures, ancient Buddhist religious articles, and brocades. Of particular interest is a miniature shrine that belonged to Lady Tachibana, mother of the Empress Komyo. The shrine is only a little over 9 feet in height, and the Buddha image inside is about 20 inches tall.

As you leave the exit of the Daihozoden, turn left, walk a short distance until the path ends, and turn left again. You will be at the **Todaimon** (Great East Gate), which leads to the eastern precincts of the temple complex. The octagonal building is the **Yumedono** (Hall of Dreams). This building is so named because Prince Shotoku used to meditate in this hall. *Admission to all temple buildings: ¥700. Open daily 8–5 (8–4:30 in winter).*

In the rear of the eastern precinct of the Horyuji Temple is an exit that leads to **Chuguji Temple.** As you enter, notice the carefully raked pebbles on which you must walk to approach the entrance. Chuguji was originally the home of Prince Shotoku's mother. After she passed away, it became a temple dedicated to her memory. This quiet nunnery houses a graceful wooden image of the Miroku Bodhisattva, the Buddha of the Future. The famous statue dates to the Asuka period (552–645), and its gentle countenance offers an ageless view of hope for the future. Also of interest is the oldest example of embroidery in Japan, which dates as far back as the Asuka period (552–645). The framed cloth depicts Tenjukoku (Land of Heavenly Longevity). In front of the temple is a carefully tended small pond in which rocks are artfully arranged. Although this nunnery is a peaceful and interesting place to visit, it is not worth seeing if you are pressed for time. *Admission: ¥300. Open daily 9–4:30 (9–4 in winter).*

Get back on bus #52 and get off at the Yakushiji-mae stop. **Yakushiji Temple** was originally founded in 680 and was transferred to its current location in 718. As you enter the temple grounds, on your right you will see the **East Tower,** a pagoda that dates back to 1285. The pagoda has an interesting asymetrical shape, so startling that it inspired American scholar Ernest Fenollosa (1853–1908) to remark that it was as beautiful as "frozen music." Although it appears to have six stories, in fact it only has three; it consists of three roofs with smaller ones attached underneath. The **West Tower,** to your left, was built in 1981. The new building in the center is the **Kondo Hall,** which was rebuilt in 1976 and is painted in garish vermilion. These newer buildings are not nearly as attractive as the older structures, and they look out of place in the otherwise attractive temple complex. *Admission: ¥400. Open daily 8:30–5.*

From the rear gate of Yakushiji Temple, it is a 10-minute walk to **Toshodaiji Temple** down the "Path of History," trod by important dignitaries and priests for centuries. The path is lined with clay-walled houses, gardens, and small shops selling antiques, crafts, and *narazuke* (vegetables pickled in sake), a popular local specialty. There are also several good restaurants here (*see* Dining, below). Toshodaiji Temple was founded in 751 by Ganjin, a Chinese priest who traveled to Japan at the invitation of Emperor Shomu. At this time, Japanese priests had never received formal instruction from a Buddhist priest. The invitation was extended by two Japanese priests who traveled to China in search of a Buddhist priest willing to undertake the arduous and perilous journey to Japan. Ganjin agreed to go but was unsuccessful in his first attempts to reach Japan.

On his first journey, some of his disciples betrayed him. His second journey resulted in a shipwreck. During the third trip, his ship was blown off course, and on his fourth trip, he was refused permission to leave China by government officials. Before his next attempt, he contracted an eye disease that left him blind. Nevertheless, he persevered in his goal of reaching Japan and finally arrived in 750. Ganjin shared his knowledge of Buddhism with his adopted country and served as a teacher to many Japanese priests as well as Emperor Shomu; he is also remembered for bringing the first sugar to Japan.

In order to enter the temple complex, you pass through the **Nandaimon** (Great South Gate), which is supported by entastic pillars, also seen in the gate of Horyuji. The first building you see is the **Kondo** (Main Hall), which is considered to be one of the finest remaining examples of Nara architecture. Inside the hall is a lacquer statue of Vairocana Buddha, the same incarnation of Buddha that is enshrined at Todaiji Temple. The halo surrounding this figure originally was covered with 1,000 Buddhas, though only 864 remain today. In back of the Kondo is the **Kodo** (Lecture Hall), which was originally an assembly hall of the Nara Imperial Court and was moved to its current location when Toshodaiji was founded. Because all the other buildings of the Nara imperial court have been destroyed, the Kodo is the only remaining example of Nara palace architecture. In the back of the temple grounds is the **Mieido Hall,** in which there is a lacquer statue of Ganjin that dates back to 763. This image is on public display only once a year, on June 6, in commemoration of the birthday of the illustrious priest. *Admission: ¥300. Open daily 8:30–5.*

Dining

Nara cuisine resembles that of its neighboring city, Kyoto. The specialty of this region is *kaiseki*, carefully prepared and aesthetically pleasing Japanese full-course meals (usually 7–12 courses). Another local specialty is *chagayu*, rice porridge flavored with green tea and served with vegetables in season. Nara boasts the lowest rate of stomach cancer in Japan, and local wisdom attributes this to the healthfulness of chagayu. An unforgettable gourmet experience is your first bite of *narazuke*, tangy vegetables pickled in sake, often served as a side dish with traditional meals in Nara. Most visitors to Nara are day-trippers and do not necessarily plan to dine here, but an elegant Japanese meal in a traditional Nara restaurant is an appropriate and enjoyable way to conclude a day of temple viewing. Those who do not have time to partake of dinner may prefer to have a leisurely lunch in one of the restaurants located near a temple. One word of warning—many of the Nara restaurants are small and offer limited menus with set courses and no à la carte dishes, so it is often a good idea to make reservations in advance. Restaurants tend to close early in Nara, so plan accordingly. Some places may not have an English-speaking staff or menus in English, so ask someone from your hotel to help make your arrangements. This may seem a lot of trouble for the sake of a meal, but the quiet atmosphere and the hospitality of the local residents make this a memorable place to enjoy a fine traditional meal.

A 3% federal consumer tax is added to all restaurant bills. Another 3% local tax is added to the bill if it exceeds ¥5,000. At more expensive restaurants, a 10%–15% service charge is added to the bill. Tipping is not necessary.

The most highly recommended restaurants are indicated by a star ★.

Category	Cost*
Very Expensive	over ¥7,000
Expensive	¥5,000–¥7,000
Moderate	¥3,500–¥5,000
Inexpensive	under ¥3,500

Cost is per person without tax, service, or drinks

Credit Cards The following credit card abbreviations are used: AE, American Express; DC, Diners Club; MC, MasterCard; V, Visa.

★ **Onjaku.** Located near the Nara Hotel, this restaurant offers exquisitely presented kaiseki meals in a serene Japanese-style room with gentle lighting. The exterior, with its faded wood walls, is in keeping with the architectural style of Nara. The menu consists only of kaiseki set meals of varying prices. *1043 Kita-tenma-cho, tel. 0742/26–4762. Reservations required. Jacket and tie required. No credit cards. Lunch 12–1:30, dinner 5–8. Closed Tues. Very Expensive.*

Tsukihitei. A quiet Japanese restaurant set in the hills in back of the Kasuga Taisha Shrine, Tsukihitei serves formal kaiseki Japanese cuisine. Your dining experience begins when you walk up the shaded, wooded path leading to the restaurant. When you make your reservation, ask for a kaiseki set meal. As you dine on delicate morsels of fish, vegetables, and rice, and sip on sweet plum wine, you will look out on the forests surrounding the restaurant. *158 Kasugano-cho, tel. 0742/26–2021. Reservations required. Jacket and tie required. DC. Open daily 11:30–7. Very Expensive.*

Bekkan Kikusuiro. For those who want to try kaiseki, but do not want a formal and complicated meal, Bekkan Kikusuiro offers what it calls "mini kaiseki," an abridged version with fewer courses. Unlike standard kaiseki, where each course is served separately, your whole meal will be served on one tray. You can either sit at a table, which is less expensive, or in a Japanese-style room with tatami. *1130 Takahata-cho, tel. 0742/23–2001. Reservations advised. Dress: informal. No credit cards. Open daily 11–8:30. Expensive.*

Musashino. Located on the road from the Todaiji Temple complex leading to Kasuga Taisha Shrine, Musashino is a good place to have a traditional Japanese meal while seeing the various temples in Nara-Koen Park. Various set meals are available here, most of them consisting of tempura, steamed vegetables, soup, sashimi, and rice. *90 Kasugano-cho, tel. 0742/22–2739. Reservations advised. Dress: informal. No credit cards. Lunch 11–2, dinner 5–7. Moderate.*

Tempura Asuka. Directly south of Sarusawa Pond in Naramachi, Asuka offers full-course tempura meals and reasonably priced bento or tempura soba noodle lunches. Take a seat at the counter, reserve a tatami room, or sit at a table overlooking the garden. *11 Chonanin-cho, tel. 0742/26–4308. Dress: informal.*

AE, MC, V. Open 11–2 and 5–10, Sun. 5–9. Closed Tues. Moderate.

★ **Uma no me.** Kaiseki is not the only Japanese food available in Nara. Uma no me prides itself on home cooking, featuring roast fish, tofu, and other home-style Japanese dishes. The atmosphere is friendly and informal, with dark wood walls decorated with attractive pottery. This restaurant is within a few minutes' walk of the Nara Hotel. *1156 Takahata-cho, tel. 0742/23–7784. Reservations advised. Dress: informal. No credit cards. Lunch 11–2:30, dinner 5:30–8:30. Closed Thurs. Moderate.*

Van Kio. Outside the south gate of Yakushiji Temple, this traditional restaurant is famous for its "hot stone steam cookery" and its exotic meat dishes, including costly Nara venison and duck. Sushi and vegetarian dishes are also available. The resident landscape gardener, Kawatake-san, offers a selection of stone lanterns, basins, and other garden ornaments, as well as a variety of Nara antiques on the premises. *410 Rokujo-cho, tel 0742/33–8942. Reservations advised. Dress: informal. AE, MC, V. Open 11–10. Closed Mon. Moderate.*

★ **Yanagi-chaya.** Yanagi-chaya specializes in excellent *bento* meals, served in basic black-lacquer boxes. The food is Nara style: elegantly simple, with sashimi, stewed vegetables, and tofu. There are two branches of this revered old teahouse: (the elder) Yanagi-chaya is on the north bank and overlooks Sarusawa Pond. *49 Noborioji-cho, tel. 0742/22–7460. The younger sister is just east of Kofukuji Temple. 48 Teraoji-cho, tel. 0742/22–7560 (both locations). Reservations required. Dress: informal. No credit cards. Open 11:30–7:30. Closed Wed. Moderate.*

Ginsho. Across from the Nara Shiryokan (Historical Library) on a tiny side street in Naramachi, this soba noodle shop has a strikingly contemporary Japanese-style interior in a traditional building that harmonizes with the old neighborhood around it. Great ten-zaru soba (cold noodles and tempura) or tempura soba (hot tempura noodle soup) is served. *18 Nishishinya-cho, tel. 0742/23–1355. Dress: informal. No credit cards. Open 11–2. Closed Mon. Inexpensive.*

To-no-chaya. One distinctive Nara meal is *chagayu*, a rice porridge flavored with green tea. To-no-chaya offers a light meal of this special dish, combined with some sashimi and vegetables, plus a few sweetened rice cakes for dessert. From the restaurant you can see the Five-Story Pagoda of Kofukuji Temple. Appropriately, the name of this restaurant means the "tearoom of the pagoda." *47 Tera-oji, tel. 0742/22–4348. Reservations required. Dress: informal. No credit cards. Open 11:30–6. Closed Tues. Inexpensive.*

Lodging

There is much to see and do in Nara, but surprisingly few people plan to stay overnight. The city has fine accommodations in every style and price range, and because most people think of Nara as a day-trip destination, the streets are deserted at night, allowing those wise enough to tarry a chance to stroll undisturbed beside the ponds and in temple grounds. A 3% federal consumer tax is added to all hotel bills. Another 3% local tax is added if the bill exceeds ¥10,000. At most hotels, a 10%–15% service charge is added to the total bill. Tipping is not necessary.

The most highly recommended accommodations are indicated by a star ★.

Category	Cost*
Very Expensive	over ¥15,000
Expensive	¥10,000–¥15,000
Moderate	¥6,000–¥10,000
Inexpensive	under ¥6,000

Cost is for double room, without tax or service

Credit Cards The following credit card abbreviations are used: AE, American Express; DC, Diners Club; MC, MasterCard; V, Visa.

Edo-San. A night in this ryokan is an experience of being entirely enveloped by Japanese tradition. The accommodations here consist of small cottages with complete privacy. The cottages, old-fashioned Japanese structures with thatch roofs, are all surrounded by lovely trees, flowers, and other greenery. Deer from Nara-Koen Park occasionally wander onto the grounds of the inn. The excellent food, served in your private cottage, is included in the cost of your stay and consists of a variety of seafood dishes. *1167 Takahatake-cho, tel. 0742/26–2662. 11 rooms. AE, DC. Very Expensive.*

★ **Kankaso.** Elegance reigns at this ryokan, located near Todaiji Temple, right in the heart of Nara-Koen Park. The rooms have all been exquisitely decorated with Japanese scrolls, pottery, and other artwork. Great care is taken with the flower arrangements set in the alcove of each room. The communal bath looks out on a lovely garden. *10 Kasugano-cho, Nara-shi, tel. 0742/26–1128. 10 rooms. No credit cards. Very Expensive.*

★ **Nara Hotel.** Set right in the heart of Nara Park, this establishment is in fact a site of historical interest. Built in the Meiji period (1868–1912), the architectually delightful Nara Hotel has a graceful Japanese tiled roof and a magnificent lobby with high wood ceilings. The rooms, many of which overlook the temples of Nara-Koen Park, are spacious and also feature high ceilings. Ask for a room in the old wing, and enjoy the wonderful Old World charm of this grand turn-of-the-century hotel. *1096 Takahakate-cho, Nara-shi, tel. 0742/26–3300. 160 rooms. Facilities: Japanese and Western restaurants, tearoom. AE, DC, MC, V. Expensive.*

Nara Hotel Annex. Located in the Kintetsu Nara Station Building on the 6th through 8th floors, this hotel is extremely convenient for those who have to catch an early train. The rooms, slightly on the small side, are clean and comfortable. The restaurant has a good panoramic view of Nara. Service is exemplary. *28 Higashi-muki Nakamachi, Nara-shi, tel. 0742/26–3101. 34 rooms. Facilities: grill restaurant. AE, DC, MC, V. Expensive.*

Hotel Fujita Nara. This hotel, situated on the main road running from the JR Nara Station to the Nara-Koen Park, offers attractive rooms, simply decorated in beige colors. The Japanese restaurant serves excellent food. *47-1 Shimo Sanjo-cho, Nara-shi, tel. 0742/23–8111. 118 rooms. Facilities: Japanese restaurant, coffee shop. AE, DC, MC, V. Expensive.*

Hotel Sun Route Nara. With clean and comfortable rooms, this hotel is a cut above business hotels. Its location near the

Kintetsu Nara Station makes it a convenient place to stay. *1110 Takahatake Bodai-cho, Nara-shi, tel. 0742/22–5151. 95 rooms. Facilities: French restaurant, coffee shop. AE, DC, MC, V. Moderate.*

Kotton Hyakupasento. The name of this pleasant little hotel is a play on words written with Chinese characters that mean 100% Old Capital (rather than 100% Cotton). Popular with young Japanese, it is located on a side street near Sarusawa Pond, a short walk south of Nara Park. *1122–21 Bodaiji-cho, Nara-shi, tel. 0742/22–7117. 14 rooms. No credit cards. Moderate.*

People's Inn Hanakomichi. This attractive, reasonably priced establishment is located near Kintetsu Nara Station; it is also close to shops and within walking distance of Nara Park. The first and second floors feature boutiques, a gallery, and a café. *23 Konishi-cho, Nara-shi, tel. 0742/26–2646. 28 rooms: 20 Western-style, 8 Japanese-style. AE, DC, MC, V. Moderate.*

Seikanso. This family-run Japanese-style inn, located in the heart of the old Naramachi district, has a relaxed atmosphere, with most rooms overlooking a central garden. The bath is shared. *29 Higashikitsuji-cho, Nara-shi, tel. 0743/22–2670. 14 rooms. AE, MC, V. Moderate.*

9 Osaka

Introduction

In terms of industry, commerce, and technology, Osaka is definitely Japan's "Second City," next to Tokyo. It has a long history as a center for trade. Until the Meiji Restoration (1868), the merchant class was at the bottom of the social hierarchy, even though many of this class were financially among the richest people in Japan. Osaka expanded as a trading center at the end of the 16th century. Denied the usual aristocratic cultural pursuits, merchants sought and developed their pleasures in the theater and in dining. Even today, Osaka is known for its Bunraku (puppet theater) and its superb restaurants. Indeed, it is often said that many a successful Osaka businessman has eventually gone bankrupt by spending so much on eating.

In the 4th and 5th centuries, the Osaka-Nara region was the center of the developing Japanese (Yamato) nation. It was through Osaka that knowledge and culture from mainland Asia filtered into the fledgling Japanese society. During the 5th and 6th centuries, several emperors maintained an imperial court in Osaka, but the city lost its political importance after a permanent capital was set up in Nara in 694.

For the next several hundred years, Osaka, then known as Naniwa, was just another backwater port on the Inland Sea. Then, at the end of the 16th century, Hideyoshi Toyotomi (1536–1598), a great warrior and statesman, had one of Japan's most majestic castles built in Osaka as part of his successful unification of Japan. Hideyoshi encouraged merchants from around the country to set up their businesses in the city, which soon prospered. The castle took three years to build and was completed in 1586.

After Hideyoshi died, Ieyasu Tokugawa usurped power from the Toyotomi clan in 1603. However, the Toyotomi clan still maintained Osaka as their base. In 1614, Ieyasu sent his troops from Kyoto to Osaka to oppose rebellious movements in support of the Toyotomis. Ieyasu's army defeated the Toyotomi clan and their followers and destroyed the castle in 1615. Even though the Tokugawa Shogunate rebuilt the castle after they had destroyed it, Osaka was once again apart from Japan's political scene. Nevertheless, the Osakan merchants, left to themselves and far from the shogun's administrative center in Edo (Tokyo), continued to prosper, and they sent products from the hinterland through the city to Kyoto and Edo. During this time of economic growth, some of Japan's business dynasties were founded, whose names we still hear of today— Sumitomo, Marubeni, Sanwa, and Daiwa. Their growing wealth also gave them the means to pursue pleasure, and, by the end of the 17th century (the Genroku Era), Osaka's residents were giving patronage to such literary giants as the dramatist Chikamatsu (1653–1724), often referred to as the Shakespeare of Japan, and the novelist Saikaku Ihara (1642–1693). Chikamatsu's genius as a playwright elevated the Bunraku to a dignified dramatic art. Also at this time, Kabuki was patronized and developed by the Osakan merchants.

With the opening of Japan to Western commerce in 1853 and the end of the Tokugawa Shogunate in 1868, Osaka stepped into the forefront of Japan's commerce. At first Yokohama was the major port for Japan's foreign trade, but when the Great Kanto earthquake leveled that city in 1923, foreigners looked to Kobe and Osaka as alternative gateways for their import and export business. Osaka's merchant heritage placed the city in a good position for industrial growth—iron, steel, fabrics, ships, heavy and light machinery, and chemicals all became part of Osaka's output. Today, the region accounts for 25% of the country's industrial product and 40% of the nation's exports. Since the building of its new harbor facilities, Osaka has become a major port in its own right, as it relies less on the facilities in Kobe.

Osaka is also still a merchant city, with many streets devoted to wholesale business activity. For example, medical and pharmaceutical companies congregate in Doshomachi, and fireworks and toys are found in Matchamachi-suji. Anyone over 50 in Japan remembers Osaka as an exotic maze of crisscrossing waterways that provided transportation for the booming merchant trade. All but a few of the canals were destroyed, along with most of the traditional wood buildings, during the bombings of World War II. With all the present-day high-rise buildings and broad avenues, it is hard to visualize what the vivacious city must have been like 50 years ago.

Today, however, the city is working hard to restore some of the beauty that was lost. A greening campaign has been under way for the past few years, culminating in the 1990 International Flower Exposition.

Although Osaka may not have many sites of historical interest, it is a good starting point for trips to Nara, Kyoto, and Kobe. As a visitor, you can also participate in one of Osaka's leading pleasures: the pursuit of fine dining.

Essential Information

Arriving and Departing

By Plane   All domestic and international flights arrive at Osaka International Airport, about 30 minutes from central Osaka. Flights from Tokyo, which operate frequently throughout the day, take 70 minutes. Regular domestic flights from major Japanese cities to Osaka are handled by Japan Airlines (JAL), All Nippon Airways (ANA), and Japan Air System.

Between the Airport and Center City   Airport buses operate at intervals of 15 minutes to one hour, 6 AM–9 PM, and take passengers to seven locations in Osaka: Shin-Osaka Station, Umeda, Namba (near the Nikko and Holiday Inn hotels), Uehonmachi, Abeno, Sakaihigashi, and Osaka Business Park (near the New Otani Hotel). Buses take 25–50 minutes, depending on destination, and cost ¥320–¥410. Airport limousine schedules, with exact times and fares, are available at the information counter at the airport.

The following hotels operate shuttle bus service to and from Osaka International Airport: Osaka Dai-ichi Hotel, Hanshin Hotel, Nikko Osaka Hotel, New Otani Osaka Hotel, and the Holiday Inn Nankai.

Taxis between the airport and hotels in central Osaka take about 30 minutes and cost approximately ¥5,000.

By Train   The Tokaido Shinkansen super express trains from Tokyo to Osaka's Shin-Osaka Station take just under three hours and cost ¥13,480 for reserved seats, or ¥12,980 for nonreserved. The Shin-Osaka Station, which is located on the north side of the Shin-Yodo River, is linked to the center of the city by the JR Tokaido Line and the Midosuji Subway Line. The ride, which takes 6–20 minutes, depending on your mid-city destination, costs ¥170–¥200. Train schedule and fare information can be obtained at the Travel Service Centers in the Shin-Osaka Station. A taxi from the Shin-Osaka Station to central Osaka costs ¥1,000–¥2,500.

Getting Around

By Train Osaka's fast, efficient subway system offers the most convenient means of exploring the city, because the complicated bus routes display no signs in English, and taxis, while plentiful, are costly. The various lines converge at the Osaka Station at Umeda, where they are linked underground. The main line is the Midosuji, which runs between Shin-Osaka and Umeda in six minutes; Shin-Osaka and Shinsaibashi in 12 minutes; Shin-Osaka and Namba in 14 minutes; and Shin-Osaka and Tennoji in 20 minutes.

Trains run from early morning until nearly midnight at intervals of three to five minutes. Fares are determined by the distance traveled. A one-day pass for unlimited municipal transportation can be obtained at the commuter ticket windows in major subway stations and at the Japan Travel Bureau office in Osaka Station (cost: ¥800 adults, ¥400 children). A subway network map of Osaka is available from the Japan National Tourist Organization.

By Bus Economical one-day transportation passes for Osaka are valid on bus lines as well as subway routes, and the service operates throughout the day and evening, but bus travel is a challenge best left to local residents or those fluent in Japanese.

By Taxi You'll have no problem hailing taxis on the street or at specified taxi stands. (A red light in the lower left corner of the windshield indicates availability.) The problem is moving in Osaka's heavy traffic. Fares are metered at ¥480 for the first two km, plus ¥90 for each additional 450 meters. It is not customary to tip the driver.

Important Addresses and Numbers

Tourist Information **Osaka Tourist Information Center** (tel. 06/305–3311), located on the east side of the main exit of the Japan Railways Shin-Osaka Station, is open daily 8–8; closed December 29–January 3. Another branch (tel. 06/345–2189) at the east gate of the JR Osaka Station operates daily 8–5; closed December 29–January 3.

The **Information Center** in the Osakajo Castle (tel. 06/94–0546) is open daily 9–5.

Tourist Information Service, Osaka Prefectural Government (tel. 06/941–9200), is located in the lobby of the International Hotel (58 Hashizumecho, Uchihonmachi, Chuo-ku), a five-minute walk from Sakaisuji Hommachi Subway Station (open noon–7; closed Tues.).

Japan Travel-Phone (tel. 0120/444–800) will provide free information service in English 9–5 daily.

Consulates **U.S.,** 2-11-5 Temma, Kita-ku, tel. 06/315–5900.
Canadian, 28 Hachiman-cho, Chuo-ku, tel. 06/212–4910.
U.K., The Hongkong and Shanghai Bank Bldg., 4-45 Awajicho, Chuo-ku, tel. 06/231–3355.

Emergencies **Police,** tel. 110; **ambulance,** tel. 119.

Doctors **Tane General Hospital,** 1-2-31 Sakaigawa, Nishi-ku, tel. 06/581–1071; **Sumitomo Hospital,** 15 Nakanoshima, 5-chome, Kita-ku, tel. 06/443–1261; **Yodogawa Christian Hospital,** 57 Awaji-Honmachi, 1-chome, Higashi Yodogawa-ku, tel. 06/322–2250; **Osaka University Hospital** (accepts emergency patients by ambulance only), 1-50 Fukushima, 1-chome, Fukushima, tel. 06/451–0051.

English Bookstore **Kinokuniya Book Store Co., Ltd.** (Hankyu Sanban-gai 1-1-3, Shibata, Kita-ku, tel. 06/372–5821) is open 10–9, except for the third Wednesday of the month.

Travel Agencies **Japan Travel Bureau,** Foreign Tourist Division, 1-3-7 Tosabori, Higobashi, Shimizu Bldg., Nishi-ku, tel. 06/449–1071; **Hankyu Express International,** 8-47 Kakuta-cho, Kita-ku, tel. 06/373–5471; **Kinki Nippon Tourist Co.,** Shokusanjutaku Bldg., 2-26 Uehonmachi 6 chome, Kita-ku, tel. 06/768–4821; **Nippon Express Co., Ltd.,** 3-16 Sonezaki Shinchi 1-chome, Kita-ku, tel. 06/345–1841; **Nippon Travel Agency Co., Ltd.,** Dojima Bldg., 6-8 Nishi Tenma 2-chome, Kita-ku, tel. 06/364–1681; **Tokyu Tourist Corp.,** Kansai Foreign Tourist Center, Nakamuraya Bldg., 4th Fl., 1-2 Dojima 2-chome, Kita-ku, tel. 06/344–5488.

Business Assistance Contact **Information Service System Co., Ltd. (I.S.S.)** (Hotel Nikko Osaka, 1–3–5 Nishi Shinsaibashi, Chuo-ku, tel. 06/245–4015) for business-related assistance, including quick-print business cards and interpreting.

Guided Tours

Orientation Tours The **Municipal Bus System** (tel. 06/311–2995) operates regular sightseeing tours of the city on its double-deck "Rainbow" bus. The tours are in Japanese. The five different tour routes start at the Umeda Sightseeing Information Center. They vary in length from three to four hours and cost about ¥3,000.

The **Aqua Liner** (tel. 06/444–5000) operates a 60-minute tour through Osaka's waterways, departing every hour 10–7 from three piers at Osakajo, Tenmabashi, and Yodoyabashi. The hours are extended somewhat in spring, summer, and fall (cost: ¥1,600 adults, ¥800 children). This is the only tour of Osaka conducted in both Japanese and English.

Special-Interest Tours **Japan Travel Bureau** (tel. 06/449–1071) conducts Osaka Industrial Tours that include visits to a variety of factories and are operated periodically during March, April, July, August, and October. Japan's **Home Visit System,** which enables foreign visitors to meet local people in their homes for a few hours and learn more about the Japanese lifestyle, is available in Osaka. Visitors should apply in advance through the **Osaka Tourist Information Center** (tel. 06/305–3311) at the JR Shin-Osaka Station; at the **Osaka Tourist Association** (tel. 06/208–8955) at Sumitomo Seimei Yodoyabashi Bldg.; or at the Osaka **City Tourist Information Office** (tel. 06/345–2189) at the JR Osaka Station.

Excursions **Japan Travel Bureau** (tel. 06/343–0617) operates daily afternoon tours to Kyoto and Nara. Pickup is available at several hotels. **Fujita Travel Service** (075/222–0121) offers a full-day
Kyoto-Nara tour, departing from the Osaka Hilton Hotel and
including train transfer to Kyoto.

Exploring

*Numbers in the margin correspond with points of interest on
the Osaka map.*

Visitors often arrive in Osaka at Shin-Osaka Station, which is
the terminal for the Shinkansen super express trains. Located
two miles north of Osaka's main railway station amid some of
Osaka's most modern architecture, it is also close to the Expo
Memorial Park. If you should arrive at Shin-Osaka, take the
commuter train to Osaka Station, which is on the edge of central Osaka.

Osaka is divided into 26 wards, and, though the official city
population is only 2.6 million, if one were to include the suburbs, this number would be around 6 million. Central Osaka is
predominantly a business district, but there is shopping and
entertainment. This is also the area with hotels and most of the
sights that will interest the visitor.

Central Osaka is bounded by the JR Osaka Kanjo (Loop) Line.
The main railway station, Osaka Station, is at the northern
part of this loop. In front of this station and to the east of the
Hankyu Umeda Station is the center of the Kita (north) district. While ultramodern skyscrapers soar above the streets,
underground is a maze of malls (Umeda Chika Center),
crowded with shops that sell the latest fashions, dozens of restaurants, and department stores that offer every modern gadg-
et. This district is one of the two major shopping areas in
Osaka. Just to the south of the station are some major hotels,
such as the Hilton, the Dai-ichi, and, farther south, the ANA-
Sheraton Osaka.

If you continue south, you come to two rivers, the Dojimagawa
and the Tosaborigawa, with Nakanoshima Island separating
them. Here is Osaka's oldest park, which is home to many of the
city's cultural and administrative institutions, including the
Bank of Japan and the Museum of Oriental Ceramics.

Beyond these rivers and south of Nakanoshima Island are the
Minami (south) and Shinsaibashi districts. They are very close
together and are surrounded by the JR Osaka Kanjo (Loop)
Line. Shinsaibaishi is Osaka's expensive shopping street, with
stores featuring high-fashion merchandise. The nearby America-Mura, with American-style boutiques, and the Europe-
Mura, with Continental fashion shops, appeal to the hip Osaka
young. Minami has a wonderful assortment of bars and restaurants, especially on Dotonbori Street. The Bunraku National
Theater is also close by, a few blocks to the southeast, near the
Nipponbashi Subway Station.

In the eastern part of Osaka, just within the area surrounded
by the JR Osaka Kanjo (Loop) Line, is Osaka's main tourist attraction, Osakajo Castle. Just north of the castle are the futuristic Twin 21 towers of Osaka Business Park. The other major
landmark, Shitennoji Temple, is in the southeast corner of the

JR Osaka Loop Line. The number of tourist attractions in the city are limited and can easily be visited in less than a day.

❶ The most famed sight in Osaka is **Osakajo Castle** in the eastern part of the city. The easiest way to reach the castle is to take the Tanimachi Subway Line from Higashi Umeda Station (just to the southwest of Osaka Station) to Tanimachi Yonchome Station. From there, it is a 15-minute walk up the hill to where Osakajo stands. An alternative route, and one that is slightly easier, is to take the JR Osaka Kanjo (Loop) Line (if you have just arrived at Osaka Station, walk over to Umeda Station for the Kanjo Loop Line) to Osakajo Koen-mae Station. You'll still have a walk up the hill from the other side.

Osakajo was one of Hideyoshi Toyotomi's finest buildings. The first stones were laid in 1583, and for the next three years as many as 100,000 workmen labored to build a majestic and impregnable castle. Note the thickness and the height of the walls. In order to demonstrate their loyalty, the feudal lords from the provinces were requested to contribute immense granite rocks. The largest piece of stone is said to have been donated by Hideyoshi's general, Kato Kiyomasa (1562–1611), and brought from Shodo Island. Known as Higo-Ishi, the rock measured a gigantic 19 feet high and 47 feet wide.

Hideyoshi was showing off with this castle. He had united Japan after a period of devastating civil wars, and he wanted to secure his western flanks. He also wanted to establish Osaka as a vibrant merchant town that could distribute the produce from the surrounding wealthy territories. The castle was intended to demonstrate Hideyoshi's power and commitment to Osaka, so as to attract merchants from all over Japan.

Hideyoshi's plan succeeded, but within two years of his death in 1598, Ieyasu Tokugawa, an executor of Hideyoshi's will, took power and got rid of the guardians of Hideyoshi's son. However, it was not until 1614 that Ieyasu sent his armies to defeat the Toyotomi family and their allies. In 1615, the castle was destroyed, and Ieyasu Tokugawa was victorious.

Over a 10-year period, Osakajo was rebuilt according to its original plan by the Tokugawa Shogunate and was completed in 1629. This version remained standing until 1868. The Tokugawa Shogunate's power was at an end. Rather than let the castle fall into the hands of the forces of the Meiji Restoration, the Tokugawa troops burned it. In 1931, the present five-story (8 stories inside) *donjon* (main stronghold) was built in ferro-concrete for the prestige of the city. An exact replica of the original, though marginally smaller in scale, it stands 189 feet high (including 46-foot-high stone walls). At night, when it is illuminated, it becomes a brilliant backdrop to the city.

Inside the castle is a museum with artifacts of the Toyotomi family and historical objects relating to Osaka prior to the Tokugawa Shogunate's reign. Unless you are a Hideyoshi fan, these exhibits perhaps have marginal interest. The castle's magnificent exterior and the impressive view from the eighth floor of the donjon are the reasons to see Osakajo. If you are really fortunate, your visit may coincide with cherry-blossom time, when the lovely castle gardens are at their best. *1-1 Osaka-jo, Chuo-ku, Osaka, tel. 06/941-3044. Admission: ¥400 adults, ¥50 children 5–15. Open 9–5 (enter by 4:30), 9–8:30 July 15–Aug. 31 (enter by 8). Closed Dec. 28–Jan. 1.*

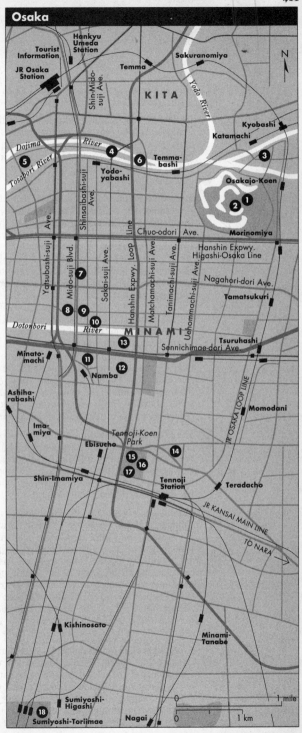

Osaka

❷ The **Osaka City Museum** is also located on the castle grounds. This museum is a storehouse of municipal memorabilia. On display are books, photographs, and other records of the city's history. *1-1 Osaka-jo, Chuo-ku, Osaka, tel. 06/941-7177. Admission to the permanent collection: ¥200 adults, ¥150 college and high school students, ¥100 younger students. Admission to special exhibitions varies. Open 9:15-4:45 (enter by 4:15). Closed 2nd and 4th Mon. of each month.*

Leave the castle and, facing north, walk down the hill past Osakajo Hall (a center used for sport competitions and concerts), and cross the overpass near the Aqua Liner (water-bus) pier. On the other side of the Hiranogawa River, you'll come to the New Otani Hotel and, just behind it, the Twin 21 towers of ❸ **Osaka Business Park.**

Panasonic Square, on the second floor of one of the Twin 21 structures, the **National Tower Building,** features displays of the Matsushita Electric Group's high-tech developments. Both fun and educational, the exhibits are divided into four zones: Knowing, Learning, Experiencing, and Creating with Electronics. On any given day, you'll see crowds of Japanese schoolchildren absorbed in testing the TV telephone that allows them to see the person they're talking to on a monitor screen, or donning Superman costumes to star and direct in their own mini-TV shows. Other displays allow you to check your golf, baseball, or tennis skills on a video camera at the Swing Check Corner; have your portrait drawn by a robot; and test what you've learned via a computerized question-and-answer session—a computer will even calculate your score. Moderately priced food shops serve sushi and other light fare, and there is also a souvenir shop. *Twin 21, National Tower Bldg., 2nd floor, 1-61 Shiromi 2-chome, Chuo-ku, tel. 06/949-2122. Admission: ¥300 adults and high school students, ¥200 junior high and elementary school students. Open 10-6 (enter by 5:30).*

❹❺ **The Museum of Oriental Ceramics** is in Nakanoshima Park, on **Nakanoshima Island,** between the Dojimagawa and Tosaborigawa rivers. From Osaka Business Park, take the JR train at Katamichi Station to the Kyobashi stop and transfer to the Keihan Line, which you take to the Yodoyabashi stop. It's a five-minute walk from the station.

The museum opened in 1982 and houses about 1,000 pieces of Chinese and Korean ceramics. The artworks come from the priceless Ataka Collection, which belonged to a wealthy Japanese industrialist, and were donated to the museum by the giant Sumitomo Group conglomerate. The ceramic collection, rated as one of the finest in the world, includes 14 works that have been designated as National Treasures or Important Cultural Properties. *1-1 Nakanoshima, Kita-ku, tel. 06/223-0055. Admission: ¥500 adults, ¥400 high school students, ¥200 junior high and elementary school students. Admission to special exhibitions varies. Open Tue.-Sun. 9:30-5 (enter by 4:30).*

❻ After your visit to the museum, take some time for a stroll in Osaka's oldest park, **Nakanoshima-Koen,** which opened in 1891 and is located at the eastern end of Nakanoshima Island. Also on the island are **Osaka University** and **Osaka Festival Hall,** which is considered the city's best concert hall. Major Japanese and international musicians regularly appear here. The **Royal Hotel** is at the far end of the island. If you linger till after dark, you'll be able to enjoy the illuminated view of **Osaka City Hall,** near the ceramics museum, and of the bridges that link the island with the mainland.

7 Take the Midosuji Subway Line from Yodoyabashi to Shinsaibashi Station. When you emerge, you'll be on **Midosuji Boulevard.** Shinsaibashi and Ebisubashi, which run parallel to Midosuji, are two of Osaka's best shopping and entertainment **8** streets. East of Midosuji Boulevard, you'll find **America-Mura** (American Village), a group of streets that feature stores with youth-oriented American clothes. Bright neon signs with the Japanese version of American shop names hang over the shop doors as the sound of rock music booms from inside. The stores carry an assortment of U.S.-made jeans and sportswear, and they are tended by Japanese youth who wear punk hairstyles.

9 West of Midosuji Boulevard is **Europa Mura** (European Village), with its boutiques of fashionable clothes from European capitals. The sidewalks in this area, which are made of cobblestone, attempt to re-create the feeling of a traditional Continental city. Located here are Parco, Sogo, and Daimaru department stores, some of Japan's top chain stores.

10 If you continue walking south on Midosuji Boulevard, you'll come to **Dotonbori,** a broad cross street that runs alongside the river of the same name. The street and the area around it are filled with a cornucopia of restaurants and nightclubs.

A virtual feast for neon connoisseurs, this is the place to stroll in the evening for a glimpse of nightlife, Osaka-style. Locate the giant, undulating Kani Doraku crab sign, a local landmark, walk in any direction, and prepare yourself for a unique sensory experience.

11 Two blocks from Dotonbori Street is the **Namba Rainbow Town** shopping mall, which extends six blocks east–west. About two blocks from Rainbow Town is **Nan Nan Town,** another underground mall, which runs eight blocks south from the southern end of Midosuji Boulevard. Both malls offer a good selection of clothes, appliances, and unpretentious restaurants. At the far southern end of Midosuji Boulevard are the Kabukiza Theater and the Takashimaya department store. East of the southern **12** terminus of Namba Station is **Den Den Town,** where, amid its nearly 300 specialty shops, you can purchase discounted electrical appliances. About a block south from Den Den Town is **Osaka Stadium,** where the local baseball teams square off.

13 From Namba Station, if you take the Sennichi-mae Subway Line, it is just one stop east to the Nipponbashi Station and the **National Bunraku Theater.** Take exit #7 and you will be right outside the theater. Osaka is known for Bunraku, and, if you are in the city at the right time, this is an opportunity you shouldn't miss. Osakans have helped make it a sophisticated art form. This puppet form of drama began during the Heian period (794–1192), but it was not until the late-17th and early 18th century that the genius of playwright Chikamatsu elevated Bunraku to a dignified dramatic art. A typical Bunraku play deals with themes of tragic love or stories based on historical events. The story is chanted in song by a *joruri* singer who is accompanied by ballad music played on a three-stringed *shamisen.* Although you may not understand the words, the tone of the music certainly sets a mood of pathos.

Bunraku's actors are puppets, about two-thirds human size. Elaborately dressed in period costume, each puppet is made up of interchangeable parts—a head, shoulder piece, trunk, legs, and arms. For example, various puppet heads are used for roles of different sex, age, and character, and a certain hairstyle will indicate a puppet's position in life. Each puppet is operated by three puppeteers, who must act in complete unison. The *omozukai* controls the expression on the puppet's face and its right arm and hand. The *hidarizukai* controls the puppet's left arm and hand, and any props that it is carrying. The *ashizukai* moves the puppet's legs. This last task is the easiest. The most difficult task belongs to the omozukai. It takes about 30 years to become an accomplished expert. A puppeteer must spend 10 years as ashizukai, a further 10 as hidarizukai, and then 10 years as omozukai.

These master puppeteers not only skillfully manipulate the puppets' arms and legs, but also roll the eyes and move the lips so that the puppets express fear, joy, and sadness in a most life-like manner. Although they are puppets, their expressions of happiness and anguish are not difficult to understand. *12-10 Nipponbashi 1-chome, Chuo-ku, Osaka, tel. 06/212–2531. Admission: ¥3,600 and up. Bunraku performances are scheduled 7 times a year (Jan., Mar., Apr., June, July, Aug., Nov.). Each run starts on the 3rd of the month and lasts about 3 weeks.*

After you leave the Bunraku Theater, walk east for about 10 minutes to the Tanimachi-Kyuchome Subway Station. If you take the Tanimachi Subway Line going south, it is only one stop to the Shitennojimae Station and from there only a few minutes' walk to Shitennoji Temple. If you wish to come directly here from Osakajo Castle, take the JR Kanjo (Loop) Line from Osakajo-Koen Subway Station or Kyobashi Subway Station going south. If you exit at Tennoji Subway Station, you'll see the street going north up to Shitennoji Temple; Tennoji-Koen Park will be on the left.

⓮ Shitennoji Temple, popularly known as Tennoji, is one of the most important historical sights in Osaka. Architecturally, the temple has suffered. The ravages of fire have destroyed it many times. Maintaining the original design and adhering to the traditional mathematical alignment, the last reconstruction of the Kondo (Main Hall), Kodo Taishiden Hall, and the five-story pagoda was after World War II, in 1965. What has managed to survive is the stone *torii* (arch) gate that was built in 1294 and stands at the main entrance. One does not often see a torii gate at a Buddhist temple. Shitennoji Temple claims that it is the oldest Buddhist temple in Japan. Outdating the Horyuji Temple in Nara (607), Shitennoji Temple was founded by Prince Shotoku in 593.

Umayado no Mikoto (573–621), who is posthumously known as Prince Shotoku or Shotoku Taishi, was one of early Japan's most enlightened rulers. He was made regent over his aunt, Suiko, and set about instituting reforms and establishing Buddhism as the state religion. Buddhism had been introduced to Japan from China and Korea in the early 500s, but it had been seen as a threat to the aristocracy, who claimed prestige and power based upon their godlike ancestry. Prince Shotoku recognized both the power of Buddhism and how it could be used as a tool for the state. His swords and a copy of his Hokkekyo Lotus Sutra, made during the Heian period (897–1192), were stored at Shitennoji, though today they are kept in the National Museum of Tokyo. On the 21st of every month, the temple has a flea market that sells antiques and baubles; it shouldn't be missed if you're in town at this time. *1-11-18 Shitennoji, Tennoji-ku, Osaka, tel. 06/771–0066. Admission: ¥200 adults, ¥120 children. Open 8:30–4:30 Apr.–Sept., 8:30–4 in winter.*

⑮
⑯ To the southwest of Shitennoji Temple is **Tennoji-Koen Park,** where the **Municipal Museum of Fine Art** is located. This museum is best known for its collection of classical art from the 12th to the 14th century. An exception to this are the special exhibitions that feature the works of an Edo period artist, Ogata Korin. Some modern art is also included in its permanent collection (though these seem to appeal more to the Japanese than to foreigners), as well as a collection of Chinese paintings and archaeological artifacts. *1-82 Chausuyama-cho, Tennoji-ku, tel. 06/771–4874. Admission to the permanent collection: ¥200 adults, ¥150 college and high school students, ¥100 younger students. Admission for special exhibitions varies. Open 9:30–5 (enter by 4). Closed Mon.*

⑰ Adjacent to the Municipal Museum is **Keitakuen Garden,** with flowers, trees, and a pond. The garden, originally constructed in 1908, was given to the city by the late Baron Sumitomo. An example of the Japanese circular garden, its cherry trees and azaleas are lovely to behold when in bloom. The garden offers a welcome respite from the rest of the city. *Admission: ¥150 adults, ¥50 children 6–12. Open Tues., Thurs., Sun. 9:30–4:30 (enter by 4).*

The park also contains the **Tennoji Botanical Gardens** (open 9:30–5). If you are traveling with children, next to the Keitakuen Garden is the **Municipal Zoological Gardens.** The zoo is one of the largest in Japan and has some 22,000 animals caged. *6-74 Chausuyama-cho, Tennoji-ku, tel. 06/771–8401. Admission: ¥400 adults, ¥200 college and high school students, children under 15 free. Open 9:30–4:30 (enter by 4). Closed 3rd Mon. of each month and Dec. 29–Jan. 1.*

Before you leave Tennoji-Koen Park you may also notice **Chausuyama Hill,** a prehistoric burial mound and the site of Ieyasu Tokugawa's camp during the siege of Osakajo Castle in 1614–1615.

⑱ The final site on this exploring tour is the **Sumiyoshi Grand Shrine.** Most of the Shinto shrines in Japan today were built after the 8th century and were heavily influenced by Buddhist architecture. The three shrines that were built prior to the arrival of Buddhism in Japan are the Ise Jingu (Grand Shrines) at Ise, the Izumo Taisha Shrine near Matsue, and the Sumiyoshi Shrine in Osaka. To reach this latter shrine, take the 20-minute ride on the Nankai Main Line to the southern suburbs of Osaka.

Sumiyoshi Grand Shrine is dedicated to the goddess of sea voyages, Sumiyoshi, and, according to legend, was founded by Empress Jingu in 211 to express her gratitude for her safe return from a sea voyage to Korea. In those days, the shrine faced the sea rather than the concrete urban sprawl that now surrounds it. On the shrine's grounds are many stone lanterns donated by sailors and shipowners as dedications to Sumiyoshi and other Shinto deities that also guard the voyages of seafarers. Note the arched bridge on the grounds, said to have been given by Yodogimi, the consort of Hideyoshi Toyotomi who bore him a son. Of the three ancient shrines (Ise Jingu, Izumo Taisha, and Sumiyoshi), only Sumiyoshi has a Japanese cypress structure that is painted vermilion; the other two are left unpainted with their natural wood showing. According to the Shinto custom, shrines were torn down and rebuilt periodically to the exact specifications of the original. Sumiyoshi, which, incidentally, is also the name given to the style of architecture of this shrine, was last replaced in 1810. Sumiyoshi Matsuri, one of the city's largest and liveliest festivals, is held on July 30 and August 1. A crowd of rowdy young men carries a two-ton portable shrine from the Sumiyoshi Shrine to the Yamato River and back; this event is followed by an all-night street bazaar. *2-9-89 Sumiyoshi, Sumiyoshi-ku, tel. 06/672-0753. Admission free. Open daily 6-6 Apr.-Oct., 6:30-5 Nov.-Mar.*

Additional Attractions

The following lists include additional places of interest that were not covered in the preceding exploring tour:

Historical Buildings and Sights

Nintoku Mausoleum. The 4th-century mausoleum of Emperor Nintoku is in Sakai City. Archaeologists calculate that the central mound of this site is 1.3 million square feet; the mausoleum was built on an even larger scale than that of the pyramids of Egypt. Its construction took more than 20 years and required a total work force of about 800,000 laborers. Surrounding the emperor's burial place are three moats and pine, cedar, and cypress trees. Visitors may walk around the outer moat to get an idea of the size of the mausoleum and the grounds. However, entry into the mausoleum is not allowed. To get to the mausoleum, take the JR train from Tennoji Station to Mozu Station (½-hour ride). From there, the sight is a five-minute walk away. *2 Mozu-Yugumo, Saki-shi, tel. 0722/41-0002.*

Temples and Shrines

Fujiidera Temple. A 1,000-handed seated statue of Kannon, the Goddess of Mercy, made in the 8th century, is the main object of worship here. The statue, a National Treasure, is the oldest Buddhist sculpture of its type. To reach the temple, get on the Midosuji Subway Line from Umeda Station to Tennoji Station, then transfer to the Kintetsu Minami-Osaka Line and take it to Fujiidera Station. The temple is a few minutes' walk from the station. *1-16-21 Fujiidera, Fujiidera-shi, tel. 0729/38-0005. The statue is on view the 18th of each month 8-5.*

Temmangu Shrine. A short walk from the Minami Morimachi Station on the Tanimachi line, this 10th-century shrine is the main site of the annual **Tenjin Festival,** held July 24-25, one of the three biggest and most enthusiastically celebrated festivals in Japan. During the festival, dozens of floats are paraded through the streets, and more than 100 vessels, lighted by lanterns, sail along the canals amid a dazzling display of fireworks. A renowned scholar of the 9th century, Michizane Sugawara, is enshrined at Temmangu; he is now considered the God of Aca-

demics. 2-1-8 Tenjinbashi, Kita-ku, tel. 06/353–0025. Admission free. Open daily 5:30–5.

Museums and Galleries

Japan Folk Art Museum. Located in Expo Park, the museum contains outstanding examples of traditional regional handicrafts. On view are ceramics, textiles, wood crafts, bamboo ware, and other items. To get to the museum, take the Midosuji Subway Line at Umeda Station to Senri-Chuo Station (30-minutes); then change here to bus #114 or #115 at stop #6 to Expo Park. *10–5 Banpaku-koen, Senri, Suita-shi, tel. 06/877–1971. Admission: ¥360 adults, ¥310 college and high school students, ¥100 junior high and elementary school students. Admission to special exhibitions varies. Open 9–4. Closed Wed.*

Mint Museum. This money museum displays about 16,000 examples of Japanese and foreign currencies. It also exhibits Olympic medals, prehistoric currency, and ancient Japanese gold coins. Near the museum is the Mint Garden, part of which is open to the public for a short period during the cherry-blossom season (usually Apr.); a visitor can stroll on a pathway, shaded by blossoms, along the Yodogawa River. The museum is a 15-minute walk from Minami Morimachi or Temmabashi Station on the Tanimachi Subway Line. *1 Temma, Kita-ku, tel. 06/351–8509. Admission free. Open 9–3:30. Closed weekends and holidays.*

National Museum of Ethnology. This building, also in Expo Park, offers a range of exhibits on comparative cultures of the world, with displays arranged according to regions. Automatic audiovisual equipment, called Videotheque, provides close-up views of the customs of the peoples of the world. To reach the museum, take the Midosuji Subway Line at Umeda Station to Senri-Chuo Station (30 min); then change here to bus #114 or #115 at stop #6 to Expo Park. *Senri Expo Park, Senri, Suita-shi, tel. 06/876–2151. Admission: ¥360 adults, ¥230 high school and college students, ¥100 junior high and elementary school students. Open 10–5 (enter by 4:30). Closed Wed. and Dec. 28–Jan. 4.*

Parks and Gardens

Expo Park. On the former site of Expo '70, this 647-acre park houses the three museums listed above, an amusement park called Expo Land, sports facilities, and several gardens, including a Japanese garden with two teahouses. To reach the park, take the Midosuji Subway Line at Umeda Station to Senri-Chuo Station (30 min); then change here to bus. #114 or #115 at stop #6 to Expo Park (15 min). *Senri Expo Park, Senri, Suita-shi. Admission free to park, but the individual facilities within the park impose separate entrance fees, which vary. Open daily 9–5. Closed Wed.*

Hattori Ryokuchi Park. This recreation park has facilities for horseback riding and tennis, a youth hostel, and a museum of old farmhouses. To reach the park, take the Midosuji Subway Line from Umeda to Esaka stations, then the Kita Osaka Kyuku Line to Ryokuchi Koen Station. The park is a 10-minute walk from the station. *Admission to the park is free. Admission to the Farmhouse Museum: ¥300. If you plan on riding,* *the charge is ¥3,500 for one ride. The cost is ¥600–¥700 for 1 hr. of tennis. Have your hotel make a reservation for you a day in advance for horseback riding; no reservation necessary for tennis during the week; if you're going on a weekend, you may need as much as a week's advance reservation, and selection is then made by lottery. Open 9:30–5 Apr.–Oct. (enter by 4:30), 9:30–4 Nov.–Mar. (enter by 3:30).*

Mino Park. Osakans come here in autumn to admire the dazzling fall foliage, especially the maple trees, whose leaves turn to brilliant crimson. The path along the river leads to the Mino Waterfall. Monkeys reside in a protected habitat. The park is 30 minutes from Hankyu Umeda Station on the Mino Line, north of the Mino Station. *Admission free. Open 24 hours year-round.*

Takarazuka Excursion

A trip to Takarazuka allows visitors a view of the mountains outside Ozaka. If you are visiting Japan with young children, this is an excursion you won't want to miss. Takarazuka is best known as the theatrical home of an all-girl, Broadway-style revue. The **Takarazuka Grand Theater** was founded in 1914 by Ichizo Kobayashi, who ingeniously mixed theatrical elements from East and West. The theater has a large following, especially among young Japanese girls who dream of growing up to become a Takarazuka star.

To reach the theater from Takarazuka Station, follow the crowds and walk along the tracks on the opposite side from the zoo. It is a 10-minute walk. *Tel. 0797/84–0321. Tickets: ¥800–¥4,100. Performances weekdays at 1, Sat.–Sun. 11 and 3.*

Apart from the theater, you may visit the **Takarazuka Family Land,** which includes a zoo, a botanical garden, and an amusement park. *Admission: ¥1,000. Open 9:30–5 (9:30–9 in Aug.). Closed Wed.*

Getting There **By Train.** To reach Takarazuka, take the Hankyu Takarazuka Line from Osaka's Umeda Station. The express train to Takarazuka Station takes approximately 40 minutes. To reach the theater from the train station, follow the crowds and walk along the train tracks on the opposite side from a zoo. The walk to the theater is about 10 minutes.

Shopping

Osaka's role as a transportation hub for more than 1,500 years has enabled it to prosper first as a merchant town and today as a center of business and commerce. Osakans are known for driving hard bargains, but at the same time, they are practical in their approach to life. Osaka has two main shopping areas: one is centered on Namba Station in the Minami (southern) district, the other on Osaka and Umeda stations in the Kita (northern) district. Minami is the older of the two, but the merchandise sold here is a mixture of traditional and modern goods.

To the northeast of Namba Station are the Ebisubashi Street shopping area and the Nijinomachi (Rainbow Town) underground shopping mall. To the southeast are Namba City and Nan Nan Town underground shopping malls. Farther east from Namba Station, but still within walking distance, is Den Den Town (*see* Electronic Goods below).

Near Osaka and Umeda stations, which connect with underground concourses, are the Umeda Chika Center and the Hankyu Sanbangai and Hankyu Higashidori malls. This complex of stores is the largest underground shopping area in all of Japan and perhaps the world, complete with man-made streams and its own version of the Fountain of Trevi.

Located over Osaka Station is the Acty Osaka Building, a newly opened 27-story shopping and office building. To the west of this complex, near Nishi-Umeda Station on the Yotsubashi Subway Line, are the Dojima and Nakanoshima underground malls.

Osaka's most elegant shopping arcade, however, is Shinsaibashisuji. This covered arcade with marble pavement is located near Shinsaibashi Station on the Midosuji Line, halfway between the Minami and Kita districts. To the east of the arcade is yet another shopping arcade, called Europe-mura (European Village), with trendy, European-influenced clothing. Across Midosuji Boulevard to the west is America-mura (American Village), with clothing styles, inspired by U.S. designers, for both the young and old.

Specialized wholesale areas can be found throughout the city. A few retail shops are located in these areas so it is worth a visit. Dobuike is the wholesale area for clothing and accessories (located near Honmachi Station on the Chuo, Tanimachi, and Yotsubashi subway lines, or Sakaisuji-Honmachi Station on the Sakaisuji Subway Line). Matchamachisuji is famous for its rows of toy and doll shops.

Department Stores

All major Japanese department stores are represented in this ultramodern city. Many of them, such as Hankyu, Hanshin, and Kintetsu, are headquartered here. Hours are 10–6:30, with food halls open until 7. The following are some of Osaka's leading department stores: **Hankyu,** 8-7 Kabutacho, Kita-ku, tel. 06/361–1381, closed Thurs.; **Hanshin,** 1-13-13 Umeda, Kitaku, tel. 06/345–1201, closed Wed.; **Matsuzakaya,** 1–1 Temmabashi Kyomachi, Chuo-ku, tel. 06/943–1111, closed Wed.; **Mitsukoshi,** 2-63-1 Koraibashi, Chuo-ku, tel. 06/203–1331, closed Mon.; **Daimaru,** 1-118 Shinsaibashisuji, Chuo-ku, tel. 06/271–1231, closed Wed.; **Sogo,** 1-38 Shinsaibashisuji, Chuo-ku, tel. 06/281–3111, closed Thurs.; **Takashimaya,** 5–1–5 Namba, Chuo-ku, tel. 06/631–1101, closed Wed.; **Kintetsu,** 1–1–43 Abenosuji, Abeno-ku, tel. 06/624–1111; closed Thurs. There is also a Kintetsu branch at 6–1–55 Uehonmachi, Tennoji-ku, tel. 06/779–1231, closed Thurs.

Gifts

At one time famous for its traditional crafts, particularly its ornately carved *karaki-sashimono* furniture, its fine *Naniwa suzuki* pewter ware, and its Sakai *uchihamono* cutlery, Osaka lost much of its fine traditional industry during World War II. The simplest way to find a wide selection of Osaka crafts is to visit one of the major department stores, many of which carry a selection of locally made crafts.

For folk crafts from all over the country, including ceramics, basketry, paper goods, folk toys and textiles, visit the **Nihon Kogeikan Mingei Fukyubin,** located near the Umeshin East Hotel in the popular gallery district, within walking distance of the U.S. Consulate. *4-7-15 Nishi-Tenma, Kita-ku, tel. 06/362–9501. Open 10–6.*

Electronic Goods **Den Den Town** (Den Den is a take-off on the word *denki,* which means electricity) has about 300 retail shops that specialize in electrical products; it also has stores for cameras and watches. The area is located near Ebisucho Station on the Sakaisuji Subway Line (exit #1 or #2), and Nipponbashi Station on the Sakaisuji and Sennichimae subway lines (exit #5 or #10). Shops are open 10–7 daily. Take your passport, and make your purchases in stores with signs that say "Tax Free."

Dining

Not only are the residents of Osaka known to be passionate about food; they also insist on eating well. Osakans expect the restaurants they frequent to use the freshest ingredients available from the area; this habit developed over the centuries because of the city's proximity to the Inland Sea, which allowed all classes (not just the aristocracy) easy access to fresh seafood. Today Osakans have discriminating palates and demand their money's worth. In fact, Osakans are famous for their gourmet appetites. "Osaka *wa kuidaore,*" the old saying goes—Osaka people squander their money on food.

Osaka cuisine is flavored with soy sauce that is lighter in color, milder in flavor, and saltier than the soy sauce used in Tokyo. One local delicacy is okonomiyaki, a pancake which may be filled with cabbage, mountain yam, pork, shrimp, and other ingredients; okonomiyaki is made to order on an iron grill at the table.

Osaka-zushi (Osaka-style sushi), which is made in wood molds, has a distinctive square shape, with pieces of fish or broiled eel placed on top of rice and then pressed together. Another variation of Osaka-zushi is wrapped around an omelet and filled with pickles and other delights. Eel, prepared in several different styles, remains a popular local dish; grilled eels are often eaten during the summer months for quick energy. **Fugu** (globefish), served boiled or raw, is a gourmet fish that is less expensive in Osaka than in other Japanese cities.

Another Osaka invention is **tako-yaki,** griddle-cooked dumplings with bits of octopus, green onions, and ginger smothered in a delicious sauce. Sold by street vendors in Dotonbori, these tasty snacks and their lively makers are also in evidence at every festival and street market in the Kansai district.

Osaka's shopping arcades and underground shopping areas abound in affordable restaurants and coffee shops, but when in doubt, head to Dotonbori and Soemoncho, two areas along the Dotonbori River that specialize in restaurants, nightclubs, and bars. If money is not a problem, walk to the northern part of Osaka to Kita Shinchi, the city's most exclusive dining quarter, but be prepared to pay a stiff price for an elegant meal. This area is somewhat similar to Tokyo's Ginza district.

A 3% federal consumer tax is added to all restaurant bills. Another 3% local tax is added to the bill if it exceeds ¥5,000. At more expensive restaurants, a 10%–15% service charge is also added to the bill.

The most highly recommended restaurants are indicated by a star ★.

Category	Cost*
Very Expensive	over ¥6,000
Expensive	¥4,000–¥6,000
Moderate	¥2,500–¥4,000
Inexpensive	under ¥2,500

Cost is per person without tax, service, or drinks

Credit Cards The following credit card abbreviations are used: AE, American Express; D, Discover; DC, Diners Club; MC, MasterCard; V, Visa.

Very Expensive

Benkay. For those who appreciate Japanese-style red snapper (served with stewed plums), Benkay is the place to go. Sea urchin, squid, and prawns are staples on the menu here; tempura and sushi are popular as well. The restaurant utilizes the traditional Japanese decor of blond wood paneling, and there's a sushi bar on one side. *Hotel Nikko Osaka, 7 Nishinocho, Daihoji-machi, Chuo-ku, tel. 06/244–1111. Reservations advised. Jacket and tie preferred. AE, DC, MC, V. Lunch 11:30–2:30, dinner 5:30–10.*

Les Célébrites. On the menu at Les Célébrites are French items identified by their association with such painters as Cézanne, Degas, Renoir, and Toulouse-Lautrec. The gourmet selections include such dishes as terrine of eel and spinach, dodine of stuffed wild duck with foie gras, chilled consommé flavored with tomato, tenderloin steak with morels, and a host of other items, such as French cheeses, green and mixed salads, and, of course, espresso. The atmosphere is best described as smartly casual or semiformal, with most, but not all, of the male patrons wearing ties. The two intimate dining rooms (only 33 seats total) are decorated in lavender and pink, and they feature fresh flowers and beautiful chandeliers. You can also come here for breakfast. Les Célébrites is located in the Hotel Nikko, which also has the distinction of hosting another class act: Benkay, a gourmet Japanese restaurant (*see* above). *Hotel Nikko Osaka, 7 Nishinocho, Daihoji-machi, Chuo-ku, tel. 06/244–1111. Reservations advised. Jacket and tie preferred. AE, DC, MC, V. Lunch 11:30–2:30, dinner 5:30–10.*

★ **Chambord.** Named for an elegant French castle in the Loire Valley, the Chambord restaurant is French in every way, from the crystal chandeliers to the chef's innovative cuisine. Specialties served by tuxedoed waiters include tenderloin with chestnuts and mushrooms, boiled lobster with tomato and cream sauce, and roast lamb with green peppers. Situated on the 29th floor of the Royal Hotel, the restaurant treats guests to a panoramic view of Osaka's flickering night lights and river activities. *Royal Hotel, 5-3 Nakanoshima, Kita-ku, tel. 06/448–*

1121. Reservations usually required. Jacket and tie required at dinner. AE, DC, MC, V. Lunch 11:30–2:30, dinner 5:30–10.

Chikuyotei Honten. Unless you're adventurous or want to wing your dinner selection, you might want to either bring a translation or memorize a few choice Japanese phrases on your way to Chikuyotei. Owner Teruyo Tsuda and her staff speak little or no English, but don't let that deter you. Possibly her son, Tsuda, who does speak English, will be on hand to help out. The food is excellent, the service will pamper you, and the atmosphere is classic Japanese. Specialties include grilled eel and tilefish. Housed in a Japanese mansion that once belonged to a tobacco merchant, Chikuyotei features handsome private dining rooms and a beautiful garden. *Nakanoshima 3–5–3, Kita-ku, tel. 06/441–1883. Dinner reservations advised. Dress: casual. AE, DC, MC, V. Lunch 11–2, dinner 4–9. Closed Sun.*

Le Rendezvous. Located atop the Plaza Hotel, Le Rendezvous offers guests not only an elegant meal but also expansive views of the city. A regal French restaurant with lovely wood paneling and formal place settings, it features French nouvelle cuisine and a fine selection of wines. Chef Paul Bocuse has an established reputation in Japan for presenting eye-pleasing gourmet dishes ranging from beef cuts to choice salmon. *2-2-49 Oyodo-minami, Oyodo-ku, tel. 06/453–1111. Reservations advised. Jacket and tie required. AE, DC, MC, V. Lunch 11:30–2, dinner 5:30–11.*

Ron. This establishment bills itself as having the best steak in the world; if its bustling business on three floors is any indication, the kudos are not off base. A five-minute walk from Osaka Station, Ron is housed in a five-story brick building. On the menu you'll find fried prawns, fried vegetables, boiled rice, tossed salad, and, of course, prime Kobe-beef steak. The setting is casual and homey with only 13 tables on three floors. Your beef and other delectables will be prepared on the iron grill table around which you sit—the preparation is half the experience. *1-10-2 Sonezaki Shinchi, Kita-ku, tel. 06/344–6664. Reservations advised. Dress: informal. AE, DC, MC, V. Open Mon.–Sat. dinner 5–2; Sun. and holidays 4–10.*

★ **Rose Room.** Yet another elegant hotel restaurant, this one is dressed up in green marble and has color-coordinated furnishings. The Rose Room features a formal atmosphere, enhanced by candlelit tables, fresh flowers, and a mirrored ceiling. This intimate establishment seats only 59 guests and serves Continental cuisine. Fish and beef dishes are the specialties, which include grilled sea bass with onion-flavored vinegar, steamed turbot with ravioli, grilled sirloin steak, and Châteaubriand. *ANA Sheraton Hotel, 1-3-1 Dojimahama, Kita-ku, tel. 06/347– 1112. Reservations usually required. Jacket and tie required. AE, DC, MC, V. Lunch 11:30–2, dinner 5:30–10.*

★ **The Seasons.** This grand, elegant dining room in the Hilton International is located in the bustling restaurant and retail sector around Osaka Station. Subtle colors, lustrous marble, and shining chandeliers blend together in The Seasons to create a lovely, warm ambience. The Continental menu offers selections you'll recognize from home: Maine lobster, fine wines, and the local favorite, Kobe beef. Seating less than 100 guests, the restaurant's formality assures patrons a dining event. Specialties include duckling terrine with goose liver, sliced beef in red wine sauce, and fillet of beef with goose liver in a puff pastry. The quick, lower priced lunch menu is ideal for a sampling of what the Hilton chef has to offer; at night, a pianist entertains.

A jacket is required, but a tie is not; management is more lenient in the summer. *Hilton International Osaka, 8-8 Umeda 1-chome, Kita-ku, tel. 06/347–7111. Reservations strongly advised. Jacket required. AE, DC, MC, V. Lunch 11:30–2:30, dinner 5:30–11.*

Expensive–Very Expensive

Kobe Misono. This dining spot is a branch of a restaurant in Kobe, and the chefs have managed to transfer the successful Kobe-beef recipe to Osaka. Located close to dozens of other less distinguished restaurants, Kobe Misono stands out for its attentive service and casual ambience. Besides the Kobe beef dinners with all the fixings, the other dishes include a chef salad, scallops, and fried vegetables. One family or couple is seated at each iron grill table; there are only six tables, which seat a maximum of 43 persons. *Near Osaka Station, Star Bldg., 1-31-2 Sonezakishinchi, Kita-ku, tel. 06/341–4471. Reservations advised. Dress: informal. AE, DC, MC, V. Open Mon.–Sat. lunch 11:30–2, dinner 5–10; Sun. noon–9.*

Osaka Joe's. First came Miami Joe's, then Tokyo Joe's; now here is the third version of that formidable institution for stone crabs. The obvious specials are the crabs (with melted butter and mustard mayonnaise) flown in from Florida and, for dessert, Keye- lime pie. Also on the menu are baked prawns, T-bone steak, and lamb chops. The setting is casual, with a distinctive American flair—even the music is from the States. A cozy, rustic bar at the entry seats only eight people; the two dining rooms seat a total of 99. Lunch is served until 3. *IM Excellence Bldg., 2nd floor, 1-11-20 Sonezakishinchi, Kita-ku, tel. 06/344–0124. Reservations advised. Dress: casual, but jacket and tie preferred. AE, DC, MC, V. Open 11:30–11:30 (last order at 10:30).*

Moderate

★ **La Bamba.** You'll find this casual Mexican restaurant and bar hidden down an otherwise old-fashioned Osaka shopping arcade near the #1 exit of the Nakazakicho subway station. Nothing on this little street forewarns you that you are about to enter perhaps the only *real* Mexican restaurant in all of Japan. The owner-chef learned his craft in Mexico. The fact that probably everyone from south of the U.S. border who stays for more than a few days in Japan not only finds it—but also signs his name with kudos to the chef on La Bamba's blackboard—should be testimony enough to the superior quality of its tacos, guacamole, burritos, quesadillas, and magnificent pitchers of margaritas. *8-2 Kurozaki-cho, Kita-ku, tel. 06/372–4224. Reservations advised weekends. Dress: casual. No credit cards. Open 6–midnight. Closed Mon.*

Fuguhisa. This no-nonsense little restaurant specializes in *fugu ryori*, the blowfish delicacy for which Osaka is famous. Extremely expensive almost everywhere else, Chef Kato's *tessa* (raw blowfish) and *techiri* (one-pot blowfish stew) are the most reasonable and delicious around. What the place lacks in glamour, it makes up for in down-to-earth Osaka-style good food. It's located across from the west exit of Tsuruhashi Station on the JR Osaka Loop Line. *3-14-24 Higashi-ohashi, Higashinari-ku, tel. 06/972–5029, Dress: casual. No credit cards. Open noon–10:30. Closed Wed.*

Kani Doraku. The most famous restaurant on Dotonbori, Kani Doraku is noted for its fine crab dishes at reasonable prices. The giant mechanical crab above the door is a local landmark. As you sit at tables or on tatami mats overlooking the Dotonbori Canal, you have a perfect view of the ultranew Kirin Plaza Building glittering across the water. Full-course crab lunches and dinners are served, as well as a wide selection of crab dishes à la carte. The menu is in English. *1-6-18 Dotonbori, Chuo-ku, tel. 06/211–8975. Reservations advised weekends. Dress: casual. AE, DC, MC, V. Open 11–11.*

Kanki. *Akachochin*, or red lanterns, are the symbol of inexpensive eating in Japan, but the wonderful combination of Western and Japanese dishes offered at this friendly place makes it different from most *nomiya*, as these inexpensive drinking places are called. Order "*Kyo no osusume,*" the daily special. You might end up with Florentine-style scallops. Table seating is available on the second and third floors. *1-3-11 Shibata-cho Kita-ku (on the northeast end of Hankyu Umeda Station), tel. 06/374–0057. Reservations advised. Dress: casual. No credit cards. Open 6–11. Closed Sun.*

Kirin City. This beer hall is located on the second floor of the fantastic Kirin Plaza Building designed by architect Shin Takamatsu, one of Japan's most controversial new architects. This hypertechno postmodern extravaganza presides over the old Narubashi Bridge on the Dotonbori Canal. Stop here for a cold-draft beer and a bite to eat in the Shinsaibashi district. The menu features fried chicken, "city potatoes" (french fries), and chorizo, among many delights. *2F Kirin Plaza Bldg., 7-2 Shuzaemon-cho, Chuo-ku, tel. 06/212–6572. Dress: casual. Open weekdays 11:30–1; weekends 11–11. AE, DC, MC, V.*

Mimiu. Udon-suki was born here, the thick, white noodle stew simmered in a pot over a burner at your table—with Chinese cabbage, clams, eel, yams, *shiitake* mushrooms, *mitsuba* greens, and other seasonal ingredients. The dish is an old favorite in Osaka, particularly when served in this traditional restaurant. *3-20 Yokobori, Chuo-ku (near Honmachi Station on the Dojima-suji Subway Line), tel. 06/231–5770. Dress: casual. No credit cards. Open 11:30–8:30. Closed Sun.*

★ **Tako-ume.** Take a rest from the glitter of Dotonbori nightlife at this 200-year-old traditional dining spot, which specializes in *oden*, a mixture of vegetables, and things like fish cakes, hard-boiled eggs, and fried tofu, cooked in a broth they say has been simmering here in the same pot for the past 30 years (just add liquid . . .). Sake is poured from pewter jugs, handmade in Osaka. The hot Chinese mustard dip is mixed with sweet miso bean paste, a house recipe. *1-1-8 Dotonbori, Chuo-ku, tel. 06/211–0321. Reservations advised weekends. Dress: informal. No credit cards. Open 4:30–10:30. Closed 1st and 3rd Sun. of each month.*

Inexpensive–Moderate

★ **Kushitaru.** Specializing in dinners served up piping hot on skewers, Kushitaru is an Osaka favorite. Your possible selections include chicken meatballs, celery with sea eel, quail egg with half beak (a Japanese dish), Chinese mushrooms, pineapple with sliced pork, and oysters with bacon. The restaurant is informal and has two dining rooms; the one upstairs is a throwback to the 1970s, with furniture and music of that period—young people love it here. *Located behind the Nikko Hotel,*

Sander Bldg., Shinsaibashi, 56-2, Nishinocho, Unagidani, Chuo-ku, tel. 06/281–0365. Reservations advised for upstairs, open seating on 1st floor. Dress: informal. AE, DC, MC, V. Lunch 11:30–1:30, dinner 5–11 (last order at 10:30), upstairs opens at 6. Closed Sun. and late Dec.–early Jan.

★ **Little Carnival.** Across the Plaza from Studebaker's (*see* below), tucked on the lower level of the Umeda Center Building, you'll find Little Carnival, where singing waiters serve up lobster, salmon, crab, and raw fish. The restaurant's library theme and multiwood paneling combine with dining areas on levels to create a casual, friendly atmosphere. Little Carnival also features a big buffet and salad bar, and from 6 to 10 in the evening, a piano player accompanies the singing servers. *Umeda Center Bldg., 2-4-12 Nakazaki-nishi, Kita-ku, tel. 06/373–9828. Dress: casual. AE, DC, MC, V. Open weekdays lunch 11:45–2:30, dinner 5–11:30; weekends 11:45–11:30.*

★ **Studebaker's.** The music, the food, and the neon lighting is all-American. A clone of the successful U.S. group of restaurants, Studebaker's attracts young, Western-influenced Japanese with its ice-cream soda fountain, classic Studebaker car, good-size dance floor, and DJ who spins bebop. On the menu are chicken fingers, onion rings, fried crabs, Spanish sausage, the American Burger, and ice-cream sodas. A happy hour falls from 5 to 7; the food is free, but there is a cover charge of ¥1,500. The design is, of course, red, white, and blue; the domed ceiling, booths, and counter service complete the scene. *Umeda 2-4-12 Nakazaki-Nishi, Kita-ku, tel. 06/372–1950. Reservations accepted for 4 or more. Dress: casual day, collar shirt and no jeans at night. AE, DC, MC, V. Lunch 11:30–5, dinner 5:30–midnight. Closed 3rd Sun. of each month.*

Inexpensive

Country Life. The current health boom has at last started to dispel the notion left over from less prosperous days in Japan that brown rice is something only poor people eat. Country Life, with its <u>inexpensive yet gourmet vegetarian meals</u>, has Early American decor; the food (no meat, fish, eggs, or milk) is served buffet-style—all you can eat, and all delicious for very reasonable prices. The restaurant is across the river to the southeast of the Museum of Oriental Ceramics. *3-11 Kyobashi, Chuo-ku, tel. 06/943–9597. Dress: casual. No credit cards. Open 11–3. Closed Sat.*

Lodging

Osaka is known more as a business than as a tourist destination. Although the trend for tourists is still to stay in nearby Kyoto and visit Osaka on a day trip, Osakans would like to see this pattern reversed. Among the city's assets are sparkling new Western-style hotels, some of which have gone up as recently as in the last two years; these have been constructed with comfort and luxury in mind. Osaka bills itself as the premier city of the 21st century; every new building appears to resemble a prototype for future architecture.

Osaka has accommodations for almost every taste, from first-class hotels to more modest business hotels, which unfortunately aren't very distinctive. You may be somewhat disappointed if you expect guest quarters to be along the same lines as the better hotels in the United States. The Japanese hotel designers are often more concerned with being efficient and functional rather than being elegant and flamboyant. However, discriminating travelers will appreciate the individual attention provided by the solicitous staff at most hotels.

You'll be relieved to discover that a hotel room costs less in Osaka than does one of comparative size in Tokyo. Osaka also has more hotels to choose from than does Kyoto, which is especially important to keep in mind during the peak tourist seasons.

A 3% federal consumer tax is added to all hotel bills. Another 3% local tax is added to the bill if it exceeds ¥10,000. At most hotels, a 10%–15% service charge is added to the total bill. Tipping is not necessary.

Category	Cost*
Very Expensive	over ¥20,000
Expensive	¥15,000–¥20,000
Moderate	¥10,000–¥15,000
Inexpensive	under ¥10,000

Cost is for double room, without tax or service

The most highly recommended accommodations are indicated by a star ★.

Credit Cards The following credit card abbreviations are used: AE, American Express; D, Discover; DC, Diners Club; MC, MasterCard; V, Visa.

Very Expensive

ANA Sheraton Hotel Osaka. One of only a half-dozen Osaka hotels to be classified as deluxe, the ANA Sheraton overlooks the city's picturesque Nakanoshima Island. A handsome 24-story white-tile structure, it is characterized by unusual architectural features, such as the six-story rock sculpture behind the main stairway and the huge fluted columns in the lobby. There is underground parking, and also an enclosed court where live trees add a note of color. Guest rooms are done in pastel shades and have all the extras, such as remote-control TV and baths with phone extensions and travertine marble. Each room is furnished with twin or double beds; some rooms have extra sofa beds. The hotel's fine restaurants include the elegant Rose Room (*see* Dining, above). *1-3-1 Dojimahama, Kita-ku, Osaka 530, tel. 06/347–1112. 500 rooms. Facilities: several restaurants (including Chinese, Japanese, and French), coffee shop, indoor pool, sauna, business center, several lounges. AE, DC, MC, V.*

★ **Hotel New Otani Osaka.** Osaka's newest hotel, the New Otani is ideally situated next to Osakajo Castle Park on the JR line. Popular with Japanese and Westerners alike, it offers such amenities as indoor and outdoor pools, tennis, superior rooms, and a sparkling marble atrium lobby. The rooms, large by Japanese standards, afford handsome views of Osakajo Castle and the Neyagawa River. The room decor is modern, with twin or double beds, light color schemes, dining tables, lined draperies, and excellent bathrooms with decent counter space. A large selection of bars and restaurants offers enough diversity to suit almost any taste. The New Otani is also near Osaka Business Park. If you need to go to midtown Osaka, the Aqua Liner water bus stops right in front of the hotel. *4 Shiromi, 1-chome, Chuo-ku, Osaka 540, tel. 06/941–1111. 610 rooms. Facilities: top-floor lounge and Japanese restaurant, Western grill, 4 additional restaurants, bars, health club with activities. AE, DC, MC, V.*

Hotel Nikko Osaka. An impressive and rather striking white tower in the colorful Shinsaibashi Station area, the Nikko Osaka is within easy reach of Osaka's nightlife. The hotel's atmosphere is lively and even exciting: As you enter, you'll probably be greeted by a doorman in top hat and tails. Some rooms offer contemporary furnishings with Japanese touches and traditional light decor. Higher price rooms have expensive furniture, thick carpets, bedside controls, and cable TV featuring the CNN news station. On the executive floors, the tile baths come complete with hair dryers and phones. The drinking and dining establishments are numerous and varied, and the hotel's management has elevated service to an art. *7 Nishinocho, Daihojicho, Chuo-ku, Osaka 542, tel. 06/244–1111. 650 rooms. Facilities: 3 bars, including the Jetstream on top floor; French, Japanese, Chinese, and Western restaurants, among others; shopping arcade. AE, DC, MC, V.*

★ **Osaka Hilton International.** Glitz and glitter draw both tourists and expense accounters to the Hilton International, Osaka's leading hotel. Located across from Osaka Station in the heart of Osaka's business district, it is a typical Western-style hotel, replete with marble and brass. The high-ceiling lobby is dramatically luxurious, and the hotel's arcade boasts several designer boutiques. Standard rooms are first-rate, with almost all the extras, and the three executive floors offer higher price rooms if you desire even more comfort. The staff is very helpful. *8-8 Umeda, 1-chome, Umeda, Kita-ku, Osaka 530, tel. 06/347–7111. 550 rooms. Facilities: 4 restaurants, top-floor bar where lunch is served weekdays, café, coffee shop, health club with indoor pool and outdoor tennis, business services, designer shops. AE, DC, MC, V.*

★ **Royal Hotel.** With a host of restaurants and bars from the basement to the top floor of its tower, the Royal is a self-contained city. The lobby is the perfect spot for people-watching, with crowds going in and coming out of the hotel's many lounges. Rooms in the main building are somewhat routine, with traditional somber decor, but the tower offers first-class accommodations with such extras as the CNN news station on TV, in-room minibars, and marble bathrooms with phones and hair dryers. Guests staying in the VIP tower have access to an extensive health club. A shuttle runs from the hotel to the Grand Hotel (nearby) and to the subway. Considered by many travelers to be the best hotel in Osaka, the Royal has a high reputation among the Japanese. *5-3-68 Nakanoshima, Kita-ku, Osaka 530, tel. 06/448–1122. 1325 rooms. Facilities: 16 restaurants, including Chambord, a well-known French dining room, health club with 2 pools, tanning beds, sauna, steam, massage, lounges. AE, DC, MC, V.*

Expensive–Very Expensive

Holiday Inn Nankai Osaka. Although it is located in the midst of the popular restaurant and nightlife neighborhood around

Nankai Station, the 14-story Holiday Inn Nankai is actually fairly quiet inside. Americans will recognize the familiar Holiday Inn touches—the rooms are a bit bland, with twin or double beds, modern baths, and a television with standard Japanese stations. The best rooms are found on the 10th floor. Restaurants range from a grill room to a coffee shop with a garden promenade. This is not the best value in the city. *28-1 Kyuzaemoncho, Chuo-ku, Osaka 542, tel. 06/213–8281. 229 rooms. Facilities: 3 floors of shops, Chinese and Japanese restaurants, pub, coffee shop, grill, outdoor rooftop pool. AE, DC, MC, V.*

★ **Hotel Osaka Grand.** A sister to the superior Royal Hotel, the Grand is a lively first-class commercial hotel with free shuttle service every few minutes to the Royal and to a nearby subway stop. Everything is neat and clean; the staff is large and hard-working. Housekeeping is very good, and the rooms bigger than average for Japan. The decor is somewhat dated but in good repair, and all the food and beverage areas are very popular. *2-3-18 Nakanoshima, Kita-ku, Osaka 530, tel. 06/202–1212. 350 rooms. Facilities: French, Western and Japanese restaurants; basement lounge; coffee shop; shopping arcade. Guests may use health club at Royal Hotel for a fee. AE, DC, MC, V.*

Miyako Hotel Osaka. A relatively new, 21-story high rise, the Miyako is filled with expansive public rooms such as the lobby, which rises two stories and is decorated with marble columns and attractive pastel color schemes. The rooms are also pastel; they are modern and inviting, with such extras as bedside television controls, and dining tables. Executive rooms occupy two floors and have plusher appointments. The Miyako is near the Uehonmachi subway stop, and trains for Kyoto on the Kintetsu Line leave from an adjacent building, which makes the hotel convenient for travelers. The National Bunraku Theater is also fairly close. *6-1-55 Uehonmachi, Tennoji-ku, Osaka 543, tel. 06/773–1111. 600 rooms. Facilities: 6 restaurants, including a roof room, grill, and coffee shop; lower-level shopping arcade, roof lounge, bars, health club with indoor pool and retractable roof, Japanese bath, racquetball courts. AE, DC, MC, V.*

Osaka Terminal Hotel. Across from the Osaka Station (not to be confused with the Shin-Osaka Station, where Shinkansen trains arrive and depart), the Osaka Terminal is housed in a skyscraper and shares floors with offices and shops. It ranks as a minimally first-class hotel but has many restaurants, including a grill and coffee shop. Rooms have minibars, bedside TV controls, and small but modern bathrooms. *3-1-1 Umeda, Kita-ku, Osaka 530, tel. 06/344–1235. 660 rooms. Facilities: 4 restaurants, 2 lounges, underground shopping access. AE, DC, MC, V.*

Moderate–Expensive

Hotel Do Sports Plaza. Situated in the heart of Osaka's colorful nightlife district, the Do Sports Plaza earned its reputation by catering to sports enthusiasts and athletic teams. Most of the rooms are small, but fairly bright, singles; doubles are not much larger. Located on a commercial block off a sidestreet, the hotel is easily accessible to subway lines. Fitness activities are the main attraction here. *3-3-17 Minami Semba, Chuo-ku, Osaka 542, tel. 06/245–3311. 193 rooms. Facilities: gym, sauna, pub, coffee shop. AE, DC, MC, V.*

Hotel Hanshin. Located near the underground shopping center at Umeda and Osaka stations, the Hanshin is a pleasant 15-story commercial hotel. Popular mostly with Japanese businessmen, it does manage to attract a few tourists. The moderately priced rooms are found between the 10th and 15th floors. Furnishings are mostly Scandinavian; the tile baths are so small you might say they are claustrophobic. Waterbeds are available. *2-3-30 Umeda, Kita-ku, Osaka 530, tel. 06/344–1661. 243 rooms. Facilities: Japanese–Western restaurant, coffee shop, 2 bars, sauna, small shopping arcade. AE, DC, MC, V.*

International Hotel Osaka. This massive L-shape hotel may be a bit hard to reach in traffic, but it's a reliable choice. The best rooms are located in an annex where most of the units are situated; if you're on a budget, ask for a room in the back. The color scheme can best be described as reserved and uninspiring. Popular mostly with Japanese clientele, the International's lobby and public areas are often busy with groups coming or going. *58 Hashizumecho, Uchihonmachi, Chuo-ku, Osaka 540, tel. 06/ 941–2661. 393 rooms. Facilities: 2 lounges, 5 restaurants, including Japanese, coffee shop, grill. AE, DC, MC, V.*

Mitsui Urban Hotel. Under renovation for quite some time, the Mitsui Urban now boasts a new lobby, a remodeled bar, and several new guest room furnishings. The decor in the new rooms is the ever-popular pastels; autumn-colored rooms (soon to be renovated) offer coffee makers and other extras. Some of the carpeting in the rooms is new, and the baths are fairly modern, though a bit small. There's also a 17th-floor restaurant. The staff's English is fairly good, considering the hotel receives mostly Japanese guests. The Mitsui Urban is accessible to the Midosuji Subway Line at Nakatsu Station. *18-8 Toyosaki, Oyodo-ku, Osaka 531, tel. 06/372–8181. 400 rooms. Facilities: remodeled lounge, bar, Western–Japanese restaurant. AE, DC, MC, V.*

New Hankyu Hotel and New Hankyu Annex. This busy hotel complex is located in the popular area around Osaka Station, with its restaurants and shopping. The 17-story Annex, a block from the main hotel, houses the newest, largest, and best rooms; it also offers a café, three other eateries, and an indoor pool. The single rooms in the main hotel, however, are about as roomy as telephone booths. Guests are permitted the use of facilities in both buildings. *1-1-35 Shibata, Kita-ku, Osaka 530, tel. 06/372–5101. 990 rooms. Facilities: 5 restaurants in main building, 3 more in annex; health club, indoor pool, several bars. AE, DC, MC, V.*

Osaka Airport Hotel. For those with an early flight out of Osaka Airport, this place is located right inside the airport terminal building. These are not the most luxurious rooms for the price, but the location saves time and trouble for the busy traveler. *3F Osaka Airport Building, Toyonaka, Osaka-fu. tel. 06/855– 4621. 105 rooms. Facilities: large variety of Japanese and Western restaurants, gift shops, and bars serving the airport and hotel. AE, DC, MC, V.*

Osaka Dai Ichi Hotel. As Japan's first cylinder-shape skyscraper, known as the Maru-Biru (Round Building), the Dai Ichi is easy to locate amid the Osaka cityscape. Now somewhat overshadowed by the Hilton, it still receives many groups. The rooms are wedge-shape, and half are small singles that are usually taken on weekdays by Japanese businessmen. The hotel has a coffee shop, which is open around the clock, and an underground shopping arcade. The Dai Ichi is conveniently located across from Osaka Station. *1-9-20 Umeda, Kita-ku, Osaka 530, tel. 06/341-4411. 475 rooms. Facilities: Chinese, Japanese, and Western restaurants; bar, 2 shopping promenades. AE, DC, MC, V.*

Moderate

Hotel Echo Osaka. This hotel is recommended for those seeking good budget accommodations. Though near the JR station, the Echo Osaka is far from other major parts of the city. The 83 plain rooms offer air-conditioning and routine furnishings, such as double or twin beds, uncoordinated carpeting, and small baths. The hotel is neat and clean, if nothing more, and has an accommodating young staff. *1-4-7 Abeno-suji, Abeno-ku, Osaka 545 (near Tennoji Station), tel. 06/633-1141. 83 rooms. Facilities: Chinese restaurant, coffee shop, 2 bars. AE, DC, MC, V.*

Osaka Castle Hotel. Noted for its proximity to Osakajo Castle and its park, this square mid-rise building is unexceptional and receives its name for its location, not for any majestic manner. It boasts a rooftop beer garden in summer and a subway stop in the basement. Rooms are small and not very light; the furniture, which may have been bought from a catalogue, is uninspired. Some rooms in front have good views, but all have dwarf-size baths. You may have to bone up on your Japanese with the front desk. *2-35-7 Kyobashi, Chuo-ku, Osaka 540 (at Temmabashi Station on independent subway line), tel. 06/942-1401. 120 rooms. Facilities: Japanese, Chinese, and French restaurants; café, beer garden, a handful of shops. AE, DC, MC, V.*

Umeshin East Hotel. In the antiques shop and art gallery neighborhood near the U.S. Consulate, this small brick hotel has an attractive modern design, with a lush green interior garden café, a restaurant, and a bar in its tiled lobby. Rooms are small, but comfortably furnished. *4-11-5 Nishi-Tenma, Kita-ku, (a 10-minute walk from Midosuji Subway Line and Umeda Station), tel. 06/364-1151. 140 rooms. AE, DC, MC, V.*

10 Kobe

Introduction

by Kiko Itasaka

Kobe has been a prominent harbor city throughout Japanese history. In the 12th century, the Taira family moved the capital from Kyoto to Fukuhara, the western part of modern Kobe, with the hope of increasing Japan's international trade. Fukuhara remained the capital for a mere six months, but its port, known as Hyogo, continued to flourish. Japan opened her ports to foreign trade in 1868 after a long period of isolationism. In order to prevent foreigners from using the profitable and active port of Hyogo, the more remote port of Kobe, located slightly northeast of Hyogo, was opened to international trade. Within a few years, Kobe eclipsed Hyogo in importance as a port.

Now a major industrial city, Kobe has an active port that serves as many as 10,000 ships a year. A century of exposure to international cultures has left its mark on Kobe, a sophisticated and cosmopolitan city. In the hills above the port area is a residential area where foreign merchants and traders have settled over the years. Many Western-style houses built in the late 19th century are still inhabited by Kobe's large foreign population, while others have been open to the public as buildings of historical interest. Many sailors passing through Kobe, beguiled by the charm of this city, have settled here. As a result, Kobe boasts remarkable diversity in its shops and restaurants.

This port city is extremely popular with young Japanese couples and women on vacation, who enjoy the numerous shops, countless restaurants, the active nightlife, and the romantic harbor views. Travelers searching for exotic or traditional Japan will be disappointed by the very modern Kobe, but visitors will be satisfied by the city if they are eager to relax in a cosmopolitan setting with excellent places to shop and a variety of international cuisines to sample.

Essential Information

Arriving and Departing

By Plane

The airport for Kobe is Osaka International Airport, approximately 40 minutes away. Frequent service from Tokyo to Osaka is available, as well as direct service from international destinations to Osaka.

Between the Airport and Center City

The airport bus to Kobe Sannomiya Station (Kobe's main train station) leaves from the domestic airlines terminal's main entrance and from a stop between the domestic and international terminals approximately every 20 minutes, 8 AM–9 PM. The trip takes about 40 minutes and costs ¥680.

Because public transportation is excellent, a taxi is not a practical alternative for getting into Kobe from the airport.

By Train

Japan Railways offers frequent Shinkansen super express service between Tokyo and Shin-Kobe Station. From Tokyo, the trip to Kobe takes about three hours, 30 minutes (cost: ¥14,000). The trip between Osaka Station and Kobe's Sannomiya Station is a 30-minute run on the JR Tokaido Line rapid train, which leaves at 15-minute intervals throughout the day (cost: ¥390). Japan Rail Passes may be used for these trains.

Two other private lines, the Hankyu and Hanshin lines, offer service between Osaka and Kobe for ¥350.

Getting Around

By Train Within Kobe, Japan Railways and the Hankyu and Hanshin lines run parallel from east to west and are easy to negotiate. Sannomiya and Motomachi are the principal downtown stations. Tickets are purchased from a vending machine and surrendered upon leaving the train. Fares depend upon your destination.

The city's subway system runs from Shin-Kobe Station west to the outskirts of town. Fares start at ¥140 and are determined by destination. A ride between Sannomiya Station and Shin-Kobe Station costs ¥160.

By Bus The city bus service is frequent and efficient, though it might be somewhat confusing to a first-time visitor. At each bus stop, you will find a pole that displays a route chart of official stops. Enter at the rear or center of the bus; pay your fare as you leave at the front (cost: ¥180 adults; ¥100 children, regardless of the distance). Exact change is needed.

By Taxi Taxis are plentiful and can be hailed on the street or at taxi stands. The fare starts at ¥540 for the first two km and goes up ¥90 for each additional 375 meters.

By Portliner The Portliner is a computerized monorail that services the recently built man-made Port Island, located in the middle of Kobe Harbor. The monorail central station is connected to the JR Sannomiya Station; the ride from the station to Port Island takes about 10 minutes (cost: round-trip between downtown Kobe and Port Island ¥220 adults, ¥120 children).

Important Addresses and Numbers

Tourist Information The **Kobe Tourist Information Center** (tel. 078/392–0020), located on the second floor of the Kobe Kotsu Center Building, on the west side of the JR Sannomiya Station, is open daily 9–5:30. Here you can pick up a free detailed map of the city in English. The Tourist Information Center has a branch at the Shin-Kobe Station (tel. 078/341–5277) that is open daily 10–6.

The **Japan Travel-Phone** number for information in English on Kobe and other points in western Japan, tel. 0120/444–800.

Consulates The closest U.S., U.K., and Canadian consulates are located in Osaka (*see* Chapter 9).

Emergencies **Police,** tel. 110; **Ambulance,** tel. 119.

Doctors **Kobe Adventist Hospital** (4-1 Arinodai 8-chome, Kita-ku, Kobe, tel. 078/981–0161); **Kobe Kaisei Hospital** (11-15 Shinohara-Kitamachi, Nada-ku, tel. 078/871–5201).

Pharmacies The **Daimaru Department Store** Chuo-ku (40 Asahi-cho, tel. 078/331–8121), located within a three-minute walk of the Motomachi JR Station (40 Akashico), has a pharmacy department.

English-Language Bookstores **Bunyodo** (Kobe Kokusai Kaikan 1st fl., 8 Goko-dori, Chuo-ku, tel. 078/221–0557); **Maruzen** (1-4-12 Motomachi-dori, Chuo-ku, tel. 078/391–6001).

Travel Agencies **Japan Travel Bureau,** Sannomiya JR Station (tel. 078/231–4701).

Guided Tours

Orientation Tours Between March 21 and November 30, the City Transport Bureau offers several ½-day tours of major attractions in the city and surrounding areas. While the tours are conducted in Japanese, they do give you a satisfactory overview of Kobe. Itineraries vary, depending upon the day of the week. The buses depart from the south side of the Kobe Kotsu Center Building, near Sannomiya Station (cost: ¥2,300–¥2,800 adults, ¥1,200–¥1,400 children). Tickets and information can be obtained at the **Kobe Tourist Information Office** on the second floor of the Kobe Kotsu Center Building (tel. 078/391–4755).

A series of sightseeing tours is also offered by authorized taxi services. The tours cover 11 different routes and range in time from two to five hours (cost: ¥7,830–¥19,570). The taxi tours can be reserved at the Kobe Tourist Information Center (tel. 078/392–0020).

Exploring

Numbers in the margin correspond with points of interest on the Kobe map.

The downtown section of Kobe, where most businesses are located, is near the harbor area. The rest of Kobe is built on slopes that extend as far as the base of Mt. Rokko. In the middle of the harbor is the man-made Port Island, which has conference centers, an amusement park, and the Portopia Hotel. The island is linked with the downtown area by a fully computerized monorail that is without a human conductor. The major nightlife area, Ikuta, is just north of the Sannomiya Station.

❶ A good place to start your trip to Kobe is with a visit to the **Kobe City Museum,** where you'll find out about the history of this international port town. Alongside earlier artifacts, the museum has an interesting collection of memorabilia from the old days when the old foreign settlement was in its heyday, including a scale model of the foreign concession. Three entire rooms from a turn-of-the-century Western house are on display. You'll also discover selections from the museum's famous *namban* collection of prints, screens, and paintings by Japanese artists of the late 16th to 18th century; these artworks depict foreigners in Japanese settings from that period.

To get to the museum, walk south down Flower Road from Sannomiya Station, past the Flower Clock and City Hall to Higashi Yuenchi Park. Walk through the park to the Post Office, across the street on the west side. Walk east on the road in front of the Kobe Minato Post Office toward the Oriental Hotel. Turn left at the corner in front of the hotel and you'll find the City Museum in the old Bank of Tokyo building, at the end of the block. *24 Kyomachi, Chuo-ku, Kobe-shi, tel. 078/391–0035. Admission: ¥200 (more for special exhibitions). Open 10–5. Closed Mon.*

Return to Sannomiya Station, browsing through Nankin Machi (Chinatown) and the Motomachi and Sannomiya shopping arcades (*see* Shopping, below) if time permits. Once back at

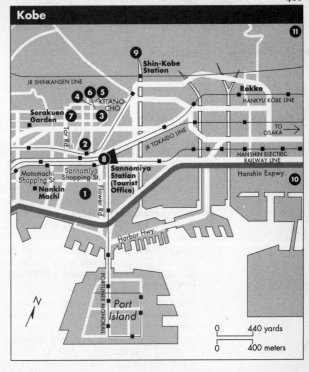

Sannomiya Station, begin your tour of the northern district by
crossing the street that runs along the tracks and turning left
at the first main intersection. You'll see the orange torii gate of
② **Ikuta Jinja Shrine.** According to legend, the shrine was
founded by Empress Jingu in the 3rd century.

The road that runs up the right side of the shrine leads up the
slope to Nakayamate-dori Avenue. Cross the avenue and continue up the slope.

Turn right at the corner of Yamamoto-dori. This road is lined
with high-fashion boutiques and restaurants. Turn left at
③ **Kitano-zaka,** which leads to **Kitano,** an area where Western
traders and businessmen have been living since the late 19th
century. The district is extremely popular with young Japanese tourists, who enjoy the rare opportunity of seeing old-
fashioned Western houses (referred to in Kobe as *Ijinkan*),
very few of which exist in Japan. Many of the residences are
still inhabited by Westerners, but some have been turned into
museums. More than a dozen Kitano 19th-century residences
are open to the public, and seeing all of them can get repeti-
tious. A few are recommended here for those who are interested. Otherwise, you may simply enjoy a walk around the hills
of this area while you admire the Victorian and Gothic architecture.

For those who want to see the interior of some of the buildings,
continue walking up the slopes from Nakayamate-dori Avenue.
The second intersection crosses Yamamoto-dori Avenue (nick-
named Ijinkan-dori Avenue). At the third intersection, just

❹ past Rin's Gallery (filled with boutiques of Japan's top design-ers), turn right and walk east to the **Eikoku-kan** (English House). This structure, inhabited until 1979, is now open to the public. The building was constructed in 1907 by an English ar-chitect and was inhabited by another Englishman, J. E. Baker. *2-3-16 Kitano-machi, Chuo-ku, Kobe-shi, tel. 078/241–2338. Admission: ¥500. Open weekdays 8:30–5, 8:30–5:15 week-ends.*

❺ Three of the Ijinkan in the Kitano area are publicly owned and free of charge. The **Rhein no Yakata** (Rhine House), opposite the English House, has a pleasant German-style coffee shop in-side. Near Kitano Tenman Jinja Shrine at the top of the hill is **❻** the **Kazami Dori no Yakata** (Weathercock House) made famous on a national TV series some years ago. It is the most elaborate of Kobe's Ijinkan, listed as an Important Cultural Property. Continue back down the slope via Kitano-zaka toward San-**❼** nomiya Station. One Ijinkan house not to miss is the **Chouéké Yashiki** (Chouéké Mansion), built in 1889. The only house still inhabited, it is filled to the rafters with turn-of-the-century memorabilia from East and West, and Mrs. Chouéké is on hand to show you her treasures and share her vast knowledge of Kobe. Her collection includes a large number of Namban wood-block prints.

❽ Return to **Sannomiya Station** and go to the **Portliner** platform. This automatic monorail, which goes out to the man-made **Port Island,** travels in a loop around the island, stopping at eight sta-tions and returning to the Sannomiya Station. From the Portliner you can get a close-up view of the harbor with its many piers, ships, and containers. The entire ride lasts about 30 minutes and is a good way to see industrial Kobe (cost: ¥220 adults, ¥120 children).

Excursions

Nunobiki Falls

❾ A quiet side trip from the city is the 20-minute walk up the hill behind Shin-Kobe Station to **Nunobiki Falls,** whose beauty has been referred to in Japanese literature since the 10th century. It is actually a series of four cascades of varying heights, to-gether described as one of the three greatest falls in Japan.

Kikumasamune Shiryokan (Sake Museum)

The district between the Oishi and Uozaki stations on the Hanshin Electric Railway line, once known as Nada, has been a sake-producing region since the Edo period (1603–1868). With pure water from the Rokko Mountains and particularly deli-cious rice available in the area, Nada was an ideal location for sake production. Because of its proximity to the ocean, sake was transported from Nada to Edo (now Tokyo), thus becoming one of the first areas in Japan to distribute its sake to other re-gions. To this day, the 50 sake companies in this brewery dis-trict produce one-third of all of the sake in Japan. For the most part, this area is full of huge concrete factories, but some old wood buildings for sake production still continue to operate.

Few tourists visit the brewery district, which is a shame, because the trip can be fascinating. A few breweries have opened up small museums. One of these is the **Kikumasamune Shiryokan.** As you enter the building, a guide will seat you and show you a video in English that describes the history of sake production. To enhance your enjoyment of the video, you will be offered a sample of Kikumasamune sake, with an opportunity for refills. After the video, a very enthusiastic guide, who speaks a modicum of English, will take you to another 330-year-old building, which was originally a sake brewery. This structure was constructed using no nails, and it is in excellent condition. On display inside are sake-producing implements, some of which date back as far as the Edo period (1603–1868). Antique posters and advertisements are also exhibited.

Getting There To get to Kikumasamune Shiryokan from Kobe, take the local train to Uozaki from the Hanshin Electric Railway Sannomiya Station located under Sogo department store, just south of the JR Sannomiya Station. When you arrive at the Uozaki Station, take the staircase on your left in the station and exit. Walk straight along the road toward the main highway and cross the footbridge on your right. At the end of the footbridge, turn left. Continue along the road before you until you get to the highway. Turn right on the street before the highway, and walk along another small road. On your left you will see a small tunnel that takes you under the highway. Continue walking along this small road for approximately five minutes. On your left, you will see an old brown wood structure, which is the Kikumasamune Shiryokan. *1-9-1 Ozaki Nishimachi, Higashinada-ku, Kobe-shi, tel. 078/854–1029. Admission free. Open 10–3. Closed Tues.*

Mt. Rokko

Mt. Rokko is a popular excursion from Kobe. The highest peak of the Rokko Mountains, it offers a magnificent view of the city and the Inland Sea. On top of the mountain are various recreational areas, including the oldest golf course in Japan, built in 1903, and the summer homes of some of Kobe's wealthier residents. The most exciting view is probably from the ropeway that runs between the Rokko-sanjo area and the Rokko-sanjo countryside.

Getting There Take the Hankyu Electric Railway Line from the JR Sannomiya Station to Rokko Station (cost: ¥170). From the latter station, take either a taxi or a bus to Rokko Cableshita Station; a cable car travels from there up the mountain to Rokko-sanjo Station (cost: ¥560).

Shopping

Kobe is a shopper's paradise. Unlike Tokyo, Osaka, and other places in Japan where shops are scattered all over the city, most of the shopping districts in Kobe are in clusters, so you can visit numerous shops with great ease. The historic shopping area of Kobe is known as **Motomachi,** which extends for one mile between Motomachi JR Station and Daimaru department store. Most of the district is under a covered arcade, so even if the weather is inclement, you can wander around from shop to shop. You can purchase nearly anything in Motomachi, ranging from antiques to cameras to electronics goods. One favorite stop for many tourists is the **Maruzen** bookstore, located right at the entrance on the Motomachi Station side of the arcade. This store has an excellent selection of books in English. At the opposite end of the arcade are two small shops that sell traditional Japanese goods. **Sakaeya** (8-5 Motomachi-dori, 5-chome, Chuo-ku, tel. 078/341–1307) specializes in Japanese dolls. **Naniwaya** (8-3 Motomachi-dori, 5-chome, Chuo-ku, tel. 078/341–6367) has an excellent selection of Japanese lacquer ware at reasonable prices. Also try **Harishin** (3-10-3 Motomachi-dori, Chuo-ku, tel. 078/331–2516) on the west end of the arcade for antiques.

Nearly connected to the Motomachi shopping arcade, and extending from the Sogo department store to the Motomachi area for half a mile, is the **Sannomiya Center Gai** shopping arcade. This mall has fewer shops and more restaurants than the neighboring Motomachi. Because of its extremely convenient location right next to the Sannomiya Station, this is a good place to have a quick bite to eat.

The famous pearl company **Tasaki Shinju** (Tasaki Bldg. 6-3-2 Minatojima Nakamachi, Chuo-ku, tel. 078/302–3321) in Center Plaza across from Sannomiya Station has a museum and demonstration hall along with its retail pearl shop.

The new **Sanchika Town** underground shopping mall, which runs for several blocks beneath Flower Road south from Sannomiya Station, has 120 shops and 30 restaurants.

Kobe's trendy crowd tends to shop in the many exclusive shops lining **Tor Road,** which extends from the north to the south of the city on a slope lined with trees. Fashionable boutiques featuring Japanese designers and imported goods alternate with chic cafés and restaurants.

Dining

Kobe beef is considered a delicacy all over Japan. Tender, tasty, and extremely expensive, it is a must for beef lovers. The beef is raised in the nearby Tajima area of Hyogo Prefecture. The cows are fed beer and are even massaged to improve the quality of the meat and give it the marbled texture that is considered to be its most attractive quality. As a result, Kobe beef is rather high in fat content, and this may disappoint lean-meat lovers.

Ethnic food fans will also appreciate the many international cuisines available in Kobe. Sailors passing through often stay on in Kobe, and some of them open restaurants that are popular not only with the large foreign community of Kobe, but also with resident and visiting Japanese. The number of international restaurants is perhaps fewer than in Tokyo, but the quality and authenticity are unsurpassed. Simply walking around north of the Sannomiya Station in the Kitano area, you are bound to come across restaurants representing nearly every cuisine imaginable. From the corner of Hanta-dori and Yamamoto-dori (also known as Ijinkan-dori), there are at least a dozen fine restaurants of every different cuisine imaginable—Italian, German, French, Swiss, Middle Eastern, Thai, American, and, of course, Japanese.

A 3% federal consumer tax is added to all restaurant bills. Another 3% local tax is added to the bill if it exceeds ¥5,000. At more expensive restaurants, a 10%–15% service charge is also added to the bill. Tipping is not necessary.

The most highly recommended restaurants are indicated by a star ★.

Category	Cost*
Very Expensive	over ¥10,000
Expensive	¥6,000–¥10,000
Moderate	¥3,500–¥6,000
Inexpensive	under ¥3,500

Cost is per person without tax, service, or drinks

Credit Cards The following credit card abbreviations are used: AE, American Express; D, Discover; DC, Diners Club; MC, MasterCard; V, Visa.

Kobe Beef

Aragawa. Japan's first steak house is famed for its superb hand-fed Kobe beef. The wood-paneled, chandeliered dining room has an old-country atmosphere. Aragawa's serves melt-in-your-mouth *sumiyaki* (charcoal broiled) steak that is worth its weight in yen—an evening here is the ultimate splurge, but this is considered *the* place for Kobe beef. *2-15-18 Nakayamate-dori, Chuo-ku, tel. 078/221–8547. Reservations advised. Jacket and tie required. AE, DC, MC, V. Open noon–3 and 5–10. Very Expensive.*

Highway. If price is no object, this small and exclusive restaurant has a reputation for serving the best Kobe beef in the area. The quality of the meat is extraordinary—it will literally melt in your mouth. *13–7 Shimoyamate-dori 2-chome, Chuo-ku, tel. 078/331–7622. Reservations advised. Jacket and tie required. No credit cards. Open 11–9. Expensive.*

A-1. This is one of the only steak restaurants among many in the neighborhood north of Hankyu Sannomiya Station that serve prime Kobe beef at anywhere near affordable prices. The teppan-style steak is served on a hot grill with a special spice and wine marinade that is as memorable as the voluptuous garlic and crisp fried potatoes. Right across from the Washington Hotel, A-1 has a relaxed and friendly atmosphere. *2-2-9 Shimo-Yamate-dori, Amashi-biru 2F, Chuo-ku, tel. 078/331–8676. Reservations advised. Dress: informal. No credit cards. Open 3–11 PM. Moderate.*

International

Totenkaku. This establishment has been famous among Kobe residents since 1945 for its Peking duck, flown in fresh from China. The building itself is worth the splurge—built at the turn of the century, it is one of Kobe's Ijinkan (foreigner's residences), the F. Bishop House. *3-14-18 Yamamoto-dori, Chuo-ku, tel. 078/231–1351. Reservations advised. Dress: informal. No children. DC. V. Open 11–9. Expensive.*

Gaylord. Just a few minutes' walk from Sannomiya Station, this

Indian restaurant, with a flashy decor, is a favorite with Kobe's foreign residents. The curries are on the mild side but are very tasty. *8-3-7 Isogami-dori, Meiji Seimei Bldg. B1, Chuo-ku, tel. 078/251–4359. Dress: informal. AE, D, V. Lunch 11:30–2:30, dinner 5–10. Moderate.*

Heidelberg. Authentic home-style German cooking is served here in a quiet location behind the courtyard on the second floor of the brick-walled Rose Garden Building. Heidelberg has enough excellent smoked pork, sauerkraut, and accordion music to appease the most discerning of Kobe's German community. Try the Kobe beef tartare. The relaxed atmosphere and abundance of good German wine and fine lager guarantee an enjoyable evening. *8-15 Yamamoto-dori, 2-chome, Chuo-ku, tel. 078/222–1424. Reservations advised. Dress: informal. AE, DC, MC, V. Open 11:30–10. Closed Wed. Moderate.*

King's Arms. Famous for its excellent platter of roast beef and its traditional atmosphere, the old King's Arms pub has become a Kobe landmark. When this pub opened 38 years ago, it was off limits to the Japanese. A portrait of Sir Winston Churchill still presides over the old wooden bar that was once the exclusive territory of some of Kobe's thirstiest Englishmen. The clientele have increased in number and kind over the years, but the flavor of the legendary roast beef, the finest Scotch whiskey, and the seriousness of the annual dart tournament haven't changed. There's much to be said for the fish and chips as well. *4-2-15 Flower Road, Chuo-ku, tel. 078/221–3774. Dinner reservations advised. Dress: informal. No credit cards. Open 11:30–9. Moderate.*

Marrakech. Elmaleh Simon, a former sailor and the Moroccan chef/owner of this restaurant, and his wife serve excellent Middle Eastern food. In this cozy little basement dining spot, it is easy to forget that you are in Japan. The couscous and kabobs are particularly delicious, and portions are generous. *Maison de Yamate B1, 1-20-15 Nakayamate-dori, Chuo-ku, Kobe-shi, tel. 078/241–3440. Reservations advised. Dress: informal. No credit cards. Open 5–midnight. Closed Mon. Moderate.*

★ **Salaam.** A light and airy restaurant with potted palms and white walls, Salaam credits itself with being the first Middle Eastern restaurant in Japan. The owner, a former ship engineer, has made an effort to offer a very complete menu with a variety of pickles, desserts, and main courses, such as kebabs, grilled seafood, and lamb. If you find the selection overwhelming, try the special dinners, in which you get a little of everything. Finish off your meal with refreshing hot mint tea served in a glass and a piece of baklava. *12-21 Yamamoto-dori 2-chome, Chuo-ku, Ijin Plaza Bldg., 2F, tel. 078/222–1780. Reservations advised. Dress: informal. AE, V. Lunch 11:30–2:30, dinner 5–10. Moderate.*

The Attic. Several years ago, former U.S. baseball player Marty Kuehnert opened this little haven for ball-park refugees and beer lovers of all sorts. Along with the Budweiser, Marty brought pizza, fried chicken, roast beef, and American-style fun to Kobe—complete with juke boxes and peanut shells. *Ijinkan Club Bldg. 3F, 4-1-12 Kitano-cho, Chuo-ku. tel. 078/222–1586 or 222–5368. Reservations accepted for large groups. Dress: casual. AE, V. Open 6–2. Closed Mon. Inexpensive.*

★ **Raja.** A former chef of restaurant Gaylord (*see* above) opened this small and unassuming place located near the Motomachi Station. Raja features home-style Indian cooking, with spicy and tasty curries and excellent saffron rice. *Sakaemachi, 2-*

chome, Sanonatsu Bldg. Bl, Chuo-ku, tel. 078/332–5253. Dress: informal. AE, D, V. Lunch 11:30–2:30, dinner 5–9. Inexpensive.

★ **Wang Thai.** Thai food is both trendy and popular in Tokyo, but it has yet to reach such heights in other regions of Japan. This is one of the few Thai restaurants in the area; it features a menu with hot Thai and slightly less spicy Chinese dishes. *14-22 Yamamoto-dori, 2 chome, Chuo-ku, President Arcade 2F, tel. 078/222–2507. Dress: informal. No credit cards. Lunch 11–2:30, dinner 5:30–9:30. Closed Wed. Inexpensive.*

Lodging

Kobe has a wide range of hotels varying in price and quality. Because this is a heavily industrialized city, many businessmen travel. As a result, the business hotels are conveniently located, and most are quite comfortable.

A 3% federal consumer tax is added to all hotel bills. Another 3% local tax is added to the bill if it exceeds ¥10,000. At most hotels, a 10%–15% service charge is added to the total bill. Tipping is not necessary.

The most highly recommended accommodations are indicated by a star ★.

Category	Cost*
Very Expensive	over ¥15,000
Expensive	¥10,000–¥15,000
Moderate	¥6,000–¥10,000
Inexpensive	under ¥6,000

*Cost is for double room, without tax or service

Credit Cards The following credit card abbreviations are used: AE, American Express; DC, Diners Club; MC, MasterCard; V, Visa.

Very Expensive

★ **Kobe Portopia Hotel.** Situated on Port Island, the Portopia is a dazzling modern hotel with every facility imaginable. The spacious rooms look over the port. The restaurants and lounges on the top floors of the hotel have spectacular panoramic views of Mt. Rokko and Osaka Bay. Because of its location, this hotel can only be reached by the Portliner monorail or by taxi. This inconvenience is counterbalanced by the fact that everything from food to clothing is available inside the hotel. *6-10-1 Minatojima Nakamachi, Chuo-ku, Kobe-shi, tel. 078/302–0111. 556 rooms. Facilities: shopping arcade, beauty salon; indoor and outdoor pools, gym, sauna, tennis courts; Chinese, Japanese, French, and sushi restaurants, coffee shops. AE, DC, MC, V.*

Shin-Kobe Oriental Hotel. The tallest building in western Japan, this luxury hotel is located in front of the JR Shin-Kobe Station where the Bullet Train arrives. Decor is sleek and modern, with Art Deco motifs in the carpeting and furnishings. The hotel is three minutes from downtown on the subway. *Kitanocho 1-chome, Chuo-ku, Kobe-shi, tel. 078/291–1121. 600 rooms.*

Facilities: shopping arcade; indoor and outdoor pools, sauna, gym, tennis courts; beauty salon; French, Chinese, Japanese, steak, and sushi restaurants. AE, DC, MC, V.

Expensive

★ **Oriental Hotel.** A small, distinguished hotel that has been in business for a century, the Oriental is a favorite with those who appreciate old-world hospitality. The rooms are comfortable, and the service is deferential. *25 Kyomachi, Chuo-ku, Kobe-shi, tel. 078/331–8111. 190 rooms. AE, DC, MC, V.*

★ **Sannomiya Terminal Hotel.** Located in the terminal building above the JR Sannomiya Station, this hotel is extremely convenient, particularly for anyone who has to catch an early train. The rooms are on the small side, but they are clean and pleasant. *8 Kumai-dori, Chuo-ku, Kobe-shi, tel. 078/291–0001. 190 rooms. Facilities: French, Japanese, and Chinese restaurants. AE, DC, MC, V.*

Moderate

Arcons. You'll need a taxi to get here from Sannomiya Station, because it's up on the hill in Kitano-cho, in the heart of the Ijinkan district. Many of the immaculate rooms at this little white hotel have a view out over the city to the sea. There's patio dining at the first-floor café when the weather is good. *3-7-1, Kitano-cho, Chuo-ku, tel. 078/231–1538. 22 rooms. Facilities: Italian restaurant, bar, gift shop; refrigerator in every room. AE, DC, MC, V.*

Green Hill Hotel. This business hotel is located about a 15-minute walk from either the Shin-Kobe Station or Sannomiya Station. Despite this slight inconvenience, this is, as business hotels go, a good place to stay. The rooms are well-kept, particularly in the new wing, and the atmosphere is pleasant; this is unusual in business hotels, which tend to be rather depressing. *5-16 Kanno-cho, 2-chome, Chuo-ku, Kobe-shi, tel. 078/222–1221. 110 rooms. Facilities: Japanese restaurant, coffee shop, sushi bar. AE, DC, V.*

Washington Hotel. A standard business hotel situated right in the heart of the nightlife district of Ikuta, the Washington Hotel offers decent rooms and efficient service. *2-11-5 Shimoyamate-dori, Chuo-ku, Kobe-shi, tel. 078/331–6111. 194 rooms. Facilities: Western and Japanese restaurants. AE, DC, MC, V.*

Inexpensive

Union Hotel. A short walk from the Sannomiya Station, the most attractive feature about this business hotel is its low rates. A 24-hour convenience store is located right next door, which comes in handy for midnight snacks. *1-9 Nunobiki-cho, 2-chome, Chuo-ku, Kobe-shi, tel. 078/222–6500. 210 rooms. Facilities: Western restaurant. AE, DC, MC, V.*

11 Western Honshu

by Nigel Fisher

Western Honshu is split through the center by mountains. On either side of this split are two distinct regions. The south side of the mountains, facing the Inland Sea, is referred to as the Sanyo region (Mountains in the Sun). The north side of Western Honshu, which faces the Sea of Japan, is called San'in (In the Shadow of the Mountains). From these descriptive names, one might think that Sanyo is the more attractive of the two, but that would be wrong. The southern coast, the route that the JR Shinkansen travels from Osaka to Hakata (on Kyushu), is heavily industrialized and visually, if not environmentally, polluted. The San'in coast, however, has so far escaped the fabricated buildings of Japan's economic miracle and retains its identity with traditional Japan.

This chapter sketches an itinerary from Osaka down the Sanyo coast, stopping at Himeji, Okayama, Kurashiki, Hiroshima, and Miyajima before reaching Honshu's westernmost point, Shimonoseki. Then the itinerary returns to Kyoto (or Osaka), traveling through San'in. Only a few places are mentioned in San'in, namely, Hagi, Tsuwano, Matsue, Tottori Dunes, and Amanohashidate, but, for the intrepid traveler, much more is left to explore.

Essential Information

Arriving and Departing

By Plane There are domestic airports at Hiroshima, Izumno, Tottori, and Yonago that connect these cities to Tokyo with daily flights. However, Hiroshima is the major airport for this region, with seven daily flights to Tokyo's Haneda airport (1hour, 15 minutes) as well as direct daily flights to Kagoshima (1 hour, 10 minutes), on Kyushu, and Sapporo (1 hour, 55 minutes), on Hokkaido.

By Train By far the easiest way to travel to Western Honshu and all along its southern shore is by the Shinkansen trains that run from Tokyo and Kyoto through southern Western Honshu to Hakata, on the island of Kyushu. The major stops on the Shinkansen line are Himeji, Okayama, and Hiroshima. It takes, for example, four hours and 37 minutes on the Shinkansen to travel to Hiroshima from Tokyo, one hour and 39 minutes from Osaka. To cover the length of southern Western Honshu from, for example, Osaka to Shimonoseki (the last city on Honshu before Kyushu) takes only three hours.

JR express trains cover both the southern and northern shores of Western Honshu, making, as it were, an elliptical loop around the shoreline, beginning and ending in Kyoto. Crossing from one coast to the other in Western Honshu requires traveling through the mountains (slow going), but there are several train lines that link the cities on the northern Sea of Japan coast to Okayama, Hiroshima, and Ogori. These are discussed later in the San'in section.

Important Addresses and Numbers

Tourist Information Centers Most major towns or sightseeing destinations have tourist information centers that offer free maps and brochures. They will also help in securing accommodations. The following telephone numbers are for the tourist information center at the major tourist destinations in Western Honshu: **Hagi Information Office,** tel. 08382/5–3145; **Hagi City Tourist Association** at Emukai, tel. 08382/5–1750; **Himeji Tourist Information Office,** tel. 0792/85–3792. **Hiroshima City Tourist Office,** tel. 082/245–2111; **Hiroshima Prefectural Tourist Office,** tel. 082/221–6516; **Hiroshima Tourist Information Office,** tel. 082/249–9329; **Kurashiki Tourist Information Office,** tel. 0864/26–8681; **Matsue Tourist Information Office,** tel. 0852/21–4034, **Miyajima Tourist Association,** tel. 0829/44–2011; **Okayama Prefectural Tourist Office,** tel. 0862/24–2111; **Okayama Tourist Information Office,** tel. 0862/22–2912; **Tsuwano Tourist Association Information Office,** tel. 08567/2–1144.

The Japan Travel-Phone The nationwide service for English-language assistance or travel information is available seven days a week, 9–5. Dial toll-free 0120/444–800 for information on western Japan. When using a yellow, blue, or green public phone (do not use the red phones), insert a ¥10 coin, which will be returned.

Emergencies **Police,** tel. 110; **Ambulance,** tel. 119.

Guided Tours

The **Japan Travel Bureau** (JTB) has offices at every JR station in each of the major cities and can assist in local tours, hotel reservations, and ticketing onward travel. Except for JTB's Hiroshima office (tel. 082/261–4131), one should not assume that any English will be spoken beyond the very basic essentials.

Japan Travel Bureau, operating through Sunshine Tours, has one-, two-, and three-day tours from Kyoto and Osaka to Hiroshima. The one-day tour covers Hiroshima and Miyajima (¥49,440 per person). The two-day (¥97,820 per person) tour also includes a hydrofoil trip on the Inland Sea to visit Omishima Island and Ikuchijima Island. The three-day tour (¥142,140 per person) adds a visit to Kurashiki and Okayama.

No guided tours of the San'in region are conducted in English, though the Japan Travel Bureau will arrange your individual travel arrangements.

The Sanyo Region

Though the Sanyo region faces the Seto Inland Sea, only glimpses of it are seen from the train traveling from Osaka to Shimonoseki. Most of the coastal plain is heavily industrialized through Hiroshima. Only from there, until the outskirts of Shimonoseki, does the postwar building diminish and open country begin. Furthermore, because the main Sanyo railway line is away from the coast, to appreciate the beauty of the Inland Sea, one must either make trips to one or more of the islands in the Inland Sea or take a cruise. There are, for example, several day-cruises from Hiroshima, or one can travel the length of the Inland Sea by ferries that ply the Inland Sea between Osaka and Beppu on Kyushu. In this chapter, one short trip on the Inland Sea goes to Miyajima, one of the most beautiful (though unfortunately tourist-filled) islands. (In the following chapter on Shikoku, an excursion is suggested to Shodo Island, the second largest island in the Inland Sea, from Takamatsu.)

Getting Around

Except for crossing over to Miyajima island, a 22-minute ferry ride from near Hiroshima, all of the following itineraries through the Sanyo region use JR trains, either the Shinkansen or the local commuter and express trains. Explanations of which trains to take between destinations are given throughout the Exploring section. Essentially, though, the itinerary follows the main trunk railway line along the southern shore of Western Honshu, and it is simply a matter of hopping on and off the trains plying between Osaka and Hakata. Local buses or streetcars are used in the major cities. Driving one's own rented car is not recommended. The roads are congested, and travel by train is faster and less expensive.

Himeji

Numbers in the margin correspond with points of interest on the Western Honshu map.

The first sight of Himeji's castle occurs from the train as it pulls into Himeji Station. Like a magnet, its incredible presence draws you off the train for closer inspection. Himejijo Castle is the grandest and most attractive of the 12 surviving feudal castles. The castle, also known as the Shirasagijo (White Egret Castle), stands on a 150-foot-high bluff and dominates the city. Visually, the castle commands respect.

Arriving and Departing ①
The city of **Himeji** is on the JR Shinkansen Line, with trains arriving and departing every 15 minutes during the day. The train journey to Himeji is three hours, 52 minutes from Tokyo, 59 minutes from Kyoto, and 42 minutes from Shin-Osaka. The Shinkansen to Okayama (to the west, it is the next destination of this itinerary) arrives and departs every hour during the day. Himeji was severely damaged in World War II and retains little to interest the foreigner. However, the castle miraculously escaped damage, and, because of the frequent train service, it is easy to disembark one train, visit the castle, and reboard another train two hours later.

Exploring
From the central exit of the Himeji JR station, the castle is a 15-minute walk or five minutes by bus (fare: ¥130), which leaves from the left-hand side of the station plaza. There is a Tourist Information Office (tel. 0792/85–3792) to the right of the station's north exit.

The present structure of **Himejijo Castle** took eight years to build and was completed in 1609. Ieyasu Tokugawa had given his son-in-law the surrounding province as a reward for his victory at the Battle of Sekigahara, and this magnificent castle was built to isolate the Osaka *daimyo* (lord) from his friends in the Western provinces. So, the castle was built not only as a military stronghold but also as an expression of Tokugawa power.

The five-story, six-floor main donjon (stronghold) stands 102 feet high and is built into a 50-foot-high stone foundation. Surrounding this main donjon are three lesser donjons. All four donjons are connected by covered passageways. This area was the central compound of the castle complex. There were also other compounds to the south and west. Enemies would therefore have to scale the bluff, cross three moats, breach the outer

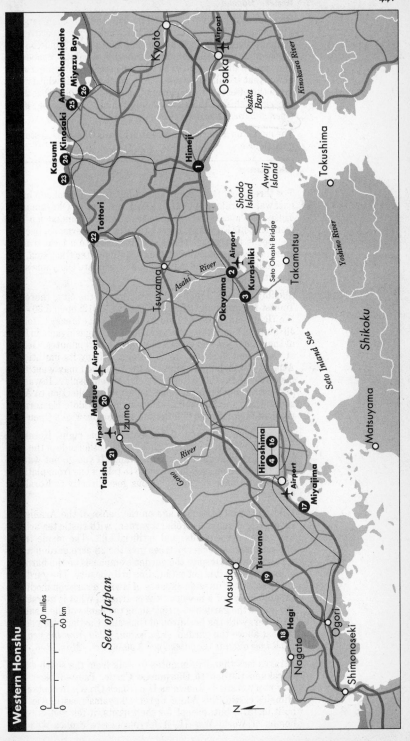

Western Honshu

Sea of Japan

Kyoto

Airport

Osaka

Osaka Bay

Kinokawa River

Amanohashidate

Miyazu Bay

Kinosaki

Kasumi

26

25

24

23

Himeji

1

Shodo Island

Awaji Island

Tokushima

Tottori

22

Tsuyama

Asahi River

Airport

Okayama

Kurashiki

2

3

Seto Ohashi Bridge

Takamatsu

Yoshino River

Airport

Matsue

20

Izumo

Seto Inland Sea

Shikoku

Matsuyama

Taisha

21

Gono River

Hiroshima

4

16

Airport

Miyajima

17

Matsuyama

Masuda

Tsuwano

19

Hagi

18

Nagato

Ogori

Shimonoseki

N

40 miles

60 km

0

0

compounds, and then be raked by fire from the four donjons. The castle existed not only to maintain military control over the Hyogo province but was also meant to impress. Note the aesthetic qualities of the donjon's dormerlike windows, cusped gables, and walls finished with white plaster, displaying a stark power that still inspires awe. From a distance, this white vision gives the effect of a silhouette of an egret, the bird that aunts the rice fields of the surrounding plains. *Admission: ¥500. Open 9–5 (grounds open to 6).*

The next stop along the Shinkansen Line is Okayama, a stop for garden lovers.

Okayama

❷ The three most famous gardens in Japan are Kenrokuen in Kanazawa, Kairakuen at Mito, and Korakuen at **Okayama;** because Okayama is only 35 minutes down the Shinkansen Line from Himeji, Korakuen is easy to visit. Furthermore, because one needs to change from the Shinkansen to a local train to travel to Kurashiki, the next destination after Okayama, it is convenient to visit the gardens and to compare Okayama's castle with Himejijo.

Exploring Should you need a map or information on the city, there is a **Tourist Information Office** (tel. 0862/22–2912; open 8:30–8) in the JR station. However, the layout of the city is easy to follow. Just hop on board the streetcar bound for Higashiyama in front of the JR station and go directly north for 10 minutes. Get out at the **Orient Museum.** You'll recognize it by its imitation of Athens' Parthenon. If you have the time, you may want to go inside to see the 2,000 items of Asian art on display. It was one of the first museums in Japan to devote its collection to Asian art and has special exhibits showing how Middle Eastern art reached Japan via the Silk Route. *Admission: ¥200. Open 9–5.*

At the Orient Museum, the streetcar turns right. **Korakuen Garden,** however, is straight ahead on the other side of the Asahigawa River (about a 10-minute walk). If you do not want to visit the museum, you may choose to take a bus from platform #9 in front of the station. This bus goes directly to Korakuen Garden.

Laid out three centuries ago on the banks of the Asahigawa River, Korakuen is a strollers' garden, with rustic tea arbors, extensive lawns, ponds, and artificial hills. The maple trees, apricot trees, and cherry trees give the 28-acre garden a seasonal contrast. Despite the garden's emphasis on the harmony of its elements, it is not astounding in its beauty. The garden is appreciated for its wide expanse of lawns, a rare commodity in Japan but less of a novelty to Westerners. What is attractive, though, is the garden's setting along the banks of the Asahigawa River, with the backdrop of Okayama Castle, which seems to float above the garden. *Admission: ¥250 from the vending machines outside the gate. Open 7:30–6; Oct.–Mar., 8–5.*

It takes less than five minutes to walk from the south exit of Korakuen Garden to **Okayamajo Castle.** Painted black, the four-story castle is known as Ujo (Black Crow), in contrast to Himeji's castle, the White Egret. Okayama's castle was first built in 1573, but, except for the turrets, it fell victim to the bombs of World War II. A ferro-concrete replica was constructed in 1966 and now houses objects of the region's history, including the usual collection of armor and swords. There is also, as behooves its modern construction, an elevator to take you between floors. *Admission:* ¥*200. Open 9–5.*

Aside from visiting Korakuen, the castle, and, perhaps, the Orient Museum, the other reason for disembarking from the Shinkansen at Okayama is to change to the local JR train for Kurashiki.

Kurashiki

❸ Kurashiki is a town in which to savor old Japan. During feudal times, the town was the center for merchants shipping rice and cotton from its port to Osaka. No longer a granary or textile town, Kurashiki has become a living museum of the past, surviving on the income produced by some 4 million visitors a year. Miraculously, Kurashiki escaped war damage and the wrecker's ball that has so often preceded Japan's industrial growth.

Arriving and Departing Commuter trains depart frequently from the Okayama JR station and take approximately 15 minutes to reach Kurashiki Station (not Shin-Kurashiki, where the Shinkansen trains stop). If you are coming directly from Tokyo, Kyoto, or Osaka, you may wish to stay on the Shinkansen until Shin-Kurashiki and take the local train back to the Kurashiki Station. There is a **Tourist Information Office** (tel. 0864/26–8681) opposite the entrance to the train platforms. The main tourist office (Bikan Historical Area, Kurashiki-kan, tel. 0864/26–8681) is located in the center of the old town. Both offices are open daily 9–5. If you telephone the day before, the main office can arrange for a volunteer guide to show you the city. The center of the old town is about 10 minutes on foot from the station and can be reached by walking down the main avenue extending perpendicular from the station; turn left at the street before the Kurashiki Kodusai Hotel.

Exploring Though one can tour Kurashiki in a half a day, the ideal way to enjoy this traditional town is to arrive in the late afternoon and stay the night in a ryokan. Being in Kurashiki on a Monday has an advantage and disadvantage. It is the day that most of the museums close, but for that reason, there are fewer visitors in town.

Amid the industrialized Sanyo coastal plains, Kurashiki is an oasis of the culture of traditional Japan. There are several museums to visit, but, in fact, all of the old town resembles a museum. The curving tiled roofs of the houses, the swaying willows lining the canal, and the stone half-circle bridges from which to watch the white swans float by transport the visitor back in time.

The major museum is the **Ohara Art Museum,** located in the old town. Magosaburo Ohara built this Greek pantheon-type building to house a collection of art that includes works by El Greco, including the Annunciation, Corot, Rodin, Gauguin, Picasso, Toulouse-Lautrec, and many more paintings by Western artists. To counter this preponderance of Western art, an additional wing was constructed in 1961 to house modern Japanese paintings and, more recently, to display Japanese tapestries, wood-block prints, pottery, and antiques. *Admission:* ¥*600.*

*Open 9–4:30. Closed Mon. and Dec. 28–Jan. 3. When Mon.
falls on a public holiday, the museum stays open.*

More Western art, this time Greek and Roman sculpture, may
be seen two minutes away at the **Karashiki Ninagawa Museum**
(Kuashiki Bijutsukan) (admission: ¥600; open 8:30–5). Around
the corner from this museum (next to the tourist office) and of
more interest to the foreign visitor is the **Kurashiki Folkcraft
Museum** (Kurashiki Mingeikan). In four converted granaries,
still with their white walls and black-tile roofs of the Edo period, are some 4,000 folk-craft objects ranging from ceramics to
rugs and from wooden carvings to bamboo wares. Especially
fascinating is the way that the museum displays similar products from different parts of the world, offering a cross-cultural
comparison of styles, design, and techniques of everyday folk
craft. *Admission: ¥500. Open 9–4. Closed Mon. and Dec. 28–
Jan. 3. When Mon. falls on a public holiday, the museum stays
open.*

Next door to the Folkcraft Museum is the **Japan Rural Toy Museum.** (Nihon Kyodo Gangukan). This museum, one of the two
top toy museums in Japan, is a pure delight. It exhibits some
5,000 toys from all regions of the country and has one room devoted to foreign toys. *Admission: ¥310. Open 8–5. Closed
Jan. 1.*

Time Out Before leaving this cluster of museums, you may care to drop
into the famous **El Greco** coffeehouse (next to the Ohara Art
Museum). It has scrumptious ice cream, milk shakes, cakes,
and other Western temptations.

All of these museums are clustered together on the north bank
of the Kurashiki River. Now cross over the bridge, and in less
than five minutes you will reach the **Ivy Square.** This ivy-cov-
ered complex used to be a weaving mill. With artful renovation,
it now contains a hotel (appropriately named Ivy Hotel), several boutiques, a restaurant, and, in the central courtyard, a
summer beer garden. The courtyard and beer garden are popular rendezvous in the early evening, when locals and tourists
gather for refreshment.

Three museums can be found in the complex. The **Kurabo Memorial Hall** retells the history of spinning and textiles, an industry that, along with the shipping of rice and cotton, was
Kurashiki's source of income. In many ways, it is a museum of
Japan's industrial revolution, and it includes a video of the factory workshop floor with its scurrying seamstresses and of the
dormitory that housed the unmarried female employees (admission: ¥100; open 9–5). The other two museums are the
Torajiro Kajima Memorial Museum, which has Western and
Asian art, and the **Ivy Gakkan,** which is an educational museum
using reproductions to explain Western art to the Japanese.
*Admission: ¥400 covers all 3 museums, though the only one of
any real interest is the Kurabo Memorial Hall. Open 8:30–5.
Closed Mon.*

For many of us, the real pleasure of Kurashiki is not the museums, but rather the ambience of the old town. Even the numerous tourists don't destroy it, but you should try to rise early in
the morning to stroll through the old neighborhood and be cap-
tivated by the pink glow of the early-morning lights dancing off

the buildings, the waterways crossed by arched bridges, and the whispers of the willows lining the streets.

The next stop down the Sanyo Line is Hiroshima, another world away, a world the 20th century first destroyed and then created. Savor Kurashiki while you can.

Hiroshima

4 **Hiroshima** will forever be etched in man's conscience as the first place where a nuclear weapon was used to obliterate man. No visitor to the city can fail to be acutely aware of the event which took place at 8:15 AM, August 6, 1945. On that morning, three B-29s flew toward Hiroshima; two planes were decoys, one flew directly over the city and cut loose a single bomb, codenamed Little Boy. In the center of the city, the bomb exploded at 1,900 feet above the Industrial Promotion Hall. Two hundred thousand people died, including 10,000 Korean prisoners forced to serve the Japanese empire as slave laborers. It was the only bomb to land on Hiroshima during World War II, and it wiped out half the city.

Only one telling reminder remains from the havoc and death that the atomic bomb wrought. Miraculously, the Industrial Promotion Hall did not completely collapse. Its charred structure remains untouched since that fated morning. It has been renamed the A-Bomb Dome and stands surrounded by the new Japan of ferro-concrete buildings.

Arriving and Departing **By Plane.** Seven daily flights run between Hiroshima and Tokyo's Haneda airport, as well as flights to Kagoshima, on Kyushu, and Sapporo, on Hokkaido.

By Train. Hiroshima is the major town in Western Honshu and a major terminal for the JR Shinkansen trains; several Shinkansen trains end their run at Hiroshima rather than continue to Hakata on Kyushu. During the day, Shinkansen trains arrive and depart for Okayama, Osaka, Kyoto, and Tokyo approximately every 30 minutes and about every hour for Hakata, on Kyushu. From Tokyo train time is four hours and 37 minutes and, unless you have a Japan Rail Pass, the fare is ¥17,700. The Hiroshima train station also serves as the hub for JR express and local trains traveling along the Sanyo Line. Coming from Kurashiki, the train ride is only an hour if you take the local JR train to Shin-Kurashiki (2 stops) and transfer onto the Shinkansen rather than doubling back to Okayama. There are also two trains a day that link Hiroshima to Matsue on the northern (Sea of Japan Coast) shore of Western Honshu.

By Ferry. Hiroshima is serviced by many ferries. Two important ones are: to and from Matsuyama on Shikoku (16 hydrofoil ferries a day that take 1 hr at ¥4,950 and 11 regular ferries a day that take 3 hrs at ¥3,710 for 1st class and ¥1,850 for 2nd class); and to and from Beppu on Kyushu (departs Hiroshima at 10:30 PM to arrive at Beppu at 6 AM and departs Beppu at 4 PM to arrive at Hiroshima at 10 PM at ¥3,600 to ¥10,070.) *Contact the Setonaikai Kisen Co., 12–23, Ujinakaigan 1-chome, Minami-ku, Hiroshima city, tel. 082/255–3344, fax 082/22–4178.*

Getting Around A **Tourist Information Office** (tel. 082/249–9329) at Hiroshima Station has free maps and brochures. The staff will also advise on accommodations. The Hiroshima International Relations has recently established a **Home Visit Program.** To make arrangements, go the day before to the International Center on the ground floor of the International Conference Center in Peace Memorial Park (1–5, Nakajima-cho, Naku-ku, Hiroshima 730, tel. 082/247–8007). The streetcar (tram) is the easiest form of transport in Hiroshima. Enter the tram from its middle door and take a ticket. Pay the driver at the front door when you leave. All fares within the city limits are ¥130. There are seven streetcar lines, and four of them either depart from Hiroshima Station or make it their terminus. Stops are announced by a tape recording, and each stop has its Romaji sign (spelled phonetically in English) posted on the platform. Buses also ply Hiroshima's streets; the basic fare is ¥170.

Taxis are available throughout the city. The initial fare is ¥460 for the first mile, then ¥70 for every 400 yards. There are also sightseeing taxis. For a three-hour tour, the charge is approximately ¥11,740. Because the taxi driver is not a guide, one may rent a taped recording describing the key sights in English. These special taxis depart from a special depot in front of the Hiroshima Station at the Shinkansen entrance. If you want to arrange for one of these taxis ahead of time, telephone the **Hiroshima Station Tourist Information Center** (tel. 082/261–1877).

Guided Tours A number of sightseeing tours are available. These include tours of Hiroshima and cruises on the Inland Sea, in particular, to Miyajima Island. A three-hour, 20-minute tour (Japanese-speaking guide only) to the city's major sights costs ¥2,830. A seven-hour tour of both the city and Miyajima costs ¥5,220. These tours are operated by the **Hiroshima Bus Company** (tel. 082/261–7104) and depart from in front of the Hiroshima Station at the Shinkansen entrance.

The **Seto Nakai Kisen Company** (tel. 082/253–1212) operates several cruises on the Inland Sea. Its cruise boat, the *Southern Cross*, operates a 5½-hour trip (9:30–3:10) every Sunday, Monday, Friday, and Saturday, March–November, which includes visits to Etajima, Ondo-no-seto, Kure Bay, and Enoshima (cost: ¥11,250, includes lunch and soft drinks). For a shorter cruise, you can take the boat (10:10 and 12:20) to Miyajima (cost: ¥960 one way, ¥1,810 round-trip). There is also the Sunset Cruise, which leaves Hiroshima Bay at 6:45 PM and returns at 8:40 PM (cost: ¥2,600), with dinner on board as an optional extra, for a total of ¥9,056.

Exploring *Numbers in the margin correspond with points of interest on the Hiroshima map.*

Entirely rebuilt after World War II, Hiroshima is a modern city. The atomic bomb is its living history. The monuments and the museum dedicated to "No More Hiroshimas" in the **Peace Memorial Park** are the key sights to visit. To reach the park from the station, take either streetcar #2 or #6 from the Hiroshima Station Plaza to the Genbaku-Domu-mae stop. On disembarking from the streetcar, your first sight will be the **A-Bomb Dome**. It is a powerful and poignant symbol. The old Industrial Promotion Hall, with its half-shattered structure, stands in sharp contrast to the vitality and wealth of the new Hiroshima. The A-Bomb Dome is the only structural ruin of the war left erect in Hiroshima, and, for that, its impact is even stronger.

From the Genbaku-Domu-mae bus stop, walk onto Aichi Bridge, the double bridge that crosses the Honkawa and

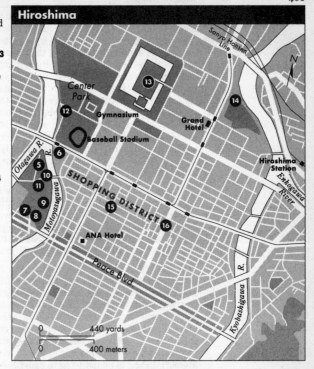

Hiroshima

❼ Motoyasu rivers. In the middle of the bridge is the entrance to the Peace Memorial Park. The **Peace Memorial Museum** is at the far end of the park. En route are statues and monuments, but, because you'll probably be returning through the park, head straight for the museum, about a 10-minute walk from the bridge. If you require more tourist information, there is a city tourist information center in the rest house located on the left-hand side of the park near another bridge crossing the Motoyasu River. A less dramatic approach from Hiroshima Station is to take the Hiroshima Bus Company's red-and-white bus #24 to Kokaido-mae, which is only a two-minute walk from the museum, or take streetcar #1 to Chuden-mae for a five-minute walk to the museum.

The Peace Memorial Museum is as disturbing as it is educational. Through exhibits of models, charred fragments of clothing, melted tiles, and photographs of devastation and contorted bodies, the story of havoc and agonizing death unfolds. Nothing can capture the reality of 12,632°F (7,000°C), the surface heat of the atomic fireball, but the remains of the melted statue of Buddha or the imprinted human shadow on granite steps is enough to unnerve our confidence in man's future existence. Most of the exhibits have brief explanations in English. However, more detailed information is given on tape cassettes, which may be rented for ¥120. *Admission to the museum: ¥50. Open 9–6; Dec.–Apr., 9–5. Closed Dec. 29–Jan. 2.*

❽ On the east side of the museum is the **Peace Memorial Hall,** where documentaries on the effects of the atomic explosion are given in English. (Times are posted at the museum's entrance.)

On the west side is the recently completed International Conference Center. In front of the museum on its north side is the **9 Memorial Cenotaph.** Designed by Japanese architect Kenzo Tange, the cenotaph resembles the primitive A-frame houses of Japan's earliest inhabitants. Buried inside the vaults of the cenotaph is a chest containing the names of those who died in the holocaust. On the exterior of the cenotaph is the inscription (in Japanese), "Repose ye in Peace, for the error shall not be **10** repeated." Before the cenotaph, the **Peace Flame** burns. The flame will be extinguished only when all atomic weapons in the world are banished. In the meantime, every August 6, there is a solemn festival in which the citizens of Hiroshima float paper lanterns on the city's rivers for the repose of the souls of the atomic-bomb victims.

11 Before you leave the park, pause before the **Statue of the A-Bomb Children.** The figure is of a young girl who died of leukemia caused by the atomic radiation. Her will to live was strong. She believed that if she could fold 1,000 paper cranes (cranes are a symbol of good fortune and long life), her illness would be cured. She died after making her 954th crane.

The Peace Memorial Park is disquieting. It does not engender hope. However, if you cross the Aichi Bridge at the park's northern entrance and walk 200 yards north and east, keeping the river on your left and the baseball stadium where the Hiro-**12** shima Carps play on your right, there is the **Hiroshima Science and Cultural Center for Children.** Aside from being a wonderfully laid out hands-on museum, the joy and enthusiasm of the youngsters here dispels some of the depression that the Peace Memorial Park is bound to have caused. Next door is a planetarium, open at the same times as the museum. *Open 9–5. Closed Mon. Admission:* ¥410.

13 Ten minutes' walk farther north is the resurrected **Hiroshimajo Castle.** The city of Hiroshima received its name from the castle, Hiroshimajo (Broad Island Castle), when Mori Terumoto built it in 1589. The castle was a Japanese Army headquarters in World War II and, as was the intent, the atomic bomb destroyed it. In 1958, the five-story donjon (stronghold) was rebuilt to its original specifications. Its interior has been used as a local museum, but since 1989, it has served as Hiroshima's historical museum, with exhibits from Japan's feudal period. *Admission to the castle grounds free; admission to the museum:* ¥300. *Open 9–6, Oct.–Mar. 9–5.*

14 The other place worth visiting in Hiroshima is **Shukkeien Garden.** Situated slightly to the east of the castle on the banks of the Kyobashigawa River, the garden was laid out in 1630 by Lord Nagaakira Asano in a design resembling that of a famed scenic lake in Hangzhou, China. The beauty of the garden stems from the streams and islets winding their way between the sculpted pine trees. Small bridges cross the streams, and, looking down into the waters, you will see exotic colored carp, so praised for their long lives. It is a fitting end for a visit to Hiroshima. *Admission:* ¥200. *Open 9–6, Oct.–Mar. 9–5.*

If you like big cities and want an urban base to explore the Inland Sea, Hiroshima combines international and Japanese urban pleasures with 4,000 bars. In its central district, around **15 Hondori,** there are the major department stores and masses of smaller shops. The major stores, Fukuya (closed Wed.),

Tenmaya (closed Tues.), Mitsukoshi (closed Mon.), and Sogo (closed Thurs.), are open 10–6. Restaurants abound, and oysters are the specialty of the region, best washed down with sake, of which Hiroshima produces some of Japan's finest. There is, of course, a range of modern hotels from which to choose (*see* Dining and Lodging, below), located in the city center to the east of the Peace Memorial Park and around the JR station. To the east of the Hondori Shopping District is **16 Shintenchi,** an all-important entertainment district.

Miyajima

Numbers in the margin correspond with points of interest on the Western Honshu map.

17 The most enjoyable part of any visit to Hiroshima is the excursion to **Miyajima.** The Japanese have what is known as the "Big Three Scenic Attractions." Matsushima, in Tohoku, is one, Amanohashidate, on the San'in coast, is another, and Miyajima, a small island in the Inland Sea, is the third. Miyajima also has the famous Itsukushima Jinja Shrine, built on wooden supports that extend the buildings into the sea; the shrine is known for its much-photographed torii gate rising out of the waters of the Inland Sea.

The island of Miyajima is only 19 miles in circumference, but its center peaks at 1,740 feet with Mt. Misen. With forested slopes on the mountain and the surrounding Inland Sea, it is a pretty, though touristy, village; Miyajima, with history and tradition everywhere, is delightful either as a day trip or for an overnight stay. Though the religious center of the island is Itsukushima Jinja Shrine, all of the island is sacred. You will note that there are no cemeteries on the island. No one is allowed to die here, or even to be born here. When either time comes, the concerned party must be taken over to the mainland.

Arriving and To reach Miyajima, sightseeing boats leave from Hiroshima **Departing** (*see* Guided Tours section for Hiroshima, above). However, the easiest, least expensive way is to take the commuter train on the JR Sanyo Line from Hiroshima Station to Miyajima-guchi Station. The train takes about 25 minutes and departs from Hiroshima every 15–20 minutes. The first train departs from Hiroshima at 5:55 AM and, for the return, the last ferry leaves Miyajima at 9:20 PM. From Miyajima-guchi Station, it is a three-minute walk down to the shore and the pier from which the ferries scoot over to Miyajima island. There are two ferry boats. One belongs to JR, and your JR Rail Pass is valid on this boat only. There are also direct ferries from Hiroshima Ujina Port. They leave seven times a day and take 22 minutes to make the trip (cost: ¥1,250). Allow a minimum of three hours to cover the major sights of Miyajima. More time is needed if you go inland up to the park.

Exploring From Miyajima's pier, follow the coast to the right (west). This leads to the village, which is crowded with restaurants, hotels, and souvenir shops selling, for the most part, the tackiest of objects to Japanese tourists. At the far end of the village is the park which leads past the **Torii Gate** and on to the **Itsukushima Jinja Shrine.** Expect to be greeted by deer as you walk through the park. The deer are protected, and they take full advantage of their status, demanding edibles and nudging you if you are not forthcoming.

The Torii Gate is located 500 feet from the shore, at an entrance to the cove in which the shrine stands. The gate is huge, rising 53 feet out of the water, making it one of the tallest in Japan. It was built in 1875 and has become a symbol not only of Miyajima but also of Japan. Especially as the sun sets over the Inland Sea, the vermilion structure and its reflection in the rippling water is an unforgetable sight. Past the torii stands the shrine. Poets write of how the shrine's building seems to float on the water. They omit that it "floats" only at high tide. At other times, the shrine stands on wooden stilts above the mud flats.

Itsukushima Jinja Shrine was created in 593 and dedicated to the three daughters of Susano-o-no-Mikoto, the Shinto god of the moon and the oceans. The structure has had to be continually repaired and rebuilt, and the present structure is thought to be a 16th-century copy of the 12th-century buildings. Most of the shrine is closed to the public, but you can walk around its deck, which gives some idea of the size of the building complex as well as a clear view of the Torii Gate. *Admission: ¥300 (or a combined ticket with the Treasure House for ¥500). Open 6:30–6 (6:30–5 in winter).*

Located across from the shrine's exit is the **Treasure House** (Home Tsu-kan). Because every victor of battles that took place on the Inland Sea saw fit to offer their gratitude to the gods by giving gifts to Itsukushima Jinja Shrine, the Treasure House is rich with art objects, 246 of which have been designated as either National Treasures or Important Cultural Properties. *Admission: ¥300 (or a combined ticket with Itsukushima Jinja for ¥500). Open 9–5.*

Adding to this uniquely Japanese scene of the floating Torii Gate and shrine are the **Five-Story Pagoda** and **Senjokaku Hall.** Senjokaku Hall (Hall of One Thousand Mats) was dedicated by Hideyoshi Toyotomi in 1587 and has rice scoops attached to the walls, symbols of the soldiers who died fighting for Japan's expansionism. The Five-Story Pagoda *(Goju-no-to)* dates from 1407. Both are situated on top of a small hill overlooking the shrine. If you climb up the steps to these two buildings for a closer look, a small street on the other side (away from the shrine) serves as a short cut back to the village.

Though many visitors spend only a half a day on the island, those with more time to enjoy its beauty may enter **Momi-jidani-Koen Park,** inland from the shrine. Here in the park is the start of the mile-long ropeway that takes you virtually up to the summit of **Mt. Misen.** A short hike at the end of the ropeway takes you to the very top. It's worth it; the views of the Inland Sea and Hiroshima beyond are splendid. *Cost: ¥800 one way, ¥1,400 round trip.*

Miyajima has become a vacation spot for Japanese families; hence, there are many hotels and ryokans in and around the village. One of these ryokans is worth remembering. It is the famous **Iwaso Ryokan** (tel. 08294/4–2233), which has been a host to pilgrims and vacationers for 130 years. Even if you are not staying in town overnight, Iwaso makes an ideal spot for lunch *(see* Dining and Lodging, below). Also, be aware that the most exciting, and the most crowded, time to visit Miyajima is in June (lunar calendar) for the annual Kangen-sai Festival, when three stately barges bearing a portable shrine, priests, and musicians cross the bay, flanked by a squadron of festooned boats.

Once back at Hiroshima, the westbound Shinkansen heads for Shimonoseki an hour away, before crossing to Kyushu and terminating in Hakata. Instead of crossing over to Kyushu with the Shinkansen, this itinerary does practically a 180-degree turn to travel east along Western Honshu's northern region, the San'in.

The San'in Region

San'in officially stretches along Western Honshu from Shimonoseki all the way to Kyoto. However, the special atmosphere of San'in ends on the Sea of Japan coast at Maizuro, just inside the border of Kyoto Prefecture. San'in means "In the Shadow of the Mountains." Whereas the coastline that faces the Inland Sea has the direct light of the sun, San'in has a misty, eerie light that diffuses to cause an ever-changing mood of flirting shadows. Also, San'in has been in the shadow of Japan's economic miracle. The presence of the mountains makes transport expensive between the north and south coasts and has staved off the pollution of sprawling factories and the modern urbanization that have destroyed so much of the Sanyo coast. The influx of tourists, both Japanese and foreigners, has also been less; San'in is off the beaten track, which adds to its appeal.

San'in is different from Sanyo in its lifestyle. Life moves slower. Trains and buses are less frequent. There is an austerity in the architecture, the crafts, and in the attitude of the people, a reflection of the cold winters and the isolation from mainstream Japan. An example of their art may help explain this. To the San'in people, a chipped tea bowl has more aesthetic appeal than the perfected symmetry used by Kyoto's craftspeople. San'in potters will create a crack in a bowl and artfully glaze it. The result is inspiring. The imagination must make the leap to what ultimate perfection could be. This is San'in—inspiring, restrained, forever conceiving perfection but never harnessing it.

Getting Around

By Train Along the Sea of Japan coast, the JR San'in Main Line runs from Shimonoseki to Kyoto. The line is the second longest in Japan, 422 miles. More to the point, it has the most stations of any line, which means frequent stops and longer traveling times. The trains are also less frequent. Only two limited express trains a day cover the Shimonoseki–Kyoto route in either direction. There are, however, local trains that go back and forth between the major cities along the San'in coast.

At several points along the San'in coast are routes through the mountains to cities on the Inland Sea. A few of the major connecting routes are:

Between Hagi and Ogori: one hour, 30 minutes on the JR or Bocho bus lines.

Between Tsuwano and Ogori: one hour on the JR Yamaguchi Line.

Between Tsuwano and Matsue, via Masuda: three hours, 20 minutes on JR San'in Main Line.

Between Tsuwano and Hagi: three hours, with a change at Masuda on the JR Yamaguchi Line and the JR San'in Main Line; or two hours by Bocho bus lines.

Between Masuda and Ogori: two hours on the JR Yamaguchi Line.

Between Yonago and Okayama: three hours on the JR Hakubi Line.

Between Matsue and Hiroshima: five hours on the JR Geibi and Kitsugi Line (one train a day, departing from Hiroshima at 8:45 AM).

Between Matsue and Okayama: two hours and 25 minutes on the JR Yakumo Limited Express (four Limited Express and five local trains a day). From Kyoto, the train takes six hours. There are also two night trains from Tokyo to Matsue; the trip takes 13 hours.

Unless you do not mind waiting around stations or being stranded overnight, before you set out to explore the San'in, ask any information office at a JR station to list the current times of the trains arriving and departing from the major towns along the San'in. Trains run so infrequently that you will need to plan your time to fit their schedule, unlike many other regions in Japan, where it rarely matters if you miss one train.

Indeed, there are not many trains that set out each day from Shimonoseki to **Hagi**, so plan ahead. The limited express takes two hours; the local takes four hours. Try not to find yourself stranded in Shimonoseki overnight. Shimonoseki is an industrial port town from which ferries leave for various ports on Kyushu, the Inland Sea, and Pusan, across the Sea of Japan in Korea. Even the first hour on the JR train heading for Hagi shows landscape built up with man's factories, but gradually the scenery becomes more natural, and the views of the coastline start setting the tone of San'in and its first major city, Hagi.

Hagi

Although the castle was dismantled in 1874 as a relic of feudalism, **Hagi** retains the atmosphere of a traditional castle town. Hagi is rich with history, one that is closely linked to the Mori family. Even though the Mori family had opposed the Tokugawa Shogunate and were defeated by Ieyasu Tokugawa in 1600 at the Battle of Sekigahara, the Mori were able to keep their fiefdom for 13 generations. The Tokugawa Shogunate had tried to isolate the Mori as much as possible, but in so doing, the Mori, who had never forgotten their defeat, became the forerunners of the movement to restore power to the emperor. It was the army from Hagi and the surrounding Nagato Province that, on the second attempt, captured Kyoto and turned the tide against the shogunate. Hagi's fame lies not simply in defeating the shogunate but also in supplying the intellectual ideas for the new Japan. Indeed, Japan's first prime minister, Hirobumi Ito (1841–1909), was born and educated in Hagi.

Hagi, too, has another claim to fame: Hagi-yaki. This pottery has been cherished for 375 years for its subtle pastel colors and its milky, translucent glazes. Mind you, the tradition of Hagi-yaki has less than noble beginnings. Returning from Japan's aborted attempt to invade Korea in the late 16th century, a Mori general brought home two Korean potters as "souvenirs." With techniques that were probably used during the Silla Kingdom, these Korean brothers, Yi Sukkweng and Yi Kyung, created Hagi-yaki for their masters. Hagi-yaki has since become second to Raku-yaki as the most praised pottery in Japan. Unfortunately, the two most famous kilns, Rikei's Saka Kiln and Miwa Kiln, do not accept visitors, but several others do. Shizuki Kiln is one; it is conveniently located on the way to the castle grounds.

Arriving and Departing Though the second part of this chapter's itinerary begins at Hagi as if we were coming from Kyushu or Shimonoseki, it is possible to cross over the mountains from Ogori, served by the Hiroshima-Hakata Shinkansen, on the Inland Sea to Tsuwano by train, and then to Hagi by bus; or you may travel directly to Hagi from Ogori by JR bus, which is the quicker way.

Hagi is surrounded by mountains on three sides and by the Sea of Japan on the fourth. The actual city of Hagi is in the V formed by two rivers, the Matsumoto gawa on the east side and the Hashimoto gawa on the west side. The major train station for entering the city is Higashi-Hagi (not Hagi), on the eastern side of town. There is a **Travel Service Desk** (tel. 08382/5-3145) at the station for free maps, sightseeing information, and help with finding accommodations.

Getting Around The ideal way to explore Hagi is by bicycle, and there are many outlets where bikes can be rented for approximately ¥1,000. Try the bicycle shop across from the Rainbow Building, left of the station plaza. Alternatively, one can hire a "sightseeing taxi" for about ¥3,500 per hour; it takes about three hours to complete a hurried city tour.

A four-hour sightseeing bus tour (Japanese-speaking guides only) operated by the **Bocho Bus Company** departs from the Bocho Bus Station, located on the eastern edge of the central city (cost: ¥2,000).

Exploring To get to the Hagi downtown area from the Higashi-Hagi Station, cross the bridge over the Matsumoto River and, bearing right, continue on the street until you reach the Hagi Grand Hotel. Then, take a left, and six blocks up on the right-hand side is the beginning of **Tamachi Mall.** Just on the corner is the **Ishii Chawan Museum.** This small, second-floor museum has a rare collection of antique tea bowls produced in Hagi, including some by the Korean potter whose creations first captured the attention of the Japanese. Also in this prized collection are Korean tea bowls made during the Koryo Dynasty (916–1392). For afficionados this museum is a pleasure, but if you are short of time you may want to skip this to be sure of visiting the Kumaya Art Museum (*see* below). *Admission: ¥350. Open 9–5. Closed Dec.–Mar.*

Tamachi Mall is the busiest street in Hagi, with a complement of some 130 shops offering both the latest fashions from Tokyo and the more interesting local products from Yamaguchi Prefecture. You may well wish to return to purchase Hagi-yaki after touring the sights and one of the kilns where the pottery is made. Two stores worth noting are Harada Chojuan and Miwa Seigado. The latter is at the top end of Tamachi, past the San

Marco restaurant. Another gallery and store is Saito-an, in which both the masters and "unknown" potters display their works for sale. If you search through the wares, you may be able to find a small sake cup for less than ¥500, or, if you have your gold credit card ready, you may choose a tea bowl by such living master potters as Miwa Kyusetsu for ¥250,000.

At the top of Tamachi Mall, a right turn toward Hagi Bay will lead you through the Teramachi section of town. Numerous temples here cry out for someone to pay heed to them. The locals just take them for granted. Each one of these temples has something to offer and all have a tranquillity rarely transgressed by tourists. There are about 10 from which to choose and explore, from the old wooden temple of **Hofukuji,** with its bibbed Jizo statues, to **Kaichoji,** with its two-story gate and veranda around the Main Hall's second floor.

Instead of walking all the way to Hagi Bay, take a left after the Kaichoji Temple. This street will lead to the **Kumaya Art Museum.** It will be on the left-hand side—look for a big metal gate. The complex was once the home of a wealthy merchant, and the warehouse has been made into a museum, which houses art objects and antiques. Of special note are the scrolls, paintings, a screen of the Kanoschool, and a collection of ceramics, which includes some of the first Hagi-yaki produced. *Admission:* ¥500. *Open 9–5.*

From the Kumaya Art Museum, take the next left (south and away from the sea) to visit the **Kikuya House.** This was once the home of the chief merchant family to the Mori clan. Though the Kikuya were only merchants, they held a special relationship with the Mori. (After the Mori defeat at Sekigahara, the Kikuya family sent their daimyo money to return to Hagi.) As a result, this house has more extravagance than merchants were normally allowed to display. *Keyaki* (Japanese cypress) was, for example, forbidden to merchants, yet notice its extensive use in this home. This is not your typical family home during the Edo period, but it does indicate the good life of the few. *Admission:* ¥390. *Open 9–5.*

The next stop is **Shizuki-Koen Park,** where the Hagijo Castle once stood and the castle remains are now located. Head west from Kikuya past the NHK broadcasting building, and keep the Sosuien Park on your left. After the next major cross street on the left, you will find the **Shizuki Kiln.** You may want to stop in here and browse over its Hagi-yaki pottery and, if the wallet can bear it, purchase some of the magnificent work. Also, most of the time, you will be welcome to enter the adjoining building where the kilns are fired.

At the next major intersection after Shizuki Kiln, take a left and walk or bicycle along the street between the **Toida Masuda House Walls.** These are the longest mud walls of the Horiuchi samurai section of town, and, for a moment, one is thrust back into feudal times. Follow the walls around and head west to the grand wooden **Fukuhara Gate.** A right turn here leads directly to the **Tomb of Tenjuin,** a memorial to Terumoto Mori, who founded the clan giving rise to 13 generations of Mori rule.

At the memorial, take a left turn and head toward the park grounds. On the left, past the Shizuki Youth Hostel, is the **Mori House,** a long (170 feet) and wide (17 feet) building that was once the home to the samurai foot soldiers. *Admission:* ¥200.

Open 8–6:30 (8–4:30 in winter). Admission to the Mori House also covers entrance to Shizuki-Koen Park and the castle grounds.

The entrance to Shizuki-Koen Park is opposite the Mori House. On the way to the castle you will pass two pottery kilns, **Shogetsu Kiln** and **Hagijo Kiln,** both of which offer the opportunity for browsing, watching the potters at work, and, of course, purchasing the products. Once inside the actual castle grounds, there is the **Shizukiyama Jinja Shrine,** built as recently as 1879; the wood used has weathered to give the shrine a comfortable, reassuring presence. Beyond the shrine is a highly recommended place to visit, the **Hananoe Tea House.** Set in delightful gardens, this thatch teahouse exudes peace and tranquillity. The attendants will make tea for you while you savor the quiet of the gardens. *Admission free, but the tea is ¥ 300.*

The actual Hagijo Castle is no more. Its demise, though, was unusual. Neither warfare nor fire destroyed it. Instead, the castle was dismantled as a gesture of support for the Meiji Restoration. Also, with the arrival of Western gunboats 15 years before the Meiji Restoration, the castle became vulnerable to attack.

In fact, the Mori family had moved from the castle in 1863 to create a new home and provincial capital at landlocked Yamaguchi. All that remains of the castle are its high walls and wide moats. But the pleasure of Shizuki-Koen Park is its space and setting.

The castle walls and moat are a few steps beyond the Hananoe Tea House. From the top of the walls, there is a panoramic view of Hagi, the bay, and the surrounding mountains inland. However, the best panoramic view is from **Mt. Shizuki,** which rises 470 feet behind the castle. It takes about 20 minutes to hike up the path to the top.

On the way back down Mt. Shizuki, you may want to stop at the **Hagi Shiryokan,** the local history museum. (Admission: ¥300; open 9–5, in winter 9–4.) If your time is limited, forgo a visit to the museum and leave the park to head for Dashoin Temple. It is a lengthy hike, so unless you have a bicycle, in which case it is about a 20-minute pedal, a taxi is advised. To reach the Dashoin, cross over the canal that marks the boundary of Shizuki-Koen Park and follow it south to the Tokiwabashi Bridge. Once over the Hashimoto gawa River, take the main road that follows the river upstream. Dashoin Temple is on the right, on the other side of the JR San'in Main Line tracks.

Dashoin Temple is the counterpart to the more frequented Tokoji Temple (covered later). Screened by the surrounding mountains, Dashoin is the final resting place for half of the Mori family. The first two Mori generations are buried at Dashoin. The third generation is buried at Tokoji Temple. Thereafter, even-numbered generations of the Mori generations are buried at Dashoin, and odd-numbered generations are buried at Tokoji. What is unusual about both Dashoin and Tokoji are the lanterns and the placement of the daimyo's wife next to her husband's tomb. Such a close affiliation, or recognition of the wife, in death was not the custom in feudal Japan. The lanterns tell another story.

When Hidehari Mori, the first Mori daimyo to be buried at Dashoin, died, seven of his principal retainers followed, dutifully committing ritual suicide. Extending this custom further, one of the retainers to one of the daimyo's retainers also killed himself. The eight graves are lined up in a row of descending rank. The Tokugawa Shogunate realized that this custom could decimate the aristocracy and decreed that such ritual suicide upon the death of one's lord was illegal. Future generations of retainers gave up their suicidal rights and, instead, donated lanterns. The path leading to the main hall of Dashoin Temple is lined with 603 lanterns. The temple is a special place to visit at any time, but in May the temple grounds burst into a purple haze with the wisteria in full bloom. Another special time to visit is on August 13, when all the lanterns are lit. *Admission: ¥200. Open 9–4:30.*

Dashoin Temple is in the southern outskirts of Hagi. We need now to move to the eastern sector of town, the same sector as Higashi-Hagi JR Station. If you are without a bicycle, then walk five minutes to the east of Dashoin Temple, catch the train at Hagi Station to Higashi-Hagi Station, and walk south to Matsumotobashi Bridge. If you are on a bicycle, return to Hashimoto gawa River, follow it upstream to Hashimotobashi Bridge, and head into central Hagi. At the Bocho Bus Center, go right and cross over Matsumotobashi Bridge.

Directly east of Matsumotobashi Bridge, the road leads to **Tokoji Temple,** the other cemetery of the Mori family. The temple was founded by the Zen priest Domio in 1691 under the auspicies of Yoshinari Mori, the third lord of Hagi. It is here that he (and every succeeding odd-numbered generation of the Mori family) is buried. You enter the temple grounds through the three-story Sanmon Gate to reach the Main Hall, which contains rather garish images of Buddha. Behind this building are the monuments of the Mori lords and their wives. Needless to say, it is easy to point to the husbands' graves. They are the grandest of all. Surrounding the monuments, amid the pine trees, are 500 lanterns donated by the lords' retainers. On August 15, all of these lanterns are lit: an impressive sight, indeed. *Admission: ¥200. Open 8:30–5:30.*

Instead of returning directly to the Matsumotogawa River, keep to the left as you leave the shrine and after a steep climb, you'll reach the **Monument to Shoin Yoshida** (1830–1859). Yoshida was a revolutionary. With the coming of Commodore Perry's Black Ships in 1853, Shoin recognized the need for Japan to step out of feudalism and accept certain Western practices. In his quest to understand the West, he attempted to slip aboard an American ship. He was caught by the shogunate, imprisoned, and later sent home to Hagi to be kept under house arrest. During his arrest, he started expounding a liberal philosophy that suggested both adapting to Western practices and introducing democratic elements into government. In the eyes of the shogunate, these preachings were outright sedition. At age 29, Shoin was executed. His execution inflamed and united the antishogunate elements of Hagi and the Namoto Province (now Yamaguchi Prefecture).

Coming down the hill from Yoshida's monument, take a left turn and you will pass the house of one of Shoin's students, Hirobumi Ito, the first prime minister of Japan. Across the street from the **Ito House** is the **Shoin Jinja Shrine,** with the

Shoka-Sonjuku, the private school that Shoin founded to teach his students his revolutionary philosophy. At the shrine's exit, there is a museum, which recounts Shoin's life depicted in three-dimensional scenes with model figures. There are, however, no English explanations of their meaning. *Admission: ¥ 300. Open 8:30–5.*

From the Shoin Jinja Shrine, you can cross the Matsu-motobashi Bridge and go straight to Tamachi Mall, or take a right before the bridge and return to the JR Higashi-Hagi Station to journey onward through San'in. The next stop in San'in is Tsuwano, situated inland and nestled in the mountains. En route between Hagi and Masuda is the small fishing village of Susa. Besides being located on an attractive bay, few gaijin ever come here, and it has one of Japan's best minshukus (*see* lodging). Some might want to stay overnight here rather than at Hagi.

Tsuwano

⑲ The castle town of **Tsuwano** is a much smaller town than Hagi; because of that, it has an intimate atmosphere. One can quickly feel part of the town and its 700-year history. Indeed, Tsuwano is occasionally referred to as a "little Kyoto" for its genteel qualities, and, like Kyoto, it has a river flowing through town. However, aside from these similarities, Tsuwano is not Kyoto. Tsuwano is a mountain town, small and compact.

Arriving and Departing To reach Tsuwano, you can take the JR train on the San'in Main Line to Masuda, where one must change trains for a 30-minute run up to Tsuwano; you can also take a bus from Hagi's Bocho Bus Center directly to Tsuwano, which takes two hours (fare: ¥1,550). You can also reach Tsuwano directly from Ogori by the JR train, which takes one hour. Ogori is 40 minutes on the Shinkansen from Hiroshima.

Getting Around All the sights are within easy walking distance, or one can rent a bicycle (cost: ¥600 for 3 hours, ¥800 for a full day). A taxi may also be used at ¥3,600 an hour, and it takes about two to three hours to visit the sights. There is a **Tourist Information Office** (tel. 08567/2–1144) at the railway station that has free brochures and will help in securing accommodations.

Exploring Except for the stone walls, nothing is left of the mountaintop castle, but Tsuwano's other attraction, the multicolored carp that fill the waters of the Tsuwanogawa River and the water-filled ditches, is still much in evidence. Indeed, the carp outnumber Tsuwano's residents by 10 to 1. Carp were originally introduced into the river and sewers as a ready source of food should the town ever be under siege. There was no siege, and because the carp live about 60 years, they have had a rather privileged existence. Life is still good for them. If you make your way from the JR station to Tonomachi Street (a 5-minute walk), you can feed these exotic-colored fellows (swimming in the man-made ditches along the street) with "carp snacks" bought at the coffee shop across from the **Catholic Church.** (Gourmands may like to dine on carp at the Yuki Restaurant on Honcho-dori Avenue, close to the post office.)

The Catholic Church, though built in 1931, is a reminder of the time when Christianity was outlawed in Japan. In 1865, in an effort to disperse Christian strongholds and cause them extreme hardship, in the hope that they would recant their faith, the Tokugawa Shogunate transported 153 Christians from Nagasaki to Tsuwano. By the time the Meiji government lifted the ban on Christianity, 53 Christians remained in Tsuwano. Thirty-six had been martyred, and the remainder had either recanted or died of natural causes. It's worth stopping at the church: Where but in Japan can one find a Catholic church with floors covered with tatami matting?

A few steps farther up Tonomachi Street, on the left-hand side, is the **Yorakan Museum.** The building was originally a feudal school where the sons of samurai would train in the arts of manhood. Today, in its fencing hall, there is a folk-craft museum. *Admission: ¥150. Open 8:30–5:30.*

At the top of Tonomachi Street, the road crosses the Tsuwano River at the Ohashi Bridge. Just on the other side is the **Kyodokan Museum,** with a collection of exhibits that recounts regional history. *Admission: ¥300. Open 8:30–5.*

However, you may want to save the time and, instead of crossing the bridge, fork to the right under the *torii* gate, cross the railway tracks of the JR Yamaguchi Line, and follow the river for approximately 250 yards. Indicative of the million visitors who make the pilgrimage each year, the number of souvenir stands and teahouses increases until you reach the **Yasaka Shrine,** where, every July 20 and July 27, the festival of the Heron Dance is held. Behind this shrine is the stepway to the **Taikodani-Inari Jinja Shrine.** The approach resembles a tunnel, because one passes under numerous red torii gates—1,174 of them—to reach the shrine high on the cliffside. (Nowadays, the weak of spirit may reach the shrine by bus along another road.)

From the shrine, you can either hike a hard 20 minutes up to the site of **Tsuwanojo Castle** or take the road down the other side of the shrine to the chair lift, which takes five minutes to reach the base of the castle grounds. To ascend the summit from the top of the chair lift requires a further eight-minute walk. Whichever way you make it to the top, it is worth every effort. The view from where this mountaintop castle once stood sweeps over the tile-roof town of Tsuwano and the valley below. What a marvelous castle it must have been! The original castle was built in the 13th century and took 30 years to build. Its demise took a lot less. Like Hagijo Castle, as a sign of good faith, this castle was dismantled during the Meiji Restoration.

You can walk back down from the castle grounds to the main street or use the chair lift. Because the views from the chair lift are so superb, you may prefer the latter. At the bottom of the chair lift, turn left and then right to cross over the Tsuwanogawa River. Immediately on crossing the river, take the right-hand street and follow it around to the left, where you will pass by the **Old House of Ogai Mori.** Ogai Mori (1862–1922) was one of the prominent literary figures in the Meiji Restoration. He spent only his first 11 years in Tsuwano (he went to the Yorokan school), but his hometown never forgot him, nor he his hometown. His success as a doctor caused him to travel overseas, and, in so doing, he tried to reconcile the differences between Western and Japanese cultures. His tomb is at the **Yomeiji Temple,** located to the east of Tsuwano's JR station. *Admission to the temple: ¥300. Open 8:30–5.*

Next door to the Mori House is **Sekishukan,** a museum displaying Japanese handmade paper *(washi)*. Demonstrations of paper-making are given, as well as a display of the Iwami-style
paper. On the second floor, there are displays of washi made
from other regions of Japan. If you have not seen the process of
making handmade paper or wish to compare different regional
types, this is a good museum to visit. *Admission free. Open
9–5.*

From this museum, continue along the street until the main
road and take a left. This will lead you back to town over the
Ohashi Bridge. If there is time before your train, and you did
not see the exhibition of papermaking at Sekishukan, in front of
the station is the **Tsuwano Industry Museum.** Demonstrations
are given of the town's traditional industries, and most of the
space is given to the craft of papermaking. There is also a section on sake brewing if you have not had the opportunity to witness it before (admission: ¥100; open 8:30–5). Also, five
minutes to the east of the JR station and up the hill through the
Pass of the Virgin is **St. Maria's Church.** The church was built in
1951 to commemorate the Christian martyrs, and their plight is
portrayed in the stained-glass windows. The Pass of the Virgin
(in Japanese, Otometoge) is the site of the graveyard where 36
martyrs have their crosses.

The next stop going east along the San'in coast is Matsue, a
three-hour, 30-minute ride on the JR limited express. However, you may want to break your journey an hour before Matsue
and visit the Izuno Taisha Shrine. If so, disembark from the
train at Izumoshi. (*see* Izuno Taisha Shrine, below).

Matsue

Of all the towns in the San'in district, the city of **Matsue** is the
most well-known as a summer vacation destination. Like the
rest of San'in, though, Matsue sees few foreigners, yet it is rich
in beauty and heritage. Only scattered archaeological remains
exist from the days when the people of "The Eightfold-Tower-
ing-Thunderhead Land of Izumo" lived here in the 2nd and 3rd
centuries, and only ruins have been left behind of Matsue's early days, when the town became the capital of the Izumo in the
8th century. However, many of today's existing shrines origi-
nate from that time, and the more recent past is still visible.
Matsue is the only town along the San'in coast with part of its
castle intact. In fact, Matsue's castle is one of the dozen castles
in Japan that are originals and not ferro-concrete replicas.

Matsue's location is unique. The city is situated inland from the
Sea of Japan at the conjunction of two small lagoons. Known as
the City of Water, Matsue lies at a point where Nakaumi Lagoon, to the east, connects with Lake Shinji, to the west. This
makes Matsue a gourmet heaven, with not only fresh fish taken
from the cold waters of the Japan Sea but also the seven delicacies—eel, shrimp, shellfish, carp, sea bass, pond smelt, and
whitebait—from Lake Shinji. The narrow isthmus between
the Nakaumi Lagoon and Lake Shinji divides the city. However, except for the JR station and the bus terminal, most of
Matsue's points of interest are on the northern side of the isthmus.

Getting Around An added delight of Matsue is that despite its population of
140,000, most of the sights are within walking distance of each

other; when they are not, Matsue has a comprehensive bus system. For those who would like to be accompanied on their tour of Matsue, the city has a Goodwill Guide Program, which offers an English-speaking volunteer to show you around the city and also escort you to Izumo Taisha Shrine. There is no charge for this, though you should pay guide's expenses, including lunch. To arrange for a Goodwill Guide, contact the **Matsue Tourist Information Office**, Asahi Machi, Matsue (tel. 0852/27–2598), a day in advance. The office is located in the JR Matsue Station and is open 8:30–7. You can also use this office to collect free maps and brochures.

Exploring   The first place to head for is **Matsuejo Castle** and its environs, located diagonally across town from the JR station. Take the bus (cost: ¥170) to Kencho-mae from either stop #1 or stop #2, both located in front of the JR station. (The same buses continue on to Matsue Onsen, should you want to go there first to your hotel.) It is about a 10-minute ride, and the Kencho-mae stop is near the Prefectural Government Office. When you leave the bus, walk a little farther to the north; the castle, located in Jozen-Koen Park, is on the left.

Made entirely out of pine, Matsuejo Castle was built in 1611, and, with a partial reconstruction in 1642, it was never ransacked or burned during the Tokugawa Shogunate. Amazingly, soon after the Meiji Restoration, the castle was put on the auction block. Sentimental locals, whose ancestors had been living under its shadow for 345 years, pooled their resources and purchased the castle for posterity.

Built by Yoshiharu Horio, the castle was built for protection. The donjon is, incidentally, the tallest (98 feet) left in Japan. Camouflaged among the surrounding trees, the castle seems to move with the shadows of San'in's opaque light. Note the overhanging leaves above the top floor, designed to cut down any glare that may prevent the spotting of an attacking force. Inside, the five-story facade contains six levels; the lower floors now exhibit a collection of samurai swords and armor. It is a climb to the uppermost floor, but it is worth it—the view commands the city, Lake Shinji, and the distant mountains. *Admission: ¥310. Open 8:30–5.*

In a Western-style building close to the castle is the **Matsue Kyodo-kan** (Matsue Cultural Museum), which displays arts, folk crafts, and implements, including such items as *bento* (box lunch) boxes and hairpins, used during the first three eras after the fall of the Tokugawa Shogunate. *Admission: ¥155. Open 8:30–5.*

If you walk out of Jozen-Koen Park at its east exit and follow the moat going north, at the top of the park will be a road leading to the right. A little way up this road, no more than a five-minute walk, is the **Meimei-an Tea House.** Lord Fumai Matsudaira of the Matsue clan built this teahouse in 1779, and it is one of the best preserved teahouses of the period. You must walk up a long flight of stairs to this thatch-roof teahouse, but your effort will be rewarded by both a fine view of Matsuejo Castle and, if you request, tea. *Admission: ¥200; ¥300 for Japanese green tea. Open 9–5.*

If you return down the side street on which Meimei-an is located to the main road, and take a right (keeping the castle moat on your left), you will reach four historical sights next door to each other. The first is **Buke Yashiki,** a samurai house built in 1730. Samurai at this time lived fairly well, depending on their rank. This house belonged to the Shiomi family, a chief retainer to the daimyo, and you'll notice the separate servant quarters, a shed for the palanquin, and the slats in the walls to allow the cooling breezes to flow through the rooms. *Admission:* ¥205. *Open 8:30–5.*

Next door to the Buke Yashiki is the **Tanabe Art Museum,** dedicated mainly to objects of the tea ceremony and ceramics from the region. The museum also exhibits works of wood-block prints by local artists. *Admission:* ¥500 *(though it varies according to the exhibition). Open 9–4:30. Closed Mon. and Dec. 28–Jan. 3.*

The next house is the **Koizumi Yakumo Residence** (1850–1904), unchanged since he left Matsue in 1891. Koizumi was born of an Irish father and a Greek mother, and was christened Lafcadio Hearn. His early years were spent in Greece, but he left there to study in Britain before traveling to the United States, where he became a journalist. In 1890, he traveled to Japan and soon became a teacher in Matsue. During his tenure he met a samurai's daughter, who nursed him when he fell sick. Recovered, he married her and later became a Japanese citizen, taking the name Yakumo Koizumi. He spent only 15 months in Matsue, but it was here that he became enthralled with Japan, and, in his writings, he helped introduce Japan to the West. He died at the age of 54, while working as a professor at Waseda University in Tokyo. *Admission:* ¥150. *Open 8:30–5.*

Adjacent to Yakumo Koizumi's former home is the **Yakumo Koizumi** (Lafcadio Hearn) **Memorial Hall.** The hall contains a good collection of his manuscripts and other items, including his desk, that reflect his life in Japan. If it is at all possible, you should read his essay "In a Japanese Garden," contained in the volume *Glimpses of Unfamiliar Japan,* in which he writes his impressions of Matsue. You will surely be asked by every local resident whether you are familiar with his work. *Admission:* ¥205. *Open 8:30–5.*

Two minutes from the Memorial Hall is the Hearn Kyukyo bus stop, where you can catch a bus back to Matsue's center and the JR station. The main shopping street is Kyomise Shopping Arcade, located just before the bridge to the JR station. However, you may prefer to shop for crafts at the **Matsue Meisan Center** (open 9–9), located next to the smartest hotel in town, the Ichibata, and on the north shore of Lake Shinji in an area known as Matsue Onsen. At the center, products from all over the Shimane Prefecture are on display and for sale, and, on its fourth floor, performances of folk dances are given four times a day. The Tourist Information Office at the JR station has the current schedule. *Admission to performances:* ¥500.

Should sunset soon be falling, set yourself up for a position to see the sun decline over Lake Shinji. Each sunset is memorable. You can watch one from the Matsue Meisan Center or from the Shinjiko Ohashi, the first bridge over to the south side of Matsue, the same side as the JR station.

The railway station at Matsue Onsen is the most convenient setting-off point for Izumo-Taisha Shrine, the second (after the Grand Shrines at Ise) most venerated shrine in Japan.

Izumo Taisha Shrine

Arriving and Departing ㉑
To go from Matsue Onsen to **Taisha,** the location of the Izumo-Taisha Shrine, it only takes 55 minutes on the Ichibata Electric Railway (fare: ¥750). You will need to change trains at Kanato Station for the Izumo-Taisha-mae Station. The shrine is just a five-minute walk from there.

You can also arrive there by taking the JR train from Matsue Station. First take the train on the San'in Main Line to Izumoshi, then transfer to the JR Taisha Line to Taisha Station, where you can either take a five-minute bus ride to Taisha-mae Station or walk directly to the shrine in about 20 minutes. The only two advantages of using the JR trains are to use the JR Rail Pass and to see the ornate, palace-style JR Taisha Station—it is quite an oddity.

Exploring
The Izumo-Taisha Shrine has the oldest site for a shrine in Japan, though the contemporary shrine was built in 1874. Entrance to the shrine is under a giant torii arch; then take a 15-minute walk along the path shaded by pine trees. At the end stands the impressive Main Hall, shielded by a double fence so that one can only have glimpses of the architectural style, representative of Japan's oldest shrine construction. The shrine is dedicated to a male god, O-Kuni-Nushi. He is known as the creator of the land. Over time, his role has broadened to include managing fruitful relationships such as marriage and, even more recently, business mergers.

Notice the very steep gabled roof of compressed bark descending from the ridge line, which runs from front to back rather than from side to side. Notice, too, that the ornately carved beams at the roof peak have their ends beveled perpendicular to the ground. This indicates that the shrine is dedicated to a male god. (Shrines dedicated to female gods have their crossed beams beveled parallel to the ground.)

On either side of the compound are two rectangular buildings. These are said to be the home of the Shinto gods, who meet annually at the shrine in October (the lunar month, which often falls in our Nov.). That is why in the rest of Japan, the lunar October is referred to as Kannazuki (Month Without Gods), while in Izumo, October is called Kamiarizuki (Month With Gods).

Despite the shrine's veneration, the buildings are not as worthwhile to see as the experience of the spiritual heritage of the Japanese. Remember, too, that this area predates Nara. It is where Japan was born, where her mythology was founded, and where the invading and successful Yamato and the Izumo peoples accommodated each other's gods during the 2nd and 3rd centuries.

If you would like to go out to Cape Hinomisaki, exit the temple grounds to the west and take the bus (they go every hour) from the Ichibata Bus Terminal for the 25-minute ride. The seascape contains more of the beauty one sees all along the San'in coast when traveling between Hagi and Matsue. The lighthouse on the cape is open to the public, and one may climb up the 127 feet to the top (remove your shoes first). Built in 1903, **Cape Hinomisaki Lighthouse** is Japan's tallest and beams its light 21 nautical miles out to sea. And for climbing to its top, you will receive a certificate of ascent. *Admission: ¥80. Open 8:30–4.*

The next destination up the San'in coast is the Tottori Sand Dunes, two hours by JR train from Matsue. En route you will pass by the town of **Yasugi,** best known for the Adachi Museum of Art (320 Furukawa-cho, Yasugi City, tel. 0854/28–7111), which exhibits the works of both past and contemporary Japanese artists. (Admission: ¥2,300; open Tues.–Sun. 9–4:30). Yonago is the next major town where buses leave every hour for the 50-minute ride to **Daisen** (fare: ¥590). Mount Daisen, a volcanic cone, which locals liken to Mt. Fuji, is popular with hikers. But only during the autumn is the beauty of the region worth a detour. On the slopes above the town of Daisen is the ancient Tendai sect temple, Daisen-ji. A few subtemples offer lodgings, such as Domyo-n (tel. 0859/52–2038) and Renjo-in (tel. 0859/52–2506) where novelist Shiga Naoya stayed and used the location for the ending of his *A Dark Night's Passing.* These are about ¥6,300 per person with two meals. There are also several overpriced minshukus such as the well-worn and dormitorylike Hakuun-so (25 Daisen, Daisencho, Saihaku-gun, Tottori Pref., tel. 0859/52–2331) for around ¥8,000 per person, including two meals. After Yonago comes **Kurayoshi,** where a 25-minute bus ride takes you to **Misasa Onsen,** a famous 1,000-year-old hot-spring resort claiming the hottest, highest radium waters in the country. Then comes Tottori.

Tottori Dunes

Exploring 22 The reason for stepping off the train at **Tottori** is to visit the dunes (*Hamasaka* in Japanese). To reach them, take a #20, 24, 25, or 26 bus; they depart from gate 3 at the bus terminal in front of the JR station for a 15-minute ride (fare: ¥250) to the north of Tottori City. The dunes are a unique feature of the San'in coast. They stretch along the shore for 10 miles and are a mile wide. Some of the crests rise up to 300 feet, and they are always in motion. Endlessly, the sands shift and the shadows change. Each dune has wavy rivulets that seem to flow in the wind. The Tottori Dunes are an unexpected phenomenon, and therein lies their interest for the Japanese, though world travelers are likely to be disappointed. The dunes have appealed to the Japanese for making man seem so temporal and insignificant. Literary men would come to be mesmerized by the continually changing patterns of the dunes and the isolation they offered. Now tourists come in droves during the summertime. Camel rides are for hire, and there is a "kiddieland" to appeal to families. You must walk farther to escape the crowds and find your solitude. Better yet, rent a bicycle from the Cycling Terminal, Kodomono-koni, (near the entrance to the dunes) and work your way east to the Uradome Seashore. At the pier near the Iwanoto Bridge, you can board the San'in Matsushima Yuran sightseeing boat for a 50-minute trip along the coast to see the twisted pines and eroded rocks of the many islands that stand offshore (cost: ¥1,100).

Though Tottori is the prefectural capital, it has only marginal points of interest, so rather than stay in Tottori, continue on the JR San'in Main Line up the coast to either Kasumi or Kinosaki. The train parallels the shoreline, offering glimpses of the beautiful seascapes. One particular attraction is **Kasumi Bay,** where, on the east side, the sleepy fishing village of **23 Kasumi** is located. To the left of the harbor is a small headland, **Okami-Koen Park,** which used to be popular for lovers' suicides. Now there is a small restaurant in which to slurp noodles while contemplating the cliffs. Various sightseeing boats also leave from the quay. If you have time while you are in Kasumi, be sure to visit **Daijoji Temple**, located directly inland from the JR Kasumi Station. The temple's origins began in 746, but its fame did not occur until the 18th century, when Okyo Maruyama, a leading artist of the time, came from Kyoto on a field trip with his students. Apparently Maruyama felt inspired, and he designated his students to paint various themes in several rooms of the temple. Some of these themes took a long time to paint, especially the Gilded Peacock. The field trip lasted eight years. *Admission: ¥500. Open 8:30–4:30.*

An even more picturesque village is Kundani, two stations (use Satsu Station) farther down the track on the local train from Kusumi. This small town of 300 people and two bars is a quiet haven on a horseshoe-shaped bay. There is nothing to do here but relax.

The alternative to spending the night at Kasumi or Kundani is to visit **Kinosaki.** There are a couple of small temples in Kinosaki, **Onsenji** and **Gokurajuji,** to interest the visitor, but the real reason for staying here is the thermal baths. Virtually every inn and hotel has its own springs, but join in the traditional custom of visiting the seven public baths. Don't bother about dressing up. It is perfectly correct simply to wear your yakuta and join the procession from one bath to another. Each of these public baths charges about ¥300 and closes at 11:30 PM (2 close at midnight, the Mandata-yu and the Sato-no-yu). Before taking the baths, you may want to visit the **Mugisen Folkcraft Shop,** at the top of the village's main street, to look at the wickerwork of baskets and cases for which the area is known.

Amanohashidate

The next and final major attraction on the San'in coast is **Amanohashidate.** This is one of the Japanese "Big Three" scenic wonders. Most Westerners are slightly disappointed by it, and, indeed, the younger Japanese are, too. However, in the past, Japanese literati have waxed poetic about Amanohashidate, so you may want to disembark from the train at Amanohashidate Station, rent a bicycle from one of the stores in front of the station, and go and see what all the fuss is about.

Amanohashidate is a two-mile-long sandbar that stretches across **Miyazu Bay.** Its width varies from 100 to 350 yards, and it is lined with those contorted pine trees that so stir the Japanese imagination. The best vantage point is to take the cable car from the northwest side of **Kasamatsu-Koen Park** (cost: ¥ 200). To reach there, take the 15-minute bus ride from Amanohashidate Station to Ichinomiya, or the ferry boat from Amanohashidate Pier. (There are also bicycles for rent at the stores in front of the JR station.) When you have finally reached the top of Kasamatsu-Koen Park, don't be surprised to see masses of people standing on stone benches with heads between their legs. This is the "proper" viewing stance to see Amanohashidate. It is even more amusing to watch them take photographs.

The San'in coast continues north as far as Maizuru, and though this chapter ends by reboarding the train at Amanohashidate

Station and returning to Kyoto, that does not mean there are not other sights to see. San'in is rich with places to explore, most of which have yet to be inundated with tourists. This chapter covers the highlights of the San'in, but San'in is the area that any traveler seeking the traditional Japan should leisurely explore.

Dining and Lodging

Dining In most of Japan outside of the large cities, one is usually advised to eat Western-style food in the dining rooms of the larger hotels. However, we strongly recommend that you eat out at local Japanese restaurants. Most reasonably priced Japanese restaurants will have a visual display of their menu in the window. On this basis, you can decide what you want before you enter. If you cannot order in Japanese and no English is spoken, after you secure a table, lead the waiter to the window display and point.

Unless the establishment is a *ryotei* (high-class, traditional Japanese restaurant), reservations are usually not required at restaurants unless they are the formal restaurants at a hotel or a ryokan. Whenever reservations are advised or required at any of the restaurants listed, this is indicated.

A 3% federal consumer tax is added to all restaurant bills. Another 3% local tax is added to the bill if it exceeds ¥5,000. At more expensive restaurants, a 10%–15% service charge is added to the bill. Tipping is not the custom.

Category	Cost*
Very Expensive	over ¥6,000
Expensive	¥4,000–¥6,000
Moderate	¥2,000–¥4,000
Inexpensive	under ¥2,000

*Cost is per person without tax, service, or drinks

Lodging Accommodations cover the broad spectrum of pensions and *minshukus* to large modern resort hotels that have little character but offer all the facilities of an international hotel. All of the large city and resort hotels offer Western as well as Japanese food. During the summer season, hotel reservations are advised.

Outside the cities or major towns, most hotels quote prices on a per-person basis with two meals, exclusive of service and tax. If you do not want dinner at your hotel, it is usually possible to renegotiate the price. Stipulate, too, whether you wish to have Japanese or Western breakfasts, if any. For the purposes here, the categories assigned to all hotels reflect the cost of a double room with private bath but no meals. However, if you make reservations at any of the noncity hotels, you will be expected to take breakfast and dinner at the hotel—that will be the rate quoted to you unless you specify otherwise.

A 3% federal consumer tax is added to all hotel bills. Another 3% local tax is added to the bill if it exceeds ¥10,000. At most hotels, a 10%–15% service charge is added to the total bill. Tipping is not the custom.

Category	Cost*
Very Expensive	over ¥20,000
Expensive	¥15,000–¥20,000
Moderate	¥10,000–¥15,000
Inexpensive	under ¥10,000

Cost is for double room, without tax or service

The most highly recommended restaurants and accommodations in each city are indicated by a star ★.

Credit Cards The following credit card abbreviations are used: AE, American Express; DC, Diners Club; MC, MasterCard; V, Visa.

Hagi

Dining **Higaku-Mangoku.** This small restaurant has the best selection of seasonal seafood in town. *Shimo Goken-machi, Hagi, tel. 08382/2–2136. Jacket and tie suggested. Open 11–8. V. Moderate.*

★ **Fujita-ya.** This is a casual restaurant, full of color, where locals delight in handmade *soba* (buckwheat noodles) and hot tempura served on handmade Japanese cypress trays. *Kumagaicho, Hagi, tel. 08382/2–1086. Dress: informal. Open 11–7; closed 2nd and 4th Wed. of each month. No credit cards. Inexpensive.*

Lodging **Hokumon Yashiki.** This elegant ryokan with luxurious rooms overlooks a garden. The gracious and refined service makes one feel pampered in the style to which the ancient Mori clan were surely accustomed. The location of the inn is in the samurai section, near the castle grounds. *210 Horiuchi, Hagi, Yamaguchi Prefecture 758, tel. 08382/2–7521. 21 Japanese-style rooms. Facilities: Japanese food served in room. AE. Expensive.*

Hagi Grand Hotel. Convenience to the Higashi-Hagi JR station makes this the number one choice for an international-style hotel in Hagi. The staff here is helpful and friendly, and the guest rooms are relatively spacious. *25 Furuhagicho, Hagi, Yamaguchi Prefecture 758, tel. 08382/5–1211, fax 08382/5–4422. 190 rooms; half are Western-style. Facilities: Japanese and Western restaurants, shops, travel desk. AE, DC, MC, V. Moderate–Expensive.*

Hotel Royal. Located in the Rainbow Building above Higashi-Hagi JR station, this business hotel is friendly and efficient. The guest rooms are on the small size, but they are clean and comfortable. Businessmen and tourists stay here, and the front desk will arrange bicycle rentals for you. *3000-5 Chinto, Hagi, Yamaguchi Prefecture 758, tel. 08382/5–9595. MC, V. Moderate.*

Higashi-Hagi Minshuku. The price and the convenience of being two minutes from the JR station make this small minshuku worth remembering. None of the rooms have private baths, but they are larger than many minshukus in this price range. However, over the past year the rooms have become a little shoddy though the owners are keen to make your stay in Hagi enjoyable. *3064-1, Shin-Kuwaminami, Hagi, Yamaguchi Prefecture 758, tel. 08382/2–7884. 11 Japanese-style rooms. Facilities: Japanese dinner and Western or Japanese breakfast offered. AE. Inexpensive.*

Hiroshima

Dining
★ **Mitakiso Ryokan.** For a kaiseki lunch, or an elaborate kaiseki dinner in a private tatami room, the Mitakiso Ryokan is superb. The inn is one of the most respected ryokans in Hiroshima. It makes an excellent place to entertain Japanese guests. It is not necessary to stay at the ryokans in order to enjoy its cuisine. If do you stay, it is worth splurging and choosing a room with sliding doors onto the private garden. *1-7 Mitakimachi, Nishi-ku, Hiroshima 733, tel. 082/237–1402. Reservations required. Jacket and tie required. AE. Open for lunch and dinner. Expensive.*

★ **Kanashi Restaurant.** For tempura using the freshest possible ingredients, this unpretentious restaurant on Chuo-dori Avenue is a favorite with local businessmen. *204 Mikawa-cho, Naka-ku, Hiroshima, tel. 082/247–0138. Reservations required for private tatami room for business meetings. Jacket and tie suggested. No credit cards. Open 11–9. Closed 2nd and 4th Sun. of each month. Moderate.*

★ **Kanawa Restaurant.** Hiroshima is known for its oysters, especially in the winter, when they are fresh and sweet. Kanawa is Hiroshima's most famous restaurant for this shellfish. The restaurant is a barge moored on the Motoyasu River, near the Peace Memorial Park. Dining is on tatami matting, with river views. Only oysters are served here, in at least 10 different ways. *Moored on the river at Heiwa Bridge, Naka-ku, Hiroshima, tel. 082/241–7416. Jacket and tie suggested. AE, V. Open 11–10:30. Closed 1st and 3rd Sun. of each month except Dec. Moderate.*

Suishin Restaurant. Famous for its sashimi and sushi, this restaurant offers the freshest fish from the Inland Sea—rockfish, globefish, oysters, and eel, to name but a few. *6–7 Tatemachi, Naka-ku, Hiroshima, tel. 082/247–4411. Dress: informal. DC, V. Open 11–10. Closed national holidays. Moderate.*

Lodging **ANA Hotel Hiroshima.** Opened in 1983, this is Hiroshima's largest international hotel. Located in the business district on Peace Boulevard, the hotel is within walking distance of the Peace Museum. With glittering chandeliers, the pink-carpeted lobby looks onto a small garden with a waterfall. The tea lounge facing the garden is an excellent place to rest after visiting the Peace Memorial Park. The furnishings of the guest rooms are uninspired, but the rooms have all the extras of a first-class hotel, including English-speaking channels on the television. The Unkai restaurant on the fifth floor has not only good Japanese food but also a view onto a Japanese garden of dwarf trees, rocks, and a pond of colorful carp. However, many second-time visitors, as well as the local tourist office, consider the Hiroshima Grand the city's top hotel. *7-20 Nakamachi, Hiroshima 730, tel. 082/241–1111, fax 082/241–9123. 431 rooms; all but 4 are Western-style. Facilities: Chinese, Japanese, and Western restaurants, summer rooftop beer garden, free delivery of Ja*pan Times *newspaper, indoor pool, sauna, fitness center, shopping arcade. AE, DC, MC, V. Expensive.*

★ **Hiroshima Grand Hotel.** The other major hotel in Hiroshima is operated by Japan Airlines. It is slightly more moderate in price than the newer ANA Hotel. Located downtown, four blocks from the Peace Memorial Park and between Hiroshima Castle and Shukkeien Garden, the Grand has established a reputation for fine service and comfort. It has less glitter than the ANA Hotel and appeals to the traveler who is looking for quiet refinement. The guest rooms are pleasantly furnished, though the views from their windows on the street below are unappealing. *4-4 Kami-Hatchobori, Naka-ku, Hiroshima 730, tel. 082/ 227–1313, fax 082/227–6462. 381 rooms, only 6 are Japanese style. Facilities: Chinese, Japanese, and Western restaurants, beauty parlor, post office, shopping arcade. AE, DC, V. Moderate–Expensive.*

Hiroshima Terminal Hotel. This is the smartest and largest hotel near the station—located at the back, not the front—and it still has a feeling of newness. An expansive vaulted marble lobby greets you as you enter. By Japan standards the rooms are spacious, and are furnished in subdued pastels and ochres. The staff is briskly efficient and many employees speak English. On the penthouse (21st) floor, the Japanese, Chinese, and French restaurants offer panoramic vistas. *1–5, Matsubara-cho, Minami-ku, Hiroshima 732, tel. 082/262–1111, fax 082/262– 4050. 440 rooms, mostly Western style. Facilities: 4 restaurants, coffee lounge, 2 bars, travel desk, florist, modest business center (copier, fax, word processor, business cards, data bank), meeting rooms. AE, DC, V. Moderate–Expensive.*

Mikawa Ryokan. This simple ryokan offers the basics—tatami rooms, coin-operated television, air-conditioning, but no rooms with private baths. There are too many guests for the limited toilet facilities. However, the inn has a good location halfway between downtown and the JR station and is within walking distance of both. Advance reservations are requested. *9-6 Kyobashi-cho, Minami-ku, Hiroshima 730, tel. 082/261–2719. Located 7 minutes on foot south of the JR station; turn right on the street before Aori-dori. 13 Japanese-style rooms. Facilities: breakfast only. AE. Inexpensive.*

Riyo Kaikan. For a no-nonsense place to stay close to the Peace Memorial Park, this accommodation offers the best value for money in Hiroshima. It is strictly a business hotel, with small rooms and tiny bathrooms, but the decor is cheerful and refreshing, and the bathtubs are deep enough for a good soak. Riyo Kaikan has neither lobby space nor lounges, but it does have an inexpensive cafeteria. Check-in is at 4 PM, and advance reservations are recommended. *1-5-3 Otemachi, Hiroshima 730, tel. 082/245–2322. 200 rooms. Facilities: cafeteria with Western and Japanese food. V. Inexpensive.*

Kasumi

Lodging **Marusei Ryokan.** Located between the JR station and the harbor, this small, quiet inn in the center of the town is both a place
★ to stay and eat. Hospitality and the owner's English-speaking son, who is also the chef, make this an ideal base for exploring the area. This is the best place in the area to eat *kani-suki* (succulent crab casserole). *Kasumi-cho, Kinosaki-gun 669, tel. 07963/6–0028. 15 Japanese-style rooms, 4 with private bath. Facilities: excellent restaurant. No credit cards. Moderate.*

Kinosaki

Lodging   **Mikaya Ryokan.** This three-story wood inn reflects traditional
★   Japan. It is delightfully old-fashioned, with creaking timbers
and spacious tatami rooms. It has its own thermal baths, which
look out onto the garden. *Kinosaki-gun, Hyogo Prefecture, tel.
07963/2–2031. 35 Japanese-style rooms. Facilities: Japanese
restaurant and thermal baths. AE, DC, V. Expensive.*

Kundani

Lodging   **Minshuku Genroku Bekkan.** This private guest house is a true
★   find. The eight tatami guest rooms are spacious and freshly
decorated. None of them, however, have private baths. Excellent Japanese dinners are served. The husband speaks English—his wife tries—and he will likely invite you to the local
bar after dinner. The house is in the center of the quiet fishing
village, two streets from the sea front. *Kundani Kasumi,
Kinosaki-gun, Hyogo Prefecture, tel. 07963/8–0018. (Closest
JR station is Satsu. Call on arrival and the owners will collect
you at the station.) 5 rooms. Facilities: dinner and breakfast
served. No credit cards. Inexpensive.*

Kurashiki

Dining   **Hamayoshi.** Only three tables (tatami seating with a well for
your legs beneath the table) and a counter bar make up this personable restaurant specializing in fish from the Seto Inland
Sea. Sushi is just one option; another is sashimi sliced from a
live (very ugly-looking) fish! A less adventurous dish is filleted
fish lightly grilled. Another delicacy is *shako*, chilled boiled
prawns. No English is spoken, but the owner will help you order and instruct you on how to enjoy the chefs' delicacies. Located on the main street leading from the station and just
before the Kurashiki Kokusai Hotel. *Chuo-dori, tel. 0864/22–
3420. Dress: informal. No credit cards. Open 11–2 and 5–10.
Moderate.*

Kiyutei. For the best grilled steak in town, one should come to
this attractive restaurant, where chefs work over the fires
grilling your steak to order. The entrance to the restaurant is
through the courtyard, just across from the entrance to the
Ohara Museum. *1-2-20 Chuo, Kurashiki, tel. 0864/22–5141.
Dress: informal. No credit cards. Open 11–9. Closed Mon.
Moderate.*

Lodging   **Ryokan Kurashiki.** In the atmosphere of the Edo period, this
★   delightful ryokan is made up of a merchant's mansion and three
converted rice and sugar storehouses. Close to the Ohara Museum, with the Kurashiki flowing gently before it, this elegant
ryokan maintains its serenity, no matter how many visitors are
walking the streets in town. The cuisine is famous for its regional dishes, making the most of the oysters in the winter, fish
straight from the Inland Sea in spring and autumn, and freshwater fish in the summer. There is a wonderful inner garden on
which to gaze while sipping green tea in the afternoons. Here is
Japanese hospitality at its best. Even if you are not staying
here, you can still experience the ryokan by having lunch
(¥10,000 per person) or dinner (¥14,000 per person). *4-1
Honmachi, Kurashiki, Okayama Prefecture 710, tel. 0864/22–*

0730. 20 rooms, not all with private bath. Facilities: Japanese restaurant and tea-house. AE, DC. Expensive.

★ **Kurashiki Kokusai Hotel.** Owned by Japan Airlines, this is the best Western hotel in town. Next to the Ohara Art Museum in the old town, the location is perfect. Every attempt has been made to make this hotel blend in with the environment, with black tiles on the walls and wood-block prints by Shiko Munakata adding drama to the lobby. Rooms are on the small side, but they're trim and neat. The Aichi Japanese restaurant serves good seafood from the Seto Inland Sea; tempura is prepared at the table. *1-1-44 Chuo, Kurashiki, Okayama Prefecture 710, tel. 0864/22–5141, fax 0864/22–5192. 70 rooms, 4 Japanese style. Facilities: Western, Japanese steak, and tempura restaurants, beauty parlor, parking facilities. AE, DC, MC, V. Moderate–Expensive.*

Hotel Kurashiki. Above the station, this is an efficient business hotel that is useful if you have an early-morning train to catch. It is rather dreary and worn, but at least the bathrooms are custom-made, and not the usual plastic cubicles. Though it's time Japan Railways refurbished their hotel, it is better than the adjacent Kurashiki Terminal hotel, where the rooms are downright shabby. *1-1-1 Achi, Kurashiki, Okayama Prefecture 710, tel. 0864/22–5141. 139 Western-style rooms. Facilities: Japanese/Western restaurant. AE, DC, MC, V. Moderate.*

Kamoi. Located an eight-minute walk from the Ohara Museum, this minshuku is close to Tsurugatayama-Koen Park and the Achi Jinja Shrine. The rooms are simple and tatami-style, but they are very clean. This hostelry is the best bargain in Kurashiki. The food here is very good, too. It should be; the owner is also the owner and chef of Kamoi Restaurant, located across from the Ohara Museum. A visual display in the window shows what is offered, and, inside, the walls are decorated with artifacts such as cast-iron kettles and ancient rifles. *6-21 Hinmachi, Kurashiki, Okayama Prefecture 710, tel. 0864/22–4898. 17 Japanese-style rooms, none with bath. Japanese breakfast (Western breakfast on request) and dinner served. No credit cards. Inexpensive.*

Matsue

Dining **Ginsen Restaurant.** Close to the Tokyu Inn and not far from the north exit of the Matsue JR station, this restaurant is popular with the locals for its fresh seafood casseroles. The season determines what these are, and with Lake Shinji on hand, the fish is superb and the prices are reasonable. *Asahimachi, Matsue, tel. 0852/21–2381. Dress: informal. No credit cards. Open 11–10. Moderate.*

Hi-daka-toshi-yuki. For fun and socializing with the locals, this yakitori bar with counter service offers a delightful evening's entertainment, good grilled chicken, and flowing sake. *Asahimachi Shimane, Matsue, tel. 0852/31–8308. Located 2 doors from Ginsen restaurant and easily recognized by its red lanterns outside. Dress: informal. No credit cards. Open 11–11. Inexpensive.*

Lodging **Minami-kan.** This is Matsue's most elegant and prestigious
★ ryokan, tastefully furnished and with refined service. It also has the best restaurant in Matsue for kaiseki haute cuisine and *tai-meshi* (sea bream). Even if you do not stay here, make reservations for dinner. *Ohashi, Matsue, Shimane Prefecture 690,*

tel. 0852/21–5131. 27 Japanese-style rooms. Facilities: superb Japanese restaurant. AE. Expensive.

Hotel Ichibata. Located in the spa section of town, next to Lake Shinji, the Ichibata appeals to those on a restful vacation who want to enjoy the thermal waters. For a long time, the hotel has been the leading place to stay in central San'in and, consequently, shows signs of wear. The guest rooms facing the lake are the nicest but are also the most expensive. Still, if you do not mind the 20-minute walk from the station or downtown, the Ichibata is still Matsue's first choice, if only to watch the sunsets from its vermilion lounge on the penthouse floor. *30 Chidoricho, Matsue, Shimane Prefecture 690, tel. 0852/22–0188. 137 rooms, ½ are Western-style. All of the Japanese-style rooms face the lake; not so with the Western ones. Facilities: Japanese/Western restaurant, thermal baths, summer beer garden. AE, DC, MC, V. Moderate–Expensive.*

Tokyu Inn. This business-type hotel has the best location for the overnight visitor with its location across from the Matsue JR Station. The rooms are basic, furnished only with the essentials, but are clean and of reasonable size for a moderate hotel. *590 Asahicho, Matsue, Shimane Prefecture 690, tel. 0852/27–0109. 181 Western-style rooms. Facilities: Japanese/Western restaurant, rooftop beer garden during summer. AE, V. Moderate.*

Miyajima

Lodging
★ **Iwaso Ryokan.** For tradition and elegance, this is the Japanese inn at which to stay or dine on the island. The inn has a newer wing, but the older rooms have more character. Two cottages on the grounds with Japanese suites are superbly decorated with antiques. The prices at the inn vary according to the size of the guest room, its view, and the dinner that you select. Be sure, when you make reservations in advance, to specify what you want and fix the price. Breakfast and dinner are usually included in the tariff. *345 Miyajimacho, Hiroshima Prefecture 739, tel. 08294/4–2233. 45 Japanese-style rooms. Facilities: Japanese restaurant, but Western breakfast served on request. AE. Expensive–Very Expensive.*

★ **Kamefuku Hotel.** The name of this hotel in English is "Happy Turtle," and the name seems to create a friendly, joyful atmosphere. The subdued lighting, a back-lit garden, and the use of split-level floors make the lobby a comfortable and intimate place to relax. There is a pleasant coffee-shop area, a cozy bar, and a restaurant that has superb seafood, especially its succulent oysters. *849 Miyajimacho, Hiroshima Prefecture 739, tel. 08294/4–2111. 71 Japanese-style rooms. Facilities: Japanese restaurant, but Western breakfast served on request. AE. Expensive–Very Expensive.*

Jyukeiso Ryokan. For a more modest place to stay, this family ryokan (the owner speaks English) makes a pleasant home. However, it is to the east of the ferry pier (away from the town and shrine), which may not be what you want. Breakfast and dinner are usually included in the tariff. *Miyajimacho, Hiroshima Prefecture 739, tel. 08294/4–0300. 20 Japanese-style rooms, 2 with private bath. Facilities: Japanese restaurant, but Western breakfast served on request. AE. Moderate.*

Shimonoseki

Lodging **Bizenya Ryokan.** Should you have to spend the night in this town waiting for a ferry to Pusan or the morning train up the San'in coast, this small ryokan has clean tatami rooms and offers either Continental or Japanese breakfasts before you leave in the morning. *3-11-7 Kamitanaka-machi, Shimonoseki, Yamaguchi Prefecture 750, tel. 0832/22–6228. To reach the ryokan, take bus at bus stop #2 from the JR station to Nishinohashi bus stop. The ryokan is a 2-minute walk from there. 13 rooms, not all with bath. Facilities: Japanese food served, as well as Continental breakfast. AE, V. Inexpensive.*

Susa

★ **Minshuku Susa.** Often the decision to stay at a minshuku is the price, not its food, comfort, or decor. That's not so with this minshuku, yet the price is still reasonable. Rooms are huge, at least 10-tatami, and with an alcove for a coffee table and two chairs—some are even larger. The best rooms look onto the harbor. The bathroom is splendid, with an iron Goemon tub (Goemon Ishikawa, a Japanese version of Robin Hood in the 13th century, was boiled alive). Service is more in the style of a traditional ryokan and such niceties as an orange in the bath to scent the water are not overlooked. No English is spoken, but the staff's friendliness overcomes any language barrier. Dinner served in a tatami-floor dining room is an occasion to try the region's delicacies from the sea. *Irie, Susa-cho, Abu-gun, Yamaguchi Pref., 690, tel. 08387/6–2408. 6 rooms. Facilities: Japanese meals served in the dining room. No credit cards. Inexpensive–Moderate.*

Tottori

Lodging **New Otani.** This multistory red-concrete building across from the JR station is the most modern hotel in town. The guest rooms are compact and are smartly decorated in cream-and-red color schemes. *Hinmachi 2-153, Tottori-shi 650, tel. 0857/23–1111. 150 rooms. Facilities: Western and Japanese restaurants, bookstand, meeting rooms. AE, DC, MC, V. Moderate–Expensive.*

Tsuwano

Dining **Yuki.** A small stream runs through the center of the dining room. While the decor could be smarter, this restaurant is famous for its carp dishes (such as carp sashimi and carp miso soup) and mountain vegetables. *Honcho-dori, Tsuwano, tel. 0856/2–0162. Open noon–2 and 6–8, No credit cards. Moderate.*

Lodging **Tsuwano Kanko Hotel.** This pleasant establishment is the most centrally located hotel in town, with fair-size guest rooms and a friendly staff. The furnishings have become worn and drab, however, and the Japanese restaurant is only passable. *Ushiroda, Tsuwano-machi, Kanoashi-gun 699, tel. 08567/2–0332. 30 Japanese-style rooms. Facilities: Japanese restaurant, but will cook a Western breakfast. AE, V. Moderate.*

★ **Wakasagi-no-Yado.** This is a small minshuku run by a friendly family who speak very limited English. They are, however, eager to help overseas tourists and will meet guests at Tsuwano Station. *Mori, Tsuwano-cho, Kanoashi-gun 699-56, tel. 08567/ 2–1146. Located 8 minutes on foot from the JR station. 8 rooms, all without bath. Japanese and Western breakfasts offered. No credit cards. Inexpensive.*

12 Shikoku

Introduction

by Nigel Fisher

The smallest of Japan's four major islands, Shikoku is often omitted from tourist plans by both Japanese and foreigners. This is due in part to the fact that, despite the many ferries available, the Inland Sea is perceived as hampering easy access. Instead of recognizing the pleasure of crossing the island-studded Inland Sea by boat, many travelers regard the trip to Shikoku as being a handicap. However, this may change with the new Seto Bridge, which now links Shikoku at Sakaide (slightly west of Takamatsu) to Kojima (south of Okayama) on Honshu by both road and rail.

Shikoku's isolation may also be traced to the rugged mountain ranges that run east to west and divide Shikoku into two halves, each with a different climate. The northern half, which faces the Inland Sea, has a dry climate, with only modest rains in the autumn during the typhoon season. The southern half, which faces the Pacific, is more likely to have ocean storms sweep in, bringing rain throughout the year; with its shores washed by the Black Current, it has a warmer climate and especially mild winters. The mountain ranges of the interior are formidable, achieving heights up to 6,400 feet, and are cut by wondrous gorges and valleys. In these valleys, small farming villages nestle; they appear unchanged since the Edo period (1603–1868). Shikoku is an island worth exploring, where travelers are greeted more as welcome foreign emissaries than as income-bearing tourists.

Despite the fact that Shikoku has been part of Japan's political and cultural development since the Heian period (794–1192), the island has retained an independence from mainstream Japan. There are some eyesores of factories littering the northern coast, but, to a great extent, Shikoku has been spared the ugliness of Japan's industrialization. The island is still considered by many Japanese as a rural backwater where pilgrims trek to the 88 sacred temples.

The Buddhist saint Kobo Daishi was born on Shikoku in 774, and it was he who founded the Shingon sect of Buddhism that became popular in the shogun eras. (During the reign of the Tokugawa Shogunate, travel was restricted, except for pilgrimages.) Pilgrims visit 88 temples to honor Kobo Daishi. To successfully complete visiting and praying at all 88 temples can release the pilgrim from having to go through the cycle of rebirth. Many Japanese wait until they have retired to make this pilgrimage, in part because the time is right and in part because it used to take two months on foot to visit all the temples. In modern times, however, most pilgrims now scoot around by bus in 13 days.

Essential Information

Arriving and Departing

By Plane   Takamatsu is serviced by seven daily flights from Tokyo and by 10 daily flights from Osaka. Tokushima has five daily flights from Tokyo and 10 daily flights from Osaka. Kochi is serviced by five daily flights from Tokyo and by 23 daily flights from Osaka. Matsuyama has six daily flights from Tokyo and six daily flights from Osaka.

By Train With the 1989 opening of the 9.3-kilometer (5.83-mile) long Seto-Ohashi Bridge, Shikoku is now linked by road and rail to Honshu. Instead of the hour-long ferry ride that was once necessary to cross the Inland Sea, the train takes a scant 15 minutes to traverse a series of double-decker suspension bridges, 93 meters (307 feet) above the water.

Shikoku can be reached by taking the JR Shinkansen to Okayama (3 hours, 50 minutes from Tokyo; 1 hour, 20 minutes from Kyoto), then transferring onto the JR Limited Express bound either for Takamatsu (1 hour), Matsuyama (3 hours), or Kochi (3 hours).

Matsuyama can also be reached by taking the JR Shinkansen to Hiroshima (5 hours, 10 minutes from Tokyo; 2 hours, 20 minutes from Kyoto). From Hiroshima's Ujina Port, the ferry takes two hours, 45 minutes to cross the Inland Sea to Matsuyama. The hydrofoil takes one hour.

By Ship Takamatsu can also be reached by the Kansai Kisen steamship, which takes five hours, 30 minutes from Osaka's Bentenfuto Pier, and four hours, 30 minutes from Kobe's Naka-Tottei Pier. The boat leaves Osaka at 8:30 AM and 2:20 PM, Kobe at 9:50 AM and 3:40 PM; it arrives at Takamatsu at 2 PM and 8:10 PM. The cost is ¥2,370 and up from Osaka, slightly less from Kobe. Passenger ships travel to Kochi from Osaka (depart at 9:20 PM and arrive in Kochi at 6:40 AM, returning to Osaka with departures at 9:20 PM and arriving in Osaka at 7 AM. Kochi can also be reached from Tokyo by a ship that departs at 7:40 PM, stops in Katsuura, Wakayama Prefecture at 8:50 AM, and arrives in Kochi at 5 AM.

Getting Around

By Train/Bus All the major towns of Shikoku are connected either by JR express and local trains or by bus. Because of the lower population density on Shikoku, transportation is not so frequent as on the southern coast of Honshu. So before you step off a train or bus, find out how long it will be before the next one departs for your next destination.

The main routes are from Takamatsu to Matsuyama by train (2 hours, 45 minutes); from Takamatsu to Kochi by train (3 hours), from Takamatsu to Tokushima (90 minutes); from Matsuyama to Kochi by JR bus (approximately 3 hours, 15 minutes); from Matsuyama to Uwajima by train (2 hours); and from Kochi to Nakamura by train (2 hours).

By Car Since traffic is light, the scenery marvelous, and the distances relatively short, Shikoku is one region in Japan where renting a car makes sense. (Remember that an international driving license is required.) **Budget Rent-a-Car** has rental offices in Maysuyama, Takamatsu, and Kochi, as do other car-rental agencies.

Important Addresses and Numbers

Tourist Information Centers Major tourist information centers are located at each of Shikoku's main cities: **Takamatsu,** tel. 0878/61–4119; **Kochi,** tel. 0888/23–1434; and **Matsuyama,** tel. 0899/31–3914.

The Japan Travel-Phone The nationwide service for English-language assistance or travel information is available seven days a week, 9 to 5. Throughout Shikoku, dial toll-free 0120/444–800 for information on western Japan. When using a yellow, blue, or green public phone (do not use the red phones), insert a ¥10 coin, which will be returned.

Emergencies **Police,** tel. 110. **Ambulance,** tel. 119.

Guided Tours

No guided tours covering the island of Shikoku are conducted in English, though the **Japan Travel Bureau** will arrange your individual travel arrangements. The Japan Travel Bureau has offices at every JR station in each of the prefectural capitals and can assist in local tours, hotel reservations, and ticketing onward travel. There are also local city tours, conducted in Japanese, that cover the surrounding areas of each of the four major cities in Shikoku. These may be arranged through your hotel.

Exploring

Numbers in the margin correspond with points of interest on the Shikoku map.

There are three major cities on Shikoku: Takamatsu, Kochi, and Matsuyama. To these three, one may possibly add Tokushima, on the island's east coast. Few overseas visitors travel to Tokushima, but if you can visit there during August 12–15, you will witness one of the liveliest, most humor-filled festivals in Japan. The Awa Odori Dance is an occasion for the Japanese to let all their reserves fall away and act out their fantasies. Prizes are even given to the "Biggest Fool" in the parades, and foreigners are welcome to compete for these awards. Also, near Tokushima are the Naruto Straits, which attract visitors to see the giant whirlpools. At each ebb and flow of the tide, the currents rush through this narrow passage to form hundreds of foaming whirlpools of various sizes.

A short and popular itinerary for the overseas visitor to Shikoku is to arrive at Takamatsu and travel along the north coast to Matsuyama, with one short detour to Kotohiragu Shrine. Such an itinerary could be accomplished in two nights and two days. However, we recommend continuing on from Kotohiragu Shrine, crossing through the mountains to Kochi on the Pacific Coast and traveling around the island's west coast before reaching Matsuyama. From Matsuyama, there is a hydrofoil to Hiroshima.

Traditionally, the major gateway to Shikoku has been Takamatsu. Even with the new Seto Bridge, it has the easiest access to and from Honshu.

Takamatsu

❶ The JR station and the pier at **Takamatsu** share the same location at the north end of Chuo-dori, Takamatsu's main avenue, where most of the large hotels are located. The Takamatsu Information Office is located at the station. The maps and brochures are limited to Kagawa Prefecture, of which Takamatsu is the capital. If you need information on the entire island,

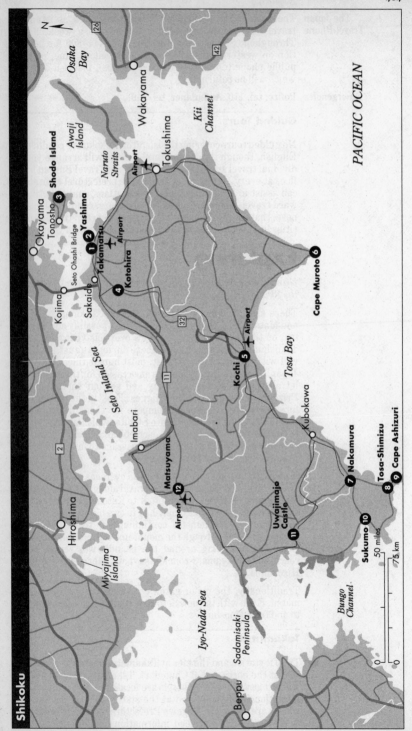

Shikoku

N

Osaka Bay

26

42

Wakayama

Kii Channel

PACIFIC OCEAN

Shodo Island

Awaji Island

3 Tonosho

Naruto Straits

Okayama

Tokushima

Airport

Seto Ohashi Bridge

1 2 Yashima

Takamatsu

Airport

Kojima

Sakaide

4 **Kotohira**

Cape Muroto **6**

Seto Inland Sea

32

Airport

11

5 Kochi

Tosa Bay

Imabari

Kubokawa

2

Matsuyama

Nakamura **7**

Tosa-Shimizu **8**

Hiroshima

Airport **12**

Uwajimajo Castle

Cape Ashizuri **9**

Miyajima Island

11

Sukumo **10**

50 miles

75 km

Iyo-Nada Sea

Bungo Channel

Sadamisaki Peninsula

0

Beppu

make sure that you visit the Tourist Information Center in Tokyo or Kyoto before you set out for Shikoku.

Three hundred yards down Chuo-dori Avenue, on the left-hand side, the shopping arcades begin. The east–west arcade is intersected by another arcade running north–south (parallel to Chuo-dori). Department stores, shops, and larger restaurants are located in these malls. The small streets off the arcades are crowded with bars, cabarets, and small restaurants.

A bus tour (Japanese-speaking guide only) departs at 8:45 AM from Takamatsu-Chikko Bus Station (near the JR station) and covers Takamatsu's Ritsurin-Koen Park, Kotoshira, and other sights. The tour takes about eight hours, 45 minutes.

The number one attraction in Takamatsu is **Ritsurin-Koen Garden,** once the summer retreat of the Matsudaira clan. The garden is located at the far end of Chuo-dori Avenue. To reach it, take a 10-minute ride (cost: ¥190) on any bus that leaves from in front of the Grand Hotel from stop #2. (The bus makes a short detour from the main avenue to include a bus depot on its route. Don't disembark from the bus until it rejoins the main avenue—Chuo-dori—and travels two more stops.) An alternate route is to take the JR train bound for Takushima and disembark five minutes later at the second stop, Ritsurin-Koen. Ritsurin-Koen was completed in the late 17th century after 100 years of careful planning, landscaping, and cultivation. The garden is actually two gardens. The north garden is more modern and has wide expanses of lawns. The more appealing south garden is traditional, with a design that follows a classical layout. The garden's six ponds and 13 scenic mounds are arranged so that as one walks the intersecting paths, at virtually every step there is a new view or angle to hold the focus of attention. One cannot hurry through this garden. Each rock, each tree shape, each pond rippling with multicolored carp has a fluidity of motion enhanced by the reflections of the water and the shadows of the trees. *Admission: ¥310. Open 5:30 AM–7 PM (5:30–5 in winter).*

Within Ritsurin-Koen's north garden is an **Exhibition Hall,** displaying and selling local products from the Kagawa Prefecture—these include wood carvings, masks, kites, and umbrellas. Another museum exhibits work by local artists, and the **Folk Art House** displays local handcrafts and folk crafts.

However, Ritsurin's gem is in the south garden. It is the tea house, **Kikugetsutei,** looking as if it were floating on water. Here, just as the lords of Matsudaira did in previous centuries, you may enjoy a cup of green tea and muse on the serene harmony of the occasion. *Admission: ¥310; tea is an additional ¥310, or you can get a combination ticket for ¥590.*

Ritsurin-Koen is the reason to visit Takamatsu. The bombing of World War II left Takamatsu with few other visible attractions. However, if you are waiting for a train or ferry, across from the station and behind the Grand Hotel are the castle grounds of Tamamo Park. The Tamanojo Castle, built in 1588, had been the home of the Matsudaira clan, who ruled Takamatsu during the Edo period. Now, only a few turrets of the castle are left, but its setting, with the Inland Sea in the background, makes it a pleasant place in which to relax. *Admission: ¥100. Open 8:30–6.*

The reasons to stay overnight in Takamatsu are its modern hotels, the openness of the city, and the opportunity to make excursions to Yashima and Shodo Island.

Yashima

JR trains from Takamatsu Station make the 20-minute run every hour to **Yashima,** or you can take the commuter Kotoden tram from the Chikko terminal (across from the JR station and behind the Grand Hotel). These run 10 times a day; the tourist office can supply a schedule. When you arrive at Yashima Station, simply walk up the hill and that will lead you to the reconstructed village of **Shikoku Mura** and the battle site where, in 1185, the Minamoto clan defeated the Taira family; this allowed Yoritomo Minamoto to establish Japan's first shogunate, in Kamakura.

In this open-air museum village, 21 houses have been relocated from around the island of Shikoku to represent what rural life was like during the Edo period. The village may be artificial, but in this age where ferro-concrete has replaced so much of traditional Japan, Shikoku Mura provides an opportunity to see traditional thatch-roof farmhouses, a paper-making workshop, a ceremonial teahouse, a rural Kabuki stage, and other buildings used in the feudal age. Similar to the Hida Village near Takayama, Shikoku Mura presents a picture of what life was like 200 to 300 years ago. *Admission: ¥500. Open 8:30–5; Nov.–Mar., 8:30–4:30.*

Close to Shikoku Mura's entrance is a cable car, which takes five minutes to travel up to **Yashima Plateau.** Yashima was once an island (it's now connected to Shikoku by a narrow strip of land), and on its summit, nearly 1,000 feet above the Inland Sea, the Minamoto and Taira clans clashed. Relics from the battle are on view in the Treasure House at the Yashimaji Temple (originally constructed in 754, it is the 84th of the 88 sacred temples), but the major reasons for ascending this plateau are the expansive vistas over the Inland Sea and views of Shodo Island.

Shodo Island

A longer excursion from Takamatsu is to **Shodo Island** (Shodoshima, in Japanese), the second largest island in the Inland Sea. The ferry (fare: ¥ 430) takes an hour from Takamatsu Pier to reach Tonosho, the island's major town and port. A hydrofoil also makes the same run, but it does so in 35 minutes (fare: ¥1,000). Tonosho may also be reached by a 40-minute hydrofoil ride from Okayama Pier. Sightseeing bus tours depart from Tonosho to cover all the island sights, or you can simply use the public buses—they cover the island efficiently and thoroughly. Motor bicycles may also be rented at ¥3,000 a day, including insurance, from Ryobi Rent–a–Bike (tel. 62–6578, open 8:30–5) near Tonsho's pier.

The major attraction on Shodo is **Kankakei Gorge,** an hour's bus ride (fare: ¥610) from Tonosho. The gorge is 3.7 miles long and 2.4 miles wide, hemmed in by a wall of mountainous peaks with weather-eroded rocks. The thick maple and pine forest lining the gorge creates a splash of color in the autumn; in the spring, the profusion of azaleas makes for an equally colorful spectacle.

If the grandeur of the gorge is not thrilling enough, you can take an aerial tramway to the summit that travels scaringly close to the cliffs' walls. Then take a bus back to Tonosho via Kusakabe.

The other principal attractions on Shodo are **Kujukuen** (15 minutes by bus from Tonosho), where 3,000 peacocks roam; **Choshikei Gorge** (25 minutes by bus from Tonosho), which extends along the upper stream of the Denpo River; and the nearby **Monkey Park,** where 700 wild monkeys cavort.

On returning to Takamatsu from Shodo Island, you may travel to Kotohiragu Shrine and then on to Kochi, or, if you are pressed for time, to Matsuyama.

Several minshukus offer accommodation on the island. Try Churchi (tel. 0879/62–3679) with 10 rooms or Maruse (tel. 0879/ 62–2385) with six rooms, both in Tonosho.

Kotohira

From Takamatsu, the JR train takes 55 minutes to reach **Kotohira** Station, from which it is an eight-minute walk to the steps that lead up to **Kotohiragu Shrine.** (If the JR train is not convenient, you can take the 70-minute tram ride that departs from the other side of the Takamatsu Station plaza.) This shrine may not rank quite as high in importance as do the Grand Shrines at Ise or the Izumo Taisha Shrine near Matsue, but it is one of Japan's oldest and grandest. It is also one of the most popular shrines in Japan. Four million visitors come to pay their respects each year.

Founded in the 11th century and built on the slopes of Mt. Zozu, the shrine is dedicated to Omono-nushi-no-Mikoto (Kompira, as he is fondly known), the guardian god of the sea and patron of seafarers. Traditionally, fishermen and sailors would come to visit the shrine and solicit godly help for their safe passage at sea. However, their monopoly on seeking the aid of Kompira has ended. His role has expanded to include all travelers, including tourists, though it is uncertain whether messages written in English will be understood.

To reach the main gate of the shrine, you must first mount 365 granite steps. On either side of the steps are souvenir and refreshment stands. However, don't dawdle. There are another 420 steps to the main shrine. Once through the main gate, the souvenir stands are replaced by stone lanterns. The climb becomes more of a solemn, spiritual exercise. Just before the second torii gate is the shrine's **Treasure House,** (Homotsu-kan), with an impressive display of sculpture, scrolls, and, despite their Buddhist origins, Noh masks. *Admission: ¥200. Open 9–4.*

Shoin is the next important building. It will be on your right. The building dates from 1659, and its interior is covered in paintings by the famous 18th-century landscape artist Okyo Maruyama. Maruyama (1733–1795) came from a family of farmers and, not surprisingly, looked to the beauty of nature for his paintings. Such was his talent that a new style (the Maruyama school) of painting developed, which may be best termed "Return to Nature."

Onward and forever upward, you'll see the intricate carvings of animals on the facade of **Asahino Yashiro,** and, at the next landing, you'll finally be at the main shrine, a complex of buildings that were rebuilt 100 years ago. Aside from the sense of accomplishment in making the climb, the views over Takamatsu and the Inland Sea to the north and the mountain ranges of Shikoku to the south justify the climb of 785 steps, even more perhaps than a visit to the shrine itself. That is, unless you ask Kompira for good fortune, and, after climbing 785 steps, you may want to.

You should allow a total of an hour from the time you start your ascent up the granite stairs until you return. Just as the feudal lords once did, you may hire a palanquin to porter you up and down (cost: ¥4,500 one way, ¥6,000 round-trip). Riding in a palanquin has a certain appeal, and it most certainly saves the calf muscles, but the motion and narrow confines are not especially comfortable.

It is worth making the time to visit the oldest Kabuki theater in Japan. Located in Kotohira Park, it is only a 10-minute walk from Kotohira Station and is near the first flight of steps leading to the Kotohiragu Shrine. The theater, called **Kompira O-Shibai,** is exceptionally large and was moved from the overcrowded center of Kotohira in 1975. At the same time, the theater was completely restored to its original grandeur. Kabuki plays are now performed only once a year, in April, but throughout the year, the theater is open for viewing. Since the theater was built in 1835, one of the interesting aspects is how the theater managed its special effects without electricity. Eight men in harness, for example, rotate the stage. Within the revolving stage are two trap lifts. The larger one is used for quick changes in stage props, the smaller one for lifting actors up to floor level. Equally fascinating are the sets of sliding shoji screens used to adjust the amount of daylight filtering onto the stage. *Admission: ¥300. Open 9–4. Closed Tues.*

From Kotohira Station, the JR Limited Express train continues on to Kochi, the principal city of Shikoku's southern coast. (Or, you can return to the north coast of Shikoku and travel west to Matsuyama.)

Kochi

⑤ The views from the train en route from Kotohira to **Kochi** are stunning, though the tunnels through which the train passes sometimes become frustrating. The train goes up the inclines to follow the valleys, cut deep by swift-flowing rivers. The earth is red and rich, and the foliage is lush and verdant. It is an area of scenic beauty that could happily lend itself to exploration by car, though once you are off the main roads, a small knowledge of Japanese will help your navigation.

From Kotohira, the train takes about 2½ hours to reach Kochi. The **Tourist Information Office** (tel. 0888/82–1634) is located to the left of the station's exit. Should you need language assistance while in Kochi, you may telephone the Nichibei School (tel. 0888/23–8118) weekdays 9–5, Saturday noon–5. The JR bus terminal for direct JR buses to Matsuyama (there is no train line) is on the left wing (as you exit the station) of the station plaza.

The train station is a 20-minute walk from the city center. A taxi ride from the station to downtown is about ¥550. There are also buses.

There are ½-day and full-day sightseeing tours (tel. 0888/82–3561) of Kochi and the surrounding area. These leave from the area around the JR bus terminal at Kochi Station. There are also full-day sightseeing tours (tel. 0880/35–3856) that travel down to Cape Ashizuri. These leave from Nakamura Station and are not available throughout the whole year, so be sure to call ahead.

For residents of Kochi, fishing and agriculture are the mainstays. For the tourist, the major attraction is **Kochijo Castle,** one of the 12 feudal castles to have survived the course of time. The castle is easy to find; its location dominates the center of Kochi.

Kochi's castle is unique in that it is the only one in Japan to have kept both its donjon (stronghold) and its daimyo's residence intact. The donjon, admittedly, was rebuilt in 1753, but it faithfully reflects the original (1601–1603). The stone foundation of the donjon seems to merge into the cliff face of the bluff on which the structure is built. The donjon has the old style of watchtower design, and, by climbing up to its top floor, one can appreciate its purpose. The commanding view is splendid. The daimyo's residence, **Kaitokukan,** is located to the southwest of the donjon and is worth entering to see the formal main room, so elegantly laid out in the Shoin style, a style known for its decorative alcove, staggered shelves, decorative doors, tatami-covered floors, and shoji screens reinforced with wooden lattices. In the castle grounds, beneath the donjon, is Kochi University. It must be inspiring to look up through the library windows to see this feudal structure tower above. *Admission: ¥300. Open 9–4:30.*

Except for the castle, Kochi is not architecturally the most exciting of towns. However, perhaps because of its warm climate, the people of Kochi are full of humor. Even their local folk songs poke fun at life, such as, "On Harimayabashi, people saw a Buddhist priest buy a hairpin. . . ." Because priests in those days were forbidden to love women, and they shaved their heads, some naughty business was afoot. Kochi is friendly, and fun-loving, and people congregate every evening in the compact downtown area for pleasure. Several streets in the heart of downtown are closed off from traffic to form shopping arcades. Every day of the week seems to be a market day; however, should you be in Kochi on a Sunday morning, be sure to visit the thriving **Sunday Open-Air Market** on Otesuji-dori Avenue, just north of Harimayabashi in downtown Kochi, where farmers bring their produce to sell at some 650 stalls. It is a tradition that has been maintained for 300 years. As an added bonus, you may also see the incredibly long-tailed (more than 20 feet) roosters for which Kochi is known. The actual village where these roosters are raised is Oshino, though the easiest place to see them is outside of Kochi at the **Long-Tailed Rooster Center** at Shinohara, Nankoku City. *Tel. 0888/64–4931. Admission: ¥300. Open 9–5. Closed Mon.*

During the summer months, residents of Kochi flock to **Katsurahama Beach,** 8 miles southeast of town. Buses depart from the Kochi station plaza and take 35 minutes (fare: ¥530).

The beach consists of gravelly white sand, but the swimming is good, and there are pleasing scenic rock formations offshore. There is also the **Tosa Fighting Dog Center** (tel. 0888/42–3315), where the victor of a bout is paraded around the ring dressed in a sumo wrestler's apron, and given the same ranking title as his human counterpart. To get to Katsurahama Beach, either catch the bus from the Kochi station or from the Harimayabashi stop, just before the bridge.

If you prefer to spend an afternoon amid lawns, greenery, and an old temple, take the bus to Mount Godai and **Godaisan-Koen Park.** The 20-minute bus ride departs from the Toden bus stop, next to the Seibu department store on Harimayabashi (fare: ¥ 300). First visit the **Chikurinji Temple,** which has an impressive five-story pagoda that, despite beliefs to the contrary, is fairly uncommon in Japan. This one can stand up to those of Kyoto; the people from Kochi say it's more magnificent. The temple belongs to the Shingon sect of Buddhism and, founded in 724, is the 31st temple in the sequence of the 88 sacred temples. Down from the temple is the **Makino Botanical Garden,** built to honor the botanist Dr. Tomitaro Makino (1862–1957). The greenhouse has an exotic collection of more than 1,000 plants, and the gardens are full of flowers, which have been planned so that in all seasons something is in bloom. *Admission: ¥300. Open 9–5.*

East along the coast from Kochi, the road follows a rugged shoreline, marked by frequent inlets and indentations. Most of the coast consists of a series of 100- to 300-foot terraces. Continuous wave action, generated by the Black Current, has eroded these terraces. The result is a surreal coastline of rocks, surf, and steep precipices. It is about a 2½-hour drive along the coast road out to **Cape Muroto,** a popular sightseeing tour destination to watch the sea crash against the cliffs.

West of Kochi, in the southwestern tip of Kochi Prefecture, is Ashizuri National Park. The JR Dosansen Line goes to Kubokawa Station, where, if you were going straight to Uwajima, you'd change trains. For Nakamura usually there is no change. This last leg of the journey is on the Kuroshio Tetsudo Line, and JR Rail Pass holders will be charged an additional ¥170. At **Nakamura** you continue by JR bus to **Tosa-Shimizu,** where you can catch another bus out to **Cape Ashizuri.** (There are also sightseeing buses that depart from Nakamura JR Station to Cape Ashizuri, tel. 0880/35–3856.) It is wonderfully wild country, with a skyline-drive road running down the center of the cape. At the end of the cape is the lighthouse and the Kongofukuji Temple, the 38th of the 88 sacred temples, whose origins trace back 1,100 years, though what you see was rebuilt 300 years ago.

Returning from Cape Ashizuri, you can reboard the bus at Tosa Shimizu and follow the coastline to **Sukumo** (four ferries a day depart from here for Saeki on Kyushu. Fare: ¥1,650. Sukumo can also be reached directly by an hour's bus ride from Nakamura. Fare: ¥1,100.) With a change of bus, continue north to **Uwajima,** the terminal for JR lines arriving from Matsuyama and Kochi. Ferries depart from Uwajima for Usuki, on Kyushu.

Shikoku has three of the surviving 12 feudal castles; one of these is **Uwajimajo Castle,** though the first castle was torn down and replaced with an updated version in 1665. It's a friendly castle, without the usual defensive structures such as a stone drop, which suggests that by the end of the 17th century, war, at least those fought around castles, was a thing of the past. Most people however, do not come to Uwajima to see the castle. They come for the **Togyu Bullfights.** Though there are very similar bouts in the Ogi Islands, Uwajima claims these bullfights are a unique tradition that goes back for 400 years (good for tourism). Tournaments are held five times a year (dates vary, except for the Wareisai Festival on July 23–24, but usually they are January 2, the first Sunday in March and April, the third Sunday in May). In these tournaments, two bulls lock horns and, like sumo wrestlers, try to push each other out of the ring. The Togyujo, where the contests are held, is at the foot of Mt. Tenman, about a 30-minute walk from the JR station.

From Uwajima, it is a two-hour ride on the JR train to Matsuyama. You can also take a JR bus directly to Matsuyama from Kochi (3 hrs, 50 mins). There is frequent JR train service to Matsuyama from Takamatsu and also a hourly hydrofoil (60 minutes at ¥4,950) and ferry (three hrs at ¥3,710 for first class and ¥1,850 for second class) service from Hiroshima.

Matsuyama

⑫ The two most popular attractions of **Matsuyama** are its castle and the nearby Dogo Onsen.

Matsuyama is Shikoku's largest city, and it bristles with industries ranging from chemicals to wood pulp and from textiles to porcelain. It's a useful town for replenishing supplies—to change traveler's checks, for example—but with the exception of the castle, it lacks character. At the station, you may want to stop in at the City Tourist Information Office (tel. 0899/31-3914), located just inside the JR station, for a map and brochures. Downtown Matsuyama, often defined as the Okaido Shopping Center, which is at the foot of the castle grounds, is best reached by taking streetcar #5, which departs from the plaza in front of the train station.

Matsuyamajo Castle is on top of Matsuyama Hill, right in the center of the city. Originally built in 1603, the castle is the third feudal castle in Shikoku to have survived—though barely. It burned down in 1784 but was rebuilt in 1854, with a complex consisting of a major three-story donjon and three lesser donjons. The lesser ones succumbed to fire during this century, but all have been reconstructed. Unlike other postwar reconstructions, these smaller donjons were rebuilt with original materials, not with ferro-concrete. The main donjon now serves as a museum for feudal armor and swords owned by the Matsudaira clan, the daimyo family that lorded over Matsuyama (and Takamatsu) during the entire Edo period. The castle is perched high on the hill; unless you are very energetic, take the cable car that shuttles visitors up and down every 10 minutes. *Cost of cable car and admission to the castle: ¥550. Open 9–4:30.*

Because Matsuyama has no special character of its own, rather than stay in town, many visitors spend the night at **Dogo Onsen.** It is only 18 minutes away by streetcar, which you can take from the JR Matsuyama Station or catch from downtown—there is a stop before the ANA Hotel. In either case, take streetcar #5. With a history that is said to stretch back for more than two millennia, Dogo Onsen boasts of being one of Japan's oldest spas. It hasn't outlived its popularity, either. There are more than 60 ryokans and hotels, old and new. Most of these now have their own thermal waters, but at the turn of the last century, visitors used to go to the public bathhouses; the grandest of them all was, and still is, the municipal bathhouse *(shinrokaku)*, the **Dogo Onsen Honkan.**

Indeed, even if your hotel has the fanciest of baths, to stay at Dogo Onsen or even downtown Matsuyama and not socialize at the shinrokaku is to miss the delight of this spa town. The grand old three-story, castlelike wood building was built in 1894 and, with its sliding panels, tatami floors, and shoji screens, appears as an old-fashioned pleasure palace. It is, in many ways. Two thousand bathers or more come by each day to pay their ¥250 and take the waters. Some of them pay a little more and lounge around after their bath, drinking tea in the communal room. Bathing is a social pastime, and the bath has the added benefit of scalding water that has medicinal qualities, especially for skin diseases.

There are different price levels of enjoyment. A basic bath is ¥220; a bath, a rented *yukata* (cotton robe), and access to the communal tatami lounge is ¥780; access to a smaller lounge and bath area away from hoi polloi is ¥1,000; and a private tatami room is ¥1,300. A separate wing was built in 1899 for imperial soaking. Most of the time it is not used, but visitors are allowed to wander through this royal bathhouse. *Admission: ¥200. Open 6 AM–10 PM.*

Matsuyama has eight of the 88 sacred temples. The one of note is **Ishiteji Temple,** located 10 minutes on foot from Dogo Onsen Honkan. Representative of the Kamakura-style architecture, the temple has its origins early in the 14th century. It may not be that grand, but its simple three-story pagoda is a pleasant contrast to the public bathhouse. Note the two statues of Deva kings at the gate. One has his mouth open, representing life, and the other has his mouth closed, representing death. Praying at the Ishite Temple is said to cure one's aching legs and crippled feet. The elderly, in fact, hang up their sandals in the temple as an offering of hope.

Dining

The delight of Shikoku is the number of small Japanese restaurants that serve the freshest fish, either caught in the Seto Inland Sea or in the Pacific. Noodle restaurants abound, too. We have not singled out particular restaurants because they rarely differ in terms of ambience or quality of food. You may want to control your adventure in eating by choosing those restaurants that offer visual displays of their menus in the windows. However, if you have been in Japan for a week, you'll probably feel comfortable going into a small restaurant, even without a visual display of the menu in the window, and ordering what the chef recommends. That dish is always the best. Just tell them that you wish to keep the price within certain limits.

In each of the three major cities—Takamatsu, Kochi, and Matsuyama—the entertainment districts have innumerable Japanese restaurants, and the fun of these areas is selecting your own restaurant. However, if you are staying at the Grand Hotel in Takamatsu or are waiting for the train or the next ferry at the JR station and have time enough for a good meal, there are nine excellent Japanese restaurants from which to chose on the second floor of the Grand Hotel's building. All the restaurants have their menus visually displayed in the windows, so you can select the dish and price your meal before you enter. If you are feeling more ambitious, there are dozens of good, small restaurants on and around Nakahonmachi—an arcade that runs parallel to the main boulevard, Chuo-dori. A particularly good restaurant is Maimai-tei (tel. 0878/33–3360, closed Sun.) which serves excellent Sanuki cuisine at approximately ¥4,700 for two.

In Matsuyama, the Okaido shopping arcade near the ANA Hotel has numerous good restaurants serving Western and Japanese food in all price ranges—the local specialty is *ikezukuri*, a live fish with its meat cut into strips. In Kochi, the entertainment district is crammed with appealing small restaurants and nomiya.

For Western-style cuisine, you are better off eating at the top hotels. The Hankyu, in Kochi, for example, has an excellent French restaurant, as does the ANA Hotel in Matsuyama. If you're on a budget, these hotels have Western-style coffee shops, and the ANA Hotel in Matsuyama also has a delightful rooftop beer garden, open in the summer, where one can also eat well and inexpensively.

Lodging

Accommodations cover a broad spectrum, from pensions and minshukus to large modern, resort hotels that have little character but offer all the facilities of an international hotel. All of the large city and resort hotels offer Western as well as Japanese food. During the summer, reservations are advised.

Outside the cities or major towns, most hotels quote prices on a per-person basis with two meals, exclusive of service and tax. If you do not want dinner at your hotel, it is usually possible to renegotiate the price. Stipulate, too, whether you wish to have Japanese or Western breakfasts, if any. For the purposes here, the categories assigned to all hotels reflect the cost of a double room with private bath and no meals. However, if you make reservations at any of the noncity hotels, you will be expected to take breakfast and dinner at the hotel—that will be the rate quoted to you unless you specify otherwise. A 3% federal consumer tax is added to all hotel bills. Another 3% local tax is added to the bill if it exceeds ¥10,000. At most hotels, a 10%–15% service charge is added to the hotel bill. Tipping is not the custom.

The most highly recommended accommodations in each city are indicated by a star ★.

Category	Cost*
Very Expensive	over ¥20,000
Expensive	¥15,000–¥20,000

| Moderate | ¥10,000–¥15,000 |
| Inexpensive | under ¥10,000 |

Cost is for double room, without tax or service

Credit Cards The following credit card abbreviations are used: AE, American Express; DC, Diners Club; MC, MasterCard; V, Visa.

Kochi

★ **Hotel Hankyu.** Located in the center of town, within sight of the Kochijo Castle, the Hankyu opened in late 1985 and is indisputably the best hotel in Kochi. On the ground floor is the modern open-plan lobby, with a lounge away from the reception area and a small cake/tea shop to the side. On the second floor, there are several excellent restaurants. The best omelets on Shikoku are offered at breakfast in this hotel. The spacious guest rooms, decorated with light pastel furnishings, create a sense of well-being, and the staff are extremely helpful to foreign guests. *4-2-50 Honmachi, Kochi-shi, Kochi 780, tel. 0888/ 73–1111. 201 rooms, mostly Western style. Facilities: Chinese, Japanese, and French restaurants. AE, DC, MC, V. Expensive.*

Ikawa Ryokan. English is not spoken here, but the genteel hospitality and sophistication of this inn make a stay relaxing and comfortable. Elegant simplicity achieves harmony. Even the few Western guest rooms are simply adorned. Dinner is kaiseki-style and uses the produce of the sea to full advantage. *5–1 Nichu-dai cho, Kochi 780, tel. 0888/22–1317, fax 0888/24– 7401. 40 rooms, mostly Japanese style. Facilities: meals served in one's room, small banquet room, Japanese garden. AE, DC, V. Expensive.*

Washington Hotel. On the street leading to Kochijo Castle and a 20-minute walk from the station, this is a small, friendly business hotel in downtown Kochi. It has a small restaurant, and the rooms are a good size for this kind of lodging. *1-8-25 Otesuji, Kochi-shi, Kochi 780, tel. 0888/23–6111. 62 Western-style rooms. Facilities: Japanese/Western restaurant. AE, V. Moderate.*

Hotel Sunroute Kochi. This business hotel has slightly larger rooms than the average of its kind and is close to the station. *1–1–28 Kitahon-cho, Kochi-shi, Kochi 780, tel. 0888/23–1311. 64 rooms. Facilities: breakfast room. AE, DC, V. Inexpensive.*

Matsuyama

★ **ANA Hotel Matsuyama.** If you don't wish to stay out at Dogo Onsen, this is the best international hotel in town. It caters to the business executive—half its rooms are singles. The location downtown is excellent, within five minutes on foot to the cable car that travels up to Matsuyamajo Castle. The streetcars that go out to Dogo Onsen pass by the front of the hotel. The first four floors of the hotel are banquet rooms and shopping arcades, with some 50 boutiques, and a summer beer garden is located on the hotel's roof. On the 14th floor is the Castle Grill restaurant, serving well-prepared Continental food and offering a view of Matsuyama. Japanese cuisine, specializing in seafood from the Seto Inland Sea, is offered at the Unkai restaurant on the 6th floor overlooking a Japanese garden. The guest rooms are well maintained, reasonably spacious, and ful-

ly equipped, with everything but a hair dryer. *3-2-1 Ichi-
bancho, Matsuyama 790, tel. 0899/33–5511. 334 rooms. Facilities: Chinese, Japanese, and Western restaurants; rooftop beer
garden open May–Sept. AE, DC, V. Expensive.*

Funaya Ryokan. The best Japanese inn in Dogo Onsen, this is
where the imperial family stays when it comes to take the waters. The ryokan has a long history, but the present building
was built in 1963. The best rooms look out on the garden.
Breakfast and dinner are included in the tariff. *1-33, Godo
Yumo-machi, Matsuyama 790, tel. 0899/47–0278. 43 rooms;
most are Japanese style, but a few are combination style (Western beds and a tatami area). Not all rooms have private bath.
Facilities: Japanese cuisine, thermal baths. AE, V. Expensive.*

Hotel Sunroute. This business hotel has no particular charm,
but its rooms are not too small, and it is located within a five-
minute walk from the JR station. The best part of the hotel is
its rooftop beer garden (open summer only), from which you
can catch a glimpse of the castle. *Miyata-cho, Matsuyama 790,
tel. 0899/33–2811. 110 Western-style rooms. AE, V. Inexpensive.*

Takamatsu

Kawaroku Ryokan. This is the best hotel in the center of town,
amid the shopping arcades, and offers Western- and Japanese-
style rooms, all with private bath. The original Kawaroku was
bombed out in World War II. This replacement is unappealing
from the outside but is pleasantly furnished on the inside. The
rooms have a light, refreshing decor. *1-2 Hyakkencho, Takamatsu, Kagawa Prefecture 760, tel. 0878/21–5666. 70 rooms, 21
Western style. Facilities: French restaurant. Japanese food is
available and will be served in your room, ryokan style. AE,
V. Moderate–Expensive.*

Keio Plaza Hotel. The staff is shy but friendly at this efficient
hotel. However, its location, at the far end of Chuo-dori Avenue
and near Ritsurin-Koen Park, places it a good 10 minutes by
taxi from the JR station, but within easy walking distance from
Nakahonmachi, the shopping arcade mall, and entertainment
district. Guest rooms are reasonably spacious and comfortable,
though the rooms facing Chuo-dori do suffer slightly from traffic noise. *11-5 Chuocho, Takamatsu, Kagawa Prefecture 760,
tel. 0878/34–5511. 180 rooms; 2 Japanese style. Facilities: Japanese and Western restaurants. Moderate–Expensive.*

★ **Takamatsu Grand Hotel.** The Grand is the best hotel in Takamatsu. It is within a five-minute walk from the JR station and is
located on the main avenue, Chuo-dori. It is within five minutes
of the shopping arcades and entertainment quarter. The lobby
is on the third floor (there are nine independently owned restaurants on the second floor), and the main restaurant is on the
seventh floor. Because the hotel faces Tamamo Park and the
Tamamojo Castle, the views are quite splendid. The guest
rooms on the side of the building facing the park are the choicest, rather than those looking over Chuo-dori Avenue. All the
guest rooms could use refurbishing, but they are clean. *1-5-10
Kotobukicho, Takamatsu, Kagawa Prefecture 760, tel. 0878/
51–5757. 136 Western-style rooms. Facilities: penthouse restaurant serving Western food, wonderful specialty Japanese
restaurants on the 2nd floor. AE, DC, MC, V. Moderate.*

Tokiwa Honkan. Though it was constructed in 1954, this is a traditional ryokan that faces an inner courtyard laid out with a carp-filled pond, stone lanterns, and dwarf trees. All the rooms have private toilets, though not all have their own bathtub. You may choose whether or not to dine at the ryokan. *1-8-2 Tokiwa-machi, Takamatsu, Kagawa Prefecture 760, tel. 0878/61–5577. 21 Japanese-style rooms. Facilities: Japanese cuisine, Western breakfast available on request. AE, V. Moderate.*

13 Kyushu

Introduction

by Kiko Itasaka

Kyushu, the quiet island southwest of the main island of Honshu, offers a mild climate, lush green countryside, hot springs, and eerie volcanic formations. This island, however peaceful it may be now, was for centuries the most active and international island in all of Japan. To this day, it is considered to be the birthplace of Japanese civilization. The cities of Kyushu are full of sights of historical and cultural significance.

Legend has it that the grandson of Amaterasu, the sun goddess, first ruled Japan from Kyushu. Another tale relates that Jimmu, Japan's first emperor, traveled from Kyushu to Honshu, consolidated Japan, and established the imperial line that exists to this day.

From the 4th century on, Kyushu, as a result of its geographic proximity to Korea and China, was the first area of Japan to be culturally influenced by its more sophisticated neighbors. Through the gateway of Kyushu, Japan was first introduced to pottery techniques, Buddhism, the Chinese writing system, and other aspects of Chinese and Korean culture.

Not all outside influence, however, was welcome. In 1274, Kublai Khan led a fleet of Mongol warriors in an unsuccessful attempt to invade Japan. The Japanese, in preparation for further attacks, built a stone wall along the coast of Kyushu; remnants of it can still be seen today outside Fukuoka. When the Mongols returned in 1281 with a force 100,000 strong, they were repelled by the stone wall and by the fierce fighting of the Kyushu natives; the fighters were aided by a huge storm, known as *kamikaze* (divine wind), which blew the Mongol fleet out to sea. This term may be more familiar in its revived form, used in World War II to describe suicide pilots.

In the mid-16th century, Kyushu was once again the first point of contact with the outside world, when Portuguese ships first landed on the shores of Japan. The arrival of these ships signaled Japan's initial introduction to the West and its knowledge of medicine, firearms, and Christianity. The Portuguese were followed by other European powers, the Dutch and the Spanish. The Tokugawa Shogunate was not entirely pleased with the intrusion of the Westerners and feared political interference. In 1635, the shogunate established a closed-door policy that permitted foreigners to land only on a small island, Dejima, in the harbor of Nagasaki. As a result, until 1859, when Japan opened its doors to the West, the small port town of Nagasaki became the most important center for both trade and Western learning for Kyushu and the entire nation. To this day, the historical influence of Europe is apparent in Nagasaki, with its 19th-century Western-style buildings and the lasting presence of Christianity.

Whether you visit the castle in Kumamoto or the ancient temples of Fukuoka, a visit to Kyushu is a tour of Japan's past. This island is no longer a center of power in Japan; many cities and their sights have remained untouched and have not been replaced by skyscrapers.

A visit to Kyushu's major attractions requires travel around the island. Fortunately, the journeys between the points of interest in Kyushu afford beautiful views of Kyushu's rich green rice fields, mountains, and the ocean. The starting point of any

visit to Kyushu is Fukuoka City, where there is a major airport
and a JR Shinkansen train station. Of course, it is possible to
travel to the different sights of Kyushu in any order, but in this
chapter, a tour that is a circular route is suggested for your convenience; it starts in Fukuoka, proceeds to Nagasaki, Kumamoto, and Mt. Aso, and concludes with a visit to the relaxing
hot-spring resort of Beppu (from which you can return to Fukuoka).

Essential Information

Arriving and Departing

By Plane The only international airport in Kyushu is Fukuoka Airport
(*see* Arriving and Departing in Fukuoka, below). Nagasaki,
Kagoshima, Oita, Miyazaki, and Kita Kyushu all have airports
serviced by domestic airlines.

By Train The JR Shinkansen trains travel only as far as Fukuoka (*see* Arriving and Departing in Fukuoka, below). JR trains connect all
major destinations in Kyushu.

By Ferry The Kansai Kisen Line operates ferries connecting the cities of
Kobe and Osaka with Beppu (*see* Arriving and Departing in
Beppu, below).

Ferries have scheduled runs between the Hakata Pier Ferry
Terminal at Fukuoka and Yosu and Pusan, both in Korea. At
press time, a hydrofoil service to Pusan was planned for scheduled service before the end of 1991.

Fukuoka

*Numbers in the margin correspond to points of interest on the
Kyushu map.*

❶ **Fukuoka** is the second-largest city in Kyushu and the starting
point for most travel around the island. Many people visiting
Kyushu spend at least a day or two here. If you are planning to
stop in Fukuoka en route to other cities, you'll discover a few
places of particular historical and cultural interest. Although it
is the major industrial city of Kyushu, you will immediately
sense a slower pace of life compared with that of Japan's other
main cities. People in Kyushu are known for their straightfor-
wardness and warmth, and visitors often find this city to be
less cosmopolitan but more pleasant than Tokyo or Osaka.

Arriving and Departing

By Plane Japan Airlines (JAL), All Nippon Airways (ANA), and Japan
Air System have 1½-hour flights between Haneda Airport in
Tokyo and Fukuoka City. Twenty flights are offered daily. JAL
provides service (1 hour, 45 minutes) between Narita International Airport and Fukuoka Airport daily. JAL and ANA also
offer a total of eight direct flights between Osaka and Fukuoka
(1 hour, 45 minutes) making it convenient for travelers to begin
or end their Japan travels in Kyushu.

*Between the Airport
and Center City* The Fukuoka Airport is located very near the center of the city.
A regular bus service connects the airport with Hakata Station
in 15 minutes (cost: ¥240).

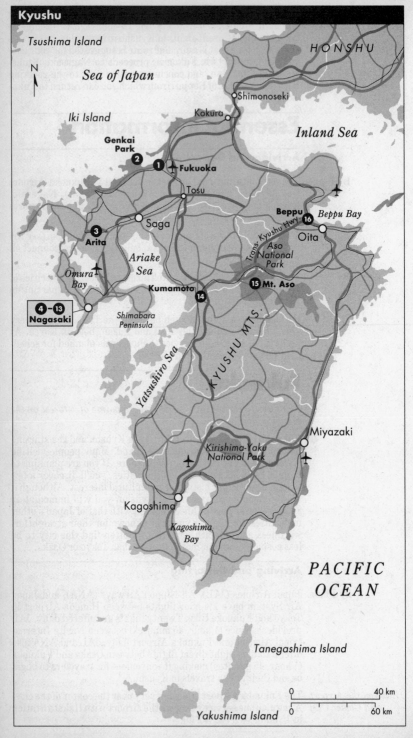

Kyushu

Tsushima Island

Sea of Japan

Iki Island

H O N S H U

Shimonoseki

Kokura

Inland Sea

Genkai Park

②

① ✦ **Fukuoka**

Tosu

③ Arita

Saga

Ariake Sea

Beppu
⑯
Beppu Bay

Oita

Omura Bay

Kumamoto

⑭

Trans-Kyushu Hwy.

Aso National Park

⑮ Mt. Aso

④ – ⑬ Nagasaki

Shimabara Peninsula

Yatsushiro Sea

K Y U S H U   M T S.

Miyazaki

Kirishima-Yaku National Park

Kagoshima

Kagoshima Bay

PACIFIC OCEAN

Tanegashima Island

| 0 | 40 km |
| 0 | 60 km |

Yakushima Island

By Train JR Shinkansen Hikari trains travel between Tokyo and Hakata Station in Fukuoka (time: 6 hours, 26 minutes to 7 hours, 24 minutes). There are 15 daily runs. Shinkansen trains travel between Osaka and Hakata, and also between Hiroshima and Hakata. Other JR express trains travel these routes but take twice as long.

Getting Around

The easiest way to get around Fukuoka is by bus or by one of the two subway lines (the minimum fare is ¥160). The two major transportation centers of Fukuoka are located around Hakata Station and in the downtown area known as Tenjin, the terminal station for both of the subway lines. Buses leave from the Kotsu Bus Center just across the street from the Hakata Station, and from the Fukuoka Bus Center at Tenjin.

Important Addresses and Numbers

Tourist Information **The Fukuoka City Tourist Information Office** (tel. 092/431–3003) is located in Hakata Station. Some of the office staff speak English and have excellent maps of the city and neighboring areas are available. Open daily 9–7. If you plan on staying in Fukuoka for more than a day or two, you may wish to contact The Fukuoka International Association (Rainbow Plaza, IMS 5F, 1–7–11 Tanjin, Chuo–ku, Fukuoka City 810, tel. 092/733–2220, fax 092/733–2215) which serves as an information resource and center for networking.

U.S. Consulate (5-26 Ohori 2-chome, Chuo-ku, tel. 092/751–9331).

Travel Agencies **Japan Travel Bureau.** (Daiwa Seimei Kaikan Bldg., 1-14-4 Tenjin, Chuo-ku, tel. 092/771–5211).

Guided Tours

You can take sightseeing bus tours of the major historic sights of Fukuoka City from the **Tenjin Bus Center** (tel. 092/771–2961) or the **Kotsu Bus Center** (tel. 092/431–1171). Not all tours are in English, so it is better to have your hotel call for further information or to ask at the tourist information office.

Exploring

Fukuoka is the commercial, political, and cultural center of Kyushu and the island's largest city. With 1.2 million inhabitants, it is the eighth largest city in Japan. In comparison to Tokyo, it is small and provincial, but there is a dynamic quality to Fukuoka whose city council is determined to position the city as Japan's gateway to Asia. Most activities and entertainment events happen around the two city centers, Hakata Station and the downtown Tenjin district. (Use the subway—fare: ¥160—to travel between them.) Most of the places you visit in Fukuoka, whether they are restaurants, shops, or sights, are near these two centers, or can be reached easily from them. The city is divided in two parts by the Nakagawa River. All areas west of the river are known as Fukuoka, and everything east of the river is known as Hakata. Along the Naka and Hakata rivers is Nakuse, the nightlife district, with 3,000 bars, restaurants, and street vendors. Fukuoka was originally a castle town founded at the end of the 16th century, and Hakata was the place for commerce. In 1889 the two districts were officially merged as Fukuoka City, but the historical names are still used.

Start your tour of Fukuoka at the **Shofukuji Temple,** where Zen Buddhism was first introduced to Japan. The temple can be reached by a 15-minute walk from Hakata Station, or a five-minute Nishitetsu bus ride from the Hakata Kotsu Bus Center to the Okunodo stop.

Zen Buddhism was initially brought from China to Japan through Kyushu. One of the first Japanese priests to introduce Buddhism to Japan was Eisai (1141–1215). Upon his return to Kyushu after years of study in China, he founded the Shofukuji Temple in 1195 and commenced with his introduction of Zen Buddhism to Japan. Eisai, in addition to introducing Zen, is also said to have brought the first tea seeds from China to Japan. Note in particular the Korean-style bronze bell in the belfry, which is designated an Important Cultural Property by the Japanese government. *Admission free. Open daily 9–5.*

From the Shofukuji Temple, return to Hakata Station. Either walk or take a bus from the Hakata Kotsu Bus Center to Sumiyoshi Station and visit the **Sumiyoshi Jinja Shrine.** Buddhism and Shintoism, the indigenous religion of Japan, coexist in Japan; it is common to be married in a Shinto ceremony but buried in a Buddhist rite. It is therefore not at all unusual to have a Shinto shrine within walking distance of a Buddhist temple. Sumiyoshi, the oldest Shinto shrine in Kyushu, founded in 1623, is dedicated to the guardian gods of seafarers. An annual festival is held at this shrine October 12–14, complete with sumo wrestling. The temple is located on top of a hill with a lovely view of both the Nakagawa River and the city, and the grounds are dotted with camphor and cedar trees. *Admission free. Open 9–5.*

For a recreational break, take the subway from Hakata Station to Ohori-Koen Park Station, about a 20-minute ride. **Ohori-Koen** is a spacious park, built around a lake that was once part of a moat surrounding Fukuokajo Castle. Bridges connect three small islands in the center of the lake. In early April, the northern portion of the park is graced with the blossoms of 2,600 cherry trees. On weekends you will see many Fukuoka residents taking advantage of this oasis in the middle of an otherwise grim and gray industrial city, just as New Yorkers cherish Central Park. Bring a picnic and enjoy a leisurely walk, or boat and fish on the lake.

If you get bored with the pleasures of relaxation in the park, go to the **Fukuokajo Castle** grounds on the outskirts of Ohori Park. The castle was originally built in 1607. Little remains here—only a turret, gates, and a small portion of the castle—but the grounds are on a hill with a lovely panoramic view of the city.

Shopping

Fukuoka is famous for two local products—**Hakata dolls** and **Hakata obis** (sashes for kimonos).

Hakata dolls, popular throughout Japan, are made with fired clay and are hand painted with bright colors and distinctive expressions. These dolls are mostly ornamental and depict such figures as children, women, samurai, or geisha.

Hakata obis are made of an interesting local silk textile that has a rougher texture than most Japanese silk, which is usually perfectly even and smooth. For local young girls, the purchase of their first Hakata obi is an initiation into adulthood. Other products, such as bags and purses, are made of this Hakata silk.

The main area for shopping is the downtown district of Tenjin, which can be reached by subway from Hakata Station. It is the third stop from Hakata Station. This shopping district features many boutiques, department stores, and restaurants.

Iwataya Department Store (2-11-1 Tenjin, Chuo-ku, tel. 092/721–1111) carries the most complete selection of merchandise in the area, including Hakata dolls, Hakata silk, and an excellent china department that features some of the distinctive pottery of Kyushu. The store is in the center of the Tenjin shopping area.

Hakusen, also located in the Tenjin shopping district, is a specialty shop with an extensive selection of Hakata dolls. *Tenjin-2-chome, Shirai, Chuo-ku, tel. 092/712–8900. Open 9–8:30.*

Another store that specializes in Hakata silk is **Hakata Ori Kaikan** (Hakataeki Minami, Hakata-ku, tel. 092/472–0761), a store that is acknowledged locally as the best place to get obis and bags. This shop is small, but everything is neatly organized and attractively displayed.

Excursions from Fukuoka

Genkai Park ② This park extends from Hakata Bay along the coast of Fukuoka and Saga. It offers long beaches with white sands and eerie Japanese black pines. The waters of Hakata Bay facing the Genkai Nada Sea are surprisingly clean and relatively uncrowded. You can combine a swim in the bay with a visit to the *boheki*, the ruins of stone walls (next to a beach) that were built in the 13th century to stave off the invasions of the Mongols.

Getting There **By Bus.** Take the Nishi-no-ura bus from the Fukuoka Kotsu Center. The trip takes about two hours.

Arita ③ **Arita** is a small town, south of Fukuoka, that has been a leading pottery center for centuries. In 1616, a Korean potter introduced the art of making white porcelain to Japan to the artisans of Arita. After this, color-decoration techniques were introduced by Chinese artists. The wonders of Arita pottery have long been appreciated in the West. Early Dutch traders first noticed the pottery in Nagasaki early in the 17th century, but it was at the Philadelphia Exhibition of 1876 that Arita ceramics became renowned. The pottery is known for its delicate patterns, which incorporate flowers and birds.

Arita is a small village with one main street that is entirely lined with small pottery shops. These shops all have their own kilns and have been run by the same families for generations. Prices depend on the quality of the ceramic, but you can get a beautiful handmade teacup for around ¥1,000, or a set of five cups and a teapot for ¥5,000. Once a year, at the end of April or early May, there is a large pottery fair, where everything in all the shops goes on sale. At these times, many of the ceramic pieces are priced as low as ¥100.

Getting There **By Train.** To get from Fukuoka to Arita, take the Nagasaki Line from the Hakata Station in Fukuoka to the Arita Station. The trip will take approximately 1 hour and 15 minutes.

Nagasaki

❹ Nagasaki, a quiet city of hills with a peaceful harbor, is often called the San Francisco of Japan. The harbor, now serenely dotted with a few fishing boats, was once the most important trading port in all of Japan. In 1639, when Japan decided to close its ports to all foreigners, it appointed the small island of Dejima in Nagasaki Harbor as the one place where foreigners were allowed to land. The only Japanese allowed to have contact with the foreigners were merchants and prostitutes. The Tokugawa Shogunate established this isolationist policy to prevent Western powers from having political influence in Japan. With Nagasaki as the focal point, however, knowledge of the West, particularly in fields such as medicine and weaponry, began to spread throughout Japan. Japan reopened its doors to the West in 1859, thus ending Nagasaki's heyday as the sole international port. Many of the original buildings and churches from the 19th century still stand as testaments to this unique period in Japanese history.

After more than two centuries of prominence, Nagasaki was not the center of world attention until the atomic bomb was dropped on it in 1945. Although the bomb destroyed one-third of the city, enough remained standing so that, to this day, Nagasaki has an atmosphere that mixes both Eastern and Western traditions.

Travelers to Nagasaki will want to pick up a copy of *Harbor Light*, a monthly publication in English that provides detailed information on various activities in the city.

Arriving and Departing

By Plane Omura Airport is approximately one hour by bus or car from Nagasaki. ANA and Japan Air System offer direct flights from Haneda Airport in Tokyo to Omura Airport (1 hour, 45 minutes). There are five daily flights. From Osaka the flights are 1 hour and 10 minutes.

Between the Airport A regular shuttle bus travels between Omura Airport and Na-
and Center City gasaki Station in 55 minutes. The cost is ¥1,100.

By Train Take the JR Nagasaki Line Limited Express train from Fukuoka (2 hours, 30 minutes). To get to Kumamoto from Nagasaki by train, take the Kamone Line from Nagasaki to Tosu Station (2 hours). From Tosu, board the Kagoshima Main Line and get off at Kumamoto (1 hour).

By Bus The Kyushu Kyuko Bus Company offers bus service between Fukuoka and Nagasaki (3 hours, 20 minutes; the bus leaves from the Fukuoka Bus Center in the Tenjin downtown district). A bus service also runs between Nagasaki and Kumamoto (4 hours).

Getting Around

By Streetcar Streetcars are the most convenient way of getting around Nagasaki. Although they are slow, they appropriately reflect the relaxed atmosphere of Nagasaki and echo another century. The streetcars stop at most of the major sights, and most stops have signs in English. You can purchase a one-day pass for unlimited streetcar travel for ¥500 at the City Tourist Information Center or at major hotels. Otherwise, you pay ¥100 as you get off the streetcar. If you wish to transfer from one streetcar to another, take a transfer ticket (*nori ka ay ken*) from the driver of the first streetcar as you alight and drop your ¥100 in the box.

By Bus Bus routes exist in Nagasaki, but they are complicated and not very convenient.

Important Addresses and Numbers

Tourist Information The **City Tourist Information Center** (1-88 Onoue-cho, tel. 0958/23–3631) is on the left hand corner (as you leave the station) of the station plaza. There is no sign written in English, so it takes perseverance to find, but the office is useful for maps and directions. Open Monday–Saturday 9–6, closed Sunday. **The Nagasaki Prefecture Tourist Office** (2nd floor, Nagasaki Kotsu Sangyo Bldg., 3–1 Daikoku-machi, tel. 0958/23-4041) is across the street from the JR station one floor above street level in a department store. To reach it from the station, use the pedestrian bridge. The staff is not very helpful, but maps and bus schedules to various areas within the prefecture are available. Open weekdays 9–5:30, Saturday 9–12:45. **Japan Travel Bureau,** 1-95 Onoue-cho, tel. 0958/24–2400.

Guided Tours

By Boat A 50-minute port cruise of the Nagasaki Harbor departs at 11:40 and 3:15. Fare: ¥770. Take a streetcar to the Ohato Station, then go to Pier No. 1.

By Ricksha For a unique tour, though rarely ever taken, you can ride on a ricksha through the streets of Nagasaki. Rickshas, though once ubiquitous, are now a rare sight in Japan. Prices vary according to the course you take, but the minimum is ¥2,000 per person. Ask your hotel or the tourist information office to call in Japanese to arrange your tour (tel. 0958/24–4367).

City Tours **Japan Travel Bureau** offers a few city tours with English-speaking guides. Tel. 0958/24-3200. A three-hour tour of the city's major sights costs ¥2,710.

Exploring

Numbers in the margin correspond with points of interest on the Nagasaki map.

Nagasaki is a beautiful harbor city that is small enough to walk around if you have the energy to face some of the steep inclines, which are similar to those in San Francisco. Most of the sights of interest and restaurant and shopping areas are located south of Nagasaki Station.

❺ The Glover Gardens, with its panoramic view of Nagasaki and the harbor, alongside 19th-century European-style buildings,

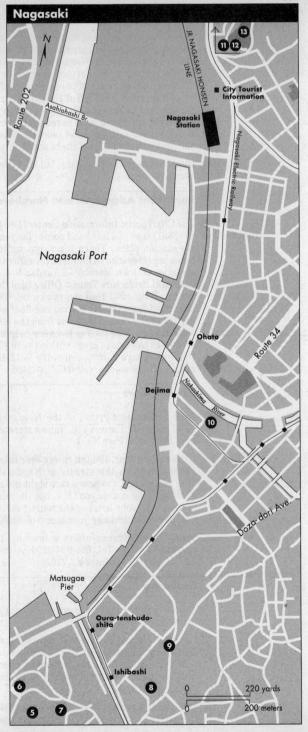

Nagasaki

City Tourist Information

Nagasaki Station

JR NAGASAKI HONSEN LINE

Nagasaki Electric Railway

Route 202

Asahiohashi Br.

N

Nagasaki Port

Ohato

Route 34

Dejima

Nakashima River

Doza-dori Ave.

Matsugae Pier

Oura-tenshudo-shita

Ishibashi

11 12

13

10

9

8

6

7

5

0   220 yards

0   200 meters

is a good place to begin your tour of Nagasaki. To get here, board the No. 1 streetcar from the JR station to the downtown stop, Tsuki-machi, and transfer (don't forget to collect a transfer ticket) to streetcar No. 5. Get off at the Oura-Tenshudo-shita stop (the last but one on the line). Take the side street to the right and then the second on your left up the hill. On your left, is the Tokyu Hotel, a place to keep in mind for afternoon tea, and on the right is an array of souvenir shops. Facing you, as you turn a corner on the hill will be the Oura Catholic Church. We will return here shortly.

The gardens feature Western-style houses built in the late 19th century. The main attraction is the Glover Mansion itself. This house, built in 1863, was the home of Thomas Glover, a British merchant who married a Japanese woman, settled in Nagasaki, introduced the first steam locomotive, and established the first mint in Japan. The house remains as it was in Glover's time, and his furniture and possessions are on display. The story for Puccini's opera *Madame Butterfly* is said to have been set here. Escalators going up the slopes toward the Glover Mansion are somewhat incongruous, but otherwise the grounds seem unspoiled and evoke the atmosphere of Japan's opening to the West in the 19th century. *Tel. 0958/22–8223. Admission:¥600. Open Mar.–Nov. 8–6 ; Dec.–Feb. 8:30–5 .*

Located just outside the exit of the Glover Gardens is the
❻ Jurokuban Mansion. Built in 1860 as accommodations for the American consular staff, it is now a museum that displays Dutch and Portuguese objects related to the history of early trade between these countries and Japan. *Tel. 0958/23–4260. Admission:¥400. Open Mar.–Nov. 8:30–6; Dec.–Feb. 8:30–5 .*

After you leave the Jurokuban Mansion, continue down the same street past the Glover Mansion for a few minutes; you will come across another 19th-century European-style structure,
❼ the **Oura Catholic Church,** the oldest Gothic-style building in Japan. The church was constructed in 1865 by a French missionary and was dedicated to the memory of the 26 Christians who were crucified in 1597 after Christianity was outlawed. The church, in addition to its architectural importance, features beautiful stained-glass windows. *Admission: ¥250. Open 8:30–6.*

As you leave the church and walk past the Ishibashi streetcar stop, you will see evidence that the Europeans were not the
❽ only foreign influence in Nagasaki. The **Tonjin-kan Chinese Mansion** was built in 1893 by the Chinese residents of Nagasaki. The hall now houses a gallery of Chinese crafts and souvenir shops. Although this is a favorite with many Japanese tourists, it is probably more popular for its many little shops than for its historic interest. *Admission:¥515. Open 8:30–5.*

After seeing the interiors of these 19th-century buildings, perhaps you may want to take a stroll. Head toward the station and pass it. Walk on the street behind the station, and you will no-
❾ tice a cobblestone slope known as the **Orandazaka** (Hollander Slope). It is a pleasant walk alongside wood houses built by 19th-century Dutch residents.

The walk along this slope will lead you to the Shimin Byoin Mae streetcar stop, located just in front of Nagasaki View Hospital. Board the streetcar and go to the Tsukimachi stop, where you

⑩ can see the original site of **Dejima,** the man-made island where the Dutch were allowed to land in the years when Japan maintained its isolationist policy. It is no longer an island, because the area has been land-filled, but there is a miniature reconstruction of the entire village and community of Dejima, as part of the **Dejima Historical Museum.** *Admission free. Open 9–5. Closed Mon.*

After viewing all of these picturesque sights, Nagasaki may seem to be a quaint port town that time and progress have somehow passed by, but it is important to remember that Nagasaki, along with Hiroshima, was one of the two places where atomic bombs were dropped. In order that the memory of this tragedy will live on, a **Peace Park** was built on the exact site of the epicenter of the August 9, 1945 atomic blast. In a blinding flash, 2.59 square miles were obliterated and 74,884 people were killed, with another 74,909 injured out of an estimated population of 204,000. And it was only a small bomb compared to present day atomic weapons. To get to this park, return to the Tsukimachi stop and take streetcar No.1 to the Matsuyamachi stop (If you are going to the Peace Park directly from the JR Station, take either streetcar No. 1 or No. 3 to the Matsuyamachi stop, about a 10-minute ride.) At one end of the park is a black pillar, grimly denoting the exact center of the blast. At the other end is a 32-foot statue of a male figure with one arm pointing horizontally, the other pointing toward the sky. The statue is rather ugly, and the message of the positioning of the arms is rather unclear. Every year on August 9 there is an antinuclear war demonstration at the Peace Park. *Admission free.*

⑫ Standing on the hill above the Peace Park is the **Nagasaki International Cultural Hall.** To reach it, climb the steps at the southern end of the park, past the Flame of Peace. Inside the hall, which looks like a prefabricated building from early post-war days, are displays of photos and objects demonstrating the devastation caused by the atomic bomb. The museum is far more impressive than the Peace Park itself. Walking through the hall is a sobering experience. Note the tiny corner on the third floor given to the foreign victims of the bomb dropped by the American B29 *Bockstar.* It notes that there were 500 Allied POWs interned in the middle of a factory site, although 200 of them had died of disease, malnutrition, and torture before the bomb was dropped. *Admission:* ¥ *50. Open 9–5.*

⑬ An appropriate finale to your visit to Nagasaki is **Nishizaka Hill,** a short walk from the Nagasaki train station. As you leave the front of the station, turn left and walk along the road next to the train tracks for a few minutes. Turn right on the first major road and you will be at Nishizaka Hill. In the early 16th century, Christian missionaries successfully converted many Japanese to Christianity. Japanese leaders feared the potential influence of Christianity and banned its practice in 1587. In 1597, 20 Japanese and six foreigners were crucified on Nishizaka Hill for refusing to renounce their religious beliefs. A monument was built in 1962 dedicated to the memory of the 26 martyrs, and a small museum documents the history of Christianity in Japan. *Admission:* ¥ *250. Open 9–5.*

Shopping

Hamanomachi, located not far from Dejima, is the major shopping district in the downtown area of Nagasaki. In this area you can find traditional crafts, antiques, and restaurants.

Gift Ideas **Castella cake.** Based on a Dutch cake, this dessert has long been the most commonly known Nagasaki product. The cake resembles a pound cake, has a moist top, and was popular in Nagasaki when baked goods were still unknown in the rest of Japan. **Fukusaya** is a bakery that has been in business since the beginning of the Meiji period (1868–1912). When you say "castella," most people think of this famous shop with its distinctive yellow packaging of the cake. Tokyoites would never return from a trip to Nagasaki without their Fukusaya castella. *3-1 Funadaikumachi, tel. 0958/21–2938. Open 8:30–8. Closed every 2nd Thurs.*

Glassware. Biidoro Bijutsukan is a museum featuring exhibits documenting the history of Nagasaki glassware, an art that was introduced by the Dutch during the Tokugawa period. Located near the Peace Park, the museum has a small gift shop. The museum annex has a more extensive selection of items for sale. *16-10 Hashiguchimachi, tel. 0958/43–0100; annex: 5-19 Hamanomachi, tel. 0958/27–0100. Open 9–5.*

Tortoiseshell items. Nagasaki has always been well known for its tortoiseshell accessories. Hair ornaments, cuff links, and tie pins are popular souvenirs from Nagasaki. The best-known store in Hamanomachi for tortoiseshell is the **Ezaki Bekko-ten.** This store has a history of 270 years. In addition to a store, it has a workshop where you can see how tortoiseshell is crafted into various accessories, and a gallery that displays tortoiseshell items, old and new. (U.S. citizens should keep in mind that tortoiseshell items may not pass through U.S. customs.) *7-13 Uonomachi, tel. 0958/21–0328. Open 9–8.*

Kumamoto

Numbers in the margin correspond with points of interest on the Kyushu map.

⑭ In the years of the Tokugawa Shogunate (1603–1868), **Kumamoto** was one of Japan's major centers of power. The main attractions in Kumamoto, the castle and the landscaped gardens of Suizenji-Koen Park, date from this period and are among the most famous in Japan. Kumamoto may no longer be a major political center, but, with its broad avenues lined with countless trees, it is an extremely attractive city and is one of considerable historic interest.

Arriving and Departing

By Plane Five daily flights connect Haneda Airport (Tokyo) with Kumamoto Airport (1 hour, 40 minutes). ANA and Japan Air System (JAS) fly between Tokyo and Kumamoto. From Osaka Airport, ANA has four flights daily (1 hour).

Between the Airport and Center City A regular bus service connects the airport with the JR Kumamoto Station. The bus takes 55 minutes and costs ¥670.

By Train Japan Railways offers a limited express train that stops in Kumamoto en route to Kagoshima (1½ hours). From Nagasaki, take the train to Shimabara, board a one-hour ferry across the Ariake Bay to Misumi, then take the train to Kumamoto. JR Rail Pass holders may prefer to take the train to Tosu, change, and go to Kumamoto (3 hours total).

By Bus From Nagasaki Bus Terminal, you can take a four-hour bus trip to Kumamoto. The bus goes as far as Shimabara, after which you board a ferry across the Ariake Bay for one hour to Misumi, then take the bus directly to Kumamoto Kotsu Center. The cost of this journey, which takes you through some of Kyushu's most beautiful scenery, is ¥2,650 including the ferry ride.

Getting Around

By Streetcar The easiest way to get around Kumamoto is by streetcar. There are two streetcar lines that connect the major areas of the city. When you board the streetcar, take a ticket. When you get off, you will pay a fare that depends on the distance traveled. The chart of the fares is displayed at the front to the left of the driver. A streetcar stop, Kumamoto Eki-mae, is in front of the JR Kumamoto Station, and it is a good 10-minute ride into downtown. Fare: ¥160.

By Bus The main bus terminal is the Kotsu Center, located within a few minutes' walking distance of Kumamoto Castle. Although the buses travel all over the city, the routes are more complicated than those of the streetcars.

Important Addresses and Numbers

Tourist Information City Information Office, 3-15-1 Kasuga, tel. 096/352–3743. This office is in a booth in front of the JR station, next to the streetcar stop. Open 9–5.

Exploring

Unlike many other Japanese cities, there is very little activity around the JR station. Shops, restaurants, and hotels cluster downtown under the shadow of the castle. The heart of the town is a broad shopping arcade from which small streets branch off. It comes alive at night with neon lights advertising restaurants and bars.

Kumamotojo Castle, located in the heart of downtown Kumamoto, is where most people begin their tour of Kumamoto City. To get to the castle, board streetcar #2, get off at the Kumamoto-jo-mae stop and walk up a tree-lined slope toward the castle. Kumamotojo was first built in 1607 under the auspices of Kiyomasa Kato, feudal lord of this region. Especially famous for its unique and massive curved walls, which warded off many an attack, it is often referred to as Ginkojo Castle, named after a giant ginko tree that was supposedly planted by Lord Kato. Much of the original castle was destroyed in 1877, when it was attacked by an army from Kagoshima led by Saigo Takamori. It was rebuilt in 1960.

Often, reconstructed buildings are of little interest, but this castle of concrete is an excellent example of reconstruction that manages to evoke the magnificence of the original. By walking around the expansive grounds, you can get a true sense of the grandeur of feudal Japan. Inside Kumamotojo is a museum for those who are interested in feudal history. It exhibits relics such as samurai armor and palanquins. As you look at the displays, you cannot help but imagine samurai in full regalia, protecting their lord. From the top floor there is an excellent view of Kumamoto. If time permits further exploration of the grounds, go to the Higo Gardens; they are filled with lovely flowers and are a peaceful place to conclude your visit. *Admission: ¥200 (grounds), ¥300 (castle). Open Apr.–Sept. 8:30–5:30; Oct.–Mar. 8:30–4:30.*

To the west of the castle in a modern, redbrick building is the **Kumamoto-keuritsu Bijutsukan** (Prefectual Art Museum) that in the spring and autumn exhibits the famous Hosokawa collection. Be sure to see the full-scale models of the burial chambers with Kumamoto's design of painted geometrical shapes. *Admission: ¥300. Open 9:30–4:30. Closed Mon.*

From the castle, take either the #2 or #3 streetcar to the Suizenji-Koen-mae stop, in front of the **Suizenji-Koen Park.** It features a 300-year-old garden that is a tribute to the art of landscape gardening. The garden was originally created in 1632 by the Hosokawa clan as part of the grounds of their villa. Although the park is often crowded with tour groups and lacks a certain serenity, there are still elements of beauty where the artistry of man has worked with nature. A part of the garden with ponds and small artificial mounds recreates the 53 stations of the Tokkaido (the route between Edo and Kyoto) and its prominent features such as Lake Biwa and Mt. Fuji. *Admission: ¥200. Open 7–6.*

On the hill to the west of town is Honmyo-ji, a Nichiren temple built by Kato Kiyomasa. It is reached by streetcar from the Kumamoto JR station. Kiyomasa is buried here in the tomb at the top of a flight of stairs so that his spirit may look across at eye level to the donjon of his castle, Kumamoto-jo. The temple's museum contains Kiyomasa's personal effects, including the helmet that he wore while campaigning in Korea for his master, Toyotomi Hideyoshi. *Admission to museum: ¥200. Open 9–4:30. Closed Mon.*

Time Out Take a break in the park at the small, old-fashioned teahouse located by the garden's pond. Here, for a small fee, you can sip green tea as you sit on tatami mats and appreciate the exquisite view. If you get hungry, numerous food stalls in the park offer light snacks. You may very well be in need of refreshment, because a visit to Suizenji-Koen takes at least several hours; it is possible to spend an entire day here.

Off The Beaten Track

If you have time, you may want to go south from Kumamoto to Kagoshima. The scenic, three-hour train ride to Nishi-Kagoshima passes mountains on the left and the sea on the right. Downtown is a five-minute walk from the JR station.

The modern city of *Kagoshima* has few sightseeing attractions. It is usually a jumping-off point to the surrounding country and Okinawa islands, or a stopover on the train ride across to Kyushu's east coast. The **Park Hotel,** two minutes from Nishi-Kagoshima Station, has reasonable rates, clean, efficient rooms, a pleasant coffee lounge, a Japanese restaurant, and a helpful staff. (15-24 Chuo-machi, Kagoshima 890, tel. 0992/51-1100.) In the downtown entertainment district you'll find **Edo-ko Sushi**, an excellent sushi bar (counter seating and two tables with tatami seating) with a very hospitable owner. *Bunka St., 2–16 Sannichi-cho, tel. 0992/25–1890. Take the 1st right off Yubudo (the wide shopping-arcade street), and Edo-ko is the last restaurant on the left. Moderate.*

Shopping

One of Kumamoto's most famous products is **higo zogan,** a form of metalwork consisting of black steel inlaid with silver and gold, creating a delicate yet striking pattern. Originally an ornamentation technique for samurai armor, it is now used mostly in jewelry and other accessories. Another popular local product is the **Yamaga doro,** a lantern of gold paper. On August 16, as part of an annual festival, young women carry these gold lanterns through the streets of Kumamoto.

Shimatori Shopping Arcade, located by the Kumamotojo Castle, is a good place to find everything from toothpaste to local crafts. One of the best places to get higo zogan, Yamaga doro, and other local crafts is the **Kumamoto Traditional Crafts Center.** A combination gallery and shop, the center displays crafts from all over Kumamoto Prefecture. It is located next to the Kumamoto Castle Hotel. *3-35 Chiga-jo, tel. 096/324–4930. Open 9–5. Closed Mon.*

Mt. Aso

⓯ On the way to **Mt. Aso** you pass through Kyushu's radiant green countryside. As you look upon farmers bent over their rice fields, bamboo groves, and other idyllic sights, you have a sense of the peaceful relationship between man and nature. This serene image quickly fades when you arrive at the smoking and rumbling volcano of Mt. Aso; here you become aware of the power of nature and the mortality of man.

Mt. Aso is, in fact, a series of five volcanic peaks, one of which, Mt. Nakadake, is still active. The five peaks, along with lakes and fields at its base, all form a beautiful national park. Mt. Aso can be seen either on a day trip from Kumamoto or on a stop on the way from Kumamoto to Beppu. If you are interested in spending more time relaxing in the beautiful national park, you can stay in the many mountain pensions on the other side of Mt. Aso (*see* Lodging, below).

Arriving and Departing

By Train The JR Hohi Line runs between Kumamoto Station and Aso Station (1 hour). From the Aso Station to Beppu there are three JR express trains daily (2½ hours). From the Aso Station, you must board a bus outside the JR station to get to the Aso Nishi Ropeway Station (40 min; fare: ¥570). The ropeway leads you to the top of the crater in four minutes. Fare: ¥820.

By Bus Buses leaving from the Kumamoto Kotsu Bus terminal go directly to the Aso Nishi Ropeway Station (1½ hours).

Exploring

Although Mt. Aso National Park is very pleasant, the main reason to come here is to see the crater of the one active volcano, Nakadake. In order to get to the crater, board one of the seven daily buses from in front of the Aso JR station. It is better to begin your trip well before noon, because the last buses for the Aso Nishi Ropeway Station leave mid-afternoon. The 40-minute scenic ride leads you to the Aso Nichi Ropeway Station. From there you board the ropeway that takes you in a matter of minutes to the top of Mt. Nakadake.

From the inside of the largest crater of Mt. Nakadake, which is 600 meters (1,968 feet) across and 160 meters (525 feet) deep, you hear the rumblings of the volcano and see billowing smoke. It is fascinating and yet terrifying to look at this crater and realize that someday it could erupt. Sometimes the volcano does become overexcited, and visitors can't view it up close, so check at Kumamoto or Beppu before you make this excursion. Instead of taking the ropeway back, you can walk along a path that leads you back to the ropeway station. If you are really up for a hike taking several hours, you can take a path that takes you to Mt. Nakadake and down to the Sensuikyo Gorge. From there you walk to the Miyaji JR station, the next stop after Aso Station. Because most visitors to the mountain do not choose to take this arduous route, the paths are delightfully uncrowded, and the views of the live crater from afar and of the gorge are awe-inspiring.

Beppu

After all your travels, an enjoyable way to rest your weary body is by soaking in a hot spring. One of the most popular hot-spring resorts in all of Japan, **Beppu** provides over 3,000 sources of hot water not only to the hotels and inns but also to private homes. Beppu is a garish town with neon lights, amusement parks, Pachinko halls by the dozen, and souvenir shops. These ingredients, its location—the sea in the foreground and mountains to its rear—and the variety of hot mineral springs make it a favorite vacation spot for the Japanese. Many tourists come here and do not leave their hotel or inn to see any of the local sights. The leisurely pace of this resort is indicated by the many Japanese tourists walking around the streets in their *yukata* cotton kimonos, casually strolling and looking as though they have not a care in the world.

The more sophisticated Westerner is likely to find Beppu irritatingly expensive, tawdry, and over–commercialized and might prefer to experience a hot springs resort in more elegant surroundings, such as Yufuin, situated on a highland plateau, 60 minutes by bus from Beppu or 90 minutes by the JR Kyudai line from Hita. Yufuin has one of the country's charming traditional inns, Tamanoyu (tel. 0977/84–2158, Very Expensive) as well as several other ryokans and minshukus, such as Minshuku Nakaya (tel. 0977/84–3835).

Arriving and Departing

By Plane The closest airport to Beppu is the Oita Airport, which is served by ANA and JAS domestic flights from the Haneda Airport in Tokyo (1 hour, 40 minutes) and from Osaka Airport (1 hour).

Between the Airport and Center City Buses leave regularly from the airport to Beppu City. The one-hour trip costs ¥1,300 and terminates at Kitahama bus stop on the bay side of Beppu's main street.

By Train The Hohi Main Line travels between Kumamoto and Beppu (3 hours, 20 minutes). On the way, you can stop on the Hohi Main Line at Mt. Aso. The Nichirin Limited Express Train runs between Beppu and Hakata Station in Fukuoka. Over 10 trains travel the route daily (2½ hours).

By Bus Buses travel between Kumamoto and Beppu (3½ hours) and between Mt. Aso and Beppu on the Trans-Kyushu Highway (3 hours). Sightseeing buses operated by the Kyushu Kokusai Kanko Bus Company travel regularly between Beppu and Kumamoto, stopping at Mt. Aso.

By Boat Three ferries (two of which make calls at Matsuyama and Imabari or Takamatsu and Sakaide, all on Shikoku), connect Beppu with Osaka and Kobe on the Kansai Kisen Line (in Tokyo, tel. 03/274–4271; in Osaka, tel. 06/572–5181); (in Beppu, tel. 0977/22–1311). These overnight ferries leave in the early evening (the direct ferry for Osaka leaves at 7:20 PM and arrives at 8:20 AM. Fare: ¥5,870, second class). Reservations are necessary for first class. A ferry to Hiroshima leaves Beppu at 2 PM and arrives at Hiroshima 7 PM and leaves Hiroshima at 9:30 PM, arriving in Beppu at 6 AM. Fare: ¥3,600–¥5,550.

Getting Around

By Bus Regular buses travel to most places of interest in Beppu. The main bus terminal, Kitahama Bus Station, is just down the road from the JR Beppu Station.

By Taxi Because most of the sights in Beppu are relatively close to one another, this is one of the few places in Japan that it may be worthwhile simply to hop in a taxi. Fares range from ¥1,000 to ¥3,000. Hiring a taxi for two hours to visit the major thermal pools would run approximately ¥5,000, after negotiation.

Important Addresses and Numbers

Beppu City Information Office (12-13 Ekimae-cho, tel. 0977/24–2838) is located in Beppu Station and has very limited information for foreign tourists. Open 9–6. **Foreign Tourist Information Service** (Furosen 2F, 7–16 Chuomachi, Beppu City, 874 Oita-gun, tel. 0977/23–1119) is located four minutes from the station—use the map posted on the City Information Booth in the JR station. This office has an enthusiastic volunteer staff. Open Monday–Saturday 10–4.

Guided Tours

A regular sightseeing bus service, leaving from Kitahama Bus Station, located just east of the Beppu JR station, covers most of the major sights in the area. The tour lasts about 2½ hours. Although an English-speaking guide is not always available, most of the sights are self-explanatory.

Exploring

Beppu is a resort area; the main attractions are the hot springs. A few sights in Beppu are worth seeing, though many people choose to bypass them, and just recline and relax.

If you are tired of inactivity and want to see the sights, the first recommended stop is the **Eight Hells,** the Kannawa section of Beppu. Take bus Nos. 15, 16, 17, 41, or 43 from the stop across from the JR station for the 30-minute trip to Kamenoi Bus Station. Fare: ¥310. This mandatory sight for all tourists consists of eight distinctive hot springs. One of the springs, **Chino-ike Jigoku** (Blood Pond Hell), is a boiling spring with red gurgling water. The vapors from this spring are purported to have curative powers for skin diseases. **Umi Jugoku** (Sea Hell) features not only water the color of the ocean, but also tropical plants. **Oniyama Jigoku** (Devil Mountain Hell) is a place where crocodiles are bred. An entertaining aspect of the Eight Hells are the many vendors nearby who try to sell their wares, such as eggs placed in baskets and boiled in the water. Although it is fascinating to see just how *hot* hot springs can be, keep in mind that this very popular attraction is crowded year-round. Each hot spring charges ¥300 admission, but a combined ticket for ¥1,300 will admit you to all eight. Do not bother with Hon Bozu Jigoku. It is having a period of inactivity. After your tour of the springs, take a bath at Hyotan Onsen, across the road from Kamenoi Bus Terminal for buses returning to Beppu. This is one of the more interesting thermal baths. The pool is outdoors, with waterfalls, hot stones, and sand. *Admission: ¥500. Open daily 7 AM–9 PM.*

The other main sight near Beppu is **Takasakiyama Monkey Park,** the home of 1,900 monkeys. To get there, take a bus from Kitahama Bus Station, located just down the road from the Beppu JR station. The bus ride lasts about 10 minutes. These once-wild monkeys were a problem for local farmers, but now they are domesticated. The monkeys are divided into three groups, each carefully guarding their territory. Observation of the hierarchy within each group is fascinating: for example, it is easy to determine which monkey is the leader because he stands on higher ground than his subordinates. This park is particularly fun for children who are not put off by the striking resemblance in the behavior of monkeys and humans. *Tel. 0975/ 32–5010. Admission: ¥500. Open 8–5.*

All hotels and inns in Beppu will have baths, but if you want to spend a day in a veritable amusement park of hot springs, the **Suginoi Palace,** a part of the Suginoi Hotel, is quite a spectacle. A variety of hot springs to soak in are available at this indoor complex, such as a sand bath, a saltwater bath, and many others. There is also a vast souvenir-shopping complex, with electronic games—quite ghastly, but a place to visit once. *Admission: ¥2,000 (see* Lodging, below).

Other attractions in Beppu include the **Beppu Ropeway** up to Mount Tsunumi for views over the city and bay (take bus 2, 34, 36 or 37 from Beppu Station and then the 10-minute ropeway to the top. Cost: ¥1,400. Open 9–5) and the **Marine Palace Aquarium** (Admission: ¥1,000. Open daily 8–5). Both have more appeal for Japanese vacationers than for foreign tourists. The small **Take-no Museum** in the center of town exhibits Beppu's celebrated crafts made from bamboo (tel. 0977/25–7776. Admission: ¥300. Open 8:30–6). You can purchase bamboo objects in Kishi-mae, the adjoining shop.

Dining

Until the 20th century, Kyushu was the international center of Japan. Certain Kyushu dishes, not surprisingly, show the influence of China and Europe. Tempura, for example, is often thought of as a standard Japanese dish; in fact, it was introduced by Europeans to Kyushu in the 17th century.

Particularly in Nagasaki, the influence of foreign cuisines is still apparent. In addition to these international dishes, many regions in Kyushu have special dishes that incorporate the food available in that locale.

Beppu is famous for its delicious seafood. Because it is a hot-spring resort town, most people tend to remain in their hotels or inns even for meals. Many of the lodgings available provide fresh, locally caught fish. One particularly popular local dish is **fugu** (blowfish).

Fukuoka, Kyushu's largest city, has a wide range of excellent Japanese and Western restaurants. Many of the best Western restaurants are located in hotels. Fukuoka is well known for its **Hakata ramen,** noodles with a stronger flavored soup than in other parts of Japan. It is also known for its *ikesu* restaurants, places that have a fish tank from which you can select the fish you want to eat, guaranteeing its freshness.

Adventurous eaters will enjoy the challenge of the regional specialty of Kumamoto, **horse meat.** The horse meat is served roasted, fried, and even raw. Another Kumamoto delicacy is called **dengaku,** tofu or fish covered by a strong bean paste and grilled. Dengaku is a good example of Kyushu cuisine with strong flavors, unlike the very delicate taste of food from Kyoto, for example.

Nagasaki is really the place where one gets a sense of the many cuisines that have influenced Kyushu dining. One dish, available only in Nagasaki, and with distinct Chinese, European, and Japanese influences, is **shippoku.** Shippoku is actually a variety of dishes that, when combined, make a full meal. Dinners center on a fish-soup base with European flavorings, to which many foods are added, including stewed chunks of pork cubes prepared Chinese-style, marinated in ginger and soy sauce; rice cakes; and a variety of vegetables. Usually, shippoku is served as one large communal dish, which is unusual in Japan. (In the traditional way of serving and eating Japanese food, individual portions are prepared.) Another distinctive Nagasaki dish is **champon,** heavy Chinese-style noodles in a soup. Not surprisingly, Nagasaki also has some of the best Western restaurants in Kyushu.

A 3% federal consumer tax is added to all restaurant bills. Another 3% local tax is added to the bill if it exceeds ¥5,000. At more expensive restaurants, a 10%–15% service charge is also added to the bill.

The most highly recommended restaurants for each city are indicated by a star ★.

Category	Cost*
Very Expensive	over ¥9,000
Expensive	¥6,000–¥9,000
Moderate	¥3,000–¥6,000
Inexpensive	under ¥3,000

*Cost is per person without tax, service, or drinks

Credit Cards The following credit card abbreviations are used: AE, American Express; DC, Diners Club; MC, MasterCard; V, Visa.

Beppu

Fugumatsu. This small, popular restaurant, with a simple, Japanese-style interior, has counters, tables, and private rooms. Its specialty is *fugu* (blowfish), which is a favorite in the area. Fugu is a potentially poisonous fish that restaurants must be licensed to serve. In the summer a type of *karei* fish is served that can only be caught in Beppu Bay. Fugumatsu has courses starting at ¥5,000. Upon your request you can have less- or more-expensive food; the restaurant will adjust to your budget. It is one block north of the Tokiwa department store and one block from the bay. *3-6-14 Kitahama, tel. 0977/21–1717. Reservations for parties of 10 or more only. Dress: informal. No credit cards. Moderate–Expensive.*

Fukuoka

Ikesu Kawataro. Picture a large tank full of edible fish in the middle of a restaurant, and you've imagined Ikesu Kawataro. This large establishment offers counters, Japanese-style rooms with tatami mats, and regular tables. The tatami section, if you can bear sitting on the floor for the duration of the meal, is the most pleasant, because the other areas of the restaurant tend to be rather noisy. Try any of the sashimi (raw fish) dishes; they will be remarkably fresh. If you order certain kinds of fish and shrimp, they will still be wriggling on your plate when served. *1-6-6 Nakasu, Hakata-ku, tel. 092/271–2133. Reservations not required. Dress: informal. DC, MC, V. Very Expensive.*

Gyosai. This restaurant has an excellent selection of seafood. The humble atmosphere of this place belies the quality of the food. Order any of the sashimi dishes or steamed fish. Although the staff do not speak much English, they are very helpful, and gestures and a smile will go a long way. This restaurant has the added advantage of being within walking distance of the Hakata Station. *2-2-12 Ekimae, Hakata-ku, tel. 092/441–9780. No reservations. Dress: informal. No credit cards. Moderate.*

Ichiki. If you are interested in checking out Japanese nightlife but are not sure where to go, try this bar/restaurant and see how many Japanese spend their recreational evenings. The atmosphere is relaxed and friendly, and as the evening wears on, it is more likely than not that one of your Japanese neighbors will attempt to make your acquaintance. Try the *kushi yaki*, a sort of Japanese shish kebab with fish, meat, and vegetables, fried on a hot flat grill and served on a wood skewer. This is not a restaurant where you just sit down and order your meal, but rather a place where you relax for the evening, have a few beers, and order a few small dishes at a time. The price range for each dish is ¥400–¥1,000. *1-2-10 Maizara, Chuo-ku, tel. 092/751–5591. No reservations. Dress: informal. No credit cards. Inexpensive.*

Kumamoto

Loire. If you are tired of Japanese food and want a good French meal, try this elegant, spacious restaurant located on the 11th floor of the Kumamoto Castle Hotel. Loire has an excellent view of Kumamotojo Castle. The set-course meals, which feature fish or meat dishes, change every month. During some months, special all-you-can-eat buffets are available. The desserts are varied, and are recommended. Those who do not feel like paying so much for the view can instead sample the reasonably priced lunches. *4-2 Jotomachi, tel. 096/326–3311. Reservations advised. Dress: informal. AE, DC, MC, V. Very Expensive.*

★ **Togasaku Honten.** Formal Japanese cuisine is at its best in this restaurant, which serves a set menu. The dinners, served at low, Japanese-style tables, consist of several small courses of fish, meat, tofu, and vegetables, which add up to a very filling meal. The prices are high, but your yen is well spent, because the meals not only are tasty but are presented with exquisite beauty. Togasaku Honten overlooks a peaceful garden, and the staff is formal and polite without being stiff. Ask for a table with a view when you make your reservations. *1-15-3 Hamazuno, tel. 096/353–4171. Reservations required. Jacket and tie required. DC, MC, V. No lunch. Very Expensive.*

A branch of Togasaku Honten with good food at slightly lower prices is located right by the Suizenji-Koen Park. This restaurant is more informal and has Western-style tables. *Togasaku Suizenji-koen, Tsuchiyama Bldg., 2F. 3-4 Suizenji-koen, tel. 096/385–5151. Reservations recommended. Dress: informal. DC, MC, V. No lunch. Expensive.*

Mutsugoro. This casual dining spot, with light-color paper-and-wood walls, is located in the basement of the Green Hotel. Curious, adventurous eaters will note that this restaurant serves horse meat in 40 different ways, including raw horse-meat sashimi and fried horse meat. If you go and decide that these specialties are not to your taste, you can choose from a variety of seafood dishes. As is the case with many informal Japanese restaurants, you order many small dishes. Each dish is about ¥800–¥1,000; for a full meal, you will probably want four or five dishes. *12-11 Hanabata-cho, tel. 096/356–3256. No reservations. Dress: informal. No credit cards. No lunch. Moderate.*

Senri. Couple a visit to the beautiful Suizenji-Koen Park with lunch or dinner at Senri, situated right in the gardens. Senri serves a wide variety of dishes, including seafood, eel, and horse-meat sashimi. Although Western-style tables and chairs are available, the tatami rooms and low tables are really more in keeping with the ambience of the gardens. Even if you do not choose to have a meal here, you can get a light snack or an appetizer. *7-17 Suizenji, tel. 096/384–1824. No reservations. Dress: informal. No credit cards. Moderate.*

Nagasaki

Harbin. This establishment serves Continental cuisine in a dark, romantic setting. The sauces are a bit heavy, and the food is slightly overcooked, but perhaps the chef is only trying to re-create the dishes as they would be served in Europe. It is not hard to imagine the residents of the 19th-century Western-style houses of Nagasaki eating at this restaurant. *2-27 Kozen-machi, tel. 0958/22–7433. Reservations advised. Dress: informal, although most guests wear jackets. AE. Very Expensive.*

Kagetsu. This quiet establishment, set on top of a hill, is Nagasaki's most prestigious restaurant. Dishes are served in the kaiseki manner, but the menu combines Japanese and Chinese cuisine. The building that houses Kagetsu was visited long ago by the Meiji Restoration leader, Ryoma Sakamoto. According to local legend, Sakamoto, while involved in a fight, slashed his sword into a wood pillar and left a gash that is still visible in the restaurant today. *2-1 Maruyama-cho, tel. 0958/22–0191. Reservations advised. Jacket and tie required. AE, DC, MC, V. Very Expensive.*

Fukiro. In this roomy Japanese restaurant with tatami mats and shoji screens, some of the best shippoku in Nagasaki is served. The shippoku combines tasty morsels of Chinese and Japanese food, all presented in an aesthetically pleasing way. To get to Fukiro, you must first walk up a steep set of stone steps. The restaurant is an old Japanese-style building, with a tiled roof and long wooden beams. *146 Kami-nishiyama-machi, tel. 0958/22–0253. Reservations advised. Jacket required. DC. Closed Sun. Expensive.*

★ **Shikairo.** This large restaurant, with its garish decor, is the birthplace of the well-known Nagasaki champon noodles, which are the house specialty. With a capacity to seat 1,500, Shikairo has an extensive menu. The seafood dishes are particularly good, and the beef with bamboo shoots is recommended; the menu features many excellent Chinese dishes from the Fukien region—a surprise, because most Chinese food in Japan is rather bland. The service is somewhat brusque by Japanese standards. *4-5 Matsugae-machi, tel. 0958/822–1296. Dress: informal. Reservations accepted. DC. Inexpensive–Moderate.*

Hamakatsu. Fans of the Japanese dish *tonkatsu* (fried pork cutlets) will enjoy the Nagasaki version, which uses ground pork mixed with scallions. Hamakatsu specializes in this local treat. Other dishes are available, but most diners stick with the tonkatsu, especially because it is one of the lower-priced dishes on the menu. *1-14 Kajiya-machi, tel. 0958/23–2316. No reservations. Dress: informal. No credit cards. Inexpensive.*

Lodging

Accommodations in Kyushu are plentiful; because the number of tourist and business travelers is limited, it is nearly always possible to get reservations. Fukuoka has major hotels with excellent facilities. Nagasaki features grand old hotels and ryokans that, like the city itself, seem to be frozen in the 19th century.

Travelers looking for a more active vacation may choose to spend a few days in the Mt. Aso region at a pension. Pensions are similar to bed-and-breakfasts, with supper served as well.

The pensions near Aso are set in the mountains and are located near trails for hiking. Some also offer tennis courts.

A 3% federal consumer tax is added to all hotel bills. Another 3% local tax is added to the bill if it exceeds ¥10,000. At most hotels, a 10%–15% service charge is added to the total bill. Tipping is not the custom.

The most highly recommended accommodations for each city are indicated by a star ★.

Category	Cost*
Very Expensive	over ¥20,000
Expensive	¥15,000–¥20,000
Moderate	¥10,000–¥15,000
Inexpensive	under ¥10,000

Cost is for double room, without tax or service

Beppu

Suginoi Hotel. More than just a hotel, this is a miniresort. Once you arrive and check in, you may not feel any need to go anywhere else. The hotel is situated on a hill with a panoramic view of the city and the ocean. The Suginoi Palace is a building connected to the hotel, which features a variety of hot springs, such as the "Dream Public Bath" and the "Flower Public Bath." The baths are located in huge buildings, with unique types of hot springs. Once you wash off, you proceed into a room full of plants and trees. You can soak in a standard hot spring, bury yourself in warm sand, or, if you get bored with hot water, move to the swimming pool. Breakfast and dinner are included in the price of the accommodations, and there are both Western- and Japanese-style buffets where the food is bountiful. Guests tend to wander around the hotel and attend meals in their *yukata* (cotton kimono). The rooms are a welcome break from the opulence of the rest of the hotel—they are rather austere in decoration. If a quiet and refined experience is what you seek, this is not the right choice. It feels a little bit like a Japanese Las Vegas. Nevertheless, this is the most popular hotel in all of Beppu. A labor dispute shut down the hotel for 1989 and part of 1990. However, the hotel was able to reopen in 1991. *Kankaiji-onsen, Beppu, tel. 0977/24–1141, fax 0977/21–0010. 600 rooms (80 Western style). Facilities: shopping arcade, conference room, beauty parlor, bowling, restaurant, Japanese banquet hall, pool, children's playground. AE, DC, MC, V. Very Expensive.*

Beppu Kankaiso. This ryokan used to be a hotel with many Japanese-style rooms. It now serves two meals, inclusive in the price of accommodations. The rooms are large and clean. The Japanese rooms can sleep as many as five, which cuts down on the cost per head. Although the baths here are nothing special, the ryokans are close enough to the Suginoi Hotel that it is easy to pay the daily admission of around ¥2,000 and take advantage of their facilities. The food in the Japanese restaurant Orion is excellent. *Kankaiji-onsen, Beppu, tel. 0977/23–1221, fax 0977/21–6285. 51 rooms (9 Western style). Facilities: Japanese restaurant. AE, DC, V. Expensive.*

★ **Sakaeya.** Many minshukus are drab concrete buildings that are different from youth hostels only in that they have private rooms. This minshuku is a rare gem in a beautiful old wooden building with surprisingly low rates, which include meals. The meals consist of straightforward Japanese food with fish and rice, but they are prepared in the oven in the backyard, which is heated from the hot springs. Only one public bath is available, but as you relax in it with your fellow guests, you have a sense that this is how the Japanese have been enjoying the wonders of hot springs for centuries. This minshuku is small and is gaining popularity quickly, so make reservations. To reach the inn, take bus Nos. 16, 17, 24, or 25 from Beppu Station. *Idonikumi, Ida, Kannawa, Beppu, tel. 0977/66–6234. 10 rooms. No credit cards. Inexpensive.*

Fukuoka

Hotel New Otani Hakata. As is the case with the New Otani hotels throughout Japan, this is a luxury hotel. The rooms are spacious and are decorated in muted tones. This is one of the few hotels in all of Kyushu where you can expect most of the staff to speak English. One very unusual feature is that they offer free baby-sitting services. *1-1-2 Watanabe-dori, Chuo-ku, Fukuoka, tel. 092/714–1111, fax 092/715–5658. 423 rooms. Facilities: bars, Chinese, Japanese, and French restaurants, barber shop, beauty parlor, massage room, shopping arcade, travel agency, florist, art gallery, tea-ceremony room, indoor pool. AE, DC, MC, V. Very Expensive.*

Fukuoka Yamanoue Hotel. The name of this hotel means "on a mountain," and it is on a hill above Fukuoka, with excellent views of the ocean on one side and the city on the other. The hotel is a little out of the way—10 minutes from Hakata Station by taxi or bus (catch the Nishitetsu #56 or #57)—but the spectacular views make the travel time worthwhile. The service is quietly polite and extremely helpful. The rooms are on the small side, but not uncomfortably so. *1-1-33 Terakuni, Chuo-ku, Fukuoka, tel. 092/771–2131, fax 092/771–8888. 55 rooms. Facilities: tennis courts, large public bath, Japanese and Western restaurants. AE, DC, MC, V. Expensive.*

★ **Clio Court Hotel.** The new hotel is the best value in Fukuoka. Conveniently located across the street from Hakata Station (Shinkansen–side), it has remarkably attractive rooms furnished with great care. They are decorated in a variety of styles, such as art deco and early American. Request a room with a window—rooms #1202 and #1203 are good choices. Some tea-ceremony rooms are modeled on designs by Kamiya Sotan and Hosakawa-Sansai, both disciples of the founder of the tea ceremony, Sen-no Rikyu. Another tea-ceremony room is designed with Western-style chairs for foreigners. You can request the type of room decor you prefer when you make your reservation. One of the hotel's most pleasant features is the courtyard on the 13th floor that serves as a beer garden in the summer. One floor higher is the hotel's revolving restaurant serving steak and seafood cooked Western of Japanese style. In 60 minutes, you've seen all of Fukuoka! *5-3, Hakata-eki-chuo-gai, Hakata-ku, Fukuoka, tel. 092/472–1111, fax 092/474–3222. 194 rooms. Facilities: French, Chinese, and Japanese restaurants; steak house, English-style bar, café bar, sushi* *bar, florist, art gallery, rooms for the handicapped. AE, DC, MC, V. Moderate.*

Hakata Green Hotel. This is a standard business hotel with clean rooms that are small and characterless; it's nevertheless a good value. The advantage of this establishment is that it is just a few minutes' walk from Hakata Station. It has a Japanese restaurant called Ginroku that has decent food at low prices, and a Western restaurant that should be avoided, except for the breakfast, which at a mere ¥600 is quite good. *3-11 Hakata-eki-chuo-gai, Hakata-ku, Fukuoka, tel. 092/451-4111, fax 092/451-4508. Facilities: Japanese- and Western-style restaurants. AE, DC, MC, V. Inexpensive.*

Suehiro Inn. For inexpensive lodgings, this member of the Japanese Inn Group offers small tatami rooms, three with private bath. Only Japanese food is served in the small dining room, but guests are not required to eat at the inn. The two-story wooden inn, across from Nishitetsu Zasshonokuma Station, is four subway stops from downtown. *2-1-9, Minami-Honmachi, Hakata—ku, Fukuoka City 816, tel. 092/581-0306. 12 rooms. Facilities: Japanese food available. AE, MC, V. Inexpensive.*

Kumamoto

Kumamoto Castle Hotel. This hotel is conveniently situated near the Kumamotojo Castle and the downtown district. Request a room with a view of the castle, if possible. The Kumamoto Castle is quiet with rooms a cut above those of business hotels. However, not much of the staff speaks English. *4-2 Jotomachi, Kumamoto, tel. 096/326-3311, fax 096/326-3324. 208 rooms. Facilities: Chinese, Japanese, and French restaurants; coffee shop. AE, DC, V. Moderate.*

New Sky Hotel. Managed by the ANA group, in many ways the New Sky is the best lodging Kumamoto has to offer. In addition to several good restaurants, the hotel maintains a relationship with a health club down the street so that its guests can use the pool for ¥700, or all facilities for ¥1,500. The rooms are small, but they are bright and cheerful. *2 Amidajicho, Kumamoto, tel. 096/354-2111, fax 096/354-8973. 358 rooms. Facilities: Chinese, Japanese, and French restaurants; beauty salon, barber shop. AE, DC, MC, V. Moderate.*

Fujie. On the main street leading directly away from the station, this is a smart business hotel with Western single rooms and attractive Japanese double rooms. The lobby lounge faces a Japanese garden and the restaurant serves well-presented Japanese food. Service is personable and friendly, though the English language in not the staff's strong point. *2-2 Kasuga, Kumamoto 860, tel. 096/353-1101, fax 096/322-2671. 47 rooms. Facilities: restaurant, garden. AE, V. Moderate*

Kumamoto Station Hotel, a three-minute walk from the station (tel. 096/325-2001) is marginally less expensive and strictly utilitarian. *1-16-14 Kumamoto-shi 860, tel. 096/325-907. 55 rooms. Facilities: small restaurant. AE, DC, V. Inexpensive.*

Mt. Aso

Flower Garden. This small Western-style lodging is surrounded by gardens. The owners also fill the rooms with blossoms of the season. This cheerful place serves bountiful meals and attracts a young crowd. The nearest station is Takamori, and someone from the pension will come and pick you up if you call. *Taka-*

mori-machi, Ozu, Takamori 3096-4, tel. 09676/2–3012. 9 rooms, a few with private bath. No credit cards. Moderate.

Pension Cream House. The rooms at this pension are on the small side, but they are light and airy. The owners do not object to squeezing a group of people into one room, and lowering the costs per head accordingly. As a result, Pension Cream House is a particularly good choice if you go with a group of friends. *Takamori-machi, Ozu, Takamori 3096-1, tel. 0976/2–3090. 9 rooms. No credit cards. Moderate.*

Nagasaki

★ **Sakamoto-ya.** This ryokan, started in 1895, seems to have changed very little from its founding days. Cedar baths are offered in which to soak, and the wood building is a testament to the beauty of the simple lines of Japanese architecture. The restaurant specializes in shippoku food (a meal consisting of various dishes), and the cost per night includes breakfast and dinner. The inn is very small and has extremely personalized service. The cost of the rooms varies depending on size and location. *2-13 Kanaya-machi, Nagasaki, tel. 0958/26–8211, fax 0958/25–5944. 15 rooms. AE. Very Expensive.*

Hotel New Nagasaki. Losing its pre-eminence to the new Prince Hotel, this three-year-old hotel still has the advantage of being just a two-minute walk from Nagasaki Station. The standard twin guest rooms, the largest in the city, have enough space for a couple of easy chairs and a table. The lobby lounge is sparkling fresh and the French restaurant, Hydrangea, has the airy, light ambience of a conservatory. On the 13th floor is a Chinese restaurant and the Moonlight Lounge for evening drinks; the Steak House serves beef from Goto Island. Many staff members are fluent in English. *14-5 Daikoku-Machi, Nagasaki 850, tel. 0958/26-8000, fax 0958/26–6162. 149 Western-style rooms. Facilities: 5 restaurants, indoor pool, gym, sauna, business center, shopping arcade. AE, DC, MC, V. Very Expensive.*

Nagasaki Prince Hotel. This is the city's newest, grandest, and most expensive hotel. Despite its ugly block tower exterior, the inside is relaxing even if it slightly overdoes the "opulent-look" so popular with new Japanese hotels. The long, rectangular lobby shimmers with glass, marble, and ponds, but the warm red carpet softens the glare. Guest rooms are decorated in the ubiquitous pastels and have natural-colored processed wood furniture. Each room has bedside panels and is equipped with the amenities of a first class hotel. Restaurants run the gamut from the New York Steak and Seafood dining room on the 15th floor to a Japanese sushi bar. One drawback: the Prince is a 10-minute walk from Nagasaki Station but in the opposite direction from downtown, though the streetcar passes by the front entrance and taxis are plentiful. *2–26, Takaramachi, Nagasaki–cho, Nagasaki 850, tel. 0958/21–1111, fax 0958/23–4309. 183 rooms. Facilities: 5 restaurants, room service from 7–midnight, beauty salon, florist, parking. AE, DC, MC, V. Very Expensive.*

Nagasaki Grand Hotel. This hotel is small and quiet, with a dignified atmosphere. Best of all is the outdoor beer garden. The rooms are compact, but are pleasantly decorated in pastels. *5-3 Manzai-machi, Nagasaki, tel. 0958/23–1234, fax 0958/22–1793. 126 rooms (3 Japanese style). Facilities: French, Japanese, and Western restaurants. AE, DC, MC, V. Expensive.*

Yataro. On top of a mountain, about 20 minutes by taxi from the center of Nagasaki, is this ryokan and its annex, which is a hotel. Yataro has an excellent view of all of Nagasaki, and the meals at the ryokan are plentiful and presented with great care. The view from the shared bath is particularly good. It is a pleasure to relax in a large hot tub, taking in the sights. Because Yataro is a little distance from the city, it is probably advisable to stay in the ryokan as opposed to the hotel, as your meals are included and you will not have to go out as much. Nearly all of the rooms have good vistas, but to ensure that you are not disappointed, request a room with a view when you make your reservation. The hotel is less expensive than the inn. *2-1 Kazagoshira-machi, Nagasaki 850, tel. 0958/22–8166, fax 0958/28–1122. Ryokan: 56 rooms. Hotel: 169 rooms. Facilities: steak bar and grill. AE, DC, MC, V. Moderate.*

Ajisai Inn One. At this small establishment near the station, opposite the Hotel New Nagasaki, the rooms are small, but they are clean. The staff is friendly, and speaks a few words of English. *11-4 Daikoku, Nagasaki 850, tel. 0958/27–3110. 42 rooms. Facilities: breakfast room. V. Inexpensive.*

14 Tohoku

Introduction

by Nigel Fisher

Few foreign tourists make it farther north from Tokyo than Nikko. It is their loss. Tohoku, the name given to the six prefectures of northern Honshu, has country charm, rugged mountains, small villages, its share of temples, and some glorious coastline. For a long time the area was known as Michinoku, which, translated, means the "end of the line" or "backcountry." That image of remote rusticity is still held by many Japanese, and the result has been that Tohoku is one of the areas least visited in Japan. Yet the image is far from the truth. Tohoku has some of the country's greatest attractions, not the least of which is its people.

In a land where politeness is paramount, it seems that the people in Tohoku are actually more friendly than their fellow citizens who live in the industrial Tokyo–Osaka corridor. With the exception of Sendai, Tohoku's cities are small, and the fast pace of urban living is foreign to their inhabitants. Also, because of the lack of good transportation, the residents of Tohoku live their lives independent of Western industrialism and other changes that swept through the southern ⅔ of Honshu.

The consequence has been that many of the traditional ways and folk arts have been maintained, as well as an independence of spirit, much like one finds in Hokkaido farther north. Visiting Tohoku gives a glimpse into old Japan. All of the large cities are prefectural capitals (prefectures are similar to states in the United States or counties in Great Britain) and have all the amenities of any international community. However, none of these six cities has particular merit as a tourist attraction, with the possible exception of Sendai.

Tohoku's climate is similar to New England's. The winters are cold; in the mountains, snow blocks off some of the minor roads. However, in Sendai and Matsushima, and along the Pacific coast, snow is rarely seen, and temperatures rarely fall to freezing. Spring and autumn are the most colorful seasons. Summer is refreshingly cool and, consequently, attracts Japanese tourists escaping the summer heat and humidity of Tokyo and points south. August is the month for big festivals in Akita, Aomori, Hirosaki, and Sendai, all of which draw huge crowds.

Tohoku, like all of the island of Honshu, has mountain ranges running along its spine. Most of the island's trains and highways run north–south on either side of the mountains. Hence, when traveling the major roads or railway trunk lines, one tends to miss some of the grandest mountain scenery. This chapter, laid out as an itinerary up the Pacific side of Tohoku's spine and down the Sea of Japan side, embraces the best of Tohoku using the JR trains as much as is possible, but it also takes the traveler to more remote areas.

In brief, the itinerary starts with Tohoku's unofficial capital, Sendai. It then continues on to Matsushima and travels north to Aomori, with detours to Hiraizumi, the Tono Basin, the Pacific Kaigan coast, Morioka, and the Towada-Hachimantai National Park. Those wishing to continue on to Hokkaido from Aomori should jump to the chapter devoted to that island, and then return to this chapter for the journey south. The journey south goes down to Akita and Tsuruoka, where it then turns inland to Yamagata and Fukushima prefectures; from here one can return to Tokyo, continue south to Nikko, or go west to Niigata and the Japan Alps.

Essential Information

Arriving and Departing

By Plane Akita has four daily flights from Tokyo's Haneda Airport by ANA (All Nippon Airways) and two flights from Osaka International Airport by Japan Air System.

Aomori has two daily flights from Tokyo's Haneda Airport by ANA. Aomori also has flights to Sapporo's Chitose Airport.

Morioka (whose Hanamaki Airport is 50 minutes by bus from downtown) has two flights from Osaka International Airport by Japan Air System. Morioka also has flights to Sapporo's Chitose Airport and to Nagoya Airport.

Sendai has three daily flights from Osaka International Airport by Japan Air System. Sendai also has flights to Sapporo's Chitose Airport.

Yamagata has four daily flights from Tokyo's Haneda Airport by ANA and two flights from Osaka International Airport by Japan Air System.

By Train The most efficient method to reach Tohoku from Tokyo is on the Tohoku Shinkansen trains, which run as far north as Morioka. The Shinkansen makes a total of 71 runs a day between Tokyo (leaving from Ueno Station) and Sendai (two hours) and Tokyo and Morioka (2 hours and 45 minutes). Some Shinkansen trains stop on route to Sendai at Fukushima (one hour). North of Morioka, conventional trains continue on to Aomori (two hours and 35 minutes). To reach Akita, the limited express from Morioka takes two hours. To reach Yamagata, the limited express from Sendai takes one hour.

On Tohoku's western side (facing the Sea of Japan), the train from Niigata takes four hours to travel along the Sea of Japan coast to Akita, and an additional three hours to reach Aomori. From Niigata inland to Yamagata, the train takes 3½ hours. (Niigata is connected to Tokyo's Ueno Station by the Joetsu Shinkansen, which makes the run in two hours.)

Any extensive traveling through Tohoku justifies use of the Japan Rail Pass, which costs ¥27,800 for a week's unlimited travel. For example, the one-way economy fare on the Shinkansen train from Tokyo to Sendai is ¥10,200; to Morioka, ¥12,360.

By Bus While the Tohoku Kyuko Express Night Bus from Tokyo to Sendai is inexpensive (¥4,950), it takes 7 hours and 40 minutes. It leaves Tokyo Station (Yaesu-guchi side and in front of Tobu Travel on Yaesu Street) at 10 PM and arrives in Sendai at 5:40 AM. The bus from Sendai departs at 10 PM and arrives in Tokyo at 5:40 AM.

By Car The Tohoku Expressway now links Tokyo with Aomori, but the cost of gas, tolls, and car rental makes driving an expensive form of travel. It is also considerably slower to drive than to ride on the Shinkansen. Assuming one can clear metropolitan Tokyo in two hours, the approximate driving time is five hours to Fukushima, six hours to Sendai, eight hours to Morioka, and 10–11 hours to Aomori.

Getting Around

Transportation in the country areas of Tohoku was, until recently, limited. That is why Tohoku still has been undiscovered by modern progress and tourists. However, that is changing rapidly. Now, using a combination of trains and buses, most of Tohoku's hinterland is easily accessible, except during the heavy winter snows.

By Train Trains are fast and frequent on the north–south runs. They are slower and less frequent (more like every 2 hours rather than every hour during the day) when they cross Tohoku's mountainous spine. Most of the railways are owned by Japan Railways, so Rail Passes are accepted. Be aware that most trains stop running before midnight.

By Bus Buses take over where trains do not run, and, in most instances, they depart from the JR train stations. Though English may not be widely spoken in Tohoku, there is never any difficulty at train stations in finding someone to direct you to the appropriate bus.

During the summer tourist season, there are also scenic bus tours operating from the major tourist areas. The local Japan Travel Bureau at the train station in each area, or the major hotels, will make the arrangements.

By Boat Three sightseeing boats are especially recommended: at Matsushima Bay, near Sendai; at Jodogahama on the Pacific coast, near Miyako; and at Lake Towada. Keep in mind that these boats offer constant commentary in Japanese over the loudspeaker; this can be particularly annoying if you do not understand what's being said. (*See* appropriate Exploring sections for details.)

By Car Once in the locale you wish to explore, a rented car is ideal for getting around. All major towns have car-rental agencies. The Nippon-Hertz agency is the one most frequently represented. Bear in mind, though, that except on the Tohoku Expressway, few road signs are in Romaji (Japanese words rendered in English). However, major roads have route numbers. With a road map in which the towns are spelled in romaji and kanji (Japanese pictographs derived from Chinese characters), it becomes relatively easy to decipher the directional signs. Maps are not provided by car-rental agencies. Be sure to obtain your bilingual maps in Tokyo or Sendai.

Important Addresses and Numbers

Tourist Information Centers Tourist information centers are available at all the train stations at the prefectural capitals. The two largest tourist centers that give information on all of Tohoku and not just the local area are at Sendai's train station (tel. 022/222–3269) and at Morioka's train station (tel. 0196/25–2090). The telephone numbers of each prefectural government tourist department are: Akita, tel. 0188/80–1702; Aomori, tel. 0177/22–1111; Fukushima, tel. 0245/21–1111; Iwate, tel. 0196/51–3111; Miyagi, tel. 022/221–1864; and Yamagata, tel. 0236/30–2371.

The Japan Travel-Phone This nationwide service for English-language assistance or travel information is available seven days a week, 9–5. Dial toll-free 0120/222–800 for information on eastern Japan. When using a yellow, blue, or green public phone (do not use the red phones), insert a ¥10 coin, which will be returned.

Emergencies **Police,** tel. 110. **Ambulance,** tel. 119.

Guided Tours

The Japan Travel Bureau has offices at every JR station in each of the prefectural capitals and can assist in local tours, hotel reservations, and ticketing onward travel. Though one should not assume that any English will be spoken, there is usually someone whose English is sufficient for your basic needs.

The Japan Travel Bureau also arranges a three-day tour of Tohoku out of Tokyo. For ¥225,000, the tour includes Sendai (overnight), Matsushima, Togatta, Mt. Zao, Kaminoyama Spa (overnight), Yonezawa, and Fukushima. Only one breakfast and one dinner are included, and there is a ¥17,000 single supplement. These tours operate daily May 6–October 20.

Sendai

Numbers in the margin correspond with points of interest on the Tohoku map.

1 With a population of nearly 900,000, **Sendai** is the largest city between Tokyo and Sapporo, in the northern island of Hokkaido. The city is very modern because American firebombs left virtually nothing unscorched by the end of World War II. The buildings that replaced the old ones are not particularly attractive, but Sendai is an open city with a generous planting of trees that justifies its nickname *mori no miyako* "the city of trees." With 10 colleges and universities, including the prestigious Tohoku University, the city has intentionally developed an international outlook and appeal. This has attracted many foreigners to take up residency. For the visitor, the blend of old customs and modern attitudes makes Sendai a comfortable southern base from which to explore Tohoku.

Sendai is a city in which it is easy to find one's way around. Even the major streets have signs in romaji (Japanese words rendered in Roman script). The downtown area of Sendai is compact, with modern hotels, department stores with the latest international fashions, numerous Japanese and Western restaurants, and hundreds of small specialty shops. Three broad avenues, Aoba-dori, Hirose-dori, and Jozenji-dori, head out from the station area toward Sendai Castle and cut through the heart of downtown, where they are dissected by two wide shopping arcades, Ichiban-cho and Chuo-dori. Between these two malls and extending farther east are narrow streets, packing in the bars, tea shops, and restaurants that make up Sendai's entertainment area.

While it is easy to get one's bearings in Sendai, public transport is not so convenient. There is no useful subway for the tourist, and the bus routes are not easy to follow. Fortunately, the center of the city is within easy walking distance from the train station, and all hotels are between the center and the station.

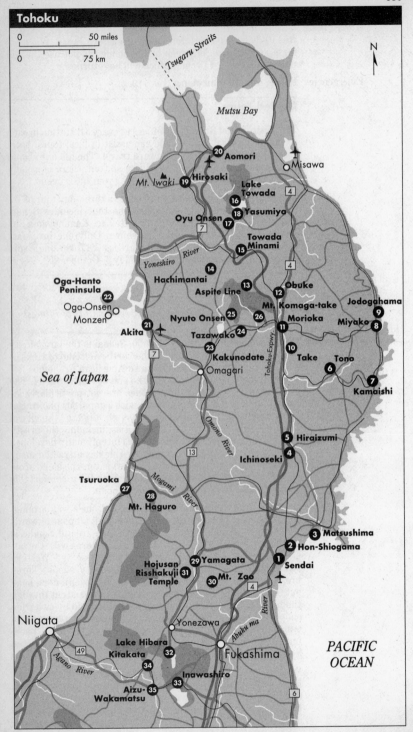

Tohoku

0 — 50 miles
0 — 75 km

Tsugaru Straits

N

Mutsu Bay

20 Aomori

Misawa

Mt. Iwaki **19** Hirosaki
Lake Towada

16
18 Yasumiya
Oyu Onsen **17**
7
4

Towada **15** Minami

Yoneshiro River

14 Hachimantai
4

13 Obuke
Aspite Line **12**
Mt. Komaga-take
Oga-Hanto Peninsula **22** Nyuto Onsen **25** **26** Morioka Jodogahama **9**
Oga-Onsen **24** **11** Miyako **8**
Monzen **21** Tazawako **23**
Akita Kakunodate **10** Take Tono
Omagari **6**
Kamaishi **7**

Sea of Japan

7

Omono River

13

5 Hiraizumi
4 Ichinoseki

Tsuruoka **27**
28
Mt. Haguro

Mogami River

3 Matsushima
2 Hon-Shiogama
1 Sendai
Hojusan **29** Yamagata
Risshakuji **31**
Temple **30** Mt. Zao
4

Niigata

Yonezawa

Abukuma River

PACIFIC OCEAN

Lake Hibara
Kitakata **32**
34
Agano River
49 Inawashiro
Aizu- **35** **33**
Wakamatsu
Fukashima

6

Tohoku-Expwy

For sightseeing, taxis are the best means of travel, except for the 10-minute bus ride from the JR station to Sendai's castle.

Like all the urban centers of Tohoku, Sendai has a limited number of sights worth visiting, and these can easily be covered in a morning's tour. The tour is made easier, too, because Sendai's history focuses almost entirely on a fantastic historical figure, Masamune Date (1567–1636). Affectionately called the "one-eyed dragon" for his valor in battle and the loss of an eye from smallpox when he was a child, Masamune Date established a dynasty that maintained its position as one of the three most powerful daimyo (feudal lord) families during the shogun period. But aside from his military skills and progressive administration (he constructed a canal linking two rivers, thus improving the transport of rice), he was also an artist and a scholar who did not close his eye to new ideas.

Getting There

Sendai is the largest city in Tohoku and, hence, is the most accessible base in Tohoku from which to explore northern Japan.

By Plane Sendai has three daily flights from Osaka International Airport on Japan Air System. Sendai also has flights to Sapporo's Chitose Airport; however, from Tokyo it is probably more convenient to take the train.

By Train The most efficient method to reach Sendai from Tokyo is on the Tohoku Shinkansen trains, which make 71 runs a day between Tokyo's Ueno Station and Sendai (2 hours). Shinkansen trains from Sendai continue north to Morioka (45 minutes). There are also Shinkansen trains from Fukushima (1 hour). Coming from Yamagata, the limited express takes one hour to reach Sendai.

By Bus The Tohoku Kyuko Express Night Bus from Tokyo to Sendai costs ¥5,450. It takes 7 hours and 40 minutes. It leaves Tokyo Station (Yaesu-guchi side and in front of Tobu Travel on Yaesu Street) at 10 PM and arrives in Sendai at 5:40 AM. The bus departs Sendia at 10 PM and arrives in Tokyo at 5:40 AM.

By Car The Tohoku Expressway links Tokyo with Sendai, but the cost of gas and tolls (and car rental) makes it an expensive form of travel. It is also considerably slower to drive than to ride on the Shinkansen. Assuming one can clear metropolitan Tokyo in two hours, the approximate driving time is six hours to Sendai. You are better off taking the train to Sendai and renting a car after you arrive.

Exploring

Before starting your city tour, you may want to stop at the tourist information office in the Sendai railway station. The staff is very helpful and generous with free maps and brochures about Sendai and the region. While you are waiting for a train, be sure to explore the tempting arrays of prepared foods and numerous restaurants in the underground mall aptly named Restaurant Avenue. *Tel. 022/222–3269. Open daily 8:30–8.*

Masamune Date's presence is everywhere. His statue dominates the hill, **Aobayama-Koen Park,** on which his mighty castle, Aobajo, stood and served as the Date clan's residence for 270 years. To get to Aobayama, take bus #9 for the 15-minute ride from Sendai station. The hill is easy to spot because it rises 433 feet above the city and is guarded by the high rock walls of the Hirosegawa River to the east and the deep Tatsunokuchi Valley to the south. No wonder Date's castle was considered impregnable when it was built in 1602.

The castle was destroyed during the Meiji Restoration, though the outer gates survived an additional 73 years, until firebombs destroyed them in 1945. Now the **Gokoku Shrine** covers most of the area where the castle stood. The shrine is a rather grandiose building, heavy and cumbersome, but a small rock garden to its right is quite delightful in its simplicity. To the rear of the castle grounds, a 360-foot-long bridge over the deep Tatsunokuchi Valley leads to the **Yagiyama Zoo**. *Admission: ¥ 400. Open 9–4:15.*

Even though these antiquities of Masamune Date no longer exist, Aobayama-Koen Park and the Gokoku Shrine are good starting points on a sightseeing tour of Sendai. Just by Masamune Date's statue is an observation terrace from which you can look down over the city and plan your next route, a 15-minute walk to **Zuihoden Hall.** To reach it, you must cross back over the Hirosegawa River and then take a right; you will walk past sports ground and over another bridge, which brings you back on the same side of the river as Aobayama. Zuihoden Hall is up the hill and to the left.

Zuihoden Hall, the Date family's mausoleum, was also bombed in 1945, but a five-year reconstruction project was begun in 1974 to re-create the original. During the excavation, Masamune Date's well-preserved bones were found and are now reinterred in what appears to be a perfect replica of the original hall. Two other mausoleums for the remains of the second (Tadamune Date) and third (Tsunamune Date) lords of Sendai were also reconstructed. These mausoleums cost in excess of ¥800 million to rebuild and are astounding in their craftsmanship and authenticity in the architectural style of the Momoyama period (16th century). Each mausoleum is the size of a small temple, and the exterior is inlaid with figures of people, animals, and flowers in natural colors, which are sheltered by elaborate curving roofs. Gold leaf is used extravagantly on the pillars and in the eaves of the roofs, creating a glinting golden aura. Some funeral plot! *Admission: ¥515. Open 9–4.*

For those who become fascinated with the history of the Date family, whose rule over the region lasted 270 years, the **Sendai Municipal Museum** contains several thousand artifacts connected with the clan, including a collection of armor. To get there from Zuihoden Hall, follow the Hirosegawa River back to the grounds of Aobayama-Koen Park. It's about a 15-minute walk. *Admission: ¥400. Open 9–4. Closed Mon. and the days following national holidays.*

Next, visit the **Osaki-Hachimangu Shrine,** located in the northwest section of the city, about 10 minutes by taxi, either from downtown or Aobayama. This is the only historic building in Sendai to have survived the war. It was actually built in 1100 by a warrior general of the Minamoto clan. Masamune Date liked it, and, in 1607, had it moved from its original site in Toda-gun to be rebuilt in Sendai. Its free-flowing architectural form has a naturalness similar to the architectural style in Nikko, and its rich, black-lacquered main building more than justifies its designation as a National Treasure. *Admission:* ¥*300. Open sunrise to sunset.*

A 10-minute walk from Osaki-Hachimangu Shrine and to the left (west) of Sendai Station is the **Rinnoji Temple garden.** Of the several gardens in the neighborhood, this Zen-type garden is the most peaceful. A small stream leads the eye to the lotus-filled pond, the garden's focal point. Flowing around the pond and creating a balance are the waving, undulating hummocks covered with clusters of bamboo. In June the garden is a blaze of color, with irises everywhere, but there are so many visitors that much of the tranquillity is lost. *Admission:* ¥*200. Open daily 8–5.*

Bustling activity should be, and is, found downtown. Sendai is a shopper's paradise. For one, the downtown shopping area is compact, and many of the stores and small shops are in, or are connected to, the two main shopping arcades, **Ichiban-cho** and **Chuo-dori.** Second, as the unofficial capital of the Tohoku region, Sendai is the major marketplace for many of the regional crafts made outside the Miyagi Prefecture. Then, as the shops begin to close around 7 PM, the restaurants start filling up with their patrons. All along the two shopping arcades are Japanese and Western restaurants with menus posted. Down the side streets, between the two arcade streets, is the **Sendai entertainment area,** where there are many small, traditional Japanese restaurants and an even larger number of clubs.

Sendai's big festival is **Tanabata** (Aug. 6–8), and, while similar festivals are held throughout Japan (usually on July 7), Sendai's is the largest, swelling the city to three times its normal size with Japanese tourists. The celebration stems from a poignant Chinese legend of a weaver girl and her boyfriend, a herdsman, represented by the stars Vega and Altair. Their excessive love for each other caused them to become idle. The irate king of heaven exiled the two lovers to opposite sides of heaven. However, he permitted them to meet one day a year— that day is now celebrated as Tanabata, highlighted with a theatrical onstage performance of the young lovers' anguish. For the festival, houses and streets are decorated with colorful paper and bamboo streamers fluttering from poles.

If you want a bird's-eye view of the city, the SS 30 Building, 30 stories high, is the tallest building in town since it opened in 1989. The top three floors are reserved for restaurants and viewing galleries. At night, riding up in the outside elevator, with the city lights descending below, is quite a thrill.

Excursions Around Tohoku

From Sendai to Matsushima

Matsushima and its bay are the most popular coastal resort destinations in Tohoku and are only 35 minutes by train from Sendai. Hence, one can easily visit Matsushima as a day trip from Sendai or, because there are many hotels and ryokans, stay on the coast rather than return to cosmopolitan Sendai. The Japanese have named three places as their Three Big Scenic Wonders—Amanohashidate on the Sea of Japan in Western Honshu, Miyajima in Hiroshima Bay, and Matsushima Bay. Matsushima made it into the big three because the Japanese are infatuated with oddly shaped rocks, which are featured at Matsushima. Counts differ, but there are about 250 small, pine-clad islands scattered in the bay. Some are mere rocks with barely room for a couple of trees, while others are large enough for a few families to live on them. Each of the islets has a distinctive shape; several have tunnels through them large enough for a rowboat to pass through. It is indeed a beautiful bay and a pleasant day's excursion from Sendai.

Getting There
By Train to Shiogama

Though one can go directly by train, the prettiest way to arrive at Matsushima is by sea. First, however, we suggest you take the JR train (Senseki Line), whose platforms are reached from the Sendai Station basement, for a 30-minute trip to **❷ Hon-Shiogama** Station. (The same train goes on to the Matsushima-Kaigan Station [kaigan means "coast"], so this itinerary may be done in reverse.) **Shiogama** is the port city of Sendai and has little appeal, except for one shrine, **Shiogama-jinja,** whose buildings, with bright orange-red exteriors and simple, natural wood interiors, are well worth the climb up the hill before you catch the boat to Matsushima.

To reach Shiogama-jinja Shrine, turn left from the station for about a 10-minute walk. You'll easily spot Shiogama-jinja because it is on a wooded hill overlooking the town. To avoid clambering up the 223 stone steps, don't use the main entrance. Instead, when you see the flashing neon signs of a *pachinko* (Japanese pinball machine) hall in front of you at a "T" junction, go right, and then left down a wide street running along the shrine's grounds. You'll see the entrance and a large gate on your left.

There are actually two shrines, the Shiogama-jinja and the **Shiwahiko-jinja.** The former is the second one you'll reach and is the main building of the complex (admission free). Two other reasons for the climb up to Shiogama-jinja are the view of Shiogama Bay and a 500-year-old holly tree on the temple grounds. You'll usually be able to recognize it by spotting the Japanese taking photographs of themselves standing before it. Near the Shiwahiko-jinja Shrine is a modern building that houses swords, armor, and religious articles on its first floor and whaling exhibits on its second. *Admission: ¥309. Open Apr.–Nov. 8–5; Dec.–Mar. 8:30–4.*

By Ferry to Matsushima

In the summer, sightseeing ferries leave from Shiogama every hour (every 2 hours in the winter) for Matsushima. Whether you catch the gaudy "Chinese dragon" ferry or one that is less ostentatious, the route through the bay will be the same. So will the incessant and distracting loudspeaker naming (in Japanese) the islands. The first 10 minutes of the trip are dismal. Don't fret! Shiogama's ugly port and the oil refinery on the promontory soon give way to the beauty of Matsushima Bay and its islands. *Cost: ¥1,400 one way, second class for the hour long trip; ¥2,400 for the upper deck in first class. The dock is to the right (seaward side) of the Hon-Shiogama train station.*

Exploring
❸

Once you are in **Matsushima,** the key sights are within easy walking distance of each other. The first sight, **Godaido Hall,** is just to the right as you step off the boat on the Matsushima-Kaigan Pier. Constructed at the behest of Masamune Date in 1600, the temple is on a tiny islet connected to the shore by two small arched bridges. Weathered by the sea and salt air, the small building's paint has peeled off, giving it an intimacy often lacking in other temples. Animals are carved in the timbers beneath the temple roof and among the complex supporting beams. *Admission free.*

Across the street from Godaido Hall is the main temple, **Zuiganji.** Its origins date from 827, but the present structure was built on Masamune Date's orders in 1606. Designated as a National Treasure, Zuiganji Temple is the most representative Zen temple in the Tohoku region. The Main Hall is a large wood structure with ornately carved wood panels and paintings (faded with age) from the 17th century. Surrounding the temple are natural caves filled with Buddhist statues and memorial tablets that novices carved from the rock face as part of their training. The grounds surrounding the temple are full of trees, two of which are plum trees brought back from Korea in 1592 by Masamune Date after an unsuccessful military foray. *Admission:* ¥*500. Open 7:30–5; shorter hrs Sept. 15–Mar. 31.*

If you want to know all about how people looked and dressed during Masamune Date's time, a new wax museum, **Ro Ningyo Rekishi Hakubu Thukan,** has opened close to Zuiganji. With life-size figures, the museum displays scenes from the feudal period—battles, tea ceremonies, and processions. *Admission:* ¥*700. Open daily 8:30–5.*

On the opposite (south) side of the harbor from Godaido Hall is **Kanrantei,** translated as "Water Viewing Pavilion." Originally, the structure was part of Fushimi-Momoyamajo in Kyoto, but when that castle was demolished, Hideyoshi Toyotomi gave it to Masamune Date, who then brought it to Matsushima. Here, the Date family held their tea parties for the next 270 years. Next to Kanrantei is the **Matsushima Museum,** with its full collection of the Date family's armor, swords, pikes, and more genteel items, including an array of lacquer ware. *Admission:* ¥*300 for both Kanrantei and the museum. Open daily 8–5.*

Time Out   Matsushima is a vacation town, and at its many snack bars and restaurants, one can choose anything—eels, noodles, even burgers. However, the **Ryokan Matsushimajo** (Matsushima Miyagi 981, tel. 022/354–2121) is the place to dine, for it is full of character. This enchanting building is straight out of the Edo period with its curved roofs and its castlelike structure next door, housing some of the guest rooms. It is one of the famous old ryokans of Japan. Inside there are ancient relics from armor to scrolls to faded paintings. Lunch can be relatively modest or a variety of dishes. To make the selection easier, the six options that focus on tempura, sashimi, or veal cutlet are pictured in the menu. The view from the dining-room window overlooks Matsushima Bay. Just fantastic!

From Matsushima-Kaigan Station it is a 30-minute train ride on the JR line back to Sendai. In the opposite direction from Sendai the train goes to Nobiru, two stops down the line. A 10-minute walk from the station brings you to the beach where, on weekends, the young cruise in their cars trying to attract the attention of the opposite sex. It's a good place to go for youthful company if you know a few words of Japanese. The road follows the shore, and it is a 30-minute hike to Ogatani peninsula for spectacular views of Matsushima.

North of Sendai to Hiraizumi

Another day's excursion from Sendai is north to Hiraizumi. In the 12th century, Hiraizumi came close to mirroring Kyoto as a cultural center. Hiraizumi was the family seat of the Fujiwara clan, who for three generations were powerful lords dedicated to promoting peace and the arts. The fourth-generation lord became power hungry, and his ambition wiped out the Fujiwara dynasty. Not too much remains of the great age under the first three generations of the Fujiwara clan, but what does, in particular the Chusonji Temple, is a tribute to Japan's past.

Getting There To reach Hiraizumi, take the JR express train on the main Tohoku Line going north to **Ichinoseki.** At Ichinoseki, there are ❹ ❺ two options. There is a local train to **Hiraizumi;** from Hiraizumi Station you can walk to the two major temples. Then a short bus ride is required to reach Gembikei Gorge, southeast of town. After returning to town, another bus is required to get to Geibikei Gorge, east of Hiraizumi. The better and quicker way is to use a taxi and bus combination from Ichinoseki Station, described below.

However, if your time is short and you wish to limit your sightseeing to Motsuji and Chusonji, simply take the local train from Sendai for the nine-minute run to Hiraizumi. You can obtain maps at the tourist office (tel. 0191/46–2110) on the town's main street—take a right from the JR station plaza. To reach Motsuji, walk 1,000 yards up the street leading directly away from the JR station. For Chusonji, you can either walk along a narrow road from Motsuji or return to the JR station and take a short bus ride.

Exploring By taxi from Ichinoseki, it's less than 10 minutes to the first stop, **Gembikei Gorge.** It's a miniature gorge—only a thousand yards long and less than 20 feet deep, but with all the features of the world's best gorges. Once, rushing water carved its path into solid rock; now it is quiet. Because of its miniature scale, you can walk its entire length and appreciate every detail of its web of sculptured patterns; the circular holes (Jacob Wells) scoured into the rock side become personal discoveries.

From Gembikei, either by bus or by taxi, it is a mile ride to **Motsuji Temple.** En route is **Takkoku-no-Iwaya,** a cave with a small temple dedicated to Bishamonten, the Buddhist deity of warriors, at its entrance. To the side of the cave and etched into the rock face are faint traces of an imposing image of Dainichi-Nyorai, a pose of Buddha said to have been carved in the 11th century. The temple is a 1961 rendition of the 17th-century temple.

During the 12th-century dynasty of the Fujiwara clan, Motsuji Temple was the most venerated temple in northern Honshu. The complex consisted of 40 temples and some 500 lodgings. Eight centuries later, only the foundations remain. The current buildings are of more recent vintage, including the local youth hostel. However, what have survived in good condition are the Heian period Jodo-style (paradise-style) gardens, laid out according to the Buddhist principle some 700 years ago. Off to the side of the gardens is the Hiraizumi Museum, with artifacts of the Fujiwara family. *Admission: ¥500 for the gardens, ¥300 for the museum. Gardens and museum open 8–5.*

Now for the major sight, **Chusonji Temple.** From Motsuji, walk into Hiraizumi and up the main street, stopping at the tourist office for a local map and brochure. The walk to Chusonji is not far, less than a mile up the road from there. Buses make the trip frequently, or you can take a taxi from Motsuji to Chusonji for ¥800.

Set amid thick woods, Chusonji Temple was founded by the Fujiwara family in 1105. At that time, there were more than 40 buildings. War and a tremendous fire in 1337 destroyed all but two halls, **Kyozo** and **Konjikido.** The other buildings in the complex are reconstructions from the Edo period.

Of the two original buildings, Kyozo Hall is the less interesting. It once housed the greatest collection of Buddhist sutras (precepts), but fire destroyed many of them, and the remainder have been removed to the Sankozo Museum next door. Konjikido Hall, on the other hand, may be considered one of Japan's most historic temples.

Konjikido (Golden Hall) is small but magnificent. The exterior is black lacquer, and the interior is paneled with mother-of-pearl and gold leaf. In the Naijin (Inner Chamber) are three altars, each with 11 statues of Buddhist deities. Beneath the central altar are the remains of the three rulers of the Fujiwara family—Kiyohira, Motohira, and Hidehira. The power-seeking fourth member's remains are not there. His head was sent to Kyoto so that Shogun Minamoto no Yoritomo could look at his face! *Admission: ¥500 (includes Sankozo Museum). Open 8–5.*

The other major attraction of the area is **Geibikei Gorge.** To get to the gorge from Chusonji Temple by rail, you must return to the center of Hiraizumi, take a train back to Ichinoseki, and then change for the train to Rikuchu-Matsukawa. However, the direct route is only about 13 miles, so a taxi (about ¥2,000) is much more convenient.

Geibikei Gorge is Gembikei Gorge's big brother. Flat-bottom boats, poled by two boatmen, ply the river for a 90-minute round-trip through the gorge. The waters are peaceful and slow moving, relentlessly washing their way through silver-streaked cliffs. The climax of the trip is reaching the depths of the gorge, faced with 300-foot cliffs. Coming back downstream would be an anticlimax if it were not for the boatmen, who, with little to do but steer the boat, sing their traditional songs. The boat trip makes a marvelous rest from the temples (cost: ¥1,000).

From Hiraizumi, you can return to Sendai and Tokyo, continue on the train north to Morioka, or, as we do, go east to the Pacific coast before returning inland to reach Morioka.

To the Tono Basin and the Pacific

This itinerary to the Pacific coast requires approximately two days for you to enjoy traditional pastoral Japan and the southern Kaigan coastline. Tono is rich in traditional ways and folklore, and the Kaigan coast is an ever-changing landscape of cliffs, rock formations, and small coves.

Getting There From Hiraizumi, take the train north in the direction of Morioka to Hanamaki. If you take the Shinkansen from Ichin-

oseki, disembark at Shin-Hanamaki. Then take the JR train to
Tono for a 70-minute ride. The same train continues to Kamaishi and Miyako. From there, take the train up to Morioka.

Exploring

6 The people of **Tono** like their old ways. The town itself is not
particularly remarkable, but in the Tono Basin are old buildings and historical remains that take us back to old Japan and
allow the ugliness of modern offices and factories be temporarily forgotten. The Tono Basin is surrounded by forest-clad
mountains, so the setting for this enclave of rusticity is picture-
perfect. Along the valley on either side of Tono are several L-
shaped *magariya* (thatch-roof Nambu-style farmhouses).
Families live in the long side of the L, and animals are off to the
side. One of these has been made into a family-run hotel, the
Minshuku Magariya (without the animals). To the southeast of
Tono is a *suisha* (waterwheel), one of the few working ones left
in Japan. In a peaceful, wooded area above the Atago-jinja
Shrine are the *gohyaku-rakan* (disciples of Buddha) images
carved by a priest on boulders in a shallow ravine. The priest
wanted to appease the spirits of the quarter of Tono's inhabitants who starved to death in the two-year famine of 1754–55.

The Tono Basin has much more—temples (including Fuku-
senji, with Japan's tallest wood Kannon [Goddess of Mercy]
built by priest Yuzen Sasaki to boost morale after World War
II; an abundance of shrines; mysterious rocks [the Tsuzuki
Stone]; and a *kappa* pool [kappas are demons that impregnate
young girls, who then give birth to demikappas]—all of which
are listed on two maps given out by the Tono Tourist Office in
the village. There is also a redbrick museum and a folk village
exhibiting Tono's heritage. *Joint admission: ¥500. Open daily
9–4:30. Closed last day of each month, Sept. 21–30, and Mon.
Nov.–Mar.*

Distances between points of interest are too far to walk; unless
you have a car, a rented bicycle is necessary. Finally, to make
the most of the Tono experience, you should read *Tono
Monogatari*, translated into English as the *Legends of Tono* by
Robert Morse.

7 From Tono the train runs down (90 minutes) to the Pacific
seaport of **Kamaishi.** Note the 48.5-meter statue of Buddha
built in 1970 that stands on Kamazaki Point. Then, with a
change of trains, the journey turns north to run along the coast
8 (another 90 minutes) to **Miyako,** a busy, prosperous town that is
pleasantly compact and has several reasonable places to stay.
9 However, the reason for staying over is to enjoy **Jodogahama,** a
20-minute bus ride (from bus stop #1 at Miyako Station) up the
coast. Jodogahama (Paradise Beach) was given its name by a
priest who thought it was what the hereafter must look like.
The combination of glinting white-quartz beach, the peculiarly
shaped rock formations, and the pine trees on the cliffs bending
to the wind makes Jodogahama a special place. Two rock formations to spot are **Rosoku Iwa** (Candle Rock) and **Shiofuki Ana**
(Salt Spraying Hole).

The best way to appreciate Jodogahama is from the water.
Rowboats are for hire, but the easier way to get around is to
take a 40-minute cruise around the bay. The boats leave from
Jodogahama Pier and are operated by the Iwate Kenhoku
Jidosha Company. *Tel. 01936/2–3350. Cost: ¥820. 9 trips a day
mid-Mar.–mid-Nov.*

Alternatively, you may want to use Taro as your base (16 min up the coast from Miyako by the Sanniku Railway. Fare: ¥340). There are several minshukus and hotels offering hospitality in this small fishing village. Walk along the left side of the harbor and you will find a marked, paved nature trail that curves around the jagged, rock-strewn shore. Notice the marks some 100 feet above your head on the side of the cliff at the harbor entrance. These indicate the highest waves recorded. The trail leads to a series of steps that climb to a parking area outside the Sanokuku Hotel. From there it's a downhill walk along the road back to the village.

Further up the Senniku Railway Line is Kuji (fare from Miyako: ¥1,510), where, in the summer, the most northern Ama (women divers) search for oysters. At Kuji the JR line starts again, heading north to Hachinoche, where it connects with the JR Aomori-Morioka route. It is a slow ride up the coast from Miyako to Hachinoche, and much of the beautiful shoreline is missed owing to frequent tunnels.

A Special Detour
❿ If you do not go down to the Kaigan coast from Tono, consider a trip to **Take.** It is especially worth considering if you are traveling at the end of July, when there is a delightful Shinto festival to visit. The road from Tono winds through picturesque hills to reach the village of Take, situated on the slopes of Mt. Hayachine. For centuries Mt. Hayachine has been regarded as a sacred mountain, and every July 31 to August 1 there is the festival of Hayachine-jinja. For two days the stories of Yamabushi-kagura are acted out in masked dance performances. However, the most colorful part of the festival is on August 1, when a procession of townspeople, wearing lion costumes and wood lion masks, parade through the village en route from the main shrine to a lesser shrine nearby. Because the festival has grown in popularity, it is advisable to telephone the local festival authorities (tel. 0198/48–5864) to secure accommodations.

From Take, the road goes east to Fujima, a major railway stop on the Tohoku Line. Morioka is 20 minutes up the line.

Morioka

⓫ **Morioka** is a busy commercial and industrial city ringed by mountains. Because it is at the northernmost end of the Shinkansen Line, it has become a transfer point for destinations to northern Honshu and Hokkaido. However, despite the city's attempt to appeal to visitors, there is little to keep the tourist interested. Once it had a fine castle built by the 26th Lord of Nambu in 1597, but it was destroyed in the Meiji Restoration and all that remains are its ruins. Its site is now the **Iwate-Koen Park,** the focus of town and the place to escape the congestion of traffic and people in downtown Morioka.

Getting There Morioka is the last stop on the Tohoku Shinkansen Line. From here, all trains going north are "regular" JR trains. So while it can take less than one hour to travel between Sendai and Morioka, the same distance to Aomori (north Honshu) takes two hours and 20 minutes. Morioka also has a JR line, via Tazawako, to Akita on the Sea of Japan coast, as well as the line down to the Pacific coast at Miyako.

Exploring The tourist office, Kita-Tohuku Sightseeing Center, in Morioka JR station, has useful maps and other information on Morioka and Iwate prefectures. It can also help arrange accommodations. To reach downtown take Nos. 5 or 6 bus from the terminal in front of the JR station. *Tel. 0196/25–2090. Open daily 8:30–8.*

Should you wish to take a tour of the city, the Iwate Kanko Bus Company offers full-day and ½-day tours with Japanese-speaking guides. *Cost: full-day tour ¥3,600, departs 10:45 Morioka Station, returns 4:45; ½-day tour ¥2,100, departs 9:30 and 1:45 Morioka, returns 3 hrs later. Tours operate Apr. 20–Nov. 20.*

The major attraction of Morioka is its special craft, *nambutetsu* (ironware). The range of articles, from small wind-bells to elaborate statues, is vast, but the most popular items are the *nambutetsubin* (heavy iron kettles), which come in all shapes, weights, and sizes. Hundreds of shops throughout the city sell nambutetsu, but the main shopping streets are Saien-dori and O-dori, which run by Iwate-Koen Park. Across the river from the park is **Gozaku,** an area of small shops that look much as they did a century ago—a more interesting place in which to browse for nambutetsu. On the other hand, if you are just changing trains at Morioka with little time to spare, the basement floors of the department store under the JR station have a wide selection of nambutetsu.

To reach Gozaku from the park use the Nakano-hashi bridge and take the first main street on the left. A short way down, just past the Hotel Seito, you will find the large Nambu Iron shop and the narrow streets of the Gozaku section on your left. Beyond Gozaku is another bridge, Yonogi-hashi. At the street corner you'll see a very Western-looking firehouse, built in the 1920s and still in operation. The next bridge, Morioka's pride, is the Kamino-hashi, one of the few decorated bridges in Japan. Eight specially crafted bronze railings were commissioned in 1609 and ten bronze posts added two years later.

If there is time to spare in Morioka, visit the **Hashimoto Museum,** reached by a 35-minute bus ride from the station. (Buses run infrequently, especially during the winter, so verify the time of the return bus before you set out.) Buses Nos. 8 and 12 (fare: ¥210) go up to the observation tower on Mt. Iwayama, and the museum is halfway up the small mountain. The museum was created by Yaoji Hashimoto, himself an artist, from a traditional Nambu *magariya* (L-shape thatch-roof farmhouse), rescued from a valley drowned by a dam. The building itself is worth a visit, and the works of Hashimoto and other Iwate artists are an added pleasure, but you could skip the room exhibiting 19th-century paintings by French naturalists of the Barbizon school. There is also one room devoted to ironware and pottery in case you have not had your fill. *Admission: ¥700. Open 10–5. Closed Dec. 29–Jan. 3.*

Back at the JR station on the Shinkansen platforms, a special *bento* (box lunch) is sold. The content (mostly tuna sushi) is less interesting than the container; it's made of pottery in the shape of a *kokeshi*, the folk-craft doll that is so popular throughout Tohoku.

From Morioka Through Towada-Hachimantai Park to Aomori

From Morioka, the main railway line runs north to Aomori (and Hokkaido). It veers west and then east and entirely misses Tohoku's rugged interior, the Hachimantai Plateau. The Towada-Hachimantai National Park is rugged mountains, with gnarled and windswept trees, sweeping panoramas over the gorges and valleys (forming wrinkles in which natives shelter during the region's harsh winters), mountain cones, and crystal-clear lakes.

Getting There From Morioka, you take the JR Hanawa Line for a 40-minute ride to Obuke. From there, travel is by bus for a distance of about 100 kilometers (62 mi) before rejoining the train at Hachimantai for Hirosaki and Aomori. The travel time is less than a day, but you should plan on spending at least one night en route.

Exploring Coming from Morioka, **Obuke** is at the southern entrance to the **⑫** Towada-Hachimantai National Park. A bus leaves from Obuke Station for the 50-minute trip to **Higashi Hachimantai,** the resort town where hikers and skiers begin their ascent into the upper reaches of the mountains. A few miles farther on is **Gozaisho Onsen,** a popular spa resort that can be a useful overnight stop. Aside from several large hotels, there is a village complex (Puutaro-mura) of wood cabins with private thermal pools. A huge youth hostel also accommodates skiers in the winter and hikers in the summer.

The left-hand fork leads to **Matsukawa Onsen** (noted for its pure waters), which has a youth hostel and also the Kyoun-so ominshuku. This spa town is on the backside of Mt. Iwate, amid the eerie barrenness left by the volcano's eruption 250 years ago. A faster way of reaching Hachimantai and Matsukawa is to take a bus direct from Morioka (2 hrs; fare: ¥1,020). The last stop of this bus is the Hachimantai Kanko Hotel. For Matsukawa, change buses at the stop before in Higashi Hachimantai.

⑬ Past Gozaisho is the entrance to the **Aspite Line** toll road, which is a 17-mile scenic road that skirts Mt. Chausu (5,177 feet) and Mt. Hachimantai (5,295 feet). The toll road twists, and with every turn there is another view of evergreen-clad slopes and alpine flowers. From the Hachimantai-chojo (bus stop) it is a 20-minute walk up a path to **Hachiman-numa Pond,** originally a crater lake of a volcano. There is a paved esplanade around the crater, and in July and August the alpine flowers bloom at their best.

The road turning left after Hachimantai-chojo leads to **Toshichi Onsen,** which, at a height of 4,593 feet and located at the foot of Mt. Mokko, is a popular spring skiing resort and a year-round spa town. On the northern side of Toshichi is **Horaikyo,** a natural garden with dwarf pine trees and alpine plants scattered among strange rock formations. In early October, the autumn colors are resplendent.

Just before the end of the Aspite Line toll road is another spa town, **Goshogake Onsen,** noted for its abundance of hot water. This spa and Toshichi are the best spas for overnight stays, especially Goshogake if you want to try Ondoru (Korean-style) steam baths and box-type steam baths. Just outside of Gosh-

ogake is a mile-long nature trail highlighting the volcanic phe-
nomena of the area, including *doro-kazan* (muddy volcanoes)
and *oyunuma* (hot-water swamps).

After Goshogake Onsen, the toll road joins Route 341. A left
turn here leads south to Lake Tazawa, discussed later in this
chapter. A right turn at the junction heads north for an hour's
⑭ bus journey to the town of **Hachimantai,** where you can rejoin
the Hanawa JR line either to return to Obuke and Morioka or to
travel north toward Aomori.

Twenty minutes north of Hachimantai on the JR Hanawa Line
⑮ is **Towada-Minami.** From here, buses leave to make the 60-min-
⑯ ute trip to **Lake Towada** (fare: ¥980). (If scarcity of time dictates it, you could forgo the Hachimantai Plateau and arrive at
Towado-Minami directly from Obuke and Morioka.)

The area around Lake Towada is one of the most popular resorts in northern Tohoku. The main feature is the caldera lake,
which fills a volcanic cone with depths of up to 1,096 feet, the
third deepest in Japan and which, strangely enough, had no
fish in it until Sadayuki Wanoi stocked it with trout in 1903.
Since buses frequently travel between Towada-Minami and
⑰ Towadako, you may want to get off the bus at **Oyu Onsen** and
change for a local bus to travel 14 miles to visit Japan's Stone-
henge, **Oyu Iseki**—a circle of stones with another center ring of
upright stones, one of them shaped like a sundial. Oyu Iseki
was discovered only in the 1930s, but studies have estimated
that the ring is 4,000 years old.

After Oyu Onsen, the road snakes over **Hakka-toge Pass**—
some of the best views of the lake are from here—and through a
series of switchbacks it descends to circle the lake along the
shore. Taking a right at the lake leads to the village resort of
⑱ **Yasumiya,** from which pleasure boats depart (from mid–Apr.
to early Nov.) every 30 minutes for a run across the lake to
Nenokuchi. The one-hour trip on the boat (fare: ¥1,100) covers
the most scenic parts of the lake, and at Nenokuchi there are
bicycles to rent for further exploration. (Rental bicycles are
also available in Yasumiya and Nenokuchi.) From Nenokuchi
there is a bus that continues around the lake's northern shore
to **Taki-no-zawa**—more superb views of the lake—and then to
Hirosaki.

⑲ **Hirosaki** is one of northern Tohoku's friendliest and most attractive cities, said to be the home of Japan's most beautiful
women. Its major (and really only) sight is **Hirosakijo** (Hirosaki
Castle), but the town has an intimacy that makes it appealing.

Located at the northwestern end of the town in the opposite direction from the JR station and across the river, the castle is an
original—a pleasant change from admirable replicas. Built in
1610, it is relatively small but perfectly proportioned, and it is
guarded by moats. The gates in the outlying grounds are also
original, and, when the 6,000 *someiyoshino*, cherry trees, blossom (festival, Apr. 25 to May 6) or the maples turn red in autumn (festival, early Oct.–early Nov.), the setting is
marvelous. Even in the winter, when a thick carpet of snow
covers the ground, the princely castle, unblemished by time,
has a virgin freshness no one can resist (snow festival, early
Feb). *Admission: ¥200. Open daily 8:30–5.*

Also, don't miss the five-story pagoda, **Saishoin Temple,** built in 1672. It is located by the river on the southwest edge of town.

At any time, Hirosaki is a pleasant overnight stay, but during the first week of August the city comes even more alive with its famous **Nebuta Festival.** Each night different routes are followed through the town, with floats displaying scenes from Japanese and Chinese mythology represented by huge fanlike paintings that have faces painted on both sides. With lights inside the faces, the streets become an illuminated pantomime.

If you are heading directly to Aomori from Lake Tozako, rather than spend the night in what is a large, sprawling, unattractive city, choose a Japanese experience by overnighting at **Sukayu Onsen,** near the Hakkoda Ropeway. Buses depart from Towada-Minami, pass by Lake Towada, and stop at Sukayu en route to Aomori. Unfortunately, because of winter snows, the only route to Sukayu Onsen between November 11 and March 31 is an hour-long bus ride from Aomori and the last bus departs at 3:30 PM.

It is known that more than 300 years ago a hunter shot and wounded a deer. Three days later he saw the deer again, miraculously healed. He realized that the deer had cured himself in the sulphur springs. Since then, people have been coming to Sukayu for the water's curative powers. The inn, and there is nothing but the inn, is a sprawling wooden building with highly polished creaking floors. The main bath, known as Sen Nin Buro (Thousand People Bath), is made of Hiba, a very strong wood. It is not segregated—men and women bathe together. Two big tubs fill the bath house: one pool called Netsu-no-yu is 42° C degrees and feels hotter than the other, Shibu rokubu, which is one degree colder. The other two bathtubs, called Hie–no–yu, are for cooling off by pouring water only on your head so you don't wash the minerals off your body. (*See* Lodging, below.)

Hirosaki is a compact little town where you can walk everywhere. In the evening, the small entertainment area is the cluster of narrow streets flanked to its north and east by Hirosaki's two main streets, which cross each other. Near the intersection is a *pachinko* (Japanese pinball machine) center, an easy landmark to spot with its flashing lights, and the next street left leads into the entertainment center. One extremely friendly, inexpensive yakitori restaurant, the **Isehiro,** is the second restaurant on the left after the first cross street. But there are numerous choices for dining, from small *izakayas* (small bars) to restaurants with visual menus in their windows, and after dinner there are coffeehouses, *nomiya*, and more expensive clubs for further pleasure. Perhaps because of the large resident foreign population in Hirosaki, foreigners are accepted, understood, and welcomed, seemingly more so than in other Tohoku small towns. You'll even find an excellent bookshop, **Kinokuniya** (tel. 0172/36–4511), next door to the Hotel Hokke Club on Hirosaki's main street; the shop stocks a wide selection of English-language books.

The Civic Sightseeing Museum opened in late 1990 to display local industry, crafts, and regional art. *Open 9–4:30. Closed Sun. Admission free.*

From Hirosaki it is a 40-minute local train ride to Aomori.

Aomori **Aomori** is another of Tohoku's prefectural capitals that have
⑳ more appeal to their residents than to travelers. Foreign visitors used to stop here while waiting for the ferry to cross over
to Hokkaido. Now, the traveler can stay on the express train
and ride through the Seikan Undersea Tunnel (33.66 miles
long, with 14.5 miles of it deep under the Tsugaru Straits) to
Hokkaido. The Seikan tunnel is, by the way, the world's longest tunnel under the sea.

Exploring Aomori has only marginal interest unless you can be there for
its **Nebuta Festival** (Aug. 3–7). The festival is similar to
Hirosaki's (the two festivals are celebrated at the same time).
Three-dimensional representations of men and animals parade
on floats through the streets at night. Because the figures are
illuminated from the inside, the spectacle might be ghostly but
for the flaming colors used, which make everything festive.

If you are in Aomori at another time than during the festival,
you can take the JR bus from gate 8 or 9 (cost ¥575; 35 minutes)
to **Nebuta-no-Sato** (Nebuta Museum) in the southwest of town,
where 10 of the figures used in Aomori's festival are stored and
are on display. (The same JR bus continues on from Nebuta-no-
Sato to Sukayu Onsen, so if you are coming from that spa, you
may wish to get off and visit this museum before continuing
into downtown Aomori.) *Nebuta-no-sato. Admission: ¥620.
Open 9–8 July–Sept., except during the Nebuta Festival, beginning of Aug., mid-Apr.–June 30, open 9–5:30; and Oct. 1–
Nov. 30, 9–5:30. Closed Dec.–mid-Apr.*

Munakata Shiko Kinenkan is a museum that opened in 1974 in
dedication to the locally born artist Shiko Munakata (1903–
1975). To reach the Munakata Shiko Kinenkan requires taking
a bus from the JR station in the direction of Tsutsui and getting
off at Shimin Bunka Senta-mae. Then walk back over the crossing and take a left. You will see the museum on the left. The
building is constructed in the attractive azehura-style. Inside,
the two-floor gallery displays the prints, paintings, and calligraphy of this internationally known artist. *Admission: ¥300.
Open Apr.–Sept. 9:30–4:30; Oct.–Mar. 10–4. Closed on the
last day of the month and national holidays.*

You may also wish to visit the **Prefectural Museum** (Kyodo-
Kan—a five-minute bus ride from the station), which displays
folk crafts and archaeological material. *Admission: ¥300.
Open Apr.–Sept. 9:30–4:30; Oct.–Mar. 9:30–4. Closed Mon.*

The **Museum of Folk Art** (Keikokan), also five minutes away
from the station, has a larger display of local crafts, including
fine examples of Tsugaru-nuri lacquer ware, which achieves its
hardness through 48 coats of lacquer. Dolls representing the
Hamento dancing girls of the Nebuta Festival are also on display. *Admission: ¥300. Open 9:30–4:30. Closed Thurs. Nov.–
Apr.*

For a quick overview of Aomori, there is the ASPAM
(Asupamu) Building down by the waterfront, where the ferry-
boats once docked. The 15-story ultramodern eyesore is easy to
recognize by its 76-meter (249-foot) tall pyramid shape. An outside elevator whisks you 13 floors up to an observation deck.
*Admission: ¥300. Open 9 AM–10 PM. Inside are a number of
restaurants and exhibits on Aomori's tourist attractions and
crafts.*

Aomori ends this excursion north through Tohoku. Now, we go south down Tohoku's Sea of Japan coast. For those of you going first to Hokkaido, either take the train under, or the ferry across, the Tsugaru Straits to Hakodate.

South from Aomori to Akita on the Sea of Japan

So far, our travels have been on the central and Pacific sides of Tohoku. The return journey travels south down the Sea of Japan side to Akita before moving back into Tohoku's mountainous central spine at Tazawako. From there, staying within the mountains, our excursion continues on to Yamagata. Then comes the final leg through the southern Tohoku prefecture of Fukushima.

Exploring Leaving Aomori for Akita (a 3-hour ride), the train goes back through Hirosaki and past **Mt. Iwaki** (5,331 feet high), which dominates the countryside. A bus (40 minutes) from Hirosaki travels to the foot of this mountain. From there, one can take the sightseeing bus up the Iwaki Skyline toll road (open late Apr.–late Oct.) to the eighth station. The final ascent, with the reward of a 360-degree view, is by a seven-minute ropeway, followed by a 30-minute walk to the summit. Back on the train and soon after Mt. Iwaki, the mountains give way to the rice fields and flat plains that surround Akita.

㉑ **Akita,** the prefectural capital (pop. 300,000), is not a particularly appealing city. Essentially, Akita is a built-up and commercial city whose major attraction for the tourists is its famous **Kanto Festival** (Aug. 5–7). In this festival, young men balance a 30-foot-long bamboo pole that supports as many as 50 lit paper lanterns on its eight crossbars. The area around Akita is said to grow the best rice and have the purest water in Japan. The combination of these two produces excellent dry sake and local women with fair complexions.

If you have time between trains, **Senshu Park** is a 10-minute walk from the station by following the train tracks to the north. It was the site of the now-ruined Kubota Castle, and today it is a pleasant spot of greenery, with cherry blossoms and azaleas adding color in season. Aside from the prefectural art museum, the park includes the **Hirano Masakichi Art Museum,** with a noted collection of paintings by Tsuguji Fujita (1886–1968), as well as works by van Gogh and Cézanne. The building itself is architecturally interesting for its Japanese palace-style roof covered with copper, which slopes down and rolls outside at the edge. *Admission: ¥400. Open 10–5. Closed Mon.*

For regional arts and crafts, make a visit to the **Akita Sangyo Kaikan,** which is a five-minute walk from the park toward the city center. Though this is a museum, there are also crafts for sale (open 10–5; closed Wed.). Two streets to the west of the crafts center is Kawabata Street. This is where everyone comes in the evening to sample the regional hot-pot dishes *shottsuru-nabe* (made with pickled sand fish) and *kiritampo-nabe* (made with rice cakes and chicken), drink the local ji-sake, and be entertained at one of the many bars lining Kawabata.

㉒ Only 30 kilometers (19 miles) to the north and west of Akita is the **Oga Peninsula,** a promontory indented by strange rock formations and reefs, mountains clad with Akita cedar, and grassy green hills. Though there are toll roads that trace Oga's coastline, public transport is infrequent. The easiest way to tour the peninsula is by using the services of the Akita Chuo Kotsu bus lines (tel. 0188/23–4411). The tour buses leave from Akita Station, Oga Station, and Oga Onsen. They depart daily late April–early November. However, the tour is conducted in Japanese.

Instead of continuing south along the Sea of Japan coast from Akita and going directly to Tsuruoka, this excursion turns inland up to **Tazawako.** After that, the excursion goes south, offering the detour to Tsuruoka en route to Yamagata.

On the way to Tazawako, with a change of trains at Omagari, is the small and delightful town of **Kakunodate.** Founded in 1620 by the local lord, the town has remained an outpost of traditional Japan that, with cause, boasts of being Tohoku's little Kyoto. Within a 15-minute walk northwest from the station are several 350-year-old samurai houses, all well-preserved and maintained. The most renowned of the samurai houses is Aoyagi, with its sod-turf roof. The cherry tree in Aoyagi's garden is 280 years old. The whole town is full of weeping cherry trees, some 400 in all, which are direct descendants of those imported from Kyoto three centuries ago. *Admission: ¥515. Open 9–4:30 daily in summer. Closed late Nov.–mid-Apr.*

If there is time before the next train to Tazawako, visit the **Denshoken Hall** located in front of a cluster of samurai houses. The hall serves as a museum and a workshop for cherry-bark handicrafts. *Admission: ¥310. Open 9–5. Closed Thurs. Nov.–Mar.*

From Kakunodate it is a 16-minute ride on the train to **Tazawako.** (The total journey from Akita to Tazawako takes about 2 hours.) You will need to take a 15-minute bus ride (fare: ¥190) from the JR station to Tazawako Kohan on the lake shore, but first drop in at the tourist information office to the left of the JR station for maps and bus schedules. *Tel. 0187/34–0307. Open daily 8:30–5:15.*

Tazawa is Japan's deepest lake (1,394 feet). Its waters are the second most transparent in Japan (after Lake Mashu in Hokkaido). Like most of Japan's lakes, Tazawa is in a volcanic cone, but its shape is a more classic caldera than most. With its clear waters and forested slopes, it captures a mystical quality that appeals so much to the Japanese on vacation. It helps to know that the legendary beauty from Akita, Takko Hime, now sleeps in the water's deep as a dragon. Apparently, that is why the lake never freezes over in winter. Takko Hime and her dragon husband churn the water with their passionate lovemaking. Or, perhaps, as scientists say, the water doesn't freeze because of a freshwater source that enters the bottom of the lake.

An excursion boat makes 40-minute cruises on the lake during late April–November (cost: ¥980). There is also regular bus service around the lake (halfway around in winter), and bicycles are available for rent at the Tazawa-kohan bus terminal as an alternative to the cruise boat. The better way is to rent a bike (or use a rented car) and make the drive around the lake yourself. That way, more time can be spent appreciating the beauty of Takko Hime, whose bronze statue is on the western shore.

A 40-minute bus ride (fare: ¥540) from the Tazawako JR station via Tazawa-kohan takes you up to the **Tazawako Kogen Plateau.** Located to the northeast of Lake Tazawa, the journey offers spectacular views of the lake, showing off the full dimensions of its caldera shape. The same bus then continues on for

25 another 10 minutes to **Nyuto Onsen.** These small, unspoiled, mountain hot-spring spas are some of the few traditional spa villages left in Tohoku. Most of these villages have only one inn, so it is advisable to arrange accommodations before you arrive if you wish to stay the night. *(See* Lodging, below.)

26 A few miles east of Lake Tazawa stands **Mt. Komaga-take.** At 5,370 feet, it is the highest mountain in the area. Yet Mt. Komaga-take is one of the easiest mountains to climb. A bus from Tazawako Station runs up to the eighth station, from which it takes less than an hour to reach the summit; you'll walk through clusters of alpine flowers if you choose June or July for your hike.

Another old traditional spa town, **Tamagawa Onsen,** is to the north of Tazawako on Route 381. There is frequent bus service between the two towns (90 minutes; fare: ¥1,120). The spa is quaint and delightfully old-fashioned, with wood buildings surrounding the thermal springs. However, think twice before staying here overnight. The inns are a little ramshackle, but the elderly who come to take the waters are very serious about the curative qualities of the mineral waters. Beyond Tamagawa Onsen, the road joins the Aspite Line toll road described earlier in the Hachimantai excursion. Since direct JR train service runs between Morioka and Tazawako, an alternative itinerary to the one described in the earlier section is to go first to Tazawako from Morioka and travel up Route 381 to Hachimantai.

Heading south from Tazawako, you can either travel directly down the middle of Tohoku to Yamagata or make a detour to visit Tsuruoka and Mt. Haguro by returning to the Sea of Japan coast. Then turn inland again to Yamagata.

South of Akita and along the Sea of Japan coast are, for the most part, small fishing villages, noteworthy only for the fact

27 that few tourists stop over en route. The one exception is **Tsuruoka,** the religious center of Shugendo, an esoteric religious sect that combines Buddhism with Shintoism. Though Tsuruoka itself is famous for its temple, **Zempoji,** a pagoda containing images of Buddha in every pose that could possibly be attributed to him, the city serves as the gateway for visiting

28 **Mt. Haguro,** the most accessible of the three mountains in the Dewa-san range. All three mountains are sacred to the *yamabushi,* the popular name given to members of the Shugendo sect, but it is the thatch-roof shrine **Haguro-san Jinja,** on the summit of Mt. Haguro, that attracts pilgrims throughout the year.

Nowadays most pilgrims take the easy way up to the summit—a direct bus from Tsuruoka Station along the toll road. The old way, the one that the more devout or foolhardy tourists take, is by train from Tsuruoka to Haguro; from there, they walk up the 2,446 stone steps to the summit. The climb is not for the faint at heart, but the route along avenues of 300-year-old cedar trees—with shafts of sunlight filtering through, the occasional waterfall, the tiny shrines, and the tea shop halfway up—is the reason for reaching the summit. The actual shrine, Haguro-san Jinja, surrounded by souvenir stands, is not so impressive; you'll be glad to get on the bus to return to Tsuruoka, leaving behind on the slopes of Mt. Haguro the numerous small huts used by yamabushi pilgrims engaged in their penance. Once back in Tsuruoka, it is a two-hour train ride to Yamagata.

Yamagata

29 **Yamagata,** with a population of 250,000, is the capital of the prefecture of the same name. For visitors to Japan, Yamagata is more a transportation hub than a destination in itself, but it is a friendly town. Pick up free maps and brochures from the tourist information office inside the JR railway station. *Tel. 0236/ 31–7865. Open daily 10–6.*

Getting There Coming to Yamagata directly from Tokyo, the best method is to take the Shinkansen to Fukushima and transfer to the JR Ou Honsen Line. The total time is about three hours and 15 minutes. There is also direct train service on the JR Senzan Line to Sendai (about 1 hour). To the Sea of Japan coast, a train on the JR Yonesaka Line running between Niigata and Yamagata takes 3½ hours; the train on the JR Rikuu West Line to Tsuruoka, which connects with the JR Uetsu Honsen Line to Akita, takes three hours. Finally, going north, the JR Ou Honsen Line travels up to Tazawako and then over the mountains to Morioka.

Yamagata is also serviced by All Nippon Airways (ANA) flights from Tokyo's Haneda Airport (55 minutes) and by Japan Air System from Osaka (80 minutes). Yamagata's airport is 40 minutes by bus from the city center.

Exploring Yamagata is a small, country town whose major attraction is summer hiking and winter skiing in the nearby mountains. The main event is the August **Hanagasa Festival,** in which some 10,000 dancers from the entire area dance their way through the streets in traditional costume and *hanagasa* hats, so named for the safflowers used to decorate them. For anyone interested in pottery, take a taxi ride (the route is very difficult by bus unless you speak Japanese) to **Hirashimizu** on the outskirts of the city. This small enclave of traditional buildings and farmhouses is a step back in time and a sharp contrast to the modern urban sprawl of Yamagata. About six pottery families live here, each specializing in a particular style. The pottery of Seiryugama is the best known, and, with exhibitions of its wares in America and Europe, its prices are high. Other potteries available are more simple wares, and are more affordable. Seek out the reasonably priced Nanaemon pottery.

30 Most visitors come to Yamagata, though, to make their way to the prefecture's largest draw, **Mt. Zao,** where 1.2 million alpine enthusiasts come December–April to ski its eight slopes. (During the winter, there are direct buses from Tokyo to Zao Onsen.) The mountain's resort town, **Zao Onsen,** is only 12 miles (45 minutes by bus) from Yamagata Station. From Zao Onsen, the first cable car leaves from the base lodge to climb 1,734 feet, and the second one makes the final ascent of an additional 1,839 feet. Even nonskiers make the round trip in order to see the heavy snow on the conifers. The weight of the snow causes the trees to form weird cylindrical shapes, making them look like legendary monsters. In the summer hikers come, though in fewer numbers than the winter skiers, to walk among the colored rocks and visit Zao Okama, a caldera lake with a 900-foot radius.

Another attraction, 20 kilometers (12 miles) outside Yamagata, (30 minutes on the JR Senzan Line toward Sendai) is **Hojusan Risshakuji Temple,** more commonly known as Yam adera Temple. Built 1,100 years ago, Yamadera's complex of temples with steeply pitched slate roofs on the slopes of Mt. Hoju is the largest one of the Tendai sect in northern Japan and attracts some 700,000 pilgrims a year. The small town at the base of the hill has become very touristy with hotels and souvenir shops, but once through the entrance to the temple grounds, a modicum of serenity prevails. Just inside the entrance and to the right is Konponchudo, the temple where the sacred flame has been burning constantly for 1,000 years. The path continues on and up. The ascent is relatively easy, but the path is strewn with fallen rocks, and some of the 1,000 steps are crumbling. On the way to the top is a statue of the Japanese poet Basho Matsuo (1644–1694), who wrote of his wanderings throughout Japan in his 17-syllable poems (haiku). Finally, after a steep ascent, there is the Niomon, the gate leading to Kaisando, where the temple founder is buried.

Into Fukushima Prefecture and Out of Tohoku

From Yamagata, there are three possible routes: directly across the mountains by JR trains to Sendai; south and west to Niigata, Sado Island, and the Japan Alps *(see* Chapter 6); or continuing down Tohoku's mountainous spine to the fifth prefecture of the region, Fukushima, from where one can cross over to Nikko *(see* Nikko in Chapter 4).

Fukushima Prefecture is tamer both in scenery and in attitudes than the rest of Tohoku; it was the first region in northern Honshu to become a popular resort area for Japanese families, especially around the Bandai-Kogen Plateau. During 15 minutes, 101 years ago, Mt. Bandai erupted, wiping out over 40 small villages, killing 477 people, and resculpturing the landscape. The result was nature's damming of several streams to form hundreds of lakes, the largest of which is **Lake Hibara,** with its crooked shoreline and numerous islets.

Getting There From Yamagata, the Bandai-Kogen Plateau is reached by taking the train to **Yonezawa,** and then taking a two-hour bus ride over the Nishi-Azuma Sky Valley toll road. The whole mountain resort is, in fact, crisscrossed by five scenic toll roads. A direct bus to Bandai-Kogen from Fukushima City departs from near the Shinkansen station and travels over the Bandai-Azuma Skyline drive, offering splendid views of mountains by climbing up through **Jododaira Pass** at 5,214 feet.

All buses from Fukushima City, Inawashiro, Yonezawa, and Aizu-Wakamatsu arrive at **Bandai-Kogen** bus stop, the tourist center on Lake Hibara, where the Japanese vacationers disperse to their campgrounds, bungalows, or modern ryokans.

Exploring While the Bandai-Kogen Plateau area is somewhat spoiled by the hordes of tourists, a particularly pleasant two-hour walk, the Goshikinuma Trail, meanders past the dozen or more tiny little lakes (ponds, really) that are collectively called **Goshikinuma** (five-color lakes), because each throws off a different color. The trail begins across from the Bandai-Kogen bus station and in the opposite direction from Lake Hibara.

A bus that departs from Bandai-Kogen goes straight to Aizu-Wakamatsu, taking 90 minutes. En route, the bus makes a stop at **Inawashiro,** the town on the northern edge of the Lake Inawashiro. The lake is Japan's fourth largest, but, unlike Tohoku's other large lakes, Towada and Tazawa, Inawashiro is not a caldera lake but instead is formed by streams. Hence, its flat surrounding shore is not particularly attractive. The Japanese like the lake, though, for the gaudy sightseeing swan-shape cruise boats that circle on the water. Of more cultural interest (only 10 minutes by bus from Inawashiro Station) is **Hideo Noguchi's** birthplace and a Memorial Museum in honor of his extraordinary life and his research of yellow fever, which eventually killed him in Africa in 1928.

An alternative route to Aizu-Wakamatsu is via **Kitakata.** Kura (storehouses) are to be seen all over Japan, but for some reason Kitakata has over 2,000 mud-wall storehouses. But Kitakata's kura are not only simple places to store rice, miso, soy sauce, and sake, the products of the town, they are also status symbols of the local merchants. The kura fascination spread in the past so that shops, homes, and inns were built in this architectural style, as each citizen tried to outdo his neighbor. One can quickly use up a couple of rolls of film taking photographs of the many different kura—some are black-and-white plaster, some simply of mud, some with bricks, and some with thatch roofs; still others have tiles.

Aside from the major architectural attractions—**Kai's Kura,** an elaborate mansion that took seven years to build, and the **Aizu Lacquer Museum** (both have admission of ¥300 and are open daily 9–5, Apr.–Nov.)—your final goal should be the **Yomatogawa Sake Brewery** (tel. 0241/22–2233). Located in the center of town near the Lacquer Museum, the brewery consists of several kura buildings. One building serves as a small museum to display old methods of sake production. The other buildings are still used for making sake. After a dutiful tour, you are offered the pleasurable reward of tasting different types of sake. *Admission free. Open daily 9–5.*

The tourist office at the local station has a kura walking-tour map for the city, but, if you are short on time, the area northeast of the JR station has a selection of storehouses, including Kai Shoten, a black kura storefront of an old miso and soy sauce factory.

The train from Kitakata to Aizu-Wakamatsu takes 20 minutes. **Aizu-Wakamatsu,** with its **Tsurugajo castle,** was the most powerful stronghold of the northeast during the shogun period. Because the castle is located on the opposite side—south—of the JR station, take the bus from the station plaza (gate #6 but check with the information booth first) that loops around the city to include the castle and the Byakkotai monuments. The Aizu clan was closely linked to the ruling family in Edo and remained loyal until the end. When the imperial forces of the Meiji Restoration pressed home their successful attack in 1868, that loyalty caused the castle, which had stood for five centuries, to be burned down, along with most of the city's buildings. The five-story castle was rebuilt in 1965 as a museum (admission: ¥310; open 8:30–5) and is said to look like its original, but without the presence it must have had 121 years ago, when 19 teenage warriors committed ritual suicide. Every Japanese knows this story, so it bears telling.

These young warriors, known as Byakkotai (White Tigers), had been soundly beaten by pro-Restoration forces in a battle outside the city. The surviving 20 boys retreated to a nearby hillside, Iimoriyama. Then, to their horror, they saw smoke rise from the castle and mistakenly believed the castle to be overrun by the enemy. As good samurai, all 20 boys began a mass suicide ritual. One boy was saved before he bled to death and spent the rest of his life with a livid scar and the shame of having failed to live up to the samurai code. There is now a monument to the 19 on the hill next to their graves. The **Byakkotai monuments,** a small memorial museum, and a strange octagonal Buddhist temple, Sazaedo, are reached by a 15-minute bus ride from the station. You may want to visit Iimoriyama September 22–24, when a special festival is held in memory of the Boshin civil war and the Byakkotai. *Admission: ¥200. Open daily 8–6.*

To the east of the castle is **Aizu Bukeyashiki,** an excellent reproduction of a wealthy samurai's manor house (open 8:30–5). The 35-room house gives some idea how well one could live during the shogun period. A museum on the grounds displays Aizu craft, culture, and history. Access to Aizu Bukeyashiki is by Higashiyama bus from the JR station.

Higashiyama Onsen is a spa town 15 minutes beyond Aizu Bukeyashiki and is, with several modern ryokans, an alternative layover to Aizu-Wakamatsu, especially if one enjoys hot mineral baths. The town itself is modern and not particularly attractive, but there is one traditional and simple ryokan, the Mukaitaki, that retains the feeling of an inn.

The unfortunate aspect about Aizu-Wakamatsu is that, for our excursions throughout Tohoku, it is the end of the line. Routes south, by train and bus, go to Nikko. Traveling east by train to Koriyama puts you on the Tohoku Shinkansen for Sendai to the north and Tokyo to the south. The train going east leads you to Niigata and the Sea of Japan.

Dining and Lodging

Dining

In most of Japan, outside the large cities, one is usually advised to eat Western-style food in the dining rooms of the larger hotels. However, we strongly recommend that you eat out at local Japanese restaurants. Most restaurants that are reasonably priced will have a visual display of their menu in the window. On this basis, you can decide what you want before you enter. If you cannot order in Japanese, and no English is spoken, after you secure a table, lead the waiter to the window display and point.

Unless the establishment is a *ryotei* (high-class, traditional Japanese restaurant), reservations are usually not required except for formal restaurants at a hotel or a ryokan. Whenever reservations are recommended or required at any of the restaurants listed, this is indicated.

Some of the regional Japanese dishes of Tohoku are special, and you should make a point of enjoying them:

Akita is famous for its clean water and its rice. These two ingredients make good sake; Akita is known for its **kara-kuchi** (dry sake). Akita's **kiritampo** is made from boiled rice, pounded into cakes and molded on sticks of **sugi** (Japanese cedar).

Sendai miso is a red and salty version of fermented soybeans. **Mochi,** found in Sendai, is a tiny ball covered with **yuzu** (Japanese citrus) flavored sugar. When put into a cup of hot water, the ball floats and imparts sweetness and fragrance, creating a delicious drink. Sendai's **dagashi** are traditional candies and cakes, usually made with rice, soybean flour, and sugar.

Sensai ryori, from Yamagata Prefecture, refers to a variety of dishes made from mountain vegetables and fish (mostly carp and sweet fish) caught in the streams and rivers.

A 3% federal consumer tax is added to all restaurant bills. Another 3% local tax is added if the bill exceeds ¥5,000, At more expensive restaurants, a 10%–15% service charge is added to the bill. Tipping is not the custom.

Category	Cost*
Very Expensive	over ¥6,000
Expensive	¥ 4,000–¥6,000
Moderate	¥ 2,000–¥4,000
Inexpensive	under ¥2,000

Cost is per person without tax, service, or drinks

Lodging

Tohoku has a broad spectrum of accommodations, from inns and minshukus to modern, large resort hotels. However, because the region has only recently opened itself up to tourists, most of the accommodations are of recent vintage. That means the hotels are utilitarian and functional. The difference between them is that the more expensive the tariff, the larger the lobby area and the guest rooms. Do not expect to find a hotel with character. Moreover, because the Japanese are renowned for their service, politeness, and cleanliness, these characteristics do not differentiate between hotels. Hence, the hotels listed below are chosen because their locations have certain advantages, their prices are in line for what they offer, and they welcome foreign visitors. There are Japanese hotels which are timorous of accepting foreign guests because of the differences in language and customs.

All of the large city and resort hotels offer Western and Japanese food. During the summer season, hotel reservations are advised.

Outside the cities or major towns, most hotels quote prices on a per-person basis with two meals, exclusive of service and tax. If you do not want dinner at your hotel, it is usually possible to renegotiate the price. Stipulate, too, whether you wish to have Japanese or Western breakfasts, if any. For the purposes here, the categories assigned to all hotels reflect the cost of a double room, with private bath but no meals. However, if you make reservations at any of the noncity hotels, you will be expected to take breakfast and dinner at the hotel—that will be the rate quoted to you, unless you specify otherwise.

A 3% federal consumer tax is added to all hotel bills. Another 3% local tax is added if the bill exceeds ¥10,000. At most hotels, a 10%–15% service charge is added to the total bill. Tipping is not the custom.

Category	Cost*
Very Expensive	over ¥20,000
Expensive	¥15,000–¥20,000
Moderate	¥10,000–¥15,000
Inexpensive	under ¥10,000

*Cost is for double room, without tax or service

The most highly recommended restaurants and accommodations are indicated by a star ★.

Credit Cards The following credit card abbreviations are used: AE, American Express; DC, Diners Club; MC, MasterCard; V, Visa.

Aizu-Wakamatsu

Lodging **Mukaitaki Ryokan.** The Mukaitaki is one ryokan in this spa town of Higashiyama-onsen (nearby Aizu-Wakamatsu) that retains a traditional ambience, thanks to its plank floors, shoji screens, and screen prints. *200 Kawamukou, Yumoto, Higashiyama-machi, Fukushima-ken 965, tel. 0242/27–7501. 25 Japanese-style rooms. Facilities: Japanese dining only, thermal (public) baths. MC. Moderate.*

Akita

Dining **Restaurant Bekkan Hamanoya.** This establishment is the local favorite for *hata-hata* (sand fish), which is a regional specialty and is especially good in the wintertime. *4-2-11 Omachi, Akita, tel. 0188/23–7481. Dress: informal. MC, V. Open lunch and dinner. Moderate.*

Lodging **Akita View Hotel.** This hotel has clean, fresh rooms, though they are slightly on the small side. On the upper floors of a department store, and located seven minutes by foot from the JR station, it is convenient to shopping; it also has a swimming pool. *2-6 Nakadori, Akita 010, tel. 0188/32–1111. 115 Western-style rooms. Facilities: Western and Japanese restaurants, coffee shop, 2 bars, indoor pool, health center, shops. AE, DC, MC, V. Expensive.*

★ **Akita Castle Hotel.** With the best location and the most professional service in Akita, the Castle Hotel has well-maintained rooms, but be aware that the larger double rooms (normal American size) fall in the expensive category. The more commodious Japanese-style rooms (only 3 in the hotel) are the same price as the Western-style ones. The bar and the French restaurant offer a park view. *1-3-5 Nakadori, Akita 010 (opposite the moat and a 15-min walk from the station), tel. 0188/34–1141. 206 rooms, mostly Western style. Facilities: Western,*

Japanese, and Chinese restaurants. AE, DC, MC, V. Moderate–Expensive.

Kohama Ryokan. No rooms in this small inn have a private bath. However, it is friendly, homey and priced right. Moreover, it is conveniently located across from the Akita JR station and 100 yards to the right of Mr. Donut. *6-19-6 Nakadori, Akita 010 (15 min walk, bearing left from the station, past Mr. Donut), tel. 0188/32–5739. 10 rooms without bath. Facilities: Japanese dining, but Continental breakfast is offered. AE, V. Inexpensive.*

Aomori

Lodging   **Aomori Grand Hotel.** Close to the station, this establishment is the best in town for an overnight stay. Its recent refurbishing has made the lobby personable. The lounge for morning coffee has superbly comfortable armchairs, and the Continental Bellevue restaurant on the 12th floor is an enjoyable place to spend an evening. Guest rooms tend to be small. *1-1-23 Shinmachi, Aomori City 030, tel. 0177/23–1011. 148 rooms, mostly Western style. Facilities: Japanese and Continental restaurant. AE, DC, MC, V. Moderate.*

Hachimantai

Matsukawa so. The ryokan is popular for its rustic flair and the rejuvenating spa waters. It is simple, clean, and traditional, with highly polished wooden floors. Two meals are included, and all rooms are Japanese style. *Matsukawa Onsen, Matsuo-mura, Iwate-gun 028-73, tel. 01957/8–2255. 25 rooms. Facilities: dining room, thermal baths. AE. Inexpensive–Moderate.*

Kyounso. Just the basic essentials are offered at this little inn: small tatami rooms and shared bathroom facilities. Meals (optional) are served in a communal room. The owners are always delighted to have a Westerner stay. *Matsukawa Onsen, Matsuo-mura, Iwate-gun 028-73, tel. 01957/8–2256. 18 rooms. Facilities: dining room. AE, V. Inexpensive.*

Sukayu Onsen. In a vast, rambling wooden building in the mountains, this traditional Japanese Inn is one of the few left in the country where men and women are not separated in the main baths. (There are smaller baths that are segregated.) The sulphur mineral waters have been used for their curative powers for three centuries. The guest rooms are small and only thinly partitioned from each other, so light sleepers may find it hard to fall asleep. A fixed, multi-dish dinner is served in your room. Japanese breakfasts are served in a large dining room. There is no village nearby, but ski slopes and hiking trails are close. *Sukayu Onsen, Hakkoda-Sunchu, Aomori, tel. 0177/38–6400; fax 0177/38–6677. 134 rooms. Facilities: thermal baths, Japanese food served in one's room. AE, DC, MC, V. Moderate–Expensive.*

Hirosaki

Lodging   **Hotel New Castle.** A smart business hotel, on a par with the Hokke Club, the New Castle is fractionally more expensive, though no better. It is, however, a good alternative if the Hokke is full. The restaurant here offers formal and elegant Japanese meals. *24-1 Kamisayashi-machi, Hirosaki 036 (located on the* *castle side of downtown Hirosaki), tel. 0172/36–1211. 59 rooms, mostly Western style. Facilities: Japanese and Continental restaurant. AE, DC, MC, V. Moderate–Expensive.*

★ **Hokke Club Hotel.** This modern, efficient hotel uses sparkling marble for its public rooms. These rooms are small, with an open design giving an illusion of space. Bedrooms tend to be small, so you may want to upgrade your room. Surrounded by shops and restaurants, the Hokke Club begins two flights up a moving escalator. The Kasen Japanese restaurant has excellent formal dining. *126 Dotemachi, Hirosaki 036 (located in the center of town), tel. 0172/34–3811. 65 rooms, mostly Western style. Facilities: tearoom, American-style bar (The Jolly Dog), Finnish sauna. AE, V. Moderate.*

Matsushima

Lodging
★ **Ryokan Matsushimajo.** This very traditional ryokan is in the center of the town and just up from the shore road. The main building has antique objects of art on its walls, including woodblock prints done by the famous artist Hiroshige. The ryokan, creaking with age, has ancient banisters and polished wood floors. Its sloping tiled roof and adjoining tower make the Matsushimajo look like a castle, but the ryokan is only about 100 years old. Guest rooms only have overhead fans, and most of them do not have private baths, but a room overlooking the bay is quite marvelous. Come here for lunch if you are only visiting Matsushima for the day. *Matsushima, Miyagi 981, tel. 022/354–2121. 28 Japanese-style rooms. Facilities: Japanese dining room serving lunch and dinner. AE, V. Moderate–Expensive.*

Koganesaneo. The advantage of this minshuku which is in Nobiru, a village situated on the far (north) side of Matsushima Bay, is its location—an easy six-minute-walk from the Nobiru JR station and a block from the beach. Otherwise, the rooms are tiny (six tatami) and the paper-thin walls permit you to hear every guest's footfall. Avoid the room next to the toilet! Food is served in your room in a perfunctory manner, but the fresh Pacific seafood—mussels, crab, oyster, and shrimp—especially in the colder months, is a redeeming feature. *68–46 Aza Minami-yogei, Nobiru, Naruse-machi, Monoo-gun, Miyagi Pref., tel. 0225/88–2183. 12 rooms, none with private bath. Facilities: Japanese food served in one's room. V. Inexpensive.*

Miyako

Minshuku Obata. Sixteen minutes on the Senniku Railway from Miyako is Taro, a small village well-located for sightseeing. This large minshuku provides fair-size (8 tatami) rooms, two meals a day, and clean public bath and toilet facilities. The food is adequate, not special, but you will usually have the opportunity to taste the local specialties, scallops and abalone. *60–2 Nokara, Tarocho, Shimohei–gun, Iwate Pref. (15 min walk from Taro railway station, but owners will collect you by car if you phone them), tel. 0193/87–2631. 16 rooms, none with private bath. Facilities: Japanese breakfast and dinner included. Hosts' son will give guests tour of area. Inexpensive.*

Morioka

For *wanka soba* (buckwheat noodles), there are at least 16 restaurants in the city, some directly across the road from the JR station plaza. Try **Azumaya** (tel. 0196/22–2233) one flight up in a building on Ekimae Kita-dori, right across from the taxi stand on the corner of Ekimae-dori.

Dining **Restaurant Nambu Robata.** Recognized for its regional specialties cooked over charcoal, the Nambu Robata is like an old country farmhouse with a traditional hearth. Try the grilled fish, which are first filleted and then reassembled. The restaurant is near the Hachiman Firewatch Tower, a five-minute walk from the bus center. Its popularity has grown since we first mentioned it; prices now run close to ¥7,000 per person. *Hachiman-cho, Morioka City, tel. 0196/22–5082. Dress: informal. No credit cards. Open 11:30–9:30. Expensive.*

Restaurant Wakana. This dining spot is within an eight-minute walk from the station—cross the river, fork left and take another left after the Kawatoku Department Store. The Wakana offers good *teppanyaki* (food cooked on a flat grill) and claims the best beef in the city. *1-3-33 Osawakawara, Morioka City, tel. 0196/53–3333. Jacket and tie required. AE, DC, MC, V. Open 11–8. Closed Tues. Moderate.*

Lodging **Morioka Grand Hotel.** The most personable and smartest mod-
★ ern hotel in town, the Grand is situated on a small hill on the edge of the city, 10 minutes by taxi from the station. Its views are broader, the air is cleaner, and its rooms are slightly larger than most hotels in the area. Do not confuse this hotel with the cheaper Morioka Grand Hotel Annex. *1-10 Atagoshita, Morioka, Iwate 020, tel. 0196/25–2111. 36 rooms, 21 Western style. Facilities: Japanese and Continental restaurants. AE, DC, MC, V. Expensive.*

Hotel Higashi-Nihon. This is the largest hotel in town and bustles with groups, wedding parties, and banquets. It caters to all and has all the amenities of an international, but impersonal, hotel, including eight restaurants of various international cuisines. The two Japanese-style rooms are slightly larger and no more expensive than the Western-style ones. *3-3-18 Odori, Morioka. Iwate 020, tel. 0196/25–2131. 209 rooms, 207 Western style. Facilities: indoor tennis courts, Japanese and Continental restaurants. AE, DC, MC, V. Moderate.*

Morioka Terminal Hotel. Convenient to the station and located just to the left of the station plaza and one flight up the escalator, this hotel has clean and utilitarian rooms. The combination Chinese/Japanese and Western buffet at breakfast is the best value in town. The staff is extremely helpful, despite the language barrier. Though the hotel has a good Chinese restaurant on the 4th floor, ask the reception clerk to take you across the street and introduce you to Umacho, a tiny *nomiya*, or pub. No English is spoken here, so point to what you want or have the clerk order for you. The Kin Kin, a slowly grilled fish, is delicate and succulent. *1-44 Morioka Ekimae-dori, Morioka, Iwate 020, tel. 0196/25–1211. 194 rooms. Facilities: Western, Japanese, and Chinese restaurants. AE, MC. Inexpensive–Moderate.*

Ryokan Kumagai. In a two–storey wooden building, this simple hostelry is a member of the inexpensive Japanese Inn Group offering basic tatami rooms. None of the rooms have a private bath, but there is a small dining area where Japanese or Western breakfasts and Japanese dinners are optional. Located between the station and center city, it is a 10-minute walk from the Morioka JR station—cross the river and walk along Kawinbashi-dori two blocks and turn right (a gas station is on the left and a bank on the right). Cross over one block and the ryokan is on the left. *3-2-5 Oosawakawara, Morioka City, Iwate Pref. 020, tel. 0196/51–3020. 11 rooms, none with private bath. Facilities: breakfast and dinner served. Inexpensive.*

Nyuto Onsen

Lodging Nyuto consists of six small spa villages. The following are the telephone numbers to be called for reservations at each of the villages' inns: **Tsurono Onsen,** *closed in winter, tel. 0187/46–2438.* **Taeno-yu Onsen,** *tel. 0187/46–2740.* **Ohgama Onsen,** *tel. 0187/46–2438.* **Kaniba Onsen,** *tel. 0187/46–2021.* **Magoroku Onsen,** *tel. 0187/46–2224.* **Kuro-yu Onsen,** *closed in winter, tel. 0187/46–2214.*

Sendai

Dining Sendai abounds in restaurants. Many of the Japanese restaurants are along Chuo-dori Avenue and most of them display their menus in their windows, along with the prices for each dish. The following are just a sampling of the many restaurants from which to choose:

Iwashiya. This restaurant is famous for its fresh sashimi. The specialty is five slivers of meat taken from the back of the fish, while it is still alive. The slivers and the tail-twitching fish are presented on a plate before you. Grilled-fish dishes are also available and perfectly done. Service is either at the counter or at tables placed on tatami matting. *4-5-42 Ichiban-cho, tel. 022/222–6645. (Take the alley left [east] just before the Gateaux Boutique on Ichiban-cho, and then the first right. The restaurant is on the right, with a fish tank in the window.) Jacket and tie suggested. No credit cards. Open 5–11. Expensive–Very Expensive.*

Aka-Beko. This small izakaya has an excellent array of foods—sushi, grilled meats on skewers, grilled fish, and tasty soups. There is both a counter and seating on tatami mats. Close to the SS 30 Building and to Ryokan Aisaki, this is one of the friendliest local restaurants in town. *91 Yagamouchi-dori, Sendai, tel. 022/224–2966. Dress: casual. No credit cards. Open 5–11. Moderate.*

Isahachi. On the ground floor the restaurant hums with activity and offers yakitori-style cuisine (grilled skewers of chicken). Downstairs in a slightly quieter ambience, the restaurant offers a range of regional dishes *(kyodo ryori)* as well as beef dishes, including sukiyaki. *4-3-7 Ichiban-cho, tel. 022/222–7080. (Located on Chuo-dori, just north of Hirose-dori; Isahachi has a sign outside and one enters the building through a corridor.) Dress: informal. No credit cards. Lunch 11–2:30, dinner 6–10:30. Inexpensive–Moderate.*

Robata. A fun drinking place, Robata has decorations from traditional folklore. Order the herring *(nisshin)* with your beer—it's a meal in itself. *Next to the Hotel Rich (2-2-2 Kokubucho), tel. 022/23–0316. Dress: informal. No credit cards. Inexpensive.*

SS 30 Building. Inside the tallest building in town, the restau-

rants on the top three floors of the SS 30 do a brisk trade. There
are plenty to choose from—**Saboten** (tel. 022/267–4083), on the
28th floor, serves inexpensive fried fish and salads; **Le Monde**
(tel. 022/224–2181), also on the 28th floor, serves French food;
Toh–Ter–Koh (tel. 022/267–0841), on the 30th floor, serves innovative Japanese cuisine with a distinct French influence. Or,
if you prefer just a cocktail with your view, drop into **Ermitage**
(tel. 022/261–4777), a cozy, Western-style bar.

However, one is really better off for serious French-style cuisine at either **Hotel Sendai Plaza** or **Koyo Grand Hotel**.

Lodging **Sendai Kokusai Hotel.** The newest of Sendai's hotels (com-
★ pleted in 1990, next to the new SS 30 complex), immediately
won attention as the town's leading hotel. The lobby glistens
with marble and stainless steel; guest rooms are furnished in
light pastels, and larger rooms have stucco arches to exagge-
rate their size. Fresh flowers add a touch of color. Lighting is
subdued—not so good for late-night reading. Competing with
the dozen restaurants in the SS 30 Building, the hotel offers
French, Chinese, and Japanese fare and two bars. *4-6-1 Chuo,
Aoba-ku, Sendai, Miyagi 980, tel. 022/268–1112, fax 022/268–
1113. 190 rooms. Facilities: 3 restaurants, sushi bar, 2 bars,
coffee shop, children's room, banquet/conference rooms, shopping arcade. AE, DC, MC, V. Expensive–Very Expensive.*
Koyo Grand Hotel. The Koyo Grand must be the most weirdly
furnished hotel in Japan. The hotel combines objects of art
from China and Europe with a predominance of Louis XV reproductions. The total assemblage is a mismatch of statues,
mounted deer heads, Regency upholstered furniture, gold
painted chandeliers, and ceiling murals. Thankfully, the guest
rooms have more simple and standard furniture (though with
turn-of-the-century French reproductions); otherwise one
would have horrendous nightmares. The hotel has a small but
good French restaurant, and also a Chinese restaurant, the
Lou-Lan, offering Szechuan and Cantonese cooking. *1-3-2
Hon-cho, Sendai, Miyagi 980, tel. 022/267–5111. 149 Western-
style rooms. Facilities: Japanese, French, and Chinese restaurants. AE, DC, MC, V. Moderate–Expensive.*
Sendai Hotel. The decor is refreshingly light, using modern,
pale colors and cheerful prints for wall decorations. This modern hotel is popular with businessmen wishing to stay near the
station. The service is attentive to foreign guests, including
the delivery of an English-language newspaper, the *Japan
Times*, in the morning. *1-10-25 Chuo, Sendai, Miyagi 980 (located 2 min. on foot from the station), tel. 022/225–5171. 123
rooms, mostly Japanese style. Facilities: Chinese, Japanese,
Western, and French (with a garden view) restaurants, shopping arcade. AE, V. Moderate–Expensive.*
Sendai Terminal Hotel. Brand-new in 1989 and located adjacent
to the railway station, this upscale business traveler's hotel has
reasonably large guest rooms that are decorated in light colors.
The 21st-floor Sky Lounge restaurant offers the best city
view—and French food to go with it. Simpler fare at more reasonable prices is found in the coffee shop, Pal Phony, on the second floor. *1-1-1 Chuo-dori, Sendai 980, tel. 022/261–2525. 300
rooms, including 3 suites and 4 Japanese-style rooms. Facilities: restaurants, coffee shop, indoor pool, gym, small business center, banquet rooms. AE, DC, MC, V. Moderate–
Expensive.*

★ **Ryokan Aisaki.** This inn has been run by the same family since 1868. However, the present building is post–World War II, and the rooms have recently been newly wall-papered. Only two rooms have private bathrooms, but the public bath has the added benefit of a sauna. Still, the hostelry is enjoyable for friendly companionship with other guests, and the owner welcomes foreigners. He speaks fluent English and often will take guests on sightseeing trips. *5-6 Kitame-machi, Sendai, Miyagi 980, tel. 022/264–0700. 20 rooms, 8 Western style. Facilities: sauna, meals (Japanese) are optional. AE, MC. Inexpensive–Moderate.*

Tazawako

Lodging **Tazawako Prince.** A modern white hotel on the edge of Lake Tazawa, the Tazawako Prince has views of Mt. Komaga-take. Most of the hotel's rooms have balconies. The rooms are: large with a lake view; small with a lake view; or small with a mountian view. Aside from the main dining room, there is a garden room down near the lake. *Katajiri, Saimyoji, Nishiki-mure, Senboku-gun, Akita 014-05, tel. 0187/47–2211. Facilities: shops, game room, Japanese and Western dining, boat rentals. AE, DC, MC, V. Moderate.*

Tono

Lodging **Fukuzanso Inn.** Highly polished creaky floors characterize this
★ friendly, old-fashioned ryokan. Rooms have a dressing room/ closet area, a main area, and a small enclosed balcony with Western-style table and chairs. Dinner, served in your room, is a marvelous array of a dozen dishes, ranging from sashimi to steamed beef. No English is spoken, but the hospitality is all smiles; the staff lends bikes for sightseeing. *5-30 Chuo-dori, Tono City 028, tel. 01986/2–4120. 25 rooms. Facilities: dinner and breakfast included, Japanese public baths. MC. Moderate.*

Towada

Lodging **Towada Grand Hotel.** The Towada Grand is on the beach, but the main reason for staying here is its own thermal baths; at least, that's the reason for its popularity with Japanese summer vacationers. *16 Yaumiya, Aza-Towada, Kauni-gun, Akita 018-55, tel. 0176/75–2121. 57 rooms, about ½ Western style and ½ Japanese style. AE, V. Expensive.*

Yamagata

Lodging **Hotel Castle.** A modern and utilitarian hotel, the Castle is smartly efficient and conveniently located. The rooms are on the small side. There are always a lot of guests milling around the lobby area, where there is a coffee/tea lounge (refills on coffee are free), but for views try the Kega pub/restaurant or the Chateau Reine French restaurant on the 12th floor, which offers the best dining in town. *2-7 Toka-machi, 4-chome, Yamagata 990 (a 7-minute walk from the railway station), tel. 0236/31–3311. 160 Western-style rooms. Facilities: Western, Chinese, and Japanese restaurants, pub. AE, DC, MC, V. Moderate.*

15 Hokkaido

Introduction

by Nigel Fisher

Hokkaido is untamed Japan. In the rest of the country it may be said that the cities dominate the countryside—not so in Hokkaido. Its cities and towns are modern outposts of urban man that are surrounded by wild, untamed mountains, virgin forests, crystal-clear lakes, and surf-beaten shores. Hokkaido is Japan's last frontier, and the attitudes of the inhabitants are akin to the pioneers of the American West.

Hokkaido was not even mentioned in books until the 7th century; even then, for the next millennium, it was discounted as the place where the "hairy Ainu" lived. The Ainu, the original inhabitants of Japan, were always thought of as the inferior race by the Yamato Japanese. As the Yamato spread and expanded their empire up from Kyushu through Honshu, the peace-loving Ainu retreated north to Hokkaido. There they lived, hunting and fishing in peace, until a hundred years ago.

With the Meiji Restoration in 1868, Japan changed its policy toward Hokkaido and opened it up as the new frontier to be colonized by the Yamato Japanese. The Tokyo government encouraged immigration from the rest of Japan to Hokkaido but made no provision for the Ainu peoples. Indeed, the Ainu were given no choice but to assimilate themselves into the life and culture of the colonizers. Consequently, the Ainu have virtually disappeared as a race. A few elders still speak Ainu, but when they die, so will their language. Long gone are Ainu communities. Only Ainu villages, constructed as tourist attractions, remain, and they are depressing places.

The Ainu are not the only Japanese aborigines. There was also another race, the Moyoro, which lived before the Ainu, but little is known about these mysterious peoples. From anthropological evidence found on Hokkaido's east coast in the Moyoro Shell Mound, now displayed in the Abashiri Museum, it is thought that their civilization ended in the 9th century.

With no visible past and with newly born cities, Hokkaido is a respite from temples, shrines, and castles. For the tourist, Hokkaido is a geographical wonderland. Bears still roam the forests, snagging rabbits and scooping up fish from mountain streams, and deer wander the pastures, stealing fodder from cows. Lava-seared mountains, imposing in their dominance, hide deeply carved ravines. Hot springs, gushers, and steaming mud pools boil out of the ground. Crystal-clear caldera lakes fill the seemingly bottomless cones of volcanoes. As recently as 1945, the volcano Showa Shinzan rose from a potato patch before the eyes of a bewildered farmer. Half of Hokkaido is covered in forests. Wild, rugged coastlines hold back the sea. All around Hokkaido, islands surface offshore. Some are volcanic peaks poking their cones out of the ocean, and others were formed aeons ago by the crunching of the earth's crust.

May and early summer bring the blossoming of alpine flowers and lilacs. Also, the cherry trees in Hokkaido are the last to bloom in Japan—in late April and early May. Summers are drier and cooler than in the rest of Japan, and thus a trip to Hokkaido allows an escape from the humidity. Hotel space becomes relatively difficult to find, and the scenic areas become crowded with tour groups and Japanese families. September brings autumn, and the turning leaves offer spectacular golden colors, reaching their peak in early October. November and April are the least desirable months; the first falls of snow in November just dirty the roads, and in April the snow melts into a brown mess. The winter makes travel more difficult (some minor roads are closed), and, especially on the east coast, the weather is frigid. Yet the winter is also beautiful, with crisp white snow lying everywhere.

One of the delights of traveling through Hokkaido is meeting the people, who are known as the Dosanko. Since virtually all of the Japanese in Hokkaido are "immigrants to a new frontier," a Dosanko places less emphasis on tradition and more on accomplishing the matter at hand. He is still very Japanese, sharing the same culture as the rest of Japan, but he is also open to new customs and other cultures.

Hokkaido was born during the Meiji Restoration, a time when the Japanese government turned to the West for new ideas. Hokkaido, especially, sought advice from America and Europe for its development. In the 1870s, some 63 foreign experts came to this island, including an American architect who designed Hokkaido's principal city, Sapporo. Around the same time, agricultural experts from abroad were brought in to introduce dry-farming as a substitute for rice, which could not grow in the severe winter climate. This has left the Dosanko with a peculiar fondness for Europeans. In Sapporo, there is an open warmth displayed to Westerners. In the country, the Dosanko is shy but not timid in coming to the aid of Westerners.

Because Hokkaido consists of more countryside than cities, foreigners appear reluctant to visit the island. Only 23,000 foreigners come each year (16,500 are Westerners), in contrast with the several million Japanese who choose Hokkaido for winter skiing and summer hiking. Because Hokkaido is Japan's northernmost and least developed island, there is a strong sense shared by resident and visitor alike of discovering uncharted territory. It's untrue, of course. Hokkaido has a road and rail network that crisscrosses the island, but the feeling of newness still remains.

Essential Information

Arriving and Departing

For most visitors to Hokkaido, the points of entry are either Sapporo (by plane) or Hakodate (by train).

By Plane Japan Airlines (JAL), Japan Air System, and All Nippon Airways (ANA) link Hokkaido to the island of Honshu by direct flights from Tokyo's Haneda airport to Hakodate, Sapporo, Asahikawa, Mombetsu, and Kushiro. Several other major cities on Honshu (Sendai, Aomori, Akita, Niigata, Nagoya, Osaka, and Hiroshima) have flights to Sapporo. Sapporo's airport is Chitose, 25 miles south of Sapporo. There are frequent trains and buses connecting the city with the airport. (*See* Sapporo, below). The cost by air from Tokyo to Sapporo is ¥23,850, compared with ¥21,070 by train. Although the policy is subject to change, travelers arriving in Japan on Japan Airlnes from overseas can, with a change of planes at Tokyo, fly at no extra charge to Sapporo.

By Train   With the 33.66-mile Seikan Tunnel (opened March 1988) permitting train travel between Hokkaido and Honshu, the train journey from Tokyo to Sapporo is 10 hours, 21 minutes; this trip involves a combination of the Shinkansen train to Morioka, the northernmost point on the Tohoku Shinkansen line, and a change to an express train for the remaining journey. Alternatively, there is the Blue Train (the blue-colored long-distance sleeper) from Tokyo to Sapporo, which takes 16 hours. The Japan Rail Pass covers the train fare in either case, but an additional charge is made for a sleeping compartment on the Blue Train.

By Ferry   The inexpensive form of travel to Hokkaido is by ferry from Honshu. From Tokyo to Kushiro (33 hours), there is the luxury ferryboat *Marimo*, which sails twice weekly and is operated by the Kinkai Yosen Company. (Cost: ¥28,000 first class, ¥14,000 second class.) From Tokyo to Tomakomai (31 hours), another large ferry, the *Shiretoko*, is operated by the Japan Coastal Ferry Company. (Fare: ¥29,660 first class, ¥11,840 second class.) The same company also operates an overnight ferry (15 hours) from Sendai to Tomakomai. The ferry between Aomori and Hakodate (4 hours), which was the way to cross from northern Honshu to Hokkaido before the Seikan Tunnel, plans to stay in operation for those not wishing to take the train through the tunnel.

Getting Around

By Plane   The two domestic airlines that connect Sapporo with Hakodate, Kushiro, and Wakkanai are Japan Air System and Nippon Kinkyori Airways. There is also air service from July to October between Wakkanai and both Rebun and Rishiri.

By Train and Bus   Japan Railways (JR) has routes connecting most of the major cities. For the most part, the trains travel the unscenic routes and are simply efficient means to travel to the areas that you want to explore. Buses cover most of the major routes through the scenic areas, and all the excursions in this chapter may be accomplished by bus.

By Car   Cars are easy to rent, and the Nippon-Hertz agency has offices at all major railway stations. An international driving permit, obtainable from any AAA office in the United States, is required for driving in Japan. Driving is on the left-hand side of the road, and speed limits are frustratingly low. For the most part, the Japanese are cautious drivers and obey the rules of the road. International traffic signs are used and are easy to understand. Directional signs are often sufficiently given in romaji (Japanese written in Roman script) to enable non-Japanese readers to navigate, and all major roads have route numbers. Also, the Dosanko are extremely helpful in giving instructions and directions to the Western tourist. The limitation to renting a car is the expense. A day's rental is about ¥11,000, with limited free mileage. Gas and tolls on the few expressways are three times as much as you would find in the United States. The best plan is, wherever possible, to travel long distances by public transport and then rent a car for local trips.

Important Addresses and Numbers

<table>
<tr><td>Tourist Information</td><td>The Japan National Tourist Organization's **Tourist Information Center (TIC)** in Tokyo (the Kotani Bldg., 1–6–6 Yurakucho, Chiyoda-ku) has free maps and brochures on Hokkaido. Within Hokkaido, the best place for travel information is in Sapporo (*see* Sapporo, below).</td></tr>
</table>

Tourist Information

The Japan National Tourist Organization's **Tourist Information Center (TIC)** in Tokyo (the Kotani Bldg., 1–6–6 Yurakucho, Chiyoda-ku) has free maps and brochures on Hokkaido. Within Hokkaido, the best place for travel information is in Sapporo (*see* Sapporo, below).

Other important regional tourist information centers are: **Akan Lake** (tel. 0154/67–2254); **Noboribetsu Onsen** (tel. 01438 /4–2068); **Sounkyo Onsen** (tel. 01658/5–5530); **Lake Toya** (tel. 01427/5–2446).

Bus and train travel information centers are available at all the major train stations to help. The main Hokkaido office of the **Japan Travel Bureau** is in Sapporo; this office is where you are most likely to find English spoken (tel. 011/241–6201).

The Japan Travel-Phone (the nationwide service for English-language assistance or travel information) is available from 9 to 5, seven days a week. Dial toll-free 0120/222–800 for information on eastern Japan. When using a yellow, blue, or green public phone (do not use the red phones), insert a 10-yen coin, which will be returned.

Emergencies

Police, tel. 110; **ambulance,** tel. 119.

Guided Tours

The Japan Travel Bureau operates four-day tours of Hokkaido from Tokyo. For ¥195,700, the tour includes Sapporo (overnight), Nakayama Pass, Lake Toya (overnight), Noboribetsu (overnight), Shiraoi, and back to Chitose. Three breakfasts, one lunch, and two dinners are included, and there is a ¥28,000 single supplement. These tours operate daily from April 15 through October 31.

Hakodate

When traveling by train from Honshu, the first town in Hokkaido to be reached is **Hakodate.** Whereas prior to 1988, crossing over to Hokkaido required taking the four-hour ferry trip from Aomori to Hakodate, the new Seikan Tunnel lets trains make the passage in less than two hours. En route through the tunnel is a railway station 400 feet beneath the sea, where there is a museum dedicated to the construction of the tunnel. You can get off the train here and stretch your legs, take in the museum, and catch the next train 90 minutes later. However, the first stop in Hokkaido proper is Hakodate; because there are still four hours on the train before reaching Sapporo, Hakodate may be a better place to stretch your legs. Stop at the Information Office just to the right of the Hakodate JR station to collect maps in English. If you only want a short stopover and have arrived in the morning, take a visit to the colorful morning fish and vegetable market, **Asa Ichi,** just a three-minute walk south of the station (open every morning, except Sunday, from 5 AM to noon, peaking at 8). Recently, it has grown to be more than just a market, with 400 shops selling anything from Kegani crabs to sea urchins, asparagus to cherries.

Exploring

Hakodate's peak was in 1859, when it was one of the three ports in Japan opened to trade with the West. This heritage supplies the attractions for visitors today. Old (sometimes rather decrepit) buildings with definite European- and American-style architecture cluster around the section of town known as **Motomachi.** To get there from the JR station, take the streetcar to the Suehirocho stop and walk 10 minutes toward **Mt. Hakodate,** the mountain that rises above the city. There is no one particular building that stands out, though a useful spot to start in is the **Orthodox Church of the Resurrection,** founded in 1862 by a Russian prelate and rebuilt in Byzantine style in 1916. A large-scale restoration project was completed here in 1989, and it has become an important tourist attraction for the city. Then head for the **Kyodo-shiryokan** (three minutes away), built in 1880 and now a local museum with artifacts from Hakodate's past. Close to the museum is the building that served as the city's public hall, but with its classical columns and antebellum architecture, it looks as if it should be a manor house in America's Deep South.

In the center of the city is **Goryokaku,** a Western-style fort completed in 1864. The fort's design is unusual for Japan, especially with its five-pointed-star shape, which enabled its defenders to rake any attackers with murderous cross fire. However, the Tokugawa shogunate's defenders were unable to hold out against the forces of the Meiji Restoration, and its walls were breached. Nothing of the interior of the castle remains today, though there is a small museum with relics from the battle. Now the fort area is a park with some 4,000 cherry trees, which, when they bloom in late April, make the stopover in Hakodate worthwhile. There is also an observation tower in the park, but at ¥520 admission, it is not worth the climb for the view. *Open May–Oct., daily 8–8; Nov.–Apr., daily 9–6.*

Behind, as if guarding the city, is Mt. Hakodate, a volcanic hill rising 1,100 feet. The panoramic views of the city from the top are good at any time, but especially at night, with the lights of the buildings and street lamps below. A bus, which takes 20 minutes, goes to the top of Mt. Hakodate from the JR station. For a more interesting trip, there is the streetcar (Line 2) to the Horaicho stop, where a ropeway makes the five-minute haul up the mountain. A restaurant at the top is particularly appealing for its nighttime view. *Cost: ¥620, one way; ¥1,130, round-trip. Operates daily 9–9 (Mar. 1–Oct. 21); 10–6 (Oct. 22–Feb. 28). The road is closed late Nov.–late Apr.*

Finally, should you need a bath before leaving Hakodate, take the streetcar from the JR station for a 20-minute ride to Yachigashira Onsen. Here there is a mammoth public bathhouse accommodating 600 people. *Admission: ¥400. Open 6 AM–9:30 PM (Apr.–Oct.); 7 AM–9:30 PM (Nov.–Mar.).*

From Hakodate there are two ways by train to Sapporo. The slow way cuts through the west side of Shikotsu Toya National Park and heads up to the north coast of Hokkaido to Otaru before veering east for Sapporo. The fast way travels along the southern coast before turning north to Sapporo. On this route, one may disembark from the train for visits to Lake Toya and/or Noboribetsu Onsen before continuing on to Sapporo. *(See* Lake Toya, below.) For the purposes of this book, both Lake

Toya and Noboribetsu Onsen are covered as excursions out of Sapporo.

At the Hakodate train station, you can purchase something to eat. Try the local *eki-ben* (box lunch), the *nishin-migaki-bento*. It consists of *nishin* (herring) boiled in a sweet, spicy sauce until the bones are soft enough to eat. Then, when your appetite returns at Mori station, an hour's distance from Hakodate en route to Sapporo, you can have another well-known ekiben, *ika-meshi*. This box lunch is made by stuffing a whole *ika* (squid) with rice and cooking it in a sweet, spicy sauce. Each meal includes two or three ika.

Sapporo

Sapporo is not just Hokkaido's capital; it is also the island's premier city. With 1.6 million inhabitants, it is three times larger than the second largest city (Asahikawa) in Hokkaido. It continues to expand, as Hokkaido's unemployed from the economically depressed shipbuilding towns in the southwest and the farms in the central plains migrate to Sapporo for work. The result is that Sapporo, in just over 100 years since its birth, has the benefits of a large city without the street confusion and congestion; however, it also lacks the pre-Meiji historical sights. In 1870, the governor of Hokkaido had visited President Grant in the United States and requested that American advisers come to Hokkaido to help design the capital on the site of an Ainu village. As a result, the city was built on a 100-meter grid system with wide avenues and parks. Sapporo, then, is not the exotic and cultured city one expects to find in Japan. Despite its ever-increasing population, the city has had room to spread. One can walk the sidewalks or underground shopping malls without being swept away in a surge of humanity. Sapporo is architecturally boring, yet it is comfortable; within a couple of hours of walking around, your knowledge of its layout is clear.

By hosting the 1972 Winter Olympics, Sapporo made itself an international city and developed a cosmopolitan attitude. Numerous international-style hotels and restaurants came into being at that time and have stayed. Banks here are used to traveler's checks, and there is always someone on hand to help you out in English. Sapporo readily becomes the base from which to make excursions into the wild, dramatic countryside. The actual time spent exploring Sapporo can be minimal—a day, perhaps two at the most.

Arriving and Departing

By Plane Sapporo's airport, at Chitose, 25 miles south of Sapporo, is Hokkaido's main airport. Since it is new and one of Japan's better ones, attempts are underway to divert some of the air traffic from Narita to Chitose. Japan Airlines (JAL) (tel. 011/231–4411 international; tel. 011/231–0231 domestic), All Nippon Airways (ANA) (tel. 011/251–4231), and Japan Air System (tel. 011/231–5131) use this airport. For information on arrival and departure times, call the individual airlines. For the airport itself (Hokkaido Airport Terminal Co.), dial 0123/41–5311.

Between the Airport Japan Railways (JR) has frequent train service between the
and Center City airport terminal (Chitose Airport Station—Chitosekudo—not Chitose City Station) and downtown Sapporo. The trip takes 35

minutes and costs ¥720 for the local and ¥920 for the express (a difference of 10 minutes in travel time). ANA runs a shuttle bus (¥700) that connects with its flights at Chitose and its hotel, the ANA Zenniku, in Sapporo. The Chuo Bus (¥700) runs a shuttle between the airport and Sapporo's Grand Hotel. Taxis are available, but the distance between Sapporo and the airport makes them ridiculously expensive, so they are rarely used.

By Train All JR trains come into the central station, located on the north side of downtown Sapporo. Trains arrive and depart for Honshu about every two hours. Trains to and from Otaru run every hour, as do the trains for Asahikawa, in central Hokkaido.

By Car Sapporo has three expressways: to Chitose and points south and west; to Otaru; and east, halfway to Asahikawa.

Getting Around

Sapporo is a walking city with wide sidewalks; it's easy to find your way around. The **Sapporo Tourist Office** at the Sapporo railway station has a city map, and most hotels have a smaller map marking their hotels and the major points of interest.

By Subway Sapporo's subway is a pleasure. As in Toronto and Moscow, the trains have rubber wheels and run quietly. There are three lines, which makes it easy to use. One (the Nanboku Line) runs from the station south to north past Susukino to Nakajima. A second (the Tozai Line) bisects the city from east to west. They cross at Odori Station. A third subway line (Toho Line), opened in 1989. It parallels the Nanboku Line from Odori Station to the JR station before branching off into the northeastern suburbs. The trains stop running at midnight. The basic fare covering about three stations is ¥160. There is a one-day open ticket at ¥700 that gives unlimited trips on the subway and bus. These tickets are available at the JR Station Underground Commuter's Ticket Office (open 9–6) and at the Odori Station Underground Commuter's Ticket Office. (open Mon.–Sat. 9–6).

By Bus Buses follow the grid system; they stop running at midnight.

By Taxi Taxi meters start at ¥470; an average fare runs about ¥600.

Important Addresses and Numbers

Tourist Information **Sapporo City Tourism Dept. Office,** Nishi-2-chome, Kita 2, Chuo-ku, tel. 011/211–2376. Open 9–5; Sat. 9–1; closed Sun. and holidays. **Hokkaido Tourist Association,** Keizai Center Building, Nishi-1-chome, Kita 2, Chuo-ku, tel. 011/231–0941. Open 9–5; Sat. 9–12:30; closed Sun. and holidays. **Sapporo City Tourist Office,** Sapporo Station, tel. 011/213–5062. Open 9–5, except closed on the 2nd and 4th Wed. of every month.

Travel Agencies The Japan Travel Bureau (tel. 011/241–6201).

U.S. Consulate Kita 1, Nishi 28, Chuo-ku, tel. 011/641–1115.

Emergencies Police (tel. 110). **Ambulance** (tel. 119).

Doctors **City General Hospital** (tel. 011/261–2281). **Hokkaido University Hospital** (tel. 011/716–1161).

Dentists **The Emergency Dental Clinic** (tel. 011/511–7774); open evenings only, 7–11.

Road Travel For road-condition information during the winter, call 011/281–6511.

Exploring

The comforting fact about Sapporo is the ease with which one can understand the city's layout. Streets running north to south are called *jo*, and those running east to west are called *chome*. These streets are numbered consecutively, and one block consists of about 100 meters square (100 yards by 100 yards).

Numbers in the margin correspond with points of interest on the Sapporo map.

Sapporo's few major sites of interest can easily be seen in a day. A good place to start one's visit is at Sapporo's landmark, the **①** **Clock Tower.** Built in 1878 in the Russian style, with a clock from Boston added three years later, the Clock Tower is where Japanese tourists take photographs of one another to prove that they were in Sapporo. However, other than being on every Sapporo travel brochure, it is very ordinary to a Westerner's eyes and has little architectural value. Inside the building, a small museum recounts the local history of Sapporo and includes such items as horse-drawn trams, but it lacks information about the Ainu village that preceded present-day Sapporo and from which the city takes its name. (Sapporo is made up from a combination of Ainu words meaning "a long, dry river.") *Admission free. Open 9–4. Closed Mon.*

② Across the street from the Clock Tower is the **Sapporo International Communication Plaza** on the third floor of a white office building. The center has recently been established to facilitate commercial and cultural relations with the world beyond Japan. It is the best place (far better than the tourist office) for helpful suggestions on travel in Hokkaido and for meeting people who speak English. It is also a useful place to have something translated from Japanese into English. The center has a reading room with books, newspapers, and brochures in English. *Kita 1, Nishi 3, Chuo-ku, tel. 011/221–2105. Open 9–7.*

③ On the other side of the Clock Tower is the **Hokkaido Tourist Association Office.** No English is spoken here, and the staff is limited in the amount of useful advice it has to offer, but maps and brochures in English are available. (The same maps and brochures may be obtained from the information center inside the Sapporo railway station.) *Keiza; Center Bldg., Nishi-1-chome, Kita 2, Chuo-ku, tel. 011/231–0941. Open weekdays 9–5, Sat. 9–12:30. Closed Sun. and holidays.*

④ Two blocks south of the Clock Tower is **Odori-Koen Park,** a broad, 345-foot avenue that runs east and west, bisecting the city center. The median of the avenue is the park. Here, in the summer, office workers buy lunch from various food vendors and take in the sun, so long absent during the winter months. For the out of towner, it is a place to people watch and to try Hokkaido corn. The corn is overpriced, but as a tourist, one must sample it. It's first boiled, then roasted over charcoal and, just before it is handed to you, given a dash of soy sauce. In February the park displays large and lifelike snow sculptures made for the Sapporo Snow Festival, which has made the city famous.

Aurora Town, **6**

Batchelor Museum, **12**

Botanical Gardens, **11**

Clock Tower, **1**

Grand Sapporo Hotel, **9**

Hokkaido Migishi Kotaro Museum, **13**

Hokkaido Museum of Modern Art, **14**

Hokkaido Tourist Office, **3**

Hokkaido University, **15**

Nakajima-Koen Park, **4**

Odori-Koen Park, **4**

Old Hokkaido Government Building, **10**

Pole Town, **7**

Sapporo Beer Brewery, **17**

Sapporo International Communication Plaza, **2**

Sapporo JR Railway Station, **16**

Susukino, **8**

TV Tower, **5**

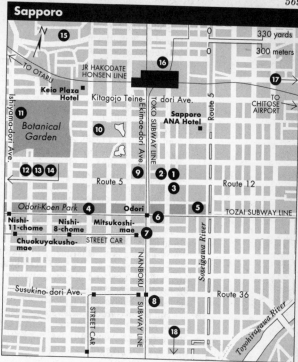

(See Nightlife, below, and Festivals and Seasonal Events in Chapter 1.)

5 At the east end of Odori-Koen Park is the **TV Tower,** which stands at 470 feet. It's ugly, but the Sapporo Tourist Association promotes it for the view from its observation platform. Open daily 9–8. Don't be persuaded. It costs ¥500 for a view of the city that is better, and free, from any of the high-rise hotels.

Odori-Koen Park is actually at the heart of Sapporo's downtown shopping center, where many of the shops are underground rather than lining the park. The shopping center is located at the intersection where the main avenue (Nishi 4-chome) heads south from the JR station and where the two subway lines intersect at the Odori Subway Station. Aboveground are large department stores. At all times of the year, two underground shopping malls (especially welcome during the seven-month winters) attract shoppers and diners who come to browse as much as to buy or to eat. Underneath Odori-Koen

6 Park, from the TV tower to Odori Station, is the **Aurora Town** arcade of shops and restaurants. **Kinokuniya** (tel. 011/231-2131) has opened up a branch here should you wish to browse through a good selection of English-language books. At Odori

7 Station, Aurora Town turns south to **Pole Town,** a long mall that continues all the way to Susukino.

8 **Susukino,** Sapporo's entertainment district, is a nighttime reveler's paradise with some 4,200 bars and restaurants offering the Japanese equivalent to bacchanalian delights. *(See*

Nightlife, below.) Because Susukino is for the night (until 4 AM, if you have the yen and stamina), let's return to the Odori Station and walk up the main street toward the JR station. Along this street are the major banks and airline offices. Here you can change your traveler's checks and confirm plane reservations. Once out of Sapporo, such matters are more difficult to accomplish.

From Odori-Koen Park walk up Sapporo's main street toward the train station; on your left (west side) will be the side entrance of the **Sapporo Grand Hotel.** As the name implies, the Grand is built in a traditional European style with substantial pillars and majestic lobbies. Because it appears so out of place in Japan, especially in modern Sapporo, it seems even more of a landmark than the Clock Tower. The hotel has a bustling café looking out to the street, making it a convenient tea or coffee stop. Another good reason for stepping inside is to see the nimble bellgirls scurrying to open doors and heft guests' luggage, which is sometimes nearly the size of themselves.

If you leave the Grand Hotel by its front entrance and go left, the street leads to a large, redbrick building, the grandest structure in Sapporo. It's the **Old Hokkaido Government Building,** built in 1888 and now containing exhibits displaying the early development of Hokkaido. (Open weekdays 9–5, Sat. 9–1, closed Sun.) Beyond this pleasing Western-style building are the **Botanical Gardens,** with some 5,000 plant varieties. This is a cool retreat in the summer, both for its green space and its shade from the sun. *Admission: ¥350. Open in the summer 9–4; only the greenhouse is open Nov. 4–Apr. 28, 10–3. Closed Sun.*

Within the gardens are two museums. The one that is worthwhile is the **Batchelor Museum.** Dr. John Batchelor, an English missionary in Sapporo during the late 19th century, made it his hobby to collect handicrafts and artifacts used by the Ainu people. Since the Ainu culture was virtually wiped out with Hokkaido's colonization by the Yamato Japanese, this museum takes on more value each year. The University Museum, which offers poor displays of stuffed animals, should only be used as a last resort to occupy children on a rainy day.

Continuing farther west is the **Hokkaido Migishi Kotaro Museum** (admission: ¥300), which exhibits the works of a native son, Migishi. This museum was built in 1968 for the sole purpose of housing 220 of the 20th-century artist's paintings. It was designed to reflect the many changes of style that characterize his career. On the next block is the attractive **Hokkaido Museum of Modern Art,** built in 1977, with local and foreign exhibits (admission: ¥250). Both museums, though not holding priceless works of art, enable foreigners to see what in Japanese art is appreciated by the Japanese and, in that sense, are worth visiting. *Both museums open 10–5. Closed Mon. and national holidays.*

Retracing one's steps to the Botanical Gardens and then left (north) for ½-mile, one arrives at the spacious grounds of **Hokkaido University,** Japan's largest campus, with over 12,000 students. The beautifully designed grounds make the campus another summer escape from the concrete to greenery and blossoming flowers. During the warmer months, the numerous green and open spaces connected by wide, lilac-lined avenues make Sapporo a particularly pleasant city.

16 Cutting back southeast from the university campus, one returns to the downtown area at the **Sapporo JR station.** Underneath the station is another comprehensive shopping mall with one mouth-watering section devoted to food stalls and restaurants.

17 About a 15-minute walk east from the station and past the Governor's residence (about a ¥900 taxi ride from downtown) is the **Sapporo Beer Brewery.** During the day, free tours around the brewery are offered, but the fun of coming here is the huge beer garden and the cavernous, three-tier beer hall. The beer hall is where most of the action occurs in the evening until closing at 9 PM. It is similar in atmosphere to a German beer hall (it was a German, after all, who, when finding wild hops growing, taught the Japanese to make beer) but instead of bratwurst, *genghis khan* (strips of mutton and vegetables cooked on a hot iron grill) is the favored meal. It's Sapporo's favorite dish, and the beer hall is the perfect place to try it. In the summer, the beer garden is both a day and evening gathering place for locals and visitors. Mugs of beer are downed with gusto amidst exclamations of "Kampai!" In the winter, around February, the beer garden is transformed into a huge igloo to become a temporary restaurant. *Brewery tours 8:30–11:30 and 1–4, May–Sept.; 9–11 and 1–3, Oct.–Apr., except for weekends and holidays. Reservations advised. Request a guide who speaks some English. Tel. 011/731–4368.*

18 The last place to visit is **Nakajima-Koen Park,** a little less than 2 miles from the railway station. The easiest way to get there is by the Nanboku subway from the JR station to the Nakajima-koen stop; from here it's a couple minutes' walk to the park. Nakajima-Koen Park has a playground with a small lake for boating, a beautiful rose garden, and the Nakajima Sports Center. The park also features two national cultural treasures, one Japanese and one Western. **The Hasso-an Teahouse,** harmoniously surrounded by a Japanese garden, is virtually the only traditional Japanese structure in Hokkaido and is in stark contrast to the new frontier style of architecture on the rest of the island (open 9–4; May–Nov.). The other national treasure is **Hohei-kan,** a Western-style building, originally constructed as an imperial guest house (open 9–5). Hoheikan is symbolic of an age when Hokkaido was colonized by Japan, a time when the Meiji government looked to the West for the country's modern transformation.

Nightlife

Susukino is Sapporo's entertainment area and the largest of its kind north of Tokyo. Some 4,200 bars, restaurants, and nightclubs, all lit by lanterns and flashing signs, crowd into a compact area. It is mind-boggling and, in itself, justifies an overnight stay in Sapporo to experience it. Most of the bars stay open until 4 AM, though the restaurants often close soon after midnight. Just make sure you know the type of bar before you enter. Aside from all kinds of restaurants, from the relatively inexpensive to expensive, there are several kinds of bars: the clubs (the three exclusive ones are **Mino's, Chickary,** and **Saroma**) with many conversational hostesses (¥10,000 and up); the snack bars, with a few conversational hostesses (they don't offer food, as their name suggests, only expensive *auduburus*— bar tidbits); *izakayas*, for different kinds of food and drink; bars with entertainment, either taped video music *(karaoke* bars) or live bands; and "soaplands," which is the new name for Turkish baths or houses of pleasure.

If at all possible, go to the clubs and snack bars with a Japanese acquaintance. For a quiet drink, try the **Prosperity** bar in the Mitsuwa Building (Minamo 5, Nishi 5) on the fifth floor. The owner is friendly, and so is the clientele. For beer, an extensive menu, and hearty companionship, the **Mykirin Beer Entertainment Hall** in the Urban Building (Minamo 5, Nishi 4) has the *Kuma-Daiko* (bearskin drums) beating nightly. Down a small alley (Minamo 7.5, Nishi 4), a wonderful small izakaya bar called **Godai** has an open charcoal hearth for cooking and a bar/ counter around it, with a few tables off to the side. No English is spoken, so a few words of Japanese are needed, and most of the food served is grilled fish and seafood. A friendly karaoke bar is **Nakimushi Pierrot**, on the fifth floor of the Japanland Building (Minamo 5, Nishi 5, open to 5 AM), where you can get by on ¥2,500 per person.

Though not nightlife per se, mention should be made here of Sapporo's best-known annual event. In the first week of February, the **Sapporo Snow Festival** is held, and it is the greatest of its kind. Approximately 300 lifelike sculptures, as large as 130 feet high, 50 feet deep, and 80 feet wide, are created each year. The history of the festival began in 1950 with seven statues as a way to entertain the local citizens, whose spirits were depressed by the aftermath of the war and the long winter nights. Now the event is so large that sculptures may be seen in three sections of the city—Odori-Koen Park, Makomanai, and Susukino. The festival attracts some 2 million visitors each year.

Excursions Around Hokkaido

Because Sapporo is such a comfortable and reassuring city, albeit architecturally boring, it serves as a convenient base for making excursions into Hokkaido's interior. Following are three which cover the best of Hokkaido:

The first excursion is to Otaru and the Shakotan Peninsula to the northwest of Sapporo; it requires a minimum of a day to complete with a rented car, or two days by public transport.

The second excursion travels southwest of Sapporo through the Shikotsu-Toya National Park and includes crystal-clear caldera (crater) lakes surrounded by mountains and hot-spring resorts. To complete the itinerary of this excursion takes a minimum of two days by car, three by public transport, though one can shorten the itinerary to make it a day trip out of Sapporo.

The third and final excursion heads into central Hokkaido through Daisetsuzan National Park, Akan National Park to the east coast, and the Sea of Okhotsk. From there, the itinerary goes along the coast to Hokkaido's northernmost point at Cape Soya and over to the islands of Rebun and Rishiri before returning to Hokkaido. Together, the three excursions take at least six days, but it can be divided, as in this chapter, into three separate trips.

Otaru and the Shakotan Peninsula

This first excursion goes northwest of Sapporo to Otaru on the coast. West of Otaru is the Shakotan Peninsula, which offers a taste of Hokkaido's rugged coastal scenery.

Getting There Otaru is 50 minutes by train from Sapporo. By car on the expressway, Otaru is only 40 kilometers (24 miles) from Sapporo. Less than an hour beyond Otaru, the Shakotan Peninsula begins at Yoichi.

One can take the train as far as Yoichi. From there, buses travel around the peninsula as far as Yobetsu. The road then ends, but ferries travel down the coast to Iwanai, where one can take the train back to Sapporo. In many ways, using a combination of train, bus, and ferry is a better way to tour the Shakotan Peninsula, because part of the western coast has no usable road and a ferry is used. Cars need to backtrack and cross the center of the Shakotan Peninsula via Tomaru Pass.

Numbers in the margin correspond with points of interest of the Hokkaido map.

Exploring

❶ **Otaru** is described as "famous for its canals and old Western-style buildings" by the Hokkaido Tourist Office. In truth, Otaru is a commercial city in the shadow of Sapporo. Very few of its 19th-century, wood-frame houses are left standing, and those are sandwiched between modern concrete structures. Instead, what you find is a traffic-congested center city with shops and office buildings, a busy port area from which ferries depart for Niigata to the south and the Rebun and Rishiri islands off Hokkaido's northwest cape, and some ramshackle suburbs.

The major attractions in Otaru are available only in the evening. Otaru has two of Hokkaido's best sashimi restaurants, **Uoisshin** (1-11-1 Hanazono, Otaru-shi, tel. 0134/32–5202) and **Isshintasuke** (1-5-3 Hanazono, Otaru-shi, tel. 0134/34–1790). Connoisseurs of sashimi from Sapporo will make a special trip to these two restaurants, and, because there is frequent train service to and from Sapporo, you can do the same. Your Sapporo hotel will be happy to make reservations at either restaurant; reservations are essential.

❷ We recommend not dallying in Otaru but continuing west along the coast road leading to **Yoichi** and the Shakotan Peninsula. Before Yoichi are some of Hokkaido's best sandy beaches; once through Yoichi, these beaches soon give way to cliffs rising vertically out of the sea. This is the beginning of the **Shakotan Peninsula.** Two mountain peaks, Yobetsu at 4,019 feet and Shakotan at 4,258 feet, dominate the peninsula's interior. On the north coast are two capes, Shakotan and Kamui, on its eastern and western tips. Sentimental Japanese go to Kamui for the sunsets; the colors fading into the Sea of Japan are romantic.

The Shakotan is a sample of the real Hokkaido. Stalwart cliffs stave off the endless surging sea, while volcanic mountains rise up majestically to dominate the interior. Thick forests blanket the imperial slopes with dark, rich greens, and ravines crease

36 Cape Soya

38 Rebun Island   **37** Wakkanai

40 Kafuka

42 **41** Oshidomari

Kutsugata   **39**

Rishiri
Island

KITAMI MTNS.

Mombetsu **3**

Sea of Japan

Mt. Teshio

Asahikawa   Sounkyo

17 Mt. Asahi   **20**

Asahida Onsen   **18**   Mt.
Ishikari

Daisetsuzan   **16**
National Park

19   **21**

Shirogane   Lake
Onsen   Shika

Furano

*Ishikari
Bay*

Yobetsu   Furubira

3   **4**   Yoichi   Mt. Yubari

Tomaru Pass   **5**   **2**   **1** Otaru

6   **8** Sapporo

Kamoenai   Mt.

Iwanai   Tempu

7   Jozenkai   **9**   Nakayama Pass

Mt. Yotei Onsen   **10**

Mt. Niseko-annupuri   **11**   *Shikotsu*   Chitose   Obihiro

Toya

National Park

Toyako   **15**

Onsen   Lake

12   Shikotsu

14 Shiraoi

13 Noboribetsu
Onsen

*Uchiura
Bay*   Mt. Apoi

Muroran   Hiroo

Mt. Kamagatake

Oshima Peninsula

HIDAKA RANGE

Hakodate

N   *Tsugaru Straits*

HONSHU

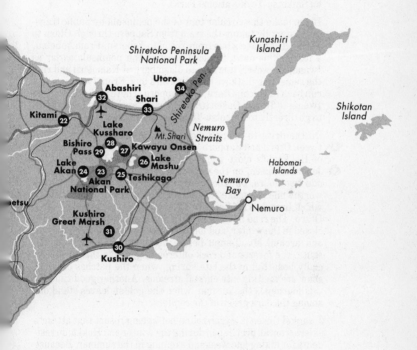

Sea of Okhotsk

Kunashiri Island

Shiretoko Peninsula National Park

Utoro 34

Abashiri 32

Shari

Shiretoko Pen.

Kitami 22

Lake Kussharo

Shikotan Island

Nemuro Straits

Mt. Shari

Bishiro Pass 29

28

27 Kawayu Onsen

26 Lake Mashu

Habomai Islands

Lake Akan 24

23

25 Teshikaga

Nemuro Bay

etsu

Akan National Park

Nemuro

Kushiro Great Marsh

31

30

Kushiro

PACIFIC OCEAN

0   20 miles

0   60 km

the regal mountainsides. The Shakotan Peninsula is nature in full drama.

The road from Yoichi circles the peninsula, keeping to the coast ❸ as much as the cliffs allow. At **Yobetsu,** near Cape Kamui, the corniche road is even more spectacular as it heads south to Iwanai. Unfortunately, soon after Yobetsu the road becomes a track, unsuitable for cars at the time this book goes to print. Unless you can pass through the barrier, you have to drive back ❹ to **Furabira** and cross the peninsula by taking the hairpin road ❺ through **Tomaru Pass** for a thrilling drive that skirts Mt. ❻ ❼ Yobetsu to **Kamoenai** and then goes down to **Iwanai.**

From Iwanai there is a straight road cutting across the base of the peninsula back to Otaru. There is also the alternative, at Iwanai, to go south and combine this excursion with one through Shikotsu-Toya National Park *(see* the following section on Shikotsu-Toya National Park).

If you make this circular tour of the peninsula by public transport, start by taking the train from Sapporo through Otaru to Yoichi. Then take a bus from Yoichi to Yobetsu. From Yobetsu, a ferry skips down the east coast of the peninsula as far as Iwanai. However, it is best to disembark at Kamoenai and ride the remaining distance to Iwanai on a bus. From Iwanai, trains run back to Yoichi, Otaru, and Sapporo. There is also a bus from Iwanai to Toyako Onsen *(Onsen* means "spa"), should you want to go directly to Shikotsu-Toya National Park.

On the drive to Sapporo you'll find a picturesque detour be- ❽ tween Otaru and Sapporo via **Mt. Tempu,** passing through one of Hokkaido's most scenic mountain passes before reaching ❾ **Jozankei Onsen,** on the outskirts of Sapporo. The detour will add two hours, but the scenery up through the mountains is worthwhile. To make this detour via Jozankei, take Route 3, which branches off Sapporo Road 5 kilometers (3 miles) after Otaru. The road heads straight into the mountains (the road is closed in the winter) and follows a ravine that winds its way up and around Mt. Tempu before descending to Jozankei. En route, the forests and rock outcroppings make this trip especially beautiful in the late spring, when the patches of white snow are melting into crystal streams. Another good time for this journey is the autumn, when the golden leaves stand out among the dark green of the conifers.

Jozankei Onsen is a year-round hot-spring resort that attracts skiers from all over Japan during the winter and Hokkaido residents for hiking and weekend camping in the summer. Because Jozankei is virtually an extension of Sapporo's sprawling suburbs, the weekends are crowded with day-trippers. The actual ski area, which is in full swing by the beginning of December (the season lasts through May), is at the **Jozankei Kogen International Skiground,** 25 minutes by bus from the spa. The resort town itself is wedged in a small valley in the foothills beneath the mountains of Shikotsu-Toya National Park. Were it not for the modern, square-block hotels, the village would be beautiful. Unfortunately, while it has all the creature comforts of a resort, plus the hot springs, the hotels' architects have managed to deface nature's beauty. Still, refreshment at a hot spring will be rewarding before heading back to Sapporo.

Shikotsu-Toya National Park

The second excursion loops around the Shikotsu-Toya National Park and includes traveling through Jozankei Onsen, up through Nakayama Pass, down to Lake Toya, and on to the hot-spring spa resorts of Toyako Onsen and Noboribetsu Onsen before returning to Sapporo via the Ainu village at Shiraoi and the beauty of Lake Shikotsu. The area of Shikotsu-Toya National Park, about 100 kilometers (60 miles) southwest of Sapporo, is full of old and young volcanoes, mountains, forests, lakes, hot springs, and several hotels. Shikotsu-Toya National Park is a Japanese playground with activities for all ages.

Getting There The itinerary described below is by road from Sapporo and can be accomplished by bus and train, even though we describe the car route. Nor does one have to complete all of this excursion, since there are direct buses from Sapporo to Lake Toya, Noboribetsu Onsen, and Lake Shikotsu, as well as from Lake Toya to Noboribetsu Onsen.

By Train Toyako Onsen and Noboribetsu Onsen are easily accessible by train from Sapporo on the JR Sapporo–Hakodate Line. For Lake Toya, disembark from the train at the Toya JR station for a 15-minute bus ride to the lake. For Noboribetsu Onsen, disembark from the train at Noboribetsu and then take the shuttle bus (a 20-minute ride) to Noboribetsu Onsen. Because this excursion lies on the Sapporo–Hakodate train line, if you are either going to or arriving from Honshu by train, consider joining this itinerary at Toyako Onsen or Noboribetsu Onsen.

By Bus The direct bus service from Sapporo to Lake Toya (Toyako Onsen) via Nakayama Pass takes two hours and 45 minutes. *Fare: ¥2,600; reservations necessary.*

Direct bus coaches, the Chuo and the Donan lines, also run from Sapporo to Noboribetsu Onsen; this trip also takes two hours and 45 minutes.

Between Toyako Onsen and Noboribetsu via the Orufure Pass, a one-hour-and-40-minute bus ride operates from June 1 to late October. *Fare: ¥1,450; 4–6 buses a day; reservations necessary.*

Exploring Leaving Sapporo by car to the first destination, Jozankei, is easy. Take the road running along the west side of the Botanical Gardens; it is a straight run to Jozankei, less than 45 minutes away. All along this itinerary, there are sufficient signs in romaji (Japanese written in Roman script) to give you directional confidence, and the road number is frequently displayed.

Once through Jozankei Onsen (*see above*), the twisting, winding road up through the ravine warns of the high drama of the mountains ahead. The final ascent to 2,742 feet is through a tunnel that opens out at **Nakayama Pass,** where the traveler discovers wide, sweeping panoramas of lonely mountains and peopled plains. In the distance, beyond the surrounding mountain peaks, stands **Mt. Yotei,** rising out of the plains. Mt. Yotei's near-perfect conical shape leads to automatic comparisons to Mt. Fuji, but any native worth his salt would say his Mt. Yotei has no competition.

There is a lodge restaurant (Nakayama Lounge) to the side of the road at Nakayama Pass that serves food (of inferior quality) and refreshments to help you get your breath back after the drive up and before the descent.

Lake Toya   The road descends from the pass to Kimobetsu and Rusutsu, where soon after a flat stretch **Lake Toya** suddenly appears. The lake is almost circular and is contained in a collapsed volcanic cone. Just after the first glimpse of the lake, a souvenir shop and food market on the left stand out like a sore thumb. Just beyond them is a coffee shop; the best view of the lake is from its balcony. The view embraces the northern circumference of the lake and its small islands, which are the peaks of smaller volcanoes that pop up in the lake's middle.

⑫ The road from the coffee shop descends to the lake and follows the shore to **Toyako Onsen**, at the southwestern edge of the lake. This spa town is the chief holiday center for this part of the Shikotsu-Toya Park and, consequently, is loaded with hotels, inns, and souvenir shops. The hotels are open all year, but the busiest time is the summer (June through August), when Japanese families come by the droves for trout fishing, hiking, boating, visiting Nakanoshima island (in the center of the lake), and, of course, taking the curative waters of the hot springs.

Indeed, Toyako Onsen is famous for its curative waters, but the geographical wonder is **Showa Shinzan**, Japan's newest volcano, born in July 1945. Showa Shinzan was a surprise to everyone, but no one was more surprised than the farmer who witnessed the volcano's birth in his potato patch. The volcano grew eight inches a day for seven months and then erupted to form its peak of 1,312 feet. By this time the farmer had had enough. He gave up potatoes and became a civil servant, and a small museum took its place at the base of the volcano and chronicles both Showa Shinzan's development and the volcanic activity of the entire area.

Perhaps not to be outdone, one mountain over from Showa Shinzan, **Mt. Usu**, erupted in 1978. It did so with flair, sending out 200 tremors an hour before blowing its top. This advance notice allowed local residents to flee and photographers to set up their cameras. Their photographs are shown amid sound effects of thunder and lightning at the **Abuta Kazan Kagaku-kan Museum**, located at the foot of Mt. Usu. The presentation is dramatically realistic and better seen after, rather than before, taking the cable car to the top of Mt. Usu for the superb views of Lake Toya.

From Toyako Onsen, the road continues around the lake through Sobetsu Onsen, a quieter version of Toyako Onsen. Here the road splits: One branch continues around the lake; the other (closed in the winter) heads east to clamber over the mountains to **Noboribetsu**. This east road is the one to take. The 90-minute trip climbs up **Orofure Pass** (3,051 feet) and offers tremendous views of soaring mountains, hidden valleys, and, in the distance, Lake Toya, Mt. Yokei, Lake Kuttara, and the Pacific Ocean. The Donan Bus Line goes between Toyako Onsen and Noboribetsu Onsen along this road and stops at Orofure Pass to let passengers enjoy the view.

(Do not confuse Noboribetsu Onsen with Noboribetsu, a city on the coast that is 20 minutes away by road from its namesake spa town. Noboribetsu is an ugly industrial city at which the JR trains stop. From the station, a shuttle bus runs up to

Noboribetsu Onsen. Indeed, the whole coastal area from Date to Tomakomai is an industrial eyesore, made worse by a sagging regional economy.)

Noboribetsu Onsen **Noboribetsu Onsen** is the most famous spa in Hokkaido, perhaps even in all of Japan. Its 11 types of hot-spring waters are **⑬** said to cure ailments ranging from rheumatism to diabetes. Most hotels have their own baths, and the grandest of them all are the baths at the **Dai-ichi Takimoto-Kan Hotel.** The hotel is a monstrosity with 365 rooms, video game halls, buffet dining rooms and evening cabarets, but its baths are the best. No longer is the bathing mixed (it was until a few years ago); this unfortunately decreases the size of the baths, but either side of the partition still covers a large, enclosed area. The 12 pools in each area have seven different waters each, at varying temperatures. Signs above each pool are in Japanese, so which minerals are in the waters and what they do to one's body remain mysteries to most foreigners. The solution is just to try them. Even for non-hot-spring fanatics, these baths are worth the ¥1,500 nonresident fee to attend, if only for the view beyond the bathhouses' plate-glass window: it looks upon the steaming, volcanic gases of Jigokudani, which seep out of the ground. On the floor beneath the baths is a swimming pool and a water chute for those who like their water straight. The baths are open to nonresidents only from 9 to 3, though once in you can stay as long as you can take it.

The other famous sight of Noboribetsu Onsen is **Jigokudani** (The Valley of Hell), a couple hundred yards from the village. It is a volcanic crater, though it looks like a bow-shape valley; it has a diameter of 1,476 feet and lots of seething, boiling mud. Boiling water spurts out of thousands of holes, sounding like the heartbeat of earth itself, though, because of its strong sulfur smell, others have described it differently. Apparently, the Dante-like inferno is a popular place for suicides. Entire families have been known to make their last leaps from here.

Other nearby places for families are the **Bear Ranch** and **Ukara no Sato,** a commercial replica of an Ainu village. Both are located on the slopes of Mt. Shirohei, and access is via the cable car from Noboribetsu Onsen. The few elderly Ainu who perform a dance or two every couple of hours at Ukara no Sato look bored to tears. The bears, all 150 of them, are tame and lethargic. The ranch and the five replica Ainu houses are solely for the tourists, but, perhaps because of its location and because the bears are not in minuscule cages, the area is less depressing than the Ainu village at Shiraoi (*see* below). *Admission (including ropeway): ¥1,550. Open 6AM–8 PM in the summer; 9–4:30 in the winter.*

The village of Noboribetsu Onsen is a tourist town, so expect masses of hotels and souvenir shops. However, though the modern hotel architecture could be far more aesthetic and in tune with its surroundings of mountains and forests, the village is not without charm. At least its main street still has cobblestones, and there is a stream that runs through the village. More important, the village buildings do not block out the presence of the mountains.

The Ainu have been systematically wiped out. Fewer than a hundred full-blooded Ainu are left, though no one knows exactly how many. First evicted from Honshu, they then lost their ancestral lands and heritage with the colonization of Hokkaido. One of the few remaining places in Hokkaido to see their culture (artificially) preserved is at the model village, **Shiraoi,** 30 minutes by car (40 minutes by bus) on Route 36 toward Tomakomai.

Shiraoi has a feeling of finality. As if in a zoo, Ainu sit in their reconstructed grass houses with their heirlooms. They appear even more lethargic than at Ukara no Sato. Here, too, are bears, even more pitiful as they sit cramped in cages. Yet, despite the depression that sets in while visiting here, one should make the trip, perhaps for reasons of conscience, definitely for the **Ainu Folklore Museum.** The museum has one of the best collections of the Ainu crafts and artifacts that were once part of their daily lives. *Admission: ¥515. Open Apr.–Oct., 8–5:30; Nov.–Mar., 8:30–4:30. Closed Dec. 30–Jan. 4.*

Your last stop before returning to Sapporo should be **Lake Shikotsu.** To reach the lake, continue from Shiraoi to Tomakomai on the freeway and take a left up to Shikotsu Onsen (or by train to Tomakomai; then a 40-minute bus ride from Tomakomai Station).

Lake Shikotsu is the deepest lake in Hokkaido (outfathomed only by Honshu's Lake Tazawa as the deepest in all of Japan). Its shape is a classic caldera except for the two active volcanoes, which have risen to crumble its periphery on both the north and south shores. The southern volcano, Mt. Tarumae, has a bus service that chugs three-quarters of the way to its top, where you can walk 40 minutes to the summit for views embracing all of Lake Shikotsu. At the base of the northern volcano, Mt. Eniwa, is **Marukoma Onsen,** one of the very few spas left in Japan where mixed bathing is still in fashion in its *rotemburo* (outdoor thermal springs) along the lake shore.

Rental boats are available for leisurely drifting around the lake, and sightseeing boats offer tours. Swimmers should remember that the lake is deep, and, while the beach shelves gently for 10 meters, it drops suddenly to an eventual depth of 1,191 feet. *½-hour trips halfway around the lake cost ¥840, and 1-hr-and-40-min trips around the lake cost ¥1,540.*

From Lake Shikotsu, the quickest route back to Sapporo (by car or bus) is via Chitose and up the expressway. You could also return to Tomakomai by bus and take the JR train back westward in the direction of Hakodate, or take the bus to Chitosekudo (Chitose Airport) and get the JR train to Sapporo.

Central Hokkaido, the Sea of Okhotsk, and the Northern Cape

The third excursion goes east from Sapporo to Daisetsuzan National Park, on to Akan National Park, and then to the Sea of Okhotsk on the east coast. From there the route quickly goes to Hokkaido's northernmost cape and to the islands of Rebun and Rishiri before returning to Sapporo.

Getting Around This journey may be accomplished by train and bus. However, because traveling between Daisetsuzan and Akan requires several bus changes, a rented car is more convenient and more enjoyable for this part of the excursion.

Even with a car, we do recommend taking the train to Asahika-wa and renting a car from there. Also, it is a long drive north of Mombetsu along the coast of the Sea of Okhotsk to Hokkaido's north cape. Hence, we recommend returning the car to Asahi-kawa, or dropping it off at Mombetsu, for travels north to Wakkanai and Rebun and Rishiri islands. Then, either take the train back to Sapporo or fly.

Exploring
16 **17**

The main gateway to **Daisetsuzan National Park** is **Asahikawa,** Hokkaido's second largest city. Asahikawa is vast and sprawl-ing, even though it was only in 1885 that the first pioneers es-tablished their base here. Now just under half a million people reside in an area of 225 square miles. The endless suburbs are depressing, but the center of town is small, easy to navigate in, and friendly. Several international hotels, including the spar-kling new Palace Hotel, are in the center of downtown, close to the pedestrian shopping mall (the first such car-free mall in Ja-pan) and the nightly scene of restaurants, izakayas, and bars.

Asahikawa's major attractions are the **Ainu Kinenkan** (memor-ial hall) and the **Ice Festival** in February. The Ainu Kinenkan is a reasonably good Ainu museum that includes a rather unin-spired dance performance by a couple of elderly Ainu in tradi-tional dress. If you have visited either Shiraoi or Akan, there is little reason to see more of the same here. (Admission: ¥100. Open 9:30–4:30; closed Mon.) The Ice Festival is a smaller ver-sion of Sapporo's Snow Festival (150 sculptures, compared with the 300 at Sapporo), but Asahikawa's has more of a country-fair feel.

There are several routes to take from Asahikawa into the Daisetsuzan National Park. However, only one road runs com-pletely through the park. That is from north to south—Asahi-kawa to Sounkyo and through the park to Shikaoi; the road is closed south of Sounkyo in the winter, forcing travelers to turn east and leave the mountains for Kitami, in the plains. Other roads, mainly from the west, make stabs into the mountains here and there and then retreat.

18
19

On the west side of the park, the spa towns of **Asahida Onsen** and **Shirogane Onsen** serve as hiking centers in the summer and ski resorts in the winter. Shirogane, located at 2,461 feet, has had especially good skiing since its mountain, Mt. Tokachi, erupted in 1962 to form a blanket of lava, making a superb ski bowl. Asahida, with Yukomambetsu Onsen close by, is where one can take a cable car part of the way up Mt. Tokachi (Hok-kaido's highest mountain) and hike to the 7,513-foot summit. In the late spring, the slopes are blanketed with alpine flowers. It

20

is also possible to hike over to **Sounkyo** from Mt. Asahi.

Daisetsuzan
National Park

Daisetsuzan is the geographical center of Hokkaido and is the largest of Japan's national parks. The park contains the very essence of rugged Hokkaido: vast plains, soaring mountain peaks, hidden gorges, cascading waterfalls, forests, wildflow-ers, a spa resort, hiking trails, and wilderness. Daisetsuzan (Great Snow Mountains) refers to the park's five major peaks, all of them towering more than 6,500 feet. Their presence domi-nates the area and controls man's entry into the park and his playgrounds.

For an excursion through the park, the first place to head for is Sounkyo, less than two hours southeast by car from Asahikawa. Alternatively, one can take the bus in front of Asahikawa's JR station, which goes directly to Sounkyo Onsen.

Sounkyo (*kyo* means "gorge") is the park's most scenic attraction, a 15-mile ravine extending into the park from its northeast entrance. For a 5-mile stretch, sheer cliff walls rise on both sides of the canyon as the road winds up into the mountains. Halfway up is the Sounkyo Onsen spa resort. How the Japanese are able to abuse scenic splendors with their ugly resort hotels is beyond belief. But they do, and Sounkyo Onsen is yet another example. One hotel in particular, the Chyo Hotel, sticks out as an eyesore of concrete. Sitting on a bluff, the hotel dominates what otherwise would be a dramatic view of the gorge. Instead, guests of the hotel do have a magnificent view but also a view of other concrete hotels down the gorge. Still, you have no option but to stay in Sounkyo Onsen if you choose to stay in this area of the park.

Resting precariously on the side of the gorge are a couple of grocery stores, some houses, and a couple of small inns and restaurants, plus the inevitable souvenir shops that make up the small village of Sounkyo. Activities take place in the resort hotels, not in the village, and during the day most people are out on the trails hiking through the park. One popular trip is to use the combination of a seven-minute ropeway (cost: ¥650 one way) and a 15-minute ride on a chair lift (cost: ¥210 one way) from Sounkyo up Mt. Kurodake for panoramic views over the Daisetsuzan mountain range. For the best views, including one looking over Sounkyo, take the hour's walk to the very top. In July or August the mountain is bedecked in Alpine flowers. The other activity is to rent a bicycle from Sounkyo's bus terminal (cost: ¥1,200 a day) and pedal through the gorge. A bicycle has the advantage over a car because the road goes through dark tunnels, blocking out the views.

Three kilometers (2 miles) up the road from Sounkyo Onsen are two picturesque waterfalls, **Ryusei-no-taki** (Shooting Star) and **Ginga-no-taki** (Milky Way). Neither is dramatic, but because they are like twins, separated only by a protruding cliff face called Heavenly Castle Rock, they form a balanced beauty. The road continues past the falls, following the Ishikawa River through perpendicular cliffs and fluted columns of rock until it reaches the dammed-up **Lake Daisetsu.** The dam is a feat of engineering, its walls constructed only of earth and rubble. In itself, the dam has no particular visual merit, but the lake behind has islands that appear to float and a surrounding backdrop of mountains clad with conifers.

At the lake the road divides. The right fork goes south and traverses the rough wilderness and least visited part of the park. The road is unpaved in parts, and there are no public buses. If you do not have a car, you must hitchhike as far as **Nukabira,** where you can catch buses and trains. This route is dramatic as it climbs up through **Mikuni Pass** (closed in winter) and drops down to lush valleys and through small ghost towns. In one such ghost town, **Mitsumata,** stop in at the only restaurant, where you will be enthusiastically welcomed with a dish of *shika* (deer) soba noodles. So fortified, it is an easy 11-mile run into **Nukabira** and civilization. Nukabira is a quiet spa town ㉑ close to **Lake Shikaribetsu,** the park's only natural lake. In the winter, toward the end of December, the lake becomes frozen over and an igloo village is established on the ice, where several weddings are generally performed with great ceremony. During March, the igloo village becomes the site of the local festival, the Shikaribetsu Kotan Festival.

22 The left fork at Lake Daisetsu veers east to **Kitami** and Abashiri on the Sea of Okhotsk. The road is well paved, and buses make frequent trips between Sounkyo Onsen and Kitami. As spectacular as the route south, this road to Kitami climbs over the forested mountains and breaks through the peaks at Sekihoku Pass. However, the distance is short, and within 20 kilometers (12 miles) from the lake the road has left Daisetsuzan National Park to descend among flat fields of peppermint that sparkle white and purple in season.

The road continues to Kitami and Abashiri on Hokkaido's east coast; however, south from Kitami is Akan National Park.

Akan National **Akan National Park** rivals Shikotsu-Toya National Park for its
Park scenic combination of lakes and mountains. And while the
23 mountains are not as high as those in Daisetsuzan, they are no less imposing. In addition, Akan has three major lakes, each of which has a unique character. And, crucial to the success of any resort in Japan, the park has an abundance of thermal springs.

Getting Around There is virtually no train service through the park except for the JR Senmo Line from Kushiro to Shari and Abashiri. Trains on this line stop at Teshikaga and Kawayu Onsen.

There are buses to Lake Akan from Kushiro and Kitami. There is also a bus from Lake Akan to Abashiri through the Bihiro Pass.

24 Coming from Sounkyo Onsen and arriving at Kitami, there is a road (and bus service) heading south to the small town of Tsubetsu, where it joins Route 240, entering Akan National Park shortly before **Lake Akan.** From the southern part of Daisetsuzan National Park at Nukabira, a road to Kamishihoro continues to Ashiyoro, which connects with Route 241; this runs directly to Akan. Bicycles may be rented from at the Akan Bus Terminal and at Akan View Hotel.

Exploring Lake Akan in the western part is surrounded by primeval forest and the smoking volcanoes **Me-kan** and **O-kan** (Mr. and Mrs. Akan). The lake itself is famous for marimo-green balls of duckweed about six inches in diameter. (Marimo are rare, and the only other areas they can be found are in Lake Yamanaka near Mt. Fuji, in Japan and in a few lakes in North America, Siberia, and Switzerland.) Marimo act much like submarines. These strange plants absorb oxygen from the water and then rise to the surface, where they exhale and sink. They also serve as weather forecasters, spending more time on the surface when the sun shines and settling on the bottom when inclement weather portends. Lake Akan is especially beautiful in the winter when it is frozen over and surrounded by snow-clad mountains. A popular sport at this time is skating between the *wakasagi* (smelt) fishermen. The wakasagi are hooked from ice holes and laid on the ice to immediately freeze. Their freshness makes them popular minced and eaten raw. Some eat them fried.

The town of **Akan-kohan** is the major resort area. This small village has expanded around the lake as new hotels are built. As is true in so much of Hokkaido, the hotels are not very attractive. The key is to obtain a room over the lake so that one looks onto nature's and not man's creation. The actual village center is fairly small and charming if you turn a blind eye to the souvenir shops with their endless rows of carved bears. The bears are great in number here because a small Ainu population lives in the village.

25 From Akan the road to **Teshikaga** is along the Akan Traverse. The distance is only 50 kilometers (32 miles), but it has more than its share of scenery. The road winds past O-kan, and at one point you can look over the drop-off to the right and its volcanic cone almost seems at eye level. It's not a road to be driven at night; not only are the views missed, but also the bears come out to play! The local bus between Akan and Teshikaga takes this road, and whether it is for the pleasure of the passengers or for the nerves of the driver, the bus stops for a rest at the Sokodail, an observational lookout.

26 Teshikaga is a small resort town with a few Japanese inns; the Mashu Hot Springs is nearby. **Lake Mashu** itself is a 20-minute drive (30 minutes by bus) from Teshikaga.

Lake Mashu is ringed by 656-foot-high rock walls. Curiously, no water has been found to either enter or leave the lake, so what goes on in its 695-foot depths is anybody's guess. Perhaps that mystery and the dark-blue water combine to exert a strange hypnotic effect and cause tourists to stare endlessly down from the cliffs into the lake. These cliff sides are really steep and have little or no foothold. One may live longer if one forgoes the pleasure of inspecting the water's clarity, said to be clear to a depth of 115 feet. Instead, appreciate the lake from its two observation spots on the west rim. You'll recognize them by the souvenir and food stands.

27 The road continues past Lake Mashu for nine miles to **Kawayu Onsen,** lined with relatively expensive hotels (with mostly Japanese-style rooms) for those who believe in its curative hot springs. Kawayu is not particularly attractive. However, just before Kawayu is **Io-san,** an active volcano that emits sulfurous steam from vents in two ravines. There is a car park and souvenir/grocery store just off the road. Buy a couple of fresh eggs from the store, then walk up to one of the saucepan-size pools and boil them.

28 The road from Kawayu goes around **Lake Kusshuro,** where various hotels and campgrounds line the shore. Lake Kusshuro (sometimes spelled Kutcharo) is Akan National Park's largest lake. Once it had nearly a perfect caldera shape, but other volcanoes have since sprung up and caused its shores to become flat and less dramatic. It is, however, an ideal area for camping and is popular with families who come for boating and paddling in the water. The lake is at its finest in the autumn, when the different shades of golds and greens on the trees extend from the lake shore into the higher mountain altitudes.

29 At the north end of the lake, the road climbs up **Bishiro Pass,** affording the last great view of Akan National Park's mountains and the green waters of Lake Kusshuro below. At Bihoro the road swings west to Ashikawa or east to Ashibiri.

An alternative exit from Akan National Park is to return from the lake to Kawayu Hot Springs and continue two miles to a "T" junction and the Kawayu JR station. There, take either Route

30 391 northeast or the train to Abashiri. Or, you can make a side trip south to **Kushiro,** either by train or car.

A word or two about Kushiro before discussing Abashiri and the Sea of Okhotsk: Kushiro is a port city of no great appeal, which used to be known for its rather seedy entertainment area for sailors and the tourists coming in off the Tokyo ferry. But the city is getting a new lease on life. Part of the old waterfront has been restored with 50 specialty shops, entertainment, and a terminal for sightseeing boats. Even the entertainment district has some revamped bars with traditional fireplaces where fish is cooked to order. Just to the north and west of Kushiro (30 **31** minutes by bus) is **Kushiro Great Marsh,** home to the red-crested crane (*tancho*). These birds were close to extinction four decades ago; they have slowly come back and now number about 400. The crane—long-legged, pointy-billed, with a white body trimmed in black and a scarlet cap on its head—is a symbol of long life and happiness. Although said to live a thousand years, the birds actually live about 80 and "marry" for life. Each March, the female lays two eggs. The husband and wife select one to nurture. Despite the fact that the birds have made something of a comeback under government protection, there are fears that not enough is being done to preserve their habitat. The Japanese are peculiarly reluctant to preserve nature, despite their avowed appreciation of it.

It is difficult to recommend a trip to see the cranes in the summer: The birds are shy and go deep into the swamps. Only a few are on view, and they are kept behind a fence. In the winter, when they come for food handouts, they are easier to spot.

The Sea of Okhotsk North to Rebun and Rishiri Islands

From Akan, the northeast coast is only two hours away. This coast has a feeling of being at the end of the world; it is located in the outer reaches of Japan, abutting the icy waters of the Sea of Okhotsk. The people make their living catching fish in the summer; in the winter, the sea is frozen, and survival depends on how successful the summer catch has been. The icy cold waters produce the sweetest shrimp you'll ever taste, and the hairy crab (best in May) may look ugly but its meat is so delicate that you forgive its looks. Except for the Shiretoko Peninsula, which the Ainu named the "World's End," the coastline is relatively flat, and the drama is in the isolation rather than the scenery. The major town on the coast, Abashiri, is not large, and the distances between points of interest become farther apart. However, all the points mentioned in this excursion can easily be reached by public transportation.

After a short detour to the Shiretoko Peninsula, the itinerary sketched below travels up the coast from Abashiri to Hokkaido's (and Japan's) most northerly point and crosses by ferry from Wakkanai to Rebun and Rishiri islands.

Getting There

By Train. On the JR railway system, a line connects Abashiri to Kushiro; the train passes through Akan National Park at Teshigawa and Kawaya. Traveling west from Abashiri, the JR train goes to Asahikawa and to Sapporo, some five hours away. North of Abashiri, trains go to Mombetsu and then swing inland, traveling up the north cape to Wakkanai. A short line also runs south from Abashiri, along the coast to Shari.

By Bus. A bus leaves Lake Akan and, with a transfer at Bihoro, goes to Abashiri.

Exploring
32

Abashiri is the main town on the Sea of Okhotsk, but it is quite small. In winter, ice floes jam up on its shores and stretch out to sea as far as the eye can see. A museum at **Mt. Tento** observes the ice floes and explains their role in nature. *Admission:* ¥*1,000. Open 8–6.*

Down the hill from Mt. Tento, toward Lake Abashiri, is the **Abashiri Prison Museum** (Abashiri Kangoku), (now part of the Municipal Museum), which recalls the days when convict labor was used to develop the region. The year-round attraction is the **Municipal Museum** itself, which houses a good collection of Ainu artifacts and anthropological findings taken from the nearby Moyoro Shell Mound that are believed to be relics from aboriginal people who predate the Ainu. The museum is located across the railroad tracks to the south of downtown and near Katsuradai Station. *Admission:* ¥*1,000. Open 8:30–5.*

Another museum is the **Oroke Kinenkan,** which opened in 1978 to keep alive the heritage of a small tribe, the Oroke, nomadic reindeer herders who, in dwindling numbers, live on Sakhalin Island. And, just south of Abashiri (five minutes on the JR Semmo Line—disembark at Hamakoshimuzu Station), swans come down from Siberia in the winter to hole up at Tofutsu Lagoon. In summertime (July and August), between the lagoon and the Sea of Okhotsk, the main attraction is the **Natural Flower Gardens.** This is where the locals take their afternoon promenades.

33
34

If you continue traveling south of Abashiri on the Kanno Line train beyond Hamakoshimuzu, you will reach **Shari.** Shari is the end of the line and the jumping-off point for the **Shiretoko Peninsula.** Not many tourists make this trip except for a few Japanese seeking to go off the beaten track. To get there by public transport, take a 55-minute bus ride from Shari to **Utoro.** There is a sightseeing boat out of Utoro that goes out to the cape. As the boat skirts the shore and rounds the cape's tip, the views are impressive, with 600-foot cliffs coming straight out of the sea and rugged mountains inland. You can also drive along the north shore to **Kamuiwakka Onsen** under Mt. Io. Along the shore are hot-water pools (*rotemburo*). They are free; just take your clothes off and hop in.

35

Returning to Abashiri and going north, the traveler finds that the road runs along the coast of the Sea of Okhotsk to **Mombetsu.** (The train takes an inland route to Mombetsu.) Small summer resort hotels dot the coast, especially along the shores of Lake Saroma, a seawater lagoon almost locked in by two sand pits. However, all you can look at here are the sea to the right and distant mountains to the left.

Mombetsu is a small port whose main industry is fishing the Sea of Okhotsk in the summer. In the winter the sea freezes, and Mombetsu is bitterly cold and is surrounded by ice floes. Yet, ironically, Mombetsu receives the most tourists in the winter. They come to see the ice floes and board a special boat, the *Gerinko Go,* which acts as an icebreaker, moving through the floes. *Reservations and tickets, tel. 01582/4-8000. Cost:* ¥*2,000.*

Mombetsu also has a small and attractive museum, with examples of Hokkaido's flora and fauna, some stone arrowheads, ancient pottery, and relics from Japan's 1905 war with Russia. *Admission free. Open 10:30–5:30 (4:30 in winter).*

That's it, aside from a small, friendly entertainment section, a few shops on the main street, and a couple of hotels. But Mombetsu is the last settlement fit to be called a town until Wakkanai, 300 kilometers (190 miles) to the north, the ferry port for Rebun and Rishiri islands.

(If you want to head straight back to Sapporo from Mombetsu, a new, well-paved highway cuts through the wooded mountain range to return to Asahikawa, a journey that takes a little over three hours by car or bus. Then, from Asahikawa, the train makes the 90-minute run to Sapporo. There is also a direct train from Mombetsu to Asahikawa.)

The journey north from Mombetsu to Wakkanai is long and tiring, passing through the occasional fishing village, but with usually only rocky promontories to interrupt the flat coastline. **36** Fifty kilometers (32 miles) before reaching **Cape Soya,** the mountains move out toward the sea. Out across the cold sea stands the Soviet Union's Sakhalin Island. Cape Soya is at the northernmost limits of Japan; just offshore is a little island with a wind-whipped monument marking the end of Japan's territory. Then, shortly thereafter and to the west, there is the first glimpse of Rishiri Island and its volcanic cone standing on the horizon. But first, one must enter the town of Wakkanai.

37 **Wakkanai** is a working-class town subsisting on farming the scrubland and on fishing the cold waters for Alaskan pollack and Atka Mackerel when the sea is not packed with ice floes. The area seems like it's at the top of the world. Wakkanai is an isolated outpost of man. In the winter, the nights are long, and in the summer there is a feeling of poetic solitude that comes from the eerie quality of the northern lights. Few visitors come to Wakkanai other than to wait for one of the three ferries that **38** daily make the 2½-hour crossing to both **Rebun Island** and **39** **Rishiri Island.** (Higashi-Nihon Ferry, tel. 0162/23–3780; fare: **40** ¥2.060. By the way, there is also a ferry between **Kafuka** on **41 42** Rebun Island and **Oshidomari** and **Kutsugata** on Rishiri Island (fare: ¥920).

Rebun is older island, created by an upward thrust of the earth's crust. The island is long and fairly skinny, running from north to south. Along the east coast are numerous small fishing villages where men bring their catch, usually *nukaboke* (a foot-long fish), to smoke in an old metal drum, while women rake in the edible yellowish-green seaweed (*kombu*) from the shore. On the west coast, cliffs stave off the waves coming in from the Japan Sea. Inland during the short summer months is a spectacle of wild alpine flowers, 300 species in all, blanketing the mountain meadows. In Momoiwa, the wildflowers are in such profusion in mid-June that one fears to walk, for each step seems to crush a dozen delicate flowers, including the white-pointed usuyo-kiso, a flower found only on Rebun.

Rishiri is the result of a submarine volcano whose cone now protrudes 5,640 feet out of the water. The scenery is wilder than on Rebun, and, though a larger island, Rishiri has fewer inhabitants. The ruggedness of the terrain makes it harder to support life, and it's less suitable for hiking than is Rebun. To see this island, it is better to take one of the buses, which make a complete circle of the island in two hours. There are six a day, both clockwise and counterclockwise. Get off at any of the several tourist stops along the way, and take the hiking routes laid out to the major scenic spots. With the tree line at about 3,000 feet, views are alpine panoramas of wildflowers, a cone-shape mountain, and wide expanses of sea. Tokyo and the industry of Honshu are not part of this Japan. These two islands remain beautiful outposts from modern industrialism.

From Oshidomari (on Rishiri), the ferry to Wakkanai takes just over two hours. From there the train takes six hours to return to Sapporo, 330 kilometers (210 miles) away. There are also flights directly back to Sapporo (Chitose airport), and there is an overnight ferry (about ¥8,000) from Kutsugata (Rishiri) and Kafuka (Rebun) to Otaru, which is 40 kilometers (25 miles) from Sapporo.

Dining and Lodging

Dining

Western food is served in all the major Sapporo hotels. Invariably, it is French-accented Continental cuisine and always fairly expensive. Sapporo also has a number of ethnic restaurants, from Italian to Russian to Indian, and there are even American fast-food chains. In the hinterlands, Western food is less common. However, almost all the large resort hotels offer a Western menu.

The joy of Hokkaido, however, is its regional food. We strongly recommend that you eat out whenever possible at local Japanese restaurants. Most restaurants that are reasonably priced will have a visual display of their menu in the window. On this basis, you can decide what you want before you enter. If you cannot order in Japanese and no English is spoken, lead the waiter to the window display and point.

Hokkaido Foods Hokkaido is known for its seafood. **Salmon** (*akiaji*), **squid, sea urchin, herring** (*nishin*), and **shellfish** are abundant.

The real treat is **kegani** (*hairy crabs*). Supposedly, it is forbidden to catch them, but not to eat them—the local people enjoy them too much for that rule to be in effect!

Genghis khan (also spelled *jingisukan*) are thin strips of mutton cooked in an iron skillet. Then, added to the sizzling mutton are seasoned vegetables—usually onions, green peppers, and cabbage.

A 3% federal consumer tax is added to all restaurant bills. Another 3% local tax is added if the bill exceeds ¥5,000. Tipping is not the custom. At more expensive restaurants, a 10%–15% service charge is also added to the bill.

Category	Cost *
Very Expensive	over ¥6,000
Expensive	¥4,000–¥6,000
Moderate	¥2,000–¥4,000
Inexpensive	under 2,000

Cost is per person without tax, service, or drinks

Lodging

With one or two exceptions, accommodations in Hokkaido consist of modern, characterless hotels built for Japanese tour groups. Large, unattractively furnished sitting areas and spacious lobbies are the norm. Usually the redeeming factor is the view. Invariably, hotel prices correlate with the views offered and with the size of the public areas and guest rooms.

Outside Sapporo and Hokkaido's industrial and/or commercial cities, hotels quote prices on a per-person basis with two meals, exclusive of service and tax. If you do not want dinner at your hotel, it is usually possible to renegotiate the price. The hotel categories below reflect the cost of a double room with private bath and no meals. Bear in mind, then, that except for city hotels, you will be expected to take breakfast and dinner at the hotel and that will be the rate quoted unless you specify otherwise. On the average, the food charges are 50%, per person, of the room cost. So, for example, if the double room is in the expensive category (¥15,000–¥20,000), then add ¥15,000 to ¥20,000 for two meals for two people.

A 3% federal consumer tax is added to all hotel bills. Another 3% local tax is added if the bill exceeds ¥10,000. At most hotels, a 10%–15% service charge is added to the total bill. Tipping is not necessary.

Category	Cost *
Very Expensive	over ¥20,000
Expensive	¥15,000–¥20,000
Moderate	¥10,000–¥15,000
Inexpensive	under ¥10,000

Cost is for double room, without tax or service

The most highly recommended restaurants and accommodations are indicated by a star ★.

Credit Cards   The following credit card abbreviations are used: AE, American Express; DC, Diners Club; MC, MasterCard; V, Visa.

Akan

Lodging   **Hotel Yamoura.** At the south end of the village and still on the lake front, the Yamoura is smaller than the area's other resort hotels. Three-quarters of the rooms are Japanese-style, and these are the better ones—they look onto the lake. The manager is friendly; though he speaks no English, he is very enthusiastic toward foreigners who stay at his hotel. *Akan-kohan, Akan 085, tel. 0154/67–2311. 70 rooms. Facilities: Continental and Japanese restaurants, thermal baths, boat rentals. AE, V. Expensive.*

★ **New Akan Hotel.** In Japanese eyes, this establishment is the most prestigious in the area, but, despite its ideal location on Lake Akan, it tends toward sterility and vastness. A recent improvement is the addition of the Annex Crystal of 72 rooms (half Japanese and half Western-style); this section is less crowded with groups. *Akan-kohan, Akan 085, tel. 0154/67–2121. 215 rooms. Facilities: Continental and Japanese dining,* *thermal baths, shops, boat rentals. AE, DC, MC, V. Expensive.*

★ **Hotel Parkuin.** The owners of this small hotel are really friendly, and the father is proud of his daughter's English (which is very limited). Because the hotel is not on the lake (it's just off the main road that skirts the village), request a room on the top floor to get a view of the lake and mountains. There are Japanese- and Western-style rooms; the Japanese restaurant, which attracts a local clientele, is especially good with its grilled fish. *Akan-kohan, Akan 085, tel. 0154/67–3211. 34 Japanese-style rooms. AE, MC, V. Inexpensive.*

Asahikawa

Dining **Claire France.** At the Palace Hotel, this is the best restaurant in town for French cuisine. Its rooftop setting is smart and formal, though the views are only of the tops of other nearby buildings. *6-6 Chome, Asahikawa 070, tel. 0166/25–8811. Jacket and tie required. AE, DC, MC, V. Lunch, dinner. Expensive.*

★ **Izakaya Yakara.** This bustling and cheerful bar is one floor up in a two-story building (next to a parking lot) and half a block south of the movie house on the main street. The chefs work in an open cooking area that allows non-Japanese speaking diners to see and point to the kind of food that takes their fancy. The main dishes are meats and fish grilled over charcoal. Guests can sit either at a counter or on tatami matting. *Tel. 0166/23–8228. Dress: informal. V. Dinner 6–10. Moderate.*

Lodging **Palace Hotel.** The Palace, Asahikawa's newest hotel, opened in
★ 1987. Decorated with mock marble, the public spaces are brightly lit and airy, with potted plants separating the registration area from the lounge. Use the Polestar lounge on the 15th floor for a skyline view. The Claire France restaurant is on the same floor. The Palace is located downtown, one block from the New Hokkai. Some English is spoken. *6-6 Chome, Asahikawa 070, tel. 0166/25–8811. 265 rooms (mostly Western style). Facilities: Japanese and French restaurants, coffee/tea lounge. AE, DC, MC, V. Expensive.*

Toyo Hotel. Opposite the Palace Hotel on the main street, this small hotel has recently refurbished its rooms with white-and-gray decor. The Toyo is used to serving Japanese guests but is friendly and helpful to Westerners. No English spoken. *7-chome, Shichijo-dori, Asahikawa 070, tel. 0166/22–7575. 107 rooms, (mostly Western style). Facilities: Japanese restaurant. AE, DC, MC, V. Moderate.*

Chitose

Lodging **Hotel Nikko Chitose.** This is the best hotel in the Chitose area if you wish to be near Sapporo airport, about two miles away. It is owned by Japan Airlines and is used by its flight crews. *4-4-4 Honcho, Chitose-shi 066, tel. 0123/22–1121. 203 rooms, mostly Western style. Facilities: Continental and Japanese restaurants. AE, DC, MC, V. Expensive.*

Hakodate

Lodging **Harborview Hotel.** Next to the Hakodate JR station and near buses to destinations within town, this hotel is very conveniently located. It maintains a fresh, cheerful ambience and a friendly staff. There is a pleasant coffee/tea lounge in the lobby and a sociable bar in the lobby. Guest rooms are standard Western style, furnished in light blue or peach—not particularly attractive but comfortable enough for an overnight. *14–10 Wakamatsu-cho, Hakodate 040, tel. 0138/22–0111, fax 0138/ 23–0154. 147 rooms. Facilities: Japanese and Western restaurants, coffee shop, bar, banquet rooms. AE, DC, MC, V. Moderate.*

Hakodate Ryokan. This small house with tatami rooms is located 10 minutes by foot from the JR station. *28-7 Omoricho, Hakodate 040, tel. 0138/26–1255. 15 rooms, 4 with bath. Facilities: Japanese and Continental breakfasts only. No credit cards. Inexpensive.*

Kushiro

Lodging **Kushiro Pacific Hotel.** This hotel is recommended simply for a night's stay because it is centrally located (five minutes by taxi from the train station). The staff is efficient, some English is spoken, and the rather small rooms are clean. *2-6 Sakaecho, Kushiro 085, tel. 0154/24–8811. 132 rooms, mostly Western style. Facilities: Continental and Japanese food served in the restaurant. AE, MC, V. Moderate.*

Lake Shikotsu

Lodging **Marukoma Onsen Ryokan.** Neither the building nor its interior furnishings have any aesthetic value, but the lobby, lounges, and restaurant face the northwest shore of Lake Shikotsu. The tatami-style guest rooms have plain, modern light-wood furnishings. If you have a room facing the lake and mountain, the view is splendid. Service is attentive and tolerant of foreigners, and dinner—served in your room—is above average. However, the real benefit of this ryokan is that besides the indoor thermal pool facing the water, there is a public *rotemburo* (outside thermal pool) on the lake shore, within yards of the hotel. *Poropnai, Bangaichi, Chitose-shi 066-02, tel. 0123/25–2341. 60 Japanese-style rooms. Facilities: coffee shop, bar, game room, thermal pool and private beach on lakefront. AE, DC, MC, V. Moderate.*

Mombetsu Area

Dining The entertainment area is located three streets up from the Harbor View Hotel (*see* Lodging, below). Though the area is small, there are plenty of bars that serve food and one or two modest discotheques (try the **New Jazz Club**). There are fewer restaurants than bars. While many of the restaurants have visual displays in their windows to indicate prices and the type of food served, the bars do not. Count on about ¥5,000 per person if you go into one of the bars that have hostesses with whom to talk, though that will be in Japanese, not English. Prices can climb steeply, so establish the costs before you gulp too much whiskey.

Lodging **Harbor View Hotel.** This is the best Western-style hotel in ★ town. Even though the Harbor View is modest, it is clean and comfortable. Request a room overlooking the harbor. The woman who owns the hotel is extremely helpful and speaks fluent English, a rarity in Mombetsu. *Mombetsu, tel. 01582/4–6171. 32 Western-style rooms. Facilities: small restaurant with Japanese and Western menu. V. Moderate.*

★ **Hotel Koen.** Located 49 kilometers (30 miles) south of Mombetsu on Rte. 238, this small hotel is steps away from the beach. It attracts the Japanese going to the sea in the summer and making snowmobile trips in the winter. This establishment has simple, clean accommodations and a cafeteria restaurant that serves marvelous fresh shrimp (¥1,000 per plate) and delicious hairy crabs. At least, stop here for lunch. *Toppushi, Sahomacho, Tokoru-gun 093, tel. 01587/2–3117. 40 rooms. Facilities: Japanese cuisine served in cafeteria-type restaurant, boat rentals, snowmobiling. V. Moderate.*

Togiya Ryokan. This ryokan is an extremely friendly, old-fashioned inn. It's not smart or elegant, but it has the warmth of rural Japan. The inn is located on a small street, one block up from the harbor road and two blocks east of the station. No English is spoken, but mama-san does wonders with your use of a dictionary. Good Japanese family fare (fish—raw and grilled) is served in your room. *Mombetsu, tel. 01582/3–3048. 15 rooms, none with private bath, but good, deep, Japanese baths are prepared for you. Facilities: Japanese food served in your room. No credit cards. Moderate.*

Noboribetsu Onsen

Lodging   **Dai-ichi Takimotokan.** This huge, famous spa hotel may have as many as 1,200 guests at one time staying here to enjoys its thermal pools, the best and most famous throughout Japan. The hotel is very expensive, yet it has zero ambience. It is like a giant youth hostel and, invariably, fully booked. Service is efficiently impersonal, and you must hike from your bedroom to the lobby and to the thermal baths. A vast dining room, the Food Plaza, serves average Japanese and Western food and features nightclub variety acts. *55 Noboribetsu-Onsen, Noboribetsu 059, tel. 01438/4–2111, fax 0143/84–2202. 336 rooms. Facilities: electronic game room, shops, thermal baths (nonguests pay ¥2,000 to use the baths). AE, DC, MC, V. Very Expensive.*

Noboribetsu Grand Hotel. This is another huge hotel with large, barren public rooms. Since it is at the bottom of the village and off to the side, its modern ugliness is well hidden. *154 Noboribetsu-Onsen, Noboribetsu 059, tel. 01438/4–2101. 350 rooms, mostly Japanese style. Facilities: Japanese restaurant, thermal baths, shops. AE, DC, MC, V. Expensive.*

★ **Akiyoshi Hotel.** This is a friendly, hospitable, modern ryokan in the center of the village. Antiques and paintings are judiciously placed to give a balance between traditional hospitality and modern amenities. If you enjoy sleeping on tatami with a futon, this is recommended as the most personable hotel in town. *Noboribetsu-Onsen, Noboribetsu 059, tel. 01438/4–2261, fax 0143/84–2263. 50 Japanese-style rooms. Facilities: Japanese food served either in the room or in the restaurant, thermal bath. AE, V. Moderate–Expensive.*

Ryokan Kiyomizu. A simple Japanese hotel that is within walking distance to the great baths at the Dai-ichi and a three-minute walk from the bus station. The big sign outside, "All Nationalities Welcome," is sincere and though the tatami rooms are small and services limited, the cost of a night's stay is the most reasonable in town. *60 Noboribetsu-Onsen,*

Noboribetsu 059, tel. 01438/4–2145, fax 01348/4–2148. 20 rooms without bath. Facilities: Japanese food, Continental breakfast served on request. AE, MC, V. Inexpensive.

Otaru

Lodging **Otaru International Hotel.** Above a shopping arcade, this modern hotel in town is reached by an escalator from the main street. The lobby area is rather bare and uncomfortable, but the guest rooms are cheerful, though small. *3-9-1 Inaho, Otaru 047, tel. 0134/33–8841. 46 rooms, mostly Western style. Facilities: Chinese, Japanese, and Continental restaurants. AE, MC, V. Moderate.*

Shikutsu Ryokan. This is a popular but slightly overrated ryokan. The furnishings are worn, and the staff does not seem to be overjoyed at having foreigners stay. *2-15 Inaho 3-chome, Otaru 047 (located just outside Otaru and toward the aquarium), tel. 0134/22–5276. 20 rooms, 10 with private bath. Facilities: only Japanese food is offered. No credit cards. Moderate.*

Sapporo

Dining Continental food is served in all the major hotels in either a formal dining room and/or coffee shop. Invariably, the formal dining room looks to French cuisine for inspiration, and the food is always expensive. Most large hotels, aside from their Japanese restaurants, have a Chinese restaurant. Most of the restaurants, whatever their culinary origin, use visual displays for their menus, so, even if you do not speak Japanese, ordering at a local Japanese restaurant is easy.

★ **The Ambrosia Room.** On the penthouse floor of the Keio Plaza Hotel, this restaurant serves ambitious French fare by an extremely attentive and personable staff. Perhaps more memorable than the cooking, though, is the view over the botanical gardens. *Keio Plaza Hotel, 7–2 Nishi, Kita 5, Chuo-ku, Sapporo 060 (downtown), tel. 011/271–0111. Jacket and tie required. AE, DC, MC, V. Lunch noon–3, dinner 6–10. Very Expensive.*

The Big Jug. In the Grand Hotel, this casual beer hall-type brasserie is good for lunch, with a limited Continental menu and an opportunity to talk. It's popular with businessmen. *Sapporo Grand Hotel, 4 Nishi, Kita 1, Chuo-ku (downtown), tel. 011/261–3311. Jacket and tie required. AE, DC, MC, V. Lunch noon–3, dinner 6–10. Expensive.*

★ **Yamatoya.** Excellent sushi and sashimi is served here, with counter service on the left and tatami seating on the right. *3 Nishi, Kita 2, Chuo-ku (downtown), tel. 011/251–5667 (located across the street from the JAL office). Jacket and tie required. V. Open 11–10. Closed Sun. Expensive.*

★ **Izakaya Karumaya.** Downstairs in Plaza 109 (on the south side of the main east–west street in Susukino), this local bar has the best yakitori in town. The elegant atmosphere makes it popular with Japanese and foreigners. (There is an English-language menu.) Aside from yakitori, Kuramaya also serves oden as one of its specialties. *4 Minamo, 5 Nishi Chuo-ku (Susukino), tel. 011/512–9157. Dress: informal. V. Open 5 PM–2 AM. Moderate.*

Sapporo Beer Brewery. Genghis khan (mutton) is popular here, though other Japanese dishes are offered. You'll find a festive atmosphere in either the garden or the cavernous halls of the old brewery (east of the station). *Nishi 6, Kita 9, Higashi-ku, tel. 011/742–1531. Dress: informal. AE, MC, V. Open 11:30–9. Moderate.*

Sasa Sushi. This small restaurant has a wide variety of sushi and is extremely popular with the local businessmen. Sit at the counter and you'll usually strike up a conversation with fellow patrons. *2 Nishi, Kita 2, Chuo-ku (downtown), tel. 011/222–2897 (close to the Hokkaido Tourist Office). Open 11–10. Closed Sun. V. Moderate.*

Shioya. In the Plaza 109 building, this popular restaurant serves grilled fish, but the side orders of sashimi and yakitori are also delicious. Seating is either at the counter or at tables. It's a casual place where talking to fellow diners is a likely possibility. No English is spoken, but sign language suffices, and the prices are not too high. *4 Minamo, 5 Nishi Chou-ku (Susukino), tel. 011/512–1241. Dress: informal. AE, V. Moderate.*

Silo. This has a countrylike decor and a menu to match. The restaurant serves only Hokkaido foods, including bear and deer. Some English is spoken. *5 Minamo, 3 Nishi, Chuo-ku in the Hokusen Bldg. (Susukino), tel. 011/531–5837. Dress: informal. No credit cards. Dinner 5–11. Closed Sun. Moderate.*

Yoyotei. A genghis khan dinner is offered in case you cannot make it to the Sapporo Beer Brewery. Young waitresses in Bavarian dresses and a large open space combine to re-create a German beer hall. *5 Minamo, 4 Nishi, Chuo-ku, on the 5th floor of the Matsuoka Bldg. (Susukino), tel. 011/241–8831. Dress: informal. No credit cards. Open 4–10. Inexpensive.*

Lodging

Since the Winter Olympics in 1972, Sapporo has had a large number of international hotels. The latest addition is the Ramada Renaissance (tel. 011/821–1111), which opens in late 1991 with 323 large rooms, seven restaurants and bars, business center, health center, and meeting rooms. However, the hotel's location in the southeast part of town next to the Toyohira gawa River makes it more suitable for business travelers than tourists who want a hotel more centrally located. They are, for the most part, without distinctive qualities, but all have courteous and prompt service. Ryokans are not Sapporo's strong point; only a modest one is listed below. Reservations are usually easy to obtain, except during the Snow Festival in February, when reservations should be made six months in advance. All the hotels in the Very Expensive category have minibars and bilingual TV programming.

Hotel Alpha Sapporo. This hotel has the best location for tourists who want to walk to the shopping and downtown area of the city and be close to the evening action in Susskino. The service is excellent and the decor of warm rust-browns and reds makes it an inviting place to return after a day of sightseeing. Smaller than most of the other top hotels, the hotel's staff soon knows you by name. Guest rooms tend to be a little ordinary, but the rooms are larger than most standard hotel rooms in Japan. The French restaurant, La Couronne, imports many of its ingredients from France and serves them in an elegant wood-paneled dining room. *Nishi 5, Minami 1, Chuo-ko, Sapporo 060, tel. 011/221–2333, fax 011/221–0819, 146 rooms. Facilities: 4 restaurants, indoor pool, beauty parlor, AE, DC, MC, V.*

The ANA Zennikku Hotel. In the heart of the business center, three blocks from the JR station, this is Sapporo's tallest high-rise hotel (26 floors). Shops and a coffee/pastry restaurant are on the ground floor, and up the escalator is an open lobby area with lounges and bars. The rooms are spacious and brightly decorated. Good views are available from the Sky Restaurant and Sky Lounge. The hotel is convenient for ANA passengers, because it runs buses to and from Chitose Airport. *1 Nishi, Kita 3, Chuo-ku, Sapporo 060, tel. 011/221-4411, fax 011/222-7624. 470 rooms, mostly Western style. Facilities: French and Japanese restaurants on the penthouse floors. AE, DC, MC, V. Very Expensive.*

★ **The Grand Hotel.** This is the oldest established Western hotel, centrally located on the main commercial street. Built in 1934 and renovated in 1984, the Grand is in the tradition of a great European hotel. It has a range of restaurants—Japanese, Chinese, French, and a pub (The Big Jug), popular for business lunches. The service is first-rate. The rooms in the new annex have a fresher, more modern tone than those in the older wing. The hotel's numerous facilities, from a cake and coffee shop to elegant restaurants, create a more lively atmosphere than you may expect from Sapporo's oldest hotel. *4 Nishi, Kita 1, Chuo-ku, Sapporo 060, tel. 011/261-3311, fax 011/222-5164. 585 rooms, mostly Western style. Facilities: Japanese, Chinese, and French restaurants, shopping arcade. AE, DC, MC, V. Very Expensive.*

Keio Plaza Hotel. A five-minute walk to the right of the JR station, the Keio is a large, modern hotel with a vast, open-plan lobby. Since it stands between the botanical gardens and the Hokkaido University campus, the views from the guest rooms on the upper floors are the best in town. The rooms are very spacious for a Japanese hotel. If you are not staying here, the views may be enjoyed from the Ambrosia (French) and Miyama (Japanese) restaurants on the hotel's 22nd floor. The 24-hour Jurin coffee shop, one of the few in town, can be a welcome respite for the insomniac suffering from jet lag. The enthusiastic and helpful staff will always find someone to help out in English, if required. *7-2 Nishi, Kita 5, Chuo-ku, Sapporo 060, tel. 011/271-0111, fax 011/271-7943. 525 rooms, mostly Western style. Facilities: Several Japanese restaurants, as well as French, Mediterranean, and Chinese restaurants, 24-hr coffee shop, health club facilities, car rental, and tour desk. AE, DC, MC, V. Very Expensive.*

Sapporo Tokyu Hotel. This clean, efficient establishment has a friendly staff. The hotel lacks any character, but its downtown location is convenient. *4 Nishi, Kita 4, Chuo-ku, Sapporo 060 (located 2 blocks off Sapporo's main commercial street, a 5-min walk from the station), tel. 011/231-5611, fax 011/251-3515. AE, DC, MC, V. Expensive.*

★ **Fujiya Santus Hotel.** Although 10 years old the Fujiya Santus has kept up a fresh appearance and appears new. The staff is wonderfully friendly, and the smallness of the hotel adds to the personal warmth. The price is at the low end of this category, too, which make it good value. *7 Nishi, Kita 3, Chuo-ku, Sapporo 060 (located next to the botanical gardens, which is pleasant, but requires a 10-min walk to downtown and the JR station), tel. 011/271-3344, fax 011/241-4182. 40 rooms, 32 Western-style. V. Moderate.*

Nakamuraya. A ryokan near the Botanical Park, it has a 90-year-old history—ancient for Sapporo—though the current building is more recent. The six tatami rooms seem larger because of the spacious cupboards, built-in minibar, and wide window shelf. Some rooms have private bathrooms, albeit tiny ones. Foreigners are tolerated rather than welcomed, though smiles do appear if you speak in Japanese. When making reservations, explain that you saw a listing in the Japanese Inn Group brochure; otherwise you may be charged a higher rate. *7 Nishi, Kita 3, Chuo-ku, Sapporo 060, tel. 011/241–2111. 32 rooms, mostly Japanese style. Facilities: Japanese restaurant. AE. Moderate.*

★ **Hotel Public.** The best and swankiest (lots of marble) business hotel in town, the Public has a friendly staff and Western-size beds, instead of the normal narrow ones found in business hotels. The Public also has a reasonable restaurant. *1 Minamo, 15 Nishi, Chuo-ku, Sapporo 060, tel. 011/644–7711. 120 Western-style rooms. Facilities: Japanese and Continental restaurants on the 2nd floor, typing service. AE, MC, V. Inexpensive.*

Sounkyo Onsen

Note: Rates tend to be 20% lower during the winter season.

Lodging **Chyohotel.** Perched on a bluff halfway up the side of the gorge, this hotel has the best views (and, because of this, spoils some of the natural beauty). Its corner window in the huge foyer lounge looks straight down the gorge; however, the hotel itself is an ugly and mammoth building, cold and sterile in the modern Japanese style. While rooms that face the gorge may merit the hotel's price, a room at the back looks onto a parking lot, another ugly building, and cliff walls. *Sounkyo-Onsen, tel. 01658/5–3241. 275 rooms, mostly Japanese style. Facilities: thermal baths, shops, electronic game room. AE, DC, MC, V. Expensive.*

★ **The Mount View Hotel.** This hotel has the nicest design around and an air of freshness to it. Built as a modern interpretation of an alpine inn, the decor is in cheerful, warm pastels. Unfortunately, as a recent newcomer to Sounkyo, it is situated down by the road and has limited views. Nevertheless it has taste, which the other hotels lack. *Sounkyo-Onsen, tel. 01658/5–3011. 40 rooms. Facilities: thermal baths. V. Expensive.*

Kumoi. This small new ryokan offers simple but clean tatami rooms. *Sounkyo-Onsen, tel. 01658/5–3553. 22 rooms, 6 with private bath. Facilities: Continental breakfast on request, thermal bath. AE. Moderate.*

Toyako Onsen

Lodging **Toya Park Hotel.** This is a sister hotel to the Toya Park Sun Palace, but it's smaller and more personal, though not quite as deluxe. The manager enjoys speaking English. Located at the head of the town and on a slight bluff, it has an unrestricted view of the lake. However, only the Japanese-style guest rooms face the lake. *Toyako-Onsen, tel. 01427/5–2445. 167 rooms, about half Western style, half Japanese style. Facilities: Continental and Japanese restaurants, thermal baths, tennis courts, electronics game room. AE, DC, MC, V. Moderate.*

Nakanoshima. This is a small hotel with a restaurant two miles farther around the lake and going west from Toyako Onsen. No English is spoken, but the owners are happy with sign language. *Sobetsu-Onsen, tel. 01427/5–2283. 30 rooms, mostly Japanese style. No credit cards. Inexpensive.*

Japanese Vocabulary

Notes on Pronunciation of Japanese

There are several different ways of representing Japanese in the Latin (our) alphabet, but for this vocabulary we have decided to use a modification of the Hepburn Romanization system. It is the most commonly seen system in Japan, and also is easiest for a speaker of English to read.

The vowels are pronounced as follows: *a* as in c*a*r, but shorter; *e* as in t*e*n; *i* as in pol*i*ce, but shorter; *o* as in n*o*se; *u* as in l*u*te. Vowels with a bar over them (ā, ē, ō, ū) and the double *i* (*ii*) are pronounced long. This is important as the length of a vowel can change the meaning of the word. Combinations of vowels are pronounced together but they retain their own sounds. A final *u* is silent. Thus, *desu* becomes *des*, and *wakarimasu* becomes *wakarimas*. The *i* in the combination *shita* is also silent, and is pronounced *shta*.

Consonants are pronounced as in English, with the exception of *r*, which is pronounced as if it were halfway between an *r* and an *l* with a little *d* thrown in. Doubled consonants require a bit of effort, as each of the consonants must be pronounced separately. Hence, *kk* is pronounced like the sound in the sound in the middle of *black coffee*.

Words and Phrases

	English	Japanese Pronunciation
Basics	Yes/No	hai/iie
	Please	o-ne-gai shi-ma-su
	Thank you (very much).	(dō-mo)a-ri-ga-tō go-zai-ma-su
	You're welcome.	dō i-ta-shi-mashi-te
	Sorry	su-mi-ma-sen
	Excuse me.	go-men na-sai
	Good morning.	o-ha-yō go-zai-ma-su
	Good day/afternoon.	kon-ni-chi-wa
	Good evening.	kom-ban-wa
	Good night	o-ya-su-mi na-sai
	Goodbye.	sa-yō-na-ra
	Mr./Mrs./Miss	-san (placed after last name)
	How do you do?	ha-ji-me-mashi-te

Numbers	The first reading is used for reciting numbers, as in telephone numbers, and the second is often used for counting things.	
	One	i-chi / hi-to-tsu
	Two	ni / fu-ta-tsu
	Three	san / mit-tsu
	Four	shi *or* yon / yot-tsu
	Five	go / i-tsu-tsu

	Six	ro-ku / mut-tsu
	Seven	na-na / na-na-tsu
	Eight	ha-chi / yat-tsu
	Nine	kyu / kokonotsu
	Ten	jū / to
	Twenty	ni-jū
	Twenty-one	ni-jū-i-chi
	Thirty	san-jū
	Forty	yon-jū
	Fifty	go-jū
	Sixty	ro-ku-jū
	Seventy	na-na-jū
	Eighty	ha-chi-jū
	Ninety	kyu-jū
	One hundred	hya-ku
	One thousand	sen
	Ten thousand	i-chi-man
Days of the Week	Sunday	ni-chi-yō-bi
	Monday	ge-tsu-yō-bi
	Tuesday	ka-yō-bi
	Wednesday	su-i-yō-bi
	Thursday	mo-ku-yō-bi
	Friday	kin-yō-bi
	Saturday	do-yō-bi
Useful Phrases	Do you understand English?	ei-go ga wa-ka-ri-ma-su-ka
	I don't understand Japanese.	ni-hon-go ga wa-ka-ri-ma-sen
	My name is . . .	. . . to mō-shi-ma-su
	What time is it?	i-ma nan-ji de-su-ka
	How?	dō yat-te
	When?	i-tsu
	Yesterday/today/ tomorrow	ki-nō/kyō/ashi-ta
	This morning	kesa
	This afternoon	kyō no go-go
	Tonight	kom-ban
	Excuse me./Sorry.	su-mi-ma-sen
	What is it?	nan de-su-ka
	What is this/that?	ko-re/so-re wa nan de-su-ka
	Why?	na-ze de-su-ka
	Who?	da-re de-su ka
	Are there any rooms?	he-ya ga a-ri-ma-su-ka
	How much is it?	i-ku-ra de-su-ka
	It's expensive/	ta-kai/ya-su-i de-su

cheap.	ne
A little/a lot	su-ko-shi/ta-ku-san
More/less	mot-to ō-ku/su-ku-na-ku
Enough/too much	jū-bun/ō-su-gi-ru
I'd like to exchange . . . dollars to yen. pounds to yen.	. . . ryo-gae shi-te i-ta-da-ke-ma-su-ka do-ru o en ni pon-do o en ni
Please call a doctor.	i-sha o yon-de ku-da-sai
Please call the police.	kei-sa-tsu o yon-de ku-da-sai
Help!	tasu-ke-te
Stop!	ya-me-te
Fire!	ka-ji da
Caution!/Lookout!/Danger	a-bu-nai

Getting Around

I am lost.	mi-chi ni ma-yo-i-ma-shi-ta
How do I get to . . .	. . . ma-de dō i-ku no de-su-ka
Where is . . . the train station? the bus stop? the taxi stand? the airport? the bank? the temple? the shrine? the park? the tourist information? the . . . hotel? the . . . museum? the hospital? the elevator?	. . . wa do-ko de-su-ka e-ki ba-su tei tak-shi-i no-ri-ba kū-kō gin-kō o-tera jin-ja kō-en kan-kō-an-nai-sho . . . ho-te-ru . . . ha-ku-bu-tsu-kan byō-in e-re-bē-tā
Where are the rest rooms?	toi-re wa do-ko de-suka
Here/there/	ko-ko/so-ko
Left/right	hi-da-ri/mi-gi
Is it near/far?	chi-kai/tō-i de-su-ka
Is this (bus, train, etc.) going to . . . ?	ko-re wa . . . ma-de i-ki-ma-su ka

Food Glossary

Bento   A box lunch; some bento can be eaten on the premises or taken out; *kaiseki bento* are excellent samplers of formal *kaiseki* cuisine; *eki-ben* are sold at every train station and feature the local specialty (a good way to check out regional foods "on the run").

Chawan-mushi   A side dish of vegetables and shrimp steamed in egg custard.

Chuka-ryori   Chinese-style food, modified to suit Japanese taste.

Fugu   Blowfish; a popular and expensive delicacy served at specialty restaurants (the liver of this delicacy is intoxicating in small doses but fatal when handled by amateurs).

Ippin-ryori   À la carte style.

Itamae-ryori   Literally, "before-the-counter cuisine"; refers to a small shop (often no more than a counter and 10 stools) run by a highly trained chef *(itamae-san)*, who specializes in a particular type of food.

Izakaya   A "watering hole" for thirsty *sake* fans; lively and comparatively inexpensive, izakayas often feature a variety of *jizake*, brewed in limited quantities by small regional brewers; also serves a variety of snacks.

Kaiseki ryori   Formal Japanese haute cuisine, served in exclusive *(ryotei)* restaurants amid traditional surroundings with as many as 15 courses.

Kare-raisu   Curried rice; more Japanese than Indian; predictable lunchtime fare in most Japanese coffee shops.

Katei-ryori   Home-style cooking, served at neighborhood restaurants called *shokudo;* a main dish of fish or meat is served with soup, rice, and pickles in a set menu called *teishoku*.

Kushi-age (or kushi-katsu)   Skewered bits of meat (particularly pork) battered and deep-fried; usually served as inexpensive snacks with beer.

Nabemono   A variety of one-pot dishes that resemble Western stew but are cooked in a lighter broth.

Ocha   Green tea served free of charge with meals at every restaurant in Japan; *matcha* (or *o-usu* in Kyoto) is the powdered, whipped tea served in the tea ceremony and at shops that sell Japanese sweets *(wagashi)*.

Oden   Vegetables and meats simmered for hours in broth; a popular winter accompaniment to *sake*.

Omakase-ryori   Table d'hôte style, a fixed set menu—the specialty of the house.

Robatayaki   Fish, meat, and vegetables cooked over an open grill (called *sumibi-yaki*, if it is a charcoal grill); popular fare at inexpensive bars or *nomiya*.

Sake   Japanese rice wine, either *karakuchi* (dry) or *amakuchi* (sweet); served hot *(atsukan)*, warm *(kan)*, or lukewarm *(nurukan*, approximately "skin temperature").

Sashimi   Slices of raw fish, served with *wasabi* (Japanese horseradish) and soy sauce as condiments.

Shabu-shabu   Thinly sliced beef boiled briefly in a light broth; the same dish is called *mizudaki* when instead of beef chicken is used.

Shojin-ryori   Zen vegetarian-style food.

Shumai   Shrimp or pork wrapped in a light dough and steamed.

Soba   Buckwheat noodles, served in a variety of combinations (like *tempura soba*); *zaru-soba* is a cold noodle dish.

Sukiyaki   Thinly sliced beef sautéed with vegetables in a combination of soy sauce and *mirin* (sweet wine) at table.

Sushi   Bite-size pieces of raw fish and seafood on balls of vinegared rice with a dab of *wasabi* (Japanese horseradish) in between is known as *nigiri-sushi*. Other kinds include *chirashi-sushi*, a mixture of seafood, vegetables, and egg with rice; *inari-sushi*, rice mixed with sweet vinegar wrapped in deep-fried tofu; *oshi-sushi*, vinegared rice pressed into a mold with a layer of fish on top; *maki-sushi*, fish and vinegared rice wrapped in a sheet of dried *nori* (seaweed).

Teishoku   A set menu served at family-style restaurants.

Tempura   Pieces of meat, vegetables, and seafood battered and deep-fried, to be dipped in a light soy sauce mixed with finely grated *daikon* radish.

Tofu   Soybean curd served cold *(hiyayakko)* with diced green onions and soy sauce, or hot *(yudofu)*, simmered in hot broth and dipped in sauce; also used in a number of one-pot dishes.

Tonkatsu   Batter-fried pork cutlets; an inexpensive family-style dish often served as the main course of a *teishoku*, or set-menu meal.

Tsukemono   Pickled vegetables served as an accompaniment for rice.

Udon   Thick white noodles served hot in a variety of soups; *yosenabe*—a combination stew of vegetables, seafood, and *udon* noodles.

Unagi   Eel; *kabayaki* is eel dipped in sauce and charcoal-broiled, served with rice and pickles; *unagi-donburi* is a less expensive version served on top of a bowl of rice.

Yakitori   Bits of chicken dipped in sauce and grilled on skewers.

Wagashi   A generic name for a wide variety of Japanese confectionery; either unbaked *(namagashi)* or baked *(yaki-gashi* or *manju)* and usually filled with sweet bean paste; *hi-gashi* refers to dry, sugary wafers.

Yoshoku   Western-style food.

Index

Personal Itinerary

Departure *Date*

Time

Transportation

Arrival *Date* *Time*

Departure *Date* *Time*

Transportation

Accommodations

Arrival *Date* *Time*

Departure *Date* *Time*

Transportation

Accommodations

Arrival *Date* *Time*

Departure *Date* *Time*

Transportation

Accommodations

Personal Itinerary

Arrival *Date* *Time*

Departure *Date* *Time*

Transportation

Accommodations

Arrival *Date* *Time*

Departure *Date* *Time*

Transportation

Accommodations

Arrival *Date* *Time*

Departure *Date* *Time*

Transportation

Accommodations

Arrival *Date* *Time*

Departure *Date* *Time*

Transportation

Accommodations

Personal Itinerary

Arrival *Date*   *Time*

Departure *Date*   *Time*

Transportation

Accommodations

Arrival *Date*   *Time*

Departure *Date*   *Time*

Transportation

Accommodations

Arrival *Date*   *Time*

Departure *Date*   *Time*

Transportation

Accommodations

Arrival *Date*   *Time*

Departure *Date*   *Time*

Transportation

Accommodations

Personal Itinerary

Arrival *Date*   *Time*

Departure *Date*   *Time*

Transportation

Accommodations

Arrival *Date*   *Time*

Departure *Date*   *Time*

Transportation

Accommodations

Arrival *Date*   *Time*

Departure *Date*   *Time*

Transportation

Accommodations

Arrival *Date*   *Time*

Departure *Date*   *Time*

Transportation

Accommodations

Addresses

Name	*Name*
Address	*Address*
Telephone	*Telephone*
Name	*Name*
Address	*Address*
Telephone	*Telephone*
Name	*Name*
Address	*Address*
Telephone	*Telephone*
Name	*Name*
Address	*Address*
Telephone	*Telephone*
Name	*Name*
Address	*Address*
Telephone	*Telephone*
Name	*Name*
Address	*Address*
Telephone	*Telephone*
Name	*Name*
Address	*Address*
Telephone	*Telephone*
Name	*Name*
Address	*Address*
Telephone	*Telephone*

Fodor's Travel Guides

U.S. Guides

Alaska
Arizona
Boston
California
Cape Cod, Martha's
  Vineyard, Nantucket
The Carolinas & the
  Georgia Coast
The Chesapeake
  Region
Chicago
Colorado
Disney World & the
  Orlando Area
Florida
Hawaii

Las Vegas, Reno,
  Tahoe
Los Angeles
Maine, Vermont,
  New Hampshire
Maui
Miami & the
  Keys
National Parks
  of the West
New England
New Mexico
New Orleans
New York City
New York City
  (Pocket Guide)

Pacific North Coast
Philadelphia & the
  Pennsylvania
  Dutch Country
Puerto Rico
  (Pocket Guide)
The Rockies
San Diego
San Francisco
San Francisco
  (Pocket Guide)
The South
Santa Fe, Taos,
  Albuquerque
Seattle &
  Vancouver

Texas
USA
The U. S. & British
  Virgin Islands
The Upper Great
  Lakes Region
Vacations in
  New York State
Vacations on the
  Jersey Shore
Virginia & Maryland
Waikiki
Washington, D.C.
Washington, D.C.
  (Pocket Guide)

Foreign Guides

Acapulco
Amsterdam
Australia
Austria
The Bahamas
The Bahamas
  (Pocket Guide)
Baja & Mexico's Pacific
  Coast Resorts
Barbados
Barcelona, Madrid,
  Seville
Belgium &
  Luxembourg
Berlin
Bermuda
Brazil
Budapest
Budget Europe
Canada
Canada's Atlantic
  Provinces

Cancun, Cozumel,
  Yucatan Peninsula
Caribbean
Central America
China
Czechoslovakia
Eastern Europe
Egypt
Europe
Europe's Great Cities
France
Germany
Great Britain
Greece
The Himalayan
  Countries
Holland
Hong Kong
India
Ireland
Israel
Italy

Italy 's Great Cities
Jamaica
Japan
Kenya, Tanzania,
  Seychelles
Korea
London
London
  (Pocket Guide)
London Companion
Mexico
Mexico City
Montreal &
  Quebec City
Morocco
New Zealand
Norway
Nova Scotia,
  New Brunswick,
  Prince Edward
  Island
Paris

Paris (Pocket Guide)
Portugal
Rome
Scandinavia
Scandinavian Cities
Scotland
Singapore
South America
South Pacific
Southeast Asia
Soviet Union
Spain
Sweden
Switzerland
Sydney
Thailand
Tokyo
Toronto
Turkey
Vienna & the Danube
  Valley
Yugoslavia

Wall Street Journal Guides to Business Travel

Europe

International Cities

Pacific Rim

USA & Canada

Special-Interest Guides

Bed & Breakfast and
  Country Inn Guides:
  Mid-Atlantic Region
New England
The South
The West

Cruises and Ports
  of Call
Healthy Escapes
Fodor's Flashmaps
  New York

Fodor's Flashmaps
  Washington, D.C.
Shopping in Europe
Skiing in the USA &
  Canada

Smart Shopper's
  Guide to London
Sunday in New York
Touring Europe
Touring USA